D1254816

| DATE DUE | | |
|---|---|---|
| FEB 0 9 1998 S | | |
| MAR 1 8 1998 S | | |
| | | |
| | | |
| | | |
| | | |
| | | |
| | | |
| | | |
| | | |
| | | |

WITHDRAWN

# fundamentals of
# the securities industry

**REVISED EDITION**

*Allan H. Pessin*

Salomon Brothers

NEW YORK INSTITUTE OF FINANCE

10   9   8   7

ISBN 0-13-343906-2

New York Institute of Finance
(NYIF Corp.)
70 Pine Street
New York, New York 10270

**About the Publisher**

The New York Institute of Finance was established more than 60 years ago as a training arm of the New York Stock Exchange. It now operates as a private institution dedicated to serving the needs of the financial community. The institute—"Where Wall Street goes to school"—

- publishes specialized material (such as this book),
- conducts adult day and evening classes in the financial district in New York City,
- publishes and distributes a number of correspondence courses to finance students throughout the free world, and
- presents customized programs to fit specific needs of corporate clients, both in the New York area and throughout the rest of the country.

Our courses are taught by men and women who are actively employed within the financial community and who teach what they do, making our presentations very practical and timely.

**About this Book**

This publication presents an overview of the securities industry. It explains the nature of many of the investment products that are actively traded—common stocks, preferred stocks, bonds, and many others. It also describes:

- how and why they are issued,
- the mechanics of trading them, both on the securities exchanges and in the over-the-counter market,
- how securities orders are processed within the brokerage community,
- the principles of technical analysis, and finally,
- how to read and understand the financial news.

Your reaction might be that this single publication presents a great deal of information for you to assimilate, and that impression is quite correct. There is a lot to know in the securities industry. In light of this simple fact, we have made every effort to present this wealth of information in as logical a sequence as possible, while retaining its factuality, timeliness, and interest.

We have prepared this publication to be a reservoir of detailed and easily accessed information. At the front of the book is a table of contents that guides you to the start of each chapter. There you will find an indexed and more detailed listing of the chapter contents. For more random access to the material, an extensive subject index is included at the end of the book.

We invite you to explore the marvelously complex world of securities—a most fascinating topic that has intrigued men and women throughout our history. We recommend that you augment the benefits of this text by scanning the financial pages of your local newspaper and the *Wall Street Journal*, every day if you can. You might also listen to the daily stock market reports on the radio and television. With a little self-training, even those mysterious "financial-type" pages will begin to make sense to you. And the specialized jargon that punctuates the newscasts will become a second language for you. In brief, we hope that this text will provide you with an appreciation of the securities industry, as well as an avenue to an enlarged perspective of the world of finance.

BENJAMIN F. RUSSELL
*President, New York Institute of Finance*

# contents

# fundamentals of corporate finance

There are three principal types of business organization in the United States today. Let us assume that you wish to go into business and have to decide on which type. We'll explore the advantages and disadvantages of each type to help you make your decision.

A.
three types of business

**individual proprietorship**

The simplest and most common form of business organization is known as an **individual proprietorship**. There are many advantages for you in the operation of your business as a proprietorship. You will be your own boss and will enjoy a great deal of freedom and flexibility in your business activities. You decide upon the type of endeavor, the location, the quality and quantity of merchandise, and the hours during which you will conduct your business, be it of a service or of a manufacturing nature.

A1.
*Type 1: Individual Proprietorship*

There are also disadvantages that preclude the individual proprietorship from developing into a big business. Foremost among these handicaps is the lack of perpetuity. If you become incapacitated for an extended period of time, there is usually difficulty in continuing operation. Worse yet, on your death, your business, penalized without your guidance, ceases to exist, too.

Still another deterrent to the individual proprietorship is the feature of unlimited liability. Under existing laws in most states, single proprietorships may be held personally accountable for the obligations incurred by their businesses. This means that if your business fails, your creditors may lay claim to your *personal* assets as well as those of the business itself.

Additional obstacles prevail, even in prosperity. To maintain or increase your competitive position in the industry, capital is necessary to improve and expand your business. As an individual, your personal resources are certainly limited, and you must, therefore, turn to outside sources for financing. Although your books and records may justify such borrowing, banks and commercial factors balk at granting credit for extended periods. In recognition of the shortcomings of an individual proprietorship, they might be willing to lend you capital, but for just a few years.

**partnership**

The second form of organization is merely a slight improvement over the first. It is called a **partnership**. A partnership is composed of two or more proprietors who band together in order to establish and conduct a business. You may wish to form a partnership with Jane Doe. You will pool your monies and your talents and strive for success collectively. Although a partnership is usually founded upon larger sums of capital and a greater diversity of abilities (compared with a proprietorship), as partners you will share the legal and physical shortcomings of the individual proprietorship. As partners, you also may have difficulty in arranging long-term financing. You will be hindered by the possibility of incapacitation or death of your partner, whose participation is essential to the continuation of the business. Furthermore, as partners, Jane Doe and you are financially responsible for each other's actions. You both, in fact, incur personal, unlimited liability on the failure of your joint venture.

A2.
*Type 2: Partnership*

**limited partners**

A partnership may include among the principals some **limited partners** who are not liable to the same degree that the general partners are. A limited partner, however, is only a *silent partner*, represented by capital, but with no voice in the management of the business. Let us assume that Jane Doe and you, as general partners, take Sam Smith into your business as a limited partner. In recognition of his equity contribution, you general partners pay him a return on his investment depending on the income or profits of the business. He has limited personal financial liability should dissolution become necessary because of failure or litigation. Ordinarily, he may be held liable only to the extent of his investment in your partnership.

Unfortunately, a partnership cannot be composed of limited partners alone. In most states, a majority of the capital must be contributed by general partners. Partnership interests, both general and limited, are not readily transferable either; to do so requires approval from the general partners even if a new investor can be found. Thus, the assets of the participants remain relatively frozen in the affairs of the business.

## A3.
## *Type 3: Corporation*

Because of the shortcomings and disadvantages associated with proprietorships and partnerships, there developed a third form of business organization known as the corporation. A **corporation** is a chartered association of individuals in a business enterprise. If you form a corporation with some other individuals, you will receive two significant advantages:

1. **continuous existence** of your business organization
2. **limited financial liability** for all investors

**corporation**

**continuous existence**

**limited financial liability**

On the retirement or death of a shareholder, the corporation's existence is unaffected. The corporation continues to function in legal perpetuity. Transferability of ownership is simple. Normally, as a shareholder (principal) in your corporation, you can be held financially liable and can suffer losses only to the extent of your investment in the corporation. Your personal assets and possessions are not subject to the claims of the creditors of your business.

These privileges are granted to the corporation and its principals by prevalent state statutes. It is the responsibility of the state secretary to validate issuance of a charter to this association and permit it to exist as a recognized legal institution. As a result, corporations can obtain long-term, more permanent forms of capital through offerings of securities, with relative ease.

The corporate form of organization has its disadvantages, too. They include

1. increased record keeping and voluminous paper work;
2. many more taxes to be paid (and at higher rates) than other forms of business enterprise; and
3. closer governmental supervision.

However, these shortcomings are outweighed by the important advantages mentioned above—continued existence and limited liability.

## B.
## establishing the corporation
## B1.
## *State Regulation of Incorporation*

The laws of incorporation vary from state to state, but there are many procedures common to all fifty states. For instance, after approval from the state secretary, a certificate of incorporation (charter) is filed with the county clerk within that state and becomes a matter of public record. At least one petitioner for incorporation must be a citizen of the United States, although not necessarily a citizen or resident of the particular state in which incorporation is petitioned for.

B2.
*Features of the Corporate Charter*

The information required within each charter also varies according to individual state laws, but once again, there are important features common to all states. All states require the following:

1. *Name of the corporation.* The corporate name must be original and precise because, once approved by the state secretary, no other corporation in that state will be permitted to operate using that name or a similar one in the same or similar line of endeavor.

2. *Names and addresses of the incorporators.* The number of persons necessary as incorporators can vary widely; it is as few as one in some states. In any event, this petition is generally filed by an attorney who represents the organizers and who frequently is cited as the principal founder in order to simplify and expedite proceedings. After approval, the lawyer assigns the stock to the true principals in proper proportion to their equity interest.

3. *Location of an office in the state of incorporation.* Although it is not required to engage in business activities from this office, a corporation must maintain an official location within the state of incorporation to receive correspondence and/or subpoena. For simplicity and for tax reasons, many corporations in this country are chartered within the state of Delaware, where they use local concerns to represent them even though they are headquartered and actually do business thousands of miles away.

4. *Purpose of incorporation.* As a legal entity, a corporation may participate only in activities specifically approved by the state secretary. In the securities industry, brokerage firms are particularly affected by this feature. To avoid almost certain litigation, they must not permit a corporation to use their services in arranging unauthorized purchases or sales of securities.

**authorized stock**

5. *Amount of capital stock authorized and issued.* The state secretary permits the corporation to issue a maximum number of shares representative of its capital. It is identified as **authorized stock** in the charter. Otherwise, if the corporation had an unlimited, unrestricted privilege, they could dilute or ''water'' the participation of the already existent shareholders. Any increase in the number of authorized shares necessitates a petition to the state secretary to amend the charter. This petition must be accompanied by evidence of overwhelming support for this proposal among the voting stockholders.

B3.
*Two Basic Types of Capital Stock*

There are actually two distinct forms of capital stock that can be authorized in a charter, preferred and common. Although common stock is *always* found in the capital structure of a corporation, the same is not true for preferred stock. Preferred stock may be likened to a silent partner in a partnership, silent in that it carries no voice in the management of that concern. Consequently, the circumstances and conditions under which such shares can be sold to investors are not applicable to all corporations or suitable for all purchasers. The "preference" these shares have relates generally to the

1. ability to command a fixed dividend payment before common shareholders receive dividends; and
2. prior claim (prior to common shareholders only) to the corporation's assets in the event of its dissolution and liquidation.

**B4.**
*Types of Common Stock*

**B4a.** *AUTHORIZED STOCK*

The directors of the corporation enjoy a good deal of flexibility with **authorized stock** because they rarely distribute all of it when initiating the firm's operation. In exchange for their capital, the investors are allocated only a portion of that authorized stock.

**authorized stock**

**B4b.** *ISSUED-AND-OUTSTANDING STOCK*

This is then called **issued-and-outstanding stock**.

**issued-and-outstanding stock**

**B4c.** *UNISSUED STOCK*

In accordance with their judgment, the directors may further utilize the authorized but **unissued stock** any time in the future for any worthwhile corporate purpose. They can, for example,

1. sell it to raise more capital;
2. distribute it to already existent shareholders as a stock dividend or stock split;
3. present it to key employees as supplementary compensation or bonuses for their good work; or
4. use it as payment for shares of another corporation they want to acquire, be it a merger or merely an investment.

**unissued stock**

The value of the original shares of the corporation is arbitrarily established by the incorporators and the concern's accountants and is usually identified as **par value**. The value of the same shares after issuance, however, is determined by the forces of supply and demand in the marketplace. It is known as **market value**.

**par value**

**market value**

**B4d.** *TREASURY STOCK*

The market price for equity securities is influenced by public psychology, often without regard to underlying basic value. When business news is uninspiring, or even pessimistic, the price of these shares can be depressed partly by the distress sales of the holders. At this time, the directors of the corporation may consider using some of the corporation's cash surplus to repurchase the shares in the open market. Shares that are reacquired through purchase, and occasionally by donation, are identified as **treasury stock**.

**treasury stock**

Let us take an example of a corporation with 1 million shares of authorized stock to see how the stock may be distributed.

| | |
|---|---|
| Issued stock .............................................. | 700,000 |
|    Issued-and-outstanding stock ................650,000 | |
|    Treasury stock................................. 50,000 | |
| Unissued stock............................................. | 300,000 |
| Total authorized stock .....................................1,000,000 | |

When reacquired by the corporation, treasury stock loses some basic privileges and gains a unique accounting characteristic in the process. Treasury stock is not considered by the corporation as outstanding stock when the accountants calculate the company's earnings performance on a per-share basis. It is certainly issued stock, but it is treated for accounting purposes as if the stock were unissued.

Thus, the same amount of net income is apportioned among fewer shares *outstanding*, giving an illusion of increased earnings to the less knowledgeable, and often unwary, investor. Although stock exchange and Securities and Exchange Commission rules do require financial statements to inform investors about the existence of treasury stock, few corporations explain the *effect* of treasury stock ownership to the average investor receiving this report.

Let us show the effect on earnings for our illustrative corporation when it has a net income of $2,500,000.

$$\frac{\$2,500,000 \text{ net income}}{700,000 \text{ shares issued (\textit{including} treasury stock)}} = \$3.57 \text{ earnings per share}$$

$$\frac{\$2,500,000 \text{ net income}}{650,000 \text{ shares issued and outstanding only (\textit{excluding} treasury stock)}} = \$3.85 \text{ earnings per share}$$

Treasury stock does not receive dividend distributions or voting privileges. It would be foolish and inefficient to pay dividends on this stock when no actual distribution ever occurs, nor would it be practical to allow voting privileges. If this practice were permissible, the present management could use the corporation's money to acquire sufficient voting control in order to perpetuate themselves in power.

Properly employed, treasury stock is a valuable tool of management to be utilized in the interest of all stockholders. The directors can use this stock in several ways:

1. They may exchange it for the shares of another corporation with whom they would like to merge.
2. They may use it to fulfill commitments they have made with respect to pension plans, profit-sharing plans, and employment contracts with key personnel.
3. They may reoffer it for sale in the marketplace—hopefully at a profit. If this can be arranged, the shareholders gain another interesting advantage. Ordinarily, the profit on such transactions is not taxable to the corporation.

When and if released or distributed by the corporation, treasury stock regains all lost privileges and once again is identified as outstanding stock of the company.

The types of common stock are summarized in Figure 1.

**Figure 1**
Types of Common Stock

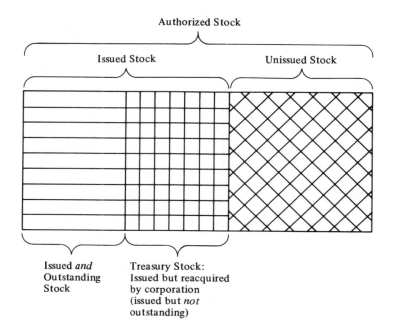

Authorized Stock

Issued Stock

Unissued Stock

Issued *and* Outstanding Stock

Treasury Stock: Issued but reacquired by corporation (issued but *not* outstanding)

*B5.*
*Par Value of Stock*

For bookkeeping reasons, each share of stock in any fledgling corporation is assigned a monetary value representative of the capital with which it has been founded. This valuation is known as the **par value**, and this figure is imprinted on the face of each certificate; for example, 100,000 shares at $2.50 par equals $250,000 value.

**par value**

*B5a.* **PAR VALUE OF COMMON STOCK**

In a few instances, where no such assignment has been made, the certificates are inscribed as **no par value**. But the accountants must, nevertheless, maintain such equity interest at a stated value in preparing financial statements for that concern. The stated value is an arbitrary one that may be closely related to the market value or may even represent money received by the corporation on the original offering of that security. In any event, a par value, or lack of one, has little significance for the common stockholder in

**no par value**

the company. As the underlying owner of the corporation, the common stockholder has the most junior claim upon dividends or assets in the event of liquidation proceedings anyway.

## PAR VALUE OF PREFERRED STOCK

B5b.

But this same commentary does not pertain to any preferred stockholders despite the fact that they too constitute a portion of a corporation's equity capital. Par value does have important significance for the preferred stockholder for the following reasons:

1.  The fixed annual dividend is often expressed as a percentage of the par value; for example, a 5% dividend on a $100 par equals $5 per share annually, while a 5% dividend on a $10 par equals $.50 per share each year.
2.  The preferred holder's claim upon the assets of a corporation in dissolution is frequently represented by that par value, *plus*
    a.  any dividends in arrears, per share; and
    b.  dividends accruable from the last payment date.

Unless otherwise specified, in accordance with state law, common stockholders in a corporation receive some advantages in return for their capital contribution via purchase of issued-and-outstanding stock.

B6.
*Six Benefits Enjoyed by Holders of Common Stock*

### BENEFIT 1: VOTING PRIVILEGE

B6a.

**voting privilege**

A **voting privilege** is the right to decide upon matters of essential interest in the affairs of the corporation. It includes mergers, reorganizations, recapitalizations, and so on, as well as the annual election of directors.

**proxy**

Prior to a meeting, stockholders receive a **proxy** from the company. The proxy is a power of attorney appointing a third party (usually a company representative) to vote for the stockholder if he/she cannot attend the meeting. Shareholders receiving a proxy may vote as they decide or may give this proxy to parties of their choice, permitting them to vote as they see fit. Practices vary among corporations as to how such proxies are applied in the voting process. Some companies employ statutory voting rules; others use cumulative voting procedures.

**statutory voting**

*Statutory voting* In **statutory voting**, you as a stockholder are allocated one vote for each share you hold. You may cast (or refrain from casting) this number for *each* proposal on the agenda or for a nominee for *each* directorship on the ballot, as the case may be. Thus, as the owner of 100 shares, you can cast 100 votes for *each* of five nominees for five directorships to be filled at that election. Majority holders in the corporation, therefore, support statutory voting because they are thus able to make all decisions. Most corporations use statutory voting.

B6a(1).

Any such combinations of vote placement are acceptable in statutory voting so long as you do not vote *more* than 100 shares in favor of any nominee.

*Statutory Voting:* Sample Voting Possibilities for a Stockholder
Owning 100 Shares

|  | Nominee A | Nominee B | Nominee C | Nominee D | Nominee E |
|---|---|---|---|---|---|
| Choice 1 | 100 | 0 | 0 | 0 | 0 |
| Choice 2 | 100 | 100 | 100 | 100 | 100 |
| Choice 3 | 0 | 100 | 0 | 100 | 100 |
| Choice 4 | 0 | 100 | 100 | 0 | 0 |

**B6a(2).**

> ***Cumulative voting***  In **cumulative voting**, you as a stockholder are allocated one vote for each share you hold. But, each share is then multiplied by the *total* number of proposals on the agenda or the *total* number of vacancies to be filled on the board of directors, as the case may be. You may then apportion your total vote as you desire. In the case of the example just given, as the owner of 100 shares you can apportion 500 votes any way you want among the five nominees for the five directorships to be filled at that election.

**cumulative voting**

*Cumulative Voting:* Sample Voting Possibilities for a Stockholder
Owning 100 Shares

|  | Nominee A | Nominee B | Nominee C | Nominee D | Nominee E |
|---|---|---|---|---|---|
| Choice 1 | 500 | 0 | 0 | 0 | 0 |
| Choice 2 | 100 | 300 | 0 | 100 | 0 |
| Choice 3 | 0 | 400 | 100 | 0 | 0 |
| Choice 4 | 200 | 100 | 0 | 0 | 200 |

Any such combinations of vote placement are acceptable in cumulative voting so long as you do not cast *more* than 500 votes for a single nominee for the entire slate of directors as a whole. It is possible, therefore, for minority holders to concentrate their votes, cast them for just a few proposals (directors) that they favor, and significantly increase the probability of passage (election) for their choices.

**B6a(3).**  ***Voting trusts***  If a corporation experiences an extended period of poor operating results, a dissident group may form with the intent of ousting company management. However, they soon discover that deterioration has been extensive and that their plans for recovery are, of necessity, very long term. If successful in a proxy contest, they do not want to risk their own removal from office after only 1 year. Therefore, the dissidents ask the stockholders to deposit their shares into a **voting trust** established by them for the purpose of gaining control of the company. After appointing a commercial bank to act as trustee, the dissidents authorize the bank to issue **voting trust certificates (V.T.C.)** in exchange for the stock deposited.

**voting trust**

**voting trust certificates (V.T.C.)**

The stockholders who deposit the shares and accept a V.T.C. in exchange retain title to any and all privileges normally granted to stockholders *except the right to vote.* They must relinquish the voting privilege for the duration of the trust.[1] The investors who surrender their stock for a V.T.C. cannot recover their certificate until the trust is dissolved by its creators. They do not, however, lose the marketability associated with their original security investment. As a consequence of this special arrangement, two separate markets for these securities are established, one for the V.T.C. and one for the common stock that was not tendered to the dissidents. As a registered representative, you must carefully ascertain which security your client wants to buy or sell before taking any market action because the two securities are not readily interchangeable after the initial appeal.

### BENEFIT 2: DIVIDENDS

B6b.

**dividends**

**Dividends** are distributions to the stockholders when earned and declared by the board of directors. The directors are not compelled to pay out any or all of a corporation's earnings in the form of cash dividends—not even to preferred stockholders. They may have other more important plans for these monies to facilitate the company's growth. The only prior claim preferred stockholders have to corporate dividends is that they must be completely satisfied, including arrearages, before any distribution of cash or stock can be made to common stockholders.

To conserve cash, the board of directors may decline to distribute anything; or they can pay dividends in the form of stock, instead. Shares may be distributed from the corporation's authorized but unissued stock or from treasury stock, if need be. Each common shareholder's percentage of ownership is unaffected, because each shareholder's proportionate interest in the company remains unchanged.

**example**

Upon declaration of a 10% stock dividend, before payment a common stockholder's proportionate interest is:

$$\frac{100 \text{ shares owned}}{1,000,000 \text{ shares issued and outstanding}} = 1/10,000 \text{ interest in the corporation}$$

After payment, percentage ownership in the corporation is:

$$\frac{110 \text{ shares owned}}{1,100,000 \text{ shares issued and outstanding}} = 1/10,000 \text{ interest in the corporation}$$

If a dividend is declared and paid to the investors, it is distributed equally per share to holders whose names appear on the company's records on a date set by the board of directors.

[1] Although voting trusts are subject to state regulation, they generally survive for extended periods, frequently for as long as 10 years.

*B6c.* ## BENEFIT 3: LIMITED ACCESS TO BOOKS AND RECORDS

This aspect of shareowner benefit, called **limited access to books and records**, is germane to compliance with federal, state, exchange, and NASD regulations. All publicly owned corporations registered with the SEC must provide their stockholders with an annual, audited copy of their financial statements prepared by an independent public accountant. Some stock exchanges also require distribution of internally prepared interim statements by the corporation to keep stockholders continuously apprised of the financial condition of their companies. To probe any deeper than the typical balance sheet and income statement usually requires either a court order and/or a close examination of the company's Forms 8K and 10K on file at the SEC. These quarterly and annual reports contain more detailed information than is normally distributed to shareholders. Management is obviously wary about revealing information that can

1. give competitors an advantage; or
2. be used by dissident groups to unseat it.

*B6d.* ## BENEFIT 4: READY TRANSFERABILITY OF SHARES

Changes in ownership may be accomplished at your instruction as the present stockholder. You may give your shares away or sell them to anyone you choose without prior consultation with the directors of the company. Legal restrictions do sometimes exist in a few instances, usually because of previous distributions of stock not registered with the SEC. However, those occasions are infrequent, last for a relatively short period of time, and affect very few shareholders.

*B6e.* ## BENEFIT 5: PROPORTIONATE SHARE OF THE ASSETS IN LIQUIDATION

If the stockholders or the public courts elect to dissolve the corporation and supervise the liquidation of its assets, a definite order of priority prevails for reimbursing the claims of the creditors and the principals. After employees' wages have been paid and federal, state, and local tax authority judgments have been satisfied, all of the corporation's secured and general creditors must be paid in full. What monies remain thereafter are made available for distribution to the stockholders according to their proportionate interest in the company.

If the company's capital structure includes preferred stock as well as common stock, the preferred stockholders must be paid their liquidation rights in the corporation before the common holders can participate. Finally, with no one else left, the common stockholders with a residual claim share in what remains of the assets, pro rata.

*B6f.* ## BENEFIT 6: SUBSCRIPTION PRIVILEGES FOR NEW SHARES

*B6f(1).* **Rights** Sometimes a company gives its stockholders a preferential opportunity to purchase any new shares or bonds it offers to raise additional capital. This is called a **preemptive right** because

**limited access to books and records**

**preemptive right**

it is offered to the stockholders before the general public has a chance to participate. To satisfy federal and stock exchange regulations, a corporation issuing rights must issue one right for each share of stock outstanding. However, the board of directors may stipulate the number of rights necessary for the purchase of one or more shares of the new stock (for example, four rights for one new share, three rights for two new shares, and so on).

The corporation encourages its shareholders to subscribe to the offering by pricing this new security below the price (or value) for the shares outstanding and already trading in the marketplace. This means that the privilege is a valuable one; it can be utilized by the holder or sold to someone who is anxious to take advantage of it by subscribing to this new security.

The price of the new security has an interesting effect on the market. Invariably, when the news of this financing circulates publicly, the market value of the old shares declines somewhat. This is probably due to the belief of some shareholders that the additional supply of stock will overhang the market, preventing a rise in price. Consequently, they sell their shares at prevailing values.

**theoretical value**   After announcement of the offering by the corporation and prior to the physical distribution of these rights to subscribe, investor inquiries usually demand determination of the **theoretical value** of this privilege. The value is *theoretical* in that no actual market for them has been established at this early date. The problem has an easy solution. Simply subtract the price of the new stock from the price of the old stock selling in the marketplace *cum rights* (with the rights attached). Then, divide this difference by the number of rights necessary for one new share *plus an additional right*. The formula for calculating theoretical value is:

$$\frac{\text{market price of old stock cum rights} - \text{subscription price of new stock}}{\text{number of rights needed to buy one share} + 1} = \text{theoretical value of one right}$$

If the stockholder receives too few rights to subscribe to a full share, the corporation normally allows him to "round up." As an example, suppose a stockholder owned 10 shares of stock and as a result received 10 rights. Suppose further, that the terms of the offer allowed the stockholder to subscribe to one share for each four rights. This would allow the stockholder to subscribe to 2½ shares. The company normally would allow the subscription for a full three shares and charge the stockholder a small fee for the "round-up." On the other hand, if the stockholder only wanted to subscribe to two shares, the company would sell the two unused rights and forward the proceeds to the stockholder.

**example**

To illustrate calculation of the theoretical value of this subscription privilege, suppose the corporation permits its stockholders to subscribe to one share of stock at $45 for each four shares of that stock currently owned and trading at $55 at the marketplace. We calculate as follows:

$$\text{Theoretical value} = \frac{\$55 - \$45}{4 + 1} = \frac{\$10}{5} = \$2$$

To prove the accuracy of this procedure, suppose that four "old" shares were purchased at $55 per share, at a total cost of $220.[2] If rights attached to those shares are then used to purchase one new share at $45, the total expenditure amounts to $265 ($220 + $45). However, the investor now owns five shares of that security. Therefore, the investor's average cost per share is $53 ($265 ÷ 5). Because the old stock originally cost $55 per share, the subscription privilege is worth $2.

Occasionally, the directors find it convenient to establish a subscription ratio expressed in a fashion other than in terms of one new share. They may decide to allow the purchase of two new shares for every three old shares held, or even three new shares for every five old shares held, and so on. Such an approach does not change the use of the prescribed formula. It merely adds an extra step by requiring the ratio to be translated into terms of subscription to one new share. The following examples use the prices from the previous example.

## examples

(1) If the ratio is three old shares for every two new shares:

$$\text{Theoretical value} \;=\; \frac{\$55 - \$45}{{}^{3}\!/_{2} + 1} \;=\; \frac{10}{2\frac{1}{2}} \;=\; \$4$$

(2) If the ratio is five old shares for every three new shares:

$$\text{Theoretical value} \;=\; \frac{\$55 - \$45}{{}^{5}\!/_{3} + 1} \;=\; \frac{10}{2^{2}\!/_{3}} \;=\; \$3.75$$

When the old stock begins trading in the marketplace without the subscription privilege attached to the price (*ex rights*),[3] it signifies that preemptive rights have been physically issued and distributed and a separate, actual market value for them has been determined. At this point, *do not* add one to the subscription ratio when dividing the difference between old and new stock prices. The old stock price already reflects the reduction in value. Let us use the original figure to illustrate this.

## example

$$\text{Theoretical value} = \frac{\$53 \text{ old stock ex rights ("rights off ")} - \$45 \text{ new stock}}{4}$$

$$= \frac{8}{4}$$

$$= \$2$$

[2]Ignoring odd-lot fees, commissions, and so on for the purpose of this illustration.

[3]This occurs on the first business day after the rights begin trading as a separate security in the marketplace.

A preemptive right is not granted to the stockholder for an indefinite time period. The holder must act to subscribe or sell these rights, generally within 30 to 60 days after issuance. If the stockholder does not act before the deadline set by the corporation, the rights expire and are worthless.

If the market price of the old shares fluctuates below the subscription price of the new shares during the effective lifetime of the offering, those rights will be mathematically worthless as long as that condition prevails. Normally, the corporation will not risk the possibility of an unsuccessful rights offering because

1. it would fail to obtain the needed capital;
2. this obvious lack of investor confidence would damage its reputation; and
3. the directors would be publicly embarrassed before their competitors for exercising such poor judgment.

If such a possibility exists, the corporation can employ the services of an investment banker to guarantee purchase of any new shares not subscribed for by the rights holders through subscription for personal account and risk. Let us assume that the corporation employs Peter Weldon as an investment banker.

Investment banker Peter Weldon does not actually know his exact commitment at the time of the agreement with the corporation. He must stand by until the expiration date and wait to see the extent of his financial responsibility. He may not need to purchase any of those shares; then again, he may need to purchase all of them. This factor is taken into consideration when the fee for this service is negotiated. The arrangement is known as a **stand-by underwriting agreement**.

**stand-by underwriting agreement**

*Warrants*  Some corporations attempting to raise capital through issuance of securities make these offerings attractive by attaching **warrants** to the new securities. They structure it as a package deal rather than tie the subscription rights to the old certificates in order to stimulate investor interest. A warrant gives its holder a *long-term* privilege to subscribe to common stock; shares are specifically reserved for this potentiality by the corporation.[4] A warrant normally has an expiration date set 5 to 10 years after date of issuance. Some warrants, however, expire after a longer interval, and a few, called *perpetual warrants*, never expire.

**warrants**

*B6f(2).*

Each warrant can be used to subscribe to one or more shares of stock, as determined by the corporation's board of directors. The number of warrants attached to each certificate offered is also determined by the board after it considers what must be done to attract capital investment. Longer-term warrants often provide for changes in subscription price and conditions every few years. This allows for opportunity to speculate or trade in them as the underlying stock appreciates or merely fluctuates in price.

What is unique about a warrant compared to a right is that the subscription price at the time of the original offering is *higher* than the current market price of the underlying stock. In terms of market value, at its initial offering a warrant is mathematically

[4]This reserve comes out of authorized but unissued stock or even treasury stock earmarked for this purpose.

> worthless. Its appeal is strictly speculative, based upon the possibility of higher percentage gain within its effective lifetime.

The opportunity to acquire warrants at no additional cost with the purchase of another valuable security issued by the corporation

1. entices speculators to risk their capital; and
2. affords the corporation an opportunity to raise long-term funds at reasonable cost.

This attachment is a very effective way to ''sweeten'' a somewhat speculative offering of securities and make it more palatable for prospective investors.

## B7.
## Preferred Stock

### B7a. REASONS FOR AND CONDITIONS

As a way of attracting investors to become owners of a corporation, the directors may decide to offer preferred stock. Preferred stock has certain attractions over common stock. Preferred stock represents equity in the corporation, but to a limited degree. The preferred stockholders have little or no voice in the management of the company. In return for their money, they must be paid a fixed dividend before any payment is made to the common stockholders. In liquidation proceedings, the preferred stockholder's claim to the corporation's assets enjoys a priority over the common stockholder's claims.

### B7b. PREFERRED STOCK TYPED BY CONCESSIONS

Admittedly, these characteristics are relatively unattractive to today's investors when, for the same money, they can enjoy a comparable return through ownership of a bond and have senior status as creditors of the company. A corporation intent upon a successful offering of preferred stock must be prepared to make further concessions to attract the investing public. These special privileges enable us to classify preferred stock into five distinct types.

### B7c. CUMULATIVE PREFERRED

> **Cumulative preferred stock** permits a stockholder to lay claim to any dividends that were omitted by the corporation in previous years. *Cumulative* means that any deferred dividends will accumulate, and it requires that this arrearage be paid in full before any distribution is permitted to the common stockholder. A noncumulative preferred stock offers no such assurance to its holders. Any dividends passed are gone forever and no longer represent a commitment by the corporation to those stockholders.

**cumulative preferred stock**

### B7d. PARTICIPATING PREFERRED

> **Participating preferred stock** offers the privilege of receiving extra dividends, if declared by the directors of the corporation.

**participating preferred stock**

After all preferred stockholders (including participating stockholders) receive their usual fixed dividend and the common stockholders have been paid their previously determined normal dividend, additional distributions must include the participating preferred stockholders equally with the common stockholders. Understandably, a corporation in need of capital is reluctant to include this feature in a preferred issue except as a last resort because it infringes upon a most attractive feature for becoming a common stockholder.

### CONVERTIBLE PREFERRED

B7e.

**convertible preferred stock**

*Attractiveness*  **Convertible preferred stock** enables the stockholders to exchange their shares for a predetermined number of shares of common stock in the company any time they choose to do so. It is understandable that the value of this type of preferred stock is influenced by the fluctuations in price of the common stock because the holder enjoys the best features of both preferred and common stock at the same time. It is a very attractive feature and enables the corporation's directors to pay a lower fixed dividend on this issue than they would without it.

B7e(1).

**conversion ratio**

*Conversion ratio*  The terms of an issue's convertibility are set at the time the corporation offers it in exchange for capital. It may state that this preferred stock shall always be convertible into 2 shares of common stock at the holder's option—or into 3.3 shares or 4½ shares or some other such number as management deems necessary to make the preferred sale a success. When expressed in this fashion, the ratio of underlying common stock available for each share of convertible preferred is called the **conversion ratio.**

Not all corporations present conversion features in those terms, however. The conversion terms of the convertible preferred stock can become complicated in the event the corporation subsequently issues more common shares in the form of stock dividends or reorganizes its capital structure through a stock split. To provide for these and other potential maneuvers involving common stock, the corporation invariably guarantees the convertible preferred stockholders against dilution of their equity interest in the concern. This means that those preferred stockholders will be entitled to a proportionately larger number of common shares. This enables them to maintain the same percentage of underlying ownership in the company if and when they convert into common. As a result, the conversion ratio may become unwieldy, perhaps extending to as many as five or six decimal places (for example, 3.21647 shares).

B7e(2).

**conversion price**

*Conversion price*  To avoid those cumbersome fractions, some corporations express convertibility in terms of a **conversion price**. The conversion price is simply a market value level for underlying common stock at which the preferred holder *may* begin to find it economically feasible to convert into common stock. At the time of a preferred stock offering, the initial conversion price is often set from 10 to 15% above the prevailing market price of the common stock. This higher price helps to avoid the prospect of immediate or near-term conversion by the preferred stockholders, which would defeat the whole purpose of the offering. The conversion price indirectly reveals the conversion ratio of that

B7e(3).

issue, too. When divided into the par value of each preferred share, the conversion price discloses the number of common shares receivable upon exchange. The formula for determining the conversion ratio based on the conversion price and par value is:

$$\frac{\text{Common shares receivable}}{\text{upon conversion}} = \frac{\text{par value of preferred stock}}{\text{conversion price}}$$

**B7e(4).** ***Conversion examples*** The problems of dilution and resulting cumbersome fractions are easily resolved with the formula above. Even with adjustments, the conversion price figure rarely extends beyond the fourth decimal place. Moreover, investors relate easily to dollar prices in making value judgments regarding conversion feasibility.

Let's look at a typical example of how this procedure is handled. Suppose XYZ Industries issued a convertible preferred stock with a $100 par value and a $40.50 conversion price. We apply the conversion ratio formula:

## example

$$\text{Common shares receivable} = \frac{\$100}{\$40.50}$$
$$\text{Common shares receivable} = 2.4691$$

Let's carry this example further. Let's assume that with the common stock at $36 the board of directors votes to split the common stock two for one. Because its preferred holders are protected against dilution, the conversion price must be halved to enable those investors to obtain twice as many shares as before, upon conversion. To determine that price, or to prove the accuracy of that statement, first multiply the former shares receivable by the number of shares to be received for each share now held. Then, divide the par value of the stock by that new number.

Step 1: $2.4691 \times 2 = 4.9382$

Step 2: $\dfrac{\$100 \text{ par value}}{4.9382} = \$20.25$ conversion price

In an arithmetically efficient marketplace, the trading level of the old stock will also be adjusted. It should revise itself to a level where the total shares now receivable upon conversion are worth the same amount of money as the old share package was worth at $36 per share. Thus:

Step 1: $\$36 \times 2.4691 = \$88.887$

Step 2: $\dfrac{\$88.887}{4.9382} = \$18$ revised market price per share

Now, let us assume the board of directors votes to pay a 10% stock dividend soon after this with the common stock price still at $18 per share. Both the conversion price and the conversion ratio must be adjusted again. Using the same approach as that described above, the new conversion ratio will be:

$4.9382 \times 1.1a = 5.4320$ new shares obtainable upon conversion

aOne-tenth of a share for each new share.

The new conversion price becomes:

$$\frac{\$100 \text{ par value}}{5.4320} = \$18.409$$

The adjusted market level per share after the distribution is effective should be:

Before: $\$18 \times 4.9382 = \$88.887$

After: $\dfrac{\$88.887}{5.4320} = \$16.36$ new market level per share

Keep in mind that although the common shares may be split up or down, stock dividends paid, or other distributions accomplished, the par value of preferred stock remains fixed for its entire lifetime. Any adjustments necessitated by those distributions are effected through changes in the preferred issue's conversion ratio and conversion price.

Determining a preferred stock's conversion ratio via its conversion price used to be a relatively simple chore; it was generally set at $100. Then, for certain sales and marketing reasons, increasing numbers of corporations began issuing $50 and $25 par value preferred stock. Since then, although the formula still works, it is difficult to calculate an accurate conversion ratio without knowing the specific par value of that particular issue.

***When to convert***    Earlier, it was stressed that the conversion price was a market level for common stock at which the convertible preferred stockholder may begin to find it economically feasible to convert into common. In practice, it doesn't often work out that way unless the preferred issue is being retired by the corporation under an option it normally reserves for that purpose. Generally, convertible preferred stockholders are better off holding their shares or selling them in the open market. Because, as the price of common stock rises up near and through the conversion price, the convertible preferred stock invariably trades at a premium price, that is, at a value above the worth of the underlying common shares. This is caused by the preferred stock's usually higher dividend rate, its status as a security senior to the common stock, and its overall ability to enjoy the best features of both securities concurrently.

*B7e(5).*

It is important, however, to be able to determine the extent of premium at which the preferred sells above *parity* at any time. The premium is a critical basis upon which value judgments are made in our efficient marketplace. We define **parity** as a price relationship between convertible preferred and common at which neither profit or loss is realized by

**parity**

1. purchase of the convertible issue;
2. exchanging it for common shares; and,
3. immediate sale of the common shares in the marketplace.

The formula for calculating parity is:

$$\frac{\text{par value of the convertible}}{\text{conversion price}} = \frac{\text{market price of the convertible}}{\text{market price of the common}}$$

**B7e(6).** **_Calculating parity_**  To apply the concept illustrated by this formula, let's calculate parity prices for the following four examples:

(1) Assume that a $100 par convertible preferred stock with a $25 conversion price is selling at $78. If it was selling at parity with the common, where must the common stock be trading?

$$\frac{\$100 \text{ par value}}{\$25 \text{ conversion price}} = \frac{\$78}{x}$$

$$100\,x = \$78 \times \$25$$
$$100\,x = \$1,950$$
$$x = \$19.50$$

This problem was relatively easy because with a $25 conversion price we recognize the conversion ratio to be a simple four shares. Then, logically, if four shares are equal to a $78 package, each share is worth one-fourth of that, or $19.50

(2) What is the parity price of underlying common stock if the $100 par convertible preferred has a $36.20 conversion price and is trading at 91¼?

$$\frac{\$100 \text{ par value}}{\$36.20 \text{ conversion price}} = \frac{\$91.25}{x}$$

$$100\,x = \$91.25 \times \$36.20$$
$$100\,x = \$3,303.25$$
$$x = \$33.03$$

(3) If a common stock is selling at 15¾, what is the parity price of the $25 par value convertible preferred stock with a conversion price of $21.40?

$$\frac{\$25 \text{ par value}}{\$21.40 \text{ conversion price}} = \frac{x}{\$15.75}$$

$$\$21.40\,x = \$25 \times \$15.75$$
$$\$21.40\,x = \$393.75$$
$$x = \$18.40$$

(4) When a $50 par value preferred stock is convertible into 2.4 shares of common stock and the preferred is trading at $56, what is parity for the common? Because the formula is dependent upon the conversion price and not the conversion ratio, we must first translate that ratio into the conversion price. We calculate the conversion price by dividing the preferred stock's par value by the conversion ratio:

$$\frac{\$50 \text{ par value}}{2.4 \text{ shares}} = \$20.83 \text{ conversion price}$$

Then,

$$\frac{\$50 \text{ par value}}{\$20.83 \text{ conversion price}} = \frac{\$56}{x}$$

$$50\,x = \$56 \times \$20.83$$
$$50\,x = \$1,166.48$$
$$x = \$23.33$$

**prior preferred stock**

**Prior preferred stock** also known as preference stock, is a somewhat ambiguous designation applied to some preferred stock issues. It generally refers to a seniority of one preferred stock over another with respect to:

1. receipt of dividends; or
2. a claim upon the assets of the corporation in the event of dissolution.

The extent of that superiority is not readily discernible from the title alone. To make such a determination necessitates a careful examination of

1. the offering prospectus when the issue was initially distributed; or
2. a manual of corporate information published by Moody's, Standard & Poor's, or some other statistical services publication.

*CALLABLE PREFERRED*

**callable preferred stock**

**Callable preferred stock** permits the corporation to retire the issue at its option. It can do so by paying these preferred stockholders a specified value for their shares. If it recalls their stock in the first few years after issuance, the corporation also pays them a small premium for their inconvenience. But, the size of the premium declines as the age of the stock increases until finally, after about 9 or 10 years, these preferred stockholders receive only the face value of their certificates if the company exercises its call privilege.                                                 *B7g.*

Exercise of a call is considered by the corporation only when (1) the terms of an older issue are economically unsuitable for it and (2) it can obtain the same funds under more favorable terms and conditions in existing money markets. Periodic partial calls of an issue are not unusual either; in this case, the certificates are selected for redemption in an unbiased lottery.

The recall value of a callable preferred stock may be

1. the *par*, or face, value appearing on each certificate (stated per share);
2. greater than par value;
3. somewhat higher than the existing market price prior to the call announcement if this action was unanticipated; or
4. lower than the existing market price prior to the call announcement if
   a. money market conditions warranted a somewhat higher market price and a call was unexpected; or

**b.** that stock was also convertible, and the present value of the preferred was comparable to the high market value of the common.[5]

Since the depression of the 1930s, most corporations insist upon some call feature in their preferred stock offerings, even if they concede to making the issue noncallable for the first 3 or 5 years. Without a call feature, the corporation could be committing itself to paying comparatively high dividends on a particular issue for the rest of its corporate life.

Not to be overlooked is the possibility of incorporating any or all of these features into the same issue. It is possible for a corporation to offer a cumulative, participating, convertible, callable, prior, preferred stock if it becomes desperate for capital and cannot obtain it another way. The various types of preferred stock are summarized in Table 1.

**TABLE 1**
FIVE TYPES OF PREFERRED STOCK

| TYPE OF STOCK | CHARACTERISTICS |
|---|---|
| Cumulative preferred | Claims previously deferred dividends before common stock can share in profits |
| Participating preferred | Can receive extra dividends beyond fixed amount |
| Convertible preferred | Can exchange shares for common stock |
| Prior preferred | Claims seniority over other preferred stocks in payment of dividends or in distribution of assets if the corporation goes out of business |
| Callable preferred | Gets premium price if stock is redeemed soon after issuance otherwise, only par value if company retires it |

**CONCLUDING COMMENTS**

We have examined how a corporation finances itself with common and preferred stock. There are definite advantages to the corporation form of business, and common stock and preferred stock each have their own advantages. The corporation's board of directors must make decisions about issuing these types of stock in terms of the status and future of the company. In the same way, investors must decide which type of stock, if any, they will purchase. There is no single, simple answer.

---

[5]In this situation, the corporation can painlessly eliminate the preferred stock by exercising its call privilege, thereby forcing conversion into common with a minimal outlay of cash on its part. What little cash is needed will pay off those few holders who neglected to convert within the time period specified. For example, a share of preferred stock is callable at $100 and convertible into two shares of common. When the common is selling at $60 per share,

$$2 \text{ shares of common} \times \$60 = \$120$$

Therefore, each share of preferred stock is also comparable to $120 in value. The corporation can call the preferred stock at $100, knowing that unless the holders converted into two shares of common, they would ''lose'' $20 in market value for their investment—in effect, forcing them to convert.

# debt securities

Bonds of all issuers have had appeal throughout U.S. history for two major reasons:

A.
introduction to bonds

*Ready marketability.* They are more liquid than real estate and most other investment mediums. This is due to the fact that (1) they can be bought or sold at minimum expense; (2) they pledge to pay a fixed amount of interest over their lifetime; (3) they must be redeemed at face value on a specific date; (4) they can be maintained in a portfolio without annual carrying charges or maintenance fees; and (5) they command a determinable investment value because of their senior securities status and the credit worthiness of their issuer.

A1.
*Reasons for Buying Bonds*

2. *Ready negotiability.* They are easily transferable from seller to purchaser. Bonds are issued in *bearer* or *registered* form. **Bearer bond certificates** do not have their owner's name imprinted on them and come with interest coupons attached. When an interest payment is due, the holder merely clips off a coupon with the appropriate date inscribed and deposits it in a bank (as would also be necessary with the deposit of an ordinary check). Bearer securities are as freely interchangeable between investors as ordinary currency in an individual's pocket.

**bearer bond certificates**

**registered**

When discussing a bond certificate, the term **registered** signifies that the holder's name and address are inscribed in the issuer's records for the purpose of (1) sending communications to the appropriate holders; (2) making direct repayment of the principal amount at maturity, or earlier, and/or, (3) disbursing periodic payments of interest on this debt. Bonds can often be issued registered as to **principal only** or **interest only**, or they may be **fully registered**. Permissibility for one form or the other, or any variation thereof, is determined by the issuer at the time of the initial offering. Bonds registered as to *principal only* have the holder's name inscribed on the certificate, with the interest coupons attached. Bonds registered as to *interest only* are bearer certificates, but the holder's name and address are registered with the issuer for the purpose of disbursing interest checks. *Fully registered* bonds look like stock certificates. This means that there are no coupons attached, and principal and interest payments are made directly to the holder recorded on the issuer's books.

**principal only
interest only
fully registered**

A2.
*Registration of Bonds*

Corporations employ various means to raise capital. As discussed in the previous chapter, corporations can sell stock. Their short-term requirements (5 years or less) may be satisfied by bank loans, promissory notes, or certificates offered privately or publicly. But for long-term borrowing of capital involving significant sums of money, corporations must turn to debt financing through an offering of bonds.

Bond offerings require considerable investor trust and confidence in the issuer's ability to honor an obligation over an extended period of years. As a result, small, relatively unknown, or asset-poor companies can be denied the ability to finance themselves by selling bonds. Sometimes, however, these small, unknown corporations are affiliates or subsidiaries of much larger businesses that may be willing to pledge their own reputation or

B.
corporate debt

assets to secure such loans. The resulting debt instruments of the subsidiary are then referred to as **guaranteed bonds**. Interest payments and/or principal repayments are thus backed or assured by the parent concern, a corporation other than the issuer. Using this technique, many local railroads were able to develop extensive trackage in the early years of the twentieth century.

## B1.
### Basic Differences between Stocks and Bonds

There are basic differences between stock and bonds that must be understood before we continue any further.

| STOCK | BOND |
|---|---|
| A share of stock represents fractional *ownership* in the corporation. | A bond certificate represents *creditorship* in a corporation. |
| An owner receives *dividends*, as earned and declared by the corporation. | A creditor receives *interest* that must be paid when due. |
| The *lifetime* of stock is *continuous* with the existence of the corporation. | The *lifetime* of a bond is *limited* to a specific maturity date when that obligation must be repaid.[1] |

Broadly speaking, it is frequently more advantageous for a corporation to borrow money than to obtain funds through the issuance of stock. If there is continuing economic inflation, capital procured under current terms and conditions can be repaid at maturity in "cheaper dollars." Furthermore, interest requirements payable on debt instruments are fully deductible from the corporation's taxable income, whereas dividend distributions to stockholders represent after-tax, nondeductible earnings. For corporations in the usual 46% tax bracket, this means that the federal government is bearing 46% of the corporation's interest burden.[2]

These reasons do not necessarily mean that corporations with a borrowing capability should exercise this privilege. Only companies with an opportunity to generate greater income than the cost of issuing and carrying debt securities should use this measure as a means of **leveraging** their capital.[3]

A company that borrows in this manner, hoping to increase significantly the return for the common stockholder, is said to be "trading on the equity." This practice may prove to be perilous in declining cycles of the economy. The corporation continually faces a significant amount of preferential fixed charges that must be satisfied from current income before any stockholders can participate. It has literally traded for capital at the expense of its stockholders.

## C.
### corporate bonds

Because bonds are debt securities, they are classified by the *type of protection* extended to creditors rather than by *concessions granted* to stockholders to make a particular stock offering appealing.

[1]Most bonds mature on a particular date 20 to 30 years after issuance. On rare occasions, a corporation may issue debt instruments without a maturity date. These are called perpetual bonds. Canadian Pacific 4% consolidated debentures are an example.

[2]Not including state and local tax requirements, if any.

[3]*Leverage* is a financial condition evidenced by a high percentage of debt in relation to equity in a corporation's capital structure. This type of capitalization is highly speculative because a company's profits and its ability to honor obligations are extremely sensitive even to minor changes in sales and income.

**mortgage bonds**

**Mortgage bonds** are the most prevalent form of secured obligation in this country today. The investor's protection rests upon the pledge of the real assets of the corporation, such as real estate. At the time of the offering, the property is valued for more than the amount of money borrowed so that the bondholder has significant protection. If the borrowing agreement has an *open-end* provision, the corporation can use that same property as collateral for future borrowing. Those future creditors will have an equal claim to that property in the event of default.

On the other hand, if the agreement is drawn with a *closed-end* provision, any future borrowing using the same property as collateral will be junior to the claims of the previous bondholders. Several heavily indebted corporations have thus issued first, second, and third mortgage bonds, all secured by the same piece of property. The first mortgage bondholder has a senior claim on this real estate if the company defaults upon payment of interest or repayment of principal.

Sometimes, when a company's financial condition deteriorates to such an extent that money becomes critical for continuing operation or even existence, the mortgage bondholders may be requested to forego their status in favor of a new class of creditors willing to lend capital. With approval, the corporation issues a new bond whose purchasers assume the seniority of the first mortgage bondholders. Accordingly, this debt instrument is identified as a **prior lien bond.**

**prior lien bond**

**indenture**

When dealing in debt securities, it is most important for investors to understand the terms of the borrowing agreement. This agreement is referred to as an **indenture.** It is merely a deed of trust established between the corporation and its creditors that specifies the full terms of the borrowing arrangement. Its provisions include such information as

1. the rate of interest, with time and means of payment clearly stated;
2. the date of maturity and any terms or conditions for repayment of principal prior to maturity;
3. a detailed description of any collateral pledged, with priorities established for the bondholders in the event of default; and
4. the name and address of the party responsible for supervisory compliance with the terms of this agreement (the trustee).

Under the Trust Indenture Act of 1939 for public offerings of debt securities, an independent trustee must be appointed by the corporation to safeguard the interest of the creditors and insure that the company abides by the terms of the borrowing agreement. The trustee is usually a commercial bank.

*TYPE 2: COLLATERAL TRUST BONDS*

**collateral trust bonds**

In the case of **collateral trust bonds,** the corporation pledges a portfolio of securities held in trust by a commercial bank, as protection for the holders of these debt instruments. This arrangement might be used by a corporation having a substantial interest in another valuable, perhaps subsidiary, corporation. Thus, if American Telephone and Telegraph Corporation wanted to issue a collateral trust bond, it could do so by pledging the shares of Western Electric Corporation, a subsidiary.

The credit rating of this type of bond is quite good because the indenture usually requires additional collateral to be deposited or immediate repayment of the loan if the pledged security value declines to a level that may jeopardize the creditors' protection.

### C1c.  *TYPE 3: EQUIPMENT TRUST BONDS*

**Equipment trust bonds** pledge machinery, such as the working equipment the corporation normally employs in its everyday operation, as collateral for the loan. Railroads, truckers, airlines, and oil companies typically turn to this means of financing for their purchases of locomotives, freight carriers, trucks, aircraft, oil-drilling rigs, and so forth.

**equipment trust bonds**

The typical equipment trust bond offering is arranged under what is known as the **Philadelphia Plan**. Its terms provide for an equity downpayment by the issuer of bonds (who is also the user of the equipment) equal to 20% of the total cost needed to buy the equipment. The issuing corporation also appoints an independent trustee (usually a large commercial bank) to

**Philadelphia Plan**

1. take title to the equipment purchased (the corporation only leases it until the entire debt is retired);
2. supervise the insuring and maintenance of the equipment;
3. disburse interest payments to the bondholders from the lease payments made by the corporation; and
4. repay principal at maturity or, if redeemed earlier, by accelerated payments from the corporation.

Title to the equipment officially passes to the corporation after the entire issue is retired. This type of issue requires repayment of a portion of the borrowing each year by setting a series of maturity dates for the entire debt over consecutive years. This self-liquidating debt arrangement is described as a **serial bond.** (See Figure 1.)

**serial bond**

Often, a significantly smaller amount comes due for redemption in the first few years after issuance than in later years. This permits the corporation to build revenues with the new equipment acquired via the borrowing. This graduated redemption procedure is called a **balloon effect**. This balloon effect offers investors a further degree of protection through constant reduction of the debt, and, as a result, these bonds are usually well rated. Moreover, because all companies in each of these industries (railroads, truckers, airlines, and oil companies) use basically identical equipment, the collateral can be sold without difficulty if the issuer defaults. This type of bondholder protection makes equipment trust securities quite appealing to most investors.

Serial bonds with ballooning maturities and ballooning interest rates are not used only for equipment trust obligations. The principle of changing rates and/or maturation amounts over the

New Issue / January 9, 1976

# $15,000,000
(Second and Final Installment)

# Norfolk and Western Railway Company

## Equipment Trust, Series No. 2

### 8% Equipment Trust Certificates
#### Non-Callable

To be dated October 1, 1975. To mature in 15 annual installments
of $1,000,000 on each October 1 from 1976 to 1990.

Issued under the Philadelphia Plan with 20% original cash equity.

MATURITIES AND YIELDS

| 1976 | 6.00% | 1980 | 7.60% | 1984 | 7.90% | 1988 | 8.00% |
|------|-------|------|-------|------|-------|------|-------|
| 1977 | 6.85  | 1981 | 7.65  | 1985 | 8.00  | 1989 | 8.00  |
| 1978 | 7.25  | 1982 | 7.70  | 1986 | 8.00  | 1990 | 8.00  |
| 1979 | 7.40  | 1983 | 7.80  | 1987 | 8.00  |      |       |

These certificates are offered subject to prior sale, when, as and if issued and
received by us, subject to approval of the Interstate Commerce Commission.

**Salomon Brothers**

**Blyth Eastman Dillon & Co.**
Incorporated

**Drexel Burnham & Co.**
Incorporated

**FIGURE 1**
Equipment trust serial bond

**TABLE 1**
A TYPICAL BALLOON INTEREST RATE SCHEDULE
(PARTIAL SCHEDULE OF A MUNICIPAL BOND)

| PRINCIPAL AMOUNT | MATURITY | INTEREST RATE (%) | YIELD OR PRICE (%)a |
|------------------|----------|-------------------|---------------------|
| $400,000 | 1973 | 4¼ | 3.00 |
| 400,000  | 1974 | 4¼ | 3.25 |
| 395,000  | 1975 | 4¼ | 3.50 |
| 395,000  | 1976 | 4½ | 3.75 |
| 400,000  | 1977 | 4½ | 3.90 |
| 410,000  | 1978 | 4½ | 4.00 |
| 405,000  | 1979 | 4¾ | 4.10 |
| 405,000  | 1980 | 4¾ | 4.20 |
| 405,000  | 1981 | 4¾ | 4.25 |

a Accrued interest to be added.

life of an issue is also typical of municipal revenue bonds discussed later in this chapter. (See Table 1.)

### TYPE 4: DEBENTURES                                                      C1d.

A **debenture** is an *unsecured* debt offering of a corporation. It promises only the general assets (sometimes referred to merely as goodwill and reputation) as protection for the holders of these securities. Debentures are most often offered as subordinated debt instruments by corporations. This means that, although they are classified as liabilities of a given corporation, they are junior in ranking (subordinate) to the claims of all other creditors in the event of dissolution. Holders of a subordinated debenture realize that as unsecured creditors of the corporation they have a claim to asset priority only over stockholders in the company.

Only companies with superior credit ratings or corporations that are fixed-asset-poor are capable of marketing debentures successfully. The corporation with a high credit rating is able to borrow at lower rates of interest than is one with no rating or no assets at all. The rate of interest on any loan is directly related to the degree of risk involved. High risk equals high interest expense for the borrower to compensate the creditors for their financial exposure.

The various kinds of protection available to holders of the four types of bonds just discussed are summarized briefly in Table 2.

**TABLE 2**
PROTECTION AVAILABLE TO BONDHOLDERS

| TYPE OF BOND | PROTECTION AVAILABLE TO BONDHOLDER |
|---|---|
| Mortgage | Pledges real assets, such as real estate |
| Collateral Trust | Pledges portfolio of corporation's securities in another company |
| Equipment Trust | Pledges machinery, such as railroad cars and planes |
| Debentures | *Unsecured*; pledges only the general assets, which are intangible assets such as goodwill and reputation |

**C2.**
**Default on payment**

If the corporation is unable to pay interest on the date prescribed in the bond's indenture or it is unable to repay the principal at maturity, the trustees, in behalf of the holders of the foregoing four instruments, can, through judicial process under Chapter X of the Bankruptcy Act, lay claim to the assets securing these loans. This action often forces the management of the company to counterclaim with its own suit in a Chapter XI petition, asking continuing control and protection from its creditors.

If management's appeal is denied, it has only two options:

1. liquidation of the assets to salvage what is left
2. continuance of the corporation through reorganization and deferral of debt repayments or, in general, holding all creditors' immediate claims in abeyance.

**C2a.** **APPOINTMENT OF A RECEIVER IN BANKRUPTCY**

One of these options will be chosen by the presiding judge in the Chapter X proceedings. Before making this decision, the judge seeks the advice of an expert in this industry and gives that expert necessary authority to direct the corporation while investigating the causes and alternatives in this predicament. The court-appointed administrator of a corporation that has failed is called a **receiver in bankruptcy**. The receiver is granted remuneration by the court from the remaining assets of the company.

receiver in
bankruptcy

**C2b.** **THE RECEIVER'S ALTERNATIVES**

**C2b(1).** ***Receivers' certificates of indebtedness*** The receiver, in immediate need of working capital to keep the corporation operating during the inquiry, can satisfy this urgency through issuance of receivers' certificates of indebtedness. These are short-term debt obligations of a bankrupt corporation that assume a priority for payment of interest and repayment of principal over all other outstanding creditors of the company. Within the 90- to 120-day lifetime of these certificates, the receiver, with support of the courts, must decide upon and implement a solution to the problem. If the receiver liquidates the assets at this time, the holders of the mortgage, collateral trust, equipment trust, and/or debenture bonds might be fortunate to get back 50 cents for each dollar of investment. Forced liquidations, like fire sales, never command top prices on an auction block.

*Income bonds*  Reorganization, on the other hand, might offer those creditors a better chance of recouping their investment over an extended period of time. Effecting a reorganization requires a greater amount of new, more permanent capital than that raised by receivers' certificates. But, at the same time, how can one acquire long-term financing for a corporation already in bankruptcy and besieged by its creditors?

*C2b(2).*

The answer to this interesting paradox rests in the receiver's ability to eliminate the immediate claims of those creditors. The receiver attempts to do this by offering them a larger principal amount of higher-interest-bearing **income bonds** in exchange for their debt issues. That is, the offer might be $1,300 of a 10% income bond for each $1,000 of a 6% mortgage bond in default.

**income bonds**

Income bonds are long-term debt obligations that promise to pay interest only when, as, and if earned by the corporation. If the earnings of the corporation do not warrant current payment of the interest, the amount accrues, similar to cumulative preferred stock, without further legal difficulty. As a natural consequence of the uncertainty of interest payments, income bonds usually trade in the marketplace without accrued interest calculable as an addition to the contract price. Thus, they are said to be trading "flat," unlike other debt securities, which normally trade on an "and interest" basis. The receiver and the successor management need not concern themselves about repayment of the principal amount because these bonds frequently carry maturity dates of 150 to 200 years after issuance.

It is true that if the bondholders agree to accept income bonds, permitting reorganization to proceed, they are, for the time being, receiving a bigger piece of nothing! But this recourse may represent their only chance of ever recovering their original investment. The corporation remains in bankruptcy under the control of a receiver until, and if, an agreement (adjustment) can be reached with those creditors. This is why income bonds are sometimes described as **adjustment bonds.** If the corporation can ever regain its former earning power, the creditors, now holding income bonds, not only receive more in interest dollars, but they also have more in principal amount as well.

**adjustment bonds**

As previously discussed, almost all bonds have a definite date of maturity. On that date, the corporation must redeem the obligation by paying those holders the principal amount due plus any interest accrued from the last interest date.

*C3.*
*Retirement of*
*Debt Securities*

### C3a.  REFUNDING

If the corporation is financially sound yet unable (due to lack of excess capital) to repay bondholders a substantial amount of money at one time, it can retire a given bond obligation through a process called refunding. **Refunding** is the issuance of a new debt security using the proceeds received to

refunding

      redeem an older bond at maturity; or

2.   redeem an outstanding bond prior to maturity via exercise of a call privilege if it was previously issued under less favorable terms.

### C3b.  SINKING FUND

The corporation can also provide enough money to meet a maturing obligation if the indenture requires the corporation to establish a sinking fund. **A sinking fund** is an annual reserve of capital set aside out of current earnings so that over a period of years sufficient money will be available to redeem that bond at maturity. It certainly represents a valuable degree of protection for the investor in the event of default.

sinking fund

      If a corporation wants to retire a portion of that debt prior to maturity, it can do so

1.   by purchasing those bonds in the open market; or

2.   via exercise of a partial call (if this feature was written into the indenture at the time of the initial offering).

### C3c.  OPEN-MARKET PURCHASE

Open-market purchase would be attempted by a corporation only if the bonds were trading below par value and only if the corporation's directors were willing to accept partial retirement. It is unlikely that a corporation would ever be able to buy back all of its debt, especially at prices below redemption value.

### C3d.  EXERCISING A CALL

call premium

The exercise of a call by the corporation requires the holders to redeem their bonds prior to maturity. This method is most frequently employed today for early debt retirement because the company enjoys the flexibility of making full or partial calls to suit its purpose. However, there *is* usually a clause in the indenture requiring payment somewhat above face value if the corporation inconveniences the bondholders by calling certificates in the first few years after issuance. It is known as the bond issue's **call premium.**

example

The certificate pays $1,020 if called in the first five years, $1,010 in the next five years, and only face value, $1,000 thereafter. The dollar amount paid above par value is the call premium.

> Conversion is a retirement privilege initiated by the bondholder that benefits the corporation at the same time. A conversion feature in a bond indenture allows the holders to exchange their certificates for a specific number of shares of stock in the corporation. Thus, the company eliminates its debt by acquiring more stockholders. When this feature is included in a bond issue, it has proved to be a very attractive incentive for investors because it permits them seniority as creditors and the advantage of potential price appreciation in the common stock at the same time.

More often than not the corporation uses several of these methods to retire a particular bond before maturity. For example, it might issue a partial call for redemption with monies available from a sinking fund or might force conversion of an exchangeable issue via full or partial calls for redemption.

The various ways of retiring a bond issue are summarized in Table 3.

**TABLE 3**
RETIRING A BOND ISSUE

| | |
|---|---|
| Refunding | New bond issue to redeem an older one |
| Sinking Fund | Annual reserve set aside, often in cash or in government securities |
| Open Market Purchase | Purchase bonds in the market below par value |
| Exercising a Call | Corporation requires bondholder to redeem prior to maturity |
| Conversion | Exchange bond for shares of stock |

*C4.*
*Listed Values and Variations*

*IN PERCENTAGES*

*C4a.*

> Equity securities customarily trade in the market in values reflected in dollars and cents. Accordingly, a stock priced at 75 is really $75 per share and a round lot (100 shares) is worth $7,500. However, corporate (and U.S. government) bonds are not normally reflected in such a fashion. These securities are priced at a percentage of face (par) amount, so that a bond represented at 75 does not mean it is valued at $75 per bond,[4] rather, it means 75% of the par value appearing on the bond certificate.

**example**

> 75% of $500 par = $375 market value
> 75% of $1,000 par = $750 market value
> 75% of $5,000 par = $3,750 market value
> 75% of $10,000 par = $7,500 market value

> Unless otherwise specified, it is safe to assume that the face amount of a bond is $1,000 per bond. This is the traditional *par* of an overwhelming number of outstanding debt securities. It is the company's principal obligation to the holder for repayment at maturity. On order tickets, trade reports, and other memoranda

> [4]Keep in mind that a *stock* quoted at 75 would be valued at $75 per share!

used within the securities industry the $1,000 par value is often abbreviated by the Roman numeral "M." Thus, an order for one bond is written as 1M, five bonds as 5M, ten bonds as 10M, and so forth. The interest requirement is also specified as a percentage of the same par value.

C4b.   **IN WHOLE NUMBERS**

Whole number bond prices are easily translated into dollar figures merely by adding a zero to the last numeral represented.

example

$$91 = \$910 \text{ per bond}$$
$$83 = \$830 \text{ per bond}$$
$$108 = \$1,080 \text{ per bond}$$

C4c.   **IN WHOLE NUMBERS AND FRACTIONS**

The introduction of a fraction, however, requires a thorough knowledge of its decimal equivalent before an accurate translation is effected. Most corporate bonds fluctuate in variations of one-eighth (⅛% of $1,000). The decimal equivalents are as follows:

⅛ = .125 or $1.25 per bond (.125 of 1% of $1,000)
¼ = .250 or $2.50 per bond (.250 of 1% of $1,000)
⅜ = .375 or $3.75 per bond (.375 of 1% of $1,000)
½ = .500 or $5.00 per bond (.500 of 1% of $1,000)
⅝ = .625 or $6.25 per bond (.625 of 1% of $1,000)
¾ = .750 or $7.50 per bond (.750 of 1% of $1,000)
⅞ = .875 or $8.75 per bond (.875 of 1% of $1,000)

Determining the dollar value for a bond priced with a whole number and fraction can be calculated by either

1. placing the decimal equivalent of the fraction next to the last whole number and then moving the decimal one place to the right; or
2. adding the dollar value of the fraction to the dollar value of the whole number.

example

| | | | | |
|---|---|---|---|---|
| 91⅛ = | 91.125 = | 911.25 or | $ | 910.00 |
| | | | + | 1.25 |
| | | | $ | 911.25 |
| 83½ = | 83.50 = | 835.00 or | $ | 830.00 |
| | | | + | 5.00 |
| | | | $ | 835.00 |
| 108⅞ = | 108.875 = | 1,088.75 or | | $1,080.00 |
| | | | + | 8.75 |
| | | | | $1,088.75 |

Any bond that trades in the marketplace below its face amount is commonly called a **discount bond,** whereas one that sells above face amount is referred to as a **premium bond.** In any event, at maturity, the holder of either security may expect to receive only its face value from the issuing company.

## IN WHOLE NUMBERS AND DECIMAL POINTS                    C4d.

Some bond issues, particularly obligations of the U.S. government, have such good marketability in a keenly competitive market that they trade in variations as small thirty-seconds or sixty-fourths rather than eighths. In practice, these fractional designations are separated from the whole number by means of a decimal point, and the denominator is dropped completely. For the decimal value equivalents of these fractions see the listing in Table 4.

**TABLE 4**
VALUE EQUIVALENTS OF THIRTY-SECONDS AND SIXTY-FOURTHS
PER $1,000

| 32NDS | 64THS | PER $1,000 | 32NDS | 64THS | PER $1,000 |
|-------|-------|------------|-------|-------|------------|
| + | 1 | .15625 | 16+ | 33 | 5.15625 |
| 1 | 2 | .31250 | 17 | 34 | 5.31250 |
| 1+ | 3 | .46875 | 17+ | 35 | 5.46875 |
| 2 | 4 | .62500 | 18 | 36 | 5.62500 |
| 2+ | 5 | .78125 | 18+ | 37 | 5.78125 |
| 3 | 6 | .93750 | 19 | 38 | 5.93750 |
| 3+ | 7 | 1.09375 | 19+ | 39 | 6.09375 |
| 4 | 8 | 1.25000 | 20 | 40 | 6.25000 |
| 4+ | 9 | 1.40625 | 20+ | 41 | 6.40625 |
| 5 | 10 | 1.56250 | 21 | 42 | 6.56250 |
| 5+ | 11 | 1.71875 | 21+ | 43 | 6.71875 |
| 6 | 12 | 1.87500 | 22 | 44 | 6.87500 |
| 6+ | 13 | 2.03125 | 22+ | 45 | 7.03125 |
| 7 | 14 | 2.18750 | 23 | 46 | 7.18750 |
| 7+ | 15 | 2.34375 | 23+ | 47 | 7.34375 |
| 8 | 16 | 2.50000 | 24 | 48 | 7.50000 |
| 8+ | 17 | 2.65625 | 24+ | 49 | 7.65625 |
| 9 | 18 | 2.81250 | 25 | 50 | 7.81250 |
| 9+ | 19 | 2.96875 | 25+ | 51 | 7.96875 |
| 10 | 20 | 3.12500 | 26 | 52 | 8.12500 |
| 10+ | 21 | 3.28125 | 26+ | 53 | 8.28125 |
| 11 | 22 | 3.43750 | 27 | 54 | 8.43750 |
| 11+ | 23 | 3.59375 | 27+ | 55 | 8.59375 |
| 12 | 24 | 3.75000 | 28 | 56 | 8.75000 |
| 12+ | 25 | 3.90625 | 28+ | 57 | 8.90625 |
| 13 | 26 | 4.06250 | 29 | 58 | 9.06250 |
| 13+ | 27 | 4.21875 | 29+ | 59 | 9.21875 |
| 14 | 28 | 4.37500 | 30 | 60 | 9.37500 |
| 14+ | 29 | 4.53125 | 30+ | 61 | 9.53125 |
| 15 | 30 | 4.68750 | 31 | 62 | 9.68750 |
| 15+ | 31 | 4.84375 | 31+ | 63 | 9.84375 |
| 16 | 32 | 5.00000 | 32 | 64 | 10.00000 |

**example**

$94.8 = 94 + 8/32\%$ of $\$1,000 = 940 + 2.50$,
                                            or $942.50 per bond

$71.12 = 71 + 12/32\%$ of $\$1,000 = 710 + 3.75$,
                                            or $713.75 per bond

$89.23 = 89 + 23/32\%$ of $\$1,000 = 890 + 7.19$,
                                            or $897.19 per bond

$97.30 = 97 + 30/32\%$ of $\$1,000 = 970 + 9.38$,
                                            or $979.38 per bond

The fraction is always reflected in terms of thirty-seconds unless it is followed by a plus sign (+), which signifies that it is denominated in sixty-fourths, instead. In this situation, double the fraction and add one to place it into its proper sixty-fourth perspective. For the decimal value equivalents of these fractions see the listings in Table 4.

## example

$$85.8+ \ = 85 + \ 17/64\% \text{ of } \$1,000 = \ 850 + 2.66,$$
$$\text{or } \$852.66 \text{ per bond}$$
$$79.20+ \ = 79 + \ 41/64\% \text{ of } \$1,000 = \ 790 + 6.41,$$
$$\text{or } \$796.41 \text{ per bond}$$
$$93.3+ \ = 93 + \ 7/64\% \text{ of } \$1,000 = \ 930 + 1.09,$$
$$\text{or } \$931.09 \text{ per bond}$$
$$98.11+ \ = 98 + \ 23/64\% \text{ of } \$1,000 = \ 980 + 3.59,$$
$$\text{or } \$983.59 \text{ per bond}$$

**C5.**
**Yield**

The purchaser of a debt security generally wants to invest capital for one reason—the rate of return earned by this money. A rate of return on capital is commonly referred to as **yield.** The concept of yield has different meanings for different investors, according to their purposes and objectives.

**yield**

**C5a.** (*NOMINAL YIELD*)

**Nominal yield** is the annual interest rate percentage payable, specified in the indenture and printed on the face of the bond certificate. It enables purchasers to determine their yearly flow of dollar income. Nominal yield is not related to market value.

**nominal yield**

Because most bonds are issued in denominations of $1,000[5] and the annual interest rate is expressed as a percentage of that amount, too, the number of interest dollars received annually by the investor is calculated by converting that percentage rate into a decimal and multiplying by $1,000.

## example

(1) a 4% nominal yield     = $1,000 × .04, or $40
(2) a 5⅝% nominal yield = $1,000 × .05625, or $56.25
(3) a 7¾% nominal yield = $1,000 × .0775, or $77.50

The nominal yield is a yearly rate that is usually paid in equal installments, semiannually. Thus a 4% nominal yield would require distribution of $20 in interest on the first or fifteenth day of January and July, or March and September, or any other calendar dates designated in the indenture, as long as the payments are separated by 6-month intervals.

[5]Recently, in order to reduce administrative effort, many corporations have begun issuing bonds in minimum denominations of $5,000, and a few have even issued them in $10,000 pieces. The only effect this has upon calculation of interest dollars is to require multiplication of the nominal yield by $5,000 or $10,000, as the case may be, instead of by $1,000. Thus, a 6¼% nominal yield for a bond with a $5,000 face value would return $312.50 annually ($5,000 × .0625).

> January and July
> February and August
> March and September
> April and October
> May and November
> June and December

---

**CURRENT YIELD**

Unless all bonds trade in the marketplace at par value, a study of nominal yield does not permit investors to compare the return on one bond with other bonds issued previously under different rates and money market conditions. This, of course, is unrealistic. To provide a means of comparison predicated upon interest rates and variable fluctuations in price most public investors rely upon calculation of current yield.

**current yield**

> The **current yield** gauges the return on an investment by relating the stated interest rate to the actual number of dollars needed to purchase that security. Current yield is calculated by dividing annual interest dollars by the current market price.

$$\frac{\text{annual interest payment}}{\text{current market price}} = \text{current yield (in decimal equivalent)}$$

Thus, a bond with a nominal yield of 5% (paying $50 annually) and a market value of $990 would have a current yield of 5.05%.

$$\frac{\$50}{\$990} = .0505 \text{ (decimal equivalent), or } 5.05\%$$

If that same bond were trading at a value of $1,100, the current yield would only be approximately 4.55%.

$$\frac{\$50}{\$1,100} = .04545 \text{ (decimal equivalent), or } 4.55\%$$

**YIELD-TO-MATURITY**

Yield-to-maturity, another way of looking at a bondholder's return on invested capital, is a more sophisticated approach to the subject of yield. It is used by institutional investors and portfolio managers who supervise pools of capital on a long-term, semipermanent basis. It is also used by professional securities traders as an accurate means of identifying the relative worth of a particular bond.

> **Yield-to-maturity** is an *average rate of return* involving collective consideration of a bond's
>
> 1. interest rate;
> 2. current price; and
> 3. number of years remaining until maturity.

Because a corporation is expected to repay holders the face value of their bonds at maturity, yield-to-maturity requires

1. *pro rata accumulation* of the capital gain to be realized on redemption, if the bond is acquired below face value; or
2. *pro rata amortization* of the capital loss to be incurred upon redemption, if the bond is acquired above face value.

C5c(1).

> **Rule-of-thumb formula for yield-to-maturity** There is a simple rule-of-thumb method used for calculating a bond's yield-to-maturity. It is inaccurate for professional use, and it becomes increasingly so with longer-term maturities. Yet it is still satisfactory for a beginning trainee's introduction to the subject.
>
> When a bond is trading at a **discount** (below face value)
>
> 1. *compute* the capital gain if bond is held to maturity;
> 2. *equally allocate* the capital gain to be established at maturity over the remaining years of life of the bond;
> 3. *add* this annual appreciation to the annual interest distribution;
> 4. *average* the redemption proceeds and the acquisition cost; and
> 5. *divide* the total by the average of the redemption proceeds and the acquisition cost.

**discount**

**example**

If a 6% debenture is purchased for $975 and matures in exactly 10 years, its yield-to-maturity is calculated thus:

(1)      $1,000 redemption price
    −   975 current market price
    $   25 gain to be realized if held to maturity

(2)   $25 gain ÷ 10-year life = $2.50 per year gain

(3)   $ 2.50 annual capital gain
   + 60.00 annual interest at 6%
   $62.50

(4)   redemption      acquisition
    proceeds          cost
   $$\frac{\$1{,}000 \;+\; \$975}{2} = \$987.50$$

(5)   $62.50 ÷ $987.50 = .06329
    yield-to-maturity  = 6.33%

When a bond is trading at a **premium** (above face value)

1. *compute* the loss if bond is held to maturity;
2. *equally amortize* the capital loss to be established at maturity over the remaining years of life of the bond;
3. *subtract* this annual depreciation from the annual interest distribution;
4. *average* the redemption proceeds and the acquisition cost;

**premium**

**5.** *divide* the remainder by the average of the redemption proceeds and the acquisition cost.

If a 7.5% debenture is purchased for $1,036.25 and matures in exactly 4 years, its yield-to-maturity is calculated thus:

(1)  $1,036.25 current market price
    − 1,000.00 redemption price
    $    36.25 loss to be realized if held to maturity

(2)  $36.25 loss ÷ 4-year life = $9.06 per year loss

(3)  $75.00 annual interest in 7.5%
    − 9.06 annual deduction
    $65.94

(4)  redemption     acquisition
    proceeds       cost
    $$\frac{\$1,000 \; + \; \$1,036.25}{2} = \$1018.13$$

(5)  $65.94 ÷ $1,018.13 = .06476
    yield-to-maturity   = 6.48%

*Alternate method*  The intermediate-level trainee calculates yield-to-maturity in a similar fashion, but with two important changes:  *C5c(2).*

1.  The annual accumulation (amortization) is subtracted (added) from (to) the redemption proceeds before averaging yields based on acquisition cost and redemption proceeds.

2.  Each equation is calculated separately in decimal form and converted to a percentage figure only in the final analysis.

The result is somewhat more accurate than the rule-of-thumb method, but still not precise enough for the professional.[6]

**discount**        When a bond is trading at a **discount** (below face value)

1.  *compute* the capital gain if bond is held to maturity;
2.  *equally allocate* the capital gain to be established at maturity over the remaining years of life of the bond;
3.  *add* this annual appreciation to the annual interest distribution;
4.  *divide* that total by the current price of the bond;
5.  *divide* that same total by the redemption proceeds minus the annual capital gain;
6.  *average* the sum of the two division results above in steps 4 and 5.

Let us apply this alternate method to the previous example.

[6]This alternate method is used to provide yield figures in the widely used, monthly *Bond Guide* published by Standard & Poor's Corporation.

For a 6% debenture selling at 97.50 and maturing in exactly 10 years, the yield-to-maturity is calculated thusly:

(1)    $1,000 redemption price
    −   975 current market price
    $    25 gain to be realized if held to maturity

(2)    $25 gain ÷ 10-year life = $2.50 per year gain

(3)    $ 2.50 annual capital gain
    +60.00 annual interest
    $62.50

(4)    $62.50 ÷ $975 (current price) = .06410

(5)    $62.50 ÷ $997.50 ($1,000 redemption proceeds − $2.50 annual gain) = .06266

(6)    $\dfrac{.06410 + .06266}{2} = \dfrac{.12676}{2} = .06338$

    yield-to-maturity = 6.34%

When a bond is trading at a **premium** (above face value)    **premium**

1. *compute* the loss if bond is held to maturity;
2. *equally allocate* the capital loss to be established at maturity over the remaining years of life of the bond;
3. *subtract* the annual depreciation from the annual interest distribution;
4. *divide* that total by the current price of the bond;
5. *divide* that same total by the redemption proceeds plus the annual capital loss;
6. *average* the sum of the two division results above in steps 4 and 5.

Let us apply this alternate method to the previous example of a bond selling at a premium.

For a 7.5% debenture selling at 103⅝, maturing in exactly 4 years, the yield-to-maturity is calculated thus:

(1)    $1,036.25 current market price
    −1,000.00 redemption price
    $    36.25 loss to be realized if held to maturity

(2)    $36.25 loss ÷ 4-year life = $9.06 per year loss

(3)    $75.00 annual interest
    −  9.06 annual capital loss
    $65.94

(4)    $65.94 ÷ $1,036.25 (current price) = .06363

(5)    $65.94 ÷ $1,009.06 ($1,000 redemption proceeds + $9.06 annual loss) = .06535

$$\text{(6)} \quad \frac{.06363 + .06535}{2} = \frac{.12898}{2} = .06449$$

$$\text{yield-to-maturity} = 6.45\%$$

---

***Professional method*** The most reliable method for determining yields-to-maturity recognizes that the capital gain or loss does not accrue in equal annual installments. It considers such accumulation or amortization as if reinvested at the coupon rate and applies these sums to the basic principles of coupon rates, acquisition price, and exact period of time until maturity.

*C5c(3).*

The mathematical formula is complicated and impractical for ordinary use even by professionals, especially in view of the almost unlimited combination of variables in the basic principles. Fortunately, however, the calculations for the most frequently found coupons, maturities, and yields-to-maturity have been printed and are sold by the Financial Publishing Company in a book of bond tables. An example of one such table is shown in Table 5. (Note that in this table, because it is for a 6.5% coupon rate, the market value is 100.00 across the entire row marked 6.50 under the column headed yield-to-maturity. As the prices above that row rise, the yield-to-maturity decreases. On the other hand, as the prices below that row decrease, the yield-to-maturity increases.

---

Bond tables may be used as a ready reference for

*C6.*
*Using the Bond Tables*

1. finding the yield-to-maturity, if you know the coupon rate, current price, and remaining years and months to date of maturation; and

2. finding market value, if you know the coupon rate, yield-to-maturity, and remaining years and months to date of maturation.

---

### FINDING THE YIELD-TO-MATURITY DIRECTLY

*C6a.*

For example, with a coupon rate of 6.50%, a bond selling at 81 and due to mature in exactly 14 years, has a yield-to-maturity of 8.90% according to Table 5. (In Table 5, a bond table for a 6.50% coupon rate, glance down the column labeled 14 years and 0 months until a price of 81 is reached. Then look across, under the column headed yield-to-maturity.)

### FINDING THE MARKET VALUE DIRECTLY

*C6b.*

For example, the market value of a bond with a 6.50% coupon rate and a yield-to-maturity of 7.80%, due to mature in 11 years and 6 months, is 90.25 according to Table 5. (In Table 5, a bond table for a 6.50% coupon rate, glance down the yield column to 7.80%. Look right, across this line, to the point where it intersects the column headed 11-6.)

### FINDING THE NEEDED DATA BY INTERPOLATING

*C6c.*

Although reading from the bond table is simple enough, note that

**TABLE 5**
BOND TABLE, 6.50% COUPON RATE, 10 YEARS, 6 MONTHS TO 14 YEARS
TO MATURITY

| YIELD-TO-MATURITY | YEARS AND MONTHS PRIOR TO MATURITY a | | | | | | | |
|---|---|---|---|---|---|---|---|---|
| | 10-6 | 11-0 | 11-6 | 12-0 | 12-6 | 13-0 | 13-6 | 14-0 |
| 4.00 | 121.26 | 122.07 | 122.87 | 123.64 | 124.40 | 125.15 | 125.88 | 126.60 |
| 4.20 | 119.37 | 120.10 | 120.81 | 121.51 | 122.19 | 122.86 | 123.52 | 124.16 |
| 4.40 | 117.51 | 118.16 | 118.79 | 119.42 | 120.03 | 120.62 | 121.21 | 121.78 |
| 4.60 | 115.68 | 116.26 | 116.82 | 117.37 | 117.91 | 118.44 | 118.95 | 119.45 |
| 4.80 | 113.89 | 114.40 | 114.89 | 115.37 | 115.84 | 116.30 | 116.75 | 117.19 |
| 5.00 | 112.14 | 112.57 | 113.00 | 113.41 | 113.82 | 114.21 | 114.60 | 114.97 |
| 5.20 | 110.42 | 110.79 | 111.15 | 111.50 | 111.84 | 112.17 | 112.50 | 112.82 |
| 5.40 | 108.73 | 109.03 | 109.33 | 109.62 | 109.91 | 110.18 | 110.45 | 110.71 |
| 5.60 | 107.07 | 107.32 | 107.56 | 107.79 | 108.01 | 108.23 | 108.45 | 108.65 |
| 5.80 | 105.45 | 105.63 | 105.82 | 105.99 | 106.16 | 106.33 | 106.49 | 106.65 |
| 6.00 | 103.85 | 103.98 | 104.11 | 104.23 | 104.35 | 104.47 | 104.58 | 104.69 |
| 6.10 | 103.07 | 103.17 | 103.27 | 103.37 | 103.46 | 103.55 | 103.64 | 103.73 |
| 6.20 | 102.29 | 102.37 | 102.44 | 102.51 | 102.58 | 102.65 | 102.72 | 102.78 |
| 6.30 | 101.52 | 101.57 | 101.62 | 101.67 | 101.71 | 101.76 | 101.80 | 101.84 |
| 6.40 | 100.76 | 100.78 | 100.81 | 100.83 | 100.85 | 100.87 | 100.89 | 100.92 |
| 6.50 | 100.00 | 100.00 | 100.00 | 100.00 | 100.00 | 100.00 | 100.00 | 100.00 |
| 6.60 | 99.25 | 99.23 | 99.20 | 99.18 | 99.16 | 99.14 | 99.12 | 99.10 |
| 6.70 | 98.51 | 98.46 | 98.41 | 98.37 | 98.32 | 98.28 | 98.24 | 98.20 |
| 6.80 | 97.77 | 97.70 | 97.63 | 97.57 | 97.50 | 97.44 | 97.38 | 97.32 |
| 6.90 | 97.05 | 96.95 | 96.86 | 96.77 | 96.69 | 96.60 | 96.52 | 96.45 |
| 7.00 | 96.33 | 96.21 | 96.09 | 95.99 | 95.88 | 95.78 | 95.68 | 95.58 |
| 7.10 | 95.61 | 95.47 | 95.34 | 95.21 | 95.08 | 94.96 | 94.84 | 94.73 |
| 7.20 | 94.90 | 94.74 | 94.59 | 94.44 | 94.29 | 94.15 | 94.02 | 93.89 |
| 7.30 | 94.20 | 94.02 | 93.85 | 93.68 | 93.51 | 93.36 | 93.20 | 93.06 |
| 7.40 | 93.51 | 93.31 | 93.11 | 92.92 | 92.74 | 92.57 | 92.40 | 92.24 |
| 7.50 | 92.82 | 92.60 | 92.38 | 92.18 | 91.98 | 91.79 | 91.60 | 91.42 |
| 7.60 | 92.14 | 91.90 | 91.66 | 91.44 | 91.22 | 91.01 | 90.81 | 90.62 |
| 7.70 | 91.47 | 91.20 | 90.95 | 90.71 | 90.48 | 90.25 | 90.04 | 89.83 |
| 7.80 | 90.80 | 90.52 | 90.25 | 89.99 | 89.74 | 89.50 | 89.27 | 89.04 |
| 7.90 | 90.13 | 89.84 | 89.55 | 89.27 | 89.01 | 88.75 | 88.50 | 88.27 |
| 8.00 | 89.48 | 89.16 | 88.86 | 88.56 | 88.28 | 88.01 | 87.75 | 87.50 |
| 8.10 | 88.83 | 88.49 | 88.17 | 87.86 | 87.57 | 87.28 | 87.01 | 86.75 |
| 8.20 | 88.18 | 87.83 | 87.50 | 87.17 | 86.86 | 86.56 | 86.27 | 86.00 |
| 8.30 | 87.55 | 87.18 | 86.83 | 86.49 | 86.16 | 85.85 | 85.55 | 85.26 |
| 8.40 | 86.91 | 86.53 | 86.16 | 85.81 | 85.47 | 85.14 | 84.83 | 84.53 |
| 8.50 | 86.29 | 85.89 | 85.50 | 85.14 | 84.78 | 84.44 | 84.12 | 83.81 |
| 8.60 | 85.67 | 85.25 | 84.85 | 84.47 | 84.10 | 83.75 | 83.42 | 83.09 |
| 8.70 | 85.05 | 84.62 | 84.21 | 83.81 | 83.43 | 83.07 | 82.72 | 82.39 |
| 8.80 | 84.44 | 84.00 | 83.57 | 83.16 | 82.77 | 82.40 | 82.04 | 81.69 |
| 8.90 | 83.84 | 83.38 | 82.94 | 82.52 | 82.11 | 81.73 | 81.36 | 81.00 |
| 9.00 | 83.24 | 82.77 | 82.32 | 81.88 | 81.46 | 81.07 | 80.69 | 80.32 |
| 9.10 | 82.65 | 82.16 | 81.70 | 81.25 | 80.82 | 80.41 | 80.02 | 79.65 |
| 9.20 | 82.07 | 81.56 | 81.08 | 80.62 | 80.19 | 79.77 | 79.37 | 78.98 |
| 9.30 | 81.48 | 80.97 | 80.48 | 80.01 | 79.56 | 79.13 | 78.72 | 78.33 |
| 9.40 | 80.91 | 80.38 | 79.88 | 79.39 | 78.93 | 78.50 | 78.08 | 77.68 |
| 9.50 | 80.34 | 79.80 | 79.28 | 78.79 | 78.32 | 77.87 | 77.44 | 77.03 |
| 9.60 | 79.77 | 79.22 | 78.69 | 78.19 | 77.71 | 77.25 | 76.81 | 76.40 |
| 9.70 | 79.21 | 78.65 | 78.11 | 77.60 | 77.11 | 76.64 | 76.19 | 75.77 |
| 9.80 | 78.66 | 78.08 | 77.53 | 77.01 | 76.51 | 76.03 | 75.58 | 75.15 |
| 9.90 | 78.11 | 77.52 | 76.96 | 76.43 | 75.92 | 75.44 | 74.97 | 74.53 |
| 10.00 | 77.56 | 76.96 | 76.39 | 75.85 | 75.34 | 74.84 | 74.37 | 73.93 |
| 10.20 | 76.49 | 75.87 | 75.28 | 74.72 | 74.19 | 73.68 | 73.20 | 72.74 |
| 10.40 | 75.43 | 74.79 | 74.19 | 73.61 | 73.06 | 72.54 | 72.04 | 71.57 |
| 10.60 | 74.40 | 73.74 | 73.11 | 72.52 | 71.96 | 71.42 | 70.91 | 70.43 |
| 10.80 | 73.38 | 72.70 | 72.06 | 71.45 | 70.88 | 70.33 | 69.81 | 69.32 |
| 11.00 | 72.38 | 71.69 | 71.03 | 70.41 | 69.82 | 69.26 | 68.73 | 68.23 |
| 11.20 | 71.40 | 70.69 | 70.02 | 69.38 | 68.78 | 68.21 | 67.67 | 67.16 |
| 11.40 | 70.44 | 69.71 | 69.03 | 68.38 | 67.77 | 67.19 | 66.64 | 66.12 |
| 11.60 | 69.49 | 68.75 | 68.06 | 67.40 | 66.77 | 66.18 | 65.63 | 65.10 |
| 11.80 | 68.56 | 67.81 | 67.10 | 66.43 | 65.80 | 65.20 | 64.64 | 64.11 |
| 12.00 | 67.65 | 66.89 | 66.17 | 65.49 | 64.85 | 64.24 | 63.67 | 63.13 |

From EXPANDED BOND VALUES TABLES, © 1970 by Financial Publishing Company, Boston, Massachusetts. Used by permission of the publisher.
a Numbers inside this bond table are market values.

the tables show yields only in increments of 10 or 20 basis points[7] and market values that are not divisible by eighths (the usual trading variation). This presents a problem in finding the yield-

[7] A basis point equals .01% (1/100% of $1,000, or 10 cents per point). It is 1/10 of 1% of a yield-to-maturity calculation.

to-maturity of a bond selling in between, say at 101½ and due to mature in 12 years and 6 months; or in finding the in-between market value of a bond selling at a 7.23 basis and due to mature in exactly 11 years.

**interpolation**  The answers to both problems can be calculated by means of a procedure known as **interpolation.** Because two of the three basic principles are known and readily identifiable from the tables,[8] a simple ratio provides an adequate solution to the problem. The ratio is formulated on the fact that proportionate changes in yield-to-maturity will be comparable to proportionate changes in bond value.

The formula for computing the *ratio* for both situations is the same:

$$\frac{\text{amount of change from next lowest market value}}{\text{increment between next lowest and next highest market values}} = \frac{\text{amount of change from next highest yield-to-maturity}}{\text{increment between next lowest and next highest yield-to-maturity}}$$

Once we have the ratio, we can determine the yield-to-maturity or the market value. To find the *yield-to-maturity by interpolating* from the bond table:

$$\text{next highest yield-to-maturity} - \text{proportionate change} = \text{yield-to-maturity}$$

Let us use the hypothetical situation mentioned above—bond at 101½, due 12 years, 6 months, 6.50%—to interpolate the unknown yield-to-maturity:

example

| | | |
|---|---|---|
| (1) | 101.50 current price | |
| | −100.85 next lowest market value in bond tables | |
| | .65 amount of change | |
| (2) | 101.71 next highest market value under 12 years, 6 months column | Computing the ratio |
| | −100.85 next lowest market value under 12 years, 6 months column | |
| | .86 increment in market value | |
| (3) | $\dfrac{.65}{.86} = \dfrac{x}{.10}$ (increment between 6.30 and 6.40 yield-to-maturity) | Finding the figures to plug into the ratio formula |
| | $.86x = (.65)(.10) = .065$ | |
| | $x = .07558$ | |
| (4) | 6.40 next highest yield to maturity | Using the ratio figure to compute the yield-to-maturity |
| | − .07558 proportionate change | |
| | 6.32442 or 6.32% yield to maturity | |

[8]Coupon rate and remaining lifetime.

To find the *market value by interpolating* from the bond table we compute similarly:

| next lowest market price + proportionate change = market value |
| --- |

Let us use the hypothetical situation mentioned above —bond selling at 7.23 basis, due in exactly 11 years, 6.5%—to interpolate the unknown market value:

## example

Finding the figures to plug into the ratio formula

(1)
$$
\begin{array}{r}
7.30 \text{ next highest yield} \\
-7.23 \text{ basis yield} \\
\hline
.07 \text{ amount of change}
\end{array}
$$

(2)
$$
\begin{array}{r}
7.30 \text{ yield} \\
-7.20 \text{ yield} \\
\hline
.10 \text{ increment}
\end{array}
$$

Computing the ratio

(3) (increment between 94.74 and 94.02 market value in the 11 year and 0 months column)

$$\frac{x}{.72} = \frac{.07}{.10}$$
$$.10x = (.07)(.72) = .0504$$
$$x = .504$$

Using the ratio figure to compute the market value

(4)
$$
\begin{array}{l}
94.02 \quad \text{next lowest market value} \\
+.504 \quad \text{proportionate change} \\
\hline
94.524 \quad \text{or } 94.524 \text{ market value, } \$945.24 \text{ per bond}
\end{array}
$$

**C7.**
***Major Factors Affecting Bond Values***

To be sure, the aggressive forces of supply and demand do play a role in determining values of debt securities, but these are only two of several factors influencing bond fluctuation in the marketplace. The availability of credit and the issuer's ability to pay interest and repay principal in accordance with the terms of its indenture are equally important considerations governing movement in corporate bond prices.

**C7a.**   ***AVAILABILITY OF CREDIT***

In the course of regulating money and credit in the United States, the Federal Reserve Board exerts a definite influence upon the secondary market for all debt instruments. When the amount of available funds is reduced, competition for these monies increases capital borrowing costs. But what about long-term debt, issued under the older and cheaper terms, that has 10, 15, 20, or even 25 years remaining until maturity? Obviously, such a security is no longer as attractive at face value as it was before. This is especially true if lenders can employ their money at higher current rates. Therefore, the older bond with the lower fixed interest rate must invariably decline in value until its yield is comparable to the newly prevailing financial conditions.

For example, a 4.5% coupon rate bond issued at $1,000 5 years ago that has 25 years from today remaining until maturity is not worth as much money as a comparable quality 6.5% coupon rate bond issued today to mature in 25 years. The former bond should *theoretically*[9] decline in value to the level at which it yields the going rate of 6.5%.

$$\frac{.045}{.065} = \frac{x}{\$1,000}$$

$$.065x = (.045)(\$1,000)$$
$$= \$45.00$$
$$x = \$692.31$$

Proof

$$\frac{\$45 \text{ (interest)}}{\$692.31 \text{ (cost)}} = .06499, \text{ or } 6.50\% \text{ yield}$$

Conversely, a 7.25% rate coupon bond issued at $1,000 2 years ago, with 23 years to wait until maturity, should be more valuable if current rates declined to 6.50% for comparable quality bonds issued today with a similar maturity. The bond with the 7.25% coupon should *theoretically*[10] appreciate in value to a level where it would then yield the going rate of 6.50%.

$$\frac{.0725}{.065} = \frac{x}{\$1,000}$$

$$.065x = (.0725)(\$1,000)$$
$$= \$72.50$$
$$x = \$1,115.38$$

Proof

$$\frac{\$72.50 \text{ (interest)}}{\$1,115.38 \text{ (cost)}} = .06500, \text{ or } 6.50\% \text{ yield}$$

### THE ISSUER'S ABILITY TO PAY                               C7b.

One or more of the three major rating services gauges a corporation's ability to honor an obligation by assigning to its publicly owned debt a letter rating that indicates its investment quality. These advisory services are:

Fitch Investors Service, 79 Wall Street, New York City
Moody's Investors Service, 99 Church Street, New York City
Standard & Poor's Corporation, 345 Hudson Street, New York City

Each organization examines the corporation's financial statistics and management policies to determine the quality of its debt and then interprets this information according to its own confidential criteria. As a result, it is not unusual to find the same corporate issue carrying a confusing "split rating" (two unequal grades assigned by different services). Nor is it necessarily an adverse reflection on a corporation for its bonds to have no rating at all. Private placements and bonds of corporations in certain industries are often unrated as a result of a particular firm's policy.

---

[9]The term *theoretically* is stressed because it is likely that too many other minor factors would interfere with the bond's fluctuation to the exact price indicated; but it should be fairly close to it, either above or below.

[10]See preceding note.

In general, an issue's rating hinges upon

1. the corporation's past earnings records;
2. the corporation's current financial position, including
   a. working capital,
   b. the amount of debt outstanding, its maturities, sinking fund provisions, and ranking, and
   c. the extent of its tangible assets;
3. the nature of the corporation's business, including
   a. the character of the industry,
   b. the necessity of its product, and
   c. the firm's position in the industry;
4. the continuity and consistency of management policies and controls; and
5. the corporation's labor relations.

In descending order of quality, each service rates corporate bonds as shown in Table 6.

**TABLE 6**
RATINGS OF BONDS

| INVESTMENT BRACKET | FITCH | MOODY'S | STANDARD & POOR'S |
|---|---|---|---|
| Top quality | AAA | Aaa | AAA |
|  | AA | Aa | AA |
|  | A | A | A |
| Medium quality | BBB | Baa $\}$ 1, 2, 3* | BBB |
| to speculative | BB | Ba | BB |
|  | B | B | B |
| Poor quality | CCC | Caa | CCC |
|  | CC | Ca | CC |
|  | C | C | C |
| Value is | DDD |  | DDD |
| questionable | DD |  | DD |
|  | D |  | D |

*The number 1 added to these ratings indicates the *high* end of the category, number 2 the *mid-range* ranking, and number 3 the *low* end.

The gradations within each investment bracket are slight compared to the quality gap between the brackets themselves. While market price is not a factor in assigning a rating to a particular issue, the rating assigned will certainly affect the market price of that security. Generally speaking, assuming equal maturity dates, lower quality bonds

1. carry higher interest coupons than issues found with higher ratings; or
2. trade at lower prices than bonds with higher ratings having identical interest coupons.

This economic fact of life provides greater compensation for investors as a reflection of the greater risk involved in owning lower rated bonds.

*C8.*
*Other Factors Influencing Bond Prices*

**CALL FEATURES**

*C8a.*    The presence of a call feature in the indenture of a bond tends to establish a ceiling for the price of that security. After all, who would buy a bond significantly above its call price knowing that the company can retire it at any time and pay holders only the redemption value specified? In fact, excluding consideration of bonds that are also convertible, the only time a bond trades significantly above face value is when interest rates are declining in the financial community. In such cases, responsible management would probably call that older, more expensive issue anyway and refinance the debt through **refunding**.[11]

**refunding**

Because of unsettled monetary conditions in recent years, investors have demanded and received ''call protection'' for the first 5 to 10 years of a bond's lifetime. That is, the bonds are noncallable for the first 5 to 10 years and then become redeemable at declining premium prices as the issue ages toward its maturation date. Consequently, if the cycle of interest rates within the economy should decline in the bond's early life, higher coupon bonds will rise above the future call price. But they never quite rise to the true level normally appropriate for a bond with that rate. The call feature looms like a spectre and to some extent restrains price advances.

Of course, on the other hand, if interest rates subsequently move higher, depressing the price of fixed debt issues, these bonds, never having experienced full appreciation, do not dramatically decline in value either. It is the moderating influence of a deferred call provision in combination with frequently changing interest rates that has provided modern securities markets with ''cushion'' bonds. A **cushion bond** is a high current coupon debt instrument with a deferred call provision in its indenture; thus, it offers a better return and minimal price volatility as compared to a bond without call protection. It has great appeal for the conservative investor seeking a somewhat higher yield on capital and is most often issued by well-rated industrial corporations and public utilities.

**cushion bond**

### SINKING FUND FEATURES

Provisions for a significant ''sinker'' will also exert an influence upon that issue's market price. When the corporation is obliged to retire a portion of its debt annually through open market purchases or exercise of a call, it provides a flexible floor in the price of that security. This built-in demand partially offsets the effect of adverse changes in the money market and provides more asset protection for the remaining holders of that issue.

*C8b(1).*

### CONVERTIBLE FEATURES

*C8c.*

*Advantages to issuer*  The conversion privilege, while considered to be the prerogative of the bondholder, is also advantageous to the issuing corporation. Because this form of dual status (creditor/stockholder) is an attractive feature for investors, a corporation can issue this obligation with a somewhat lower interest rate than is necessary for ordinary straight debt securities. Furthermore, if the company prospers, thereby experiencing appreciation in the value of its underlying stock, this debt can be eliminated with a minimal outlay of cash. The corporation merely calls the issue, thus forcing the bondholders to convert into equity or lose the economic advantage of the stock's prevailing market

*C8c(1).*

---

[11]Management would be precluded from doing this, of course, if the indenture stipulated that the bond was nonrefundable.

price. That is when the minimal outlay of cash is required. Somewhere between 1 to 5% of all convertible bondholders neglect to act in time to effect the exchange and can subsequently claim only redemption value from the corporation.

For example, if a $1,000 bond is convertible into 30 shares of stock when the underlying shares are trading at $50, the bondholders will ''lose'' $500 in paper value if they fail to convert in the time allowed following distribution of the call notice.

$$\begin{array}{r} 30 \text{ shares} \\ \times \ \$50 \text{ market price} \\ \hline \$1,500 \text{ paper value versus } \$1,000 \text{ redemption value} \end{array}$$

The bondholders usually receive 30 to 60 days' advance notice to arrange conversion. Call announcements, both partial and full, are published in most major newspapers in the United States as well as in all the financial services media. If the bonds are registered in the name of the owner (as most corporate bonds have been in recent years), the trustee sends each holder an announcement of the redemption decision, citing applicable certificate serial numbers in cases of partial calls.

**C8c(2).** *Conversion price* A convertible feature in a bond can have a dramatic effect upon the market price of that issue. This is especially true when the underlying stock reaches a price level at which it becomes economically feasible for a holder to convert into that stock. It is called a **conversion price** and is set in the indenture by the issuing corporation at the time the bond is offered for sale. For example, a conversion price of $40 means that the bondholders will not benefit financially if they convert into stock until the underlying stock begins trading at $40 and above.

**conversion price**

**C8c(3).** *Conversion ratio* The conversion price is also a means by which a corporation informs its bondholders how many shares they will receive if they decide to convert or if they are ''forced'' to convert. This information can be computed by dividing the face value (par) of the bonds by the conversion price.[12] The formula is called the **conversion ratio.**

**conversion ratio**

$$\frac{\$1,000}{\$40} \text{ (conversion price)} = 25 \text{ shares of stock}$$

Thus, the holders of this bond can, at their option, exchange each bond for 25 shares of stock. It would not be sensible for them to do so, however, if the stock is trading below $40—say at $35. They would be changing a senior security worth about $1,000 for a junior security worth $875 (25 shares × $35). But if the stock price rises to $45, then 25 shares are worth $1,125, and unless the price of the bond appreciates to at least that value at the same

[12]To protect the bondholders from dilution of their interest in the underlying equity, the conversion price is adjusted downward to reflect stock dividends, stock splits, subscription rights, or warrants to be distributed to the stockholders during the lifetime of that bond. In the illustration that follows, the conversion price would be adjusted to $20 to reflect a two for one split, to $36.36 for a 10% stock dividend, and so forth. Further protection against dilution is given the bondholders when the indenture forbids primary distributions of additional stock by the corporation *below* the conversion price.

time, there is a financial advantage in converting that security.[13]

*Conversion parity*    The ideal situation, simple in theory, is for the bond and its comparable stock to sell continuously at equal money values after the stock reaches its conversion price. Below that price, the bond should trade at its appropriate value for a debt instrument. Above that price, it would fluctuate directly with the movement of the underlying stock.

C8c(4).

The term *should* is used because in reality it does not happen that way. In fact, the conversion feature acts as a lure for investors, causing the bond to trade above its theoretical value. Even when the stock is below its conversion price, the bond usually sells higher than a comparable straight debt security with the same credit rating and maturity.[14]

As the stock approaches and exceeds the conversion price, the bond begins trading at a premium value over the market value of the stock.

| stock | convertible bond |
|---|---|
| 25 shares | $1,100 actual bond market value |
| × $40 | − 1,000 theoretical value |
| $1,000 stock market value = | $ 100 (a 10% premium) |

**conversion parity**

The textbook relationship of "equal money value" for a convertible security and its comparable stock is called **conversion parity.** The mathematical formula for conversion parity is:

$$\frac{\$1,000 \text{ par value of bond}}{\text{conversion price}} = \frac{\text{market price of bond}}{\text{market price of stock}}$$

The following problems and solutions illustrate this concept.

## problem i

What is the parity price of a bond convertible into common stock at $20 when the common stock is selling at 35?

## solution i

$$\frac{\$1,000 \text{ (par)}}{\$20 \text{ (conversion price)}} = \frac{x}{35}$$
$$20x = (35)(\$1,000) = \$35,000$$
$$x = \$1,750$$

That is, when this bond is trading at 175 ($1,750), it is worth the same amount of money as the underlying stock selling at 35.

---

[13]Unless the corporation calls their bonds for redemption, the holders are under no obligation to convert into stock at any time. An important factor for them to consider is the difference in current yield between the convertible security and the underlying stock. The holders must weigh that distinction in light of their financial circumstances and objectives. Generally speaking, the bondholder is better off owning the convertible security, even after the stock begins trading above the conversion price. The convertible security normally trades above the value of the underlying stock and offers the better current yield.

[14]Except when the stock is trading *far below* its conversion price (for example, at $16 when the conversion price is $45).

## problem ii

What is the parity price of 80 shares of common stock receivable upon conversion of a bond presently trading at 115 ($1,150)?

## solution ii

$$\frac{\$1,000}{\$12.50_a} = \frac{\$1,150}{x}$$
$$1,000x = (\$12.50)(\$1,150) = \$14,375$$
$$x = 14.375, \text{ or } \$14\frac{3}{8}$$

At $14⅜ per share, 80 shares of common stock are worth $1,150, the same value as the bond itself.

---

aConversion price is calculated by dividing $1,000 par value of the bond by the number of shares receivable. That is,
$$\frac{\$1,000}{80 \text{ shares}} = 12\frac{1}{2}, \text{ or } \$12.50.$$

---

## problem iii

What is the market price of a stock selling two points below parity when the bond has a *conversion ratio* (number of shares receivable) of 20 and is selling at 90 ($900)?

## solution iii

$$\frac{\$1,000}{\$50} = \frac{\$900}{x}$$
$$1,000x = (\$50)(\$900) = \$45,000$$
$$x = \$45$$

However, because the stock is selling two points *below* parity, the current price must be *$43!*

## problem iv

What is the market value of a bond selling 20% above conversion parity if its conversion ratio is 45 and the underlying stock is at $53?

## solution iv

First, translate the conversion ratio into the conversion price, adapting it to the parity formula by dividing $1,000 par value by the ratio.

$$\frac{1,000}{45 \text{ shares}} = \$22.22 \text{ conversion price}$$

Then,
$$\frac{\$1,000}{\$22.22} = \frac{x}{\$53}$$
$$22.22x = \$53,000$$
$$x = \$2,385.24, \text{ or a bond price of } 238.52$$

But that price is "parity." If the bond is actually trading 20% above that price it must be selling at a value equal to $2,862.29 [($2,385.24 × .20) + $2,385.24].

If a convertible bond can be purchased for $1,000 when 25 shares of comparable stock are selling at $45 per share, it would be profitable for a trader to buy it, convert it quickly into 25 shares of stock, and sell the stock immediately.

$$
\begin{array}{rll}
25 \text{ shares} \times \$45 = & \$1,125 & \text{gross sale proceeds} \\
& -\$1,000 & \text{cost to purchase bond} \\
\hline
& \$\ \ 125 & \text{gross profit (before} \\
& & \text{transaction expenses)}
\end{array}
$$

**arbitrage**  Such activity is officially referred to as an **arbitrage** and may be simply defined as the simultaneous purchase and sale of the same (or equivalent) securities to take advantage of price differences prevailing in separate markets. An arbitrage can include

1. the purchase of one security on one exchange (or over-the-counter market) and its immediate sale on another exchange (or over-the-counter market); or
2. the purchase of a convertible bond and immediate sale of the underlying stock; or
3. the purchase of a convertible preferred stock and immediate sale of the underlying common stock; or
4. the purchase of warrants or rights to subscribe in a company followed by immediate sale of the stock that is acquired by subscription; or
5. the purchase of stock in a company to be acquired and immediate sale of comparable shares in the company making the acquisition, using its own stock as payment.

The professional trader (arbitrageur), alert to these profit possibilities no matter how minute, quickly makes purchases and sales to close those gaps that develop from aberrations between supply and demand.[15] Consequently, the average investor does **bona fide** not have an opportunity to participate in a **bona fide arbitrage** **arbitrage** (locked-in profit). More likely, if such an investor participates at all, it will be in the form of a **risk arbitrage.** A risk arbitrage also **risk arbitrage** involves purchase and sale transactions, but not necessarily at the same time. The designation is derived from the fact that a participant exposes his/her capital to market risk until, and if, the positions can be closed out.

Because profit is not readily apparent in prevailing prices, the risk arbitrageurs either

1. buy the convertible security and hold it, hoping the underlying security is about to move sharply higher, at which point the underlying stock can then be sold to lock up the profit; or

[15] A critical factor to consider with the purchase of a convertible bond is the amount of accrued interest to be added to the market price. A significant amount of interest could destroy a "profitable" arbitrage by raising total acquisition expenses above net sale proceeds of the underlying stock.

**2.** sell the underlying stock short if it is believed that the stock has peaked and the convertible security is trading too close to parity with the stock itself. If the convertible security subsequently declines, they will then buy it, convert it, deliver it off to close out the short position, and lock up the profit.

Many risk arbitrages also occur with proposed corporate mergers prior to ratification by their stockholders. Uncertainty about the success of these arrangements creates wide differences in market value between the shares of the two companies. Good profits can result if the merger is completed under the announced terms and conditions. But if the proposals are altered or abandoned, a participant usually suffers heavy losses. Invariably, the security that was purchased declines sharply while the stock sold short skyrockets in value.

## D.
### u.s. government securities

As the issuer of U.S. government securities, the Treasury Department faces the same financial problems confronted by most corporate finance officers today. The Treasury Department's responsibility is primarily to pay for the cost of operating the government. In this regard, the Treasury Department is authorized to issue both marketable and nonmarketable debt securities. There is no question about the government's ability to repay any borrowing because of its unlimited powers of taxation; therefore, credit rating is not a consideration. From the investor's vantage point, however, the interest received from these securities is only partially free from taxation. Interest from U.S. government securities is exempted from state taxation but subject to full taxation as ordinary income by the federal government itself.

## D1.
### *Nonmarketable Securities*

Savings bonds are considered **nonmarketable** because they are offered publicly through an agent of the Treasury Department and redeemed directly by an agent of the Treasury Department. They do not trade freely in the open market.

**nonmarketable**

### D1a. *SERIES EE SAVINGS BONDS*

Series EE savings bonds are registered securities offered in various denominations (minimum $50) 50% below face value and redeemed at face value by an agent of the Treasury Department after 8 years. The difference between subscription and redemption prices represents *accrued interest* for the investor. The interest itself does not accrue in equal increments over the lifetime of the bond. Instead, a small amount of interest accrues in the early years and much more in the later years, providing the investor with an average rate of return on current issues equal to 9% if held until maturity.

**accrued interest**

The federal income tax payable by the holder for this interest may be declared and paid annually as it accrues, or at maturity in one lump sum—at the bondholder's choice.

### D1b. *SERIES HH BONDS*

Series HH bonds are registered securities offered in various denominations (minimum $500) at face value and are redeemed 10 years later also at the face value. Every 6 months during the lifetime of this kind of bond, the Treasury Department sends each holder a check for the interest due on that obligation. The current rate on Series HH savings bonds is 8½%.

An interesting feature of Series HH and Series EE bonds is a U.S. government regulation precluding any one owner from acquiring more than $15,000 of the Series EE bonds and $20,000 of the Series HH bonds in any one calendar year. These dollar limitations are placed upon the issue prices and not the face (par) values of those securities. Thus, for the Series EE savings bond the ceiling is actually $30,000 in face value annually because it is issued at a 50 percent discount from face value. The Series HH savings bond has a true $20,000 limitation because it is issued and redeemed at face value. (This regulation is designed to prevent draining of bank deposits when these bonds are favored by the public because of their comparatively higher interest rates.)

**marketable**

The category of marketable securities includes Treasury bills, Treasury certificates of indebtedness, Treasury notes, and Treasury bonds. These securities are classified as **marketable** because there are continuous bids and offerings for them in the marketplace, and they are freely traded there. Each of these government obligations has at least one unique feature to distinguish it from the others.

*D2.*
*Marketable Securities*

### TREASURY BILLS

*D2a.*

**Treasury bills**

U.S. **Treasury bills** are bearer obligations with maturities ranging up to 1 year in duration. Currently, the Federal Reserve, as agent for the Treasury Department, issues 3-month and 6-month bills at a weekly action. "Year Bills," bills with maturities of one-year, are generally issued at a monthly auction. The amount of issue, timing of auctions and bill maturities may vary as needs of the Treasury dictate.

**(TABs) tax anticipation bills**

Occasionally the Federal Reserve will issue **tax anticipation bills (TAB's)** which are designed to encourage corporate investors. These bills mature several days after a tax payment date (i.e. April 15, June 15, etc.); but are accepted at face value in payment of taxes. This arrangement gives the corporate investor several extra days interest.

Treasury bills do not pay a fixed rate of interest. There is no preset rate associated with them in any way. All Treasury bills are issued, and subsequently traded, at a discount from face value. The extent of the reduced purchase price determines the rate of return. The difference between the purchase cost (discounted from face value) and the redemption proceeds at maturity (face value) establishes the rate of interest received on this investment. The discount earned on a Treasury bill is taxed as ordinary interest income. If it is sold before maturity, any trading gain or loss is taxed as a capital gain or loss.

Treasury bills are the only U.S. government securities always quoted and traded at a percent discount of face value. Therefore, their bid and asked prices always distinguish them from other government obligations.

A typical quotation for a 6-month bill may appear in this form:

| Bid | Asked |
|-----|-------|
| 4.85% discount | 4.66% discount |

Note that the bid is a *numerically* higher percentage than the asked. This is indicative of a price reflected in terms of a discount from face value. The larger discount is really a lower *dollar price*. What this means is that if you buy the bill in the example on the previous page at the asked price and redeem it at maturity, the yield (rate of return) on your original investment is 4.66 percent (calculated at an *annual* rate). Treasury bills are designed for corporate and institutional investment purposes in denominations ranging from $10,000 to $1 million per bill.

### CERTIFICATES OF INDEBTEDNESS

**certificates of indebtedness**

U.S. Treasury **certificates of indebtedness** are bearer obligations with maturities ranging up to 1 year in duration, in denominations of $1,000 through $500 million. They differ from bills in that they *do* carry a fixed rate of interest, usually in the form of coupons. They are quoted and traded at a price reflecting the *average rate of return* for an investor holding them until maturity (yield-to-maturity).

**example**

The bid and asked prices of a 1 year certificate with a 4.25% coupon may appear in this form:

| Bid | Asked | Yield-to-Maturity[16] |
|---|---|---|
| 97⅛ | 97¼ | 7.20% |

Because of legal restrictions and conditions prevailing in the money market, no treasury certificates have been offered domestically for several years.

### TREASURY NOTES

**Treasury notes**

U.S. **Treasury notes** are a debt obligation of the federal government issued in registered or bearer form in denominations of $1,000 up to $500 million. Treasury notes are issued with maturities of more than 1 year and up to 10 years in duration. They carry a fixed rate of interest and are issued, quoted, and traded as a percentage of their face value.

**example**

The bid and asked prices of a 5-year treasury note with a 7.50% interest rate appears in this form:

| Bid | Asked | Current Yield | Yield-to-Maturity |
|---|---|---|---|
| 105¼ | 105½ | 7.11% | 6.20% |

Most Treasury notes are owned by commercial banks, federal reserve banks, U.S. government agencies, and trust funds.

[16]To compute yield on government securities, use the same procedures as given earlier in regard to corporate bonds.

These notes permit such groups to arrange their portfolios with coupons and maturities spaced over a limited period of years. This provides them with automatic liquidity and attractive average yields.

### TREASURY BONDS

**Treasury bonds**

U.S. **Treasury bonds** may be in registered or bearer form at the preference of the investor. They may be issued with any maturity, but they customarily range from 5 to 35 years in duration.

These obligations carry a fixed interest rate and are issued, quoted, and traded as a percentage of their face value. They are offered in denominations of $500 up to $1 million in value. The typical face value is $1,000, however.

*D2d.*

*example*

A representative quotation for this security with a 3.50% interest rate and a 20-year maturity appears in this form:

| Bid | Asked | Current Yield | Yield-to-Maturity |
|-----|-------|---------------|-------------------|
| 74¾ | 75¼ | 4.65% | 5.55% |

**term bonds**

Some Treasury bond issues carry a call feature in their indenture. This permits the government to redeem these bonds prior to maturity, but only 5 years earlier. These obligations are often referred to as **term bonds**. Their yields-to-maturity are calculated only to the call date, but it is rare to see the Treasury Department exercise its privilege. Term bonds can be identified in newspapers and offering circulars by examining the full description of the bond itself.

*example*

The description of a term bond may appear in this form:

"U.S. Treasury 4.25% due May 15th, 1989/94"

The true maturity date is May 15, 1994, but the Treasury Department reserves the right to redeem this bond at face value any time between May 15, 1989 and May 15, 1994.

Prior to April 1971, from time to time the Treasury Department issued bonds with a special provision in their indentures designed to make them attractive to wealthy individuals with sizable estates. Those particular issues, when owned by decedents at the time of their death, could be redeemed by heirs at face value in satisfaction of federal estate taxes, even though they had a current market value at the time substantially below face value.

The Treasury Department's purpose was well served because, as a result of this feature, it was able to arrange financing at interest rates below those prevailing for similar issues without it. A provision of the tax code eliminated this tax advantage from

**E.**
**u.s. government-sponsored corporations and agency obligations**

Some securities are not direct obligations of the U.S. government but enjoy federal sponsorship or guarantees to some extent. Thus, a brief comment is in order here.

*E1.*
*Banks for Cooperatives*

Under supervision of the Farm Credit Administration, Banks for Cooperatives ("Co-op") make and service loans for farmers' cooperative associations and issue debt instruments to arrange for this financing. The federal government does not guarantee these obligations, but they are secured by banks organized under federal charter operating under government supervision. The bearer securities issued by the "Co-op" pay interest that is fully taxable to the recipient under federal regulations but exempted from state and municipal tax levies. They are legal investments for, and are most popular with, other banks and state and local governments.

*E2.*
*Federal Home Loan Banks*

Federal Home Loan Banks (FHLB) operate as a credit reserve system for savings and loan associations, homestead associations, savings banks, and insurance companies that qualify and apply for membership. FHLB issues obligations to finance the home building industry in the United States by granting mortgage loans with the monies generated from the offerings. Such debt is a legal investment for fiduciary, trust, and public funds. It is issued in bearer form with interest payable to holders subject to federal taxation but exempted from state and municipal taxes.

*E3.*
*Federal Intermediate Credit Banks*

Federal Intermediate Credit Banks (FICB), under supervision of the Farm Credit Administration, makes loans to agricultural credit corporations and production associations through issuance of debt obligations maturing within 5 years. Interest paid to the holders of FICB obligations is fully taxable to them under federal regulations but exempted from state and municipal taxes.

*E4.*
*Federal Land Banks*

Federal Land Banks (FLB) arrange loans secured by first mortgages on farm or ranch properties for general agricultural purposes. The obligations of these banks are created from an offering of bonds. They provide the holder with exemption from state and municipal taxes on interest received therefrom, but such interest is subject to full federal tax liabilities. The bonds are not guaranteed by the U.S. government but are backed by participating banks organized under federal charter operating under government supervision. They are lawful investments for fiduciaries, trust funds, federal credit unions, federal savings and loan associations, savings banks, and commercial banks organized under a national charter. Denominations of certificates range from $1,000 to $100,000.

*E5.*
*Federal National Mortgage Association ("Fannie Mae")*

Federal National Mortgage Association (FNMA) is a publicly owned, government-sponsored corporation established to provide liquidity for mortgage investments in the marketplace. The corporation purchases and sells mortgages insured by the Federal Housing Administration (FHA) or Farmers Home Administration

(FHDA) or guaranteed by the Veterans Administration (VA) using monies generated in part from short-term notes and debenture obligations offered publicly. The balance of its funds is realized from direct purchase of its capital stock by qualified buyers and sellers with whom it deals in these mortgages. Those institutional investors whose names appear on an approved list are obligated to subscribe to FNMA common stock pursuant to a prescribed formula. The stock as well as the association's bonds are readily marketable. The debentures are issued only in bearer form with interest coupons attached. The interest paid on the association's bonds is fully taxable to investors despite the fact that its common stock and bonds are clearly defined as an "exempted security" under the Securities Exchange Act of 1934.

Government National Mortgage Association (GNMA) is an offshoot of the FNMA. It is a wholly owned government corporation operated by the Department of Housing and Urban Development (HUD) to provide liquidity in home and federal agency mortgage financing. The corporation offers investors a participation in pools of qualified mortgages on private enterprises that are fully guaranteed by the U.S. government. These obligations, however, enjoy no specific tax exemption with respect to interest or repayment of principal thereon.

*E6.*
*Government National Mortgage Association ("Ginnie Mae")*

Tennessee Valley Authority (TVA) obligations are authorized by Congress to promote economic development of the Tennessee River and adjacent areas. The debt created by the TVA has a senior claim upon the income derived from power projects in the region that were built with the proceeds of these bond offerings. The interest paid to investors is subject to federal taxes but exempted from state and local taxes.

*E7.*
*Tennessee Valley Authority*

The Post Office Department was reorganized as an independent entity in 1971 and is now known as the U.S. Postal Service. Its founding legislation authorizes it to issue debt securities (not to exceed $10 billion) to finance capital expenditures and conduct operations of a postal system within the United States. These securities may be guaranteed as to payment of principal and interest by the U.S. government if petitioned to by the Postal Service and if the Secretary of the Treasury deems it in the public interest to do so. The initial offering of 6⅞% debentures due February 1, 1997 does not carry such guarantees although it is widely assumed that the Postal Service's obligations offer an implied, if not actual, guarantee. Interest received by the holders of these bonds is taxable by the federal government but exempted from state and local taxes.

*E8.*
*U.S. Postal Service*

The Student Loan Marketing Association is a U.S. government-sponsored private corporation founded in 1972. It provides liquidity to lenders engaged in the Guaranteed Student Program fostered by the Higher Education Act of 1965. Liquidity is accomplished by the following programs:

*E9.*
*Student Loan Marketing Association ("Sallie Mae")*

1. *Warehousing Advance Program.* This consists of making loans to qualified lending institutions using student loans, insured by the U.S. Commissioner of Education or a duly authorized state or nonprofit institutional representative, as underlying collateral.

2. *Loan Purchase Program.* This consists of purchasing insured student loans from qualified lending institutions at rates determined through negotiation. "Sallie Mae" obtains its capital through periodic offerings of debt obligations as well as from offerings of common stock in the company. Until July 1, 1982 debt obligations may be guaranteed as to payment of principal and interest by the Secretary of the Department of Health, Education and Welfare (HEW) and is backed by the full faith and credit of the U.S. government, making it an exempted security. As such, interest paid to holders is not subject to income taxation by state or municipal authorities but is fully taxable by the federal government. The common stock carries no government guarantees whatsoever and is therefore not an exempted security. Moreover, there are restrictions placed on ownership and transferability of the common stock, limiting it to eligible holders, as defined by the Secretary of HEW. Eligibility is confined to institutions or organizations making student loans or who are parties to insuring student loans. They include colleges, universities, state agencies, national banks, financial or credit institutions (that is, federal savings and loan associations and credit unions), and some insurance companies.

**F.**
**international securities**

Various international institutions have been organized throughout the world to facilitate pooling and investment of capital for productive purposes. Debt instruments issued by these institutions are characterized by principal and interest payments denominated in currencies of the country in which such financing is arranged. Therefore, investors with specific currency preferences or requirements may choose from a variety of issues available in English pounds sterling, German marks, Dutch guilders, Swiss francs, and so forth. Consideration is further complicated by the variety of rates, maturities, and other terms and conditions specified in the indenture of those notes and bonds.

**F1.**
***International Bank for Reconstruction and Development (The World Bank)***

The International Bank for Reconstruction and Development is popularly known as the World Bank and often identified by professional dealers and traders simply as the "IB" (International Bank). The bank makes and guarantees loans to assist in the reconstruction and development of resources in countries which subscribe to its capital stock and play a role in the management of this institution. Through its sizable subscriptions, the United States controls about 25% of the voting power so that changes in the bank's Articles of Agreement[17] (drawn and founded in July 1944) necessitate this nation's consent before they become effective.

From the start of its operations in 1946, the bank's loans have been made to develop and modernize industry, agriculture, transportation, communications, education, electric power, and water supply facilities in over 90 member countries and territories.

The International Bank supplements its capital funds periodically through offerings of debt obligations to institutional investors in various countries. These obligations are denominated in

[17]Amendments require 80–100% membership approval for adoption, the variance dependent upon the nature of the change.

various currencies throughout the world. Interest paid on World Bank bonds to U.S. residents is fully taxable by federal, state, and local authorities. However, it is exempted from federal taxation if paid to nonresident aliens and most foreign corporations, whether or not engaged in business in the United States.

The Inter-American Development Bank, founded in 1959, is another international institution intent upon promoting economic and social development and modernization by financing capital projects in its member countries. Only government members in the Western Hemisphere are eligible for such loans, although the bank's own borrowings are worldwide and denominated in various international currencies. Interest paid to holders of its debt obligations is fully taxable by federal, state, and local authorities.

*F2.*
*Inter-American Development Bank (IADB)*

**money market instruments**

**Money market instruments**, as contrasted with capital notes, bonds, or debentures, are debt securities that are issued and will mature in a relatively short period of time; usually within 1 year. Bankers' acceptances, certificates of deposit, and commercial paper are some securities that fall into this classification.

G.
money-market instruments

**bankers' acceptances**

**Bankers' acceptances** are credit instruments designed to finance shipment and/or storage of merchandise by manufacturers, both domestically and abroad. They are merely drafts (bills of exchange) that have been accepted (guaranteed) by a bank or trust company for payment on a specific date in the future (1 to 6 months). Bankers' acceptances provide manufacturers and exporters with capital liquidity during the period between time of manufacture (or export) and payment by the purchasers of the goods. These short-term, guaranteed drafts may be marketed several times before maturity by the relatively few securities dealers who maintain a market for them. Bids and offerings are reflected at discounted prices from face value, the method used in the trading of U.S. Treasury bills. The rate of interest, calculated on an annual basis and adjusted for the exact number of days involved, is reasonably low, reflecting the relative safety of this investment. Profits earned and interest received on a bankers' acceptance are taxable for American investors.

*G1.*
*Bankers' Acceptances*

**certificates of deposit (CDs)**

**Certificates of deposit (CDs)** are negotiable securities issued by commercial banks against money deposited with them for a definite period of time. A time deposit cannot be withdrawn until expiration of a specific period, in contrast with the privilege of a demand or savings deposit. If the depositors want to convert their certificates to cash before the maturity date, they must sell them in the secondary market to other people or institutions. Actual interest realized by resale of a CD in the secondary market depends upon prevailing monetary conditions. When short-term money rates are higher than the fixed percentage specified in the CD, realized interest will be less than the stated rate. If short-term money was available at a lower percentage, that CD's resale would result in higher realized interest. The maximum interest paid by commercial banks on CDs of less than $100,000 is fixed by the Federal Reserve Board and is usually set somewhat higher than that paid on savings deposits. The interest rate varies, depending upon the size of the deposit and the length of time involved.

*G2.*
*Certificates of Deposit*

**G3.**
*Commercial Paper*

**Commercial paper** represents unsecured short-term corporate obligations with maturities ranging up to 270 days in duration. It is 270 days because a debt instrument redeemed more than 9 months later requires time-consuming, expensive registration proceedings with the SEC, under the terms of the Securities Act of 1933. Therefore, extended maturities for a commercial paper offering are rare. Corporations issue this paper to satisfy monetary requirements in connection with their current operations, and this I.O.U. efficiently serves this purpose. Finance companies and commercial factors in particular find this means an effective way to raise money.

Some commercial paper is issued at face value with a fixed interest rate. Most companies, however, issue paper without a particular rate, offering it at a discount from face value to reflect prevailing money market conditions.

The issuers of commercial paper tailor the maturities to the needs of the investors. Therefore, most investors hold commercial paper to maturity and no secondary market is required. Typical denominations range from $100,000 to $1 million, in bearer form.

**H.**
**tax-exempted securities**

One other type of security deserves attention in this chapter, the **tax-exempted security**. Generally speaking, a tax-exempted security is an obligation of a state, municipality, or local government. It is so named because *interest* paid to the holder of this debt instrument is exempted from federal income taxes. This privilege, however, does not apply to *profits* established via purchase and sale of these securities, nor does it necessarily exempt interest from state and local income taxes. Typically, the exemption from taxes applies in full only if a state resident buys an obligation issued by that state or by a municipality within that state.

*H1.*
*Advantages*

The tax privilege is an especially attractive one for individuals or institutions in high federal tax brackets. A taxpayer in the 50% bracket must seek a taxable yield *twice* that which is necessary for a comparable return on tax-exempted bonds to retain an equal number of dollars. For example, interest paid on an ordinary $1,000 corporate bond with a 5% coupon rate equals $50 annually. However, the investors in a 50% tax bracket must pay half of that in federal taxes, leaving them with only $25 net. If they purchase tax-exempted bonds with a 2.5% coupon rate, annual interest is $25, but it is tax free.

To calculate comparable yield required on a taxable investment so as to provide an equal number of dollars for persons holding tax-exempted securities, take the *difference* between the investor's tax bracket and 100 percent and divide that into the tax-exempted yield.

**example**

---

If investors in a 42% federal tax bracket hold a tax-exempted bond with a 4.64% yield, they must seek a taxable return of 8% to retain an equal number of dollars after paying those taxes.

$$100\%$$
$$-42\% \text{ (tax bracket)}$$
$$\overline{58\%} \text{ (decimalized } = .58)$$

$$\frac{.0464}{.58} = .08, \text{ or } 8\%$$

Information concerning events, conditions, and credits of forthcoming municipal financings is often available in *The Wall Street Journal* (published by Dow Jones & Co., Inc., 22 Cortlandt St., New York City 10007). For full coverage the professional municipal analyst, salesperson, or trader refers to *The Daily Bond Buyer, the Authority on Municipal Bonds* (published daily except Saturdays and Sundays at 1 State Street Plaza, New York City 10004).

Although tax-exempted securities are instrumentalities of a government, they do not have equal ranking with the U.S. government's willingness and ability to pay interest and principal. The U.S. government has sovereignty[18] and an unlimited power of taxation. Although state governments generally have similar powers, municipalities and local governments certainly do not. Therefore, these obligations ordinarily carry lower credit ratings as a result. All other factors being equal, *lower ratings mean higher yields* for investors, which compensates them for the greater risk involved, however minor it may be.

Tax-exempted securities are subclassified as *general obligation, special tax, new housing authority* or as *revenue* bonds in accordance with terms and conditions established in their indentures.

*H2.*
*Types of Tax-Exempted Securities*

### GENERAL OBLIGATION BONDS

*H2a.*

**General obligation bonds (GOs)**

**General obligation bonds (GOs)** pledge good faith and full taxing power of the issuer to pay interest and repay principal on the dates indicated in the agreement.

### SPECIAL TAX BONDS

*H2b.*

**Special tax bonds**

**Special tax bonds** promise payment of principal and interest from a tax or special assessment levied upon persons who benefit from facilities built with the proceeds of a bond sale. Examples of such facilities include roads and highways paved with financing supported by a gasoline tax and a community sewer system constructed with financing facilitated by a special assessment upon local property owners.

### NEW HOUSING AUTHORITY BONDS

*H2c.*

**New housing authority bonds**

**New housing authority bonds** are backed by annual net rental incomes received from lessees of apartments in projects built with the proceeds of such bond sales. Although administration of these housing projects is within the jurisdiction of a local housing au-

---

[18]*Sovereignty* is broadly defined as the legal authority to be sued only if it consents to be sued.

thority, it is most important to note that under an annual contributions contract with the Public Housing Administration (PHA) of the United States the PHA will unconditionally pay the principal and interest on these bonds, if necessary, by satisfying deficiencies in the rental revenues and other monies realized by the local housing authority. Consequently, these bonds pledge the faith of the U.S. government and represent minimal principal risk for investors able to hold them to maturity.

### H2d.  REVENUE BONDS

**Revenue bonds** pledge only the income from a particular project, financed with capital raised on the sale of that issue, to satisfy interest and principal requirements. This type of financing is often used by governmental entities to build highways, bridges, tunnels, and power plants. The tolls and fees collected from the users of these facilities are anticipated to be adequate to cover the semiannual interest requirement and to repay the principal on the loan at maturity.

**revenue bonds**

Until the early 1960s, when the Internal Revenue Service closed a loophole, municipalities often used their ability to issue federal tax-exempted securities to lure industrial corporations to their localities. They issued revenue bonds whose funds were employed to build factories and other facilities that were then leased to an industrial concern that agreed to provide jobs to area inhabitants. The rental amount was calculated to pay interest and principal on the underlying debt. Thus, the company enjoyed indirect, lower-cost financing because of the tax-exempted feature of this appropriately named *industrial revenue bond*. That is, because the revenue bonds were tax-exempt, they paid a lower interest rate. Because the rent was calculated to pay only a small amount of interest and the principal, the company benefited. Now, however, monies used for such purposes do not qualify for tax-free interest to the holders of debt securities unless the underlying funds build or improve

1. airports;
2. harbors;
3. waterways;
4. mass transit facilities; or
5. pollution control proficiencies.

Further, the IRS places restrictions on the amount of money which can be raised. Today, bonds that are designed to help improve the environment in which we live are called **industrial development bonds (IDBs).** As before, they are revenue bonds issued by industrial or utility corporations offering tax-exempted interest. The holder of such a bond looks to the issuer for satisfaction of the obligation, not to the municipality.

**industrial development bonds (IDBs)**

Ordinarily, revenue bonds are riskier investments than general obligation bonds. Consequently, they command higher interest rates and yields. Another typical characteristic of revenue bond issues is a balloon maturity for this serial-type debt. Its indenture requires the issuer to redeem bonds on a systematic basis and thus provides investors with an increasing amount of protection as the debt ages. These issues customarily employ a balloon interest rate, too. Because it is not certain how much revenue the project will be able to generate in the early years, the issuer imposes a smaller interest requirement upon that project in the first few years and a higher interest requirement in the middle and latter years.

Figure 2 shows the cover of a circular announcing an offering of tax-exempted securities. Significant information regarding this issue is summarized on its title page. The following text explains the information to which the circled numbers in the figure refer.

H3.
*Illustrative Circular for Tax-Exempted Securities*

1 The total borrowing amounts to $75 million, $33.7 million, in serial bonds and $41.3 million in term bonds.[19] Such an offering is, therefore, sometimes called a **split offering.**

**split offering**

2 These are revenue bonds and do not constitute an obligation of the state of Arizona or any of its municipalities. Payment of interest and repayment of principal is wholly dependent upon revenues paid by the users of electric power generated by the system.

3 Whereas the offering commences on June 20, 1973, the bonds are not deliverable and need not be paid for by the initial purchasers until July 1, 1973. Consequently, interest accrues to the holder's benefit beginning on July 1 and will be paid semiannually on January 1 and July 1 thereafter, until maturity.

4 The bonds are available in coupon or fully registered form but will only be issued in denominations of $5,000 or multiples thereof.

5 The term bonds may be redeemed at par beginning on January 1, 2000, whereas the serial bonds are callable at the issuer's option any time after January 1, 1983. Holders of bonds retired at that date will receive a 2.5% premium over face value to compensate them for the inconvenience of surrendering their bonds prior to maturity. The percentage of premium is scaled down thereafter until January 1, 1993, at which time holders of called bonds will be repaid only face value plus accrued interest to the call redemption date.

6 Principal amounts repayable in the early years are smaller than for the later maturities, a classic illustration of ballooning.

7 Although the early coupon interest rate schedule is higher percentagewise than for the later maturities, this modification merely reflects the unusual monetary conditions prevailing at the time of the offering. The issuer will still pay fewer *total interest dollars* to the shorter maturities than to the longer maturities to preserve the concept of ballooning interest typical of serial bonds.

8 Whereas the earlier maturities carry a 6.5% interest rate, they are offered at a price that provides the purchaser with a much lower rate of return on this investment. Because 6.5% is expressed as a function of the par value, the offering market price must be at a significant premium above that par value.

To compute the price we use the formula given earlier in this chapter:

$$\frac{\text{annual interest}}{\text{invested dollars}} = \text{yield}$$

---

[19]Serial bonds are obligations of the same issuer offered at the same time but with various interest rates and maturities arranged over a period of years. Term bonds are obligations with a single interest rate and a maturity that falls due on a date well off into the future.

# $75,000,000①

## SALT RIVER PROJECT AGRICULTURAL IMPROVEMENT AND POWER DISTRICT, ARIZONA

### Salt River Project Electric System Revenue Bonds,②

### 1973 Series B

**To be dated July 1, 1973③**　　　　　　　　　　　　**To mature January 1, as shown below:**

Principal and interest (January 1 and July 1) payable at the principal offices of the First National Bank of Arizona, Phoenix, Arizona, and First National City Bank, New York, New York. Coupon Bonds in the denomination of $5,000 registrable as to principal only and exchangeable for fully registered bonds in any integral multiple of $5,000. First National Bank of Arizona, Phoenix, Arizona, is the Trustee.④

⑤The 1973 Series B Bonds maturing on January 1, 2011, are subject to redemption on January 1, 2000 and any interest payment date thereafter from amounts accumulated in the Debt Service Fund with respect to Sinking Fund Installments at the principal amount thereof plus accrued interest to the redemption date. The 1973 Series B Bonds may be redeemed as a whole, or in part in inverse order of maturities, at any time on or after January 1, 1983, at prices ranging from 102½% for the period January 1, 1983, to and including December 31, 1984, to 100% on and after January 1, 1993, plus accrued interest to the date of redemption, as further described herein.

Interest exempt, in the opinion of Bond Counsel, from Federal income taxes under existing laws, and from income taxes within the State of Arizona.⑩

The 1973 Series B Bonds are being issued for the purpose of financing improvements to the Electric System of the District. The 1973 Series B Bonds and the presently outstanding Electric System Revenue Bonds are payable from and secured by a pledge of and lien on the net revenues of the District's Electric System, subject to a prior lien of Prior Lien Bonds, as defined in and more particularly described in the Official Statement. The 1973 Series B Bonds are also secured by a pledge of a debt reserve and other funds.

### Amounts, Maturities, Coupon Rates and Price or Yield
### $33,700,000 Serial Bonds ①

| Amount | Maturity | Coupon Rate | Yield | Amount | Maturity | Coupon Rate | Price or Yield |
|---|---|---|---|---|---|---|---|
| $　790,000⑥ | 1977 | 6½%⑦ | 4.35%⑧ | $1,455,000 | 1989 | 5　% | 100% |
| 830,000 | 1978 | 6½ | 4.40 | 1,535,000 | 1990 | 5 | 5.05 |
| 875,000 | 1979 | 6½ | 4.45 | 1,615,000 | 1991 | 5.10 | 100 |
| 920,000 | 1980 | 6½ | 4.50 | 1,700,000 | 1992 | 5.10 | 5.15 |
| 965,000 | 1981 | 6½ | 4.55 | 1,785,000 | 1993 | 5.20 | 100 |
| 1,020,000 | 1982 | 6½ | 4.60 | 1,880,000 | 1994 | 5¼ | 100 |
| 1,070,000 | 1983 | 6½ | 4.65 | 1,980,000 | 1995 | 5.30 | 100 |
| 1,125,000 | 1984 | 6½ | 4.75 | 2,085,000 | 1996 | 5.30 | 100 |
| 1,185,000 | 1985 | 6½ | 4.80* | 2,195.000 | 1997 | 5.30 | 5.35⑧ |
| 1,250,000 | 1986 | 6 | 4.85* | 2,310,000 | 1998 | 5.40 | 100 |
| 1,315,000 | 1987 | 5 | 4.90 | 2.430,000⑥ | 1999 | 5.40⑦ | 100 |
| 1,385,000 | 1988 | 5 | 4.95 | | | | |

* Priced to First Call.

### $41,300,000 5⅜% Term Bonds Due January 1, 2011 ①
### Yield 5.60%
### (Accrued Interest to be Added)

## Salomon Brothers⑨

Members New York Stock Exchange
One New York Plaza
New York, N.Y. 10004
Atlanta / Boston / Chicago / Cleveland / Dallas / Los Angeles
Philadelphia / St. Louis / San Francisco

*The 1973 Series B Bonds are offered when, as and if issued and received by us, and subject to the approval of legality by Mudge Rose Guthrie & Alexander, New York, New York, Bond Counsel.*⑩

June 20, 1973③

**FIGURE 2**
Cover Page of Circular Announcing an
Offering of Tax-Exempted Securities

Hence:

$$\frac{\$65}{x} = .0435$$

$$.0435x = \$65$$

$$x = \frac{\$65}{.0435} = \$1,494.25$$

Simple arithmetic reveals that each $1,000 par value with a 6.5% coupon must be priced at $1,494.25 to result in a 4.35% rate of return. Note the changes in relationships in coupon rate and offering price yields depicted in the scale of these serial bonds. Up through the 1988 maturities, the initial offering was set at a premium. This is identifiable by the fact the yield is *lower* than the coupon rate. But the 1989 series is priced at par (100%), making the yield equal to the coupon rate. It obviously follows that the 1990, 1992, and 1997 series are offered at a slight discount because the yield is *higher* than the coupon rate.

This is an important concept to recognize from an offering scale of serial bonds. If the yield is shown as a return that is lower than the coupon (interest rate), the bond is priced at a premium. If it is equal to the coupon rate, it is priced at par. If it is higher than the coupon, the bonds are offered at a discount from par value. Furthermore, those yields are calculated on the assumption that those bonds will be held to maturity and redeemed at par value. If the issuer calls those bonds prior to maturity and pays par value or more, an investor's effective rate of return on premium bonds will be lower (and on discount bonds higher) than this figure. This is caused by the necessity to amortize the capital loss or accumulate the capital gain over a shorter time frame than anticipated.

9 The principal investment banker offering this issue is Salomon Brothers. The contents of the circular, not just the title page, must be consulted for the names of other participants, if any.

10 General counsel retained by the issuer is expected to give its opinion about the legality of any tax-exempted security offering. Contrary to corporate offerings of debt securities, it is not always permissible under prevailing statutes for a municipality, or even a state, to incur general or revenue obligations. Laws must be examined and attested to by attorneys to discourage potential litigation by dissatisfied citizens or purchasers. The attorneys also examine IRS and state codes to determine whether interest paid to purchasers of this issue qualifies for exemption from federal and/or state income tax requirements effective at the time of such an offering.

## H4. Trading Tax-Exempted Securities

Because of the financial circumstances of those for whom tax-exempted securities have appeal, there is considerably less trading activity in most issues in the municipal market as compared to corporate bonds and stock. Banks, insurance companies, and wealthy individuals, particularly, acquire these securities for tax reasons and generally hold them for many years. Coupled with this is the fact that a typical tax-exempt issue is also significantly smaller in amount than a typical corporate or U.S. Treasury issue. Consequently, the tax-exempted securities marketplace is somewhat illiquid and is characterized by fewer bids and offerings and wider price gaps between those values.

When a secondary offering of bonds is made available, an announcement usually appears in the "Blue List," a publication widely read among municipal dealers. Officially, its full title is "The Blue List of Current Municipal Offerings," and it is sold via subscription by The Blue List Publishing Company (a division of Standard & Poor's Corporation), 345 Hudson Street, New York City 10014. Prospective purchasers are invited to call the dealer advertising bonds for sale to arrange an acceptable price. Municipal securities most often trade via telephone in an environment of personal negotiation between buyer and seller. To be sure, some issues are listed and do trade occasionally on some stock exchanges, but for the most part tax-exempted activities occur over the counter.

## H5.
### Original Issue Discount Bonds

Ordinarily, when an issuer offers a debt security for sale it does so at par value ($1,000 per certificate) or very close to it, with interest payments stated in accord with then current money market conditions. Sometimes, however, technical or legal limitations on interest payments can hinder the issuer's attempts to raise capital.[20] At those times the issuer may be able to circumvent its rate ceiling by offering its $1,000 par value bonds at a significantly lower price to compensate investors for the lower annual interest payment. The result, from the purchaser's viewpoint, is the same; an identical yield from invested dollars.

For example, let us take the case of an issuer who is limited to an annual interest of 5% per $1,000 obligation. If the issuer wishes to attract a purchaser for a $1,000 bond at par value when the prevailing yield is 6%, then the annual payment must be $60.

$$\frac{\$60 \quad \text{annual interest}}{\$1,000 \quad \text{par value}} = 6\% \text{ yield}$$

However, the $60 interest exceeds the limit of $50 annual interest. To circumvent this 5% limit, the issuer can maintain both the $50 annual interest limit and the prevailing yield of 6% by discounting the $1,000. The bond price must be $833.

$$\frac{\$50 \quad \text{annual interest}}{\$833 \text{ offering value of } \$1,000 \text{ par}} = 6\% \text{ yield.}$$

Although the issuer and purchaser may be satisfied with these arrangements, both parties must nevertheless be familiar with the Internal Revenue Service's position in this matter. The $167 discount from par in the example above is considered to be compensation paid by the issuer for borrowed dollars. It is therefore the equivalent of interest for federal tax purposes; the $167 discount is really no different from interest paid on the security itself. Thus, if the issuer is a corporate entity, the discount represents fully taxable interest to the bondholder. Moreover, the interest-discount is prorated monthly over the life of the bond, and the appropriate income tax is paid annually by the investor. In the example above, if the bond was scheduled to mature in 10 years (120 months), and an investor purchased one bond on the offering, taxable interest after the first year equals $66.70 ($50 plus

[20]The issuer may be restricted to annual interest payments of 5% per $1,000 obligation when the prevailing rate demands 6%.

$16.70, which is 10% of the $167 discount). If the issuer is a state, municipality, or other such political subdivision, the discount is tax-exempted interest under federal law.

Additionally, the purchaser of an *original-issue discount* bond must amortize that discount over the life of the bond. This increases the cost by the monthly interest accretion and precludes an automatic capital gain if held to maturity. For example, in the illustration above, if the investor held the bond for exactly 5 years (60 months out of a possible 120) his tax cost would be $916.50 ($833 plus $83.50 which is half of the $167 discount). A capital gain is realized only if the bond is sold for more than $916.50.

# the mechanics of distributing securities

A. The Securities Act of 1933
- A1. Purpose
- A2. Securities To Be Registered
- A3. Securities Exempted from Registration
- A4. Transactions Exempted from Registration
- A5. Private Placement

B: Issuers
- B1. SEC Rule 504
- B2. SEC Rule 505
- B3. SEC Rule 506
- B4. SEC Rule 147

C. Affiliated Persons
- C1. When Can They Distribute Securities?
- C2. Checklist of Cautionary Questions
- C3. SEC Rule 144

D. Underwriters
- D1. Voluntary
- D2. Involuntary

E. The Role of an Investment Banker
- E1. Services Performed
- E2. Investigation and Analysis

F. Registration of the Public Offering
- F1. Filing and SEC Examining
- F2. Effective Data
- F3. Delay after a 20-day Period
- F4. Purchasers' Protection

G. The Trust Indenture Act of 1939
- G1. Purpose
- G2. Conditions
- G3. Indenture Registration

H. Activities during the 20-Day Cooling-Off Period
- H1. The Preliminary Agreement
- H2. Forming a Syndicate
- H3. Soliciting Indications of Interest
- H4. SEC Rule 10b-6
- H5. Preliminary Prospectus
- H6. Due-Diligence Meeting

> The purpose of the Securities Act of 1933 is to protect the public against the issuance and distribution of fraudulent securities.[1] The act does so by requiring the filing of a registration statement with the Securities and Exchange Commission. This statement sets forth, in a public record, all relevant information pertaining to the specific offering. (See Figure 1.) This is the reason why this law is sometimes called the "Full Disclosure Act" by persons in the securities industry.

**A.**
the securities act of 1933
**A1.**
*Purpose*

If a securities issuer fails to furnish complete and accurate information, purchasers of that security may sue to recover realized losses. For example, someone who subscribes for a security based upon incomplete or erroneous facts, at $50, and subsequently sells it at $30, can institute suit for recovery for the amount of the loss ($20). Willful violators of this act can suffer a $10,000 fine and/or 5 years in jail.

Any security that is sold in interstate commerce or through use of the U.S. Postal Service must be registered with the SEC before a public offering or distribution can be made by

**A2.**
*Securities To Be Registered*

1. its **issuer**;
2. **affiliated persons**,[2] or
3. people who acquire unregistered securities from an issuer or from an affiliated person with a view to their immediate resale.[3]

> Some *issues,* however, are *exempted from registration* under the Act of 1933. They include
>
> 1. obligations of, or guaranteed by, the U.S. government;
> 2. obligations of, or guaranteed by, any state or municipality of that state;
> 3. issues of domestic banks or trust companies (securities issued by a *bank holding company* are not exempted from the registration requirement);
> 4. commercial paper or bankers' acceptances maturing within 270 days of issuance;

**A3.**
*Securities Exempted from Registration*

5. issues of building and loan associations;
6. securities of farmers' cooperative associations;
7. securities of a common or contract carrier (rails, airlines, truckers, and so on);
8. receivers' or trustees' certificates issued with court approval;
9. issues of small business investment companies (SBIC);
10. securities offered and sold exclusively intrastate;

[1] The term *securities* is broadly defined to include any note, stock, bond, evidence of debt, interest or participation in a profit-sharing agreement, investment contract, voting trust certificate, fractional undivided interest in oil, gas, or other mineral rights, or any warrant to subscribe to, or purchase, any of the foregoing.

[2] An affiliated person is someone who can influence management decisions in that corporation. This category *may* include officers, directors, principal stockholders, and members of their immediate families. Their shares in the company are often described as "control stock."

[3] These people are defined as *statutory underwriters,* even though they may be individuals and even though they may not be fully engaged in the securities business.

11. issues of religious, educational, charitable, or nonprofit institutions;

12. insurance policies or mixed annuity contracts (variable annuities and variable life insurance policies are not exempted); and

13. offerings that qualify under Regulation A of the Securities Act of 1933.

Regulation A permits offerings under an abbreviated statement when the value of all securities issued by that corporation in the preceding year *does not exceed* $1,500,000. Offerings by an affiliated person must not exceed $100,000 to qualify for the privilege offered under Regulation A. Although Regulation A does grant a qualified registration exemption to securities offerings of limited value, it requires the use of an offering circular containing much of the same information presented in a full registration statement. However, it does take less time and costs considerably less money in legal and SEC filing fees to accomplish a distribution under Regulation A.

14. offerings that qualify under Regulation D of the Securities Act of 1933.

SEC Rules 501-506, under Regulation D, set forth terms and conditions within which issuers can offer unregistered securities for sale in limited dollar amounts to a limited number of investors and/or to defined "accredited persons." For the most part these unregistered offerings are called *private placements*.

**A4.**
**Transactions Exempted from Registration**

To avoid burdensome paperwork and expense, certain *transactions are also exempted* from registration requirements. They include

1. transactions by anyone other than the issuer, a dealer, or an underwriter;

2. brokers' transactions executed on the unsolicited request of customers;

**FIGURE 1**
Information Prescribed for Inclusion in Registration Statements Filed with the Securities and Exchange Commission

1. The name of the issuer.
2. The name of the state or sovereign power under which the issuer is organized.
3. The location of the issuer's principal office.
4. The names and addresses of the directors and other senior officials.
5. The names and addresses of the underwriters (if any).
6. The names and addresses of persons owning 10% or more of any class of stock of the issuer.
7. The amount of securities owned by the directors, senior officials, underwriters, and 10% holders.
8. The general character of the issuer's business.
9. A statement of the issuer's capitalization.
10. A statement of securities reserved for options outstanding, with names and addresses of persons allotted 10% or more of these options.
11. The amount of capital stock of each class included in this offer.
12. The issuer's funded debt.
13. The purposes to which the proceeds of this offering will be applied.
14. Remuneration payable to the issuers directly, naming them specifically when annual payments exceed $25,000.
15. The estimated net proceeds to be derived from the offering.
16. The price at which the public offering will be attempted.
17. Commissions, fees, and so on, to be paid to the underwriters.
18. Itemized detail of expenses incurred by the issuer in connection with this offering.
19. The net proceeds derived from any securities sold by the issuer in the preceding 2 years and the pertinent details of that sale.

20. Any consideration paid to a promoter in the preceding 2 years.
21. The names and addresses of any vendors of property or goodwill to be acquired with the proceeds of this offering.
22. Full particulars of any dealings between the issuer and its officers, directors, and holders of 10% or more of its stock that transpired in the preceding 2 years.
23. The names and addresses of counsel passing upon the legality of the issue.
24. The dates and details of material contracts created outside the issuer's ordinary course of business within the preceding 2 years.
25. A certified, detailed balance sheet of the issuer drawn within the preceding 90 days.
26. A certified profit-and-loss statement of the issuer for the latest fiscal year and the preceding 2 years.
27. Certified financial statements of any issuer or business to be acquired with proceeds of this offering.
28. A copy of the underwriting contract or agreement.
29. A copy of the law firm's written opinion attesting to the legality of the issue.
30. A copy of all material contracts referred to in item 24.
31. A copy of the issuer's charter, bylaws, trust agreement, partnership agreement, and so forth, as the case may be.
32. A copy of the underlying agreement or indentures affecting any security offered or to be offered by the issuer.

3. transactions by an issuer that do not involve a public offering (such as a *private placement,* which is an offering to a limited number of purchasers).
4. transactions by securities dealers, *except for*
    a. those pursuant to an effective registration statement that are traded within
        (1) 90 days of an *initial* public offering of securities by the issuer, and
        (2) 40 days of subsequent public offerings of securities by that issuer;
    b. those representing an unsold allotment or subscription by a dealer participating in a distribution by an issuer or underwriter.

A5.
*Private Placement*

Note carefully that the transactions in subitems (a) and (b) are *exceptions* to exemption from registration. In other words, transactions that fall within these parameters *must* be qualified with the SEC. Generally, this means that purchasers and expected purchasers must be furnished with a prospectus for that issue before settlement of their transaction, even after the underwriter's group has been dissolved and most participants have disposed of their commitment.

**private placement**

A **private placement**, referred to in item 3 above, is the distribution of securities to a "limited number" of purchasers made without the filing of a registration statement. If you are such a purchaser, customarily you certify to the issuer, in a written agreement known as an **investment letter**, that your purchase is for investment purposes, without immediate intention to reoffer the securities publicly. If your financial circumstances change in a relatively short period of time thereafter, you may transfer title to this so-called "letter" security to another investor, but only in another private placement. In such secondary private placements, you as seller should obtain an investment letter from the new purchaser for your own protection. Otherwise, if the new buyer reneges on the promise to hold for investment and attempts a public sale soon after, you can be defined as a statutory underwriter and be liable for penalty under the Securities Act of 1933. The procurement of an investment letter may not always enable you to avoid a penalty, but it can surely mitigate it. Moreover, it will allow you to sue the buyer who placed you in that position and gain legal and financial satisfaction as a result.

**investment letter**

Securities placed privately may be represented by either equity or debt instruments. Although *letter stock* usually gets most of the publicity in the press and various trade journals, substantial quantities of *letter bonds* are also subject to the SEC rules, too.

Each certificate is imprinted with a legend that warns the holder of the prevailing distribution restrictions under the law. However, the absence of such a legend is no assurance of the certificate's legal transferability.

**issuer**

An **issuer** of a security is a corporation, trust, or association engaged in a distribution of its securities. Public offerings of its certificates may be attempted if a registration statement on file with the SEC has become effective.

B.
issuers

There are several ways in which issuers can avoid the time, expense, and paperwork, associated with a registered securities offering to raise capital. All of them are identified as private placements. Specific SEC rules set forth qualifications permitting unregistered distributions by eligible issuers.

**B1.**
**SEC Rule 504**

Issuers who are not investment companies or subject to the public reporting requirements of the 1934 Securities and Exchange Act have limited assets and/or few shareholders. Those small companies can publicly sell to any number of investors unregistered securities valued up to $500,000 during any 12-month period. There are no information disclosure requirements under this rule.

**B2.**
**SEC Rule 505**

Any issuer who is not an investment company or disqualified from selling under Regulation A can publicly offer unregistered securities valued up to $5 million during any 12-month period. However, in accord with this rule, that distribution may be made to no more than 35 nonaccredited investors. No limitation is imposed on the number of accredited investors who may subscribe.

As defined in regulation D, ''accredited investors'' are any of the following:

1. financial institutions (such as banks, insurance companies and investment companies, or even employee benefit plans);
2. private business development companies;
3. colleges or university endowment funds, as well as other nonprofit organizations with assets of $5 million or more;
4. corporate or partnership ''insiders'';
5. purchasers of at least $150,000 of the securities being offered, with the total purchase price not exceeding 20% of the purchaser's net worth at time of sale;
6. individuals with a net worth in excess of $1 million;
7. individuals with income in excess of $200,000 in each of the last two years, with a reasonable expectation of having income in excess of $200,000 in the year of purchase; and
8. any entity 100% owned by accredited investors.

**B3.**
**SEC Rule 506**

Any issuers, whether or not a reporting company under the 1934 Exchange Act, entitled to make private placements under Section 4(2) of the 1933 Act, can use the registration exemption available in this rule. The Rule permits offerings with no value restrictions in any time period to as many as 35 nonaccredited persons. The issuer must reasonably believe, prior to making the distribution, that these nonaccredited persons, individually or with a purchaser representative, understand the merits and risks of the investment. There is no limitation on the number of accredited persons who may subscribe, although the offeree's sophistication in such matters is nevertheless relevant.

TABLE 1
SUMMARY OF SEC RULES 504, 505 & 506

|  | RULE 504 | RULE 505 | RULE 506 |
|---|---|---|---|
| Aggregate Offering Value within 12 months | $500,000 | $5 million | Unlimited |
| Number of investors | unlimited | 35 non-accredited unlimited for accredited | |
| Issuer Qualifications | no reporting or investment companies | no investment co. or Reg. A ineligible issuer | None |
| Limitations on Resale | Restricted unless registered in states that require delivery of a disclosure document | Restricted certificates are legended and reregistration blocked | Restricted |

Intrastate offerings of securities by resident corporations to purchasers located within those same borders are also exempted from registration under the Securities Act of 1933. SEC Rule 147 defines and describes the ways and means by which this exemption may be achieved and maintained. For example, to qualify for the exemption the issuer, if incorporated, must be chartered under the laws of that state and must also be doing business therein. "Doing business" is defined as deriving 80% of gross revenues from sales in that state, having at least 80% of its assets within that state, and applying at least 80% of the offering proceeds to purchase property or facilitate sales within that state. In addition, the issuer must maintain a principal office in that state. Moreover, not only must purchasers be state residents at the time of the offering, but any resales within the following 9 months must also be to qualified residents. To prevent contravention of these procedures, thus forfeiting the exemptive privilege, the issuer is obliged to place a restrictive legend on each of the certificates, to block reregistration of those securities on the books of its transfer agent, and to obtain written representation from each purchaser as to residence.

The provisions of SEC Rule 147 are summarized in Table 2.

**TABLE 2**
SUMMARY OF SEC RULE 147

SEC RULE 147

An issuer's intrastate offering is exempted from SEC registration if the following requirements are met:
1. 80% of the issuer's business must take place within the state.
2. The issuer must have a principal office in the state.
3. The purchasers must be residents of the state.
4. Resales within 9 months must be to state residents.
5. The issuer must put a restrictive legend on certificates, block reregistration, and verify residence of purchaser in writing.

Normally, affiliated persons, with their ability to influence management policies, can distribute their controlling securities only

1. if a registration statement has become effective;
2. via a secondary private placement; or
3. if a special exemption can be found, such as contained in SEC Rule 144 (see below).

It is essential that registered representatives exercise extreme caution in dealing with customers who can be classified as affiliated persons. Questionable situations about control, restriction, or marketability should be referred to legal counsel before executing any sell order. A good checklist to use in making this determination is to obtain answers to the following questions:

1. Is the issuing corporation or trust closely held?
2. Does the proposed sale involve a large amount of stock in relation to the number of shares outstanding?
3. Did the seller acquire these securities via an option plan, merger, reorganization, or conversion of a privately placed debt security?
4. Is the seller an officer, director, trustee, beneficiary, or principal stockholder of the issuer?
5. Is the seller a relative by birth or marriage of an officer, director, trustee, beneficiary, or principal stockholder of the issuer?

6. Is the seller an estate of a deceased person who was an officer, director, trustee, beneficiary, or principal stockholder of the issuer? Or, is the seller related to someone who is?

7. Is there a restriction relating to the transfer of ownership for these certificates?

8. Is this sale part of a distribution registered with the SEC?

9. Has the seller participated in any distribution of these securities within the past year?

10. Is the seller a participant in a group that may be classified as an affiliated person?

11. Are there any other circumstances related to this sale that would lead you to suspect a control relationship exists?

If the answer to *any* of these questions is *yes*, the registered representative should contact legal counsel immediately.

**C3.**
***SEC Rule 144***

SEC Rule 144 permits sales of restricted securities which are currently subject to terms of an investment letter by affiliated and nonaffiliated persons in modest amounts and in an occasional transaction without first registering them with the SEC. Issuers or underwriters (generally broker/dealers) cannot make use of this privilege; it may be used only by

1. affiliated and nonaffiliated persons who are not broker/dealers and who acquired these securities in a private transaction; and

2. affiliated persons who acquired their securities in the public marketplace. These are unregistered but nonrestricted securities that can be sold under Rule 144 in the absence of an effective registration statement.

To qualify for the exemption, the seller and the issuer must scrupulously abide by the following conditions and guidelines:

1. If the issuing corporation is subject to the reporting requirements of Sections 14 or 15(b) of the Securities Exchange Act of 1934, it must have filed with the SEC all necessary reports due within the past 90 days, as well as its most recent annual report. That this requirement has been met must be verified prior to sale of the securities.

2. If the issuing corporation is not subject to these reporting requirements, it must make publicly available
   a. its exact name and predecessor company, if any;
   b. the address of its principal executive offices;
   c. the state of incorporation;
   d. the title, class, and par or stated value of its securities;
   e. the total amount of securities outstanding;
   f. the name and address of the transfer agent;
   g. the nature of the product, services, facilities, and business of the corporation;
   h. the name of the corporation's chief executive officer and the directors on the board;
   i. complete financial statements for the most recent period and the 2 immediately preceding years; and

  j. the names of broker/dealers or associated persons affiliated directly or indirectly with the corporation.

3. Securities to be sold under this rule must be fully paid for and owned for at least 2 years prior to the intended transaction.[4]

4. If securities to be sold under this rule

  a. exceed 500 shares, or

  b. aggregate more than $10,000 in value,

a notice of sale must be filed with the SEC *at the same time the order is entered.* Figure 2 shows a copy of Form 144. If the security is listed on one or more stock exchanges, it is also necessary to file a concurrent report with the principal exchange where it is traded. Securities not completely distributed within 90 days thereafter require submission of amended notices at the time of further sale.

5. To avoid being classified as a public distribution, thus negating the exemption offered under this rule, the amount of any stock sold by the customer, including sales for persons in concert with that customer *within the preceding 3 months,* must not exceed

  a. 1% of the shares outstanding (for over-the-counter securities); or

  b. if traded on registered stock exchanges, *the greater of*

    (1) 1% of the shares outstanding; or

    (2) the average weekly volume of that security on all exchanges in the 4 weeks prior to receipt of this order.

Non-affiliated persons do not have a volume limitation to contend with. They may sell their entire holdings within the 90 day effective period for a Form 144 filing without regard to the number of shares outstanding or activity on the stock exchanges. Affiliated persons must, however, abide by these volume requirements for their unregistered shares.

If the order is executed on an exchange, there is no need to advise the buyer that this is unregistered stock. It will automatically become registered after the transaction. But if it is traded over the counter, the market-maker should be advised of the status of the stock because there is a possibility the firm may become a statutory underwriter as a result of this transaction. That possibility may be realized if the market-maker acts as a principal for its own account instead of as an agent for a customer.

6. There must be no solicitation of buy orders in anticipation of this sale.[5] If the registered representative's employer is a market-maker in that security, the firm may continue its activity in that issue during the distribution *only* if it published its quotations in an interdealer system on at least 12 of the preceding 30 days, with a gap of no more than 4 business days between publication of such quotations.

7. A broker/dealer organization distributing these securities for its customers may act in an agency capacity, charging only

[4]There is no holding period for nonrestricted securities owned by affiliated persons, but they too must be fully paid for and fully owned securities.

[5]A dealer firm having made a written bid or offer in the pink sheets or NASDAQ communication system within the past 60 days may be queried as to possible interest. So, too, may customers who indicated a bona fide unsolicited interest in that issue within 10 business days prior to receipt of the Rule 144 order.

the customary brokerage commission for the service rendered. That commission must represent the sole expense borne by the customer to promote the sale of this security.

8.  The broker/dealer may purchase the securities for its own account only if it is a market maker in that security. It may subsequently solicit buy orders from its customers to dispose of these shares.

The provisions of SEC Rule 144 are summarized in Table 3.

TABLE 3
SUMMARY OF SEC RULE 144

### SEC RULE 144

1. allows the sale of restricted securities (investment letter) or unrestricted but unregistered securities

2. by affiliated and nonaffiliated persons

3. within any 90-day period

4. but the sale is limited to the greater of

   a. 1% of shares outstanding, or

   b. average weekly volume for previous 4 weeks

**D.
underwriters**

An underwriter, as described in the Securities Act of 1933, may be broadly sub-classified as *voluntary* or *involuntary* (see Section H1).

**D1.
*Voluntary***

A **voluntary underwriter** is an individual or an organization that purchases a security from an issuer or affiliated person and subsequently reoffers it for public sale under a registration statement that has become effective.

**voluntary underwriter**

**D2.
*Involuntary***

An **involuntary underwriter** may be an individual or an organization that purchases an unregistered security and subsequently offers it in a public distribution without benefit of an effective registration statement. Such parties are officially identified as **statutory underwriters** and are subject to fine and/or imprisonment as a result. Brokerage firms can be considered to be statutory underwriters even if they merely act as agent for a customer in a public distribution of securities not exempted under the Securities Act of 1933 or pursuant to SEC Rule 144.

**involuntary underwriter**

**statutory underwriters**

U.S. SECURITIES AND EXCHANGE COMMISSION
WASHINGTON, D.C. . 549

**FORM 144** (4-72)

SEC 1147

# NOTICE OF PROPOSED SALE OF SECURITIES
## Pursuant to Rule 144 under the Securities Act of 1933

ATTENTION: *Transmit for filing 3 copies of this form concurrently with placing an order to execute sale.*

SEC USE ONLY
DOCUMENT SEQUENCE NO.
CUSIP NUMBER
WORK LOCATION

1(a) NAME OF ISSUER

(b) IRS IDENT. NO.    (c) S.E.C. FILE NO.

1(d) ADDRESS OF ISSUER    STREET    CITY    STATE    ZIP CODE

(e) TELEPHONE NO.   AREA CODE   NUMBER

2(a) NAME OF PERSON FOR WHOSE ACCOUNT THE SECURITIES ARE TO BE SOLD

(b) SOCIAL SECURITY NO. OR IRS IDENT. NO.

(c) RELATIONSHIP TO ISSUER

(d) ADDRESS   STREET   CITY   STATE   ZIP CODE

INSTRUCTION: *The person filing this notice should contact the issuer to obtain the I.R.S. Identification Number and the S.E.C. File Number.*

| 3(a) Title of the Class of Securities To Be Sold | (b) Name and Address of Each Broker Through Whom the Securities Are To Be Offered | (c) Number of Shares or Other Units To Be Sold (See instr. 3(c)) | SEC USE ONLY Broker-Dealer File Number | (d) Aggregate Market Value (See instr. 3(d)) | (e) Number of Shares or Other Units Outstanding (See instr. 3(e)) | (f) Approximate Date of Sale (See instr. 3(f)) (MO. DAY YR.) | (g) Name of Each Securities Exchange (See instr. 3(g)) |
|---|---|---|---|---|---|---|---|
| | | | | | | | |
| | | | | | | | |
| | | | | | | | |

**INSTRUCTIONS:**

1. (a) Name of issuer
   (b) Issuer's I.R.S. Identification Number
   (c) Issuer's S.E.C. file number, if any
   (d) Issuer's address, including zip code
   (e) Issuer's telephone number, including area code

2. (a) Name of person for whose account the securities are to be sold
   (b) Such person's Social Security or I.R.S. identification number
   (c) Such person's relationship to the issuer (e.g., officer, director, 10% stockholder, or member of immediate family of any of the foregoing)
   (d) Such person's address, including zip code

3. (a) Title of the class of securities to be sold
   (b) Name and address of each broker through whom the securities are intended to be sold
   (c) Number of shares or other units to be sold (if debt securities, give the aggregate face amount)
   (d) Aggregate market value of the securities to be sold as of a specified date within 10 days prior to the filing of this notice
   (e) Number of shares or other units of the class outstanding, or if debt securities the face amount thereof outstanding, as shown by the most recent report or statement published by the issuer
   (f) Approximate date on which the securities are to be sold
   (g) Name of each securities exchange, if any, on which the securities are intended to be sold

**FIGURE 2**
Form 144 (front)

the mechanics of distributing securities    81

## TABLE I - SECURITIES TO BE SOLD

*Furnish the following information with respect to the acquisition of the securities to be sold and with respect to the payment of all or any part of the purchase price or other consideration therefor:*

| Title of the Class | Date Acquired | Nature of Acquisition Transaction | Name of Person from Whom Acquired | Amount of Securities Acquired | Date of Payment | Nature of Payment |
|---|---|---|---|---|---|---|
| | | | | | | |

**INSTRUCTIONS**

1. If the securities were purchased and full payment therefore was not made in cash at the time of purchase, explain in the table or in a note thereto the nature of the consideration given. If the consideration consisted of any note or other obligation, or if payment was made in installments describe the arrangement and state when the note or other obligation was discharged in full or the last installment paid.
2. If within two years after the acquisition of the securities the person for whose account they are to be sold had any short positions, put or other option to dispose of securities referred to in paragraph (d)(3) of Rule 144, furnish full information with respect thereto.

## TABLE II - SECURITIES SOLD DURING THE PAST 6 MONTHS

*Furnish the following information as to all securities of the issuer sold during the past 6 months by the person for whose account the securities are to be sold.*

| Name and Address of Seller | Title of Securities Sold | Date of Sale | Amount of Securities Sold | Gross Proceeds |
|---|---|---|---|---|
| | | | | |

**REMARKS:**

SEC 1147 (4-7:

**INSTRUCTIONS:**
See the definition of "person" in paragraph (a) of Rule 144. Information is to be given not only as to the person for whose account the securities are to be sold but also as to all other persons included in that definition. In addition, information shall be given as to sales by all persons whose sales are required by paragraph (e) of Rule 144 to be aggregated with sales for the account of the person filing this notice.

ATTENTION:
*The Person for whose account the securities to which this notice relates are to be sold hereby represents by signing this notice that he does not know any material adverse information in regard to the current and prospective operations of the Issuer of the securities to be sold which has not been publicly disclosed.*

DATE OF NOTICE

(SIGNATURE)

*The notice shall be signed by the person for whose account the securities are to be sold. At least one copy of the notice shall be manually signed. Any copies not manually signed shall bear typed or printed signatures.*

ATTENTION: Intentional misstatements or omission of facts constitute Federal Criminal Violations (See 18 U.S.C. 1001).

**FIGURE 2**
Form 144 (back)

Ordinarily, in a public offering of securities by an issuer, especially one involving substantial amounts of certificates or dollars, the corporation employs the services of an investment banker. The investment banker, a broker/dealer registered with the SEC, plays an essential role in behalf of American industry. The investment banking firm is an important factor in the capital market because it arranges long-term financing for businesses. Commercial banks, on the other hand, are primarily involved in money-market activities, that is, short-term financing.

E.
the role of an investment banker

E1.
*Services Performed*

Investment bankers do more than merely raise capital. Their many other services include

1. counseling companies in the management of their money;
2. advising companies about merger and acquisition opportunities;
3. examining and analyzing corporate documents and financial statements with a view toward modernization of outdated practices;
4. providing marketability for corporate securities after public distribution; and
5. public relations work.

When a company finds itself in need of capital, it consults with an investment banker to establish a means of raising such funds. Management often relies upon the investment banker's expertise and experience in determining the means and type of financing to be employed. Important factors influencing the investment banker's judgment and recommendations are

E2.
*Investigation and Analysis*

1. the amount of money needed by the corporation;
2. the availability of money in the marketplace;
3. the cost of money in the marketplace (interest rates and so on);
4. financial restrictions in the charter and/or bylaws;
5. existing capital structure of the corporation;
6. the popularity of that industry in the investment community;
7. recent experiences by the company's competitors in raising capital;
8. pending legislation or litigation having an important bearing on the company's (or industry's) immediate future;
9. the quality of management in that corporation; and
10. the purpose for which this capital is needed.

If the investment banker concludes it is worthwhile to proceed, an immediate decision is reached about the type of security to be issued (common stock, preferred stock, or bonds). Then the corporation and investment banker must decide whether the offering will be attempted by means of private placement or public distribution.

If the security to be offered represents authorized but previously unissued stock or bonds, it is identified as a **primary distribution.** If the offering repres nts securities held by stockholders or bondholders or securities held by the corporation itself in its treasury, it is called a **secondary distribution.** The issuer is, therefore, capable of making both primary and secondary distributions whereas a stockholder or bondholder can only make a secondary distribution. Some offerings of securities are comprised of both types of distributions. Such offerings are called **split offerings.**

**primary distribution**

**secondary distribution**

**split offerings**

## F.
### registration of the public offering

Because we have already discussed requirements and procedures for private placement, we shall treat the procedures for a public offering here.

### F1.
### *Filing and SEC Examining*

Unless grounds for exemption can be established, a public offering of securities requires the filing of a registration statement with the SEC before that offering commences. That registration statement, described earlier, includes all pertinent information and documents relative to the affairs of that company and to this offering in particular. The SEC examines the registration statement for at least 20 days, trying to determine whether there are obvious omissions or misrepresentations of the material facts. If the SEC finds omissions or misrepresentations, it sends the corporation a **deficiency letter** explaining its position on the matter. The *effective date* of a registration statement is delayed or postponed indefinitely until that deficiency has been corrected. No distribution may proceed prior to the effectice date, and even subtle offers to sell the issue to be offered before that time constitute a violation of the law.

**deficiency letter**

### F2.
### *Effective Date*

In the absence of a deficiency letter, a registration statement automatically becomes effective on the twentieth calendar day after filing. SEC rules do allow for an earlier effective date if requested by the issuer or its underwriter and approved by the SEC's staff. Approval of an earlier effective date generally depends on such factors as the following:

1. whether the issuer has been a reporting company under the Securities and Exchange Act of 1934 for at least three years;
2. whether the issuer is up to date in its reporting requirements to the SEC;
3. the type and amount of publicly owned securities of the same issuer already outstanding;
4. the extent of information furnished in the registration statement.

Well known and significant issuers of securities to public investors may, under the proper circumstances, be permitted to begin their public offerings as soon as 48 hours after filing of its registration statement with the SEC.

### F3.
### *Delay Past a 20-Day Period*

On the other hand, the effective date can be delayed merely because the SEC is unable to properly examine the pertinent information within the 20-day period. The commission then notifies the issuer that its workload has overwhelmed the staff's capability to perform its function. In the busy underwriting years of 1960 and 1961, it was not uncommon for issuers of securities to encounter 4- to 6-month delays for this reason. Unfortunately, there wasn't much they could do except wait, and by the time their registration statements were allowed to become effective, market conditions had changed dramatically.

It is important to remember that despite its vigilance and conscientiousness *the SEC never guarantees the adequacy or accuracy of any registration statement*. The public's assurance of protection is found under sections of the Securities Act of 1933 regarding civil liability. The law, as mentioned before, gives an investor the opportunity to bring suit for reimbursement of financial losses sustained. The investor has authority to collect from

1. the officers of the corporation;
2. the directors of the corporation;
3. the principal stockholders in the corporation (holders of 10% or more of the outstanding common stock);
4. the investment bankers who act as underwriters; and
5. anyone whose name *voluntarily* appears in the registration statement.

Purchasers must be prepared to prove that they lost money because of the incomplete or distorted material information presented in this solicitation. Omission of material fact and/or misrepresentation of fact are the two bases under which purchasers of a public offering can recoup their investment. Disgruntled investors cannot collect on "paper losses" (unrealized), nor can they collect under this act unless purchase was effected from this particular distribution. Transactions in the open market after the offering are not usually subject to the terms of the Securities Act of 1933, but may fall instead within the jurisdiction of the Securities Exchange Act of 1934.

*F4.*
*Purchasers' Protection*

The Trust Indenture Act of 1939, although separate and distinct, was enacted as an amendment to the Securities Act of 1933. It provides additional protections for public investors. The basis for its passage was the discovery by Congress that the 1933 act did not safeguard the rights of investors in debt securities after the public offering was completed. Moreover, it found that purchasers of issues exempted from the registration requirements often did not even have the minimum protections accorded to investors in offerings required to be registered with the SEC.

G.
the trust indenture act of 1939

*G1.*
*Purpose*

Consequently the Trust Indenture Act of 1939 (1) integrated its own requirements with those of the 1933 act for debt issues registered under that law and (2) imposed unique requirements for issuers of public or private debt securities exempted from provisions of the 1933 act.

*G2.*
*Conditions*

Generally, the terms of the 1939 act extend to issuers of any debt security with a principal amount of $5 million or more. The issuer of a debt security subject to this law must appoint one or more trustees responsible for ensuring that the terms of the indenture are scrupulously adhered to by all parties to the agreement. At least one of those trustees must be a corporation empowered with authority to act as a fiduciary and must be subject to supervision or examination by a governmental body or agency. It must also have a combined capital surplus of at least $150,000. The trustees cannot have "conflicting interests"[6] and must provide an annual

[6]The term, "conflicting interests," is meticulously explained in the law itself. Broadly defined, the term means that the trustees may not be prejudiced, economically or otherwise, toward any party in its administration of the loan arrangement.

report to the SEC reaffirming their continued qualifications to serve in this capacity.

**G3.**
***Indenture Registration***

Most corporate debt issuers satisfy the Trust Indenture Act of 1939 by making a full disclosure in a formal registration statement submitted to the SEC for its scrutiny. Thus, both the security and its contingent indenture will be fully registered commencing on the effective date. Debt securities exempted from the 1933 act's registration requirement comply with the terms of the 1939 act by presentation of an **indenture qualification statement** to the SEC. Although the issue itself is not registered, its indenture will be registered on the effective date. The effective date is generally the twentieth calendar day after the statement has been received by the SEC.

**indenture qualification statement**

Whether the debt security is registered with the SEC or not, its indenture must set forth the full terms and conditions under which the loan will be maintained during its lifetime. Such facts include

1. the amount, frequency, and method by which interest will be paid;
2. the maturation date and means by which the principal amount of the loan will be repaid;
3. earlier redemption privileges, if any, reserved for use by the issuer or the debt instrument holder;
4. convertibility features and terms, if any;
5. a full description of the collateral, if any, securing this loan;
6. the powers and responsibilities of the trustees in the event of a default by the issuer on any portion of the indenture agreement;
7. any agreements, concessions, or waivers that will be an integral part of the financing;
8. the duties and responsibilities of the trustees;
9. rights of the bondholders; and
10. obligations of the issuing corporation.

**H.**
**activities during the 20-day cooling-off period**

**H1.**
***The Preliminary Agreement***

Within the 20-day period prior to the anticipated effective date, the officers of the corporation work to finalize arrangements to implement the public offering. They can attempt the distribution themselves if they have the necessary expertise and are willing to assume the financial risk, but generally thise does not happen. Instead, even prior to the time a registration statement will be prepared, the corporation's officials contract with an investment banker to assist in the offering through a procedure known as **firm commitment underwriting**. This means that the investment banker *guarantees* the corporation its money by agreement to purchase this issue and reoffer it publicly at a price somewhat higher than that paid to the corporation. Thus, the issuer's risk of failure is eliminated and is assumed by the investment banker. For example, the underwriter may guarantee the corporation $28.25 per share of stock, while attempting to sell it publicly at a fixed price of $29.50. If successful, the underwriter earns a gross profit of $1.25 per share. However, if it is unable to market it at $29.50, it must still pay the corporation $28.25 on the closing date of their contract.

**firm commitment underwriting**

**best-efforts offering**

Realistically, however, a young corporation with no proven "track record" (experience) is unable to negotiate such an arrangement. It is usually presented with a deal in which the investment banker firm agrees merely to devote its best efforts in making this offering a success but will *not* guarantee the corporation payment for any unsold portion of the issue. In a **best-efforts offering**, the investment banker acts only as an agent of the corporation. (This is different from a firm commitment underwriting, in which, by virtue of the absolute guarantee, the investment banker assumes status as a principal.) The unsold portion of a best-efforts offering is returned to the issuer without further liability for the investment banker firm. It pays the corporation only for those shares it has managed to distribute.

**all-or-none offering**

Of course, the corporation can counter a best-efforts proposition with, "If you can't sell it all, cancel the entire offering, including the portion already distributed." This type of agreement, sometimes linked to a best-efforts offering, is called an **all-or-none offering**. The corporation may choose this approach because it may simply be uneconomical to complete such a distribution unless the entire amount of capital required can be financed. No customer purchases can be finalized until the issuer determines that the entire offering was marketed successfully. This can take several days, weeks, or even months. (A registration statement relating to a particular offering may continue to be effective for two years thereafter, provided no material changes occur in the affairs of the corporation.)[7]

An investment banker firm interested in underwriting an issue on a guaranteed basis frequently does not have enough capital to make good on such a commitment. Even if it does have enough capital, it may well be reluctant to risk it all on a single offering. Instead, it generally contacts other investment bankers to organize a group (with itself appointed as manager), to *collectively* ensure the legitimacy of the corporation's guarantee. These underwriting groups, commonly called **syndicates**, are traditionally formed along historic or social ties within the financial community. It is usually difficult to break into these fraternal arrangements and even more difficult for members to increase their percentage of participation within the group itself. The organizational stratum (bracket) is often fixed according to the past distribution and performance record of each investment banker in the syndicate.

**syndicates**

Thus, if a prominent investment banker has traditionally participated in syndicates with certain other well-known investment bankers, it is safe to assume that this association will continue for all future underwritings in which any one of them acts as manager. Moreover, once established as a significant distributor of securities in such offerings, that investment banker becomes recognized as a "major-bracket" participant. Its name will be publicized near the top of all of that group's advertisements. The percentage of its underwriting commitment continues to rank equally with other major-bracket firms. Other investment bankers in those syndicates become stereotyped as sub-major-, middle-, and minor-bracket underwriters accordingly, depending upon the amount of their participations.

*H2.*
*Forming a Syndicate*

[7]If an offering is not attempted within 3 days after the effective date, the SEC must be notified immediately.

## H3.
### Soliciting Indications of Interest

Before investment bankers contractually commit themselves to the corporation, they seek assurance of reasonable opportunity for success. They are allowed under law to contact their customers, and with only preliminary information available at this time, solicit indication of interest from them. An **indication of interest** (referred to in slang as a "circle") is merely an expression of consideration for that issue and is not a binding commitment upon the customer or the investment banker. Prior to the effective date, customers may modify their indications any number of times without penalty as their investment monies or intentions change because of prevailing market conditions.

**indication of interest**

## H4.
### SEC Rule 10b–6

Once an investment banker accepts an invitation from the manager to participate in a syndicate, it becomes bound by law to comply with SEC Rule 10b–6. Rule 10b–6 is a segment of the SEC's interpretation of Section 10 of the Securities Exchange Act of 1934. The rule decrees it unfair and improper for any issuer, broker, dealer, or underwriter, having agreed to participate in a public offering of securities, *prior to the effective date of that offering,* to

1. bid for that security or a similar security of the same issuer or purchase it for an account in which it has a beneficial interest; or
2. induce anyone to purchase that security or a similar security of the same issuer.[8]

Because there are exceptions to this interesting rule and because some consideration has been given to bona fide broker/dealers in the normal conduct of their business, Table 4 is presented to summarize acceptable practices. The activities encompass those of the firm as well as its employees and affiliates *from the time a public offering is agreed upon until the distribution is completed.*

## H5.
### Preliminary Prospectus

In compliance with SEC rules governing purchases before the effective date, it is often necessary to send customers a preliminary prospectus to solicit their indications or even to accept unsolicited indications within the provisions of state or federal securities laws. A *red herring,* as it is often called because of a red-lettered caveat in the border of the front page,[9] is a summary of pertinent details from the registration statement. It contains most facts known about the offering to that moment. Admittedly, it is incomplete because it lacks a final price and other pertinent

---

[8]This restriction also applies to any security for the same class or series and to any right or warrant to purchase that security during this time.

[9]SEC regulations require the following commentary to appear in red print in the border of every preliminary prospectus: "A registration statement relating to these securities has been filed with the Securities and Exchange Commission, but has not yet become effective. Information contained herein is subject to completion or amendment. These securities may not be sold nor may offers to buy be accepted prior to the time the registration statement becomes effective. This prospectus shall not constitute an offer to sell or the solicitation of an offer to buy nor shall there be any sale of these securities in any state in which such offer, solicitation, or sale would be unlawful prior to registration or qualification under the securities laws of any such state."

**TABLE 4**

GUIDELINES FOR DISTRIBUTION OF SECURITIES IN COMPLIANCE WITH SEC RULE 10b–6

|  | STOCK EXCHANGE TRANSACTIONS | OVER-THE-COUNTER TRANSACTIONS |
|---|---|---|
| Purchases as *principal* | | |
| a. until 3 days prior to effective date | Yes | Yes |
| b. within 3-day period | No | No |
| Sales as *principal* | | |
| a. until 3 days prior to effective date | Yes | Yes |
| b. within 3-day period | No | No |
| Purchases as *agent* | | |
| a. buy order is solicited | No | No |
| b. buy order not solicited | Yes | Yes |
| Sales as *agent* (sell order is solicited) | | |
| a. contra buy order is solicited | No | No |
| b. contra buy order not solicited | Yes | Yes |
| Sales as *agent* (sell order *not* solicited) | | |
| a. contra buy order is solicited | No | No |
| b. contra buy order is not solicited | Yes | Yes |
| Publish quotations in the pink sheets or in NASDAQ communication facilities | | |
| a. until 3 days prior to effective date | No | Yes |
| b. within 3-day period | No | No |
| Circulate research information or literature | No | No |

information; it may even contain some unintentional inaccuracies. This is why it must never be used as a means of *soliciting orders,* even in this preliminary stage of negotiation. In recent years, the SEC has also requested inclusion of a "maximum" offering price in the red herring to give the reader an idea of value for the issue, even though the final price is generally set below this ceiling.

Solicitation of orders, or even acceptance of unsolicited orders prior to the effective date, is a violation of the Securities Act of 1933. The red herring is the only form of written communication permissible between a participating investment banker and a potential purchaser while the registration statement for that security is pending at the SEC.

The process of soliciting and accepting indications of interest enables investment bankers to gauge the extent of consideration their customers may have for investment purposes at this time. If they find too many customers are disinterested, they can cancel their participation in the underwriting group without financial loss or penalty.

**due-diligence meeting**

*H6.*
*Due-Diligence Meeting*

Some time before the effective date, a meeting is arranged between the corporation's officials and the members of the underwriting group. Attendance by all syndicate participants is mandatory. Awareness of personal liability, as set forth in the Securities Act of 1933, stimulates a willingness and a necessity for the participants to pay serious attention to the arrangements under discussion. Hence, this convention is often identified as a **due-diligence meeting.** An investment banker who is dissatisfied with any terms or conditions discussed at this forum still has sufficient time to withdraw from the meeting and from the underwriting group with no financial or legal liability. The purposes of this meeting are

1. to discuss and review pertinent information for inclusion in, or as an amendment to, the registration statement;

2. to prepare a final prospectus (a condensation of the effective registration statement) for later use in solicitation of orders; and

3. to begin negotiation for a formal underwriting agreement between the corporation and the investment bankers.

One of the few items in the formal agreement not fixed at this meeting is the payment price to the corporation and the price at which the public offering will be attempted. These values are usually set the night before, or even in the early morning hours of, the effective date. It is done at this time in order to adjust to market conditions prevailing at the time of the offering. To be sure, price ideas can be discussed at a due-diligence meeting, but they are not truly binding for any of the participants.

*H7.*
*Blue-Skying the Issue*

Most state governments have their own securities laws that are separate and distinct from federal regulations. To engage in securities activities within their borders requires compliance with their laws as well as with the federal statutes.

While a security is in the process of being registered with the SEC, the managing underwriter's attorneys try to qualify that issue for sale under the laws of the various states in which the offering will be attempted. Some states permit public offerings of securities simply on the basis of an effective SEC registration statement. Other states require qualification through submission of an effective registration statement filed with their own securities commissioners.

This is what the lawyers want to ascertain before the underwriters irrevocably commit themselves to the corporation. The practice of analysis, investigation, and qualification with these state laws is known as **blue-skying the issue**.[10] If the lawyers find that the security cannot qualify for sale in too many of the "big money" states, they advise the investment bankers either to defer or cancel their plans to underwrite this issue. After all, why should they jeopardize their capital and potential success in an offering because of legal restraints prohibiting solicitation of significant investors?

**blue-skying the issue**

It should also be pointed out that securities sales people who deal with purchasers residing in these states must also be registered with the securities commissioners. Failure to comply with this particular blue-sky provision enables customers to rescind the transaction anytime in the future. Such failure also can subject the representatives and their firms to civil and criminal penalties by those states.

[10]The origin of this expression stems from the enactment day of the nation's first state securities law, in Kansas, in the early 1900s. At that time, a legislator reputedly quipped, "Now Kansas citizens will have more of a basis for making investment decisions than merely by the shade of blue sky."

*APPOINTING THE SYNDICATE MANAGER*

A supplementary agreement among the underwriters themselves is drafted soon after the due-diligence meeting and is signed by the participants. This agreement delegates many broad powers and extra work to the managing underwriter to help ensure success. For its additional efforts, the syndicate manager receives a special fee from the gross profit of all members of the group. It can approximate 20% of the spread,[11] depending upon the size of the issue and the amount of work involved. For example, a recent debt offering showed the differential between the corporation's price and public offering price to be $8.75 per bond. The management fee was $1.75, or 20% of the spread. This left $7.00 per bond to be shared by each of the underwriters and the syndicate's selling group.

*THE SYNDICATE MANAGER'S RESPONSIBILITIES*

The syndicate manager's responsibilities include

1. forming an underwriting group;
2. appointing a selling group;
3. establishing the underwriter's retention;
4. conducting group sales;
5. stabilizing the aftermarket; and
6. allocating hot issues with skill and diplomacy.

*Forming an underwriting group*    The procedure used in forming an underwriting group was explained earlier in this chapter. Once formed, however, it is not necessarily a permanent entity. Commitments are continuously revised as the members ask for adjustments to reflect indications of interest they have solicited and/or accepted. Some members may drop out of the group entirely because of lack of response from their customers. Their commitment must be taken by another investment banker or assumed by other members of the group. The manager maintains a syndicate record book of such maneuvering.

**selling group**

*Appointing a selling group*    To help the underwriters achieve broad distribution of the securities featured in the registration statement, the manager may employ the services of a selling group. A **selling group** consists of selected members of the NASD who agree to act as the underwriters' agents and offer some of these securities to their customers under terms presented in the registration statement and prospectus. They must sign a contract with the managing underwriter that subjects them to the same terms and restrictions of the underwriting agreement. But they do not receive the full underwriter's spread because they assume no personal responsibility or financial liability to the issuing corporation. Their remuneration for services rendered is

[11]The *profit* is technically referred to as the *underwriter's spread* and represents the difference between the price paid to the corporation and the public offering price. The spread does not appear on the red herring because it is based on the public offering price, which is not known at the time of its publication and distribution.

*H8.*
*The Agreement Among Underwriters*

*H8a.*

*H8b.*

*H8b(1).*

*H8b(2).*

granted by the syndicate manager in the form of a **selling concession**, a fraction of the underwriter's spread.[12] Furthermore, selling groups are not normally allocated a sizable percentage of the issue to distribute, either; they receive merely a token amount to satisfy some of their customers and, hopefully, develop a continuing interest in the aftermarket.

It is not unusual to find some investment bankers acting both as underwriters and members of the selling group in the same securities distributions. In a popular offering, it is almost impossible to accommodate customer demands from underwriting allocations alone, and many investment bankers, using their influence with the manager, turn to both devices to satisfy their clients.

Even in obviously successful offerings, where there is seldom question about the underwriters' ability to market the securities themselves, most syndicate managers find it expedient to employ a selling group. ''After all,'' they reason, ''members of today's selling group may be tomorrow's managing underwriters in other offerings, and we may well want to participate in their deals to accommodate our customers.''

*H8b(3):*      ***Establishing the underwriter's retention***    The syndicate manager must decide how much of each investment banker firm's commitment will be made available to that underwriter for distribution to its customers. The manager withholds part of each member's commitment (1) to allocate to the selling group and (2) to have available for institutional purchasers, who deal in substantial quantities. The syndicate manager's responsibility here is a touchy one. The manager must coordinate an all-out sales effort and, at the same time, diplomatically juggle requests from members of the syndicate, selling group, and large buyers. If the underwriter's retention percentage is set too high for an offering that becomes very popular, the selling group and big institutions are dissatisfied with their inability to acquire sufficient quantities. If it is set too low, the underwriters are unhappy. They reason that if they must assume financial responsibility for a poor deal, they should enjoy the benefits of popular distributions by satisfying their own customers first.

A typical retention for participating underwriters approximates 75%. This means that each underwriter can personally decide on customer allocations for 75% of the financial commitment to the corporation. The manager decides upon the other 25%

*H8b(4).*      ***Conducting group sales***    As mentioned in the preceding paragraphs, the syndicate manager witholds a portion of each participant's share of the distribution. Part of this is offered to institutional purchasers in behalf of the underwriters, out of a common pool (referred to in slang as a *pot*) created for this purpose. Most institutions normally buy in sizable amounts and prefer dealing with only one underwriter in executing transactions for their portfolios. It is more convenient and economical for them to contract with the manager to buy 50,000 shares from the pot than to do business with ten different members of the syndicate and

[12]The selling group concession may range from 25 to 75% of the underwriters' spread, depending upon the anticipated degree of difficulty in marketing the issue. The greater the foreseen difficulty, the larger the concession needed to attract selling-dealer efforts.

buy 5,000 shares from each one. That purchaser can designate one or more specific underwriters for monetary credit on this transaction. If nothing is said, all underwriters will benefit pro rata.

Group sales also serve as a useful barometer and a profitable sales tool for the underwriters. The most stimulating news from a syndicate manager is a simple announcement that "the pot is clean!" It is indicative of institutional demand for this issue; it inspires the underwriters and the selling group members to sell out their participation quickly. The smaller, sometimes hesitant, investors generally follow suit.

H8b(5).

*Stabilizing the aftermarket*  On the effective date, or within a couple of days thereafter, the underwriters begin making their public offering. At about the same time, the security begins trading openly in the marketplace. It might trade on a stock exchange or in the over-the-counter market. This trading activity, which begins on the effective date, is called the **aftermarket.** It refers to the market for a security that develops after a public offering begins.

**aftermarket**

Unless the offering is an immediate sellout, practical problems hindering its success may develop in the aftermarket. The underwriters are bound by the terms of their agreements with the corporation and themselves to offer the security at a fixed price. But the aftermarket price is not so restrictive. It can, and does, fluctuate. Would investors purchase that issue from an underwriter or a member of the selling group at the fixed offering price if they could buy it in the open market for less money? The answer to that is obvious, and so is the solution to this problem.

The managing underwriter or its authorized representative is empowered to maintain a bid in the aftermarket at, or perhaps slightly below, the public offering price, on behalf of the syndicate. By pegging the market price to the public-offering price, the members of the syndicate and selling group have a reasonable chance of distributing that security successfully. Ordinarily, anyone found manipulating market prices of securities is subject to prosecution by the SEC under terms of the Securities and Exchange Act of 1934. The use of stabilization to facilitate a bona fide distribution of securities is exempted from this otherwise fraudulent practice. However, the actual trading must strictly conform to SEC rules designed to prevent the appearance of misleading market activity. For example, while the stabilizing party is permitted to initially bid for or buy the security at or below the public offering price (while offering and selling no higher than the syndicate's fixed distribution price) it may not raise its bid or buy above the lowest price at which it purchases that security. Thus, if an offering price was set at $26 and the manager decided to stabilize by bidding or buying at $25¾, the syndicate is precluded from subsequently bidding or buying at $25⅞ or above. Prompt notice of stabilizing activities must be filed with the SEC and at the appropriate stock exchange, if the issue is listed on an exchange.

When stabilizing aftermarket prices, stabilization may also precede the public offering providing notification is given to the SEC and the appropriate stock exchange; the syndicate manager certainly has no intention of repurchasing the entire issue. In fact, the syndicate manager performs this chore reluctantly, often notifying firms participating in the distribution that the stabilizing bid is made with a penalty attached. They are warned in the agreement among underwriters and in the selling group agreement that if their customers enter the aftermarket and sell this new security at the price of the stabilizing bid, the manager will

1.  deny the member its underwriter's spread or selling group concession on that transaction;
2.  penalize it perhaps $.125 per share or $1.25 per bond, as the case may be;[13] and
3.  reconsider that firm's participation in the syndicate or selling group for future offerings.

A *penalty syndicate bid* is written into the agreements between the underwriters and the members of the selling group to ensure that these participants strive to distribute that issue to investment portfolios and not to traders and speculators intent upon quick profits.

Although an attempt at public offering at a fixed price is required by terms of the underwriting agreement, the syndicate manager has a prerogative to refrain from stabilization or to withdraw the stabilizing bid without giving advance notice to the members of his group. If the manager sees that the task has turned hopeless, it has authority to release the groups from their obligation to offer only at the established price. When a syndicate agreement is thus broken by the manager, the security is allowed to fluctuate to its true price level, as determined by the forces of supply and demand. The members of the underwriting group who have been unsuccessful in the offering thus far can now sell this security in the aftermarket at whatever prices can be realized. Or, they can hold the security, waiting for better days and better prices. In any event, breaking the price restriction does not relieve the underwriters from their financial responsibility to the corporation.

*H8b(6)*    ***Allocating hot issues with skill and diplomacy*** A **hot issue** is a security in registration that is expected to trade at an immediate premium in the aftermarket (above the public-offering price). This situation often creates a problem for the syndicate manager, albeit a somewhat happier experience than stabilization.

hot issue

Hot issues are conceived prior to the effective date when investor interest reaches such proportions that the underwriters cannot fully accommodate their customers' indications of interest. In fact, they cannot fully satisfy any of their customers. Demand spills over into the aftermarket, causing initial transactions there to trade higher than the price fixed by the underwriters in their offering.

In accepting an overabundance of indications of interest (many of them from favored customers), the syndicate manager may eventually allocate more certificates than available for distribution. In other words, the manager may decide to sell short a portion of that offering on behalf of the underwriters. Overallocation is a typical and acceptable practice in investment banking procedures, even if the issue merely appears to be "lukewarm." Who knows whether the public's enthusiasm will turn cold by the effective date? Who knows how many indications of interest may be cancelled because of disappointment about price, market conditions, and so forth?

[13]Penalty syndicate bids are forbidden under NASDAQ rules for issues marketed via that medium.

The manager can use business judgment and, in accord with NASD rules, legitimately oversell the issue by up to 15% of the number of shares or bonds offered. If no cancellations are received when the offering commences, the manager can go into the aftermarket and purchase that security to cover (eliminate) the group's short position. This is *not* defined as stabilization, because more is paid than the syndicate's offering price.

Any loss sustained in this process, or for that matter in stabilization, too, is incurred by the manager on behalf of the members of the underwriting group and apportioned pro rata to their individual participation.

Still another device can be employed to cover the syndicate's short position, a method that does not cause aggressive buying in the aftermarket. The corporation can, and often does, grant the underwriters an option, or warrant, to purchase additional securities of the same issue below the public-offering price, exercisable within a specific time.[14] This new stock is registered with the SEC via amendment to the original registration statement. The manager then can exercise this option and use the certificates received to close out the syndicate's short position. All profit in this case is distributed among the members, once again in proportion to their participation.

### FOR CORPORATE SECURITIES

**H9.**
**The Underwriting Agreement**

**H9a.**

> The formal contract between the investment bankers and the corporation is officially signed the evening before, or on the morning of, the effective date. As mentioned earlier, it is at this time, too, that the final terms and prices are established. This contract is immediately filed with the SEC and becomes part of the registration statement via amendment.
>
> The agreement for underwriting of corporate securities is customarily signed "severally but not jointly." This means that while the investment bankers sign the contract collectively, they limit their individual liability to the corporation only to that portion of the issue they have personally agreed to purchase. As a result, any underwriter able to market its own commitment cannot be held financially accountable to the issuer for the inabilities of its co-underwriters.
>
> Note, however, that this scheme for limiting financial liability does not extend to the purchaser's protections granted under the Securities Act of 1933. The purchaser who can prove that an omission or misrepresentation of material fact caused investment loss on that offering can bring suit for recovery from any and all parties whose names appear voluntarily in the prospectus, whether or not the purchase was made from that underwriter. This limiting relationship is also referred to as a **divided account**, or even occasionally as a **western account**.
>
> ### FOR MUNICIPAL BONDS
>
> Most municipal bond offerings, on the other hand, are underwritten "severally and jointly." This means, of course, that each

**divided account**
**western account**

**H9b.**

[14]The privilege, known as a "Green Shoe" (named after the first issuer that used this technique), is generally exercisable within 30 days after the effective date at the same price as the underwriter's guarantee to the corporation.

| united account | underwriter has full financial responsibility to the issuing state or municipality for the inability of fellow participants to sell those bonds to their customers. This type of relationship is known as a **united account**, or **eastern account**, to differentiate it from the corporate syndicate arrangements. |
| :--- | :--- |
| eastern account | |

To summarize, the following activities take place *during the 20-day cooling-off period:*

1. A preliminary underwriting agreement must be arranged for full guarantee, best efforts, or all-or-none offering.
2. A syndicate of underwriters must be formed.
3. Customers must be contacted for indications of interest.
4. Customers must be sent a preliminary prospectus (red-herring) to solicit indications of interest.
5. A due-dilligence meeting with corporate officials and syndicate participants must be held.
6. The issue must be subjected to blue-skying.
7. A supplementary agreement among underwriters must be drafted, in which, among other things, a syndicate manager is appointed.
8. The syndicate manager must
   a. form an underwriting group;
   b. appoint the selling group;
   c. establish the underwriter's retention;
   d. conduct group sales; and
   e. allocate hot issues.
9. The formal contract between investment bankers and the corporation must be signed.

**I1.**
**Soliciting Orders**

When the offering is permitted to begin, the underwriters first contact customers who gave indications of interest and now solicit bona fide orders from them. Unless the offering is a very popular one, it is unlikely that all those "circles" will turn into orders. Some customers may be unhappy with the final price of the issue and others may have experienced a change in financial circumstances during the cooling-off period. Furthermore, it is probable that the underwriters and members of the selling group will also solicit parties who never expressed indications of interest and who never even received or read the red herring.

**I2.**
**The Final Prospectus**

Even if there were no other reasons, this is why the SEC requires that a final prospectus be presented to *all* subscribers to a registered distribution of securites *no later than with confirmation of their purchase*. The final prospectus, which is a condensation of material information appearing in the amended registration statement, is the only means of order solicitation recognized as acceptable by the SEC. It provides purchasers and prospective purchasers with information about the security and the issuer necessary for making an intelligent investment decision. In fact, if the customer is not given a red herring prior to the effective date, and the first opportunity to become informed about the issue occurs upon the receipt of a prospectus with the trade confirmation, the purchaser *may cancel the transaction within a reasonable time thereafter without loss or penalty*.

Delivery of a prospectus is considered to be so important that the SEC requires it be used by

1. the underwriters when they offer any portion of their commitment;

2. the selling group members when they offer any portion of their allotment; and

3. any broker/dealer acting *as principal* in a transaction involving a security highlighted in an effective registration statement, if that transaction occurs

   a. *within 40 days* after the effective date[15] if the issuer had previously distributed other securities under another registration statement and has not been filing current reports with the SEC, or

   b. *within 90 days* after the effective date[16] if the issuer has never filed a registration statement for any class of securities before and has not been filing current reports with the SEC.

Care must be taken by the underwriters and the members of the selling group to ensure they extend no credit (margin) to purchasers of this issue if it is defined as a "new issue" (that is, a primary distribution by an issuer as opposed to a secondary offering of securities by affiliated persons). The Securities Exchange Act of 1934 prohibits such extensions of credit to customers during the offering and for up to 30 days after the distribution is terminated.

When the public offering commences, the syndicate manager often publicizes this fact by advertising in one or more newspapers and periodicals. It is a somewhat nondescript notice because, by law, any written document that can be construed as a solicitation to purchase a registered security must be accompanied by a prospectus. The lackluster nature of this advertisement inspired its industry designation "tombstone." Nevertheless, this non-sales-oriented announcement, whose copy must contain no exaggeration, elaboration, or solicitation, presents useful information to a knowledgeable reader. Let us examine and analyze a typical tombstone from a recent public offering (Figure 3). Items have been numbered to facilitate your inspection of this tombstone.

*13.*
*The Tombstone*

1 This is an SEC-mandated hedge clause advising readers that this advertisement is not a solicitation and that a prospectus is available for such purpose.

2 This is the aggregate par value of these debt instruments and is not the offering or current market value.

3 The full description of this issue reflects interest rate, maturity date, and the fact both principal and interest payments are guaranteed, if necessary, by another and much larger corporate entity. These bonds are also debentures with no specific claim upon particular assets of either company in the event of a catastrophic failure.

4 Interest payments totalling 9.25% of par value ($92.50 per $1,000) will be paid each year until maturity. Mechanically, $46.25 will be disbursed each February and August 1.

5 The offering price is fixed at 99.50% of par value ($995. per $1,000) *plus* interest accruable from February 1, 1976 to settlement date of the transaction.

---

[15]Or commencement of the public offering, whichever is the later date.

[16]Or commencement of the public offering, whichever is the later date.

**6** This is a caveat advising the reader that this security may be offered by a particular underwriter only in those states in which that firm is registered to act as a broker/dealer and only in compliance with the ''blue sky'' laws of that state.

**7** The syndicate manager's name always appears at the top of the list of underwriters in any tombstone advertisement.

**8** The principal underwriters of this issue then appear in alphabetical order but subdivided into brackets of financial responsibility for marketing this issue. (Horizontal lines have been drawn by the author to help the less experienced reader identify these groupings). The ''major bracket'' underwriters at the top of the list have each committed themselves to bear greater financial liability to the issuer for failure to sell the bonds than a ''submajor-bracket'' firm just below them; and certainly greater than any ''minor-bracket'' underwriter at the bottom of the listing. In large syndicates the names of small underwriters may not even be published in the advertisement. Selling group participant names never appear in a tombstone regardless of syndicate size.

**9** This is the effective date, the earliest date on which the public offering may commence.

## J.
## competitive bidding

The foregoing discussion involved a typical underwriting where terms and conditions were negotiated between the corporation's officials and its investment bankers. But under terms of their bylaws, or because of governmental regulation in certain industries, some corporations are prohibited from making public offerings in this manner. Their underwriting contracts are awarded after competitive bidding by separate groups of investment bankers formed for this purpose.

### *J1.*
### *Procedures*

The corporation announces its intent to issue a specific security and requests bids from the various syndicates to guarantee it a price for the privilege of reoffering the issue publicly at a somewhat higher level. The mechanical processes are identical in both negotiated and competitive deals; they differ only in the manner of determining prices. Meetings of the due-diligence type are held with all the competing groups, but they are now referred to as information meetings, instead.

No price discussions are conducted with the corporation for fear of providing an advantage to one group in preference over the others. Prices are certainly discussed within the separate groups themselves in order to reach agreement on a bid to be submitted to the company. Final prices by the individual syndicates are generally not decided until an hour or so before presentation to the corporation. Each syndicate wants to bid high enough to win the award but not too high, lest they overprice the issue and discourage investors. Interestingly, when the winning group later contacts institutional investors to solicit their orders, the prospective buyers ask for the next highest competitive bid, too. If that bid is close to the winning bid, the issue will sell out quickly. But if the winners top the next highest bid by a wide margin, the professional investor believes the security has been overpriced and often balks at buying at those levels.

The bids must be submitted promptly at a designated hour and location in sealed envelopes, with all interested parties in attendance. True and tragic stories can be told about a representa-

## ② $150,000,000

# BP North American Finance Corporation

### 9¼% Guaranteed Debentures Due 2001

Payment of the principal of, premium, if any, and interest on the Debentures is guaranteed by

## The British Petroleum Company Limited

④ Interest payable February 1 and August 1

⑤ **Price 99½% and Accrued Interest**

⑥ Copies of the Prospectus may be obtained in any State from only such of the
undersigned as may legally offer these Securities in compliance
with the securities laws of such State.

⑦ MORGAN STANLEY & CO.
Incorporated

| | | |
|---|---|---|
| GOLDMAN, SACHS & CO. | | THE FIRST BOSTON CORPORATION |
| MERRILL LYNCH, PIERCE, FENNER & SMITH | | SALOMON BROTHERS |
| Incorporated | | |
| BACHE HALSEY STUART INC. | BLYTH EASTMAN DILLON & CO. | DILLON, READ & CO. INC. |
| | Incorporated | |
| DREXEL BURNHAM & CO. | HORNBLOWER & WEEKS-HEMPHILL, NOYES | E. F. HUTTON & COMPANY INC. |
| Incorporated | Incorporated | |
| KIDDER, PEABODY & CO. | KUHN, LOEB & CO. | LAZARD FRERES & CO. |
| Incorporated | | |
| LEHMAN BROTHERS | LOEB, RHOADES & CO. | PAINE, WEBBER, JACKSON & CURTIS |
| Incorporated | | Incorporated |
| REYNOLDS SECURITIES INC. | SMITH BARNEY, HARRIS UPHAM & CO. | WARBURG PARIBAS BECKER INC. |
| | Incorporated | |
| WERTHEIM & CO., INC. | WHITE, WELD & CO. | DEAN WITTER & CO. |
| | | Incorporated |
| BEAR, STEARNS & CO. | L. F. ROTHSCHILD & CO. | SHEARSON HAYDEN STONE INC. |
| SHIELDS MODEL ROLAND SECURITIES | WEEDEN & CO. | WOOD, STRUTHERS & WINTHROP INC. |
| Incorporated | Incorporated | |
| ABD SECURITIES CORPORATION | BASLE SECURITIES CORPORATION | ALEX. BROWN & SONS |
| EUROPARTNERS SECURITIES CORPORATION | ROBERT FLEMING | HILL SAMUEL SECURITIES |
| | Incorporated | Corporation |
| KLEINWORT, BENSON | | MOSELEY, HALLGARTEN & ESTABROOK INC. |
| Incorporated | | |
| NEW COURT SECURITIES CORPORATION | OPPENHEIMER & CO., INC. | R. W. PRESSPRICH & CO. |
| | | Incorporated |
| SOGEN-SWISS INTERNATIONAL CORPORATION | THOMSON & McKINNON AUCHINCLOSS KOHLMEYER INC. | |
| SPENCER TRASK & CO. | TUCKER, ANTHONY & R. L. DAY, INC. | UBS-DB CORPORATION |
| Incorporated | | |
| AMERICAN SECURITIES CORPORATION | ARNHOLD AND S. BLEICHROEDER, INC. | J. C. BRADFORD & CO. |
| FAULKNER, DAWKINS & SULLIVAN, INC. | | LADENBURG, THALMANN & CO. INC. |
| MITCHELL, HUTCHINS INC. | | WM. E. POLLOCK & CO., INC. |
| THE ROBINSON-HUMPHREY COMPANY, INC. | BUTCHER & SINGER | ELKINS, STROUD, SUPLEE & CO. |
| FAHNESTOCK & CO. | GREENSHIELDS & CO INC | JANNEY MONTGOMERY SCOTT INC. |
| KEEFE, BRUYETTE & WOODS, INC. | NOMURA SECURITIES INTERNATIONAL, INC. | STUART BROTHERS |
| C. E. UNTERBERG, TOWBIN CO. | WILLIAM D. WITTER, INC. | WOOD GUNDY INCORPORATED |

February 11, 1976. ⑨

**FIGURE 3**
A Typical Tombstone

tive of an underwriting group who arrived a few minutes too late for consideration and discovered subsequently that his bid would have won the award. When the bids are opened by the corporation's officials, their attorneys and accountants are usually present to advise on the legality and the economics of those bids before making an award to any of the candidates. As has happened, if these advisors rule against the form or the prices of the bids that have been submitted, the corporation may refrain from selling the issue to anyone at that time.

*J2.*
*Award Ceremony*

With debt issues in particular, the bidding and award ceremony may be an extremely complex affair. Not only must the syndicate contend with price, but interest-rate expenses as well. Although one group's bid may be higher than the others, it may still lose the award because the interest-rate proposal would cost the company more money over the life of the issue than the rates proposed by its competitors. The **net interest cost (NIC)** to the issuer is the principal factor influencing an *award of bonds to an underwriter*. For example, on a $20 million bond issue maturing in 30 years with the bidding as shown below, you would lose to your competitor because the issuer's NIC is higher in your case though your bid price offers the corporation more initial money:

**net interest cost (NIC)**

BIDDING ON A $20,000,000 BOND ISSUE

| | YOUR SYNDICATE'S BID | COMPETITOR'S BID |
|---|---|---|
| Corporation receives | 101 ($20,200,000) | 100½ ($20,100,000) |
| | Your Interest Rate Proposal | Competitor's Interest Rate Proposal |
| Corporation pays annually | 7% ($1,400,000) | 6¾% ($1,350,000) |
| Corporation's expense over 30 years | $41,800,000 | $40,400,000 |

CORPORATION
RECEIVES
AND PAYS

In the case of competitive underwritings, when it becomes obvious that bidding will be keen, each group usually submits its bid with a *tail* attached, hoping to gain a slight advantage. This means that it dislikes bidding in round numbers or round fractions and will instead submit a bid something like 98.4361 for a bond issue, or 18.9752 for a stock. The bid is often carried to four decimal places, although there is no rule preventing them from extending it even further.

**K.**
**closing the contract**

About a week after the effective date and commencement of the offering, the corporation and the underwriters settle up the terms of their contract. In return for the actual certificates, which the syndicate manager distributes to underwriting and selling groups, these investment bankers complete payment of the money specified in the underwriting agreement. They must do so even though the offering may not yet be completed, or even profitable. Unfortunately, that is the business risk assumed by an investment banker on a fundamental underwriting of securities.

**L.**
**standby underwriting agreements**

Broker/dealers acting as investment bankers are often asked to ensure success for a public distribution of securities offered directly by the issuing corporation.

**standby underwriting**

A corporation that gives preemptive rights to subscribe to a new issue is uncertain how many holders will actually exercise their privilege. Rather than gamble on the success of this capital project, the corporation contracts with an investment banker to guarantee subscription to any portion not purchased by the holders of those rights. The procedure is known as a **standby underwriting**, because the investment banker does not know what its actual subscription cost will be at the time the agreement is signed. The firm must literally stand by and wait until the rights expire. It may be required to purchase almost all of the issue, and then again, perhaps none of it.

Generally, during the 30–60-day life of those preemptive rights, the underwriter stays right on top of the situation and is quite busy preparing for all eventualities. For instance, if the stock offering is of significant size, the underwriter forms a syndicate with itself as manager. Then, using the standby fee negotiated from the corporation as a cushion of profit protection, the manager will often stabilize the open-market price so that the old stock continuously trades above the subscription price of the new stock. That often results in one or more of the following:

1. The rights holders are encouraged to subscribe for the new stock because the subscription price is attractive by comparison with the old stock.

2. Stock acquired via stabilization is "laid off"[17] to the members of the underwriting group. This encourages them to reoffer it to their customers at a net market price (earning for themselves a lucrative underwriting fee in the process).

3. The syndicate manager purchases rights in the open market below calculated market-value levels. Institutional holders frequently decide not to subscribe to the new stock and may agree to dispose of their valuable rights to the manager at a price just below what they are then worth arithmetically. They elect to do it this way in order to arrange a single transaction at one price for the substantial number of rights they hold. For example, assume that

   a. the subscription ratio is six rights for each new share;
   b. the subscription price is $15 for each new share; and
   c. the price of old stock, ex rights, is $17

   The market value of the rights is calculated as follows:

   $$\text{Market value} \quad = \quad \frac{\$17 \text{ old stock ex rights} - \$15 \text{ new stock}}{6 \text{ rights for 1 share}}$$

   $$\text{Market value} \quad = \quad \frac{\$2}{6}$$

   $$\text{Market value} \quad = \quad \$.333$$

   If the manager can buy the rights in the open market below $.333 per right, it would do so. The manager then lays them off to the members of the syndicate who subscribe at $15

[17]The slang expression "lay off" is used synonymously for allocation. In this regard, the syndicate manager lays off subscription rights and/or shares of stock on a first-come, first-served basis.

per share and offer the stock to their customers at a net price just below $17. For their effort, the underwriters earn the underwriting fee plus the profit on the discounted purchase of rights, subscription, and sale of stock at near-current market-price levels for that issue.

4. The manager acquires subscription rights abandoned by their owners through ignorance or neglect. There are always some rights holders who fail to take appropriate action by the stated expiration date and time. Under terms of the underwriting agreement, the manager claims those rights at no cost, subscribes for the stock, and "lays off" the new shares with members of the group who sell it to their customers at a net market price. This windfall usually results in a profit for the participating underwriters.

## M. shelf distributions

Thus far, this chapter has principally discussed registered distributions by corporations intent upon raising long-term capital. These situations involved issuers who sought an investment banker's guarantee of payment with a promise to offer those securities immediately at a fixed price.

### M1. Conditions

But this chapter also mentioned that sometimes registration statements must be filed and become effective before certain stockholders (that is, affiliated persons intent upon offering a sizable amount of securities) may dispose of their securities.

Those selling stockholders and even some issuers whose shares must be registered with the SEC may not be inclined to dispose of their holdings at one time or at one price. When issuers or affiliated persons want to sell securities over a period of time, or at a variety of prices (as compared to the one-time price at the time of a typical underwriting), they can often register those instruments with the SEC and reserve the right to sell within two years following the effective date. These are called *shelf distributions* and are registered and sold under SEC Rule 415. It permits the seller to make at-the-market-offerings from authorized capital or from a personal portfolio ("shelf") anytime over a two-year period, without further prior notice, as financial needs dictate. Information in the prospectus must be kept current during the distribution period and given to purchasers with their trade confirmations.[18] Transactions on a securities exchange are subject to the distribution rules of that exchange. Moreover, because two years is a long time and offers too many possibilities for inadvertent violation of SEC regulations, most broker/dealers request letters of indemnification from sellers before acting on their behalf. After all, SEC Rule 10b-6 applies to a shelf distribution, as well as to any other registered offering, of securities. That rule could therefore impact the further activities of participants during this period.

**shelf distribution**

### M2. SEC Rule 415

SEC Rule 415 enables sales to be made on a continuous or delayed basis, at various times and prices, for up to two years, in a single filing of a registration statement. Securities may be equity

---

[18]If material changes do occur in the affairs of that corporation while the seller is still in the process of distribution, an amendment to the registration statement must be filed and included with the offering prospectus.

or debt instruments but, if they are to be sold by an issuer (rather than by an affiliated person), the following requirements apply:

1. The securities must be SEC registered on Form S-3 or F-3. In general this means the issuer has been registered under the 1934 Act for at least the past three years, has been making timely submissions, and is current with its mandatory reports to the SEC. It is also up to date in its payments of dividends, interest, sinking funds, installment debt, and leasehold obligations;

2. the securities must be sold to or through one or more underwriters named in the registration statement and prospectus;

3. if these are equity securities, any voting stock offered under this Rule must not exceed 10% of the aggregate voting stock already outstanding and held by nonaffiliated persons and entities.

**CONCLUDING COMMENTS**

The procedures and investment banking activities described in this chapter are essential to the continued growth of U.S. industry. They are instrumental in facilitating the financing of new products and new businesses. Operating at the same time are numerous SEC controls to safeguard the integrity of this country's primary and secondary markets. Federal regulations provide this assurance by

1. necessitating full and accurate disclosures of material investment information; and

2. prohibiting unfair and inequitable price manipulation of securities.

In the final analysis, however, the judgment to buy or sell must always rest solely with the individual investor.

# over-the-counter transactions

**Maloney Act**

**National Association of Securities Dealers (NASD)**

In 1938, Congress legislated an amendment to the Securities Exchange Act of 1934 providing the legal means by which broker/dealers not subject to stock exchange authority could offer investors an equal degree of ethical and proprietary responsibility in securities transactions. This amendment (Section 15A) is commonly known as the **Maloney Act**, named after its sponsor, the late Senator Francis T. Maloney of Connecticut.

*A1.*
*The Maloney Act Requirement*

The Maloney Act requires any national securities association to register with the Securities and Exchange Commission. Based on the terms of its petition a securities association is empowered to establish operating standards designed to promote just and equitable principles of trade and to require adherence to high standards of commercial honor and integrity. Only two securities associations have ever registered under this act, the **National Association of Securities Dealers (NASD)** in 1939 and The Municipal Securities Rulemaking Board (MSRB) in 1975.

*A2.*
*Membership in the NASD*

Most broker/dealer organizations registered with the SEC in the United States have joined the NASD. It is not mandatory for them to do so. They have joined because they find it convenient and advantageous to participate in the NASD. Admission requirements and qualifications for NASD membership are reasonable and broad enough to include most individuals or organizations willing to comply with the association's rules and regulations. Any broker or dealer transacting investment banking or securities business under the laws of any state and/or the United States is eligible for new or continuing membership in the NASD, *unless*

1. that broker or dealer has had its registration suspended or revoked by the SEC;
2. that broker or dealer has been suspended or expelled from a registered securities exchange or association;
3. that broker or dealer has associated with any person who was a cause of suspension or expulsion from SEC registration;
4. that broker or dealer knowingly or willingly filed, or caused to be filed, an application, statement, or report with the NASD that was false, misleading, or incomplete with respect to a material fact;
5. that broker or dealer has been convicted of a felony or misdemeanor involving a securities transaction or misappropriation of money or securities within 10 years prior to application for membership or at any time thereafter;
6. that broker or dealer is enjoined by court order from acting as an investment advisor, underwriter, broker, dealer, or employee of an investment company, bank, or insurance company; or
7. that broker or dealer does not have proper or sufficient personnel qualified with the NASD as principal, financial principal, and representative.

Firms that do not belong to the NASD are generally small, regionally oriented in their business, or highly specialized in their securities activities. For example, many specialist concerns on the registered stock exchanges are not NASD members. There is no reason for them to join if they do not trade securities over the counter as a matter of practice. NASD nonmembers who are also not members of registered stock exchanges nevertheless do not escape the scrutiny or supervision of regulatory authorities. They may still be subject to qualification and compliance with SEC, state, and/or local government regulations, depending upon the securities activities in which they engage. SEC registered broker/dealers who are not members of principal stock exchanges and who also do not belong to the NASD are obliged to sit for a Securities and Exchange Commission examination to prove their ability to function as qualified representatives or principals. Such firms are generally identified as **SECO members**, an acronym for Securities and Exchange Commission Organization.

**SECO members**

A nonmember of the NASD, including a SECO member, must be treated by NASD members in the same way members treat their public customers. Members of the association are prohibited from granting discounts, selling concessions, rebates, or special allowances of any kind when transacting business with, or in behalf of, nonmembers.

*A3.*
*Organization of the NASD*

The National Association of Securities Dealers was incorporated as a non-stock-issuing, nonprofit, membership organization under the laws of Delaware in 1936 and registered with the SEC in 1939. Excerpts from the association's charter highlight its purposes and reflect compliance with the Maloney Act. These purposes and objectives are to

1. promote the investment banking and securities business;
2. standardize its principles and practices;
3. promote high standards of commercial honor and to promote among members observance of federal and state securities laws;
4. provide a medium through which the membership may consult with governmental and other agencies;
5. cooperate with governmental authority in the solution of problems affecting this business and investors;
6. adopt and enforce rules of fair practice in the securities business;
7. promote just and equitable principles of trade for the protection of investors;
8. promote self-discipline among members;
9. investigate and adjust grievances between members and between the public and members.

*A3a.* **THE BOARD OF GOVERNORS**

The terms and conditions of everyday operation as well as the classification, qualification, and responsibilities of members in this corporation are spelled out precisely in the NASD bylaws. The task of making, altering, or repealing these bylaws is assigned to a 31-member **Board of Governors**, most of whom are elected by the general membership of the association. The remainder are elected by the board itself.

**Board of Governors**

The Board of Governors is aided in its deliberations and policy formulations by an Advisory Council and 27 standing committees. Each of these committees is expert in a technical area of business activity in which member organizations frequently participate. (See Figure 1.) The job of directly supervising these policies for a nationwide membership of approximately 3,000 is herculean. Thus, for purposes of delegating administrative authority, the bylaws provide for partitioning the United States into 13 securities districts. The membership in each district, therefore, elects (1) a specified number of representatives to serve on the association's Board of Governors and (2) several participants to serve on a **District Committee** in order to achieve a maximum degree of local administration.

**District Committee**

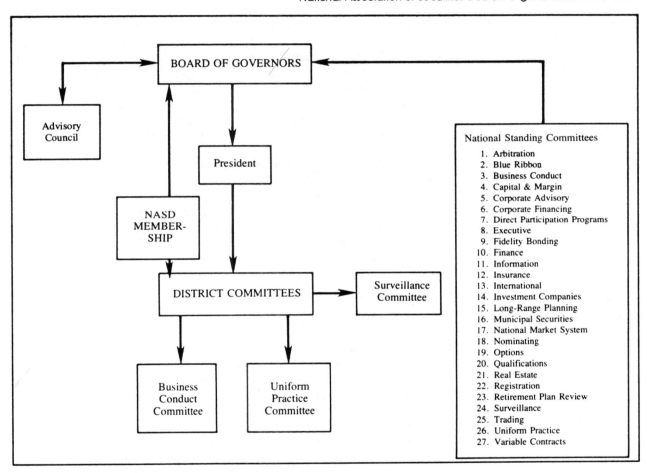

**FIGURE 1**
National Association of Securities Dealers Organizational Flow Chart

BOARD OF GOVERNORS

Advisory Council

President

NASD MEMBER-SHIP

DISTRICT COMMITTEES

Surveillance Committee

Business Conduct Committee

Uniform Practice Committee

National Standing Committees

1. Arbitration
2. Blue Ribbon
3. Business Conduct
4. Capital & Margin
5. Corporate Advisory
6. Corporate Financing
7. Direct Participation Programs
8. Executive
9. Fidelity Bonding
10. Finance
11. Information
12. Insurance
13. International
14. Investment Companies
15. Long-Range Planning
16. Municipal Securities
17. National Market System
18. Nominating
19. Options
20. Qualifications
21. Real Estate
22. Registration
23. Retirement Plan Review
24. Surveillance
25. Trading
26. Uniform Practice
27. Variable Contracts

### *THE DISTRICT COMMITTEE*

*A3b.*

The chairman of each district serves on the Advisory Council to the Board of Governors but does not vote on matters of policy. Each District Committee, in turn, then appoints at least three subcommittees to accomplish its specialized goal.

**District Uniform Practice Committee**

**Uniform Practice Code**

*District uniform practice committee* The **District Uniform Practice Committee** disseminates information and interpretations handed down by the Board of Governors regarding the **Uniform Practice Code**. This code relates to the mechanics of executing and completing securities transactions between member firms of

*A3b(1).*

the NASD.[1] In this respect, the committee may be called upon by members in its district to interpret or rule upon technical questions concerning trade contracts or the proper deliverability of certificates. It is also empowered to formulate local practice codes dealing specifically with the peculiarities of transactions within its district. These rules, of course, are subject to comment by the local membership and approval by the Board of Governors. They may not conflict with the national board's Uniform Practice Code for the entire association. Disputes arising between members from the same district concerning this code are resolved by this subcommittee. Controversies between members from different districts are mediated and resolved by the Standing National Uniform Practice Committee.

A3b(2).

> ***District business conduct committee*** The **District Business Conduct Committee** is responsible for supervising the board's Rules of Fair Practice, which concern primarily the ethics employed by members in the conduct of their business. With this objective, the committee carefully examines members' activities on a continuing basis and administers the Code of Procedure, if necessary. That code, designed to handle trade practice complaints, is a set of rules under which disciplinary proceedings are conducted.

**District Business Conduct Committee**

The District Business Conduct Committee is, in reality, the elected officials of the District Committee themselves. However, owing to varying workloads in each district, it is not uncommon to find several local business conduct subcommittees appointed to process much of the necessary hearings and accompanying paperwork. A simplified flow chart of the NASD organization is shown in Figure 1.

**A3b(3)**
***District Surveillance Committee***

The District Surveillance Committee is responsible for deciding whether remedial sanctions need be imposed upon members in that locality who may be experiencing financial or operating difficulties. Based upon information furnished it from members, customers of that firm, periodic reports filed with regulatory agencies and on-premises examination by NASD officials, this Committee determines if, and what, penalties need be employed in accordance with Section 38 of the Association's Rules of Fair Practice. These judgments to limit a member's business may be appealed in the form of an official committee hearing and subsequent review by the Board of Governors. However, the facts in such matters are usually self-evident and attempts at correcting the situation are routinely prescribed in the NASD regulation.

The District Surveillance Committee is comprised of two current or former District Business Conduct Committee members; two members of the Board of Governors National Surveillance Committee and one former member of the Board of Governors.

**A4.**
***The NASD Code of Procedure***

> The **Code of Procedure** is prescribed by the Board of Governors for administration of disciplinary proceedings stemming from infractions of the Rules of Fair Practice. All trade practice complaints are heard and passed upon initially by the District Business

**Code of Procedure**

---

[1] This code does not regulate the procedural relationships that prevail between a member firm and its customers.

> Conduct Committee of the district in which (1) the respondent's main office is located or (2) the action on which the complaint is based took place.

All complaints, whether prompted by another member of the NASD or by the District Committee itself, must be in written form and must cite the rule or interpretation allegedly violated. The respondent is allowed 10 business days in which to answer or refute these accusations, also in written form, before the District Business Conduct Committee will sit in judgment. Either party to this allegation has the right to request a formal hearing of the complaint, at which time both may be represented by legal counsel. Otherwise, the committee will determine what form of discipline, if any, will be instituted. It has the power to censure, fine, suspend, or even expel members from the association for serious violations.

If, in the opinion of the District Business Conduct Committee, the facts of the complaint are not in dispute and the infraction is a relatively minor one, the committee may offer the accused member *summary-complaint proceedings* instead of the more formalized regular complaint procedure. If accepted, the member agrees to

1. admit guilt;
2. waive formal hearings;
3. accept a penalty of censure and/or a fine of up to $2,500, and
4. waive all right of appeal to the Board of Governors.

More serious violations are adjudicated by the District Business Conduct Committee via the regular complaint procedure, which involves formal hearings and a trial. These judgments are subject to review by the Board of Governors upon appeal by any participant in this dispute or upon the board's own initiative. The board has authority to uphold, increase, decrease, or modify any penalties after careful consideration.

People aggrieved by the board's decision can then appeal to the Securities and Exchange Commission for satisfaction. If they are unable to find it there, the public court system is always available to them. Rarely does a complaint proceeding go that far, not only because of the time and expense involved, but also because of the impartiality of judgment at the intervening levels of review.

**Code of Arbitration**

As any large organization concerned with money matters must, the NASD has developed an arbitration facility for resolution of controversies arising out of, and relating exclusively to, securities transactions. NASD-sponsored arbitration under the **Code of Arbitration** is available for intramember or customer-member disputes involving securities activities. Only U.S. government securities that are exempted securities, as defined in the Exchange Act of 1934, are excluded from the association's jurisdiction.

Presenting controversies to a Board of Arbitration is strictly voluntary for the parties concerned. Nevertheless when parties agree to arbitration, they are bound to adhere to the arbitrator's decision without right of appeal. Arbitrators are appointed by an Arbitration Director, who is himself appointed by the NASD Board of Governors to perform all the administrative functions of

**A5.**
***The NASD Code of Arbitration***

this important process. The number and occupations of the arbitrators depend upon the parties involved in the dispute. Intramember controversies are resolved by three to five arbitrators, all of whom are employed within the securities industry. Disputes involving public customers, however, are resolved by five arbitrators, at least three of whom are not employed in the securities industry. Majority vote rules in all cases. The principal benefits of this process are:

1. *Impartiality.* Judgment is rendered by the disputant's peers, or disinterested parties, as the case may be.
2. *Ease and speed of operation.* A minimum of paperwork is involved, with cases heard and settled out of court, in most instances, within a few months.
3. *Reasonable cost.* Each party knows in advance the expense he must bear to support arbitration proceedings. The fee schedule is fixed by the National Arbitration Committee of the NASD and ranges from $25 per matter to $120 per hearing, depending upon the sum of money at question in the dispute.

**A6.**
*Sechedule C of the NASD Bylaws*

As a way of monitoring NASD members, the Board of Governors has established criteria whereby various persons associated with a member organization must qualify and register with the association as principal, financial principal, or representative. The differences between these roles are based on the type of work performed, the degree of responsibility enjoyed, and the type of securities sold.

**A6a.** *REGISTRATION AS PRINCIPAL*

Principal registration is the highest form of registration recognized by the NASD. A registered principal may legally participate in most areas of a member's business, including all phases of supervision, solicitation, and training. **Registration as principal** is required for the following persons who are actively engaged in the management of a member organization's investment banking and securities business other than in the area of accounting and net capital compliance:

**registration as principal**

1. sole proprietors
2. officers (titled executives with bona fide administrative responsibilities, such as vice-president, secretary, treasurer)
3. general partners of a broker/dealer partnership active in the business
4. directors of a broker/dealer corporation active in the business
5. managers of Offices of Supervisory Jurisdiction

Employees of member organizations responsible for training principals must themselves qualify as registered principals.

**A6b.** *REGISTRATION AS FINANCIAL PRINCIPAL*

The facet of the securities business denied to the typical principal is preparation or approval of the firm's financial statements and net capital computations. To be involved in these areas of the securities business, a registered principal must also be registered as a **financial principal** with the NASD. Every member organization is obliged to staff on a continuing basis at least one registered principal who can serve as a financial principal after passing a special qualifying examination. Thus, a financial principal must be a registered principal, but most registered principals are not financial principals. If a registered principal does not work in the department of his organization responsible for the firm's financial statements and calculation of net capital, he or she need not sit for this highly technical examination.

**financial principal**

## A6c. REGISTRATION AS REPRESENTATIVE

**Registration as representative** is required as a minimum qualification for the following persons:

**registration as representative**

1. solicitors of investment banking or securities business, including securities sales people, marketers of variable annuity contracts, research analysts and corporate finance department employees who communicate with customers and prospective clients of the member organization

2. traders (the employees who make decisions to buy and sell securities for the member firm's account and risk in a dealer capacity)

3. assistant officers (employees who assist principals in their supervisory, administrative, or sales responsibilities and are usually identified by such titles as assistant vice-president, assistant secretary, assistant treasurer)[2]

4. training directors and assistants (employees responsible for training solicitors, traders, and assistant officers, but who do not train principals)

### EXEMPTIONS FROM REGISTRATION

A6d.

From the foregoing commentary it may appear that all employees in a member organization are required to qualify for one registration or the other, but this is not so. The NASD recognizes the impracticality of that approach. Therefore, the following persons are specifically exempted from these registration requirements:

1. nominal officials, such as limited partners, nonvoting stockholders, or even some employees with officerial titles if those persons have no active voice in the management of their firm and their functions are related exclusively to that firm's need for capital or coordination of operation

2. persons whose functions are related *solely and exclusively* to the following activities
   a. transactions on a national securities exchange and are registered with that exchange, such as specialists and commission house brokers
   b. transactions in exempted securities, such as U.S. government obligations

[2]This category also includes any employee who merely *supervises* a function or department related to the solicitation or conduct of the firm's investment banking or securities business.

c. transactions in commodities

d. clerical or ministerial activities in the firm, such as those performed by secretaries, order clerks, margin clerks, and statisticians

3. foreign associates[3] (employees who are not citizens, nationals, or residents of the United States, its territories or possessions, and who conduct their securities activities only with noncitizens and nonresidents of the United States outside U.S. jurisdiction)

*over the counter*

*B1.*
*Location of OTC*

**B.**
**where and what is over the counter?**

When properly qualified with the NASD as a member organization, a broker/dealer may commence trading activities for itself and/or for customers in the **over-the-counter** marketplace. Over the counter is not located in a centralized area as is typical of the registered securities exchanges. In fact, over the counter is anywhere other than on a registered exchange. Over the counter is a marketplace where buyers seek out sellers (and vice versa) and then attempt to arrange terms and conditions acceptable to both parties. It is a **negotiated marketplace** that exists anywhere and everywhere as opposed to the **auction marketplace** represented by activity on the securities exchanges. All that is essential for an over-the-counter market to function is a buyer and a seller of a security.

**negotiated**
**marketplace**
**auction**
**marketplace**

The concept of the over-the-counter market is broad enough to include private transactions by public investors as well as the more frequent trading activities of professional brokers and dealers. Therefore, it is virtually impossible to pinpoint exact total trading volume in any given security. At best, figures for any given day are an estimate based on the number of existing issues related to stock exchange volume in listed securities on that day. Without a doubt, there is a greater number and variety of issues traded over the counter than on the securities exchanges.[4]

*B2.*
*Types of OTC Securities*

The types of securities traded over the counter are as follows:

1. Almost all transactions in U.S. government, state, municipal, and foreign country obligations are effected over the counter.

2. The overwhelming majority of industrial, rail, and utility debt issues are traded over the counter.

3. The equity issues of smaller, regional, or closely held corporations are traded over the counter primarily because they cannot or will not meet the stock exchanges' listing requirements.

4. Most banks and insurance companies fall into this category, although with recent popular trends toward mergers, holding companies, full disclosure, and overall projection of public image, many of these companies have obtained listing privileges on the major securities exchanges.

5. All open-end investment company shares (mutual funds) are also found over the counter.

[3]An application to serve as a foreign associate must be filed with the National Association of Securities Dealers.

[4]About 50,000 stocks and bonds trade over the counter versus approximately 4,000 stocks and bonds on all securities exchanges collectively.

6. Primary distributions of corporations offering their shares publicly trade in this market too, at least for a while, even if the company can qualify for a listing on the New York Stock Exchange or the American Stock Exchange. This occurs because at least 30 days must elapse between filing a listing application with the exchange, a certification statement with the SEC, and the time when such documents become effective. Only then can trading on the exchange commence. This provision of the Securities Exchange Act of 1934 usually works in the best interest of the exchange, because in the interim, activity in the over-the-counter market can wring out speculative excesses frequently associated with the popular public offerings of securities.

7. Even some listed stock is traded over the counter in what is often referred to as the third market. The term **third market** alludes to over-the-counter transactions in listed stocks, warrants, and closed-end investment company shares by nonmember broker/dealers of that exchange. The first, or **primary market**, represents transactions on registered stock exchanges by members of those exchanges. The **second market** consists of over-the-counter transactions in unlisted securities by broker/dealers registered with the SEC. The **fourth market** consists of over-the-counter transactions in either listed or unlisted securities between institutional investors, without benefit of a participating broker/dealer.

third market

primary market

second market

fourth market

8. Also traded over the counter are receipts evidencing the shares of a foreign corporation on deposit or under the control of a U.S. banking institution. They are called **American Depositary Receipts (ADRs)**. ADRs are designed to facilitate transactions and expedite transfers of ownership of selected foreign securities in the United States. When a foreign company's transfer agent is located in the country of origin, which is the usual practice, an ordinary reregistration of certificates from old owner to new owner initiated from the United States can take weeks to effect. This is an unacceptable situation for our highly liquid securities markets.

American Depositary Receipts (ADRs)

Therefore, to accommodate investors and brokerage firms in this country, a U.S. bank with overseas offices and foreign correspondents creates this new security to represent shares of the underlying foreign stocks physically held in its possession, either in the United States or overseas. Morgan Guaranty Trust Company, N.A., and Citibank Corporation, N.A., both headquartered in New York City, are typical of such banking institutions. Each bank acts as an intermediary between the foreign company's transfer agent and the U.S. investor. Each is empowered to transfer ownership of the ADRs on its own books and records but continues as the official holder of record on the company's stockholder list. The actual foreign shares remain registered in the name of the bank while under the control of that bank. Of course, investors can always exchange ADRs for the underlying common stock (or vice versa) if they choose to do so, but this is rarely the case except among international traders who often need the comparable security to satisfy contractual sale commitments here or abroad. In any event, a nominal certificate fee is levied upon the party requesting an exchange into or out of an ADR.

American Depositary Receipts are available in various denominations and represent the foreign stock on a share-for-share basis; however, in the case of Japanese securities, 1 ADR generally is equal to 10 underlying shares. These certificates are subject to SEC regulation within the United States. For this reason, holders of ADRs are entitled to full protection under our laws as well as most advantages of stock ownership accorded to investors in domestic securities. For example, with cooperation from the foreign corporation and through essential agency efforts of the U.S. bank, ADR investors are accorded the following privileges of ownership:

1. They receive current financial information about the company, including an audited annual report containing a balance sheet and income statement.

2. They are accorded voting privileges by means of proxies transmitted promptly to the registered ADR holders on the bank's records.

3. They receive cash dividends when paid by the foreign corporation. The bank converts the foreign currency into dollars, deducts a processing fee, and remits the balance to the ADR holder. If a tax was withheld at the source, in accord with the laws of the issuer's country, the bank notifies the ADR investor of the amount, thus enabling the party to claim it as a credit on his U.S. tax return.

4. They receive stock dividends or stock splits as distributed by the foreign corporation. The bank converts the additional shares into new ADRs and delivers those certificates to the registered holders listed on its own records.

5. They receive subscription rights for new stock to be issued by the foreign corporation. However, this occurs only if the corporation decides to raise new capital via this method and only if it complies with the registration provisions of the Securities Act of 1933 and other applicable laws of the U.S. for the new stock. Otherwise, the rights will be sold by the bank (if they have a market value) and a check for the dollar proceeds, after currency conversion, sent to the ADR holder.

A typical over-the-counter transaction is often initiated by a customer seeking to buy or sell a security. The instruction is accepted by a registered representative who, in turn, writes it down on an

C.
how trading is conducted
over the counter

order ticket and presents it to an over-the-counter trader in the firm for execution. The entire buy or sell order can be consolidated on one ticket because it is handled by a single trader in that firm. This contrasts with the way a stock exchange order is often processed. With stock exchange orders, two tickets are generally required when the quantity involved is less than 100 shares (an odd lot) as well as 100 shares (a round lot) or multiples of 100 shares. An over-the-counter transaction may also be initiated by a broker/dealer desiring to take or eliminate a position in a security for its own account.

*C1.*
*Initiating an OTC Transaction*

The first problem is to locate someone who is willing and able to negotiate terms on the contra side of the transaction. This normally means communicating with a broker/dealer who stands ready to provide continuing bids and offerings for that security or, in other words, to act as a **market-maker**.

**market-maker**

*C2.*
*Locating a Market-Maker*

How do you find one? Where do you begin? There are various means by which experienced dealers locate market-makers or anybody interested in trading with them. Two of the most popular sources of such information are represented by the National Quotation Bureau, Inc. (NQB), and the National Association of Securities Dealers Automated Quotation system (NASDAQ).

The NQB is a subsidiary of Commerce Clearing House, Inc., a well-known private publisher of financial information and manuals. The NQB distributes to subscribers a list of broker/dealers making bids and/or offerings of securities traded over the counter. In fact, the NQB publishes and distributes several lists of such market-makers each day. The list most widely employed is comprised of broker/dealers making markets in securities of nationwide interest. (See Figure 2.) It is more popularly referred to as the **pink sheets** for stocks because of the color of the paper it is printed upon. Another list, known as the **yellow sheets**, shows market-makers for corporate debt securities. The NQB also publishes a monthly service featuring quotations and market-makers for inactively traded securities. The purpose of that booklet is to provide valuations for portfolio managers, administrators, fiduciaries, and so on, and to help potential buyers and sellers of such securities locate each other.

**pink sheets**
**yellow sheets**

*C3.*
*National Quotation Bureau Inc. (NQB)*

Examination of the pink sheets on any given day reveals almost 9,000 issues with an average of five market-makers for each listing. Alongside their names may appear a quotation, but those bids and offerings are not representative of current prices. The information for the pink sheets is collected the previous day, and so the prices that appear therein are history by the time of publication. Dealers must be contacted personally to determine their current prices and even to verify that their organization is still a market-maker in that issue. Broker/dealers are privileged to stop their activities in a particular security at any time.

Some dealers don't even bother to show their prices in the pink sheets, claiming that it is pointless to show figures for a volatile or infrequently traded stock. They merely invite contact

# THE NATIONAL DAILY QUOTATION SERVICE

*Published by* NATIONAL QUOTATION BUREAU, Inc.

P. O. Box 49, Peck Slip Station,
New York, N. Y. 10038

212-349-1800
LISTING DEPT. 212-349-2213

TWX 710-581-6560

SYMBOLS / Listings received by mail today. All other listings current today.

* Correspondent.
# "Other arrangement."

VJ In Bankruptcy or receivership or being reorganized under the Bankruptcy Act, or securities assumed by such companies.

RBA Representative Bid—Asked Quotations supplied through NASDAQ as of 11:A. M.

### N Q B OVER - THE - COUNTER INDUSTRIAL STOCK AVERAGE.

#### 35 ISSUES. DIVISOR 2.16 ADJUSTED FOR SPLITS AND STOCK DIVIDENDS.

|        | OPENED | CLOSED | CHANGED  | HIGH          | LOW           |
|--------|--------|--------|----------|---------------|---------------|
| 1975   | 282.91 | 375.07 | + 92.16  | 459.83 JUN 26 | 282.91 JAN 2  |
| 1976   | 377.64 |        |          | 461.02 FEB 26 | 377.64 JAN 2  |
| JUN    | 403.23 | 407.83 | + 4.60   | 407.83 JUN 30 | 389.93 JUN 10 |
| JUL    | 408.46 | 409.38 | + 0.92   | 413.97 JUL 15 | 406.55 JUL 21 |
| AUG    | 411.53 | 398.34 | - 13.19  | 414.47 AUG 4  | 394.34 AUG 25 |
| SEP    | 397.93 |        |          | 408.34 SEP 8  | 397.93 SEP 1  |
| SEP 2  |        | 3      | 7        | 8             | 9             |
| 404.24 + 6.31 | 404.06 - 0.18 | 406.26 + 2.20 | 408.34 + 2.08 | 408.23 - 0.11 |

### N Q B INSURANCE STOCK AVERAGE

#### 15 ISSUES. DIVISOR 6.17 ADJUSTED FOR SPLITS AND STOCK DIVIDENDS.

|        | OPENED | CLOSED | CHANGED  | HIGH          | LOW           |
|--------|--------|--------|----------|---------------|---------------|
| 1975   | 69.55  | 74.45  | + 4.90   | 87.15 JUL 18  | 65.04 JAN 15  |
| 1976   | 74.80  |        |          | 92.95 AUG 18  | 74.63 JAN 28  |
| JUN    | 76.21  | 80.18  | + 3.97   | 80.18 JUN 30  | 75.91 JUN 7   |
| JUL    | 80.75  | 88.65  | + 7.90   | 88.65 JUL 30  | 79.20 JUL 7   |
| AUG    | 89.73  | 88.74  | - 0.99   | 92.95 AUG 18  | 88.27 AUG 27  |
| SEP    | 89.22  |        |          | 90.74 SEP 8   | 89.22 SEP 1   |
| SEP 2  |        | 3      | 7        | 8             | 9             |
| 90.21 + 0.99 | 90.82 + 0.31 | 90.40 - 0.12 | 90.74 + 0.34 | 90.52 - 0.22 |

| | | | | | |
|---|---|---|---|---|---|
| A & E PLASTIK PAK CO COM | NCC PRICE AVG | 7 5/8 | A L D INC COM | | |
| AMSWISS INTL CORP J CY | 800 631 3080 | | COOK INVESTMENT CO CG | 800 621 8015 | |
| A A I CORP | NCC PRICE AVG | 5 1/4 | A M F INC 3 90 PR | NCC PRICE AVG | 40 1/4 |
| PBW STOCK EXCHANGE LISTED 215 563 4700 | | | MCMULLEN & HARD NY | 212 349 1080 | |
| AAR CORP | NCC PRICE AVG | 9 27/32 | LEHMAN BROS NY | 212 344 6627 | |
| AMSWISS INTL CORP J CY | 800 631 3080 | | SWIFT HENKE & CO NY | 212 425 0360 | |
| A A V COMPANIES | NCC PRICE AVG | 5 7/8 | M S WIEN & CO INC J CY | 800 631 3088 | |
| A B A INDUSTRIES INC | ABAI | | A M F INC COM | NCC PRICE AVG | 19 7/8 |
| VOL- N/A HB- 5 1/2 LB- 5 1/4 | | 5 1/4 6 | AMSWISS INTL CORP J CY | 800 631 3080 | |
| DPCO*HRZG,JAMS,SRCO | | | H S KIPNIS & CO CG | 800 621 6630 | |
| A B C INDUSTRIES INC | NCC PRICE AVG | 5/8 | A M I C CORP N C | NCC PRICE AVG | 13 3/8 |
| TROSTER SINGER & CO NY | 212 422 2400 | | AMSWISS INTL CORP J CY | 800 631 3080 | |
| B S LICHTENSTEIN & CO NY | 212 425 4311 | 1/8 | A M I INDUSTRIES INC COLO AMIN | | |
| A C & S CORP COM | | | VOL- 8 HB- 5 3/8 LB- 5 3/8 | | 5 3/4 6 1/4 |
| E J QUINN & CO INC J CY | 212 425 1240 | | BOET*TSCO,ILCO,WBLR | | |
| A C F INDUSTRIES INC | NCC PRICE AVG | 34 | A M I INDUSTRIES INC | NCC PRICE AVG | 2 5/8 |
| AMSWISS INTL CORP J CY | 800 631 3080 | | A P F ELECTRONCS INC COM | APFE | |
| ACS INDUSTRIES INC | NCC PRICE AVG | 3/4 | VOL- 22 HB- 10 3/4 LB- 10 1/2 | | 10 3/4 11 1/2 |
| BERNARD L MADOFF NY | 800 221 2242 | | BJCO,GALS,LOEB,MASH,MRKS,MSRO*SHWD,SHDN | | |
| M RIMSON & CO INC NY | 212 964 2634 | | CONLON DIV BAIRD PAT NY | 212 422 1130 | |
| AMSWISS INTL CORP J CY | 800 631 3080 | | MULLER & CO NY | 212 952 9444 | |
| SHERWOOD SECS CORP J CY | 212 425 0300 | 1/2 7/8 | GALLANT SECS INC NY | 212 593 2320 | |
| CARR SECS CORP NY | 212 425 8220 | 1/2 7/8 | CARL MARKS & CO INC -MRKS 212 437 7100 | | |
| A C S INVESTOR INC | NCC PRICE AVG | 1 5/8 | API TRUST SBI | APITS | |
| CARR SECS CORP NY | 212 425 8220 | | VOL- 30 HB- 3 1/2 LB- 3 1/2 | | 3 1/2 4 1/4 |
| MAYER&SCHWEITZER INC J CY 800 631 3094 | | | AMIC,LOEB,MASH,SHDN | | |
| ADA FINANCIAL SVCE CORP | NCC PRICE AVG | 1/4 | A P L CORPORATION COM | NCC PRICE AVG | 14 7/8 |
| HERZOG & CO INC NY | 800 631 3095 | | AMSWISS INTL CORP J CY | 800 631 3080 | |
| NEUBERGER SECS CORP NY | 212 732 6030 | 1/8 1/2 | A P L CORP WTS | APLCW | |
| ADM INDUSTRIES INC | NCC PRICE AVG | 21/32 | VOL- 6 HB- 10 3/4 LB- 4 3/8 | | 4 1/2 5 |
| AEG TELEFUNKEN ADR | NCC PRICE AVG | 32 1/2 | HRZG,JLSS,MASH,SGMK,WIEN | | |
| CARL MARKS & CO INC NY | 212 437 7100 | | HERZOG & CO INC -HRZG 800 631 3095 | | |
| MERRILL LYNCH PFS NY | 212 766 7820 | 34 36 | A P S INC COM | APSI | |
| AES TECHNOLOGY SYSTEMS | AEST | | VOL- 6 HB- 7 3/4 LB- 7 1/2 | | 7 1/4 8 |
| VOL- 19 HB- 1 3/8 LB- 1 1/4 | | 1 1 1/2 | BEST,EHUT,GSCO,KPCO,MASH,RMDU,SGMK,WEDB | | |

FIGURE 2

Part of Page 1 of Daily "Pink Sheet"

**BW (bid wanted)**
**OW (offer wanted)**

by interested parties willing to negotiate by listing their names next to the pertinent issues each day. Still other broker/dealers do not choose to trade on both sides of the market, and so they appear in the sheets as **BW (bid wanted)** or **OW (offer wanted)**. The BW dealer is trying to sell stock and is seeking a buyer; the OW dealer is a buyer seeking sellers.

### WHO IS A MARKET-MAKER IN THE PINK SHEETS?                    *C3a.*

The ability to proclaim yourself a market-maker in these sheets is not restricted to NASD members. Any subscriber may advertise his or her willingness to trade in specific stocks. To avoid the possibility of fraudulent representation and manipulation of price, especially for shares of small "shell" corporations that are virtually assetless, the SEC implemented Rule 15c2–11 in 1971. (The SEC acted because it, rather than the NASD, has power over these corporations.) This rule requires anyone submitting bid or offering prices to any quotation medium, or indicating a willingness to be a market-maker in a particular security, insure that *one* of the following circumstances prevails:

1. The issuer has in existence a registration statement effective within the previous 90 days (40 days for statements filed under Regulation A) that is not the subject of an SEC stop order, *and* the broker/dealer has on file a copy of the prospectus (or offering circular under Regulation A).

2. The corporation files periodic reports with the SEC, the broker/dealer has a reasonable basis for believing that the corporation is current in its filing, *and* the broker/dealer has in its files a copy of the corporation's most recent annual report required to be filed with the SEC (as distinguished from the annual report sent to stockholders).

3. The broker/dealer firm has the following information on file concerning the corporation and makes it available to any person interested in a proposed transaction. It must also furnish this information to the quotation medium at least 2 days before the quotation is to be published.

    a.   the exact name of the issuer and its predecessor
    b.   the address of its principal executive offices
    c.   the state of incorporation, if it is a corporation
    d.   the exact title and class of the security
    e.   the par or stated value of the security
    f.   the number of shares or total amount of the securities outstanding as of the end of the issuer's most recent fiscal year
    g.   the name and address of the transfer agent
    h.   the nature of the issuer's business
    i.   the nature of the products or services offered by the issuer
    j.   the nature and extent of the issuer's facilities
    k.   the name of the chief executive officer and members of the board of directors
    l.   the issuer's most recent balance sheet, profit-and-loss, and retained earnings statements

**m.** similar financial information for whatever portion of the 2 preceding fiscal years the issuer or its predecessor has been in existence

**n.** whether the broker/dealer or associated person is affiliated directly or indirectly with the issuer

**o.** whether the quotation is being published or submitted on behalf of any other broker/dealer, and if so, the name of such broker/dealer

**p.** whether the quotation is being submitted or published on behalf of the issuer, or any director, officer, or any person who is the beneficial owner of more than 10% of the outstanding units or shares of any equity security of the issuer. (If so, the name of such person, and the basis for any exemption under federal securities laws for any sales of such securities on behalf of such person, must be stated.)

However, the provisions of this important rule do *not* apply to

**1.** quotations of any security traded on a national securities exchange that same day or on the business day before submission to the quotation system;

**2.** quotations of foreign securities and ADRs exempt from compliance with the Securities Exchange Act of 1934, Rule 12(g); or

**3.** quotations of any security already reflected in an interdealer system at specified prices on at least 12 days within the previous 30 calendar days and having no more than a 4-business-day gap without a two-sided quotation.

*C3b.* **NEGOTIATING A PRICE THROUGH NQB**

Before consummating a transaction with any market-maker, a member organization of the NASD normally can vasses competing firms to determine a basis for price negotiation. The firm tries to communicate with at least two or three market-makers to insure that it will trade at fair and equitable prices. The language employed in **shopping the street** in this manner is most important in order to avoid misunderstandings between the two parties without actually revealing the terms and conditions of an order until the participants are ready to act. For example, if a broker/dealer firm contacts a market-maker asking for a "quotation" or for a "price" rather than for its market, it is subtly telling the market-maker that it wants only an evaluation, an approximation, and will not require that firm to trade with it at those prices. It is signaling that it wants information only and does not want to place an order.

To illustrate this maneuvering, let us suppose that an NASD member wants to buy 100 shares of Connecticut General Insurance Co., Inc., an actively traded over-the-counter stock, in response to a customer's order. The pink sheets show twelve market-makers for that stock on a typical day, and so the NASD member's trading department has a wide selection to choose from. They call, for example, market-maker Fred Foster and ask for his market for "Conn Gen." After the firm has properly identified

**shopping the street**

itself as a fellow NASD member, market-maker Foster reveals his **trading market**, the wholesale prices available only to NASD members as prescribed in the Rules of Fair Practice. He might say, "64½ to 65," or, "I'll trade 64½ to 65," meaning he will buy stock at 64½ from a seller or sell stock at 65 to a buyer. He is unaware of whether the caller is a buyer or seller, or even if he has an order, but he is making a **firm market**. He stands ready to trade immediately at these prices in the usual minimum quantity for activity in that stock. The normal trading unit for over-the-counter stocks is 100 shares, whereas for over-the-counter debt issues it is 10 ($1,000 face value) bonds. If that market-maker Foster is unwilling to trade in these quantities, he must disclose this fact at the time he reveals his market. He might say, "64½ to 65, odd lots," or, "It's a 50 share bid," or, "10 share offering," to indicate his position.

The trading department might try to negotiate a price between 64½ and 65. More likely, it will contact, for example, market-maker Suzanne Spire to see if she has a more favorable bid or offering price. Market-maker Spire might say, "64⅜ to 67⅞, subject." A **subject market** is one in which the market-maker is unwilling to trade immediately at those prices. In response to the inquiry, she is advising that she must first authenticate her quotation with the party whose market she represents, whether that be a correspondent broker/dealer or another trader in her own firm. Such prices are literally *subject to verification*. It doesn't take too long to firm up a subject market. A quick phone call to the correspondent or to competing market-makers can confirm that those prices are abreast of current conditions. Subject quotations are generally encountered only if the market-maker is temporarily out of touch in a sensitive or volatile market climate. Sometimes these quotations are refined to such an extent that only the bid or only the offering is subject while the other side is firm.

Some issues trade very infrequently in the over-the-counter market, and, as a result, it is difficult to discover any market-makers willing to provide continuing bids and offerings. A broker/dealer is fortunate to find more than one market-maker listed in the pink sheets for such issues. Furthermore, when queried, the market-maker firm would probably then qualify its prices as a **workout market**. This means that it is unaware of an actual market for the security, but it believes it can execute an order for you in a reasonable period of time. Its quotation may be something like "58 to 68, workout." It invites you to leave your order and allow it to try to work out a *price* somewhere within that *spread* (between bid and asked) in whatever time period you specify.

### CONSUMMATING A TRANSACTION THROUGH NQB

C3c.

NASD member firms may contact any number of market-makers trying to negotiate the best terms and prices for themselves or their customers. You can contact one, two, or all twelve of those firms in an effort to buy 100 shares of Connecticut General Insurance at the lowest price. If one of those market-makers offers stock firm at 64¾ and this is the lowest offering at the time, a trade can be consummated immediately if you as purchaser announce such intentions by stating "I'll take 100 at 64¾." The market-maker

trading market

firm market

subject market

workout market

then replies, ''Sold to you,'' to avoid confusion about which firm was the buyer and which the seller on this transaction. If you as the initiating firm are a seller instead of a buyer, you accept the bid and consummate the transaction by saying, ''Sold 100 to you at 64½,'' and the market-maker replies, ''I buy.'' On a busy day, when verbal misunderstandings are likely, costly errors can be averted in this simple manner.

**NASDAQ**

NASDAQ is an electronic data terminal device that furnishes subscribers with instant identification of market-makers and their current quotations.

**C4a.**

### DIFFERENT FROM NQB PINK SHEETS

It differs from the pink sheets in the following ways:

1. Only members of the NASD may have their quotations reflected as market-makers. In this capacity they act as dealers (principals) standing ready, willing, and able to trade for their firm's proprietary account and risk.

2. Canvassing dealers to solicit their markets is obviated because bids and offers from each market-maker registered with the NASD are continuously updated.

3. Security qualifications and market-maker capital requirements are stringently controlled.

4. While there is capacity for approximately 20,000 issues, only about 2,800 equity-type (stocks, warrants, convertible bonds) securities are presently in the system.

5. Only firm markets may be represented in this device.

6. Each participating market-maker must report daily trading volume to the NASDAQ computer center.

7. The service is much more expensive than the National Quotation Bureau's daily sheets.

**C4b.**

### AVAILABILITY OF NASDAQ SERVICE

NASDAQ service is available at three subscription levels, dependent upon the applicant's preferences and requirements.

Level 1 service provides the best quotation for each security on which market-makers are entering quotations that day. Those prices are the highest bid and lowest offering levels of those securities in effect at the time. This is also known as the ''inside market.'' They are the interdealer quotations released to, and printed in, the newspapers each day.

Level 2 service provides access to the actual prices of all registered market-makers entering quotations on a given day. Each market-maker's bid and offering price is individually identified alongside the name of the firm itself.

Level 3 service is identical to level 2 service with the added feature of enabling a qualified market-maker firm to enter, alter, or delete its own quotations into or from the system. This service is available only to NASD members, but levels 1 and 2 can be provided to nonmembers under certain conditions.

To qualify as a registered market-maker under NASDAQ rules, broker/dealers must do the following:

1. They must continuously maintain net capital of $50,000 or $5,000 for each security in which they will provide quotations, whichever is the lower amount.

2. They must honor their quotations for at least the normal unit of trading (usually 100 shares or 10 bonds, as the case may be). Failure to do so is a violation of the NASD Rules of Fair Practice and is called **backing away**.

**backing away**

3. They must maintain trading hours of at least 10 A.M.–4:00 P.M. eastern time.

4. They must agree to file daily and monthly reports of trading activities, as required by the NASD Board of Governors.

5. They must apply to NASDAQ for permission to participate as a market-maker in each security desired. Dealers may enter their own quotations at the start of business on the second business day following submission of their applications.

For a security to be authorized for inclusion in the NASDAQ system, it must meet certain initial and maintenance qualifications imposed upon it by the Board of Governors of the NASD.

***Domestic securities***   Eligible domestic securities include the following:                                                          *C4d(1).*

1. stocks, warrants, rights, and convertible debt registered with the SEC under the Exchange Act of 1934

2. bank securities registered with the Federal Reserve Board, Federal Deposit Insurance Corporation, or Comptroller of the Currency of the United States

3. insurance company and closed-end investment company securities

4. foreign securities and ADRs, when the issuer is registered with the SEC under Section 12(g) of the Exchange Act of 1934

The initial and maintenance requirements are most easily understood in the following tabular presentation. Study this important information carefully.

| QUALIFICATIONS | INITIAL REQUIREMENT | MAINTENANCE REQUIREMENT |
| --- | --- | --- |
| Corporate Assets | $ 2,000,000 | $ 750,000 |
| Persons owning security | 300 | 300 |
| Total capital and surplus | $ 1,000,000 | $ 375,000 |
| Shares publicly owneda | 100,000 | 100,000 |
| Convertible debt publicly owneda | $10,000,000 | $5,000,000 |
| Number of market-makers | 2 or more | 1 or more |

aDoes not include officers, directors, and holders of 10% or more of that class of security.

**C4d(2).** *Foreign securities and american depositary receipts* [5] The standards for authorization in these securities are the same as for domestic securities, except that

1. there must be at least *three* market-makers reflecting their bids and offering prices; and
2. the average daily volume in the first 90 calendar days after authorization must not be less than 500 shares.

The NASDAQ system expedites executions by enabling a dealer with a buy or sell order to tell at a glance the market-maker with the best prices and to contact him or her directly. The standard dialogue to consummate the transaction is the same as that described under the NQB system. There is less price negotiation with NASDAQ securities, however, because the constant disclosure of competitors' quotations tends to narrow the spread between the bids and offerings. With its advanced computerization, NASDAQ is developing over the counter from a negotiated marketplace into an electronic auction marketplace similar to the national securities exchanges.

**D.
agency versus principal transactions**

The foregoing commentary explains how an order is actually executed, but the execution does not conclude a transaction. If the firm initiating this transaction has been acting for a customer, it may then position itself in either of two relationships—as agent or as principal.

**D1.
*Transacting as Agent***

As **agent**, the securities firm reports to its customer that it executed an order in the capacity of a *broker*. That is, the firm acted as a middleman between the customer and the market-maker. Thus, referring to our example, the firm might report, "As your agent, we bought for your account and risk 100 shares of Connecticut General Insurance Company at 64¾." In addition to this price, the firm generally charges a commission, a fee for the services rendered. The commission must be shown as a separate item on the customer's report and must not be included or disguised in the execution price. Under NASD rules, the commission amount must be fair and reasonable. There is no minimum schedule of commission rates for OTC transactions. All commissions are negotiated between customer and broker.

*agent*

**D2.
*Transacting as Principal***

As **principal**, the securities firm reports to the customer that it executed this order in the capacity of a *dealer*. That is, it acted directly with the customer as a trader on the opposite side of the order. After purchasing the stock from the market-maker, the firm places it into its newly created inventory and then sells it to the customer from this position, but at a higher price. It might report to the customer, "As principal, we are selling to you for your account and risk 100 shares of Connecticut General Insurance Company at 65¾ net." The price thus established is a *net price* that includes the firm's remuneration for this transaction. No further charges are added to the price quoted to the customer when

*principal*

[5]Where the issuer is not registered under Section 12(g) of the Exchange Act of 1934, but *does* file certain financial information and reports with the SEC at designated intervals.

the firm acts as principal. The firm may not change the execution price and then add a commission, because then it is acting as broker *and* dealer on the same transaction, a relationship prohibited by regulation.

**markup**

*D3.*
*Markup and Markdown*

The difference between this firm's lower cost price and its sale price to the customer is known as its **markup.** For example, in the Connecticut General transaction, the dealer has a markup of 1 point because it bought the shares at 64¾ and sold them to the customer at 65¾. Under NASD remuneration rules, markups must be fair and reasonable. Conversely, if the customer is a seller and the firm buys as principal, the difference between the lower price paid to the customer and the sale price to the market-maker is called a **markdown**, and it too must be fair and reasonable. For example, if the dealer buys ''Conn Gen'' shares at 64¼ from Sam Smith and sells them to a market-maker at 64¾, then the firm has a ½-point markdown.

**markdown**

The customer's report of execution does not reveal the amount of markup or markdown, and, therefore, in the public interest, interpretation of the phrase *fair and reasonable* becomes a matter of ethics. *Fair and reasonable* also applies to agency transactions, but the required disclosure of commission in these cases ordinarily does not lend itself to the potential inequities of principal transactions.

E.
the nasd markup policy

The markup and markdown issue was thoroughly investigated by the NASD Board of Governors in 1943, at which time the association formulated its basic policy on the subject. This policy, subsequently interpreted and reaffirmed in several disciplinary proceedings, is not a rule or regulation because the Board of Governors realized that it is virtually impossible to define the term *fair* in a random trading situation.

**5% guideline**

*E1.*
*The 5% Guideline Policy*

Instead, the board implemented a **5% guideline**, which requires consideration of all relevant factors on each transaction. The policy does *not* mean that a member will be in violation of the guideline if its markup/markdown exceeds 5%.[6] On the other hand, it does *not* mean that a member firm will be safe from prosecution if it stays below 5% either. Rather, it requires the member to consider all of the board's suggestions as an overall package and then allow its judgment and the association's code of ethics to guide its decision. The firm must be prepared to defend that decision if a complaint is lodged against it.

The 5% guideline does not apply to transactions that require delivery of a prospectus or offering circular, after which the securities are sold at the specific public offering price stated therein. Those transactions include SEC registered public offerings of corporate securities and open-end investment company shares (mutual funds). Otherwise, it is effective for all securities transactions in the over-the-counter marketplace, including oil and gas leases, royalties, listed securities in the third market, and others. It also encompasses consideration of a wide variety of related

---

[6]The markup is calculated based on the prevailing offering price by market-makers; the markdown is calculated on the prevailing bid price by market-makers.

activities in the over-the-counter market such as *proceeds sales* and *simultaneous transactions*.

### E1a.  PROCEEDS SALES

**Proceeds sales**, more commonly referred to in the financial community as **swap transactions**, are orders from customers to sell their securities and use the proceeds of the sale to purchase other securities for them. The member organization, therefore, receives two orders from the same customer at the same time. However, whether it decides to act as principal or agent, it must treat the transaction as a single order for the purpose of establishing total profit/commission.

*proceeds sales*
*swap transactions*

### E1b.  SIMULTANEOUS TRANSACTIONS

A **simultaneous transaction**, also known as a **riskless transaction**, refers to a situation in which the broker/dealer takes a position in a security only after receiving an order from a customer. In the Connecticut General illustration cited previously, the NASD member organization, not a market-maker but still acting as principal, set a price of 65¾ immediately after execution, resulting in a markup of $100 for itself. But it had not established a position in its own account until *after* the buy order was accepted from the customer. This simultaneous activity is a legal and popular method among NASD members to provide greater profits for the firm. The commission on agency transactions is generally lower than the markup/markdown on principal trades, but it can, nevertheless, prompt criticism from customers because they see the figure as a separate item on their confirmations.

*simultaneous transaction*
*riskless transaction*

### E2.
**Considerations in Applying the 5% Policy**

There are several considerations in this situation relevant to the 5% policy.

### E2a.  TYPE OF SECURITY INVOLVED

Most stocks customarily involve a greater degree of market risk for a dealer with an inventory than for one who positions a similar amount of value in bonds. Therefore, other factors notwithstanding, stock transactions employ higher percentage markups and markdowns than do bond transactions.

### E2b.  AVAILABILITY OF THE SECURITY IN THE MARKET

Closely held or inactively traded securities, which often necessitate unusual effort or cost for purchase or sale, may permit higher than usual percentage markups and markdowns.

### E2c.  PRICE OF THE SECURITY

Arithmetically speaking, lower-priced securities usually carry higher percentage markups and markdowns, while higher-priced securities entail lower percentage profits on similar transactions. For example,

⅛-point ($.125) markup on a $ 1 stock = 12.5% profit
⅛-point ($.125) markup on a $50 stock = 0.25% profit

Yet the ⅛-point markup is allowed for the $1 stock in order to make it worthwhile for a dealer to execute transactions in such a low-priced security. For this reason a dealer may have the same ⅛-point markup on a $1 stock as on a $50 stock. Each brings the firm only a $.125 profit though the percentages are quite different.

### AMOUNT OF MONEY INVOLVED IN A TRANSACTION                    E2d.

Following similar logic, minimal amounts of money carry higher percentage markups and markdowns to cover the cost of processing such activity. Orders involving substantial sums, conversely, carry smaller percentage profits.

### DISCLOSURE                    E2e.

Revealing the amount of markup or even commission prior to a transaction is a factor to consider. However, this in itself is not sufficient cause for justifying unfair prices or excessive charges because most unsophisticated investors have no basis or knowledge for comparison.

### PATTERN OF MARKUPS AND MARKDOWNS                    E2f.

The history of a dealer organization's pricing policies is an important factor, too, although this will not condone a member's practice of gouging unsuspecting customers. What is pertinent here is an examination of a member firm's economic relationship with its customers to see that it is according them fair and equal treatment on transactions.

### NATURE OF A MEMBER'S BUSINESS                    E2g.

Owing to the wide variety of services offered by some members, the 5% guideline policy has enough flexibility to permit these organizations to pass along the expense of maintaining continuous customer conveniences. However, the NASD does not excuse the use of excessive or improper charges for services or facilities that are necessary to the performance of a member's business.

The NASD member must be prepared to defend any markup or commission charge in relation to these factors considered collectively in order to highlight extenuating circumstances peculiar to the transaction.

NASD members are not required to deal personally or exclusively with a market-maker in a security. There are times when it may prove tactically advantageous to use the services of a non-market-maker in the execution of an order to avoid disclosure of

F.
interpositioning

the firm's participation. This occurs when a firm has a reputation to favor buying or selling a particular security continuously. So, in order to avoid a change in price that others might impose on it because of the firm's reputation, a firm may find it advantageous not to contact a market-maker directly. Or, it may be wise to avoid the market-maker entirely if an offsetting order execution (*cross*)[7] can be arranged with another member organization or within the firm itself.

Nevertheless, an NASD member firm has the responsibility for insuring that an order is executed at the most favorable price under prevailing market conditions. It must exercise reasonable diligence by considering

1. the size and type of transaction;
2. the number and character of primary markets checked; and
3. its own location and accessibility to the primary markets and quotation sources.

It is a violation of the Rules of Fair Practice for a member to interject a third party between itself and the best available market if doing so causes the customer to pay more on a purchase or receive less on a sale. This practice, called **interpositioning**, is unethical and unfair.

**interpositioning**

To illustrate, let's use the Connecticut General order again. Suppose that instead of canvassing the market-makers to determine the best offering available, your firm contacted another member organization who was not a market-maker in that stock and transmitted the order to it. By canvassing the NQB and NASDAQ sources, this firm would undoubtedly uncover the primary market-maker, who is offering at 64¾, and purchase the stock from this market-maker. Then the firm might mark up the stock price and offer it to your organization at 65. You in turn would mark it up again, finally selling it to your customer at 66. The end result would be a double markup on a series of transactions stemming from a single buy order. The customer who initiated the original transaction ultimately pays more for that stock than would have been the case if the unnecessary third party had not been interposed into this situation.

Lack of facilities or lack of personnel in the firm's order department is not a valid defense for such an action. Channeling these orders to a non-market-maker as reciprocation for services or business received is not justification either.

If the member firm does not deal with a bona fide market-maker on the execution of an order for or with a customer, it must be prepared to prove that the total cost (or net proceeds, as the case may be) is no higher (or lower in the case of net proceeds) than if the primary market is utilized directly.

## G. public distributions of securities

The areas of NASD responsibility and jurisdiction are not confined to the *aftermarket*.[8] The NASD acts just as aggressively prior to, and in the process of, offering securities publicly, to

---

[7]A *cross* means to pair off a purchase order with a sell order in the same security at the same price for different customers.

[8]The *aftermarket* is the over-the-counter trading market created for a security when an initial public offering of that issue begins.

insure that members' actions are consistent with high standards of commercial honor and just and equitable principles of trade.

A national Committee on Corporate Financing must examine all appropriate documents that set forth the terms and conditions of an issue to be distributed. This must be done far enough in advance of the offering so that modifications can be made if the arrangements are deemed to be unfair or unreasonable.

*G1.*
*The NASD Committee on*
*Corporate Financing*

Appropriate documents include copies of the registration statement, preliminary prospectus, underwriting agreement, and eventually, the final prospectus. The committee may also require copies of agreements among underwriters, purchase agreements, consulting agreements, and letters of intent.

Some issues are not subject to the committee's scrutiny, however. Among those excluded from scrutiny are

1. exempt securities, such as U.S. government obligations;
2. investment company securities (except closed-end management company shares, which do require filing with the NASD);
3. variable annuity contracts; and
4. straight debt issues (nonconvertible bonds) rated B or higher by a recognized rating service such as Standard & Poor's, Moody's, or Fitch.

No member of the NASD may participate or assist in the public offering or distribution of any other securities as underwriter, selling group member, or otherwise, unless the Committee on Corporate Financing has reviewed and approved the terms and conditions of all arrangements. *The committee does not evaluate the merits of any issue or pass upon the fairness of its price.* It is concerned only with the reasonableness of the offering arrangements. For this reason, the committee looks at such factors as

1. the expected public offering price and underwriter's compensation;
2. the total amount allocated to persons situated favorably to the issuer or underwriter (this amount should *not be disproportionate*[9] to genuine public subscriptions);
3. securities or options of that issuer acquired by the underwriter and related persons within the previous 12 months, including purchase prices and dates of acquisition;
4. any private placements of that issuer's securities in the previous 18 months, detailing the identity and employment of the purchasers as well as their relationship or affiliation with the issuer and proposed distribution of this offering.

*G2.*
*Free-Riding and Withholding*
*Violations*

**hot issue**

An NASD member who participates in the public offering of securities is obliged to make a bona fide distribution of those securities. This directive is especially pertinent when the securities offered qualify as a *hot issue*. Strictly defined, a **hot issue** is

---

[9]The NASD uses 10% of a member's participation in an offering as a guideline in determining the meaning of "disproportionate." However, an allocation of 100 shares or 5 bonds will not be considered a violation even if such an amount exceeds the percentage limitation.

a security that begins trading in the marketplace at a premium over the public offering price. A member who declines to offer these securities publicly is instrumental in artificially establishing the premium by encouraging demand for the security while restricting the supply. Failure to make a bona fide distribution of a hot issue, known as **withholding**, is a violation of NASD Rules of Fair Practice. Furthermore, if the member subsequently sells that security in the aftermarket at a premium price, it is guilty of an additional unfair and unethical activity called **free-riding**. The two violations usually occur together because there is no benefit to withholding without the economic advantage of a free ride.

**withholding**

**free-riding**

### G3.
### *Allocating Hot Issues*

The NASD Board of Governors further qualifies the conditions of a bona fide distribution. Their intent is to severely inhibit allocations of hot issues to persons associated with the offering and distribution process and to members of their immediate families as well. The restrictions are meant to preclude the temptation of free-riding for people who happen to be situated favorably.

For purposes of complying with the allocation interpretation, an issue will be "hot" only if it meets the following parameters on the first day of trading in the aftermarket:

1. In the case of stock, the highest bid is 10% or $2 above the fixed offering price, whichever amount is less.
2. In the case of bonds, the highest bid is 2 points or more over the fixed offering price.

Thus, if the aftermarket price does not reach or exceed those parameters a firm may allocate that issue to customers without regard to their occupational classification. This consideration, however, does not exempt that firm from its requirement to make a bona fide public offering of that security. Withholding is always prohibited, hot issue or not.

On the other hand, if the issue meets the conditions set forth above and is considered to be "hot," a careful analysis of each subscriber's occupation and business affiliations must be made. Specifically, special attention must be paid to any subscription for a hot issue that is made by any of the following persons or groups:

1. any officer, partner, registered representative, other employee of any domestic broker/dealer organization, or members of such person's immediate family
2. any domestic broker/dealer organization not a member of the underwriting or selling groups
3. the managing underwriter's "finder" for this offering, its accountants, attorneys, financial consultants, or members of such person's immediate family
4. senior officers, securities department employees, or persons influencing securities activities in the following institutions:
   a. a domestic commercial bank or trust company (including the domestic branch of a foreign bank)
   b. a domestic savings bank or savings and loan association (including a credit union)
   c. an insurance company, registered investment company,

> registered investment advisor, pension or profit-sharing
> trust, or other financial institution
>
> or members of such person's immediate family.
>
> Any person in category 1 must unequivocally be denied an
> allocation of a hot issue in any amount.[10]

It is also obviously important to understand the NASD interpretation of the term *"immediate family."* As defined by the NASD immediate family includes (1) parents, (2) parents-in-law, (3) spouse, (4) children, (5) siblings, and (6) siblings-in-law. Also included is any relative to whom the person in a restricted category gives support directly or indirectly. These relatives must be accorded the same allocation treatment as the associated parties themselves, in line with the applicable category restriction.

The domestic broker/dealer described in category 2 above is also precluded from subscribing to a hot issue *at or above the public offering price*, unless that organization furnishes the firm with a letter testifying that (1) this security will be allocated to bona fide public customers not included in the above restricted categories, (2) at the fixed public offering price, and (3) without compensation for itself for this accommodation.

**investment history**

**disproportionate in quantity**

**insubstantial quantity**

> Persons described in categories 3 and 4 above are not prohibited from purchasing a hot issue from a NASD member, but they are subject to certain limitations and conditions. For instance, they must have established an **investment history** with the particular firm intent upon making the hot issue allocation to them. This means they must have made at least ten purchases there over 3 years with an average dollar value equal to the value of the intended allocation. Additionally, the firm's allocation to each of these persons must not be **disproportionate in quantity** as compared to bona fide nonrestricted public allocations. As explained before, such subscriptions will not be considered disproportionate if they are limited to no more than a single round lot (that is, 100 shares of stock or 5 $1,000 face value bonds). Moreover, the member firm is limited to an aggregate **insubstantial quantity** for allocation to these persons as a group. As explained by NASD officials, this means that regardless of the size of the member firm's underwriting or selling group's commitment, the quantity sold to these restricted categories collectively should be less than 2,000 shares or $25,000 par value for bonds.

Another problem encountered occasionally, but still one to beware of, is a request from the issuing company whose financing is being arranged to sell some of those securities to certain persons whose business affiliations place them in one of the restricted categories. If the offering is "hot," the member firm is nevertheless obliged by the NASD's directive to allocate those securities on the basis of consideration for investment history, disproportionate quantities, and insubstantiality. No partiality may be shown to an issuer's preferences. In fact, if the designated people fall in the first restricted category, they must be excluded from any allocation.

[10]When the issuer is a financial institution or even a member firm itself "going public," it may allocate to its own employees and associates only if those persons agree to restrict sale of the certificates for at least 12 months thereafter. Bona fide gifts of those certificates during this period merely transfer the responsibility to the recipient.

In its free-riding and withholding interpretation, the NASD also addresses itself to the possibility of a **back-door subscription** for a person in one of these categories through a financial institution acting as a *conduit*. (A **conduit** refers to a bank, trust company, investment advisory, or a similar omnibus type of account in which the underlying principal and/or business affiliations are not disclosed.) To permit an allocation to such an account domiciled in the United States, the firm must be certain the registered representative makes inquiry of the party authorized to place orders for the account and that he or she

back-door
subscription
conduit

1. makes certain that the underlying recipient of the security is not someone cited in those restricted categories;
2. notes the name of the party providing those assurances on an order ticket or some such similar document;
3. records the substance of what was said and done on the same document; and
4. has that document initialled by a registered principal of the firm.

If the conduit organization is a foreign broker/dealer or foreign bank, a slightly different approach must be employed. If it is participating in a distribution as an underwriter, there must be a provision in the agreement among underwriters prohibiting it from allocating those securities to people subject to NASD restrictions unless, of course, they can qualify under the considerations stated previously. If it is not participating as an underwriter, it must sign a blanket certification form such as NASD Form FR-1. (See Figure 3.) This form advises the institution of the hot-issue restrictions. In completing it, the organization agrees not to violate these policies. The form is completed only once (the first time a participation is agreed upon between the NASD member and the foreign broker/dealer or foreign bank) and stays in the member firm's files for the period of time prescribed under law. For each hot-issue allocation thereafter, the registered representative must prepare an order ticket or similar document that notes

1. the name of the official there who was questioned about the status of the underlying purchaser and the substance of his or her response to this query; and
2. the initialled approval by a registered principal of the firm.

The last and probably most difficult NASD hot-issue interpretation that must be complied with concerns investment partnerships and investment corporations. The difficulty is in recognizing those institutions for what they are and then securing specific information from them to permit a hot-issue allocation for those accounts. Let's look at the second aspect first. The NASD insists that before a hot issue is sold to an investment partnership or corporation (other than one registered under the Investment Company Act of 1940), the member firm must receive the names and business connections of all persons having a beneficial interest in the account. Beneficial interest includes not only ownership interests but financial interests, such as management and performance fees, as well. Consequently, if any of those persons named is employed in a capacity listed in previously mentioned restricted categories, this account must incur the same type of

# NATIONAL ASSOCIATION OF SECURITIES DEALERS, INC.

### 1735 K STREET N. W. WASHINGTON, D. C. 20006

_____

**Date**

Name of Non-United States Broker/Dealer or Bank_____

Address _____|_____

    Pursuant to paragraph 8(b) of the Interpretation of the Board of Governors with respect to "Free-Riding and Withholding", a copy of which is in its possession, the above firm represents to

Name of Member _____

Address _____

that in its disposition of shares falling within the scope of the provisions of the referred to Interpretation, the purchasing firm will not sell any of those securities to:

1. Any broker/dealer including members of the National Association of Securities Dealers, Inc. (NASD); provided, however, a purchasing firm may sell all or part of the securities acquired as described above to another member broker/dealer upon receipt from the latter in writing assurance that such purchase would be made to fill orders from bona fide public customers, other than those enumerated in paragraphs (2), (3), (4) or (5) below, at the public offering price as an accommodation to them and without compensation for such.

2. Any officer, director, general partner, employee or agent of any broker/dealer including members of the NASD, or to a person associated with any such broker/dealer or member, or to a member of the immediate family of any such person.*

3. A person who is a finder in respect to the public offering or to any person acting in a fiduciary capacity to the managing underwriter, including among others, attorneys, accountants and financial consultants, or to a member of the immediate family of any such person.

4. Any senior officer of a bank, insurance company, registered investment advisory firm or any other institutional type account within the United States or otherwise, or to any person in the securities department of, or to any employee or any other person who may influence or whose activities directly or indirectly involve or are related to the function of buying or selling securities for any bank, insurance company, registered investment advisory firm, or other institutional type account, within the United States or otherwise, or to a member of the immediate family of any such person.

5. Any account in which any person specified under paragraphs (1), (2), (3) or (4) hereof has a beneficial interest.

    If is understood by the above firm that shares falling within the scope of the Interpretation are those of an issue which immediately after the distribution process has commenced trade in the "after market" at a premium over the offering price, i.e. shares of a "hot issue."

_____        _____
       (*Signature of Executive*)                      (*Title*)

* "Immediate family" is defined in the Interpretation as including parents, mother-in-law or father-in-law, husband or wife, brother or sister, brother-in law or sister-in-law, children, or any relative to whose support the member, person associated with the member, or other person in categories (2), (3) or (4) above contributes directly or indirectly.

FIGURE 3
NASD Blanket Certification Form

restriction as those do. Those partnerships or corporations prohibited by law from revealing the names of persons with a beneficial interest therein must, nevertheless, provide written assurance that no person restricted under the NASD interpretation has a beneficial interest in the account. Without this information or assurance, no hot issue should be allocated to that account.

As for the first part of the problem, the NASD defines an investment partnership or investment corporation as an institution whose primary function consists of investing in securities. It applies to such entities as hedge funds, investment clubs, and offshore management companies. But it can also pertain to several other concerns known by a variety of different names. That is what makes them so difficult to identify and regulate pursuant to NASD requirements. A well-managed NASD member firm should therefore insist that the registered representative determine and note on a new account information form the nature or principal business of any nonindividual client introduced to the firm. Particular attention in this regard should be directed toward any account established or maintained with a title containing any of the following key words:

| advisors | club | | counsellors | investors | overseas | securities |
| agency | company (if it is an unincorporated entity whose title does not reveal the principal business) | | equity | investments | partners | society |
| associates | | | family | management | pool | syndicate |
| association | | | fund | offshore | principals | ventures |
| capital | | | group | options | proprietors | |

This list is not all inclusive, but it does serve as a guideline for suspicion. It is intended to alert the member firm and its registered representatives to the need to make a searching inquiry into the business affairs of their clients if they want to avoid NASD penalties.

Anyone who, as a person associated with a member organization, is subject to NASD jurisdiction should keep in mind that the District Business Conduct Committee will institute disciplinary proceedings against the purchaser and the seller of hot issues alike, should those issues be distributed contrary to NASD policies.

Remember, too, that this directive is pertinent to hot issues offered directly by the issuing corporation as well as to those that are underwritten by a member of the NASD.

## CONCLUDING COMMENTS

In this chapter we have presented the organization and workings of the largest marketplace for securities. It is important to keep in mind the regulations established by NASD so as to keep the over-the-counter market operating on a fair and equitable basis. In this way the NASD can accomplish its overall purposes and objectives within the American economy.

# investment companies

A. Classes of Investment Company
  A1. Definition of Investment Company
  A2. A Face-Amount Certificate Company
  A3. A Unit Investment Trust Company
    A3a. Fixed Trust
    A3b. Participating Trust
  A4. A Management Company
    A4a. Diversified Company
    A4b. Nondiversified Company
    A4c. Closed-End versus Open-End Company
      A4c(1). Capitalization
      A4c(2). Current Market Prices
      A4c(3). Redemption Characteristics
B. Types of Investment Companies
  B1. Diversified Common Stock Companies
  B2. Balanced Companies
  B3. Income Companies
  B4. Specialized Companies
  B5. Bond and Preferred Stock Companies
  B6. Dual Purpose Companies
  B7. Exchange-type Companies
C. The Continuous Offering of Mutual Funds
  C1. Definition of Mutual Fund
  C2. The Direct-Sale Approach
  C3. The Underwriter Approach
  C4. The Selling-Group Approach
  C5. The Plan-Company Approach
D. Purchase Plans for Mutual Funds
  D1. Single Payment
  D2. Voluntary-Accumulation Plan
    D2a. Definition and Purpose
    D2b. Operation
    D2c. Advantages and Services
      D2c(1). Self-explanatory Advantages
      D2c(2). Automatic Reinvestment of Distributions
      D2c(3). Redemption

**investment company**

An **investment company** has been defined as an institution primarily engaged in the business of investing and trading in securities. Within the meaning of this term as used in the securities industry, we must specifically *exclude*

— a broker/dealer or underwriter;

— a bank or savings and loan association;

— an insurance company (but not its separate account for variable annuities);

— a company regulated under the Public Utility Holding Act of 1935;

— a religious, educational, or charitable institution; and

— any organization dealing in oil, gas, or mineral royalties or leases.

The term investment company as expressed in the Investment Company Act of 1940 is employed to include *only*

1. a face-amount certificate company;

2. a unit investment trust company; or

3. a management company.

**face-amount certificate company**

A **face-amount certificate company** issues a debt instrument obligating itself to pay a stated sum of money (face amount) on a date fixed more than 24 months after issuance. The certificate is offered in consideration of deposits made by an investor, usually in periodic installments. The total money deposited is less than the face amount redeemed at maturity. The difference represents compound interest and is taxable to the individual as ordinary income. The rate of interest is predetermined and is represented on a yield-to-maturity basis. This means that the percentage is an *average* return and is accurate only if the investor holds the certificate until it matures.

The company provides a formula of cash surrender values that apply to each certificate annually should holders decide to redeem their shares prior to maturity. Normally, investors have to hold their certificates for at least 8 years before the cash surrender value is equal to the money deposited during that time period. If, of course, redemption is chosen after this period but prior to maturity, the rate of return is lower than the yield-to-maturity specified. To encourage the investor to continue making installment payments, the issuing corporation may grant additional credits of perhaps 1 to 2% each year that are then added to the cash surrender value of the certificate. These credits enable investors to reach a break-even point that much sooner and to increase the effective yield if they leave the face amount on deposit with the company until maturity.

In lieu of early surrender for cash value, a certificate holder can discontinue installments and merely retain what is owned until maturity. The company will provide a paid-up certificate representing the cash surrender value plus compound interest thereon. No additional credits are granted on paid-up certificates, however.

Face-amount certificates may be issued in consideration of a single lump-sum payment as well as installment-type deposits. The advantage of the former procedure is that investment money is employed immediately, and the schedule of cash surrender values is arranged to reach the break-even point at the end of the

**A.
classes of investment company**

*A1.
Definition of Investment Company*

*A2.
A Face-Amount Certificate Company*

fourth year instead of the eighth year. The break-even point is reduced even further if the company grants additional credits, as it is privileged to do.

To ensure the integrity of the financial arrangements required with face-amount certificates, federal and state authorities dictate the type and quality of investments employed by the issuing company. Generally speaking, this means that face-amount companies may invest in U.S. government and municipal obligations, prime real estate and mortgages, and some equity securities of the highest quality only. In fact, the nature of face-amount certificates is so similar to insurance that some states have assigned supervision of these companies to the insurance commissioner rather than to their securities regulators.

**A3.**
*A Unit Investment Trust Company*

A **unit investment trust company** is a financial institution organized under a trust indenture rather than a corporate charter. The difference between the trust and the corporate approaches is legal in nature and is distinguishable solely by the manner of administration. Otherwise, they may be considered identical in most other respects. For example:

**unit investment trust company**

1. A corporation's activities are supervised by a board of directors elected by the shareholders, whereas investment trust activities are administered by a body of trustees who appoint their own successors.

2. A corporation may issue redeemable or nonredeemable shares of stock in exchange for capital, whereas an investment trust may issue only redeemable shares of beneficial interest (SBI) to represent an undivided participation in a unit of specified securities.

There are two forms of common trust agreements—fixed trust and participating trust.

**A3a.**   **FIXED TRUST**

A **fixed trust** issues shares reflecting units of participation in a packaged portfolio of securities, such as U.S. government or tax-exempt obligations. Municipal bond funds are often represented in this fashion and were sold exclusively in this manner prior to the Tax Reform Act of 1976. Now, new funds of this type are generally organized as corporate entities and classified as management companies. In a fixed trust, investors can purchase an interest in a prearranged but risk-diversified portfolio composed of many municipal bonds (mostly revenue type) geared to their personal requirements. Because the portfolio is fixed for the life of the trust, there is no trading or management activity or expenses for investors to bear after the start-up costs are satisfied.

**fixed trust**

The fixed trust municipal bond funds provide subscribers with interest exempted from federal income taxes and are characterized by the following unique features:

1. The fund inevitably must decline from its original size as its component issues are retired pursuant to maturation or to exercise of sinking fund provisions in their indentures. Holders electing to redeem shares in the fund by tendering them back to the trustees also cause the fund's size to diminish.

2. When the fund's asset value declines to a predetermined level (by means of issuer- or subscriber-directed redemptions), the trustees will liquidate the trust and distribute the value of its net assets pro rata among the remaining shareholders.

A3b.

*PARTICIPATING TRUST*

**participating trust**

> A **participating trust** is a legal entity that issues shares reflecting an interest in another investment company, an institution generally organized as a management company. It is the trust's only investment security. As money comes into the trust through a continuous offering of these shares of beneficial interest, it is immediately invested in more shares of the management company. Thus, purchasers of trust units acquire an indirect interest in the diversified portfolio of the management company. Their personal investment is limited to a single holding, a share in the participating trust itself. As the value of the underlying portfolio fluctuates, the value of the trust unit is similarly adjusted for purchase and redemption purposes. Most contractual purchase-plan arrangements for mutual funds are organized in this fashion, with a participating trust serving as the investment intermediary for the fund.
>
> Any investment company conducting its business in a manner other than as a face-amount certificate company or unit investment trust company is identified as a **management company**. An overwhelming majority of investment companies registered with the SEC are classified as management companies. These institutions employ the corporate approach to organization and, for the most part, have obtained their charters from the secretary of state of one of the 50 states in the United States.
>
> Management companies are further divided into diversified companies and nondiversified companies.

A4.
*A Management Company*

**management company**

*DIVERSIFIED COMPANY*

A4a.

**diversified management company**

> A **diversified management company** is one that has at least 75% of its assets represented by
>
> 1. cash and cash items (receivables); and/or
> 2. government securities; and/or
> 3. securities of other investment companies; and/or
> 4. other securities, limited to
>     a. all securities of one issuer having a value not greater than 5% of the management company's *total* assets,' and
>     b. no more than 10% of the voting securities of the issuing corporation.

For example, if a diversified management company has total assets of $100,000, it must invest at least $75,000 of these assets in such a way so as *not* to acquire $5,000 worth (5% of total assets) in any one company's stocks and bonds combined. In addition, such monies may not purchase more than 10% of the voting stock of the corporation. However, the remaining 25% of the assets may be invested without regard to the 10% limitation. Thus, the diversified company could acquire full control of other corporations.

A management company will not lose its status as a diversified company if the mixture or value of its securities and other assets subsequently changes to such an extent that it no longer conforms to the formula above. This statement assumes, of course, that the discrepancy did not result from a *voluntary* acquisition by the investment company.

### A4b. NONDIVERSIFIED COMPANY

A **nondiversified management company** is one that declares itself not subject to the limitations above. Such a statement is filed at the time of registration with the SEC and is usually preferred by **venture capital companies** and **holding companies**.[1] The comparatively few nondiversified companies so registered have great flexibility for concentration of investments. As a result, their asset value may prove to be extremely volatile. They have great appeal for speculators who wish to express confidence in management's ability to perform wisely. There are also special tax considerations influencing the decision to register as diversified or nondiversified.

**nondiversified management company**

**venture capital companies**

**holding companies**

### A4c. CLOSED-END VERSUS OPEN-END COMPANY

Management companies are more popularly subclassified as **closed-end** or **open-end** companies, with three characteristics of operation serving to differentiate between them. These characteristics refer to their means and methods for

1. capitalization;
2. determining current market prices for their shares; and
3. redeeming shares previously issued.

**closed-end**

**open-end**

### A4c(1). *Capitalization*

A closed-end company obtains substantially all its capital through a one-time public offering of its shares. Although it is not precluded from occasional future offerings, such offerings are not a general practice and certainly cannot compare with the capitalization activities of the open-end companies.

An open-end company acquires capital from an initial public offering similar to that made by a closed-end company but then proceeds to offer additional shares continuously and perpetually. It may issue as many shares as necessary to meet current demand (subject to the registration requirements of the Securities Act of 1933). An open-end company does have the ability to restrict its size by terminating its offering for a specific or indefinite period. If it does so, it must amend its registration statement, thus making full disclosure of this fact. If the restriction is to be permanent, it may then be reclassified as a closed-end company.

[1]*Venture capital companies* specialize by investing solely in new corporations and/or fledgling industries. *Holding companies* concentrate sizable investments in a few firms hoping to gain control of those concerns or a significant voice in their management. The typical investment company is diversified and does not try to influence management decisions of companies whose shares it acquires.

Thus, a closed-end company more or less has a fixed capitalization, whereas the open-end company's capitalization is constantly changing.

A4c(2).

***Current market prices*** After the initial offering has been completed at a fixed price, the shares of a closed-end company will fluctuate in value, reflecting the aggressiveness of the forces of supply and demand. Trading activity may take place in the over-the-counter market and/or on a stock exchange, if the company's shares are accepted and listed there.

The current market price of an open-end company is not determined in this manner, however. The very nature of its capitalization process reveals its unlimited supply ability, and so price structures founded upon competitive forces are impractical. Instead, the current market price of an open-end company is dependent upon, and determined by, its **net asset value per share (NAV)**.

**net asset value per share (NAV)**

The phrase *net asset value per share,* though peculiar to the investment company industry, is not unique when its meaning is carefully examined. Net asset value is merely another name for shareholders' equity. It is derived by adding the valuation of securities in the portfolio (using a method described in the offering prospectus) to all other assets, subtracting total liabilities from this sum, and then dividing the difference by the number of shares outstanding at that moment. Or, to restate this formula arithmetically:

$$\text{net asset value per share} = \frac{\begin{array}{c}\text{security} \\ \text{market value}\end{array} + \begin{array}{c}\text{all other} \\ \text{assets}\end{array} - \begin{array}{c}\text{total} \\ \text{liabilities}\end{array}}{\text{number of shares outstanding}}$$

Federal law requires each open-end management company to calculate its net asset value per share at least once daily. This is done at the close of trading on the New York Stock Exchange on days when the exchange has been open for business. Some companies make this calculation twice each day—at 1:00 P.M. New York City time and at the close of the exchange's daily trading activities. The net asset value per share is then employed as the bid price in the quotation for that company. The offering price is usually net asset value *plus* a predetermined sales charge, known in the industry as a **sales load**. The difference between bid and offering prices of an open-end company is thus the dollar amount of sales charge levied in the distribution of those shares.

**sales load**

**example**

$21.25 offering price − $20.00 bid price = $1.25 sales charge

As practiced by the securities industry, the sales charge is traditionally expressed as a percentage of the offering price; that is, it is a percentage of the price that already includes the sales charge.

$$\frac{\$\ 1.25}{\$21.25} = 5.88\% \text{ percentage of the offering price}$$

The sales load may also be shown as a percentage of the bid price, that is, the net asset value. However, this method is not popular in the securities industry. Its numerically higher percentage rate makes it a difficult selling point to use with prospective purchasers. Therefore, when it *is* used, it is shown side by side with the traditional method of disclosure and is identified as a percentage of the money actually invested in the fund.

$$\frac{\$\ 1.25}{\$20.00} = 6.25\% \text{ percentage of the bid price}$$

In any event, the prospectus of the investment company always shows the *maximum charge* that is levied before allowance for certain discounts that are generally available.

To determine the offering price under the traditional approach (sales charge as a percentage of the offering price) is not difficult. You start with knowledge of the percentage sales charge and an ability to determine the net asset value per share. Subtract the decimal equivalent of the sales charge from the decimal equivalent of 100% (1.00). Then divide the result into net asset value per share.

The formula is:

$$\text{offering price} = \frac{\text{net asset value}}{1.00 - \text{sales charge}}$$

The offering price of the XYZ Fund with net asset value of $20 and with a load of 5.88% is calculated as:

$$\frac{\$20.00}{(1.0000 - .0588)} = \frac{\$20.00}{.9412} = \$21.25 \text{ offering price}$$

Although the sales charge is expressed at the maximum rate, every distributor will reduce this percentage charge for quantity dollar subscribers. The dollar level necessary to qualify for this discount is called a **breakpoint**. In fact, a typical offering schedule provides for several breakpoints to entice substantial deposits. The precise dollar value of these breakpoints varies from company to company, but the first such discount is generally

**breakpoint**

offered at the $10,000 level. Table 1 shows a typical graduated schedule of sales charges.

**TABLE 1**
GRADUATED SCHEDULE OF SALES CHARGES FOR A TYPICAL INVESTMENT COMPANY

| | PERCENTAGE OF | |
| AMOUNT DEPOSITED | BID PRICE | OFFERING PRICE |
| --- | --- | --- |
| Less than $10,000 | 9.00% | 8.5% |
| $10,000 but less than $25,000 | 8.70% | 8.0% |
| $25,000 but less than $50,000 | 8.10% | 7.5% |
| $50,000 but less than $100,000 | 6.95% | 6.5% |
| $100,000 but less than $200,000 | 5.25% | 5.0% |
| $200,000 but less than $400,000 | 4.15% | 4.0% |
| $400,000 but less than $750,000 | 2.05% | 2.0% |
| $750,000 but less than $1,000,000 | 1.00% | 1.0% |
| $1 million or above | 0.75% | 0.75% |

Thus, for a deposit up to $10,000 according to that schedule an investor must pay a sales charge equal to 8.5% of the prevailing offering price. However, if the deposit is $10,000 or more but less than $25,000, the sales charge is levied at the rate of 8% of the current offering price. The greater the number of dollars invested, the smaller the percentage sales charge.

**letter of intent**

Many people cannot or will not make a single, substantial, lump sum investment to qualify for a discount. However, that does not necessarily prevent them from utilizing these breakpoints advantageously. They can furnish the distributor with a **letter of intent** stating their desire to invest a sufficient sum of money within the next 13 months and thus be privileged to enjoy the economy of a lower sales charge. That letter of intent is binding only upon the distributor of these shares and *not* upon the investor. Even if the charges are increased during that period, the distributor's obligation to honor the original commitment continues. On the other hand, if the charges are reduced or total deposits are more than declared in the letter, the subscribers are granted the benefit of a smaller load.

There is no penalty imposed upon investors who fail to live up to the terms of that promise. They are merely charged the load they would normally have paid based upon the money they did invest. Furthermore, if a person's financial circumstances change during this period, making it necessary to convert assets into cash, shares already owned may be sold (redeemed) immediately without penalty.

As a further attraction, the letter of intent may be predated by as much as 90 days to enable the investor to take advantage of a recent large deposit and incorporate it with future deposits. So long as the total time encompassed in the letter does not exceed 13 months, neither the SEC nor the NASD has any objections. Prec-

**back-dating**

edent for the practice of **back-dating** was established by the life insurance industry and stands to benefit the participant in such an arrangement.

As a means of obtaining lower sales charges, use of a letter of intent is restricted to

1. an individual;
2. an individual collectively with spouse or children under 21 years of age; or
3. a trustee or other fiduciary purchasing securities for a single

trust, estate, or fiduciary-type account (including pension plan, profit sharing plan, and so on, qualified under Section 401 of the Internal Revenue Code).

This limitation was imposed to prevent groups of people from pooling their funds in order to avoid proper payment of the legally established sales fees.

The average investor is most likely to use these breakpoints advantageously when the investment company offers its holders a **right of accumulation**. With a right of accumulation, consideration is given to the total value of the shares already owned when a new investment is made in additional shares. If the market value of presently held securities is sufficient to qualify under their breakpoint schedule, the distributor allows each new purchase, regardless of amount, to be made under the reduced sales charge. For competitive reasons, this practice is now common. For the exact details relative to any given investment company, a copy of the offering prospectus should be consulted.

right of accumulation

**A4c(3).**  *Redemption characteristics*   Once the initial offering has been completed, the closed-end company does not redeem shares held by its owners. Persons interested in liquidating their holdings must go into the marketplace, find a buyer, and negotiate a price acceptable to both parties.

Infrequently, it may develop that a closed-end company decides to repurchase some of its own shares for treasury or retirement purposes. Before it can repurchase shares it must

1. give each stockholder of record 6-months notice of its intent to make such a purchase in the marketplace; or
2. give all stockholders an opportunity to tender their shares pursuant to a formal offer filed with the SEC.

An open-end company always stands ready, willing, and able to redeem its shares within terms and conditions described in the offering prospectus. The government has reasoned that if the company is willing to offer as many shares as necessary to meet demand, it must also be prepared continuously to meet supply by repurchasing those shares from stockholders anxious to sell.

Most open-end companies' distributors redeem those shares from the stockholder at net asset value without further expense. They operate on the theory that the initial sales charge covers all such services. A few distributors do levy a 0.5% fee upon redemption, but those organizations also charge less on the initial load. As a result, the overall expense for the investor is about the same. In all instances, an open-end company is obliged to honor these requests promptly, using a determination of net asset value as the basis for redemption. The company is obliged to make payment for those shares within 7 business days thereafter.

For example, let us assume that you tendered for redemption 1,000 shares of an open-end investment company. If its quotation at the next calculation became $6.77–$7.30, you may expect to receive

1. $6,770 ($6.77 net asset value × 1,000 shares),
2. within 7 business days thereafter.

If there was also a 0.5% redemption fee in effect, the $6,770 proceeds would be reduced by $33.85 ($6,770 × .005) and your check would amount to $6,736.15.

From preceding discussions, it should now be obvious that shares of a closed-end company can trade at any price levels in the marketplace, without respect to net asset value per share. The shares of most closed-end companies do, in fact, sell at significant discounts from net asset value because they have been historically less popular than shares of open-end companies. The per share net asset values of closed-end companies often have no bearing upon the share's market prices. A closed-end company's net asset value per share would be an important consideration only if that company decided to go out of business and liquidate its assets. See Figure 1 for typical market price/NAV relationships for representative closed-end companies.

## Closed-End Funds

### Thursday, April 7, 1977

Following is a weekly listing of unaudited net asset values of closed-end investment fund shares, reported by the companies as of Thurday's close. Also shown is the closing listed market price or a dealer-to-dealer asked price of each fund's shares, with the percentage of difference.

| | N.A. Value | Stk Price | Diff Stock | | N.A. Value | Stk Price | % Diff |
|---|---|---|---|---|---|---|---|
| **Diversified Funds** | | | | ChaseCvB | 11.28 | 8⅝ | −23.6 |
| AdmExp | 14.29 | 12⅛ | −15.2 | Claremont | 9.25 | 6¼ | −32.4 |
| BakerFen | 54.07 | 36 | −33.4 | CLIC | (−8.28) | .... | .... |
| Carriers | 16.26 | 13⅛ | −19.3 | DrexelUt | 21.39 | 16⅞ | −21.1 |
| GenAInv | 11.72 | 10⅛ | −13.6 | Japan | 11.16 | 8½ | −23.8 |
| Lehman | 12.54 | 10¾ | −14.3 | KeysnOTC | 9.66 | 8¾ | − 9.4 |
| Madison | 16.39 | 12⅝ | −23.0 | NatlAvi& | 22.04 | 15 | −31.9 |
| NiagaraSh | 12.45 | 11 | −11.6 | NewAmFd | 17.28 | 13½ | −21.9 |
| OseasSec | 4.54 | 3⅜ | −25.7 | PetroCp | 24.39 | 24⅝ | + 1.0 |
| Tri-Contl | 24.34 | 22 | − 9.6 | RETIncC | 2.71 | 1¾ | −35.4 |
| cUnited | 12.08 | 10⅜ | −14.1 | S-GSecInc | 1.88 | 1½ | −20.2 |
| US&For | 21.03 | 16⅛ | −23.3 | Source | 16.67 | 14¼ | −14.5 |
| **Specialized Equity and Convertible Funds** | | | | StdSh | 39.68 | 26¼ | −33.8 |
| AmUtilS | 14.59 | 11⅜ | −22.0 | ValueLn | 4.24 | 2¼ | −46.9 |
| bASA | 15.88 | 19⅜ | +22.0 | | | | |
| BancrftCv | 22.38 | 17⅜ | −22.4 | | | | |
| Castle | 23.35 | 17⅝ | −24.5 | | | | |
| CentSec | 8.29 | 6 | −27.6 | | | | |

a-Ex-Dividend. c-Proposed merger with D. H. Baldwin announced. Based on C. I. Power at estimated value. z-Not quoted.

**FIGURE 1**
Prices and Net Asset Values for Closed-End Funds

On the other hand, the offering price of an open-end company's shares can be no lower than its net asset value and may be higher than net asset value only by the amount of any sales charge.

The typecasting of investment companies is generally based on an examination of the *objectives* of those companies. However, in many instances the statements of objectives are made in such broad language that it is often difficult to assign a company to a particular category. Furthermore, careful scrutiny of the *policies* employed to reach these objectives can lead to interesting debates. Nevertheless, for reasons of uniformity, this chapter will describe "types" of investment companies as they are classified in the *NASD Training Guide*.

**Diversified common stock companies**

**Diversified common stock companies** represent an overwhelming percentage of investment companies in the industry today. These companies invest virtually all their assets in a portfolio of common stocks in a wide variety of industries. But they have sufficient maneuverability to permit their officials to shift into debt securities or even into a cash position if, in their opinion, market conditions warrant it. Stated objectives are worded to stress *appreciation of capital* as the paramount concern. Investment income is of relatively minor importance to these companies. The more conservative common stock companies try to obtain reasonable current income from invested capital whereas the *"go-go" variety*[2] emphasize capital gains without regard for dividend or interest income. As a result, the performance records of those aggressive companies have proved to be more volatile than those of any other type or subcategory.

## B2. Balanced Companies

**Balanced companies** strive to minimize market risks while earning reasonable current income. They hope to achieve long-term growth of principal and income through moderate investment practices. Balanced companies are so named because they maintain varying percentages of bonds, preferred stocks, and common stocks in their portfolios. The term *balance* does not refer to equal amounts of security class when, in fact, most balanced companies maintain 60 to 75% of their assets in common stocks alone. The remainder is invested in the senior securities (bonds and preferred stocks) of better quality companies. A balanced company tends to decline less in value than common stock companies do in falling markets and to be less volatile in bull markets.

**balanced companies**

In recent years the number of balanced companies as a percentage of all registered investment companies has been steadily declining while the number of diversified common stock companies has been increasing.

## B3. Income Companies

**Income companies** stress higher-than-average current income from investments without regard to quality or class of security in their portfolios. Capital gains are a minimal consideration, so that during inflationary periods in the economy the value of these shares tends to remain stable or even to decline. An exception exists only if the income-oriented company is fortunate in finding investment media able to improve upon dividend payouts or to invest continuously in lower quality securities. This latter possibility, however, would increase the risk factor for investors.

**income companies**

## B4. Specialized Companies

**Specialized companies** concentrate their investments in one industry, in a group of related industries, or in a single geographic area of the world. Their principal objective is long-term capital growth with little regard for current income. The number of specialized companies has significantly declined in recent years, and many have diversified to such an extent that they are no longer classified as specialized. Those that still prevail restrict their investments to bank and insurance securities, foreign securities, public utilities, or to companies engaged in advanced scientific endeavors.

**specialized companies**

## B5. Bond and Preferred Stock Companies

**Bond and preferred stock companies** as a type are in the minority but are growing. Preferred stock companies are few and are often classified as income-type companies. Bond funds have been growing in popularity primarily because of the unique characteristics associated with the securities in their portfolios. For example, some bond companies provide excellent stability of principal together with a good current yield by investing exclusively in short-term debt instruments. Their portfolios hold U.S. Treasury bills, government agency notes, bankers acceptances, CD's, and high-

**bond and preferred stock companies**

[2]Companies whose investing philosophy is oriented toward frequent trading in stocks subject to dramatic price fluctuation.

quality commercial paper, all with maturities ranging up to 1 year. These "money market" funds are designed for persons seeking current income and minimal risk with investment capital available for relatively brief periods. Some bond companies invest exclusively in municipal securities and provide shareholders with interest that is exempted from federal income taxes. Most other bond company portfolios, however, are composed of many different corporate debt instruments that offer investors diversification and a good return as well as the stability of income that characterizes all bond funds.

*B6.*
*Dual Purpose Companies*

**dual purpose companies**
**leveraged companies**

**Dual purpose companies** are closed-end companies and are also known as **leveraged companies**. They publicly distribute two classes of securities in equal amounts in a single offering, with each class having different objectives and privileges.

**income shares**

One class is comparable to preferred stock and is identified as **income shares**. This class is entitled to receive the net dividends and interest earned by the company from the *entire portfolio,* with a minimum dollar amount assured. The other class

**capital shares**

is comparable to common stock and is identified as **capital shares**. This class is entitled to any appreciation in value and all established net gains from transactions effected in the securities of the *entire portfolio*. Conversely however, any decline in the value of those securities, up to 50%, is a risk experienced exclusively by the capital shareholders. Further declines involve both income and capital shareholders alike.

A leverage factor is enjoyed by the holders of each class of security because each dollar of investment actually receives a benefit from $2 worth of portfolio. If either class of shares is purchased on a stock exchange or in the over-the-counter market at a discount from net asset value, the degree of leverage for those holders is further intensified. The typical leverage factor has been approximately an effective 2.5 to 1 ratio based upon transaction prices of capital shares.[3]

At the time of the initial offering, the dual purpose company fixes a call date (10 or 15 years later), at which time the income shares must be redeemed by the company. Then, with abolition of those particular shares, the company is able to turn open-end subject to approval of the capital shareholders. Thus the company can begin issuing fully redeemable securities.

*B7.*
*Exchange-type Companies*

**exchange-type companies**

**Exchange-type companies** were created to take advantage of a tax loophole that existed prior to 1967. Until that date, an individual with a large paper profit in a security could swap those shares for an equal value of shares in this type of investment company and be able to defer payment of capital gains taxes on the transaction. The capital gains tax liability was officially established for the investor only when the shares received from this investment company were disposed of. In the meantime, however, the investor was able to convert this single security investment into a diversified portfolio of securities and lessen the risk of market price volatility. Of course, any subsequent payments of investment income or trading profits made by the investment company subjected the holder to a tax liability on that particular distribution.

[3]*Investment Companies—Mutual Funds and Other Types* (New York: Weisenberger Financial Services, Inc., 1971), p. 22.

That loophole was closed by the IRS in July 1967, effectively barring "swap funds" from offering such an advantage without future congressional legislation. However, in 1975 it was discovered that the IRS ruling pertained only to exchange-fund *corporations,* and the concept was revived for limited partnership forms of organization. The exchange-type company was barred again in late 1976 with passage of the Tax Reform Act of that year. Any exchange-type corporation or partnership, founded when the concept was legitimate, can continue to function but cannot offer the tax-deferred swap privilege for securities received after the appropriate cut-off dates.

## C.
### the continuous offering of mutual funds
### C1.
### *Definition of Mutual Fund*

The mechanics of making an initial public offering of bonds and stocks are described elsewhere in these text materials. The procedures and relationships created for continuous sales of open-end management company shares differ somewhat from an ordinary offering of securities. Their very uniqueness is responsible for labeling these open-end shares *mutual funds.*

The term **mutual fund** can technically be used to identify any investment company. It refers to a pooling of monies for investment purposes. Historically, however, it has been used to refer to open-end management companies. This is probably due to the effects of promotional advertising in the 1940s that was designed to acquaint the U.S. public with this blossoming investment medium.

**mutual fund**

There are four ways in which mutual fund shares can be offered and distributed to the public—the direct-sale approach, the underwriter approach, the selling-group approach, and the plan-company approach.

### C2.
### *The Direct-Sale Approach*

In the simplest approach, the mutual fund sells its shares directly, that is, without any sales force or organization for this specific purpose (see Figure 2).

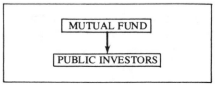

**FIGURE 2**
Direct Sale of Mutual Fund

When such a relationship is established, those shares are offered at net asset value. The offering price and the bid price will be exactly the same price—net asset value. These companies are called **no-load mutual funds**, since there is no sales charge. Such companies rely upon word-of-mouth advertising by satisfied shareholders and limited-budget media advertising to inform people of their existence. Understandably, these funds are in the minority compared to the funds with a **load** (sales charge). It is, however, a rapidly growing minority. More investors are becoming sophisticated enough to learn of and investigate the merits of mutual funds by themselves without relying solely upon the word of a salesperson.

**no-load mutual funds**

**load**

When this direct approach is chosen by a mutual fund none of the other sales methods about to be described may augment or supplement it.

Most mutual fund shares are sold to or through a broker/dealer acting as an underwriter who in turn markets them publicly (see Figure 3).

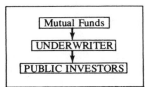

**FIGURE 3**
Mutual Fund Marketed by an Underwriter

An underwriter purchases these shares from the mutual fund at net asset value and then sells them to investors at the public offering price. The difference between bid and offering prices represents the underwriter's spread and its only source of remuneration. In this segment of the financial community, an underwriter of mutual fund shares is also often identified as a **sponsor**, or **distributor**, or even as a **wholesaler**. These terms should be thought of synonymously because the underwriter has an exclusive agreement with that fund for sales and distribution purposes.

**sponsor**

**distributor**

**wholesaler**

It is important to note that the NASD Rules of Fair Practice prohibit an underwriter (or any NASD member) from purchasing mutual fund shares for itself unless it is for a bona fide investment account. This means that NASD firms may not act as market-makers in mutual fund shares or even purchase these shares in *anticipation* of a customer's order. They may act only in *response* to an actual order initiated by, or accepted from, a customer.

A substantial percentage of mutual fund underwriters utilize the services of a selling group to gain broader distribution of these shares. The selling group is comprised of broker/dealer members of the NASD who contract with the underwriter to act as its agent. In return, the underwriter compensates these firms with a portion of the sales charge known as a **selling concession** (see Figure 4).

**selling concession**

The selling concession may be paid only to fellow members of the NASD after they sign a sales agreement that includes

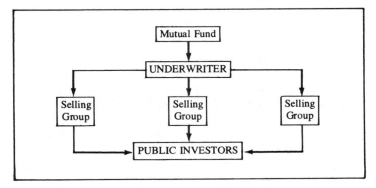

**FIGURE 4**
Selling Groups Added to Marketing Cycle of Mutual Fund

1. a provision for the amount of concession to be paid for the service rendered;
2. a promise binding the members to sell the shares *only* at the public offering price, determined as set forth in the offering prospectus (in fact, NASD rules prohibit members who are

*not* subject to a sales agreement from offering mutual fund shares at another price if that fund has an effective underwriting agreement with any NASD member);

3. a requirement to refund to the underwriter the entire concession if those shares are redeemed within 7 business days after purchase;

4. prohibitions for withholding entry of customer orders to purchase or redeem, so as to profit from such action; and

5. a stipulation barring repurchase of those shares from a customer when acting as principal, unless such purchase is made at the next established bid price quoted by that fund.

> Although the NASD member normally earns money only when a customer buys mutual fund shares, the firm can charge the customer a commission for a redemption if it acts as agent (that is, as an intermediary between the customer and the mutual fund).[4] The customer can avoid such commission expense by redeeming those shares directly to the mutual fund or its designated representative.

## C5.
## *The Plan-Company Approach*

When an underwriter offers mutual fund shares under various periodic payment plans, still another entity is often interposed between the investing public and the underwriter. That organization is called a **plan company** (see Figure 5).

**plan company**

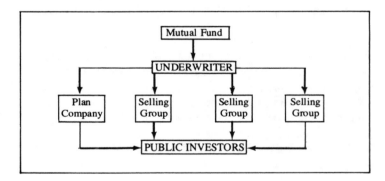

**FIGURE 5**
Plan Company Added to Mutual Fund Marketing Cycle

Officially, the plan company acts as a sales manager or coordinator for offerings of extended contracts involving purchase of mutual fund shares. As payments are received, the plan company subscribes from the underwriter for the appropriate amount and ensures proper credit to each planholder's account for valuable units of accumulation in the plan company itself. For this reason, plan companies must register with the SEC under federal law as unit investment trusts, although in reality they are merely middlemen accommodating indirect public participation in a mutual fund. Because these contractual payment arrangements use the maximum permissible load calculated under federal laws, at 9% of the total money invested, there is sufficient compensation available for all parties involved in the offering and distribution process.

---

[4]A commission redemption charge, if applicable, is separate and distinct from a redemption fee that may be levied by the fund itself.

Note that whether the mutual fund shares are sold loaded or no-load, the fund itself receives only the net asset value of those shares for investment purposes. The sales load is retained by the underwriter and any other sales organizations it employs for the marketing functions.

In summary, the offering and placement of mutual fund shares may be accomplished by mutual fund to

1. investing public; or
2. underwriter to investing public; or
3. underwriter to selling group to investing public; or
4. underwriter to plan company to investing public.

In the last case, the plan company generally uses its own sales force, bypassing the members of the selling group completely.

Mutual fund purchases may be arranged in several ways as an accommodation to the investor. Despite this fact, the underlying relationships between management company and sales organizations remain basically unchanged in each instance.

The least complicated of all procedures is the single payment. This payment is an outright purchase of shares, either directly from the fund itself or indirectly from its underwriter or participating selling-group member, as the individual cases may be. When customers enter purchase orders, they specify either

1. the number of full shares they want to acquire; or
2. the dollar amount they want to invest in full shares. (It may actually work out to be slightly above or slightly below that dollar figure if the instructions state "to the nearest full share.")

In either event, at the time of entry the customers do not know the actual execution price per share. *The purchase price is always determined after receipt of the order* by the mutual fund or its underwriter, as the circumstances may be, using a formula described in the offering prospectus. This practice, known as **forward pricing** **forward pricing**, has been in effect since 1969.[5] For example, if, at 2 P.M. Eastern time, a mutual fund's underwriter receives an order to buy 100 shares of that fund, it will be arranged based upon the offering price to be determined at 4 P.M. that day (New York Stock Exchange closing time). If the order is received after 4 P.M. Eastern time, the investor's purchase price is the offering price in the mutual fund's next determined quotation the following day. When a purchase is effected, a bona fide confirmation is prepared and sent to the customer describing the exact details of the transaction.

Regulation T of the Federal Reserve Board requires full payment for these shares on the fifth business day (no later than the seventh business day after trade date in any event). Brokers and dealers are forbidden to extend any credit to customers on

[5]The forward-pricing technique is equally applicable for redemption requests.

purchases or maintenance of mutual fund shares in a margin account because they are considered new issues and, as such, are not marginable. Nor may they help to arrange a loan elsewhere to enable a customer to pay for such a transaction. Purchases not fully paid for in the time provided must be liquidated immediately.

For customer purchases transmitted by a selling-group member, the NASD requires full payment to the underwriter promptly (no later than the tenth business day after trade date). Payment not made by this time necessitates immediate liquidation of the shares and can subject that member to disciplinary action under the NASD Rules of Fair Practice.

When fully paid for, the mutual fund certificates are registered in the purchaser's name and address and delivered to that party. The customer has become a stockholder in this management company with full rights and privileges in just about the same respects that prevail for stock ownership in any publicly held corporation.

The other two purchase plans available are somewhat more unusual because their characteristics relate to continuing purchase programs.

## D2.
### Voluntary-Accumulation Plan

#### D2a. DEFINITION AND PURPOSE

The **voluntary-accumulation plan** is an informal investment program that provides customers with the ability and facility to purchase modest quantities of mutual fund shares at their option. At the same time, it enables shareholders to enjoy certain benefits of service normally available only for substantial securities investors.

**voluntary-accumulation plan**

#### D2b. OPERATION

The plan is established with a minimum amount of money or number of shares of that fund, as prescribed by the company or its underwriter. A typical plan account may be started with $250 or $500, or perhaps 100 shares. Future deposits are made at any time as long as they meet a nominal payment schedule set, once again, by the company or its underwriter. This minimum amount, whether it is due monthly, quarterly, annually, or at some other set interval is usually $50 to $100.

A commercial bank is appointed to act as administrator of the plan in order to accomplish all bookkeeping and act as depository for investor monies and fund shares. It is usually the same bank used by the mutual fund itself for protection of the fund's monies and portfolio securities, as required by federal law.

When the investor mails in each deposit, the bank deducts a standard $.50 or $1 processing fee and purchases from the underwriter as many full and/or fractional shares of the fund as possible with the balance. The price paid for the shares is determined by the next established offering price using the forward-pricing technique previously described. Instead of registering and delivering these shares, however, the bank holds and accumulates them in this form of open account. Fractional shares are normally calculated to 1/10,000 of a share (four decimal places), although some custodians calculate to only three decimal places. Of course, if they so request, the investors can take delivery of the full shares they own at any time, provided they leave the minimum amount necessary for continuation of the voluntary plan.

## ADVANTAGES AND SERVICES

D2c.

*Self-explanatory advantages*    There are advantages and services gained by subscribing to a voluntary accumulation plan. Certain of them require no explanation.

D2c(1).

1. Professional management
2. Diversification of investment portfolio
3. Ease of operation of investment
4. Dollar-cost averaging
5. Ability to purchase full and/or fractional shares with each deposit
6. Advantageous breakpoint privileges on purchases

*Automatic reinvestment of distributions*    If and when the mutual fund makes a distribution of dividends or capital gains to its shareholders, participants in the voluntary-accumulation plan may elect to have such distributions reinvested for them automatically in more full and/or fractional shares. To encourage participants to do so, mutual funds often permit this acquisition at net asset value rather than at a loaded offering price. That privilege is not offered by all the mutual funds. Some companies require reinvested dividend purchases at the loaded offering price; only capital gains distributions can be plowed back into the fund at net asset value.

D2c(2).

Note that there is no *obligation* to reinvest any distributions. All payments can be taken by the shareholder in the form of cash. Be aware, too, that whether the investor opts for automatic reinvestment or takes the distribution in cash, the shareholder is liable for the appropriate federal tax on this distribution in the year in which the dividend or capital gain is paid by the fund.

*Redemption*    Mutual funds must be continuously prepared to repurchase shares from holders who request them to do so. Shareholders in the voluntary-accumulation plan are privileged to redeem any or all of their shares merely upon written notice to the custodial bank. Their accounts will be readjusted to reflect the reduction or withdrawal from the plan based upon the next established net asset value following receipt of notice by the bank and transmission to the underwriter.

D2c(3).

*Conversion*    Several mutual funds are participants in a "family" of funds. That is, several funds, each with a different objective, are managed by the same executive group. They allow shareholders whose personal circumstances may have changed over the years to exchange their shares for comparable value in another fund from that group having an objective more closely attuned to the investor's revised needs. The swap is accomplished at net asset value with a nominal charge of $5 or $10, levied merely to

D2c(4).

cover the paperwork expense. Thus, the customer saves sales charges on the liquidation and repurchase. However, this convenience *does not* circumvent, or even defer, the investor's tax liability to the federal government on this capital transaction.

**D2c(5).**

*Automatic withdrawal*   Many mutual funds permit shareholders to turn their accumulation program into an automatic withdrawal service. Written instructions must be given to the custodian bank to either:

1. hold all dividend distributions in the form of cash and supplement withdrawals, if necessary, with full and/or fractional share liquidations to meet dollar payments when required; or
2. automatically reinvest dividends in more shares at net asset value, then liquidate as many full and/or fractional shares, as necessary, to meet each withdrawal payment at the time intervals specified (that is, monthly, quarterly, or annually).

Hopefully, the value of accumulated holdings will appreciate more rapidly than the rate at which redemptions take place. Otherwise, in time, the shares in this account will be exhausted and the program terminated. To forestall this, most investment companies offering this privilege insist upon minimum initial value of $7,500 or $10,000 in the account and discourage annual withdrawals in excess of 6% of the total. Withdrawal amounts can be adjusted up or down from time to time.

Automatic withdrawal privileges are also available to investors making sufficient single-payment deposits in shares of that fund. Withdrawal programs are not restricted to accumulation planholders.

**D3.**
***Contractual Periodic-Payment Plan***

**D3a.**

*DEFINITION AND PURPOSE*

The **contractual periodic-payment plan** is far more formalized in operation than the voluntary-accumulation plan. Under this investment accumulation program, the participant agrees to invest a fixed sum of money at specified time intervals over a 10- or 15-year period. This plan often stipulates deposits of as little as $10 or $20 monthly over that time span with no initial down payment required.

**contractual periodic-payment plan**

This investment program is more popularly referred to as a **contractual plan** because of the implied commitment in the agreement to participate. Still, it is flexible enough to allow for late, or even deferred, payments as well as to permit advance or accelerated deposits if the investor chooses. Deferred payments extend the duration of the plan by the number of deposits omitted. Accelerated payments merely shorten the effective life of the contract. No particular consequence or advantage is attached to either action.

**contractual plan**

The typical contractual periodic-payment plan is set up to function as a unit investment trust of the "participating" variety. The payments actually purchase trust units, and the money is then invested in shares of the mutual fund. Because the distinction is strictly technical in nature, contractual plan purchases are usually thought of as direct investments in mutual funds rather than as an intermediary arrangement. Exact mechanical details vary from mutual fund to mutual fund, and a copy of the offering prospectus should be carefully scrutinized by interested parties.

*SALES CHARGES* D3b.

> The Investment Company Act of 1940 and its subsequent amendments in 1970 limit the sales charge for periodic payment plans to 9% of the total investment. Thus, a $10,000 10-year plan with a maximum load would entail $900 in sales charges deducted from deposits over that period of time.
>
> The use of a sales charge with offerings of mutual funds is rather commonplace. But the application of that sales charge in the case of contractual periodic-payment plans is what has made these plans historically controversial. The sales load is not deducted from investor deposits in equal increments. Most of the sales charge borne over the life of the contract is deducted from payments during the early years of operation. This front-end load effect, or *prepaid-charge* plan, as it is sometimes called, places it in sharp contrast with the *level-loaded* voluntary-accumulation plan and the single payment purchase arrangement.

*THE INVESTMENT COMPANY AMENDMENTS ACT OF 1970* D3c.

***Purpose of the 1970 law*** The contractual planholders who default voluntarily and redeem their shares purchased during the first few years probably lose a sizable amount of their deposited dollars. Dollars used in payment of sales charges for contractual plans are not always refundable for early redemption of shares from the investors' accounts. In past years, this consequence led **penalty plans** some critics to identify these programs as **penalty plans**. The Investment Company Amendments Act of 1970 legislated regulations to blunt or avoid such penalties for investors withdrawing from such plans in a reasonable period of time. D3c(1).

> ***Terms of the 1970 law*** Under this law, there are two distinct methods by which sales charges can be levied in an offering of periodic-payment plans. In either instance the maximum load cannot exceed 9% of the total investment. The offering prospectus must clearly state which of the two methods has been officially elected for use by the company and its sales agents. In both instances, the custodian bank servicing these contracts must send the investor (within 60 days) a notice of initiation of the plan and a statement of total charges to be incurred. The bank must also inform the subscriber about the availability of a cancellation privilege and its advantages if utilized within 45 days from the date of this notification. If the participant exercises such privilege within the 45 day period, the investor can obtain
>
> 1. the then current value of the shares in the contractual account; plus
> 2. *a full refund* of all sales charges and other ancillary charges such as custodial fees, insurance premiums, and so on.

D3c(2).

To summarize, in the case of cancellation within 45 days of notification:

> refund = current value of shares + full refund of all charges

        The 1970 law also requires the initial payment in any contractual plan to be at least $20 with minimum deposits thereafter of $10.

**D3c(3).**

> ***Method 1 for levying a sales charge***  As much as 50% of the first 12 monthly payments may be deducted in equal increments and applied toward the total requirement due on the plan contract. The remaining 50% load will then be deducted in equal proportionate increments from the balance of payments due on the contract over the remaining 9 or 14 years.

## example

An analysis of a $10,000 10-year plan with a 9% load, using this method is as follows:

| | | |
|---|---|---|
| Annual payments for 10 years | | = $1,000.00 |
|   First year's payment | = $1,000.00 | |
|   Less sales charge @ 50% | = $  500.00 | |
| Total load for 10 years (9% of $10,000) | | = $  900.00 |
| Amount of money invested in fund's shares | | |
|   in first year | | = $  500.00 |
| Remaining dollars necessary to satisfy | | |
|   total load requirement in next 9 years | | = $  400.00 |
| Approximate sales charge deductions over | | |
|   remaining annual payments | | |
|         ($400.00 ÷ 9 years) | | = $    44.44 |

>         If this method is used, the investment company, its underwriter, or the custodian bank must give written notice to investors
>
> 1. who have missed three or more payments within 15 months after issuance of the plan certificate; or
> 2. who have missed one or more payments between the fifteenth and eighteenth month after initiation of the plan
>
> advising them of their right to cancel the plan before expiration of the eighteenth month, and to receive
>
> 1. the current value of the shares in the account; plus
> 2. a refund of all sales charges paid *that exceeded 15% of total deposits* in the contract thus far.
>
>         Even investors who have kept current in their plan deposits are entitled to the cancellation privileges providing they act before the end of the eighteenth month.

        To summarize, in the case of cancellation between 45 days and 18 months of notification under method 1:

> refund = current value of shares + (amount deducted for sales charges − 15% of total invested)

To illustrate this point about cancellation, let us assume that a plan subscriber cancels the program using method 1 after depositing $100 the first month. Because the decision is within the first 45-day **full reimbursement period**, the investor will receive a refund payment of $50 worth of sales charges and the value of the shares in the account.

**full reimbursement period**

On the other hand, let us assume that the subscriber withdraws from the plan after a full year after depositing $1,000 (of which $500 was for sales charges). The investor will receive the redemption value of shares owned plus $350 of the sales charge expense. The sales charge refund is calculated this way:

(1)   $1,000      (total deposited)
      ×   .15
      $   150      (15% of deposits)

(2)   $   500      (deducted for sales charges)
      −   150      (15% of total deposits)
      $   350      (sales charge refund)

With this method, the investor is not entitled to a refund of ancillary expenses that may have been imposed—for example, custodial fees, insurance premiums, and so on—when termination of the contract is at this late date.

*Method 2 for levying a sales charge*   This method, introduced in 1970, attempts to apportion the front-end sales charge more equitably than the 50% first-year load procedure. In this second method, as much as 20% may be deducted from annual payments to cover the sales charge expense. But the deduction may not average more than 16% from each annual deposit based upon the first 4 years of operation of the plan. Let us express this rule another way: As much as 64% of the first year's deposits may be subtracted as sales-charge expense, but the amount must be apportioned over the first 4 years' required payments into this plan. Furthermore, the amount of sales charge subtracted from monthly payments during this time must also be in equal proportion to each other, calculated on a year-by-year basis. For example, if the annual sales charge requirement is determined to be $120, the fund cannot deduct it all from the first two monthly payments and take nothing more for the rest of that year. For the monthly payments to be in equal proportion to each other, the $120 requirement must be taken at the rate of $10 per month during that year. This **spread-load** application avoids concentration of sales charge deductions from any single payment and ensures that relatively similar amounts of money will be invested in fund shares with each deposit in the early years. It also gives rise to the designation of this kind of periodic investment program as a **spread-load contractual plan**.

*D3c(4).*

**spread-load**

**spread-load contractual plan**

example

An analysis of a $10,000 10-year contractual plan with a 9% load, using a typical spread-load option, is as follows:

| | |
|---|---|
| Annual payments for each of 10 years | = $1,000.00 |
| Total load for 10 years (9% of $10,000) | = $ 900.00 |
| Maximum deduction of sales charges in first 4 years (16% of $4,000, which is also equal to 64% of an annual payment) | = $ 640.00[6] |
| First year's payment = $1,000.00 | |
| Less 20% sales charge = $ 200.00 | |
| Amount of money invested in fund's shares in first year | = $ 800.00 |
| Remaining dollars necessary to satisfy load requirement in next 3 years ($640–$200) | = $ 440.00 |
| Sales charge deductions over remaining 6 years ($900–$640) | = $ 260.00 |
| Or, $\dfrac{\$260}{72 \text{ months for 6 years}}$ | = 3.61 per month[7] |

---

> The opportunity for recovery of a major portion of the sales charge within the first 18 months is *not* available when this method is used by the company or its underwriter. But the 45-day full-refund-of-load privilege *is* effective with use of this method.

To summarize, in the case of cancellation between 45 days and 18 months of notification under method 2:

refund = current value of shares only (includes *no* portion of load charges)

**TABLE 2**
CANCELLATION PRIVILEGE AFTER NOTIFICATION OF A CONTRACTUAL PERIODIC PAYMENT PLAN'S INITIATION

REFUND UNDER:

| CANCELLATION OCCURS: | METHOD 1, LAW OF 1970 | METHOD 2, LAW OF 1970 |
|---|---|---|
| Within first 45 days | Value of shares plus full refund of charges | Value of shares plus full refund of charges |
| Within period between 45 days to 18 months | Value of shares plus amount of sales charge paid that is more than 15% of total money deposited | Value of shares only |
| After 18 months | Value of shares only | Value of shares only |

Table 2 shows a summary of the cancellation privileges under method 1 and method 2 for levying sales charges according to the Investment Company Amendments Act of 1970.

**D3d.    ADVANTAGES AND SERVICES**

**D3d(1).    *Self-explanatory advantages*** The conveniences available to the contractual periodic-payment planholder generally overlap with

---

[6]Can be subtracted in equal or unequal annual increments so long as each *monthly* deduction per year is equal. For example, $200, $200, $200, and 40; or $200, $200, $120, and $120, and so on.

[7]Equal amounts of $3.61 per month must then be deducted from payments.

those available to the voluntary-accumulation plan investor. The ones that need no explanation include:

1. Professional management
2. Diversification of investment portfolio
3. Ease of operation of investment
4. Dollar-cost averaging
5. Ability to purchase full and/or fractional shares with each deposit
6. Automatic reinvestment of distributions (and at net asset value, too)
7. Conversion privileges
8. Automatic withdrawal programs
9. Advantageous breakpoint privileges on purchases

In fact, contractual plan investors frequently enjoy additional services not generally provided in the case of other mutual fund investment programs.

**D3d(2).** *Redemption* Contractual plan investors may redeem as much as 90% of their share holdings at current value and then redeposit these monies before expiration of the plan at the then prevailing net asset value. No sales charge is levied on the reinvestment of withdrawn funds. Thus, the planholder can withstand temporary financial emergencies without terminating the investment contract and losing sales charge expenses previously borne.

**D3d(3).** *Declaration of trust* Under the contractual plan, an investor may create a Declaration of Trust agreement. On the death of the investor, this agreement can provide for immediate distribution of these mutual fund shares to specified beneficiaries without subjecting those assets to time-consuming probate court proceedings.

**D3d(4).** *Insurance* The planholder also has an opportunity to purchase plan-completion insurance and thus guarantee a fully paid contract if the planholder should die before total payments have been deposited. Plan-completion insurance is declining-term life insurance whose premium, computed at group rates, is paid for by the investor as an additional monthly charge. There is no cash value in such policies. Each year the investor lives to make payments in the plan means that much less coverage on that person's life. When the contract is completed, the insurance policy is terminated.

The purpose of the insurance is to ensure satisfaction of the contractual plan in the event of the planholder's untimely death. Thus, it tempers the possibility of principal loss for the beneficiaries because of front-end load expenses in the early years. The insurance company deposits the unpaid balance due in the plan immediately upon notification of the planholder's death. The proceeds are not paid directly to the estate or to any beneficiary. Rather, they are paid to the mutual fund's custodian or plan trustee to purchase as many full and/or fractional shares at the current price, thus completing the plan. Although the details vary from company to company, maximum coverage is available from $30,000 to $45,000, despite the possible subscription to a larger-sized contractual plan.

Medical examinations are also required on most contracts above $10,000. A few states prohibit the sale of life insurance on a tie-in arrangement for mutual fund purchases. Other states, because of their blue-sky laws, will not even permit offerings of contractual plans using the terms and conditions just described.

## E.
### the investment advisor
### E1.
#### *Who Is the Advisor?*

Most open-end investment companies do not have in-house ability or facilities for deciding which securities should be bought or sold. They must rely upon the counsel of professionals to make these determinations for them. They do, in fact, enter into a contractual arrangement with such investment advisory organizations, frequently referred to as a **management group**. The similarity between the names *management company* (mutual fund) and *management group* (investment advisor) is often understandably confusing to the novice. Close examination of the circumstances reveals that the officers and directors of the investment company are usually the same persons who serve as the executives of the investment advisor and the underwriter organizations, too! The plan company, when used, is also included in this maze of interrelationships. The plan company is, after all, merely a marketing arm of the fund's underwriter specializing in promotion and sales of contractual plans. In a majority of situations, the only real distinction is a legal one, with each organization founded under separate charters or trust agreements.

**management group**

### E2.
#### *Preventing Conflicts of Interest*

The potential for conflicts of interest and other associated inequities has been recognized by the federal government. The following preventive rules have been adopted within the Investment Company Act of 1940 and its amendments of 1970:

1. Before any management group or principal underwriter may act for or serve a management company, a contract must be written and approved by a majority of the outstanding voting stock of the company. The contract
   a. must describe precisely all compensation to be paid thereunder;
   b. may be terminated without penalty upon no more than 60 days' written notice by the board of directors or by a majority of the voting stock of the company;
   c. must be approved annually by the board of directors or by majority of the outstanding voting stock; and
   d. will automatically terminate in the event it is assigned to someone else.

2. At least 40% of the board of directors of each investment company must consist of persons who are *not* the regular brokers, investment advisors, principal underwriters, investment bankers, commercial bankers, or any employees thereof for that investment company. Furthermore, the company cannot use the services provided by those persons or their affiliates, unless at least a majority of the board members are *not* persons serving in each of those respective categories.

3. Notwithstanding this requirement, an investment company will still be allowed to have a board of directors composed

solely of interested persons of its investment advisor, *plus one "outsider,"* if

  a. it is a no-load, open-end management company;

  b. it has only one class of securities outstanding, with each share having equal voting privileges;

  c. any fees levied above net asset value on the offering or discount from net asset value on redemption does not in the aggregate exceed 2%;

  d. all promotion expenses, executive salaries, and office rentals are borne by the investment advisor; and

  e. the advisor is the only such group employed, receiving an annual fee of not more than 1% of the investment company's average annual assets.

4. Unless prior approval is obtained from the SEC, no affiliated person or principal underwriter of the investment company may normally

  a. act as principal in the purchase or sale of securities or property with that investment company;

  b. borrow money or other property from that investment company; or

  c. act as joint participant in a transaction with that investment company.

5. No affiliated person or principal underwriter of the investment company may act as agent in the purchase or sale of any securities or property for that investment company in order to receive compensation

  a. from any other source, unless it conforms to that person's usual business as underwriter or broker,

  b. which exceeds—

      (1) a reasonable commission on exchange transactions,

      (2) 2% on secondary distributions, or

      (3) 1% on all other transactions,

unless a larger commission is specifically approved by the SEC.

*E3.*
*Services Performed*

The actual terms and conditions of service by management groups varies according to size and prevailing relationships. However, in broad terms, we can state that such groups always

1. analyze economic conditions in the country in general and the marketplace in particular;

2. provide research information on industries and companies in which investments are contemplated; and

3. provide advisory counsel on specific securities to be bought or sold.

In many instances the management advisory group will also

1. arrange purchase and sales transactions for the investment company;

2. pay for legal fees and contingent expenses incurred by the investment company;

3. absorb employee and director expenses of the investment company;
4. provide clerical services to conduct business in behalf of the investment company; and
5. act as public relations agent for the investment company, promoting proper images through various forms of advertisement.

The advertising responsibility is usually accorded to the principal underwriter but occasionally may be delegated to the advisory group. When practiced by the underwriter, who is a member of the NASD, the material must be sent to the Washington, D.C., office of the NASD for its approval within 10 days after publication or use. (That assumes this member has been subjected to NASD review of its advertising practices for at least one year. Otherwise, the filing requirement would call for advance submissions to the Association.) Advertising materials prepared by the management advisory group, which is not an NASD member, must be approved by the SEC *prior* to use.

*E4.*
*Advisement Fee*

In return for these services, the management group accepts a fee from the investment company as specified in their contract. Most fees are predicated on the investment company's average net assets, determined annually, scaled down from 1% for organizations with minimal assets to 0.25% for the larger, more substantial mutual funds. The standard fee approximates 0.50% of the average annual net assets, payable to the management group in monthly installments. This figure is an important component and the largest liability in the formula used to calculate net asset value per share each day.

$$\text{net asset value} = \frac{\substack{\textit{Security values plus} \\ \textit{other items of worth} \\ \text{total assets}}}{} - \frac{\substack{\textit{Management group fee} \\ \textit{plus other obligations} \\ \text{total liabilities}}}{}$$

Some analysts of investment company operations attempted to gauge the efficiency of a particular fund by examining its expense ratio and comparing it to other funds with similar objectives. The expense ratio formula is:

$$\text{expense ratio} = \frac{\text{annual operating expenses (including management fee)}}{\text{average annual net assets}}$$

Be aware, however, that for this analysis to be truly significant the comparison must be drawn between funds that are of similar *size* and that have a similar *objective*. Because the ratio is a function of the assets of the company, the larger funds normally carry smaller ratios. Operating expenses do not increase in direct proportion to the size of assets. As a form of assurance to investors, some advisory groups will refund a portion of their fee if the expense ratio exceeds a predetermined percentage of the fund's assets.

Some mutual fund management groups have even begun contracting to tie their fee to the performance of the fund instead of, or in addition to, a percentage of the annual assets. The fee is then related to the performance of a well-known index or average over an annual period. The models most frequently used in these comparisons are the Dow Jones Average, Standard & Poors Composite Index, or even the New York Stock Exchange Index. The SEC insists that if this means of compensation is employed for management advisory groups as a reward for superior service, then a penalty clause in the contract must also be included, using a like formula, for underperformance.

F.
the mutual fund custodian

F1.
*Who Is the Custodian?*

In addition to discouraging conflicts of interest, the Investment Company Act of 1940 affords protection to the shareholders of investment companies in the safekeeping of monies and securities owned by the company. With few exceptions, all money and securities must be in the custody of a commercial bank or trust company which

1. has shareholders' equity of at least $500,000;
2. publishes a report of its financial condition for public consumption at least once each year; and
3. is chartered by federal or state authorities and is subject to examination by their regulators.

F2.
*Services Performed*

Although the law does provide for other custody arrangements under circumstances requiring approval from the SEC, for all practical purposes the responsibility is enjoyed exclusively by banking institutions.

In addition to custody arrangements for the investment company itself, the bank also provides safekeeping of monies and securities for investors engaged in available accumulation programs. The shareholder pays a nominal annual fee for such service. This is, of course, supplemental to the transaction processing fee of $.50 to $1 charged on accumulation-plan purchases discussed earlier.

Other services provided by these commercial banks include

1. bookkeeping responsibilities for the mutual fund;
2. maintenance of the underwriter's sales records;
3. functioning as transfer agent, performing changes of ownership as directed;
4. functioning as registrar for the investment company, providing it with current stockholder information and ensuring against overissuance of certificates; and
5. functioning as disbursement agent for the investment company, with responsibility for distributing dividends and/or capital gains when authorized by the fund's directors or trustees.

Note that in none of these circumstances does the custodian bank play any part in determining which securities are to be bought or sold by the investment company. Nor does it have any role in arranging such purchases or sales through, or to, a broker/dealer organization. Thus, it is important for the investor to realize that the size and reputation of the custodian bank has no bearing upon the investment company's ability to achieve its objective. The use of a particular bank as custodian can be no assurance against loss of capital or decline in value of the shares of any investment company.

*G1.*
*The Securities Act of 1933*

The purpose of the Securities Act of 1933 is to protect the public against issuance of fraudulent securities. The act attempts to achieve this objective by requiring issuers or distributors of securities to furnish potential purchasers with pertinent and accurate information regarding the underlying company. Accordingly, purchasers are then able to make informed decisions on whether to invest their money.

This law is, therefore, applicable to investment companies of all three classifications and broaches a unique problem for mutual funds in particular. Prior to the issuance of face-amount certificates, unit investment trust certificates, or management company shares, a registration statement must be filed with the Securities & Exchange Commission. This statement remains with the commission for at least 20 days while it investigates the essential facts. No offering may commence until the SEC allows the registration statement to become effective. Of course, effectiveness of a registration statement does *not* signify SEC approval of the issue, nor does it even guarantee adequacy or accuracy of the information in that document. Investors who lose money as a result of a purchase and sale transaction must seek satisfaction and restitution through litigation. SEC rules, however, insist that purchasers be furnished with a prospectus (a condensation of the registration statement) prior to solicitation of an order or at worst no later than with confirmation of purchase. If the latter event prevails, the investor has a reasonable period of time to consider the information in the prospectus and to cancel the transaction at no personal loss. A mutual fund, despite all its unique sales and distribution characteristics, still must comply with federal law. But a mutual fund does require a special approach as a result of its continuous offering and unlimited capitalization.

Although its capitalization may be virtually unlimited, the fund's effective registration statement permits an offering of only a specified number of shares. Thus, when the maximum amount is approached, a new registration statement must be filed that encompasses the new shares to be issued and distributed. It is not inconceivable for a fund to postpone offering its shares when its registration is delayed at the SEC. Even while operating under an effective statement, the fund is obliged to update the essential information in its statement and prospectus *at least* once every 16 months. If material changes occur in the interim, an amended statement must be filed at that time. If a statement is not filed promptly, the fund risks exposing itself and its underwriter to liability for recovery of losses sustained by investors who used the inadequate or inaccurate prospectus to decide upon their commitment.

*G2.*
*The Investment Company Act of 1940 and 1970 Amendments*

*G2a.* **PURPOSE AND TERMS**

Many of the mechanical requirements prescribed under the Investment Company Act of 1940 have already been incorporated into the preceding discussion. The purpose of this act, along with the 1970 amendments, is to protect the investor against unfair and improper activities by the investment company, its management group advisors, underwriters, and other promoters.

To recap and highlight previous commentary, this law prescribes:

1. Registration with the SEC for investment companies doing business in the United States.

2. A declaration and adherence to diversified or nondiversified status.

3. Approval of investment objectives by the shareholders, prohibiting changes in this goal without consent of majority vote of those shareholders.

4. Formalized contracts between the investment company and its advisors and underwriters. (These contracts may be effective for 2-year periods but must be approved annually by the board of directors or by majority vote of the investment company's shareholders.)

5. Restrictions upon the composition of an investment company's board of directors, limiting the number or percentage of advisors, underwriters, brokers, and bankers serving in this capacity. Activity with, or on behalf of, investment companies by these interested persons is also closely supervised and curtailed.

6. A maximum sales charge of 9% for contractual investment programs, offering an opportunity to investors for recovery of all or a substantial portion of any sales charge levied if early cancellation is requested.

But the scope of the act and its amendments is far more comprehensive and provides even greater investor protection than we have already discussed. For instance, to ensure viability of operation, a registered investment company must have a net worth of at least $100,000 either prior to, or as a result of, an intended public offering of its securities. If it does not have a net worth of $100,000 prior to the offering, the law requires that no more than 25 responsible persons agree to purchase for indefinite investment enough shares to qualify under this provision.

### ISSUANCE OF DEBT SECURITIES AND PREFERRED STOCK      G2b.

Issuance of debt instruments is permitted under the act, although the practice is severely restricted by the SEC in the interest of the shareholders. For example, face-amount-certificate companies are limited to issuance of privately placed promissory notes in minimal amounts. Closed-end management companies are allowed publicly to offer senior securities, such as bonds or preferred stock. But these securities must have provisions for voting privileges, restrictive distributions, and continuous asset coverage included as a condition of the offering. A closed-end management company issuing bonds must ensure net asset coverage of this debt by at least 300% after the offering has been completed. The formula for net asset coverage of bonds is:

$$\frac{\text{total assets} - \text{total liabilities (excluding bonds)}}{\text{aggregate amount of debt securities}} = \frac{3 \text{ or more}}{1}$$

If coverage subsequently declines below 100% the bondholders of a closed-end company have the right to elect a majority of the board of directors until their protection exceeds 110% of net asset value again. No cash distributions may be paid to any stockholders unless the bondholders would have at least 300% asset coverage after the payment.

A preferred stock offering by a closed-end company necessitates net asset coverage of at least 200% immediately after completion of the offering. The formula for net asset coverage of preferred stock is:

$$\frac{\text{total assets} - \text{total liabilities (excluding bonds)}}{\text{aggregate amount of bonds} + \text{liquidation right of preferred stock}} = \frac{2 \text{ or more}}{1}$$

Voting privileges are extended to the preferred stockholders to elect two directors at all times and a majority of the board if dividends are in arrears for a total of 2 years' payments. No cash distributions are allowed for the common stockholder unless the preferred holder enjoys at least 200% asset coverage after such a distribution is completed.

In the case of open-end management companies (mutual funds), *no bond or preferred stock offerings are allowed under the law*. The only class of securities permitted to be issued by mutual funds is common stock. However, these companies can hold any issuer's bonds and preferred stocks in their investment portfolios. In addition they *are* permitted to contract long-term debt by borrowing from any regulated bank, provided that total borrowings are protected continuously by at least 300% net asset coverage. Should the coverage shrink below 300%, the mutual fund must reduce its borrowings and increase the ratio to the 300% level within 3 business days thereafter.

### G2c.    DISTRIBUTION OF DIVIDENDS

The Investment Company Act of 1940 requires dividend distributions to be paid solely from *net investment income*, which means from dividends and interest received from securities in the portfolio after deductions for expenses. Investment incomes does *not* mean profits or losses realized upon the sale of securities or other properties. Such distributions, if declared by the directors, represent *capital gains distributions*. Capital gains distributions may not be made more often than once every 12 months, although investment income may be disbursed more frequently.

All distributions, whether they be dividends or capital gains, must be accompanied by a statement disclosing the nature or source(s) of such payment because of tax ramifications for the investor. The tax ramifications will be discussed in detail later.

### G2d.    PROHIBITED ACTIVITIES

The SEC was given considerable latitude for deciding which activities an investment company may participate in that are appropriate to the "public interest," although they may sometimes appear to be in direct contravention of the law. For example, unless specific consent is given by the SEC, the Investment Company Act of 1940 prohibits an investment company from

1. purchasing any security in a margin account;
2. participating in a joint trading account, except for an underwriting in which they are a member of the group;
3. selling a security short, except in connection with an underwriting participation;

4. acquiring securities issued by another investment company if they would then own

   a. more than 3% of the voting stock in that company;

   b. securities issued by that company valued at more than 5% of their own total assets; or

   c. securities issued by all investment companies in their portfolio with an aggregate value of more than 10% of their own total assets;[8]

5. acquiring any security or interest in a broker/dealer, underwriter, or investment advisor, unless

   a. such an entity is a corporation whose outstanding securities will be owned by one or more other registered investment companies; and

   b. the gross income of such an entity is principally derived from the usual and related activities of broker/dealers, underwriters, and investment advisors; or

6. acquiring more than 10% of the voting stock of an insurance company unless the investment company already owns at least 25% of that stock at the time of such acquisition.[9]

### DISCLOSURE OF RECORDS

*G2e.*

> The keynote of investor protection built into the Investment Company Act of 1940 revolves around disclosure. Every investment company is required to keep the stockholders informed at periodic intervals about the relevant activities and details pertaining to the company. At least semiannually, the company must transmit to its stockholders
>
> 1. a balance sheet accompanied by a statement of the aggregate value of investments as of the balance sheet date;
>
> 2. a list of the quantity and value of each security in the portfolio as of the balance sheet date;
>
> 3. a statement of income for the period itemized with respect to each revenue and expenditure representing more than 5% of total income or expense;
>
> 4. a statement of surplus for the period itemized with respect to each debit or credit in this account representing more than 5% of total charges or credits;
>
> 5. a statement of the aggregate remuneration paid by the company during this period to
>
>    a. all officers;
>
>    b. all directors and members of any advisory board as regular compensation;

[8]An exemption from this particular prohibition, however, is generally granted to investment companies that acquire less than 3% of the outstanding stock of other investment companies and offer their own shares for sale at a public offering price that includes a sales load of not more than 1.5%. Furthermore, no mutual fund is obligated to redeem shares tendered to them by another investment company if the amount offered to them by any one company within a 30-day period exceeds 1% of their total outstanding securities.

[9]Thus, a provisional hedge is created that enables an investment company to buoy the financial condition or improve the capitalization of an insurance concern previously authorized as a permissible speculation. Still another loophole is established when this prohibition is deemed not to apply to the acquisition or promotion of a *new* insurance company.

c. each director and advisory board member as special compensation;

d. each entity of whom any officer or director of the company is an affiliated person; and

6. a statement of the aggregate dollar amounts of purchases and sales of investment securities, excluding U.S. government securities, during the period covered by the report.

To reinforce the integrity of these documents, the law requires an annual examination of the investment company's books and records by an independent accountant. Thus, one of the semi-annual transmissions to the stockholders will reflect the result of this audit and will be accompanied by a statement from the accountant certifying all findings and expressing an opinion as to the state of the company's records. Selection of the independent accountant is accomplished by a majority of the board of directors who are "disinterested" (unaffiliated) persons of that investment company. Their choice is then subject to ratification by the stockholders at the next annual meeting.

**G3.**
**The Internal Revenue Code**
**(Subchapter M)**

**G3a.** *FAVORABLE TAX TREATMENT FOR INVESTMENT COMPANIES*

Qualified investment companies and their stockholders are accorded favorable tax treatment under Subchapter M of the Internal Revenue Code. To realize the magnitude of this privilege, let us examine briefly the tax structure in the United States as it applies to other legal entities.

If an ordinary corporation earns a profit as a result of its activities, it must pay a federal tax based upon that profit. The corporation must then distribute a substantial amount of any money remaining, in the form of dividends, to its stockholders. Failure to do so without a specific business purpose in mind for that money subjects the corporation to tax penalties. Such an accumulation of income is contrary to the tax code.

The stockholders are, in turn, liable for payment of federal tax on the dividends they receive. While it is true that the first $100 of total dividends received by *an individual* annually is tax free,[10] any amount above that figure is taxed at that person's ordinary income bracket rate. Dividends received *by corporations* owning stock in a domestic concern are taxable at the regular corporate rate, but on only 15% of the dividends received. Corporate investors enjoy an exclusion from taxes equal to 85% of those dividends. For example, if a corporation received $1,000 in dividends last year, it is liable at the corporate tax rate for only $150 worth of those dividends. Then, that corporation must face the prospect of paying out dividends on its own after-tax income. This tax liability feature is passed on indefinitely as long as the original earnings continue to be distributed as dividends, in pyramid fashion, by subsequent investor-corporations.

When a recipient of such dividends is a unit investment trust or a management company that has qualified under Subchapter M, it may avoid tax liability completely, or, at worst, have a nominal

[10]If securities are owned and registered in joint names of husband and wife collectively the annual fax-tree dividend privilege is $200.

tax bill to pay to the government. This is accomplished merely by distributing those dividends to its own stockholders and thus transferring the accompanying liability as well. The terms **conduit theory** or **pipeline theory** of investment refer to this flow-through relationship between a qualified investment company, the securities in its portfolio, and its own investors (see Figure 6).

**conduit theory**
**pipeline theory**

FIGURE 6
Relationship Between Qualified Investment Company, Its Portfolio, and Its Investors

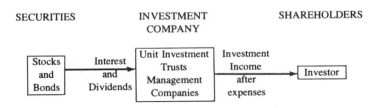

Shareholders then have an individual responsibility at their personal tax rates. However, as a result of this flow-through feature, they can also receive more money because the investment company is exempted from paying it out first in taxes on the same distribution. For example, an industrial corporation with an investment portfolio is obliged to pay taxes at a 48% rate on 15% of dividends received. It would then be able to pay its own stockholders only $928 from $1,000 in dividend income ($1,000 − [$150 × .48]). A qualified investment company on the other hand could pay out the entire $1,000 because it has no personal tax liability when it distributes its net investment income to its shareholders.

G3b.   **QUALIFICATION REQUIREMENTS FOR FAVORABLE TAX TREATMENT**

The Internal Revenue Service does not grant this privilege to all companies merely because they are investment companies. It is made available only to those organizations able to meet certain criteria for eligibility. The Internal Revenue Code identifies these companies as *regulated* investment companies. The more important requirements for qualification specify that such a company must meet the following criteria:

1.  It must be a domestic corporation—foreign (*off-shore*) mutual funds are ineligible.
2.  It must be registered with the SEC under the Investment Company Act of 1940 for the entire taxable year as a unit investment trust or management company.[11]
3.  It must be "diversified" in its portfolio investments, as defined earlier.
4.  It must derive at least 90% of its gross income from dividends, interest, and gains from the sale of securities. (Losses from securities sales are not netted out in this computation.)

[11]To be *regulated*, an investment company must be *registered*, but registration in itself does not mean the organization will also be regulated.

5. It must ensure that less than 30% of its gross income is derived from sales of securities held less than 3 months. (The purpose of these last two requirements is to provide the tax exemption to bona fide investment companies and not to speculative trading entities established specifically to circumvent the regulation.)

6. It must distribute at least 90% of its net investment income to its shareholders in the form of taxable dividends. (Net investment income considers only dividends and interest received from securities in the portfolio, less ordinary expenses. Capital gains on securities transactions are not included in this computation.)

Although the tax code prescribes distribution of at least 90%, it is common practice to pay out *all* the net investment income. Investment companies do so because if any net investment income is retained, it is taxed to the investment company at the ordinary corporate rates. Besides, most investors reinvest the dividends they receive anyway and pay the taxes due on them from personal savings.

G3c.   **LONG-TERM GAIN PRIVILEGE FOR INVESTORS**

Subchapter M further allows investors to treat long-term capital gains distributions as long-term gains on their own tax returns, regardless of their personal holding period in the shares of that investment company. That is, if the mutual fund shares were purchased last week, and a long-term gain was distributed today, the investor is taxed at the favorable capital gains rate. Short-term gains are passed along to the shareholders as short term in nature, and no advantageous treatment is allowed.

G4.
*The SEC Statement of Policy (SOP)*

G4a.   **PURPOSE AND SCOPE**

No discussion about investment companies (mutual funds, in particular) can be complete without commentary about the SEC Statement of Policy (SOP). Some officials in the financial community have always contended that investment company securities are not bought by investors; rather, they are sold by salespersons. The objective of the Statement of Policy is to provide that these securities are sold in a fair and proper manner.

The Statement of Policy was formulated in 1950 to regulate sales practices with respect to the offering of investment company shares. Because mutual funds especially are engaged in continuous offerings, much of the policy appears directed toward them. However, remember that it is just as applicable for face-amount certificates and unit investment trusts as it is for both varieties of management companies.

On March 8, 1979 the SEC repealed the Statement of Policy and its detailed provisions are no longer enforced by the Commission. However, the SEC did not repudiate the contents of the Statement because it believes many of its principles are still valid. Instead, the SEC now stresses that while the SOP does not have the status of a restrictive rule, investment companies and users of sales literature are nevertheless responsible for insuring that materials used are not, in fact, misleading. Moreover, it emphasizes that the term "sales literature" continues to include any communication used to induce the purchase of investment company shares. That is, it encompasses the spoken word as well as all written material used in connection with offerings of investment company shares.

**G4b.**   ***IMPLEMENTATION***

Although the Statement of Policy is a product of the SEC, it was formulated with the assistance of the National Association of Securities Dealers. The NASD was also delegated with authority to administer this doctrine for its own membership. The SEC supervised the activities of nonmembers.

With repeal of the Statement of Policy by the SEC, the NASD decided it would no longer enforce its provisions. The NASD has undertaken a study to determine what Association rules should be adopted to preserve and codify the important principles of this useful doctrine. In the meantime, it is necessary for NASD members to file copies of investment company sales literature for approval with the Association's Advertising Department in Washington D.C. within ten days after first use or publication. Members with less than a year of spot-check review by the Association must submit such material prior to use.

The next few pages set forth essential features of the SEC's Statement of Policy. They appear because they are considered appropriate for a student's recognition and understanding of ethical sales practices in the industry.

**G4c.**   ***DEFINITION AND RULES CONCERNING SALES LITERATURE***

The definition of sales literature includes any communication (whether in writing, by radio, or by television) used by an issuer, underwriter, or dealer to induce the purchase of shares of an investment company. Sales literature should always be thought of as *supplementary* material because federal law still requires that potential investors be provided with a formal prospectus in any event. The Securities Act of 1933 makes presentation of the prospectus mandatory no later than with confirmation of any purchase. Nevertheless, the Statement of Policy will not permit sales literature to be distributed publicly if it is materially misleading, by implication or otherwise, due to

1. a false statement of an important fact; or
2. omission of information that, in light of the circumstances, is construed as deceptive.

This standard is also applicable to sales literature prepared for circulation only among dealers or wholesale representatives. Occasionally, however, this posture is impractical. Therefore, the NASD may relax these principles if the material

1. is not directly contrary to the basic concept of the Statement of Policy;
2. is limited to single copies for each dealer office and is clearly marked "Not for Reproduction"; and
3. is labeled "Not for Use with Members of the Public" and is accompanied by a *caveat* from the underwriter explaining that use of such material with the public would constitute a violation of the Statement of Policy.

**G4d.**   ***GUIDELINES ON MISLEADING ACTIVITIES***

Under the Statement of Policy *it is considered materially misleading:*

---

[12]The nonmembers usually include the mutual fund itself, its advisory group, and the custodian bank, whereas the underwriter, plan company, and selling group participants are subject to NASD jurisdiction.

1. To refer to the effectiveness of a registration statement on file with the SEC as representing government approval of the issue. Nor may reference be made to federal or state regulation of any investment company without explaining that this does not involve supervision of management, investment practices, or policies of that company.

2. To represent or imply that shares of an investment company are similar to, or as safe as, government bonds, insurance company annuities, savings accounts, or life insurance; or that they have the fixed income, principal, or any other features of a debt security. Nor may statement or implication be made that the management of an investment company is under the same kinds of investment restrictions, or is operated under limitations similar to, or has fiduciary obligations such as those imposed by governmental authorities on savings banks and insurance companies.

3. To represent or imply that banking institutions serving as custodians of fund securities, transfer agents, or dividend disbursing agents
   a. will provide protection for investors against possible depreciation of assets; or
   b. that such institutions maintain any supervisory function over management in such matters as purchase and sale of portfolio securities or declaration of dividends, or provide any trusteeship protection.

   Any comment beyond ''The ABC Bank is custodian'' or ''The cash and securities are held in custody by the ABC Bank'' requires a complete explanation of that bank's limited role in the affairs of the investment company.

4. To represent or imply that investment companies in general are direct sources of *new* capital to industry or that a particular investment company is such a source unless the extent to which such investments are made is disclosed. (Investment companies usually buy and sell securities in the secondary market and do not often engage in corporate financing activities).

5. To make any extravagant claims regarding management ability or competence.

6. To represent or imply that investment companies are operated as, or are similar to, cooperatives.[13]

7. To represent or imply that investment company shares generally have been selected by fiduciaries. (Fiduciaries are persons or institutions to whom property is legally entrusted for the benefit of another. They are not normally buyers of mutual fund shares because state laws generally prohibit them from delegating investment authority to someone else. After all, that is what they would be doing if they invested the trust's assets in a mutual fund.)

8. To represent or imply an assurance that an investor's capital will increase, or that purchase of investment company shares involves a preservation of capital and a protection against loss in value. Unless an explanation of inherent

[13]Legal entities formed to provide low-cost services or facilities to a limited number of members.

market risks is provided, discussions of the following descriptive features are also considered misleading:

a. accumulation of capital
b. accumulation of an estate
c. preservation of capital
d. protection against loss of purchasing power
e. diversification of investments
f. financial independence or profit possibilities

9. To state or discuss the redemption features of investment company shares without explaining that the value of the shares upon redemption may be more or less than the investor's cost, depending upon the market value of the portfolio securities at the time of redemption.

10. To use any comparison of an investment company security with any other security, medium of investment, or any security index or average, without pointing out

a. that the particular security, index, or average and the period involved were especially selected;
b. that the results disclosed should be considered in the light of the company's investment policy and objectives, the characteristics and quality of the company's investments, and the period selected;
c. the material differences or similarities between the subjects of the comparisons;
d. what the comparison is designed to show; and
e. anything else that may be necessary to make the comparison fair.

This last point is particularly relevant because of human temptations to emphasize virtues while ignoring or downgrading the advantages of a competing investment. Unless full disclosure can be accomplished in a manner that is not unfair, sales literature must abstain from comparisons between dissimilar, or even similar, securities and other investment media. Indiscriminate attacks upon ordinary life insurance, for example, or to promote cancellation of such policies merely to use their cash surrender values for mutual fund shares is in poor taste and considered unfair under the Statement of Policy.

To represent or imply that the performance of any particular company may be measured by, compared with, or related to, the performance of a particular industry, unless the extent and scope of the portfolio of that company is such that its performance will generally approximate that of the industry.

12. To use any chart or table that

a. is inaccurate in factual detail;
b. tends to create a false or misleading impression as to any material aspect of the investment company's past performance or of an assumed investment of anyone in that investment company; or
c. appears to represent the investment company's past performance or investor experience will be repeated in the future.

> In this regard, it should be borne in mind that any chart or illustration of asset value performance that is not drawn to the same scale throughout, that does not encompass at least that fund's latest 10 years' results,[14] or that makes price projections into the future is deceptive and unfair. Preparation of any chart or table not specifically illustrated in a sample format appearing in the Statement of Policy should be cleared by the NASD or the SEC prior to use.

13. To fail to include in any sales literature designed to encourage investors to switch from one investment company to another or from one class of security of an investment company to another class, the substance of the following statement in a separate paragraph in type as large as that used generally in the body of the piece:

> Switching from the securities of one investment company to another, or from one class of security of an investment company to another, involves a sales charge on each such transaction, for details of which see the prospectus. The prospective purchaser should measure these costs against the claimed advantage of the switch.

The practice of switching is also called "twisting," referring to unscrupulous salespersons glibly talking customers into making frequent sales and purchases of mutual fund shares. Mutual funds are designed to be long-term investment vehicles, and frequent switching does not generally work to the investor's advantage.

14. To fail to include in any sales literature that does not state the amount or rate of the sales commission a clear reference to the prospectus for information concerning the sales commission and other related information.

15. To employ material in whole or in part from published articles or documents descriptive of, or relating to, investment companies unless such material, or the literature including such material, complies with the Statement of Policy. In addition, such material may not be taken out of context in a way that alters its intended meaning.

16. To combine into any one amount, distributions from net investment income and distributions from any other source. It is misleading to include income representing dividends and interest from securities held in portfolio with income generated as a result of purchase and sale transactions. Investment income represents a *return on capital invested,* while other distributions are indicative of a *return of capital employed.*

17. To represent or imply an assurance that an investor will receive a "stable," "continuous," "dependable," or "liberal" return, or that the investor will receive *any* specified rate of return.

18. To represent or imply a percentage return on an investment in the shares of an investment company unless it is based upon one of the following formulas:

a. *A historical basis.* Dividends from net investment in-

---

[14]If the fund is less than 10 years old the illustration must show its performance for its entire lifetime.

come paid during the preceding fiscal year are related to the average monthly offering price for that fiscal year:

$$\frac{\text{net investment income paid for fiscal year}}{\text{average monthly offering price during fiscal year}} = \text{rate of return (historic basis)}$$

**b.** *A current basis.* Dividends paid from net investment income during the latest 12 months are related to the prevailing offering price, adjusted to reflect any capital gains distribution made during this period.

$$\frac{\text{net investment income paid in preceding 12 months}}{(\text{current offering price} + \text{capital gains distributed in that 12-month period})} = \text{rate of return (current basis)}$$

It is important to note that in both instances the use of either approach is predicated upon an *annual* distribution of investment income. Applying these formulas for a lesser or even greater time period is considered misleading. Although investment companies may distribute income as often as they prefer during the year (the usual practice is quarterly), net capital gains may be distributed only once in any 12-month period.

Every such commentary, whether current or historic in nature, must be accompanied by a statement to the effect that the return is based upon dividends paid in the period covered and is not a representation of future results. In the same text material, the asset value per share at the beginning and end of the period or the increase or decrease in asset value (stated in percentage) must also appear. The current method may prove to be more advantageous for sales personnel to use if a fund has recently raised its dividend rate.

examples

Rates of return applied via formula methods:

*Historic Basis*

$$\frac{\text{(Income distributions for fiscal 1976)}}{\text{(Average monthly offering price for fiscal 1976)}[15]} \quad \frac{\$\ .24}{\$4.37} = 5.49\% \text{ rate of return}$$

[15]Usually determined on the last business day of each of 12 months involved.

*Current Basis*

Income distributions during preceding 12 calendar months=$ .31

Current offering price on 4/30/77=$4.90

Capital gains distribution in preceding 12 calendar months=$ .61

Adjusted offering price=$5.51

Therefore,

$$\frac{\$ .31}{(\$4.90 + \$ .61)} = 5.63\% \text{ rate of return}$$

19. To discuss or portray the principles of dollar cost averaging without making clear

   a. that the program will incur a loss if they discontinue their investment plans when the market value of accumulated shares is less than the amount of dollars invested;

   b. that the program is investing funds primarily in securities subject to market fluctuations and that the method involves equal dollar investments in such shares at regular intervals continuously, regardless of price levels;

   c. that investors must take into account their financial ability to continue the plan through periods of low price levels;

   d. that such plans do not protect against loss in value in declining markets; and

   e. that any such type of continuous investment plan does not ensure a profit and does not protect against depreciation in declining markets.

20. To use the phrases *"dollar averaging"* or *"averaging the dollar"* (although the phrases *"dollar cost averaging"* or *"cost averaging"* are not objectionable) in referring to any plan of constant dollar investment in the shares of an investment company periodically regardless of the price level of those shares. Despite these restrictions, the principles illustrated by this continuing deposit program have proved advantageous for most investors who are in for the long-term pull.

## example

To demonstrate this program's effectiveness, assume that monthly investments of $100 are made in shares of a no-load mutual fund[16] in the following manner.

[16]A no-load fund is utilized in this model merely to simplify the explanation for calculating an average cost price. In the majority of instances, of course, a sales charge is already included in the offering price and the deposit does not really purchase full asset value in the loaded shares.

DOLLAR COST AVERAGING PROGRAM

| MONTHLY DEPOSITS | OFFERING PRICE AT TIME OF INVESTMENT | NUMBER OF SHARES AND/OR FRACTIONAL SHARES BOUGHT |
|---|---|---|
| $100 | $ 5.00 | 20 |
| $100 | 10.00 | 10 |
| $100 | 20.00 | 5 |
| $100 | 10.00 | 10 |
| $100 | 15.00 | 6⅔ |
| $500 total investment | $60.00 aggregate offering prices | 51⅔ shares owned |

$$\text{average } \textit{price} \text{ of investment} = \frac{\text{aggregate offering price of shares}}{\text{number of deposits made}}$$

Therefore,

$$\frac{\$60}{5} = \$12 \text{ average } \textit{price} \text{ of investment}$$

$$\text{average } \textit{cost} \text{ per share} = \frac{\text{total money deposited}}{\text{total shares and fractions owned}}$$

Therefore,

$$\frac{\$500}{51⅔} = \$9.68 \text{ average } \textit{cost} \text{ per share}$$

Note that the *average cost per share is lower than the average price of investment*. This arithmetic fact is always true so long as the security has price fluctuation in the purchase program. The investor is able to buy more shares and fractions at the lower price levels with the same amount of money. Thus, the denominator (total shares) in the calculation of average cost increases and results in a lower cost per share. The formula for average price of investment alone does not include this factor in its computation.

---

If the Statement of Policy does not thus eliminate the potential inequities associated with mutual fund sales, it certainly comes a lot closer to doing so than any other regulatory aspect of investment found in the financial industry.

*G5.*
*The NASD Supplement to the*
*SEC Statement of Policy*

To supplement this SEC doctrine, the NASD Board of Governors has added its own admonitions for certain offering and sales practices that it considered to be in violation of the spirit of the Statement of Policy and the NASD's Rules of Fair Practice.

*G5a.*

**SPECIAL DEALS**

It is improper for an underwriter to give, or a member organization or registered representative to receive, anything of material value in addition to the cash discounts or concessions set forth in the offering prospectus in connection with the sale or distribution of investment company shares. Any gift valued at more than $50 per person annually, whether in cash or merchandise, is generally considered to be of "material value" and therefore in violation of this rule. However, an occasional cocktail party, dinner, ticket to the theater, sporting event, or the like is considered acceptable if

1.  it is extended infrequently;
2.  distribution is limited to relatively few persons; and
3.  there is no question of propriety about the means or manner of such an action; and
4.  it is not conditioned upon sales of shares of the investment company.

### G5b. *SELLING DIVIDENDS*

It is unfair and unethical for any NASD member or employee to solicit purchase orders for mutual fund shares *solely* on the basis of an impending distribution to be made by that company. No advantage is gained by the investor under those circumstances for the following reasons:

1.  The price of the shares is reduced by the *exact* amount of the distribution on the day the shares begin selling ex-dividend. The ex-dividend date is set by the mutual fund's board of directors, trustees, or underwriter and does not follow the usual NASD rules for such procedure. It is often fixed *after* the record date instead of prior to it.
2.  The investor is liable for taxes on the distribution received from the company.
3.  The salesperson's compensation will be higher because it is based upon the offering price—the price that includes the dividend amount prior to the "ex" date.

### G5c. *BREAKPOINT SALES*

It is contrary to equitable principles of trade to solicit mutual fund orders in dollar amounts just below the level at which the sales charge will be reduced on quantity transactions. Such practice is unfair because it forces investors to bear the burden of a maximum load, when for a little more money deposited over a 13-month period they can enjoy a lower sales charge. As a rule of thumb, the NASD will look with suspicion upon investments made within $1,000 of a mutual fund's breakpoint.

Although the use of a breakpoint is encouraged by the authorities, the practice of breakpoint sales is not! The former benefits investors, but the latter does not.

### G5d. *EXCESSIVE SALES CHARGES*

It is improper for a NASD member to participate in a public offering of investment company shares if the public offering price includes a sales charge that is excessive. Although the Investment Company Act of 1940 set a maximum sales charge requirement of 9%, this maximum pertains only to periodic-payment (contractual) plans. It has no bearing upon single-payment or voluntary-accumulation plans. Nor does the Statement of Policy address itself to this potential inequity either. It simply requires charts, tables, and sales literature in general to express any sales charge at the *highest* effective rate. The Statement of Policy assumes that if investors are apprised of the highest current charge, competition among mutual funds will keep that sales load to a minimum.

The NASD, through its Rules of Fair Practice, does not leave the subject open to chance or competition. It fixes a maximum sales charge on any single-payment, voluntary-accumulation, or contractual-plan mutual fund transaction at 8.50% of the offering price. Moreover, that maximum load may be employed by NASD members only if the fund offers its investors all three of the following benefits:

1. dividend reinvestment privileges at net asset value
2. quantity discounts at breakpoints set forth in Section 26 of the Rules of Fair Practice
3. rights of accumulation (cumulative quantity discounts) for at least 10 years from the date of the shareholder's first purchase.

If one or more of these benefits is denied to investors, the maximum sales charge must be scaled down from 8.50% to as little as 6.25% of the offering price to avoid being deemed excessive. The actual scale depends upon which of those benefits, if any, are made available.

H.
other investment-type companies

Although not thought of immediately when the subject of mutual funds arises, real estate investment trusts and annuities are types of investment companies. They are not-so-distant relatives of well-known concepts embracing investment companies. They have many of the same characteristics and are subject to many of the same federal regulations. They, too, have stated objectives regarding the performance of investments in their portfolios. They also offer subscribers advantages and risks often associated with typical mutual fund investments. These features are described in the remaining pages of this chapter.

H1.
*Real Estate Investment Trusts (REITs)*

### H1a.  DEFINITION AND PURPOSE

A **real estate investment trust**, or **REIT** as it is commonly referred to (pronounced "reet"), can be compared to a closed-end type of investment company. Whereas a closed-end company invests in a portfolio of securities, a REIT invests in various ventures, all related to the field of real estate. This includes income-producing properties, such as shopping centers and office buildings, as well as short-term construction loans and long-term mortgages. As a result, purchasers of REIT shares achieve two important goals not usually realized by the average real estate investor:

real estate investment trust (REIT)

1. *diversification*—a limited amount of capital acquires a proportionate participation in the trust's package of investments
2. *liquidity*—the investor's shares in this trust portfolio can be sold easily in the over-the-counter stock market or on an exchange where the REIT may be traded.

### H1b.  ORGANIZATION AND CAPITALIZATION

A real estate investment trust is organized according to a legal trust instrument with its business supervised by a self-appointed board of trustees. This contrasts with a closed-end company's birth by means of a charter and the use of the corporate directorship style of command. This difference between the two investment companies is strictly technical in nature. For all practical purposes the two businesses are managed alike. A way to recognize one format from the other is through description of its ownership title. Equity in a trust is called a *certificate of beneficial interest* (CBI) while that of a corporation is vested in a *share of common stock*. Both forms of business obtain a significant percentage of their capital through public offerings of such ownership interest. The similarity in their capitalization process usually ends there.

A REIT often supplements its equity capital with large borrowings from banks and insurance companies as a way of giving it a degree of leverage in its business dealings.[17] During their peak popularity in the mid-1960s, REITs sometimes borrowed two to five times the amount of their equity capital. The risk involved in this practice of heavy borrowing is that the real estate investment may not generate enough money to pay the interest carrying expenses or to repay the principal amount when it comes due. Bankruptcy and receivership then usually result as the equity capital is quickly dissipated. These investment vehicles are structured for persons capable of bearing capital risk in anticipation of receiving higher current income than that realizable from more conservative media. Because these trusts are not concerns registered under the Investment Company Act of 1940, they are not subject to its restrictive borrowing provisions.

### H1c. MORTGAGE AND EQUITY REITs

Real estate investment trusts are usually classified broadly as either mortgage or equity. A REIT's assignment to a particular category depends upon its principal investment practices. A **mortgage REIT** acts primarily as a financier for construction of commercial and residential properties. It lends money to builders and developers of real estate projects. It benefits from the difference in rates between its own borrowing expense and the interest received from holdings of these loan and mortgage contracts. An **equity REIT** is primarily a landlord or owner of commercial and residential real estate. It invests in income-producing properties such as shopping centers, office buildings, warehouses, and apartment houses. It is also the more conservative of the two categories because any borrowing it undertakes is nominal compared to its equity capitalization. If an equity REIT wants more investment capital, it is more inclined to issue additional shares of beneficial interest rather than borrow it. Therefore, its income is derived primarily from rent monies paid by the lessees of the properties it owns.

**mortgage REIT**

**equity REIT**

These classifications, as mentioned before, are broad. Often, a REIT is found to be a combination of mortgage and equity investment in order to enjoy the best of both worlds—mortgage for speculative growth opportunity and equity for a solid foundation of continuous current income. Moreover, within the field of

[17]Leverage can be defined as a high percentage of debt in relation to equity capital. It is hoped that the borrowed funds can be employed to earn a greater sum than the interest that must be paid for the use of those monies.

mortgage REITs, there is a breakdown between those trusts that invest in short-term loans and those that invest in long-term loans (so called "permanent" loans). Those trusts specializing in short-term loans finance the construction phase of real estate projects. They are frequently called **construction and development (C&D) REITs**. They provide interim credit until longer-term mortgages can be obtained when the project is completed. The **permanent mortgage REITs** are often sponsored by large life insurance companies. They extend credit on commercial and residential properties, sometimes for as long as 40 years.

**construction and development (C&D) REITs**
**permanent mortgage REITs**

*H1d.* **TAXATION TESTS FOR REITs**

> Real estate investment trusts are permitted the same conduit treatment of income as that allowed for regulated investment companies. They, too, are subject to the terms of Subchapter M of the Internal Revenue Code. Thus, if a trust is able to meet the qualifications prescribed in the Code, it avoids being taxed as a separate entity. Instead, it passes this liability on to the beneficial owners of its certificates.

In order to qualify for conduit treatment, a REIT must annually satisfy four tests regarding organizational structure, source of income, nature of assets, and distribution of income. The tests are intended to prove that

1. there is a pooling arrangement of funds invested primarily in the real estate field; and
2. income realized from these investments is passive income as opposed to monies generated from the operation of businesses involving real estate. Moreover, substantial amounts of the realized income must be paid out to the certificate holders on a current basis.

*H1d(1).* ***Organizational structure*** A REIT must be an unincorporated legal entity managed by one or more trustees. It cannot be a personal holding company. Beneficial ownership must be evidenced by transferable securities held by 100 or more persons.

*H1d(2).* > ***Source of income*** At least 75% of a REIT's income must be derived from one or more of the following:
>
> 1. real property rentals
> 2. interest from real property mortgages
> 3. gain from the sale of real property or from mortgages secured by real property
> 4. distributions from other REITs
> 5. abatements or refunds of taxes paid on real property
> 6. income and gain from foreclosure property[18]
>
> An additional 15% of a REIT's income must also come from those sources or from interest, dividends, or gains from the sale of stock or other securities. Thus, it is permissible for a REIT to have *some* of its capital invested in other than real estate ventures, should

[18]Foreclosure property is real estate acquired by a REIT through default on a lease or on an indebtedness that such property secured.

management deem it wise to do so. Furthermore, as a deterrent to frequent trading of assets, the Internal Revenue Service has decreed that no more than 30% of a REIT's income can come from sales of real property held less than 4 years and securities held for 1 year or less (requirement effective for sales in 1978 and thereafter).

*H1d(3).*     ***Nature of assets***     At the end of each quarter, a REIT must have at least 75% of the value of its assets invested in real estate, government securities, or held in cash. Not more than 5% of its assets can be in securities of any one nongovernment or non-REIT issuer. Those holdings, whatever the amount, may not exceed 10% of the voting securities of that issuer. Moreover, except for foreclosure property, a REIT may not hold real property primarily for resale to customers.

*H1d(4).*

> ***Distribution of income***     A REIT is required to distribute each year at least 90% of net investment income to its beneficial owners. Net investment income is defined as rental income and/or interest income, less expenses. But it does not include, nor does the IRS mandate distribution of, capital gains (that is, profits from sale of real property, leases, mortgage instruments, or securities). If the REIT chooses to retain any monies, capital gains, or the minimal percentage of investment income allowable, it must pay taxes on these funds at regular corporate rates. Distributed investment income is taxable for the trust's certificate holders as ordinary income. Capital gains, on the other hand, are treated by REIT investors as "long term," regardless of how long a period they have owned an interest in the REIT. This is exactly the same treatment provided for holders of regulated investment companies.

*H2.*
**Annuity Contracts**

*H2a.*     *DEFINITION*

> An **annuity** is an investment contract between a life insurance company and a subscriber. The insurance company agrees to make periodic payments to that party, as long as he or she lives, in exchange for the deposit of a specific sum of money. The deposit required depends upon the amount of periodic payment to be made as well as the individual's age and sex. The insurance company's mortality tables play a key role in this determination. An-

**annuity**

nuities are sold only by life insurance companies because only those companies can guarantee the annuity mortality risk. That is, payments are guaranteed for the lifetime of the annuity holder regardless of mortality tables of that insurance company.

*H2b.*     *FIXED OR VARIABLE OPERATION*

An annuity contract, classified according to its mode of operation, is either fixed or variable.

*H2b(1).*     ***Fixed annuity***     A **fixed annuity** (also called a **guaranteed-dollar annuity**) is one in which the life insurance company pays a set amount of money to the annuitant periodically. This sum can be increased somewhat by extra payments if the contract is also a "participating" type of agreement. That is, a participating an-

**fixed annuity**
**guaranteed-dollar annuity**

nuity agreement functions exactly like participating preferred stock. If the insurance company's investments that secure this annuity generate more money than anticipated, the contract holder will share in the excess income.

The insurance company's reserves, backing all payments to the annuitant, are invested in a portfolio comprised of fixed debt securities and real estate mortgages. In these respects the fixed annuity resembles the operation of a face-amount-certificate company. The subscriber's risk in owning a guaranteed-dollar annuity is that inflation may erode the purchasing power of the fixed payments. Consequently, buyers of these contracts are advised not to rely on this income exclusively for survival in their retirement years.

*H2b(2).* *Variable annuity*   A **variable annuity** is one in which the life insurance company makes periodic distributions to the annuitant during his or her lifetime. However, those payments vary in amount according to the investment performance of equity securities (mainly common stocks) in a special portfolio created for such contracts with the insurance company's reserves. The theory behind this approach is that, in the long run, a carefully managed portfolio of common stocks will tend to keep pace with the cost of living. This will offset fluctuations in the purchasing power of the dollar. Variable annuity payments should increase in inflationary times and decline during deflationary periods. But, the insurance company cannot guarantee that this will always be true in this plan or in any future market situation. Therefore, an obvious and important difference between the fixed and variable annuity is that with a fixed contract, investment risk is borne by the insurance company; with the variable contract, investment risk is borne by the subscriber.

**variable annuity**

*H2b(3).* *Hybrid annuity*   Life insurance companies can and do offer annuity contracts for sale that are hybrids of these basic programs. That is, these hybrids are part guaranteed-dollar and part variable; the appropriate percentage of each form in this customized annuity contract is predetermined by the individual subscriber. The annuity payments are then a combination of fixed dollars for a guaranteed base income and variable dollars for a possible hedge against inflation. For example, if the annuitant chooses an investment contract that is 50% fixed and 50% variable, half of the premium deposit is applied for purchase of a fixed annuity and half for a variable one. Then, when payments commence, the holder is assured of a constant lifetime return from the fixed annuity, supplemented by changing amounts of money from the variable contract. The specific amount receivable from a variable annuity depends upon the investment performance of an underlying portfolio of securities in which deposit premiums are invested.

*H2c.*   *ANNUITY DEPOSITS*

The rest of our discussion of annuities will emphasize the variable investment contract. The variable annuity is subject to scrutiny by the SEC because of investor reliance upon fluctuating equity values in its special portfolio. It is this feature that attracts our attention. Because it does not have this feature, the fixed annuity is of academic interest only to students in the insurance industry and is subject to the exclusive jurisdiction of state insurance commissioners.

> Deposits invested in a variable annuity are used to acquire fractional participations in a legal entity created by the insurance company and operated as a unit investment trust. It is similar in function to a mutual fund plan company. It is also registered as an investment company with the SEC. The insurance industry calls each such arrangement a **separate account**. The separate account is formed as an individual entity to avoid jeopardizing the assets of the parent company and other affiliated companies. The principal assets of a separate account are shares in a mutual fund organized and managed by the same insurance company. The mutual fund is the organization that actually invests in the common stock portfolio. However, the annuitant's participation in the separate account provides an indirect interest that is dependent on the investment performance of those securities (see Figure 7).

**separate account**

**FIGURE 7**
Relationships of Insurance Company and Annuitant to the Separate Account and Mutual Fund

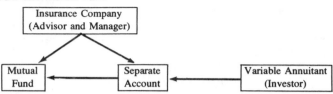

The annuitant's fractional participation purchases in a separate account are not expressed in terms of dollars invested but rather in terms of accumulation units. An **accumulation unit** is an accounting symbol that indicates the value of the separate account's reserves (net assets) during the deposit period. Each contribution by the annuitant is used to purchase these accumulation units. The value of the accumulation units varies daily relative to the investment results of the mutual fund in which the separate account, in turn, is invested. The dollar value of the subscriber's variable annuity at any time is therefore determined by multiplying the number of accumulation units purchased by the current value of one unit. For example, if you have purchased thus far in your variable annuity program 137.00321 units, and each unit today is calculated to be worth $12.153252, the dollar value of your annuity is the product of these two numbers, or approximately $1,665.03.

**accumulation unit**

*H2d.*    *ANNUITY PAYMENTS*

There are two specific programs regarding the *time* when payments will begin. These two programs, *immediate* or *deferred,* may apply to either a fixed or variable annuity contract. Under the **immediate program** the subscriber pays a single premium for the investment contract, and annuity distributions commence right away. In the **deferred program** the subscriber's deposit may be in a lump sum or paid in installments over a period of years. Whether in lump sum or in installments, the life insurance company's distributions to the contract holder are not scheduled to begin until some specified date in the future, usually at least 10

**immediate program**
**deferred program**

years hence. Most investors choose the installment procedure under a deferred program. This is because most annuity contracts are bought for future retirement income while the investor is still working. Such contracts can be, and often are, incorporated into an investors Keogh plan or Investment Retirement Account (IRA).

In choosing the *method* for payment, the investor has several options. One of these options must be selected by the annuitant at the time the contract matures. They are:

1. A **lump-sum distribution** in lieu of an annuity.

2. **Life annuity** payments that are made monthly or periodically during the contract holder's lifetime and that terminate only upon death, no matter how long that person lives.

3. **Life annuity with payments certain**—monthly or periodic payments are made to the annuitant during that person's lifetime. However, if the contract holder dies before a specified number of payments have been made (that is, 10 or 15 years' worth), the insurance company guarantees that the distributions continue and will be paid to the decedent's beneficiary. The beneficiary's payments will cease only after the minimum number of such payments has been reached.

4. **Unit refund annuity**—monthly or periodic payments are made to the annuitant during the subscriber's lifetime. However, if death occurs before that person receives payments equivalent to the contract's original purchase cost, the difference between those payments and the amount invested is refunded to the decedent's beneficiary in a lump-sum distribution.

5. **Joint and survivor annuity**—payments are made monthly or periodically during the lives of two people and continue until both have died. These contractual distributions are appealing to married couples because it assures them of an income for life for as long as either one lives.

<table>
<tr><td>When a variable annuity matures and payments are about to begin, the value of the accumulation units is used to purchase a fixed number of annuity units. An **annuity unit** is an accounting symbol that is used to measure the value of the contract holder's account during the distribution period. The annuity payments are based on the value of the annuity units. Because the annuity units are invested in a separate account with an interest in a portfolio of equity securities, the investment results, and consequently the annuitant's payments, will vary up and down.</td></tr>
</table>

**lump-sum distribution**

**life annuity**

**life annuity with payments certain**

**unit refund annuity**

**joint and survivor annuity**

**annuity unit**

*H2e.* *TAXATION OF ANNUITIES*

Deposits into an annuity contract, like purchases of mutual fund shares, are usually made with an investor's after-tax dollars. That is, the investor uses personal income remaining after payment of income taxes. Yet it need not always be that way. Because mutual funds, as well as fixed and variable annuities, are acceptable investments under the Employees Retirement Income Security Act of 1974 (ERISA) they can be an integral part of a formal retirement plan program approved by the Internal Revenue Service (IRS). If this is the case, those contractual deposits are tax deductible. This means that they are made from the purchaser's pretax income. Annuity contracts included in IRS-approved pension, profit-sharing, Keogh, or IRA retirement plans are usually identified as "qualifying annuities." Those purchased independently are called "nonqualifying annuities." Because most annuity contracts are of the nonqualifying variety, let us focus upon their tax characteristics.

Unlike a mutual fund investor, the individual annuitant pays no income tax on dividends or capital gains from realized appreciation or unrealized appreciation (paper profits) that are credited to the nonqualifying contract during the accumulation period. Income tax is handled in the same fashion as it is with IRS-approved retirement plans. All tax liabilities are deferred until payments or withdrawals begin.[19] Mutual fund shareholders, on the other hand, must pay tax on distributions made by the fund in the year in which paid even though such distributions may be automatically reinvested in additional shares. (The only exception would be if those mutual fund shares were incorporated into the individual's tax-exempted pension, profit-sharing, Keogh, or IRA plan.) This apparent heavier tax burden borne by a mutual fund investment plan participant as compared with an annuity purchaser has a counterbalance. The mutual fund itself pays no tax as a regulated Subchapter M company, whereas the separate account of the life insurance company is fully liable for whatever income or gain is realized from equities in its portfolio. That tax liability is taken into full consideration when the value of accumulation units is determined and credited to an annuitant's account.

Payments to holders of fixed or variable annuity contracts are taxed as ordinary income. This means that persons receiving payments must pay federal tax at their regular tax bracket rate on those payments. At retirement, most persons are in a lower tax bracket than when they were fully employed. Regular periodic payments are treated as earned income and are subject to a maximum tax, if appropriate, of 50%. But if a lump-sum payment is chosen, it is classified as preference income and can subject the recipient to a tax as high as 70% of that payment. In determining the amount of tax-reportable income, the annuitant first subtracts the amount of money personally deposited in that contract. Then the annuitant pays tax on the portion of the payment in excess of that amount.

### H2f. REGULATION OF VARIABLE ANNUITIES

As is the case with all insurance companies, those insurance companies selling annuities are registered with, and regulated by, the state insurance department of each state in which they do business. In addition, the individual agent must also be registered as a life insurance agent in each state in which annuity contracts will be sold. When variable annuities are to be marketed by the life insurance company and its agents, the registration and regulation function becomes a multi-responsibility because those annuity

[19]The IRS has ruled that the privilege of postponing tax liability does not apply to certain annuities. Investment contracts affected are those in which the insurance company permits policyholders to make purchase and sale decisions for securities in their personalized separate accounts. In those instances, the investor must pay taxes on income received into that account in the year in which it is received.

contracts are subject to SEC jurisdiction, too. The variable annuity represents an interest in a separate account of securities, and such interest is defined as a "security" under the law. Consequently, as a publicly owned security, it must be registered with the SEC under the Securities Act of 1933.

This registration of the annuity is preceded by registration with the SEC of the separate account itself. Because it offers accumulation and annuity units in a changing portfolio of securities, the separate account is an investment company as defined in the Investment Company Act of 1940. Thus, it must be registered pursuant to this act and classified as a unit investment trust.

The variable annuity sales arm of the life insurance company, making a continuous public offering of a registered security, must also register with the SEC. It meets the registration requirement contained in the Securities Exchange Act of 1934 and must qualify as a broker/dealer organization. It must meet the capital, filing, and reporting responsibilities associated with that form of registration. Once this is accomplished all of its sales agents must register, too, and must complete a qualifying written examination to prove their capabilities.

Moreover, because most insurance company annuity sales affiliates have elected to join the NASD, these persons are also subject to the associations' rules and standards for proper conduct. This means that the firm and its agents are subject to the terms of the NASD's Rules of Fair Practice, including the sections dealing with the terms and conditions for offering investment company shares.

## CONCLUDING COMMENTS

As you may have already concluded while studying this chapter, the topic of investment companies is detailed and complex. You may indeed buy into an investment company to avoid further specific decisions as to which underlying securities to buy and sell. "Let *them* worry about it," you may say. Yet, deciding which investment company is the appropriate one in the first place requires a solid knowledge and understanding of this topic.

Tax privileges and services of the various investment companies as well as prices, policies, and underlying portfolios must be carefully considered in advising people about this aspect of the securities industry. In addition, as the securities industry changes, new types of investment companies will probably be created so as to appeal to and attract investors. In any case, the notion that the "mutual funds" area requires little or no investment sophistication and knowledge is far from true.

# NYSE orders and round-lot stock executions

Most orders in NYSE listed stocks received by a member organization are executed on the trading floor of the New York Stock Exchange. Exceptions often occur when either

A.
what is traded on the nyse floor

1. the stock is listed on more than one registered exchange in the United States, and a member organization with comparable privileges elsewhere has chosen instead to execute the order on that exchange;

2. the stock is an inactively traded preferred issue or one of the few existing guaranteed equities;[1] appearing on a special list of stocks exempted from this requirement by the Exchange;

3. the quantity and/or terms of the order are such that the equilibrium between supply and demand would be dramatically upset and the NYSE has given its approval to execute it over the counter;

4. the customer is situated outside of the United States and wants to buy or sell that security before or after the normal hours of trading on the NYSE; or

5. after inquiry on the floor of the NYSE, the member firm finds the customer's interest can best be served by it acting *as agent* in an over-the-counter transaction.

Otherwise, orders to buy or sell listed stock are transmitted to the trading floor of the NYSE for execution by means of

1. telephone;
2. teletype; or
3. automated machinery approved by the NYSE and installed on the trading floor.

floor

The **floor** is actually comprised of four trading rooms (see Figure 1). Each of the areas is connected by short passageways on the same level, making it relatively easy for a member to walk from room to room to execute orders. The four trading rooms are as follows:

B.
the nyse facilities
*B1.*
*Trading Rooms and Assignments*

main room

1. The **main room** is where most of the listed stocks on the Exchange have been assigned trading privileges (see Figure 2).

garage

2. The **garage** is a nickname assigned to a smaller trading area positioned next to the main room. It was built to facilitate trading when space became a major consideration years ago.

blue room

3. The **blue room** is a nickname assigned to an even smaller trading area on the other side of the main room (see Figure 3). Opened in the late 1960s when the volume of activity necessitated further expansion of physical facilities, it is so named because of its colorful, attractive decor.

bond room

4. The **bond room** is a trading area beneath the main and blue rooms where debt issues listed on the Exchange have been assigned trading privileges (see Figure 4).

The assignment of trading privileges in any of these rooms is not related to the quality of a particular issue. The designation is made primarily because of space considerations, and reassignments do occur to meet changing conditions. Each of the rooms

[1] A stock whose dividend payments are assured by the promise of a corporation other than the issuer of that security.

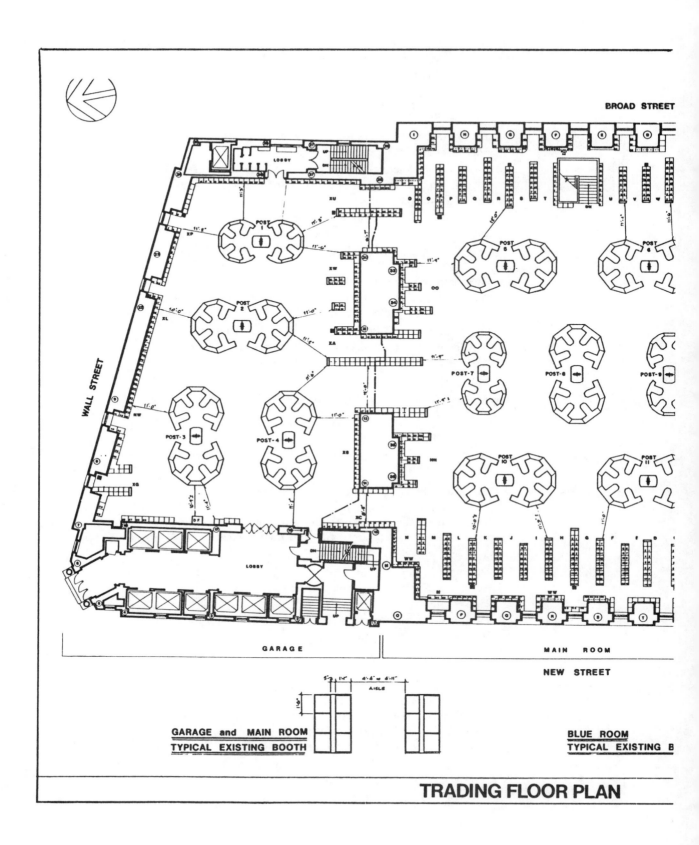

**FIGURE 1**
Floor Plan of the New York Stock Exchange, Inc.

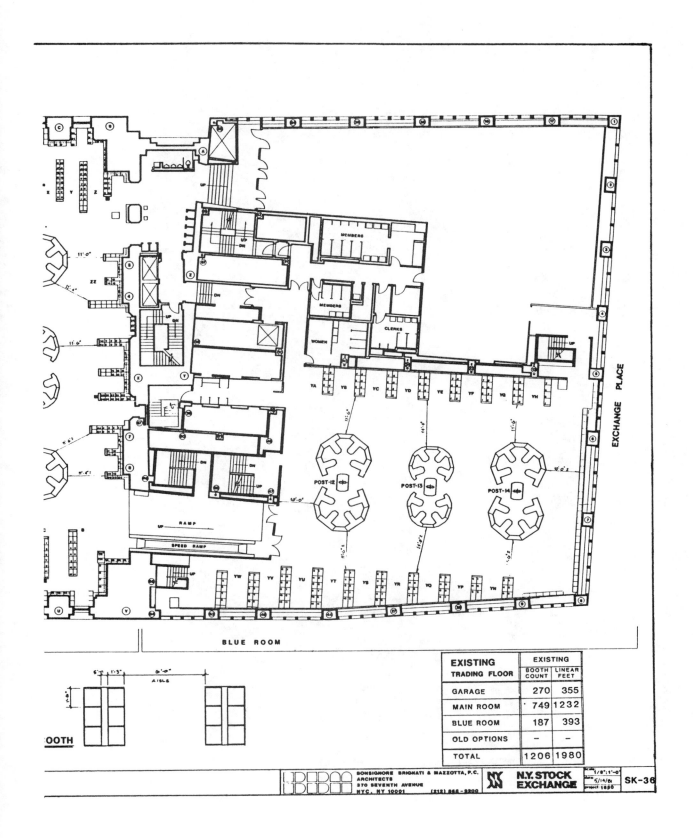

| EXISTING | EXISTING | |
| TRADING FLOOR | BOOTH COUNT | LINEAR FEET |
|---|---|---|
| GARAGE | 270 | 355 |
| MAIN ROOM | 749 | 1232 |
| BLUE ROOM | 187 | 393 |
| OLD OPTIONS | – | – |
| TOTAL | 1206 | 1980 |

BLUE ROOM

BOOTH

BONSIGNORE BRIGHATI & MAZZOTTA, P.C.
ARCHITECTS
370 SEVENTH AVENUE
NYC, NY 10001          (212) 868-8200

N.Y. STOCK EXCHANGE

Scale 1/8"=1'-0"
Date 5/14/81
project 1850

SK-36

**FIGURE 2**
Main Trading Room of the New York Stock Exchange (photograph courtesy of the New York Stock Exchange, Inc.)

**FIGURE 3**
Blue Room of the New York Stock Exchange (photograph courtesy of the
New York Stock Exchange, Inc.)

**FIGURE 4**
Bond Room of the New York Stock
Exchange (photograph courtesy of
the New York Stock Exchange, Inc.)

**FIGURE 5**
Trading Post on the Floor of the New
York Stock Exchange (photograph
courtesy of the New York Stock Exchange, Inc.)

enjoys comparable mechanical and electronic conveniences for use in the transaction of business on the floor.

**B2.**
*Trading Posts*

**trading posts**

> Transactions in the three rooms where listed stock activity occurs are consummated at specific locations known as **trading posts** (see Figure 5). With one exception, the 23 trading posts on the floor of the NYSE are 7-foot-high horseshoe-shaped structures with an outside circumference ranging from 31 to 76 feet, depending upon location.

**Post 30**

> The one exception is a large tablelike structure, located in a corner of the garage, identified as **Post 30** (see Figure 6). This trading post serves as the locale for transactions in most of the inactive preferred stocks listed on the NYSE. The unit of trading used for most stocks assigned to this post is 10 shares and multiples of 10 shares (20, 30, 40, and so forth), whereas at the other posts, stocks are typically traded in 100 share units and multiples of 100 shares (200, 300, and so forth). Some 10-share unit stocks are found at these other trading posts too, but they experience far more activity than those assigned to Post 30.

**B3.**
*"Telephone Booths"*

Ringing the perimeter of the trading rooms are booths or cubicles for use by the member organizations and from which they

1. receive orders transmitted from their offices;
2. distribute such orders to members of the stock exchange for execution; and
3. transmit back to their offices the details of executed orders and pertinent trading information.

Within the confines of existing space limitations, members may rent from the NYSE as many of these locations, strategically positioned in the various trading rooms, as they deem necessary to carry on their business. These areas are uniformly referred to as

**telephone booths**

**telephone booths**, even though the firm may use a teletype machine or another automated device for its purposes (see Figure 7).

The booths are staffed with clerks employed by the renting firm to ensure that

1. the orders received on the floor are in proper form for execution; and
2. they are disseminated to the appropriate stock exchange members for execution.

C.
order ticket information

Federal and NYSE regulations prescribe creation of an order ticket for each execution instruction entered on the trading floor of the Exchange. In fact, there is an order ticket prepared in the member firm's office by a sales person as well as one with the same instructions prepared for the Floor of the Exchange. Understandably, the information required for an order ticket written in the office of a member firm is more detailed than that prepared for execution purposes on the trading floor.

**round lot**

> The unit of trading in most stock, rights, or warrants traded on the NYSE is set at 100 shares by the Floor Department of the Exchange. This unit is known as a **round lot**. Because of their

**FIGURE 6**
Post 30 on the Floor of
the New York Stock
Exchange

**FIGURE 7**
A Typical Telephone Booth with Clerks Receiving Orders and Transmitting Reports (photograph courtesy of the New York Stock Exchange, Inc.)

> relative inactivity, some stock issues have been assigned trading units in lots of 10 shares. In these particular securities, this unit is considered a round lot. Orders for less than round lots (1–99 shares, rights, or warrants, or 1–9 shares, as the cases may be) are called **odd lots**. Because of differences in the way round lots are executed as compared with odd lots, an order for, say 225 shares, must be written on two separate instruction tickets, one for 200 shares and one for 25 shares.

**odd lots**

The unit of trading in most bonds is $1,000 face value, although some debt securities are issued and traded in minimum denominations of $5,000.

**C1.**
**Office Tickets**

Rule 17a–3 of the SEC requires noting on each order ticket

1. the date of receipt and effective lifetime (the time period during which the order instruction should be valid);
2. the time of entry (either transmitted to the floor or received from a customer);
3. the type of transaction, whether buy or sell (It is also necessary that sell orders be marked long or short. It cannot be assumed that a sale is long merely because most sales are of this nature. ''Long'' denotes that the seller owns that security and will deliver it promptly to complete the sale. ''Short'' indicates that the seller does not own that security or, if it is owned, will not deliver it to complete that transaction. In all cases of short sales, the certificate must be borrowed from someone to satisfy the requirement of that sale contract. In the case of a long sale by a customer of a stock exchange firm, it is necessary to note on the order ticket the location of the certificate at the time of execution and the means by which delivery of the security will be effected.);
4. the quantity of shares (or bonds);
5. the name or ticker symbol of the security;
6. the terms and conditions (type of order, description, tactics to be employed, and so forth);
7. the account number or name of the customer;[2]
8. any modification or cancellation of quantity, terms, or conditions;
9. the price(s) of execution; and
10. the time of execution or cancellation (to the extent feasible).

**C2.**
**Floor Tickets**

The NYSE requires members to preserve for at least 12 months each floor ticket, which must contain:

1. the date, time of receipt, and effective lifetime of the order;
2. the type of transaction (buy or sell; if sell, *long* or *short*);
3. the quantity of shares (or bonds);
4. the name or ticker symbol of the security;
5. the terms and conditions[3] (order type, tactics to be employed); and
6. the price(s) of execution.

---

[2]NYSE Rules 123 and 410 prohibit changing a customer account name after entry unless written approval is granted by a member, allied member, or authorized employee on the order ticket itself.

[3]An order entered on the floor of the Exchange without any terms or conditions is treated as a normal market order.

With few exceptions,[4] trading variations in each equity security listed on the NYSE are reflected in eighths of a dollar ($.125) or 12½¢). Stocks and warrants are always represented by valuations reflected in *dollars and cents,* so for these issues

```
⅛ point =  12½¢ per share
¼ point =  25¢ per share
⅜ point =  37½¢ per share
½ point =  50¢ per share
⅝ point =  62½¢ per share
¾ point =  75¢ per share
⅞ point =  87½¢ per share
1  point = $1.00 per share
```

Bonds, on the other hand, are generally reflected as *percentages of face value* ($1,000); so for most of those issues

```
⅛ point =  $1.25 per bond  (⅛% of $1000)
¼ point =  $2.50 per bond  (¼% of $1000)
⅜ point =  $3.75 per bond  (⅜% of $1000)
½ point =  $5.00 per bond  (½% of $1000)
⅝ point =  $6.25 per bond  (⅝% of $1000)
¾ point =  $7.50 per bond  (¾% of $1000)
⅞ point =  $8.75 per bond  (⅞% of $1000)
1  point = $10.00 per bond (1% of $1000)
```

7. the name(s) of contra broker/dealer(s);
8. the name of the member organization initiating this customer's order.[5]

If an order is cancelled prior to execution, a record of the cancellation notice indicating date and time of receipt must also be preserved for the 12-month period.

D.
types of orders

Bascially, only three types of orders are permissible for entry on the floor of the New York Stock Exchange. They are

1. market orders;
2. limit orders; and
3. stop orders.

These orders are sometimes qualified by additional instructions, but merely to adjust the tactics employed for execution. If such supplementary information is removed, what remains is a basic market, limit, or stop order, as the case may be.

D1.
*Market Orders*

**market order**

A **market order** is one in which the customer requests execution immediately at the best available price. Thus, a market order to buy stock requires purchase at the lowest offering price available at the time of entry. A market order to sell stock requires disposition at the highest bid price available at the time of entry.

**missing the market**

If a member fails to honor such instructions due to negligence, the member is guilty of **missing the market**. This oversight requires that the member promptly reimburse the customer for any loss resulting from this mistake. Missing the market cer-

[4]Exceptions are principally for subscription rights.

[5]Under certain circumstances, when the order is for an account in which the member or member organization has an interest, this too must be noted on the floor ticket.

tainly does not occur often, but it can happen if a member accidentally misplaces the order after receiving it from the telephone clerk or if the member foolishly accepts too many market orders in different securities at the same time. In the latter situation, if the member is executing an order at one end of the trading room, it is possible to miss the market in another order at the opposite end of the floor.

### D2. *Limit Orders*

A **limit order** is one in which customers set a maximum price they are willing to pay, as a buyer, or a minimum price they are willing to accept, as a seller. Under no circumstances may a member violate these instructions by paying more or selling for less than this price.

However, although the words may not necessarily appear on the order ticket, it is always understood that a price limitation includes an *"or better"* instruction.

Therefore, if a member can purchase the stock below the stated limit, or sell it for more than the specified price, as the case may be, the member must do so immediately! Failure to consummate an order that can be executed in accordance with the customer's terms and conditions holds an Exchange member financially responsible for missing the market. There is liability for missing the market just as there is liability for neglecting to obey instructions upon receipt of a market order.

**limit order**

### D3. *Stop Orders*

The term "stop order" is really a misnomer. In terms of status, a **stop order** is merely a *memorandum* that eventually becomes a market order, but only if someone else creates a transaction on the Exchange that equals or penetrates the price stated in this memorandum.

Stop orders may be used for a variety of reasons and may be entered as *buy-stop* or *sell-stop*, depending upon purpose.

**stop order**

### D3a. BUY-STOP ORDERS

A **buy-stop order** is entered with a memorandum price *above* present market levels because it is intended either to

1. curtail a loss on an existing short position;
2. preserve a profit on a short position previously established; or
3. purchase a security, but only if a transaction at the stated price level creates a technical buy signal.

**buy-stop order**

Assume that speculator Joe Smith sells a stock short (that is, stock he doesn't own) at 35 anticipating a decline in value. He can suffer a substantial loss if the price rises contrary to his expectation. To protect himself against the possibility of unlimited loss, he can enter a buy-stop order at 40 (or some other price level above the present 35). Then, if the price rises to 40 or above,[6] his memorandum becomes a market order, and he purchases the stock immediately at the best available price. This will

---

[6]Instead of trading exactly at 40, a price gap may occur; such penetration also activates the stop order (that is, 40⅛, 40¼, and so forth).

1. close out the short position; and
2. curtail his loss at *about $500* plus commissions and transfer tax expenses ($4,000 purchase *cost* − $3,500 sale *proceeds*).

It is impossible to determine the exact loss until the purchase is effected because the best available price is unknown until the stop order is activated to become a market order.

If speculator Mary Brown sells a stock short at 46 and sees it decline to 38, as she anticipated, she will have a profit of approximately $800 after purchasing stock to close out her position. But the price might decline even further if she is patient. Then again, it might move up to 46 or even higher, eliminating what paper profits she now enjoys at 38. To protect this profit, Mary Brown, instead of purchasing stock at 38, can enter a buy-stop order at 41 (or some other price level above the present 38). Then, if the price of the security continues to decline, her short position will profit further. But if it rises to 41,[7] the memorandum becomes a market order and stock is purchased immediately at the best available price. This transaction

1. closes out the short position; and
2. establishes a profit of *about $500* less commissions and transfer tax expenses ($4,600 sale *proceeds* − $4,100 *purchase cost*).

Once again, the exact profit cannot be calculated until the actual purchase price is determined.

For our final example, suppose that Ralph Babcock a *technician* (someone who plots prices of securities on charts or watches price fluctuations without regard to underlying corporate fundamentals), observes over a period of time that a particular stock has fluctuated between 71 and 74. He might be inclined to enter a buy-stop order at 74½ or thereabouts. He believes that if and when this apparent accumulation of shares by "informed sources" is completed, the price will move up through the 74 level and may rise to 80, 90, 100, or even higher. Therefore, he wants to purchase that stock, but *only* if it does move convincingly above that 74 level. As a knowledgeable technician, Ralph Babcock also realizes that instead of *accumulation*, the minimal fluctuation thus far may be reflecting *distribution*. If that is the case, the price may never move above 74 and may even soon drop below 71. Why should he waste his capital by acquiring stock somewhere between 71 and 74 under those circumstances? If it eventually trades at 74½ or above, the technician then establishes a long position. If it never trades up to that level, no purchase takes place.

### SELL-STOP ORDERS

D3b.

**sell-stop order** | A **sell-stop order** is entered with a memorandum price *below* present market levels because it is intended either to

1. curtail a loss on a present stock holding;

---

[7]Instead of trading exactly at 41, a price gap may occur; such penetration also activates the stop order (that is, 40⅞, 41⅛, and so forth).

> **2.** preserve a profit for stock previously purchased at lower prices; or
>
> **3.** dispose of the stated security via a short sale, but only if a transaction at that price creates a technical sell signal.

If, for example, investor Andrea Morse buys a stock at 15, anticipating growth in value, she can suffer a loss of capital if the price declines contrary to her expectations. To combat this possibility, investor Morse can enter a sell-stop order at 13 (or at some other price below the present 15). If the price rises or stays above 13, her position is maintained without further action required. But if the price of that security declines to 13 or below,[8] her memorandum becomes a market order and her stock is sold immediately at the best available price. This will

1. liquidate her position; and
2. curtail her loss at at *about $200* plus commissions and transfer tax expenses ($1,500 purchase *cost* − $1,300 sale *proceeds*).

The exact loss cannot be determined until the stock has actually been sold at the best available price.

If investor Ben Russet purchases a stock at 54 and watches it appreciate to 65, he will no doubt be elated. As it continues to move higher, he will certainly want to hold that security. But if it begins to decline, the paper profit will soon dissipate. A sharp decline might eventually result in a loss. Many people, unable to follow the intra-day fluctuation of stocks closely, might be inclined to enter a sell-stop order. Investor Russet can enter a sell-stop order at 60 (or some price below the present 65) and attempt to preserve most of his paper profit in case there is a violent price decline. If the price falls to 60 or below,[9] his memorandum is activated, making it a market order to sell at the best available price. This will

1. liquidate his position; and
2. officially establish his profit at *about $600*, less commissions and transfer tax expenses ($6,000 sale *proceeds* − $5,400 purchase *cost*).

The exact profit can be determined only when the actual sale is effected.

As a final illustration of the use of the sell-stop order, suppose that a technician, Bess Rinni, observes that a stock price is experiencing a great deal of difficulty in moving above 50. Apparently there are sufficient sellers available to satisfy all purchase orders. Therefore, she reasons, when buying interest peters out, the path of least resistance will lead downward. To take advantage of this movement *if and when it happens*, she enters a sell-short-stop order at 48 (or at some price level below the present 50).

---

[8]Instead of trading exactly at 13, a price gap may occur; penetration will also activate the stop order (that is, 13¼, 13⅛, 12⅞, and so forth).

[9]Instead of trading exactly at 60, a price gap may occur; such penetration will also activate the stop order (that is, 60⅛, 59⅞, and so forth).

Should that stock decline to 48 or below,[10] her memorandum is activated, directing a short sale at the first practicable opportunity, in accordance with federal regulations governing such sales. If the stock doesn't decline to that price, technician Rinni has lost nothing but time. In fact, she may have saved considerable loss by not selling short at 50 should the stock move up above that level thereafter.

### RISKS INCURRED WITH STOP ORDERS

D3c.

On the NYSE, there are several important elements of risk that should not be ignored in considering the use of stop orders. First, there is no assurance that the price of execution will resemble the price appearing on the memorandum. As it has happened with issues that fluctuate in a volatile fashion, the best available price following activation of the stop order may be several points away from the memorandum price. Consequently, the original intention to curtail a loss or preserve a profit may be defeated upon execution of that order.

**stop-limit order**

Such surprises may be avoided if a **stop-limit order** is entered instead of the normal stop order. This is a memorandum that becomes a limit order (as opposed to a market order) immediately after a transaction takes place at or through the indicated stop price. For example, suppose a customer gives you an instruction to sell long 100 XYZ at 31 stop-limit. If and when a round-lot sale takes place at 31 or below, this memorandum then becomes a limit order to sell long 100 shares at 31 or above (never below 31). The normal stop order would have become a market order and thus would have been executed immediately at the best price available—that is, at 31, higher, lower, or, in other words, at the best existing bid. But, the stop-limit order might never be executed after the stop portion has been activated because it must wait for someone to accept the minimum offering price stipulated by the customer. The risk associated with entry of any limit order is that it might never be executed! Customers entering them generally play a patient and passive role, awaiting acceptance of their price by a contra party. Market orders, on the other hand, are aggressive and must be satisfied immediately without regard to a specific price.

Although stop orders are acceptable instructions on all stock exchanges in the United States, the American Stock Exchange, in particular, requires round-lot stop orders entered there to be stop-limit exclusively. Fearful of the volatile conditions that can result from concurrent election of many stop orders in thinly capitalized stocks, the AMEX bans entry of this order variety unless it becomes the more passive limit-order type when activated. Moreover, the limit price must be identical to the memorandum price. Thus, a customer may not enter an order such as "buy 100 XYZ at 41 stop, limit 45" as a means of circumventing the AMEX's restriction. A limit price so far removed from the memorandum level is tantamount to a market order which is aggressive. The requirement for stop-limit instructions does not extend to odd-lot orders entered on the AMEX. Customers may

---

[10]Instead of trading exactly at 48, a price gap may occur; such penetration will also activate the stop order (that is, 48⅛, 47⅞, and so forth).

enter normal stop orders or stop-limit orders in odd-lot quantities, whichever suits their preference.

The second risk involved with entry of stop orders relates to the responsibilities of stock exchange specialists. The specialist is an individual appointed by an exchange to provide and promote a fair and orderly market in specific stocks. If an unusual concentration of stop orders is observed to be accumulating in those stocks, the specialist may, with approval from an official of the exchange, cancel all existing stop orders and prohibit entry of any new ones. This action is taken because

1. execution of one stop order can start a chain reaction of executions for other stop orders, thereby creating an accelerated violent price movement; or
2. execution of any order at a particular price may suddenly create market orders for many thousands of shares, thereby upsetting supply/demand equilibrium, leading to a disorderly market.

A hazard accompanying these situations exists when customers who have entered stop orders are not aware that the orders were cancelled.[11] The customers believe that their "protection" remains effective when, in fact, it does not. Subsequently, if the market price penetrates their memorandum prices, customers often cannot understand why their stop orders were not executed.

**D4.**
**The Investor's Viewpoint**

For a better understanding of the uses of market orders, limit orders, and stop orders, let us now examine these three types from the viewpoints of a prospective purchaser and a prospective seller.

**D4a.    THE PROSPECTIVE PURCHASER OF STOCK**

You ordinarily are a prospective buyer of a particular stock if you

1. believe that issue has potential for near-term or long-term growth in value; or
2. think an investment in that stock provides an attractive rate of return in the form of dividend income; or
3. have previously sold it without owning it (a short sale) and are now inclined to "cover," or eliminate, that liability by acquiring that stock in the marketplace.

If you are anxious to buy this stock at present price levels, enter a market order. The stock will be purchased immediately at the best offering price available from a seller of that issue.

If you are interested in buying the stock, but only at a price *below* the level at which the issue is now trading, enter a limit order. Specify the maximum price you want to pay if values ever decline far enough. If ever your bid becomes the highest bid, you will buy the stock from a seller anxious to dispose of it at that level.

On the other hand, you may already have a position in that stock, albeit a *short position*. Now you want to

---

[11]This information is printed on the ticker tape, reported to the major news services, and circulated to each member organization by special notice.

1. protect yourself against an unlimited loss if the price should rise above the level at which the short sale was executed; or

2. realize a profit if the value of the stock begins to rise after declining below your short sale price.

As a person with a short position, you may enter a stop order to buy at a price above the current market level. Although it is true that you can buy stock now at a cheaper price, that is not your present intention. You believe the stock will decline below the current level, and you simply want to use the stop order as "insurance" in case you are wrong. If you are wrong and the price moves up to, or through, the memorandum price specified in the stop order, the stock will be purchased at that time as if it were a market order. This purchase will eliminate your short position.

Of course, if you are fearful of market orders in a rising market, you could sacrifice your protection somewhat by entering a stop-limit order to buy. Once the stop portion of the order is elected, your instruction becomes a limit order to buy that stock. You must then take your chances that an anxious seller will appear and satisfy your bid before the price continues moving higher in its upward trend. If the latter situation occurs, your limit order to buy might never be executed.

### THE PROSPECTIVE SELLER OF STOCK                                        D4b.

You ordinarily are a prospective seller of a particular stock if you own it and

1. believe the issue has exhausted its potential for near-term or long-term growth in value; or

2. think an investment in that stock no longer provides an attractive rate of return in terms of dividend income (in comparison with other investments); or

3. need the money for other investments or for a financial emergency; or

4. realize that your inability to follow the daily price fluctuations of that stock could be costly (if the stock declined below a predetermined level).

You are also a prospective seller if you believe that the price of the stock will decline, even if you do not own the stock. You can act on your expectation about the stock's price by becoming a short seller—that is, you sell something you do not own.

If you are anxious to sell stock you own at present price levels and do not want to risk missing the market, enter a market order. Your stock will then be sold immediately to the party with the highest prevailing bid price.

If you are interested in selling the stock, but only at a price *above* the level at which the issue is now trading, enter a limit order. Specify the minimum price acceptable to you if values ever rise high enough. If ever your offering becomes the lowest prevailing offering, you will sell your stock to a buyer anxious to acquire it at that price level.

On the other hand, you may own that stock and recognize that should it decline below a certain level, contrary to your expectations, it could

1. sharply reduce or even eliminate a paper profit you have patiently accumulated; or
2. expose your capital to the potential of greater loss than that represented at this lower-than-cost-price plateau.

If so, enter a sell-stop order at a price *below* the current market. Although it is true that you can sell your stock now at a better price, that is not your present intention. You sincerely believe the stock will rise above this level, not decline. You simply are using the stop order as "insurance" in case you are wrong. If you are wrong and the price does fall to, or through, the memorandum price specified in the stop order, your stock will be sold at that time as if it were a market order.

If you are a person fearful of market orders in a falling stock market, you could sacrifice your protection somewhat by entering a stop-limit order to sell. Once the stop portion of the order is elected, your instruction becomes a limit order to sell that stock. You must then take your chances that a buyer will appear and satisfy your offering before the price continues moving lower in its downward trend. If these conditions are not fulfilled, of course, your limit order to sell will not be executed.

As a short seller, playing a role as speculator or opportunist, you can also enter market, limit, or stop orders to accommodate your belief in the imminent decline of a particular stock's price. The only difference in treatment for your short orders (as compared with your "long" orders) is that short orders are prohibited from depressing the price of the stock in the execution process. The self-serving benefit realized in forcing the price to decline with your own short sale is unfair and is considered manipulative by the SEC.

### E.
### order qualification

Each of the three types of orders may be supplemented with instructions that can affect tactics and/or time of execution of that order. It is important that you understand these qualifications not only to serve your customer effectively but, in some cases, to protect your firm from financial liability.

### E1.
### *Effective Lifetime*

Only two time qualifications are permitted for orders entered with brokers and specialists on the NYSE trading floor.

### E1a. *DAY ORDERS*

A **day order** is one that remains valid only for the remainder of the trading day on which it is entered. Unless specified to the contrary, all orders are automatically regarded as day orders.

**day order**

### E1b. *GOOD-TIL-CANCELLED ORDERS (GTC)*

A **good-til-cancelled order (GTC)** is one that remains valid *indefinitely*, until executed or cancelled. It is also referred to as an **open order**, a name that reflects the permanency of its status. A day order changed to an open order or an open order changed to a day order loses any time priority it may have enjoyed in the specialist's book until then. Such changes require that the order be treated as a brand new instruction to buy or sell.

Most brokerage firms accommodate the preferences of some

**good-til-cancelled order (GTC)**
**open order**

> customers and accept orders good-through-the-week, good-through-the-month, or good-through-a-specific-day. Because those unique qualifications may not be entered on the NYSE trading floor, they must be entered as GTC instead. The member firm assumes responsibility for cancelling that order if it cannot be executed by the close of business on the specified date. If it fails to do so, it must also accept the financial liability associated with its error.

*Lifetime of GTC orders*  The period designated by the term *indefinitely* can be an awfully long time. Techical adjustments are often implemented during this waiting period. To ensure the continued accuracy and validity of such orders on the records of each member organization, the NYSE requires these firms to compare and confirm their open orders with the specialist who holds them in the interim. Every 6 months or so, on a day determined by the Exchange, each member organization reenters its open orders under terms and conditions as they know them, resolving any differences before trading resumes the following day.

*E1b(1).*

> *Reducing prices on stocks ex dividend*  One reason for potential differences is a mandatory price reduction for certain orders on the day that a stock first begins trading without the value of a pending dividend. Prior to the opening of trading activity on such an ex-dividend date, the following orders must have their price reduced:
>
> 1. limit orders to buy
> 2. stop orders to sell

*E1b(2).*

In other words, affected by this rule are those orders originally entered at a price *below* the then prevailing market. For example, an open order to buy 100 shares at a limit of 12 when the stock is trading at 14 will be reduced. So, too, will an open order to sell 100 shares at 12 *stop*. The rationale behind this requirement is based upon the fact there is usually about a 1-month gap between the date the corporation closes its books to identify the recipients of that dividend and the date the dividend is actually distributed. During that interim period, it is unfair to oblige prospective purchasers to pay the same value for stock as before because the corporation will soon distribute a portion of its assets to other people, the former shareholders. After all, when those purchasers originally made their investment judgment, it was predicated on a company whose assets included that distribution.

The logic behind the reduction of sell-stop orders is twofold. First, persons entering such orders are already shareholders and will therefore get that dividend from the company. Second, unless that memorandum level is lowered, sell-stop orders may be elected needlessly as a result of the automatic reduction in market value. This, in turn, negates the original intent behind entry of such orders. These customers want to sell only if supply-and-demand relationships necessitate it. They do not want to sell as a consequence of dividend distributions in which they will share anyway.

> The price on pertinent orders is reduced by the *exact value* of a forthcoming cash distribution unless

1. the order is marked *do not reduce* (DNR);[12] or
2. the value is not precisely divisible by the trading variation assigned to that security by the Exchange.

Ordinarily, that trading variation is ⅛ (12½¢). Thus, if a cash distribution is made that is valued at 25¢ per share, the price for appropriate orders is lowered by ¼, a 37½¢ distribution by ⅜, a 50¢ distribution by ½, and so forth. However, if the distribution is not precisely divisible by ⅛, the price for appropriate orders must be reduced by the *next highest* ⅛. Therefore, a 26¢ distribution requires a price reduction of ⅜, a 51¢ distribution ⅝, a $1.20 distribution 1¼, and so forth.

*E1b(3).* ***Adjusting prices on stocks with forthcoming stock dividends*** Forthcoming distributions of stock, such as stock dividends and stock splits, are treated in a different fashion, and the New York Stock Exchange and the American Stock Exchange each have their own practices regarding such distributions. In the case of a stock dividend or other stock distributions, NYSE limit orders to buy and stop orders to sell are adjusted on the ex-dividend (also called ex-distribution) date to more accurately reflect the customer's intention. That is, the prices of those appropriate GTC orders are always reduced, whereas the number of shares involved may be increased so as to maintain the same proportional transaction interest. For example, if a customer had entered an open order to buy 100 shares of IBM at 270 just before it announced a 2-for-1 split (two new shares for each old share held), on the ex-distribution date the order will be adjusted as an order to buy 200 shares of IBM at 135. Because the customer's order indicated a desire to purchase $27,000 worth of IBM, after modification the customer's interest is maintained at the $27,000 level (200 × $135).

On the AMEX, *all* limit and stop orders have their prices reduced on the ex-distribution date, not just the buy-limit and sell-stop orders.

*E1b(4).* ***Calculating price adjustments for stock dividends*** Price adjustments to NYSE or AMEX good-til-cancelled orders are made by dividing the price of the original order by 100% plus the percentage value of the stock dividend or stock distribution. For instance, in the case of a 50% stock dividend, an open limit order to buy 100 shares at 42 will be reduced in price to 28 (42 ÷ 150%) on the ex-dividend date. If the calculation results in a price and fraction not divisible by ⅛ (the usual variation on the NYSE and AMEX), the fraction is reduced to the next lower variation.

**example**

Stock price adjustments based on a 3% stock dividend

| OLD PRICE | CALCULATED VALUE | | NEW PRICE AT NEXT LOWER VARIATION |
|---|---|---|---|
| 12 | 11.65 (12 | 103%) | 11⅝ |
| 23½ | 22.815 (23.50 ÷ 103%) | | 22¾ |
| 67⅞ | 65.895 (67.875 103%) | | 65⅞ |
| 87¾ | 85.19 (87.75 103%) | | 85⅛ |

[12]Some investors are not concerned with the dissipation of assets brought about by dividend payments and are interested only in buying (or selling) at their predetermined price.

*Calculating share adjustments for stock dividends or splits*     Share adjustments to GTC orders on the NYSE conform to the following rules:

**E1b(5).**

1. When a stock dividend or stock split results in *one or more full shares for each share held*, the appropriate order quantities are increased according to the exact percentage distribution. Thus, in the case of a 2-for-1 split, or 100% stock dividend, a 100-share GTC order is increased by 100% to 200 shares.

2. When a stock dividend or stock split results in *less than 100 shares for each round lot held*, the appropriate order quantities are increased but only up to the lowest full round lot. Odd lots are never tacked on to open orders when making a share adjustment. The calculation formula is:

old shares in the open order $\times$ the decimalized percentage stock distribution $=$ new shares to be added to order (but only round lots)

Thus, with a 3-for-2 split, or 50% stock dividend, a 100-share order remains unchanged, whereas a 200-share order is increased to 300 shares.

3. When a stock dividend or stock split results in *one or more round lots plus an odd lot for each round lot held*, the appropriate order quantities are increased, but only up to the lowest full round lot. Odd lots are never tacked on to open orders when making a share adjustment. The calculation formula is:

old shares in the open order $\times$ the decimalized percentage stock distribution $=$ new shares to be added to order (but only round lots)

Thus, in the case of a 6-for-5 split, or 20% stock dividend, a 300-share order remains unchanged, whereas a 600 share order is increased to 700 shares.

It is important to note that share adjustment rules do not pertain to AMEX open orders. American Stock Exchange GTC orders never have their share quantities increased. Order quantities remain the same, although price adjustments are always effected for stock distributions.

In the event the customer does not want the order automatically adjusted on the "ex" date, the order must be entered DNR (do not reduce). If the price is to be reduced but no adjustment is to be made to the quantity of a NYSE order, the customer must specify DNI (do not increase). A sample order guide for handling stock distribution on the NYSE is given in Table 1.

**TABLE 1**

| DISTRIBUTION | PRICE OF ORDER DIVIDED BY | ORDER QUANTITIES AND ADJUSTMENTS | | | |
|---|---|---|---|---|---|
| | | 100 SHARES | 300 SHARES | 500 SHARES | 1000 SHARES |
| 5 for 4 | 125% | 100 | 300 | 600 | 1,200 |
| 4 for 3 | 133$\frac{1}{3}$% | 100 | 400 | 600 | 1,300 |
| 3 for 2 | 150% | 100 | 400 | 700 | 1,500 |
| 5 for 3 | 166$\frac{2}{3}$% | 100 | 500 | 800 | 1,600 |
| 2 for 1 | 200% | 200 | 600 | 1,000 | 2,000 |
| 5 for 2 | 250% | 200 | 700 | 1,200 | 2,500 |
| 3 for 1 | 300% | 300 | 900 | 1,500 | 3,000 |
| 4 for 1 | 400% | 400 | 1,200 | 2,000 | 4,000 |

**E2.**
**Not Held (NH)**

In any reverse split (that is, 1 for 2, 1 for 3, and so forth) all GTC orders, including all limit and stop orders, are cancelled!

This instruction, when specifically stated by a customer, permits a member to use personal judgment in determining when to execute that order. Ordinarily, stock exchange members are prohibited from exercising any discretionary authority in a customer transaction. However, under these specific circumstances some leeway is allowed, and the member may decide upon

1. the price of execution, and/or
2. the time of execution

without violating the spirit or purpose of the regulation. In submitting this instruction with the order, a customer literally agrees not to hold the exchange member financially responsibile for missing the market if his or her judgment proves to be faulty. Under no circumstances may a specialist ever accept such instructions from a customer. The specialist's vantage point in the marketplace makes this form of discretion prone to claims of partiality by competitors or other public investors.

**E3.**
**Participate but Do Not Initiate (PNI)**

This instruction can be given by customers who want to enter substantial orders but who do not want to become aggressive and upset existing price equilibrium in the marketplace. It is therefore recognized as a variation of the not-held qualification with an added requirement for the executing member to avoid causing volatility. The member may buy or sell (as the case may be) so long as such activity does *not*

1. create a new price; or
2. satisfy available quantities to such an extent that a minimal order from another broker would set a new price.

The customer must realize that a few transactions may be missed in the process, but the *overall* average execution price upon completion of the order will be favorable.

**E4.**
**All or None (AON)**

All all-or-none qualification may be given by customers intent upon purchase (or sale) of *more* than one round lot (100 shares), but who stipulate that *all must be executed at the same time*. A member acting in behalf of this customer is prohibited from announcing this qualification *orally* in the trading area. In fact, an all-or-none specification requires use of a unique strategy to execute the order if at all possible.

Without revealing the terms or conditions of this customer's order, the member must inquire about the *quotation and size* for that stock. This means that the member requests information about the prevailing highest bid and lowest offering prices (quotation) as well as the number of shares wanted and offered at those respective levels (size). If the prevailing price is unsatisfactory or the size insufficient to accommodate the customer's instruction to execute at one time, the member stands by silently, doing nothing. The member has no status in the trading area. Market conditions must be watched carefully until both price and quantity available can completely satisfy that order. If it happens, *then*, and only then, does the member act to execute this order. While the member is waiting, that stock may trade at fluctuating prices and in various quantities because, after all, the Exchange is a continuous auction marketplace. This member cannot participate until, and if, that stock becomes available in sufficient quantity and at the proper price(s) to satisfy the terms of the customer's instructions. It may take all day to do it, or it may never happen at all.

This qualification is a variation of the all-or-none instruction except that it necessitates *immediate* execution or cancellation of the order. A fill-or-kill order also requires a *complete execution*, although not necessarily at one price.[13] It does not permit the stock exchange member to wait until it is possible to execute this order if it cannot be done promptly. When entering the trading area, the member simply requests a quotation and size. If the existing market precludes immediate satisfaction of the entire order, the member leaves the area and reports to the customer that nothing was done and the order is thereby cancelled.

*E5.*
*Fill or Kill (FOK)*

**immediate or cancel**

A qualification for **immediate or cancel** is a hybrid between the all-or-none and the fill-or-kill instructions. A customer entering this order wants the order executed promptly in accordance with quantity and price conditions specified but will accept consummation of *any portion* of the order, cancelling the unfilled balance *immediately*. Thus, this instruction gives the stock exchange member an opportunity to participate verbally in the trading area, albeit for a limited time period. The member can make the bid (or offering), and

*E6.*
*Immediate or Cancel (IOC)*

1. if someone promptly responds but only partially fills this order, the member accepts, cancels the unsatisfied portion of the bid (offer), withdraws from the trading area, and reports partial success to the customer; or
2. if no one promptly responds, the member merely withdraws the bid (offer), retires from the trading area, and reports to the customer that the order has been cancelled.

*E7.*
*Fractional Discretion*

**fractional point discretion**

Some limit orders are occasionally entered by customers at specific prices but with an ⅛ or ¼ **fractional point discretion** to be used by the broker if necessary for consummation of the order (such as, buy 100 V at 74¾ plus ¼ discretion, or sell 100 Q at 10 less ⅛ discretion).

These orders are always accepted on the floor of the exchange, but only at the maximum price permissible for buy orders and the minimum price permissible for sell orders. The V buy order mentioned above would be entered at 75 or better, while the Q sell order would be entered at 9⅞ or better. This type of discretion does not absolve a broker from financial responsibility for choosing *not* to utilize this leeway and, as a result, missing the market.

*E8.*
*Scale Orders*

Because of uncertainty caused by fluctuation in some volatile issues, customers intent upon accumulating (or distributing) a

[13]If an order was entered to buy 1,000 at 36 FOK, the customer would surely be satisfied to buy 400 at 35⅞ and 600 at 36 immediately.

security in volume may enter a series of limit orders at prices **scaled**

1. **down** from the value at which the initial *purchase* is contemplated (for example, a customer places a scale order to buy 100 XX at 49, scaled down 1 point for a total of 400 shares. This means that 100 shares are to be bought at 49, 100 at 48, 100 at 47, and 100 at 46[14];

2. **up** from the value at which the initial *sale* is contemplated (for example, a customer places a scale order to sell 100 at 37½, scaled up ¼ point for a total of 600 shares. This means that 100 shares are to be sold at 37½, 100 at 37¾, 100 at 38, 100 at 38¼, 100 at 38½, and 100 at 38¾.[15]

**scaled down**

**scaled up**

The principal advantage of these orders is the creation of an *average* transaction price that may prove more favorable than a single execution. The principal disadvantage is that the entire order may never be executed unless the stock fluctuates in a wide enough price range.

## E9. Cancellation

Although a **cancellation** is not really a type of order or even a qualification for execution of an order, its role can significantly influence trading activities on the floor of the exchange.

**cancellation**

Officially, prior to an actual execution of the transaction, a person entering an order on the New York or American Stock Exchange is privileged to change any of the terms or conditions of that order. That person can direct the broker to modify or negate any previous instructions and may, in fact, terminate the entire order itself.

After execution, cancellation of a transaction requires approval (and such approval is hard to get) from

1. the other party to that trade; and
2. a floor official (a member of the Exchange appointed by the Chairman of the Board of Directors to represent and assist the Exchange in the equitable conduct of business on the trading floor).

## E10. At the Close

For tactical or other reasons, a customer can request that an order be executed at the end of a particular day. This instruction necessitates processing as an ordinary market order, but only at the time a bell begins ringing to signal the end of trading that day. The bell is rung for 30 seconds, and within that time frame a member with an **at-the-close-order** completes the transaction at the best available price. There is no assurance that this will be the final trade in that security. Another member, perhaps with a similar instruction, may be more fortunate with his or her timing within those thirty seconds.

**at-the-close order**

## E11. At the Opening (Opening Only)

This qualification for a market or a limit order necessitates execution on the initial transaction for the stated security that day or the order is automatically cancelled. Obviously then, it must be en-

---

[14]With entry of any limit order, it is assumed that the price is *or better*, and thus the execution price could be more favorable than the specified limit.

[15]With entry of any limit order, it is assumed that the price is *or better*, and thus the execution price could be more favorable than the specified limit.

tered prior to the first transaction for that stock, although not necessarily prior to the opening of the NYSE at 10:00 A.M., New York City time. For one reason or another, a stock may not *open* until later in the day, if at all.

**alternative order**

*E12.*
*Alternative Order (Either/Or)*

An **alternative order** is used by a customer who is wary of price movements in a particular issue and is interested in protecting an interest or position if the issue fluctuates in an unexpected fashion. It involves entry of a limit order *and* a stop order on the same ticket for the same security at different prices.

The execution of *either* of these orders causes cancellation of the other. For example, with a stock trading at 24, a customer can enter an order to either *buy at 23 or 25 stop*. If the price drops down to 23, the limit order is executed and the stop order cancelled. But if the price moves up to 25 (or above), the stop order is elected, causing purchase at the best available price, and the limit order to buy at 23 is cancelled. If there is a partial execution of one of these orders for a multiple number of round lots, an identical quantity is automatically cancelled in the other order.

Similarly, if an investor owns XYZ Corporation stock presently trading at 46 and is interested in selling it at a slightly higher price, the following order can be entered: Sell long 100 XYZ at 50 *or* 43 stop. If the price moves up to 50, the limit order is executed and the stop order cancelled. However, if the price drops instead to 43 (or below), the stop order is elected, causing sale at the best available price and cancellation of the limit order to sell at 50. Thus, the holder is automatically able to salvage some proceeds when the market acts contrary to expectations.

*E13.*
*Sell Plus*

This instruction requests a member to dispose of the security via market or limit order, as the case may be, but at a price *higher* than the *previous different priced* transaction for that stock.

**example**

| Previous different price | Sale at this price qualifies |
|---|---|
| 75 | 75⅛ |

*E14.*
*Buy Minus*

This instruction requests a member to purchase a security via market or limit order, as the case may be, but at a price *lower* than the *previous different priced* transaction for that stock.

**example**

| Previous different price | Sale at this price qualifies |
|---|---|
| 45 | 44⅞ |

*E15.*
*Switch Order (Contingent or Swap Order)*

This order involves entry of a limit order to *sell* (buy) one stock, and when executed, entry of a limit or market order to *buy* (sell) another stock.

These orders might be worded, for example: "Sell long 100 OPQ Corporation at 41½ and when sold, buy 100 VBJ Corporation at 38⅞," or "Buy 100 KOK Corporation at 10⅛ and when bought, sell long 100 UVW Corporation at the market."

Some switch-order instructions are so sophisticated that they require purchase and sale of the security only if the swap can be executed with at least a three-point difference (or some other designated figure) between the transaction prices. No limit prices are actually specified, only the extent of a transaction price spread.

Now that we have examined the format and technicalities of orders, we shall proceed to a treatment of the mechanics of executing these orders.

## F.
## classification of NYSE members

When an order is transmitted to the floor of the Exchange, a telephone clerk examines it to see if it

1. is in the proper format prescribed by the Exchange; and
2. contains all the essential information.

The clerk must then give this order to a member of the stock exchange for execution. Only members are permitted to transact business on the floor of the Exchange. But to which member does the clerk give the order?

New York Stock Exchange members are often classified and identified by the activities in which they engage on the trading floor. However, they are not restricted to specific functions, and we frequently find many members participating in several different activities during a typical working day.

### F1.
### The Commission House Broker

Members executing orders in behalf of their own organizations and its customers are known as **commission house brokers**. Whether the firm's principals include as many as 23 members of the Exchange, such as Merrill Lynch, Pierce, Fenner & Smith Inc. (the largest member organization), or as few as one seat-holder, the minimum qualification for a member firm, there is usually a time each day when a commission house broker is unable to handle the volume of orders received. Two orders received at the same time in different securities can be enough to create a problem. If a member tries to execute both, the member may *miss the market* in one of those issues. To avoid this risk, members use the services of a two-dollar broker.

**commission house brokers**

### F2.
### The Two-Dollar broker

Members standing ready, willing, and able to execute orders in any security for any organization, are called **two-dollar brokers**. The origin of that title dates back many years when freelance activity earned these members a flat $2 for each 100 share order executed. Now two-dollar brokers receive a fee, known as **floor brokerage**, that is fully negotiated according to execution difficulty and often by the price of the security.

**two-dollar brokers**

**floor brokerage**

Some members earn their livelihood acting as independent brokers executing orders for firms in need of assistance any time during the trading day. Commission house brokers with available time can also accommodate other member firms by executing some of their orders and charging them floor brokerage for this service. Thus, when one of Bache Halsey Stuart Shields members executes an order for Bache Halsey Stuart Shields Inc., that person is acting as their commission house broker. But, if this member were to execute an order for Josephthal & Co. during the day, Josephthal classifies that person as a two-dollar broker and the fee charged would be earned in behalf of Bache Halsey Stuart Shields Inc.

**specialists**

Members appointed by the Board of Directors of the NYSE to maintain an orderly succession of prices in selected stocks are identified as **specialists**. Much of the marketability enjoyed by listed stocks today can be traced to the activities of specialists. Although specialists do not personally participate in every transaction, they do supervise and facilitate executions of orders by all brokers in the trading post area. How they satisfy their responsibilities is the subject of another part of this text.

**traders**

Members who buy and sell stock for a personal account and risk are known as **competitive traders.** They are registered with the exchange to act in this manner and must meet certain financial, trading, and reporting requirements. Restrictive regulations have been formulated to prevent competitive traders from conflicting with transactions initiated by customers of member organizations. In complying with the rules and attempting to buy and sell profitably, competitive traders frequently assist specialists in providing liquidity for listed stocks. They often satisfy aggressive customer supply or demand by acting for their own accounts on the opposite sides of these transactions. With certain limitations, competitive traders may also act as two-dollar brokers to earn brokerage fees when trading opportunities are not available.

Members who are willing and able to buy and/or sell stock in any NYSE listed issue at the request of a Floor Official or another broker holding a customer's order are called **competitive market makers.** The ability to deal in any stock differentiates them from specialists who are limited in their activities to a limited number of issues. The requirement for them to provide market depth and narrower spreads in prevailing quotations to accommodate public orders distinguishes them from competitive traders. Competitive market makers may also act as two-dollar brokers to earn brokerage fees when their services are not needed. But, they are restricted in this capacity to acceptance of only market or limited price orders. They may not handle stop orders or any orders which direct their use of discretion in the execution process. Moreover, they may not act as a competitive market maker and a two dollar broker or even act as a competitive market maker and as a competitive trader in the same stock during the same trading day.

**bond brokers**

Members who execute orders in the bond room of the NYSE as a matter of continuing practice are called **bond brokers**. Actually, any member of the Exchange is permitted to transact business in the bond room, but because this room is physically separated from the rooms where stocks are traded and competitive floor brokerage rates are nominal per $1,000 face value bond, relatively few members bother to participate there.

**annunciator boards**

Ordinarily, the telephone clerk gives orders that can be executed immediately (such as market orders or limit orders at current prices) to the firm's commission house broker to save unnecessary floor brokerage expense. If the commission house broker is unavailable, orders are given instead to an available two-dollar broker. These members can be anywhere on the trading floor at the time an order is received. To attract the attention of the appropriate party, the clerk presses one of several levers on a panel situated in the booth near the teletype machine or telephone. This activates a **radio-controlled paging device**. Brokers can rent a pocket-sized receiver from the Exchange that can be activated by the telephone clerks of as many as four different firms; the receiver uses different colored lights for each signal. A low-powered transmitter operates effectively in each of the trading rooms on the floor of the Exchange. This efficient system directs the member to the proper booth to determine the reason for that summons.

**radio-controlled paging devices**

### G2.
### *Via Pneumatic Tubes*

Of course, if an order cannot be executed immediately (such as limit or stop orders obviously away from current prices), the telephone clerk won't bother to locate the commission house broker or a two-dollar broker merely to deliver it to a specialist at a particular trading post. Instead, the clerk uses the Exchange's **pneumatic tube system**, built under the trading floor to connect the telephone booths with the trading posts. Messages, orders, and even execution reports are often placed into a plastic carrier called a **widget** and quickly transported to their proper destination.

**pneumatic tube system**

### H.
### the auction market
### H1.
### *Executing a Transaction*

When a commission house or two-dollar broker accepts an order from a telephone clerk, that person must proceed to the specific trading post assigned by the exchange for all activity in that issue. Without revealing any terms of the order, a member always asks first for the *current market* for that security. The broker might say, for example, "How is Motors?" (General Motors Corporation), or "What's the market for Big Steel?" (U.S. Steel Corporation), or "How are you making Ma Bell?" (American Telephone and Telegraph Corporation).[16]

#### *REQUESTING QUOTATION AND SIZE*

This is recognized as a request for a quotation and size. It refers to the *highest bid price* existing with the number of shares so represented, and the *lowest offering price* available with the number of shares reflected also at that level.

**example**

---

"46½ to 46¾, 300 by 100," means there are 300 shares wanted at 46½ and 100 shares available at 46¾.

"57⅞ to 58⅛, 2 up," means there are 200 shares wanted by someone at 57⅞ and 200 shares offered for sale by someone at 58⅛.

---

Although it may not be a personal bid or offering price, the specialist, acting as a coordinator, assumes responsibility for fur-

[16]Experienced brokers playfully refer to some issues by slang or amusing designations commonly accepted by the community.

nishing the quotation upon request. Brokers who are unwilling to accept these prevailing prices may verbally express their own proposals, but only if their price is *equal to, or better than,* the price in the existing quotation. Thus, if a quotation is 31⅜ bid, offered at 31¾, a broker with an order to buy stock can compete verbally in the trading area only if able to bid 31⅜ or higher. Even if that broker wants to purchase enormous amounts of stock at a lower price, a member is forbidden to interfere with anyone willing to pay a higher price and must, therefore, remain silent. An identical rule exists for sellers, prohibiting them from offering stock for sale unless their price is *equal to, or lower than,* the prevailing offering.

### WHAT IS THE RANGE?　　　　　　　　　　　　　　　　*H1b.*

range

> To plan strategy more effectively, a broker may request the **range** as well as the quotation and size. The range refers to the opening sale, high sale, low sale, and latest sale for that particular issue.

**example**

| 12¼, | 13, | 12, | 12⅝ |
|------|-----|-----|-----|
| open | high | low | last |

The first three prices are furnished by the specialist. The latest or last sale appears on an indicator at the trading post that is manually operated by the specialist or a clerk.

### THE LANGUAGE OF BIDDING AND OFFERING　　　　　*H1c.*

Brokers who want to participate actively in the auction process by stating their own bids or offers must use the phraseology prescribed by the Exchange to avoid confusion and misunderstanding. To *bid* for stock, a member must first state the intended purchase price followed by the number of shares desired. For example, "86¼ for 100," "17 for 1,000," or "48⅝ for 600," are typical of bids on the floor of the Exchange.

　　To *offer* stock for sale, a member must first state the number of shares to be disposed of, and then the price desired. For example, "200 at 21," "10,000 at 37⅞," or "700 at 45¼," are typical of offerings on the floor of the Exchange.

### ACCEPTING A BID OR OFFER　　　　　　　　　　　　*H1d.*

When a contra broker makes a bid for stock that is agreeable to the terms of the customer's order, a member shows *acceptance of that bid* at this price by saying, "Sold!"

　　This declaration consummates a transaction and leads immediately to a new series of bids and offerings for other shares of that security.

　　If the quantity on a member's order is insufficient to satisfy the entire bid, the member shows partial acceptance by saying, "Sold 100," "Sold 400," and so forth, as the case may be.

When a contra broker makes an offering of stock that is agreeable to the terms of the customer's order, a member shows *acceptance of that offer* at that price by saying, "Take it!" This statement, too, consummates a transaction and necessitates a new auction for other buyers and sellers of that security. Partial acceptance of an offering is indicated by, "Take 200," "Take 800," and so forth, as the case may be.

In this manner, price and volume fluctuate continuously, with brokers and traders accepting bids and/or offerings made by other members of the Exchange.

### H1e.  ERRORS IN EXECUTION

As the trades occur, the two members involved in the transaction approach each other to determine the name of the firm each party represents. Each member announces the name of the principal organization represented on that transaction. This is known as a **floor give-up**. The participants cannot assume the firm name that often appears on a member's white oblong identification badge is the firm represented in a specific transaction because the member may be acting as a two-dollar broker. Even with these precautions, surrounding noise and continuous psychological pressures occasionally lead to an error in execution. The member or the firm must bear the financial consequences of that mistake. The customer may not suffer a loss as a result of a broker's blunder.

**floor give-up**

It is not always easy to identify the broker who errs on a transaction. Sometimes the problem involves the number of shares actually executed. (Broker A asserts purchase of 400 shares, but Broker B claims sale of only 300 shares.) If neither member admits fault, the smaller number of shares will be binding in the contract unless that broker's original order was larger than this amount. In that case, the dispute must be submitted to a floor official for resolution.

Sometimes it may be that the price of execution is contested. (Broker C asserts purchase price of 12⅜, but Broker D claims sale of stock at 12⅝.) This kind of misunderstanding is usually resolved by researching the Exchange's official record of transactions. If it cannot be easily resolved because of the activity and price fluctuation at that approximate time

1. a compromise may be agreed to for sharing financial liability between these members; or
2. the matter must be submitted to a floor official for settlement.

Sometimes it may be the participating brokers' executing capacity at question. (Broker E claims to be the buyer, while Broker F asserts title to the purchase.) If the specialist, or some other witness in the trading area, cannot positively recall which of those members was verbally represented as the buyer, the problem must be submitted to a floor official for satisfaction.

### H2.
*Stopping Stock*

**Stopping stock** is a specialist's guarantee of price to a customer's order that enables the broker to try to improve upon that price

**stopping stock**

without fear of missing the market.[17] Under the following conditions, specialists may grant a broker the privilege of a stop, *although specialists are not obligated to do so*:

1. The order, buy or sell, must be for a public customer's account (not a member's account).
2. The broker must ask for the stop.[18]
3. There must be a spread of at least ¼ point in the prevailing quotation at the time of this request.[19]
4. The specialist must be willing and able to trade as principal if necessary,[20] to avoid defaulting on the guarantee.

For example, let us take the situation shown in Figure 8. Broker A, with a market order to buy 100 shares, is informed by the specialist that the quotation is 63 to 63¼. Broker A is obliged to buy that stock offered at 63¼ or face the risk of having someone else take it. If someone else does take it, Broker A is guilty of failing to satisfy instructions at a price that was practicable of execution (missing the market).

To avoid this exposure, Broker A asks the specialist to *stop* 100 shares at 63¼, that is, assure Broker A a price no worse than 63¼. In this case, we shall assume that the specialist agrees to "stop" the stock at 63¼. Broker A now has an opportunity to acquire the stock more cheaply without potential financial liability. Broker A is able to bid at 63⅛, in an attempt to improve the price for the customer. (Broker A must narrow the spread in the quotation by actively competing in the trading crowd.) Now, if a seller enters the area soon afterward, Broker A will buy 100 shares at this price because this bid of 63⅛ is the highest prevailing bid.

If another buyer arrives and purchases the stock offered at 63¼ before the seller appears, then Broker A will be *stopped out*[21] and forced to pay the guaranteed price (63¼). Under the rules, a broker who is stopped is allowed one transaction to improve upon the guaranteed price. If the broker cannot do better on the next sale, the order must be executed at the guaranteed price. Consequently, the customer is assured of the price of the next sale. The next sale must be at the guaranteed price or better. It cannot be worse than the guaranteed price because the specialist has someone elses' stock to offer (or bid, as the case may be) at that level. If that price is better than the stopped price, it must be this customer's transaction because that broker has priority. If the price is not better, it must be at the guaranteed price because this represents the worst possible price that can occur after the privilege is extended.

Stopping stock is a privilege that subjects specialists to trad-

---

[17]Although the expressions sound alike stop orders and stopping stock refer to two completely dissimilar practices. The stop order is a memorandum that becomes a market order when a transaction is effected at or through the indicated price.

[18]The specialist is prohibited from soliciting such requests from a broker.

[19]The spread is the difference in value between the bid and offering prices.

[20]The specialist must personally sell stock to a buyer unable to improve upon price, or buy stock from a seller in a similar position, when there is no contra customer order on the book at the stopped price.

[21]*Stopped out* is a term used to signify a broker had a chance to improve upon price but was unable to do so.

| BUY | | SELL |
|---|---|---|
| 100 - BROKER Y | **63** | |
| 100 - BROKER - A | **1/8** | |
| | **1/4** | 100 - BROKER X |
| | **3/8** | 100 - BROKER Z |
| | **1/2** | |

**FIGURE 8**
Stopping Stock: Broker A is stopped at 63¼. A sale on the bid at 63⅛ must certainly be to Broker A, who is now making the highest bid. But if, instead, the next transaction occurs at the lowest offering prevailing, it will be from Broker X at 63¼. This, in turn, requires the specialist to furnish Broker A with 100 shares at 63¼, too.

ing account uncertainties. It also provides specialists with an opportunity to earn floor brokerage for executing orders they would not ordinarily receive. Procedural etiquette on the trading floor dictates that when a specialist stops stock for a broker, the customer's order is given to the specialist to attempt improvement. If the specialist can do better, the specialist will write the execution report and receive the brokerage fee. But if the cusomer is stopped out, the specialist summons the broker to the trading crowd, allowing that member to write out the report at the guaranteed price.

This tradition serves everyone's best interest because

1. the specialist has an opportunity to handle immediately executable market and limit orders and increase earned income;
2. the commission house or two-dollar broker does not waste valuable time competing in a trading crowd and is thus free to execute possibly more lucrative orders elsewhere without concern about missing the market; and
3. the customer has a good chance to gain a better price for an order without risk.

In fact, this procedure works so well that experienced registered representatives realize occasionally that their customers have been stopped for more than one transaction in an effort to gain them better prices. This apparent violation of rules is overlooked by the exchange because it can only work to the advantage of the public customer. The customer is always guaranteed *no worse* than the price of the first transaction after receipt of the stop. The assurance is backed by the specialist's own capital and trading account. The specialist strives to do better and to keep the floor brokerage fee instead of surrendering it to the original broker, as is necessary if the order is stopped out.

### H3. Crossing Stock

**cross** Brokerage firms frequently receive orders in the same securities at the same time from different customers on opposite sides of the market. (Customer Y wants to buy 100 shares of General Motors at the same time that Customer Z enters an order to sell 100 shares of General Motors.) Because all orders are transmitted to a centralized location on the floor of the stock exchange, it appears likely that the executing broker can pair off the buy order with the sell order in that security at the same time and price. This is known as a **cross**. However, before this is accomplished, several important conditions must prevail.

1. The transaction must be effected at the trading post assigned for activity in that security, *within* the framework of the existing quotation.
2. There must be at least a ¼ point *spread*[22] in the quotation at the time the broker enters the trading area.[23] A ⅛ spread prevents a member from pairing off those orders because of inability to displace others represented at those prices (that is, brokers, representing other customers, who were in the trading area first). For example, a quotation of 21–21⅛

[22]The spread is the difference in value between the bid and offering prices.

[23]When a spread is greater than ¼ point, the broker attempts to cross stock as close as possible to the price of the last sale in order to avoid charges of discrimination from either party to the transaction.

leaves no room in between the bid and offering prices to arrange a cross. But a quotation of 21–21¼ provides an opportunity to pair off the orders at 21⅛.

3. The executing broker in a cross must give *either* the buyer or the seller a brief opportunity to improve upon the price at which the broker can pair off those orders. This is done by momentarily either bidding ⅛ point lower or offering ⅛ point higher than the price at which the cross will be arranged.

To illustrate the mechanical features of this procedure, assume that a quotation is 70–70¼ in General Electric Corp. shares when Broker A enters the trading area intent upon crossing 100 shares of stock at 70⅛. After inquiring about the current quotation, Broker A can achieve this objective by announcing *either*

1. "70 for 100, . . . . . 100 at 70⅛, take it;" or
2. "100 at 70¼ . . . . . 70⅛ for 100, sold."

In (1), the broker attempts to improve upon price for the buyer by momentarily bidding 70 for 100 shares. If another broker had a multiple round-lot sell order in the crowd, the broker could have interrupted that cross and sold the stock at 70 to the buyer represented in the trading area before the entry of Broker A and to Broker A, as well.

In (2), Broker A offers 100 shares momentarily at 70¼, trying to do better for the seller before accepting the bid at 70⅛. If a substantial buyer of that stock was in the trading crowd, that broker could have interrupted the cross by purchasing stock from the offeror represented first at 70¼, as well as from Broker A's customer.

By observing this last rule, at least one customer can enjoy a price benefit derived from a bona fide open auction market. That customer does not rely entirely on an arbitrary price set by the broker, as would otherwise be the case.

*H4.*
*The Super DOT*
*System*

**DOT** is an acronym for "designated order turnaround" and was developed by the NYSE to facilitate routing of small round-lot orders. It is a message-switching system connecting member firms subscribing to this service with the trading posts on the floor of the Exchange. Originally, only market orders of up to 299 shares could be entered through the system and within seconds be received at the appropriate trading post for immediate execution by the specialist. Through improvements over the years the DOT System was expanded in several stages until, in mid-1984, it could accommodate market orders of up to 1,099 shares and limit orders good till cancelled of up to 5,099 shares at one time from any one firm. This computerized technique enables member firms to save precious time in processing simple orders. DOT bypasses the firm's telephone clerks and eliminates the need for a commission house broker or two-dollar broker to transport that order physically and then execute it at the trading post. Transaction reports are then routed back to the originating firm through the same system. The Super DOT System also accommodates odd-lot orders of up to 99 shares separately and also when entered simultaneously with a round-lot order.

**DOT**

From time to time, a member organization may receive a customer's order that is simply too big to be handled by the normal market procedures discussed thus far. To accommodate that customer, the firm may turn to certain unique methods described in the New York Stock Exchange's *Constitution and Rules*. Because they are unorthodox, a member organization must first obtain approval from the NYSE before employing any of these measures.

In the following discussion of unusual circumstances, only the seller's viewpoint is emphasized, simply because these situations are usually initiated by a customer intent upon disposing of a large block of stock. Bear in mind that the characteristics and procedures associated with each specific sale also apply to purchases within the same framework.

After considering such relevant factors as

1. the range of prices and volume of transactions in that issue on the floor of the Exchange in the preceding month,
2. attempts to dispose of the security in question in the regular auction market,
3. amounts and prices of bids in the specialist's records and in the current auction market,
4. past and current public and member interest in that security on the floor of the Exchange, and
5. the quantity of stock to be disposed of,

**exchange distribution**

concurrent approval by the Floor Department and a floor official permits a member firm to attempt an **exchange distribution**.

In an exchange distribution, the selling customer must first give written certification to the NYSE

1. of ownership of all the shares offered for sale (short sales are prohibited because announcement and distribution of a large amount of stock for sale is likely to cause the price to decline, thus benefiting a short seller to the detriment of other investors); and
2. that this represents all the specific security to be offered for a reasonable period of time.

Then the member firm may ask a few other member organizations[24] to canvass their clients and solicit offsetting buy orders to accommodate this customer.

**special commission**

In return for this service, the seller agrees to pay the participating firms a **special commission**, a commission large enough to

1. satisfy the member firm's commission requirements for both its own and the buyer's transactions;
2. attract potential purchasers who can thereby trade *net* (no commission); and

[24]Ordinarily, only one large firm (two at most) is asked to determine confidentially whether its extensive branch office network and corresponding large number of customer accounts can develop enough interest to make the offering worthwhile. Be aware that as yet the seller has not officially entered a noncancellable order. The customer is merely reflecting an indication to become binding only *if* enough offsetting buy orders are accumulated.

**3.** encourage registered representatives in these firms to work a little harder.

Full information must be revealed to potential buyers at the time of solicitation, including the total number of shares being offered for sale.

During the time of offering and solicitation, neither the seller nor participating member organization may bid for or purchase any of that security in the marketplace for any account in which they have a direct or indirect interest. Stabilization in any form is prohibited.

When sufficient offsetting orders are accumulated by the firm coordinating the distribution, the large sell order and all of the buy orders are sent to the floor of the Exchange where they are officially *crossed at the current market price*; that is, within the prevailing quotation.

Exchange distributions are printed on the ticker tape as the sales are executed and identified by the letters *DIST* before the security symbol and volume.

**example**

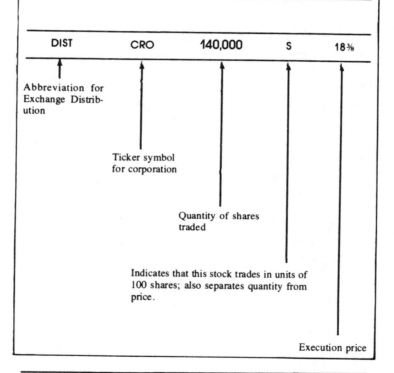

| DIST | CRO | 140,000 | S | 18⅜ |

Abbreviation for Exchange Distribution

Ticker symbol for corporation

Quantity of shares traded

Indicates that this stock trades in units of 100 shares; also separates quantity from price.

Execution price

The comparable purchase of a large amount of stock with these characteristics is called an **exchange acquisition** and is identified on the ticker tape by the letters *ACQ* before security symbol and volume.

**exchange acquisition**

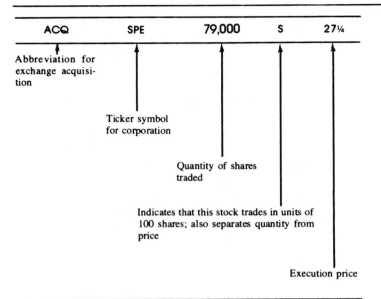

Sometimes, to facilitate the transaction and assure success for the seller of a large block of stock, a participating member organization may decide to act in a principal capacity. It can buy the stock from the seller and attempt to distribute those shares to its own customers while assuming market risk for any unsold portion. Here, too, the firm must notify potential buyers at the time of solicitation about the size of the offering; the fact that it is acting as principal; and that it may, nevertheless, be charging the buyer a commission or, if it chooses to do so under the circumstances, no commission at all.

**12.**
***Special Offerings***

When it is determined that a sizable order cannot be disposed of in a normal manner, in a reasonable period of time, and at reasonable prices, a **special offering** may be attempted.

**special offering**

A special offering is an offering of stock by a member organization from its own portfolio or in behalf of one or more customers at a *fixed price*. The fixed price may not be above the last sale or current offering price in the regular auction market, whichever is lower.

All members firms are invited to transmit their buy orders for any portion of the offering[25] to the floor of the Exchange where they can accept this price in the usual manner. The incentive for the firm and its salespeople to do so is a **special commission** (payable by the seller). Thus, the purchasing customer can trade with the offeror on a net basis (no commission expense), whereas the registered representative receives a higher than usual fee from the seller for the service provided.

**special commission**

Important points to remember about this procedure are the following:

[25]Even odd-lot orders can participate.

1. Prior approval must be granted *both* by a floor official and the Floor Department of the Exchange.

2. The regular market price may decline below the fixed special offering price and defeat the attempted sale unless a limited amount of stabilization is permitted by the Exchange.[26]

3. The special offer must remain effective for at least 15 minutes unless suspended because of a change in market conditions.

4. The party making the offering must be the owner of these shares. Short sales via this procedure are prohibited.

5. Transactions effected in a special offering do not elect stop orders or cause the execution of GTC odd-lot orders.

6. The seller must give written certification to the Exchange and the member firm that the shares offered represent all that will be distributed for a reasonable time thereafter.

7. The seller cannot offer additional shares in the regular auction market while the special offering is pending.

The terms of a special offering must be printed on the ticker tape before the offering becomes effective. At that time, too, the member organization must announce whether it has already stabilized, or intends to stabilize, the offering price in the regular auction market. Then, as each transaction is effected pursuant to this offering, an announcement is made of this fact on the ticker tape including the amount of the special commission payable.

**example**

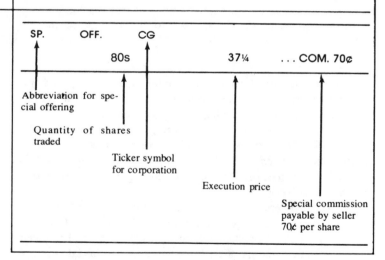

Each customer's confirmation prepared in connection with this unique execution procedure must also detail the terms and conditions of the offering.

The counterpart of a special offering is a **special bid**. Special bids are used for customers who want to buy a sizable amount of stock at a fixed price. The required approvals, written certifications, and mechanical procedures are identical to those used for

**special bid**

[26]Generally, stabilization practices may involve quantities ranging up to 10% of the amount of stock being offered.

special offerings. The exception, of course, is that the special bid takes place on the opposite side of the market. Thus, the special bid must be at the price of the last sale or the current prevailing bid, whichever is higher, in the regular NYSE auction market. Special bids are also identified on the ticker tape as they are executed.

example

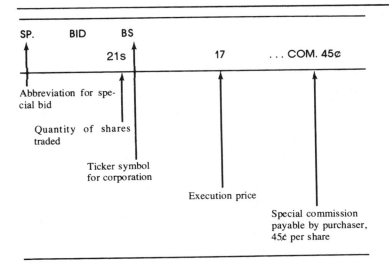

13.
*Secondary Distributions*

**secondary distribution**

A **secondary distribution** involves an amount of stock so very large that because of its overwhelming size

1.  it cannot be absorbed in the regular auction market in a reasonable time at reasonable prices; and
2.  a special offering or exchange distribution is not feasible.

It is usually an offering of a security by NYSE and NASD member organizations collectively, acting either as principal or **off-board** agent over the counter (**off-board**).

Two descriptions and procedures apply to secondary distributions in the securities industry.

**registered secondary distributions**

1.  **Registered secondary distributions**: These are offerings of stock that require an effective registration statement on file with the SEC before the sale is attempted.

**spot secondary distributions**

2.  **Spot secondary distributions**: These are offerings of stock that do not require SEC registration statements because they are sales by holders not affiliated with the issuing company. These offerings may literally be attempted on the spot, without delay.

Because a member organization of the NYSE is managing or participating in the distribution of a listed stock over the counter, approval must first be obtained from the Market Surveillance Division of the Exchange and from a floor official. The Exchange's concern centers upon whether the offering can be accomplished successfully on the floor instead of off-board. It considers such factors as

1. the price range and volume for the stock on the trading floor in the preceding 30 days;
2. the current quotation and condition of the specialist's records; and
3. the size of the offering and the degree of interest for that security exhibited in the regular auction market.

When approved, the intended offering is announced over the ticker tape, citing

1. the terms and conditions of the distribution; and
2. whether stabilization or overallotment procedures will be employed.

Contingent with approval is a requirement to satisfy all bids on the floor of the Exchange that are equal to, or higher than, the secondary offering price. Moreover, if the distribution commences after the NYSE market closes (which is usually the case), the distributor must make that privilege available for at least 30 minutes afterward.

> The ticker tape is also used to announce the completion of this distribution or its continuance from day to day if it cannot be completed on the first day offered. The Exchange ticker tape does not show the actual execution of these transactions occurring over the counter because secondary distributions are exempted from the Consolidated Tape System's reporting requirement.

The price of a secondary distribution is a **fixed price**, not higher than the last security transaction on the Exchange at the time the offering commences. The purchaser's incentive is that no commission expense is incurred because it is indirectly borne by the seller, *unless*

**fixed price**

1. the offering broker/dealer took a risk position in this issue prior to the distribution; or
2. competitive bids for the stock are required by law, in which cases buyers may be charged a commission.

## CONCLUDING COMMENT

This chapter has given a view of the NYSE from the inside. Your customers may claim justifiably that they don't care what happens between floor brokers once they place their orders. Obviously, as this chapter has shown, what occurs on the floor of the Exchange does matter to them whether they care or not and whether they realize it or not. Just as taking and writing up customer orders requires care, so does executing an order on the NYSE.

To be a professional in any endeavor means to have a broad view of an entire process, rather than a narrow view of a specific aspect of that process. This is true within the securities industry, too. You need to know what goes on with your order even after it leaves your hands In this way, you can best serve your customers who expect you to be a professional.

# transactions on stock exchanges

**short sale**

### DEFINITION

Fundamentally, a **short sale** is the sale of a security that is not owned at the time of the transaction. The short sale necessitates the purchase of the security by the seller some time in the future to eliminate the deficiency.

Obviously, people sell short to make money. They hope that their purchase expense will be lower than their sale proceeds; thus, the difference becomes their profit. If expenses are greater than proceeds, the difference represents their loss. A short sale is really not an unusual investment practice in today's markets. Typically, investors buy a security first and subsequently sell it. What is so strange if they merely reverse this procedure to take advantage of market conditions?

Selling short is sometimes maligned because of its implication of illegality (selling something not owned). However, this is a basic premise of business in the United States, not confined solely to the securities industry. Any time a manufacturer is awarded a contract for merchandise that is not immediately available, to be delivered on a future date at a fixed price, that concern is selling the merchandise short. It is speculating that it will be able to produce those goods for less money than the contract price of sale.

### USEFULNESS OF SHORT SELLER

People selling short in the securities market are, to be sure, creating an artificial supply. But at the same time, they are also satisfying an aggressive demand and thereby moderating the otherwise violent effect that demand would have upon price.

The short seller's usefulness is best demonstrated when they are needed most. During periods of falling prices, when there is a scarcity of ordinary demand, the people who are already short represent a built-in buying interest because they must eventually cover (purchase) their short position. This demand serves to cushion the depression of a bear market just as the original sale cushioned the optimism of a bull market. In fact, there is a school of thought on market theory that makes reference to this important supply-demand relationship. It is called the **cushion theory** of investment.

**cushion theory**

### CUSHION THEORY OF INVESTMENT

Persons who subscribe to this cushion theory hold that the absence of short sellers in the marketplace is detrimental to liquidity. Followers of this theory eagerly analyze monthly announcements from the New York Stock Exchange and American Stock Exchange[1] stating the short interest of individual stocks traded on their premises—that is, the number of shares already sold short which represent latent buying power for that issue (see Figure 1). These theorists believe that if an open position totals two or more times the average daily trading volume for that particular security, this situation is a bullish indicator. It forecasts imminent rising prices for that issue. On the other hand, if the short position figure

[1]The statistics are published to reflect positions as of the fifteenth day of each month.

# Short Interest Rose 6.8% on Big Board, 19.8% on Amex in Month Ended Nov. 15

*By a* WALL STREET JOURNAL *Staff Reporter*

NEW YORK—Short interest on the New York Stock Exchange increased 1,585,544 shares in the month ended last Monday, while American Stock Exchange short interest increased 529,478 shares.

On the Big Board, short interest totaled 24,777,197 shares as of the Nov. 15 settlement date, up 6.8% from 23,191,653 share in the prior month.

Amex short interest rose 19.8% to 3,199,593 shares during the period from 2,670,115 shares reported in mid-October.

A short sale is the sale of borrowed stock. The seller expects a price decline that would enable him to purchase an equal number of shares later at a lower price for return to the lender. The short interest is the number of shares that haven't been purchased for return to lenders.

Fluctuations in short interest of certain stocks also may be caused partly by arbitraging. Those that might have been so affected are marked by the symbol (t) in the table below, where the short interest in the issue exceeds 100,000 shares.

In a major method of securities arbitrage, a profit can be made when a company's stock is to be exchanged for that of another, or for a new issue, in a proposed merger. The profit opportunity arises when the stocks sell at disparate prices.

An arbitrageur may make a small per-share profit by buying stock of one company involved in the prospective merger and selling short the stock of the other.

The tables below show the Big Board and Amex issues in which a short position of at least 20,000 shares existed as of Nov. 15, or in which there was a short-position change of at least 10,000 shares since mid-October.

For the first time since some stocks have been dually listed on both exchanges, short interest figures for certain issues, such as Frigitronics Inc., Varo Inc. and Sambo's Restaurants Inc., appear slightly different as issued by each exchange. A Big Board spokesman confirmed that Big Board figures for these issues should agree with those from the Amex. However, without rechecking the computers, he said, there wasn't any way to tell which exchange was wrong. The Amex couldn't be reached for comment by the time the discrepancy was discovered.

The Big Board figures below are as received from the exchange.

| | 11-15-76 | 11-15-76 | Avg. Daily Volume |
|---|---|---|---|
| Abbott Labs | 20,908 | 37,454 | 24,204 |
| ASA Limited | 154,905 | 169,034 | 15,500 |
| Aetna Life Casualty | 34,050 | 94,700 | 58,638 |
| Air Products & Chem | 15,486 | 28,609 | 22,076 |
| Akzona Inc | 34,800 | 600 | 3,728 |
| Alcan Aluminium Ld | 29,240 | 21,040 | 27,623 |
| tAmax Inc | 118,321 | 104,872 | 21,842 |
| Allied Stores | 19,502 | 2,485 | 12,071 |
| Aluminum Co America | 43,772 | 31,172 | 31,119 |
| Amerada Hess Corp | 38,756 | 11,613 | 35,933 |
| Amer Airlines | 22,443 | 13,460 | 35,033 |
| Amer Broadcasting Co | 58,562 | 35,660 | 37,095 |
| Amer Can | 24,035 | 18,010 | 10,009 |
| Amer Cyanamid Co | 61,706 | 136,420 | 29,538 |
| tAmer General Ins Co | 102,019 | 17,163 | 19,542 |
| Amer Home Products | 11,132 | 42,532 | 53,657 |
| tAmer Hospital Supply | 118,272 | 114,901 | 23,590 |
| Amer Motors Corp | 71,267 | 73,067 | 31,776 |
| Amer Telephone & Tel | 88,752 | 55,317 | 117,557 |
| AMP Inc | 258,174 | 228,049 | 26,480 |
| Anaconda Co | 32,218 | 31 824 | 28,328 |
| Archer Daniels Midlo | 15,186 | 4,942 | 24,195 |
| tAtlantic Richfield | 336,053 | 454,069 | 100,619 |
| Atl Rich $2.83 cv pr | 25,300 | 5,600 | 21,604 |
| Auto Data Processing | 24,752 | 21,572 | 12,557 |
| Avco Corp wts 78 | 67,200 | 66,200 | 4,752 |
| tAvery Intl Corp | 108,195 | 111,690 | 7,476 |
| Avco Corp | 15,905 | 32,195 | 13,623 |
| Avnet Inc | 21,365 | 24,285 | 24,247 |
| Avon Products Inc. | 92,405 | 67,437 | 56,261 |
| Babcock & Wilcox Co | 5,126 | 48,156 | 14,238 |
| Bandag Inc | 20,510 | 23,814 | 15,452 |
| Bates Mfg Co Inc | 42,958 | 42,858 | 490 |
| Baker Intl Corp | 41,516 | 33,666 | 7,682 |
| Beatrice Foods | 32,262 | 103,538 | 77,295 |
| Baxter Travenol Lab | 46,191 | 52,526 | 15,738 |
| Beker Indus Inc | 67,809 | 90,712 | 5,552 |
| Bethlehem Steel | 44,998 | 48,872 | 45,142 |
| Black & Decker Mfg | 26,490 | 40,940 | 28,152 |
| Bally Mfg Corp. | 46,200 | 2,350 | 11,957 |
| Best Products Co | 171,337 | 23,265 | 28,066 |
| Blue Bell Inc | 29,500 | 29,000 | 15,709 |
| Boeing Co. | 90,633 | 68,497 | 44,433 |
| Bunker Hill Inc Sec | 503 | 14,870 | 4,385 |
| Boise Cascade Corp | 41,922 | 22,530 | 31,400 |
| Braniff Intl Corp | 33,602 | 26,302 | 30,157 |
| British Pete Amer sh | 98,950 | 48,423 | 35,785 |
| tContinental Group | 292,635 | 250,805 | 22,966 |
| Brunswick Corp | 19,347 | 45,590 | 26,514 |
| CBS Inc | 24,384 | 21,377 | 38,290 |
| Bucyrus-Erie | 18,500 | 4,976 | 17,390 |
| Budd Co. | 73,585 | 76,700 | 7,004 |
| Citicorp | 56,476 | 74,632 | 120,471 |
| tBurroughs Corp. | 109,708 | 97,758 | 48,747 |
| tCaterpillar Tractor | 144,588 | 72,070 | 49,666 |
| Celanese Corp | 24,305 | 19,450 | 14,757 |
| Centronics Data Comp | 73,770 | 12,825 | 22,376 |
| Champ Intl 120pr | 34,800 | 15,000 | 4,614 |
| Champion Intl | 61,775 | 10,761 | 26,328 |
| Chase Manhattan Corp | 26,640 | 24,896 | 31,357 |
| tChase Man Mtg & Rlty Tr | 148,082 | 146,000 | 4,171 |
| Chesebrough Ponds Inc | 85,675 | 67,286 | 15,733 |
| Chrysler Corp | 69,402 | 82,322 | 66,309 |
| Citizens & So Rlty Inv | 26,500 | 30,400 | 4,938 |
| City Investing | 15,975 | 4,930 | 40,133 |
| Clark Equipment | 70,683 | 6,773 | 14,195 |
| Clev Elec Illum Co | 300 | 39,000 | 14,419 |
| Clorox Co | 29,200 | 1,010 | 23,042 |
| Coca-Cola Bottling NY | 113,400 | 113,200 | 13,552 |
| tCoca-Cola Co | 112,499 | 98,258 | 26,538 |
| Colgate Palmolive | 41,712 | 50,708 | 46,357 |
| Colt Industries | 12,258 | 27,413 | 10,523 |
| Combustion Engneerng | 28,490 | 32,800 | 10,004 |
| Commonwealth Edison | 34,400 | 3,700 | 26,976 |
| Cone Mills Corp | 47,070 | 47,920 | 3,628 |
| Compugraphic Corp | 31,670 | 32,670 | 6,319 |
| Computer Sciences | 63,400 | 62,200 | 9,085 |
| Cons Freightways Inc | 20,209 | 17,196 | 7,028 |
| Continental Tel Corp | 70,657 | 48,870 | 30,371 |
| Control Data Corp | 20,680 | 14,929 | 24,014 |
| Corning Glass Works | 33,242 | 4,487 | 16,876 |
| Cummins Engine Co | 25,718 | 46,610 | 9,776 |
| Curtiss-Wright, Corp | 31,907 | 35,886 | 13,371 |
| Damon Corp | 36,700 | 36,200 | 9,747 |
| Data General Corp | 76,737 | 49,736 | 20,452 |
| Deere & Co | 65,300 | 48,735 | 55,352 |
| Denny's Inc | 23,244 | 21,825 | 11,404 |
| Delta Air Lines | 21,243 | 31,743 | 16,614 |
| Diamond Shamrock | 16,533 | 36,878 | 19,838 |
| tDigital Equip Corp | 276,822 | 149,915 | 49,952 |
| Disney Productions | 153,658 | 158,854 | 52,761 |
| Diamond M Drilling | 49,955 | 56,965 | 5,628 |
| Diversified Mtg Inv | 23,000 | 23,000 | 5,585 |
| Dr Pepper Company | 44,610 | 33,610 | 14,133 |
| Donnelley (R.R.) & Sons | 22,705 | 21,405 | 9,923 |
| Dow Chemical Co | 93,218 | 157,837 | 152,300 |
| Duke Power Co | 5,100 | 29,900 | 30,442 |
| Dun & Bradstreet Co | 40,092 | 40,692 | 8,938 |
| tDuPont | 114,797 | 123,583 | 33,376 |
| Eastern Airlines | 28,700 | 12,900 | 31,595 |
| Eastman Kodak | 86,610 | 92,640 | 90,323 |
| Eckerd (Jack) Corp | 62,300 | 36,403 | 16,757 |
| Enserch Corp | 29,807 | 10,600 | 11,204 |
| Lilly (Eli) & Co | 94,286 | 31,236 | 29,228 |
| Electronic Data Syst | 20,043 | 18,300 | 3,647 |
| Emerson Elec Co | 33,161 | 33,795 | 27,819 |
| EMI Limit am shs | 38,200 | 82,400 | 9,742 |
| Engelhard Min & Chem | 69,899 | 85,715 | 16,971 |
| Esquire Inc | 18,600 | None | 1,142 |
| Evans Products | 23,008 | 20,128 | 26,728 |
| Exxon Corp | 90,208 | 163,946 | 105,271 |
| Fairchild Camera&Inst | 79,320 | 91,537 | 27,442 |
| Farah Mfg Co | 31,461 | 33,861 | 2,809 |
| Federal Nat Mtg | 92,970 | 195,209 | 41,042 |
| tFederated Dept Stores | 121,833 | 117,132 | 28,647 |
| First Charter Fin CP | 49,008 | 31,841 | 22,238 |
| Florida Gas Co | 14,600 | None | 5,447 |
| Florida Power Corp | 16,000 | 2,759 | 9,428 |
| Fluor Corp | 20,681 | 52,523 | 23,042 |
| Ford Motor Co | 27,730 | 37,090 | 52,961 |
| t-General Electric | 1,140,208 | 577,404 | 104,442 |
| General Foods | 40,370 | 60,870 | 45,995 |
| General Host Corp | 30,325 | 30,125 | 1,800 |
| General Mills | 61,661 | 40,130 | 14,080 |
| General Motors | 135,873 | 140,704 | 145,314 |
| First Miss Corp | 12,850 | 1,354 | 28,504 |
| Gen Tel&Electronics | 53,536 | 49,886 | 44,723 |
| tGenuine Parts Co | 119,970 | 89,170 | 9,147 |

| | 11-15-76 | 10-15-76 | Avg. Daily Volume |
|---|---|---|---|
| tInter Tel & Tel | 161,053 | 336,108 | 86,728 |
| IU Intl Corp | 27,152 | 19,528 | 15,361 |
| Itel Corp | 28,050 | 22,377 | 14,738 |
| Jim Walter Corp | 16,025 | 2,795 | 19,395 |
| xEF Johnson Co | 132,286 | Not Listed | 17,752 |
| Johns Manville | 79,500 | 900 | 33,000 |
| Johnson & Johnson | 74,264 | 80,512 | 20,233 |
| Joy Mfg | 30,715 | 28,329 | 12,880 |
| tKaiser Alum & Chem | 249,727 | 224,157 | 9,857 |
| Kaiser Cement & Gypsum | 52,885 | 47,593 | 2,938 |
| Kaufman & Broad Inc | 44,700 | 45,100 | 28,109 |
| Kellogg Co | 54,917 | 22,002 | 16,776 |
| Kentucky Utilities | 17,200 | 200 | 3,457 |
| Kerr McGee Corp | 54,410 | 26,210 | 16,609 |
| tKresge (S.S.) | 107,873 | 143,518 | 78,304 |
| Lear Siegler Inc. | 26,159 | 28,176 | 14,447 |
| LTV Corp | 41,533 | 54,640 | 19,619 |
| Litton Industries | 55,532 | 80,326 | 46,752 |
| Lubrizol Corp | 54,316 | 47,016 | 11,461 |
| Lucky Stores Inc | 40,182 | 11,572 | 18.280 |
| Lykes Corp | 33,925 | 36,725 | 12,161 |
| Mobil Corp | 14,305 | 24,574 | 42,576 |
| Marriott Corp | 23,590 | 12,443 | 16,052 |
| Masco Corp | 93,000 | 83,490 | 26,252 |
| Mattel Inc | 36,238 | 36,200 | 8,966 |
| Matsushita Elec Ind | 25,300 | 25,300 | 2,023 |
| MCA Inc | 20,262 | 27,644 | 21,966 |
| tMcDonald's Corp | 205,587 | 125,679 | 51,904 |
| McDonnell Douglas | 20,121 | 9,438 | 12,204 |
| Merck & Co | 42,616 | 33,239 | 27,923 |
| Merrill Lynch & Co | 80,287 | 99,337 | 42,119 |
| Middle So Utilities | 76,900 | 7,487 | 59,519 |
| Minnesota Min & Mfg | 31,171 | 65,580 | 43,819 |
| Moly Corp Inc | 10,548 | 29,055 | 9,628 |
| Monsanto Co | 27,470 | 40,365 | 49,300 |
| Motorola Inc | 96,830 | 117,735 | 32,328 |
| NLT Corp | 10,064 | None | 16,557 |
| NCR Corp | 11,523 | 29,649 | 39,357 |
| Northern Telecom Ltd | 40,124 | 33,823 | 16,371 |
| National Can | 48,700 | 20,200 | 5,495 |
| Natl Semiconductor | 287,230 | 281,622 | 117,690 |
| Natomas Co | 29,430 | 14,640 | 64,971 |
| Occidental Pet wts | 45,680 | 38,780 | 6,433 |
| tNL Industries Inc | 268,098 | 236,359 | 21,895 |
| National Mine Svc Co | None | 40,315 | 5,771 |
| Nor Indiana Pub Serv | 38,700 | 200 | 16,866 |
| Northwest Airlines | 36,016 | 57,390 | 17,742 |
| Northwest Industries | 55,114 | 33,611 | 14,200 |
| Norton Co | 27,166 | 27,942 | 1,709 |
| Norton Simon Inc | 32,092 | 7,301 | 90,890 |
| tOccidental Petroleum | 596,468 | 699,539 | 53,519 |
| Ohio Edison Co | 21,800 | 600 | 34,452 |
| Owens-Illinois Inc | 27,168 | 9,237 | 13,680 |
| Pacific Gas & Elec | 30,122 | 1,650 | 29,871 |
| tPan Amer World Airwy | 1,402,904 | 1,622,060 | 48,495 |
| Panhandle Estrn Pipe | 42,473 | None | 17,142 |
| tPenney (J.C.) | 113,297 | 80,188 | 24,547 |
| Pennzoil Co | 3,748 | 14,862 | 27,042 |
| PepsiCo Inc | 43,193 | 56,117 | 16,895 |
| Perkin-Elmer Corp | 29,043 | 36,729 | 12,547 |
| Phila Suburban Corp | 30,006 | None | 7,014 |
| Phillips Petroleum | 16,585 | 27,185 | 27,142 |
| Pillsbury Co | 2,670 | 24,670 | 13,638 |
| Pizza Hut Inc | 23,570 | 19,670 | 15,147 |
| Pittston Co | 47,048 | 49,100 | 47,957 |
| Polaroid Corp | 312,265 | 336,972 | 159,547 |
| Ponderosa System Inc | 70,830 | 74,629 | 10,595 |
| PPG Industries Inc | 20,842 | 1,226 | 21,695 |
| Procter & Gamble | 25,176 | 24,825 | 20,080 |
| PubServ El & Gas Co | 800 | 19,500 | 29,409 |
| Pub Service Indiana | 6,717 | 21,541 | 14,580 |
| Pullman Inc | 22,008 | 12,600 | 4,761 |
| RCA Corp | 18,676 | 28,983 | 78,076 |
| Ralston Purina Co | 41,865 | 10,045 | 13,109 |
| tRapid Amer Corp | 100,035 | 100,035 | 8,695 |
| Raytheon Co | 35,750 | 51,000 | 27,728 |
| Reichhold Chemicals | 1,900 | 14,200 | 7,161 |

**AMERICAN STOCK EXCHANGE**

| | 11-15-76 | 10-15-76 | Avg. Daily Volume |
|---|---|---|---|
| Allegheny Airlines | 44,500 | 300 | 3,952 |
| Altec Corp | 73,166 | 75,166 | 2,790 |
| Atla Richfield Co ws | 102,385 | 123,565 | 2,666 |
| Atlas Cons Mng B | 52,447 | 49,311 | 7,419 |
| Bergen Brunswig A | 33,500 | 62,900 | 6,109 |
| Caressa Inc | 44,200 | 42,800 | 1,538 |
| Condec Corp | 67,137 | 59,589 | 2,161 |
| Dynell Electro Corp | 43,511 | 45,283 | 2,742 |
| Fibre Board Corp wts | 17,500 | 20,332 | 1,690 |
| Frigitronics Inc | 73,900 | 80,800 | 19,562 |
| Houston Oil & Min | 37,000 | 39,770 | 31,366 |
| Husky Oil Ltd | 42,265 | 44,047 | 1,157 |
| Intl Sys Contrl Corp | 138,650 | 135,950 | 2,014 |
| LTV Corp wts 78 | 96,700 | 91,000 | 7,476 |
| Marshall Industries | 58,200 | 58,200 | 285 |
| Miller Wohl Co | 17,630 | 20,205 | 5,238 |
| Molycorp Inc wts | 26,840 | 15,160 | 4,866 |
| Nolex Corp | 122,100 | 121,900 | 4,747 |
| Plant Industries Inc | 42,100 | 41,100 | 3,495 |
| Presley Co | 125,800 | 201,800 | 7,195 |
| Pulte Home Corp | 25,334 | 23,729 | 2,281 |
| Reliance Group wts 70 | 22,914 | 11,216 | 11,723 |
| Resort Internatl A | 391,850 | 51,900 | 52,976 |
| Resort Internatl B | 22,050 | 6,700 | 3,192 |
| Robintech Inc | 69,092 | 58,505 | 15,266 |
| xSambo's Restaurants | 23,500 | 4,383 | 18,362 |
| Syntex Corp | 270,425 | 172,175 | 57,961 |
| Sys Engin Lab Inc | 59,400 | 59,200 | 3,333 |
| UV Ind Inc wts 79 | 55,509 | 45,709 | 2,614 |
| xVaro Inc | 27,235 | 18,90 | 11,538 |
| Wang Laboratories | 92,125 | 91,200 | 2,357 |

x-Dual listing on both the American and New York Stock Exchanges.

FIGURE 1
Excerpt From Newspaper Announcement of Monthly Short Interest on the New York Stock Exchange and the American Stock Exchange

is less than 1 day's average trading volume, it means that there is little built-in demand for that security. The prospect of an immediate price decline from the current level is, therefore, to be expected.

### RISK INVOLVED

*A1d.*

The practice of selling short should be utilized only by the most sophisticated speculators; that is, only persons who understand and can afford to undertake the many risks involved should sell short. After all, when you purchase and pay for a security, you are assured you cannot lose more than the money you invested. But when you sell short, you create an unlimited financial responsibility. A rise in price means your cost of purchase to cover that sale will be that much more expensive. How high is up? Infinity!

Because of this potentially limitless financial responsibility, the New York Stock Exchange, the other major exchanges, and the NASD require all short sales to be effected only in margin accounts, where they can be under constant supervision and scrutiny. It is a necessary procedure to ensure compliance with the prescribed equity-maintenance regulations for such transactions.

### SHORT AGAINST THE BOX

*A1e.*

**short against the box**

*A1e(1).*

*Definition* **Short against the box** is an expression used to denote a situation in which a person is both long and short the same quantity of the same security at the same time. This person has thus established a fully hedged position and cannot benefit or lose from future fluctuations in price. A decline in equity in one position is offset by an increase in equity in the other position.

For example, if you sell short 100 shares of a stock you own at $40 per share and the price of that security

1. rises 5 points, the long position equity gains 5 points but the short position suffers by that amount;
2. declines 5 points, the long position equity loses 5 points but the short position gains by that amount.

To be hedged in such a fashion you must be long and short an equal amount of stock. If the long or short quantity is larger than the contra position, the net difference is subject to market risk.

*Reasons* There are a number of reasons why people sell short against the box, but the most popular one is to defer a liability for payment of a tax on capital gains until some future date, without exposure to market risk. For example, assume a customer purchased a security some time ago and had a paper profit in that issue. Unwilling to sell it now and thus become liable immediately for federal tax on the capital gain, this person can do either of two things:

*A1e(2).*

1. He or she can continue to hold the security at the risk of the market. (When ready to sell the customer can hope there will still be a profit on which to pay a tax.)
2. He or she can immediately sell that security short versus the certificate currently held by the broker in behalf of the cus-

tomer. (The customer's statement will then show that security position to be both long and short in the account.)

The second alternative permits this person to lock up (guarantee) the present gain without further risk and postpone tax liability for that profit. A person becomes liable for payment of the capital gains tax only when the long-position certificate is physically delivered to close out the short position. If this action is deferred until the following year, the customer has

1. protected a profit when prices may be most advantageous;
2. avoided paying tax on capital gains in a year when personal income may be abnormally high, thus necessitating payment of higher taxes as a result; and
3. freed some capital at the time of short sale to employ in some other investment.

WARNING: It must be borne in mind, however, that a person *cannot*

1. extend a short-term gain into a long-term gain through this technique;
2. sell short against the box unless it is done in a margin account;
3. engage in this practice unless someone else's certificate can be borrowed to facilitate delivery by the proper settlement date after sale; or
4. subsequently sell the long position and leave a net short position in that security unless the long sale is executed in the same fashion as a bona fide short sale.

For example, assume a customer is short against the box an equal number of shares in the same issue.

|  | Long | Short |
|---|---|---|
| XYZ Corporation | 500 | 500 |

To sell even as few as 100 shares of the long stock position would leave this customer in a net short position (that is, long 400, short 500 = net 100 short). Consequently, such sale must be executed mechanically as if it was a short sale; That is, the sale must be at a price not lower than the previous different-priced transaction in XYZ Corporation. The purpose of this rule is to ensure that the customer does not benefit his or her remaining short position by depressing the market value of that issue.

**A2.
Executing Short-Sale
Orders**

**A2a.**

### DEFINITIONS OF TICKS (CHARACTER OF TRANSACTIONS)

In order to understand the regulations created to prevent inequities and manipulations stemming from certain short sales, it is helpful to know about "**ticks**." A tick is securities industry jargon for a *transaction* executed on a securities exchange. Assume that after being traded at 50, a listed stock trades at 49⅞. This is obviously lower in value than the preceding transaction. This transaction is identified as a *minus tick*. If the stock trades at 49⅞ again im-

**ticks**

mediately thereafter, it is called a *zero minus tick* because, while equal to the price of the previous transaction, it is lower than the *last different price* that occurred.

> If the next sale takes place at 50, obviously a higher price than 49⅞, it is referred to as a *plus tick*. Another sale at 50 immediately thereafter is called a *zero plus tick* because, while equal in value to the last sale, it is higher in value than the *previous different-priced* transaction.
>
> ## example
>
> | 50 | 49⅞ (minus tick) | 49⅞ (zero minus tick) | 50 (plus tick) | 50 (zero plus tick) | 50 (zero plus tick) |
> |---|---|---|---|---|---|

### PLUS-TICK OR ZERO-PLUS-TICK RULES

A2b.

***SEC short-sale restrictions*** To correct inequities that occurred on stock exchanges prior to 1934, the SEC implemented Rules 10a–1 and 10a–2 relating to the mechanical processes for executing short sales. It was not unusual in those days to discover groups of speculators pooling their capital and selling short for the sole purpose of driving down the price of a particular security to a level where the stockholders would panic and unload their fully owned shares. This, in turn, caused even greater declines in value. When prices had dropped low enough, the original *bear-raiders* covered their short positions at bargain prices and pocketed a pretty penny of profit.

A2b(1).

But that is now history. With the advent of those SEC rules, it is a violation of the Securities Exchange Act of 1934 for anyone to sell a stock exchange security short if, in the execution of the sale, that party depresses the last different price of that security appearing on the consolidated ticker tape. In day-to-day terms, this means that in order to comply with federal requirements a person selling short

1. must use the last sale appearing on the consolidated ticker tape as a point of reference;[2]

> 2. must ensure that the order is executed at a price that constitutes a plus tick or a zero plus tick; and
> 3. cannot sell at a minus tick or at a zero minus tick.

The prospective short seller need not wait for someone else to create a plus tick or zero plus tick first. The seller can offer stock at a price that, if accepted by a purchaser, is identifiable as a plus or zero plus transaction. Often, this means that the short seller must play a passive role while the purchaser acts as the aggressor.

***Minus-tick example*** The last sale is at 68⅝, which is a *minus tick* from 68¾.

A2b(2).

---

[2]Instead, the SEC permits each exchange to establish as a point of reference the last sale only on its own premises. The New York and American stock exchanges are now using this privilege as their official policy.

Quotation, 68⅝ to 68⅞

The short seller can offer stock at 68¾ or at 68⅞. If a purchaser accepts, the short sale is a *plus tick*. This transaction complies with the restrictions imposed under SEC rules.

**A2b(3).**     ***Plus-tick example***    The last sale is at 53½, which is a *plus tick* from 53⅜.

Quotation, 53⅜ to 53⅝

The short seller can offer stock at 53½ (zero plus tick) or 53⅝ (plus tick). If a purchaser accepts, the short sale is either a zero plus tick or a plus tick. In either case, this transaction complies with the restrictions imposed under SEC rules.

In neither example above, can the short seller "hit" the bid prices shown. In the first instance, to do so would constitute a zero minus tick (65⅝), and in the latter instance, an ordinary minus tick (53⅜).

**A2b(4).**     ***Initial transaction on a stock exchange***    The initial transaction for a security after listing on the stock exchange is arbitrarily decreed to represent a plus tick. It can, in fact, be a short sale.

Every subsequent transaction is identified as zero plus, plus, minus, or zero minus, as the case may be. These designations continue daily, with identification of each day's first transaction dependent upon the previous day's closing price. Thus, if a stock closed at 25 on the NYSE on Monday and it was a minus tick, an opening sale on Tuesday below 25 is a minus tick; at 25, it is a zero minus tick; above 25, it is a plus tick.

**A2b(5).**     ***Ex dividends and ex distributions***    A reduction in price on the day a security begins trading ex dividend, ex rights, or *ex* any distribution necessitates a readjustment of the previous day's closing price by the value of that distribution. However, the identifying designation of that transaction is maintained, although on a lower plateau.

Thus, with a distribution of 25c per share (¼), if the previous close was at 37½ (plus tick) and if the first transaction on the ex date was at

1.  37¼, the transaction constitutes a *zero plus tick* because the difference is equal to the reduction in price (37½ − 37¼ = ¼);
2.  37⅜ or above, the transaction constitutes a *plus tick* because the difference is less than the reduction in price (37½ − 37⅜ = ⅛);
3.  37⅛ or below, the transaction constitutes a *minus tick* because the difference is more than the reduction in price (37½ − 37⅛ = ⅜).

Recall that for cash distributions not equal to the multiple of the minimum trading variation (⅛ point in most instances), the market price of that security is reduced by the *next highest ⅛ point*. Thus, if the distribution is set at 26c per share, the reduc-

> tion for dividend is ⅜ of a point. Accordingly, if the previous close was 37½ (plus tick), and if the first transaction on the ex date is at
>
> 1. 37⅛, the transaction now represents a zero plus tick;
> 2. 37¼ or above, the transaction now represents a plus tick;
> 3. 37 or below, the transaction now represents a minus tick.

*A3.*
*Ownership of Securities*
*A3a.*

### INDICATING THE STATUS OF CUSTOMER'S OWNERSHIP

In further compliance with SEC rule 10a–1 and 10a–2, each sell order entered for a stock traded on a national securities exchange must be marked *long* or *short*, as the case may be, to indicate the status of the customer's title to the security in question. It must also indicate this person's willingness and ability to settle the contract in accordance with the customs of that exchange.

If the order ticket is marked *long*, it means the customer owns that security and is prepared to make delivery of the certificate on the usual settlement date. A customer is deemed to *own* a security if that person or that person's agent

1. has title to it;
2. has entered into an unconditional contract to purchase it but has not yet received the certificate;
3. owns another security immediately convertible or exchangeable for the one to be sold, *and* has tendered this security for conversion or exchange;
4. has an option to purchase or acquire that security *and* has exercised that option; or
5. has rights or warrants to subscribe to that security *and* has exercised that privilege.

On the other hand, if the order is marked *short*, it means that the customer

1. does not own that security to be sold; or
2. owns the security but does not want to deliver that certificate to satisfy this sale (thus establishing a short against the box position).

> In either event, a *short* designation requires execution on a plus or zero plus tick and necessitates borrowing someone's certificate to complete the sale if it is executed. In fact, the entire process for selling short under any circumstances is predicated upon the seller's ability to borrow certificates to make prompt delivery to the purchaser. *If you cannot borrow the certificate, you may not sell it short.*

### BORROWING CERTIFICATES

*A3b.*

When a short sale is executed on the floor of the stock exchange or in the over-the-counter market, the selling firm does not tell the purchasing firm that it is a short sale. This item of information is of no concern to the buyer. The buyer is aware that on settlement date, in exchange for the contract money, the firm will receive a certificate. The purchasing firm doesn't really care whose certificate it is receiving.

The customer authorizing a short sale, however, must notify the executing broker that this is to be a short sale *at the time of entry*. To do so ensures compliance with the federal requirement to execute on a plus or zero plus tick. It also alerts the firm to the need to borrow that security *in this customer's* behalf. In most broker/dealer organizations, the task of borrowing certificates is delegated to the Cashiering Department. This department can utilize the period between trade date and settlement date to accomplish this service because delivery of the certificate to the purchasing firm is not made until the fifth business day after the trade date. The following sections describe some of the methods by which the Cashiering Department may obtain the needed certificates.

**A3b(1).**     *First choice*     The Cashiering Department first turns to securities available from firm-owned inventory and other margin accounts within its own firm. Margin customers must have already signed blanket hypothecation and loan-consent agreement forms when their accounts were initially established at the firm. If possible and available, it is easier to borrow their certificates than anyone else's.

Securities in a cash account are normally not available for such purposes. If the broker/dealer holds these securities for its customers, they have been fully paid for, and therefore, must be placed in *safekeeping*. Safekeeping involves physical separation and protection in a locked box or vault. Ordinarily, these certificates cannot be used in the conduct of the firm's business.

The only way that securities in a customer's cash account can be loaned or hypothecated is for the customer to give *specific written consent* per issue to do so. Needless to say, this rarely happens because there is seldom an advantage to be gained by the customer whose certificates are loaned. Securities in a margin account, on the other hand, are not usually fully paid for. When the customer signs the blanket loan-consent form, the certificates serving as collateral are made available for borrowing purposes.

Although the customer has given formal consent, regulatory authorities prohibit a broker/dealer from lending or hypothecating more of the customer's securities than the amount necessary to finance the debit balance with that firm. Thus, although a margin account may contain substantial security value, the amount available for Cashiering Department purposes depends upon the customer's debit balance. Security value in a margin account above the amount needed to finance that debit balance must be *segregated* by the firm. Segregated securities represent excess collateral in a margin account. As with securities in cash accounts, they too must be locked in a box or vault to avoid jeopardizing them in the conduct of the firm's business.

**A3b(2).**     *Second choice*     If the needed certificates are not available within its own firm, the Cashiering Department must turn to other broker/dealers for help. The cashier contacts other firms known to have many margin accounts or portfolios of many different securities in their proprietary accounts.[3] If at all possible, these firms will want to be accommodating. After all, they reason, sometime

---

[3]*Proprietary accounts* are the firm's own trading accounts or those of its principals that have been pledged to that firm as capital.

soon the situation may be reversed. They may become borrowers, and this cashier could be the lender they turn to for help. Besides, there is a valuable monetary reason for wanting to help these borrowers.

It is the custom of the industry to deposit collateral with the lender of certificates as protection for the loan. The collateral required is *cash* equal to the current value of the borrowed security. The lender can and does use this cash in the conduct of the firm's business, free of charge, until the certificate is returned. In addition, the lender can and does use this cash to reduce this firm's own borrowing needs with commercial banks, thus reducing the firm's operating costs.

The request for collateral is no real imposition upon the borrower of certificates (the short seller), either. The seller's broker merely uses the money received from the purchasing firm on the short sale and passes it along to the lending firm as the necessary collateral.

The purchasing broker/dealer pays the transaction money and receives a certificate that is then reregistered in the actual buyer's name or in the firm's name (street name) according to instructions. The buyer then steps out of the picture, fully satisfied, unknowingly leaving behind an open contract between the short seller's firm and the lending organization.

This is the most common means of borrowing certificates to accommodate short sellers. The flow of cash and certificates in these activities is shown in Figure 2.

**FIGURE 2**
A Typical Brokerage Firm Relationship Established with a Short Sale

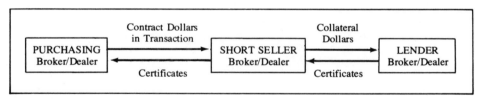

**_Third choice_** The cashier, in behalf of the short-selling customer, can approach institutions permitted by law and resolution to lend securities from their portfolios.

A3b(3).

The institutions benefit by investing the cash collateral received in short-term instruments, thereby earning additional income.

*A3b(4).*  **Desperation**  When it becomes apparent that the typical sources of supply cannot furnish enough (or any) of the needed security for the short seller, the cashier may be forced to pay a premium to entice more lenders into the marketplace. When a security is **lending at a premium**, the short seller is obliged to pay lenders a fee for the use of their certificates. This fee is paid in addition to the cash collateral deposited with the lender and is calculated on a basis of per 100 shares (or $1,000 bond) for each business day the certificate will be borrowed. It might be expressed as a $1 premium, or $2, or $3, and so on, depending upon the forces of supply and demand.

In calculating this expense, premiums do not count for weekends or holidays. They begin on the day the security is borrowed and accrue up to, but not including, the day it is returned. Thus, if a certificate is borrowed on Monday, June 7 and returned on Thursday, June 24, there are 13 days of premium money involved. (June 12, 13, 19, and 20 do not count because they are nonbusiness-day Saturdays and Sundays.)

The very mention of a premium is usually sufficient to bring a deluge of certificates into the market, which in turn eliminates the premium entirely. Obviously, then, requests for premiums are infrequent and are encountered only in the case of

1. closely held companies;
2. companies with relatively small capitalizations of stock;
3. issues with a substantial short interest; or
4. issues for which professional arbitrageurs seek assurance their stock loan will not be recalled for an extended period of time.

| JUNE | | | | | | |
|---|---|---|---|---|---|---|
| S | M | T | W | TH | F | S |
| | | 1 | 2 | 3 | 4 | 5 |
| 6 | 7 | 8 | 9 | 10 | 11 | 12 |
| 13 | 14 | 15 | 16 | 17 | 18 | 19 |
| 20 | 21 | 22 | 23 | 24 | 25 | 26 |
| 27 | 28 | 29 | 30 | | | |

In recent years, with tighter money conditions prevailing, the industry has seen more instances of a procedure that is the direct opposite of payment of premiums. The cash given to the lender organization as collateral becomes such an attractive commodity that the short seller's broker, with a choice of numerous available certificates, is able to demand *interest* from the lending firm. When a security is **lending at a rate**, the lender of the certificate pays interest to the borrower (the short seller) for the money received as collateral. The interest due is calculated on a daily basis, weekends and holidays included, until the borrowing arrangement ceases.

Under the circumstances, the lender organization doesn't often object to payment of the interest. It still represents one of the most inexpensive forms of financing its own and its customers' activities. It receives unrestricted use of cash equal to 100% of the security value loaned to the short seller. Even if the firm pays the short seller 3 to 4% for the use of this money, it is still ahead financially. If it attempts to borrow the same amount of money at a commercial bank, it must

1. deposit more in collateral value than the loan amount; and
2. pay interest to the bank at a rate somewhere between 2 to 4% higher than the rate between brokers, depending upon prevailing money-market conditions.

*Cornered* Although such instances are rare in modern times, situations have developed where one party (or a group of people) has acquired a substantial quantity of the available shares of a particular issue and, as a result, exerted influential pressure on its market price. This effect is particularly pronounced when that issue has built up a large short interest, and the borrowers suddenly find the certificates can be obtained only under exorbitant terms and conditions. The party or group who exercises such

**corner**

control establishes a powerful **corner** in the market. The premiums demanded are outrageous, and, often as not, the certificates are unavailable for any fee. It is the cornerer's intention to drive up the price by forcing the short seller to cover at any cost and at values determined arbitrarily. The classic corner created in Northern Pacific Railroad shares in the early twentieth century is recounted in the autobiography of the late Bernard Baruch and should be referred to for further information on the subject.

*A3b(5).*

As mentioned before, a broker/dealer has blanket written permission to hypothecate and to lend customers' margin securities, although it is not an unlimited authorization. Federal, exchange, and NASD authorities do not permit a customer's securities to be used beyond the amount actually needed to cover the debt to the firm.

*A4.*
*Financing Customer Activities*

When a broker/dealer finances its customer's debit balances through bank loans, it complies with the banking community's requirements. When financing is arranged by means of securities loans to dealers, it abides by the brokerage industry's customs. There are several interesting and important distinctions between these two methods.

*FINANCING THROUGH BANK LOANS*

*A4a.*

**broker's collateral loan call loan**

When using the loan facilities of a bank, a broker/dealer assumes the role of *debtor* by borrowing money to carry customer debit balances. The firm is obliged to deposit securities as the bank's protection in what is known as a **broker's collateral loan**. It is also sometimes referred to as a **call loan** because either party has the privilege of terminating the loan on 24-hour notice. Naturally, the bank requires more in securities value than the amount they are lending to the firm. The general practice of the major banks is to obtain securities worth at least 133⅓% of the money borrowed by that organization. Thus, if a broker/dealer wants to borrow $300,000 to carry customer debit balances, it must deposit customer securities worth at least $400,000 ($300,000 × 133⅓%) and pay interest to the bank on the money received.

For the purpose of financing margin account debit balances, the major stock exchanges and the NASD permit hypothecation of a customer's securities valued up to 140% of the debit balance. The cushion between the 133⅓% collateral required by the banks and the 140% in securities allowed by the authorities permits some flexibility for brokers in making and maintaining their arrangements. It is recognized that not all certificates are acceptable as collateral by the lending banks. Some banks will refrain from accepting odd-lot certificates, and some of them discourage loans having an "unusual" concentration in the securities of a single issuer.

Let us illustrate these points. Assume that a customer has a $300,000 debit balance. The broker/dealer can place as much as $420,000 ($300,000 × 140%) worth of the collateral securities into a call loan to finance that debt. Thus, the extra allowable 6⅔% (140% − 133⅓%) yields $20,000 additional ($420,000 − $400,000) funds. That excess $20,000 value can serve to forestall the bank's call for more collateral should security prices decline. Or, it can be employed to help finance another customer's debit balance if appropriate certificate denominations or issues are not readily available.

Not all customer accounts have pledged collateral at the 140% level. You will certainly find customer accounts with pledged collateral below the 140% level because of the difficulty in arranging proper denomination and value from the particular issues in the account. For example, if a customer had a $3,000 debit balance to be financed and only one certificate for 100 shares of IBM worth $27,000 available in the amount, in all likelihood the firm would not deposit it into a call loan. It is impractical to break up round-lot certificates merely to arrange short-term financing. Instead, the firm would probably utilize some of the $20,000 excess from the customer above to carry that $3,000 debit.

From an overall view of the situation there is no great advantage for the broker and no extensive jeopardy for the customers in these maneuvers. Furthermore, as the securities fluctuate in value, the broker/dealer must continuously substitute collateral to stay within the requirements. It must withdraw and segregate securities in some accounts and deliver certificates to the bank for others.

The rate of interest paid on this **call money** is influenced by    **call money**

1. the prime rate charged to the bank's best customers;
2. the broker/dealer's past credit relationship with the bank;
3. the size of the loan itself; and
4. the quality and type of collateral pledged (stock versus bonds, corporate bonds versus U.S. government bonds, and so on).

### A4b.    *FINANCING BY LENDING CERTIFICATES*

When a broker/dealer finances its customer margin accounts by means of securities loaned to other broker/dealers, the firm becomes a *creditor* in these transactions. For its protection, the firm demands and receives 100% of the market value of the certificates being loaned.

It is generally advantageous to finance a customer's debit balance by lending certificates rather than by obtaining a bank loan. The catch is that it is not always possible to lend certificates;

that is, there may be no demand for the certificate whereas bank financing is always available.

Let us expand upon this point with an illustration. Assume that a customer has a $5,000 debit in a margin account. The broker can finance this debit either by obtaining a bank loan or by lending certificates. If the broker finances the debit by a bank loan, then it deposits about $7,000 ($5,000 × 140%) worth of securities to serve as collateral for this account. On the other hand, if another firm is eager to borrow a $5,000 stock in that account to accommodate its own short-selling customer, the broker can lend the certificate to that firm. In exchange for the certificate, the lending broker receives $5,000 in cash to hold as security. It then uses this money to finance its customer's $5,000 debit balance.

The lending broker clearly benefits by using this second method rather than obtaining a bank loan. The broker charges the margin customer regular interest to carry the $5,000 debit balance, but it incurs no interest expense to obtain these funds from the other broker. In the bank-loan method, the broker's profit is the difference between the bank's interest charge to the broker and the broker's interest charge to the customer. In the case of a stock loan between brokerage firms, the broker's profit is generally the entire interest amount paid to the broker by the margin-account customer.

To see what this means in terms of monthly interest dollars on a $5,000 loan, let us use typical rates prevailing in early 1977:

|  | $5,000 Bank Loan | $5,000 Broker's Stock Loan |
|---|---|---|
| Broker charges customer 8% interest | $33.33 | $33.33 |
| Bank charges broker 6% interest | −25.00 | — |
| Broker's interest profit | $ 8.33 | $33.33 |

This may not look substantial. However, if you estimate total monthly debit balances in customer accounts at only $500,000, these dollars mean good profits for the broker.

### THE LENDER'S RIGHTS

A4c.

***Requests certificate return*** At any time, for any reason, the lender may ask for the return of its certificates. The certificates may be needed because the customer

A4c(1).

1. sold that security and must deliver it to the purchaser;
2. paid off the debit balance in the margin account or reduced it to such an extent that the firm must recall the certificates in order to segregate them and comply with regulations; or
3. has asked to withdraw that security physically from the account and is substituting another issue instead.

The short seller's firm, acting as the borrower, must then return that security within 5 business days after receiving such notice. This means it must find another lender in the interim period and establish the same relationship if it intends to remain in this short position.

A4c(2). **_Initiates buy-in procedures_**    If the short seller's firm cannot find another lender and does not return the certificates, it is placed in an unenviable position. The lender, holding the short seller's collateral, terminates the agreement and holds the firm in default. The process of termination is called a **buy-in** and, of course, is used only when all attempts at borrowing have proved futile. The lender arranges to buy that security in the marketplace, for guaranteed delivery, at whatever price is available. The lender holds the borrower financially responsible for any difference between the total cost of the purchase and the money held as collateral.

A4c(3).

> **_Marks to the market_**    In a buy-in, there probably will not be much difference between the lender's purchase cost and the money held as collateral. The reason for this is that a collateral loan is continuously adjusted during its existence to reflect any changes in the value of the security. If the security value appreciates, the certificate lender demands more money as collateral; if it declines, the certificate borrower demands a partial refund of its money. This continuous adjustment process is called **marking to the market**. A mark may be exchanged between borrowing and lending firms as often as necessary to maintain these loans equitably. Sometimes they are even exchanged when the security fluctuates as little as 1 or 2 points from the last valuation.

**marking to the market**

A4d.    *THE LENDER'S PRIVILEGES*

The lender of the security is entitled to all the privileges of ownership even though it has surrendered physical possession of the certificate. The short-selling customer thus is ultimately responsible for protection of the lender's interests. This point is clearly emphasized when consideration is given to the fact that the lender's certificate has been reregistered into the name of an unknowing third party to the transaction.

To ensure that its customers receive entitled shareholder benefits, the firm lending a stock certificate must maintain an accurate record of all securities loaned. This record is checked daily against various financial information sources subscribed to by all brokerage firms. These sources list, on a continuing basis, all essential amounts and dates relevant to the payment of interest and dividends by publicly owned companies. These sources also provide information about offerings of subscription rights. When according to these periodicals one of the firm's customers (whose certificate was loaned) should get a stockholder privilege, the lending firm creates a receivable on its records. Then the firm claims that item from the borrowing firm as soon as the benefit is distributed by the corporation. Among these privileges are interest, cash dividends, stock dividends and subscription rights.

A4d(1).    **_Interest_**    If the security in question is an interest-bearing bond, the borrowing firm must send the lending firm a check in the amount of interest so that it can credit or pay its customer. The short seller's margin account is, therefore, debited with that amount.

A4d(2).

***Cash dividend*** If the corporation declares a cash dividend, the borrowing firm must send the lending firm a check for that amount so that it can pay or credit its customer. Thus, a customer whose certificate has been loaned never realizes that the broker/dealer no longer has possession of the security. The short seller's margin account is debited with the actual amount of the dividend or interest on the *record date*, the day the short seller becomes liable for that payment.

A4d(3).

***Stock dividend*** Payment of stock dividends by corporations merely call for a simple bookkeeping entry in the offices of both borrowing and lending firms. If the original loan involves 100 shares and a 2% stock dividend is paid, internal records are adjusted to reflect an outstanding stock loan of 102 shares versus the same amount of money as collateral. The lending customer is credited with these additional shares, whereas the short seller's margin account is adjusted immediately to show a short position of 102 shares as of the record date, the date of established liability. The same technical process is employed for stock split-ups or split-downs.

A4d(4).

***Subscription rights*** When preemptive rights to subscribe are given to stockholders, the borrowing firm must immediately purchase these rights in the marketplace and deliver them to the lender to permit its customer the privilege of sale or subscription before expiration. The cost of purchasing the rights is immediately debited to the short seller's margin account.

A4d(5).

***Voting privileges*** This is the one privilege of stock ownership the lender's customer may lose. Although the borrower can manufacture all other privileges out of pocket, a short seller cannot create more votes in the corporation's affairs than actually exist. Votes are based upon the outstanding stock on the corporation's records. Ordinarily, even this is not much of a problem because so many stockholders do not bother to cast their proxies. If the lending firm's customer insists upon casting a proxy, the firm merely allows the use of another, more disinterested, customer's voting right.

In a proxy contest (a fight for control), when every vote is important and stockholders are aggressively solicited by both sides in the controversy, there is a great deal of difficulty in borrowing that stock under any condition. Every cashier who has loaned out that stock certificate immediately recalls it from the borrowers. This is the only way the firm can ensure that its customer will get a proxy and be able to vote. This, of course, places great pressure upon the short-selling customer who is literally squeezed into covering the short sale under unfavorable price circumstances. It is not unusual to see a stock skyrocketing in value merely upon rumor of a proxy contest, particularly when the stock has a large short interest and speculators have obviously panicked into covering their open positions.

The borrowing firm, acting on behalf of a short-selling customer, exposes its name and reputation to a degree of risk and financial liability. This fact is recognized by all parties concerned, as well as by the regulatory authorities. The Federal Reserve Board requires short-selling customers to deposit 50% of the net proceeds of such sales with the brokerage firm effecting those transactions. It is from this deposit that all marks to the market, cash dividends, interest obligations, and so on are deducted.

This relationship for a short sale in which the net proceeds amount to $10,000 is shown in Figure 3.

**FIGURE 3**
Short Sale with Net Proceeds of $10,000

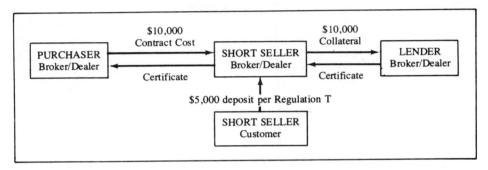

Note that the short-selling broker/dealer organization has use of the $5,000 cash deposit from its customer free of charge. It may use this deposit to finance other customers' debit balances in their margin accounts or segregate it in a special bank reserve account. In effect, whenever any customer sells short, the broker/dealer organization enjoys somewhat of a financial advantage as a result.

The New York Stock Exchange, the NASD, and other major exchanges have also established maintenance requirements for short-sale accounts as an added protection for member organizations. The firm is obliged to request more money as collateral from the customer if the equity shrinks to the minimum levels. If the customer does not deposit the funds, the firm must cover the open contract promptly. Most broker/dealers have instituted their own house rules, which are even stricter than those of the exchanges and the NASD.

**A5.**
***Closing the Contract***

Eventually, the short-selling customer will decide to cover the open position.

**A5a.**  **COVERING WHEN SHORT AGAINST THE BOX**

If short against the box, the customer merely gives instructions to deliver the long position to the lender organization. This pairs off and cancels both positions in the margin account. If the original long position had been held more than one year at the time of the short sale, the resulting profit or loss is taxed as *long term*. However, if the long position was held one year or less at the time of the short sale, it is always a short-term transaction, regardless of the date when the certificates are actually delivered back to the lender.

### COVERING A FUNDAMENTAL SHORT SALE

A5b.

> If the transaction is a fundamental short sale (that is, a short sale *not* against the box), the customer must go into the market to purchase the security and deliver it to the lender organization to satisfy the pending obligation. If the purchase expense is greater than the original proceeds, the customer suffers a capital loss, which is treated for tax purposes as short term. If the purchase expense is less than the original sale proceeds, the customer realizes a *short-term capital gain*. It is important to note that if a customer purchases a security to cover a short position at a profit, the profit is always taxed at ordinary income rates, regardless of the intervening time period involved in those transactions. Those rates can be as high as 70% of the realized profit. This contrasts with long-term capital gains, which are taxed at much more favorable rates.

Despite this tax disadvantage, a short sale can prove financially rewarding in a hurry, *if the sale is timed precisely*. Market history has proved that stock prices decline much faster than they rise, even though the longer-term trend of prices for the market, in general, has been bullish for decades.

B.
## the specialist system

The most attractive and important feature of a stock exchange listing is marketability at fair and reasonable prices. Toward this objective, one category of members has been delegated with responsibility for ensuring that each listed stock experiences an "orderly succession of prices." That member is known as the specialist. Each stock issue traded on the New York Stock Exchange[4] is assigned a specialist to supervise and conduct an equitable market for that security.

B1.
### Responsibility of the Specialist

The specialist is the lifeblood of activity transacted on the New York Stock Exchange. The specialist's knowledge, ability, skills, and capital are necessary to assure depth and liquidity for the equity securities of corporations responsible for approximately 42% of total assets, 43% of sales, and 91% of income[5] of all corporations in the United States.

To perform this function, the specialist is obliged to act in a dual capacity—as agent and as principal.

B2.
### The Specialist as Agent

> The specialist in a particular security normally receives orders to buy or sell when a firm's commission house or two-dollar brokers are unable to execute them immediately. Usually, this means that the specialist receives orders away from the current price levels of that issue. Such orders include limit orders to buy and stop orders to sell at prices below the prevailing market level, as well as limit orders to sell and stop orders to buy at prices above the prevailing market level. The specialist then enters them in a book maintained as a constant reminder to satisfy these instructions if and when market conditions favor their execution (see Figure 4).

[4]The NYSE is but one of the exchanges using the specialist system. We refer to it here as an example of those exchanges that have specialists working in this way.
[5]New York Stock Exchange, Inc., *1976 Fact Book* (New York: New York Stock Exchange, Inc. 1976), p. 35.

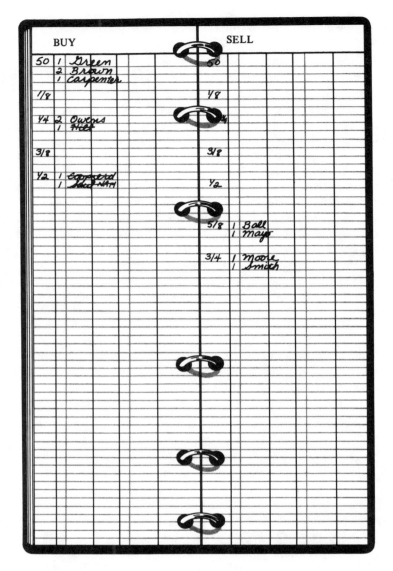

**FIGURE 4**
The Specialist's Notebook

The typical specialist's book is an informal record of orders received from various brokers on the NYSE trading floor. It fits easily into the palm of the specialist's hand; the looseleaf format allows pages to be added or removed easily.

When able to execute an order, the specialist may charge and receive a floor brokerage fee for this service[6] as can any two-dollar broker. The Brokerage fee is negotiated between the specialist and the firm for whom that order was executed. For example, when a specialist buys 100 shares of stock at 24 on behalf of a customer of a member firm, the charge may be $3.50 payable from the commission the customer owes to the member organization.

Many specialists in stocks that are popular with the public earn a substantial portion of their income acting in this riskless agency capacity. However, there is no assurance that

[6]Since May 1, 1975 specialists and other floor brokers are not obligated to charge a minimum rate. Consequently, they can execute some orders without any charge if they so choose.

1. the customers' instructions can ever be satisfied;
2. these orders will not be cancelled just prior to execution; or
3. sufficient quantities of customers' orders will be given to the specialist for execution.

In fact, the specialist's book is often empty of customer orders on the side of the quotation or at the time when they are needed most to maintain depth and price continuity. It is especially important at this time for the specialist to act as a dealer.

*B3.*
*The Specialist as Principal*

The specialist is encouraged to buy and sell for a personal account and risk in order to maintain marketability and an orderly succession of prices. The specialist is expected to personally bid or offer when the public is reluctant to do so and thus provide continuous two-sided markets in all quotations.[7]

The exchanges do not expect the specialist to act as a barrier in a rising market or as a support in a falling market. The specialist must merely try to keep these rises and declines *equitable and consistent*. Because of the variable factors influencing supply and demand for individual stocks, a specific formula for an orderly market cannot be defined.

Let us illustrate what a specialist might do in order to keep prices equitable and consistent. Take the hypothetical case of specialist Joe Brown with an absence of public orders at a particular moment. Brown may bid 50 for 100 shares of stock for himself at the same time he is offering 100 shares for sale at 50⅜ from his account. If someone then sells him 100 shares at 50, he may then bid 49¾ for 100 and offer 100 at 50⅛. If someone sells him another 100 at 49¾, he may then drop his quotation to 49½ bid and offer it at 49⅞. In this fashion, he provides liquidity for a security, although it is sometimes at personal expense to himself.

As just described, this can prove to be an expensive public service. If only sell orders prevail, and specialist Brown continually bids for stock, albeit at consecutively lower prices, there is no way for him to deal profitably. However, professional traders, including specialists, realize that prices do not fall continuously, even in bear markets, nor, on the other hand, do they rise continuously in bull markets. Prices of securities do, in fact, *fluctuate* as speculators, traders, and investors attempt to gain advantage of what they consider to be attractive values. This fluctuation enables specialists to trade out of their positions as they satisfy both supply and demand in a market-making capacity. They do not always have an opportunity to trade profitably. They often incur losses to keep their stock positions at manageable levels and still provide equitable prices for the public.

As a legally recognized market-marker, a specialist enjoys certain financing and tax advantages not available to most investors. The specialist is privileged to maintain both a specialty (trading) account and an investment account for each assigned stock. By keeping these positions physically separate and distinct, the specialist can

1. take advantage of favorable long-term capital gains rates for profits established in an investment account; and

[7]In 1975 the average specialist acted as principal in about 13% of all stock transactions on the exchange.

2. arrange financing for securities in the speciality account exempted from the restrictive provisions of the Federal Reserve Board's Regulation U. Generally, this means that the specialist can obtain credit in amounts up to 90% of the market value of the security pledged.

A specialist may also repurchase stocks sold at a loss within the past 30 days and still be able to use that loss to offset profits in calculating taxable income. That privilege, known as a wash sale, is denied to most investors under the Internal Revenue Code.

On the other hand, the government does not grant specialists any privileges to provide a tactical advantage over competing brokers in the trading crowd. Specialists must observe the unique rules about executing short sales for themselves or for customers in the same manner as do all other members. This means that when selling short, they too must sell shares short at least ⅛ point above the previous different-priced transaction. Just like everyone else, a specialist cannot depress the price of a stock when selling it short.

The New York Stock Exchange realizes that the specialist's vantage point in the marketplace provides information that could prove to be personally profitable if the specialist were permitted to use it. Because the contents of the book are generally unavailable to anyone else except NYSE officials, the specialist alone knows how many orders and shares are entered at prices just away from the prevailing quotation—orders that may serve as support or resistance levels. The specialist alone knows of the presence of stop orders and their memorandum price levels—orders that may accentuate price volatility if activated. Consequently, although the NYSE urges specialists to maintain personal trading relative to total volume in each assigned security, it must be done under restrictive regulations to avoid prejudicing the public interest.

*B4.*
*Specialist Trading Rules*

There are literally dozens of rules pertaining to conduct and activities of specialists in maintaining an orderly market. Five of them are germane to a student's understanding of specialist trading responsibilities.

When dealing for a personal account, a specialist *cannot*:

1. *Bid or offer on the same side as any customer's market order held.*[8] A specialist is not permitted to buy stock as principal until a customer's market order to buy has been satisfied; nor may the specialist sell stock as principal until a customer's market order to sell has been completed. Note that this restriction does not prevent a specialist from dealing on the opposite side of a customer's market order, provided none of the other rules in the process are violated.

2. *Bid or offer at the same price as any customer's limit order held.* A specialist may not have priority of time over any customer's limit order in the book, even if the specialist was bidding or offering as principal before receipt of the customer's order. The specialist can, of course, combine a personal bid or offering with customer orders at that price if the customer orders are given preference on executions that occur subsequently.

[8] Specialists normally receive market orders when a limit order on the book is cancelled and replaced with a market order.

3. *Activate (elect) a customer's stop order on the book.* The specialist may not be a party to any principal transaction if that trade elects a customer's stop order in the book.[9] Therefore, the specialist must carefully anticipate the possible result of a personal bid or offering if ultimately accepted by another member in the trading crowd.

4. *Act as broker* and *dealer in the same transaction.* If a specialist wants to buy stock personally from a customer's offering in the book or personally sell stock to a customer's bid in the book, the specialist must summon the broker who entered that order. That broker then executes the customer's transaction and earns the floor brokerage. The procedure is known as a **write-out**, because the specialist sends a notice to the telephone clerk of that firm requesting the appearance of its broker. The broker must reconfirm the details of the order and write an execution report. The specialist is not allowed to deal as principal and act as a customer's agent at the same time because of the inherent conflict of interest.

5. *"Stop stock" for any member's account.* This restriction means the specialist is not allowed to guarantee any member's *personal account* an execution price and thereby enable that person or firm to avoid market risk. **Stopping stock** is a specialist's guarantee of price to a customer's broker that enables the broker to try to improve upon that price without fear of missing the market.

**stopping stock**

To maintain status as fair and impartial coordinators of market activities, specialists must abide by an ethical code set down by the NYSE. It regulates a specialist's relationship to the company in whose stock this member specializes.[10]

**B5.**
**Ethical Responsibilities of a Specialist**

### CONTROVERSIES AND PROXY CONTESTS

**B5a.**

Specialists may not participate in a proxy contest of the company in whose stock they specialize. As market-makers, specialists are precluded from becoming embroiled in any controversies that may develop between management and dissident groups. However, as investors, specialists are not prohibited from assuming an active role in the affairs of other corporations.

### OFFICIAL CAPACITIES

**B5b.**

Specialists may not serve as officers or directors in a company if they specialize in its stock. They must not place themselves in a position where they can be privy to nonpublic information. Any inside revelations would surely influence their market activities and legally jeopardize them under penalties provided for by the Securities Exchange Act of 1934. Specialists may hold responsible positions in other, nonbrokerage corporations, provided that to do so does not adversely affect their specialist duties on the floor of the NYSE.

[9]In exceptional circumstances, with prior approval from a floor official, specialists may be responsible for activating stop orders. However, they must guarantee that customer an execution at the same price as the transaction that triggered this stop order.

[10]These rules also apply to partners and employees of the specialist's firm.

### B5c. OWNERSHIP OF SECURITIES

Specialists are also prohibited from owning control securities and from becoming principal stockholders in a company in which they specialize. Influential holdings represented by controlling securities would place a specialist in an insider relationship with that company, affecting and restricting any market-making ability. Similarly, as principal stockholders (owners of 10% or more of a class of stock issued by the corporation), their market judgment might be clouded or swayed by the size of their portfolios. Furthermore, by virtue of their substantial holdings, the corporations might also be tempted to accord them preferential treatment.

### B5d. REMUNERATION

Specialists may not accept finder's fees or other remuneration from a company in which they act as specialists. The old adage about a person's inability to serve two masters well at the same time is accorded some validity by this denial. The NYSE reasons that if specialists gain employment or compensation from a corporation, they are tempted to act more favorably toward it. This situation prejudices the best interests of both the NYSE and the investing public.

### B5e. BUSINESS TRANSACTIONS

Specialists may not engage in business transactions of any kind with the company in whose stock they specialize. This restriction applies not only to loans, options, contracts, and so forth, but to securities transactions in that issue for or with

1. the company itself;
2. any officer or director of the company;
3. any principal stockholder (owner of 10% or more of a class of stock) of the company;
4. any pension or profit-sharing fund;
5. any financial institution, such as a bank, trust company, insurance company, or investment company.

The obvious intent is for specialists to remain independent in their speciality stocks and avoid any conflict of interest or allegations of partiality.

## B6.
### *Managing a Specialist's Book*

#### B6a. GREEN TIGER OIL

When Broker A arrives at the trading post and asks for a quotation in Green Tiger Oil stock, the notations in the specialist's book are as shown in Figure 5. The specialist may reflect only the highest priced bid and lowest price offering with the number of shares represented at those prices (size). Other orders at various levels are strictly confidential. Therefore, the specialist announces, "26⅜ to 26½, 500 by 1,200."

If Broker A says "Take 100," it means that Broker A is accepting 100 shares of the 1,200 offered at 26½, and the specialist gives up the name of Bache Halsey Stuart to Broker A. Bache's order was entered on the book before Dean Witter's, and

| BUY | | SELL |
|---|---|---|
| | **26** | |
| 500 - PERSHING & CO. INC. | **1/8** | |
| 100 - BEAR STEARNS & CO. | **1/4** | |
| 100 - LOEWI & CO., INC.<br>400 - LADENBURG THALMANN | **3/8** | |
| | **1/2** | 200 - BACHE HALSEY STUART<br>1000 - DEAN WITTER & CO. INC. |
| | **5/8** | 100 - MERRILL LYNCH<br>600 - FERRIS & COMPANY |
| | **3/4** | |
| | **7/8** | |

**FIGURE 5**
Specialist's Book for Green Tiger Oil

Green Tiger Oil, symbol GTO. In practice, a specialist usually abbreviates entries recorded in the book, dropping the last two zeroes for volume notations and using designated code letters for member firm identification. Thus, the offerings at 26½ would be written: 2—B and 10—DW.

the specialist handles the book on a first come, first served basis. The specialist then writes a report to Bache Haley Stuart announcing sale of 100 shares at 26½ to Broker A (or perhaps to another firm given up by Broker A), leaving 100 shares remaining to be sold for Bache Halsey Stuart. At the end of the month, the specialist will send Bache a bill for floor brokerage for the execution service just performed as agent.

If, instead, Broker A says "Sold 200," it means that Broker A is accepting 200 shares of the 500 bid for at 26⅜, and the specialist gives up Loewi & Co. and Ladenburg, Thalmann to Broker A, each for 100 shares. The specialist writes execution reports to Loewi and Ladenburg, Thalmann at 26⅜, declares Broker A as the contra broker, and charges those buying firms floor brokerage as agent at month's end. Specialists may charge a floor brokerage fee only for those firms they serve as broker; that is, in an agency capacity.

| BUY | | SELL |
|---|---|---|
| | **13** | |
| | **1/8** | |
| | **1/4** | |
| | **3/8** | |
| 100-DREXEL BURNHAM LAMBERT | **1/2** | |
| 400-GOLDMAN SACHS | **5/8** | |
| | **3/4** | 100 STOP-LOEB RHOADES |
| | **7/8** | 1000-SHIELDS MODEL ROLAND<br>1000-THOMPSON McKINNON |

**FIGURE 6**
Specialist's Book for Ding-a-Ling Toys

Ding-a-Ling Toys, symbol DALT

**B6b.  *DING-A-LING TOYS***

Broker B, arriving in the Ding-a-Ling crowd, is informed that the stock is 13⅝ to 13⅞, 400 by 2,000. As shown in Figure 6, the presence of Loeb Rhoades' stop order to sell at 13¾ is not revealed because as a memorandum instruction it has no standing in the marketplace. It is a private communication between Loeb Rhoades and the specialist.

If Broker B says, "Sold 100" (to Goldman, Sachs on the specialist's book), the price level of that transaction, 13⅝, elects the stop order (at or below 13¾). Now Loeb Rhoades' memorandum becomes a market order and must be executed immediately by the specialist, in all likelihood at 13⅝, too. The specialist earns three floor commissions on these transactions, two from Goldman, Sachs and one from Loeb Rhoades.

If the specialist does not execute immediately at 13⅝ and attempts to use market judgment by offering Loeb Rhoades' stock at 13¾ instead of 13⅝, the specialist risks missing the market.

Another broker entering the crowd to sell 300 shares at 13⅝ would completely satisfy Goldman's remaining bid. This would establish the specialist's financial liability to Loeb Rhoades at that price, too.

### UNDERGROUND MINERALS UNLIMITED

*B6c.*

With the market in UMU represented in Figure 7, the specialist accepts an order to sell 100 shares *short* at the market from Broker Y. Because the previous transaction was at 41⅜ on a plus tick, the specialist can offer Broker Y's stock as low as 41⅜, changing the current offer from 41½ to 41⅜.

If a buyer accepts the offer at 41⅜, it constitutes a *zero plus tick* (equal in value to the last sale but higher than the last different-priced transaction), and complies with federal laws regarding execution of the short sale.

| BUY | | SELL |
|---|---|---|
| 100 - WHITE WELD & CO., INC. | **41** | |
| 200 - KUHN LOEB & CO. | **1/8** | |
| 100 - MITCHUM JONES TEMPLETON 300 - TUCKER ANTHONY & R.L. DAY | **1/4** | |
| | **3/8** | |
| | **1/2** | 500 - SALOMON BROTHERS 600 - OPPENHEIMER & CO. |
| | **5/8** | |
| | **3/4** | |
| | **7/8** | |

**FIGURE 7**
Specialist's Book for Underground Minerals Unlimited

Underground Minerals Unlimited, symbol UMU. Previous sale 41⅜, plus tick.

If, instead, Broker C arrives and cleans up the prevailing bid by selling 400 shares to the specialist's book at 41¼ and 200 shares at 41⅛, the specialist can then reduce Broker Y's offering price to 41¼. A subsequent sale at 41¼ would then represent a plus tick and would satisfy the short-sale regulation.

### B6d. CLEVER COMPUTER CORPORATION

The specialist's brokerage (agency) responsibility is readily identifiable, with the rules firmly fixed. If the specialist merely follows the customer's instructions, personal capital is not exposed to risk. But, as mentioned earlier, the specialist's function must often be combined with a dealer's (principal) responsibility to temper minor disparities between supply and demand.

To understand when and where the specialist may bid, offer, buy, or sell for a personal account, it is important to think ahead

| BUY | | SELL |
|---|---|---|
| 100 - REYNOLDS SECURITIES | | |
| 200 - PERSHING & COMPANY | 30 | |
| 400 - ROBINSON - HUMPHREY | | |
| | 1/8 | |
| | 1/4 | |
| 100 - BLYTH EASTMAN DILLON | 3/8 | |
| | 1/2 | 300 STOP - MERRILL LYNCH |
| | 5/8 | |
| | 3/4 | 200 - McDONALD & COMPANY |
| | | 100 - E.F. HUTTON |
| | 7/8 | 500 - THOMPSON McKINNON |
| | | 100 - BACHE HALSEY STUART |

**FIGURE 8**
Specialist's Book for Clever Computer Corporation

Clever Computer Corporation, symbol CCC. Previous sale 30⅜, minus tick. Specialist's position = none.

and project the effect of such transactions on the marketplace. For example, observe Clever Computer Corporation in Figure 8. The previous sale was at 30⅝, minus tick. The quotation resulting from public orders in the specialist's book is 30⅜ bid for 100 and 30¾ asked for 300 shares in total. With such a wide spread, this should be an ideal time for the specialist, with no position in CCC, personally to bid or offer and narrow the demand/supply gap. The question centers around permissible and appropriate prices at which to participate.

### Bids for the specialist's personal account

B6d(1).

**Below 30⅜** These bids are impractical because they do not narrow the spread in the quotation, are not reflected in the marketplace, and do not facilitate marketability.

**At 30⅜** Such bids would violate the rule about competing with a customer (Blyth Eastman Dillon) at the same price unless the specialist gave Blyth Eastman Dillon priority. Even so, this bid would be dangerous and would accomplish little. It does not narrow the spread in the quotation. Furthermore, if Blyth Eastman Dillon cancelled its order, the specialist would have to cancel, too. If the specialist's bid at 30⅜ was there alone, and a broker then sold stock at that price, the specialist would have participated in a transaction that activated Merrill Lynch's stop order (at 30½ or below). This would violate the specialist's trading restrictions.

**At 30½** Bidding for a personal account at this price would be improper for a similar reason. If a broker sold stock at 30½, the specialist would activate Merrill's stop order,[11] a practice prohibited under the trading rules.

**At 30⅝** This is a valid bid because it narrows the gap between bid and asked prices and would not be instrumental in activating the sell-stop order on the book.

**At 30¾** This is not a "bid" because of the presence of an offering at this price. To *purchase* stock, the specialist can accept an offering at 30¾. This action, however, would be suspect because normally a specialist

1. should not establish or increase a position in a stock on a plus tick (buying on a plus tick is considered a price-manipulative act and could entice public investors into buying the stock as it rises, thus benefiting the specialist's position); and
2. should never purchase more than half the quantity offered at that price (to do so would dominate trading in that issue and deny public investors a reasonable opportunity to share in a subsequent rise in price).

### Offers for the specialist's personal account

B6d(2).

**Above 30¾** Such offers are impractical because they do not improve the market. In any event, the specialist cannot compete or have priority over any public customer's order at the same price.

[11]Stop orders to *sell* become market orders if a trade occurs *at or below* the memorandum price. Stop orders to *buy* become market orders if a trade occurs *at or above* the memorandum price.

***At 30¾*** Action by the specialist at this price does not narrow the spread between demand and supply and accomplishes nothing because all public orders must be accorded priority anyway.

***At 30⅝*** This would normally be a valid offer if it weren't for one deterrent. If a broker accepted this offer at 30⅝, the specialist would be *selling short* on a zero minus tick, an act prohibited by federal regulation.

***At 30½*** The spectre of a short sale on a minus tick is also present here and must, therefore, be avoided. Additionally, a sale at this price would trigger the stop order.

***At 30⅜*** This is not an "offer" because of the presence of a bid at that price. However, an acceptance of that bid by the specialist would be illegal anyway, because

1. it would be a short sale on a minus tick; and
2. it would activate the stop order.

This illustration emphasizes the difficulty specialists experience in their market-making activities. Often they are precluded from being too aggressive because of prevailing rules and regulations. As principal in this illustration, the specialist is allowed to bid only at 30⅝ in efforts to improve marketability and also is prevented from offering stock at *any* price level.

### *B6e.* *EARTHQUAKE ERADICATORS*

When entering the Earthquake Eradicators crowd, Broker D is advised the stock is quoted 57⅜ to 57⅝, 1,800 bid for and 500 offered (see Figure 9). The confidential stop order to buy, with no active standing in the crowd, is known only to the specialist. The specialist owns 200 shares long in a personal account.

If Broker D then says "Take it," or "Take 500," the specialist gives up the names of Nesbitt, Thomson for 400 and Wood, Struthers for 100. The specialist then writes execution reports to each of these firms advising them of their sales to Broker D (or the member firm that Broker D discloses). However, as a result of that transaction at 57⅝, the stop order at 57½ has been activated. Now, with respect to that newly created market order, the specialist may

1. buy 100 shares for Advest & Co. immediately from L. F. Rothschild at 57¾, the best available offering;
2. bid 57½ for Advest & Co., using market judgment and hoping the next broker coming into the crowd will be a seller; or
3. sell 100 shares to Advest & Co., from a personal account at 57⅝, allowing Advest & Co.'s broker to write out the execution report.

### *B6f.* *VIGILANT EXAMINERS, INC.*

With Vigilant Examiners Inc., in Figure 10, quoted 83⅛ to 83½, 200 by 500 shares, Broker E asks the specialist to be stopped at

| BUY | | SELL |
|---|---|---|
| 100 - KIDDER PEABODY | 57 | |
| 200 - PAINE WEBBER J. & C. | 1/8 | |
| 1000 - SALOMON BROTHERS <br> 400 - SHIELDS MODEL ROLAND | 1/4 | |
| 300 - MERRILL LYNCH <br> 1500 - HORNBLOWER WEEKS | 3/8 | |
| 100 STOP - ADVEST & CO. | 1/2 | |
| | 5/8 | 400 - NESBITT THOMPSON & CO. <br> 100 - WOOD STRUTHERS |
| | 3/4 | 500 - L. F. ROTHSCHILD <br> 400 - BECKER SECURITIES |
| | 7/8 | 1000 - STIFEL NICOLAUS & CO. <br> 800 - STERN LAUER & CO. |

**FIGURE 9**
Specialist's Book for Earthquake Eradicators

Earthquake Eradicators, symbol EE. Previous sale 57⅜, plus tick. Specialist's position = 200 shares long.

83½ on 100 shares (see Figure 10). Broker E wants to be guaranteed a price of 83½ to buy 100 shares and have an opportunity to purchase the customer's 100 shares at a cheaper price.[12] The previous sale was at 83¼, plus tick. The specialist owns 100 shares long in a personal account.

In undertaking consideration of this request, the specialist realizes that there are two separate orders at 83½ to use as quasi-protection for any guarantee at this price. But the specialist is also aware that either or both of these sell orders may be cancelled or purchased by another broker before Broker E's customer can do better. Therefore, in granting Broker E's request, the specialist understands that as a last resort 100 shares from the specialist's personal account might have to be sold to Broker E at 83½.

Let us assume that Broker E is stopped at 83½. Broker E gives the order to the specialist for the attempt at improvement.

---

[12]Buyers are stopped at prevailing offerings; sellers at prevailing bid prices.

| BUY | | SELL |
|---|---|---|
| 100-RAUSCHER PIERCE SEC. 200-LEHMAN BROS. | 83 | |
| 100-SHEARSON HAYDEN STONE 100- E.F. HUTTON & CO. | 1/8 | |
| | 1/4 | |
| | 3/8 | |
| | 1/2 | 200-SMITH BARNEY HARRIS UPHAM 300- REYNOLDS SECURITIES |
| | 5/8 | 500—FIRST BOSTON CO. |
| | 3/4 | |
| | 7/8 | |

**FIGURE 10**
Specialist's Book for Vigilant Examiners, Inc.

Vigilant Examiners Inc., symbol VEI. Previous sale 83¼, plus tick. Specialist's position = 100 shares long.

The specialist then bids 83¼ (or 83⅜) in behalf of that customer. This bid narrows the spread in the quotation to ¼ (or ⅛) point.

A variety of circumstances can then occur. A step-by-step analysis reveals how the specialist operates under each of those possible conditions:

1. If either Reynolds Securities or Smith Barney Harris Upham cancels its order to sell, the only action called for would be a reduction in the offering size from 500 in total to 300 or 200, depending upon which firm revokes its instructions.

2. If both Reynolds Securities and Smith Barney Harris Upham cancel their sell orders, the specialist notifies Broker E that the stop is off. The specialist allows Broker E to purchase 100 shares from the specialist's account at 83½. The specialist would no longer have Reynolds Securities or Smith Barney Harris Upham stock to accommodate Broker E and therefore must terminate Broker E's opportunity to improve upon the price.

3. If a seller arrives at the post, that broker will dispose of stock to Broker E's customer who is making the best bid. In an effort to get a better price than 83½, Broker E uses the opportunity to bid 83¼ (or 83⅜, as the case may be), which is the best bid. The specialist, acting as Broker E's agent, writes the execution report and earns the floor brokerage fee.

4. If another buyer arrives instead, that broker can purchase up to the full 500 shares of the offering. This in turn stops out Broker E's customer, causing Broker E to purchase 100 shares from the stock remaining for sale at 83½ by Reynolds Securities or Smith Barney Harris Upham if there is any; in their absence Broker E buys 100 shares from the specialist's own account at 83½. Having been unsuccessful in doing better than 83½, Broker E must buy the stock at the price originally available.

In either of the latter events, the specialist summons Broker E and allows Broker E to write the execution report. Stock that has been stopped out, such as in this instance, is often identified on the ticker tape with the letters "ST" in vertical order after the execution price.

**example**

| | | |
|---|---|---|
| VEI | 83½ | S T |

*CURRENCY MANAGERS AND MANIPULATORS* **B6g.**

This last illustration involves all the complexities of a real and active trading market with the presence of a stop order and the allowance of stopped stock (see Figure 11).

The market in CMM is announced at 65¼ to 65⅝, 400 by 400 shares. The previous sale was at 65½, plus tick. The specialist owns 100 shares long in a personal account. Broker F asks to be stopped at 65¼ on the 100 shares to be sold.[13] Although most of the prerequisites are there (such as public order, minimum ¼-point spread, and so on), the specialist realizes those bids might be cancelled. If they are cancelled, then the specialist would be obliged to buy Broker F's stock at 65¼. That transaction would be responsible for activating Lehman's stop order. This normally prohibited action may be bypassed only in the public interest. The specialist would need to get approval from a floor official and to guarantee Lehman's sell-stop order, an execution at the same price as the electing sale itself. Under these circumstances, it is unlikely the specialist will stop Broker F. Probably, Broker F will sell 100 shares immediately to Lazard on the specialist's book or risk missing the market. That transaction at 65¼ now elects the stop order, and Lehman's newly created market order will be crossed by the specialist at 65¼, pairing it off with 100 shares remaining to be bought by Lazard and 100 for Evans & Co. The specialist will announce in a clear and audible voice, "65¼ for 200, 200 at 65⅜, sold."

[13]Sellers are stopped at prevailing bids, buyers at prevailing offering prices.

| BUY | | SELL |
|---|---|---|
| 100-JOHNSON LANE SPACE | | |
| 100-SHIELDS MODEL ROLAND | 65 | |
| 200-FAHNESTOCK & COMPANY | | |
| 400- DAIN KALMAN & QUAIL | | |
| | 1/8 | |
| | | |
| 200-LAZARD FRERES & CO. | | |
| 100- EVANS & CO., INC. | 1/4 | |
| 100- BEAR STEARNS | | |
| | | 200 STOP-LEHMAN BROS. |
| | 3/8 | |
| | | |
| | | |
| | 1/2 | |
| | | |
| | | 300-SHEARSON HAYDEN STONE |
| | 5/8 | 100- WOOD GUNDY & CO. |
| | | |
| | | 1000-ALEX BROWN & SONS |
| | 3/4 | 500-DONALDSON LUFKIN & J. |
| | | |
| | | 300-FAULKNER DAWKINS & S. |
| | 7/8 | 700-NEUBERGER BERMAN & CO. |
| | | |

**FIGURE 11**
Specialist's Book for Currency Managers and Manipulators

Currency Managers & Manipulators, symbol CMM. Previous sale 65½, plus tick. Specialist's position = 100 shares long.

On the other hand, if Broker G enters the original crowd instead of Broker F and asks to be stopped for 100 shares to buy at 65⅝, it is likely the specialist will do so. All the permissible factors are present, along with the added incentive of possible sale of the specialist's own 100 shares at a stabilizing price (65⅝ = plus tick).

In all likelihood, the specialist would then bid 65½ for 100 shares in behalf of Broker G's customer, trying to do better than 65⅝. Then, the following would happen:

1. If a seller appeared; Broker G's customer, with the best bid, would buy the stock at 65½. The specialist writes the execution report and earns the floor brokerage.
2. If a buyer appeared and bought stock from the lowest offeror at 65⅝, Broker G's customer would be stopped out. That customer would buy stock at 65⅝, either from
   a. one of the offerors on the specialist's book; or in their absence,

**b.** the specialist's account, in fulfillment of the guarantee obligation.

In a or b, the specialist would summon Broker G to write out the customer's execution report and thereby earn the floor brokerage. The specialist would do this because Broker G was capable of the same execution when initially entering that crowd.

| | **C.** |
|---|---|
| An odd lot is any number of shares less than a normal trading unit. Because most stocks on the New York Stock Exchange trade in multiples of 100 shares, an odd lot in those securities is less than 100 shares. For issues assigned trading privileges in units (multiples) of 10 shares, an odd lot is less than 10 shares. | **odd-lot stock executions** |

An odd lot is any number of shares less than a normal trading unit. Because most stocks on the New York Stock Exchange trade in multiples of 100 shares, an odd lot in those securities is less than 100 shares. For issues assigned trading privileges in units (multiples) of 10 shares, an odd lot is less than 10 shares.

*C1.*
*Definition and Processing Procedure for Odd Lots*

Most odd-lot orders on the NYSE are processed via computerized facilities owned by the Exchange. But the orders are actually executed on behalf of the specialist's personal trading account. The specialist accommodates odd-lot customers in addition to maintaining an orderly round-lot market, which is a primary responsibility.

Some member organizations execute their own customer's odd-lot orders by dealing directly from proprietary (firm trading) accounts. The technique they employ varies somewhat from firm to firm. For the most part these firms are geared to handle only market orders. All other orders are forwarded to the NYSE for execution. Therefore, this segment of the chapter deals only with the rules and procedures employed for odd-lot executions by the specialist on the Exchange.

*C2.*
*Role of the Specialist*

### THE SPECIALIST AS PRINCIPAL

*C2a.*

Specialist firms are always principals on all odd-lot purchases or sales transacted on the Exchange. That is, they always act as *dealer* in odd-lot transactions whether they are

1. accommodating customers in buying or selling their odd lots; or
2. adjusting inventory positions by buying or selling round lots.

With reference to accommodating "customers," bear in mind that specialists normally do not do business directly with the public. Primarily, their customers are the other member firms of the NYSE who transmit the public's odd-lot order to them for execution. Therefore, the other member firms are agents (brokers) on these transactions, whereas the specialists maintain their status as principals.

### THE SPECIALIST'S SERVICE CHARGE

*C2b.*

The specialist must accept every odd-lot order transmitted in proper form for execution. *The specialist must always buy when a customer wants to sell, and sell when a customer wants to buy, at the first possible opportunity following receipt of each odd-lot order.*

The prospect of continually trading contrary to public activity places the specialist at an obvious economic disadvantage, particularly because principal transactions preclude charging a commission to buffer potential losses. To counterbalance this inequity, the NYSE permits the specialist to levy a special charge for service on each transaction. This charge, officially called a **differential,** is added to the effective sale on a customer's purchase and deducted from the effective sale on a customer's sale. We shall treat the amount of this differential shortly.

The differential is not shown as a separate item on the trade confirmation that the customer receives from the broker. The differential has already been taken into consideration in the execution report. Therefore, if a customer is notified that an odd lot was purchased at 23¼, for example, then the customer should realize that the 23¼ price *includes* the differential charge for the specialist's service (23⅛ + ⅛ = 23¼). Similarly, an odd-lot seller notified of an execution price of 85⅞ should realize that the 85⅞ amount is the transaction price after deducting the differential (86 − ⅛ = 85⅞). In each instance, a customer may also be charged a commission by the member firm transmitting this order to the specialist for execution. The commission is shown as a separate item on the trade confirmation received by the customer.

C3a.  *AMOUNT*

**C3.**
***The Odd-Lot Differential***

> The amount of differential charged by the specialist depends upon the price of a round-lot transaction in that security executed on the floor of the New York Stock Exchange after receipt of the odd-lot order. This qualifying round-lot transaction is called an **effective sale**. An effective sale may, therefore, be defined as a round-lot transaction upon which a customer's odd-lot execution price is determined (see Table 1).

**TABLE 1**
DIFFERENTIALS ON THE NYSE

| IF THE EFFECTIVE SALE IS: | THE DIFFERENTIAL IS: |
| --- | --- |
| 1/8 point or below | One-half the price of the effective sale |
| 5/32 point | 3/32 point for sell orders, 1/8 point for buy orders |
| above 5/32 point | 1/8 point |

Almost all round-lot transactions occur on the NYSE above 5/32 point so that for practical purposes, the differential on the big board is ⅛ point for both buyers and sellers of odd lots. This means that an odd-lot buyer purchases at ⅛ point more, and an odd-lot seller sells at ⅛ point less, than the round-lot customer.

The American Stock Exchange generally uses a split differential for execution of odd-lot orders on its premises (see Table 2).

**TABLE 2**
DIFFERENTIALS ON THE AMEX

| IF THE EFFECTIVE SALE IS: | THE DIFFERENTIAL IS: |
| --- | --- |
| Below $40 per share | 1/8 point |
| At $40 or above | 1/4 point |

The exceptions to this basic rule about differentials relate to odd-lot executions

1. at the opening;
2. via the NYSE DOT (''designated order turnaround'') system, if entered as part of a round-lot order; and
3. through off-the-trading-floor facilities of a few large member organizations.

There is no differential charged to odd-lot orders entered before daily trading begins if those orders are executed on the opening transaction in that issue. Because the specialist receives these instructions in plenty of time to aggregate all odd lots, pair them off, and arrange inventory position adjustments, the customer is accorded the benefit of saving ⅛ point.

Although the DOT system is designed as an automated communications facility for processing small round-lot orders, it also accommodates odd-lot orders of up to 99 shares entered alone or as part of a round-lot order (such as an order to buy or sell 499 shares). The individual odd-lot order and a round lot with an accompanying odd lot are all executed by the specialist. A single odd-lot order is subject to the differential charge (except on opening transactions). However, if an odd-lot order is entered in the DOT system as part of a round-lot order, the round lot is executed without a floor brokerage fee and the odd lot without a differential. In fact, that entire order is executed at one price.

*C4.*
*Odd-Lot Market Orders*

### TO BUY OR TO SELL LONG

*C4a.*

Just as round-lot market orders require execution at the best available price, so, too, do odd-lot market orders, but with one modification. Because odd-lot orders have no standing in the trading crowd (that is, they may not be bid, offered, or used to initiate transactions), these orders must wait until a round-lot execution occurs. The *first* round-lot transaction after receipt by the specialist serves as the effective sale for all odd-lot market orders to buy or sell stock long (see Table 3).

**TABLE 3**
SAMPLE ODD-LOT MARKET ORDER EXECUTIONS

| ORDER | NEXT ROUND-LOT TRANSACTION | EXECUTION PRICE |
|---|---|---|
| Buy at market | 12 | 12⅛ (12 + ⅛) |
| Buy at market | 37¼ | 37⅜ (37¼ + ⅛) |
| Buy at market | 87⅝ | 83¾ (87⅝ + ⅛) |
| Sell long at market | 21⅞ | 21¾ (21⅞ − ⅛) |
| Sell long at market | 46 | 45⅞ (46 − ⅛) |
| Sell long at market | 101½ | 101⅜ (101½ − ⅛) |

### TO SELL SHORT

*C4b.*

Odd-lot market orders to *sell short* impose one additional requirement to execute such orders in compliance with federal and exchange regulations. | Specifically, in an odd-lot short sale, the effective sale must be *higher* in value than the last round-lot transaction at a different price. |

For example, assume the sequence of round-lot transactions shown on the following ticker tape:

| 40⅛, | 40, | 40⅛, | 40⅛, | 40⅛ |
|------|-----|------|------|-----|
| (1)  | (2) | (3)  | (4)  | (5) |

Trade 2 is lower in value than 40⅛ and cannot qualify as an effective sale for an odd-lot short seller. Trade 3 is higher in value than the previous transaction at 40 and can qualify as an effective sale for an odd-lot short seller. Trades 4 and 5 are also higher in value than 40 (which was the last different-price transaction), and can, therefore, also qualify as an effective sale for an odd-lot short seller. This requirement prevents an odd-lot short seller from being instrumental in depressing the price of the security. Table 4 lists some sample odd-lot market executions to sell short.

**TABLE 4**
SAMPLE ODD-LOT MARKET ORDER EXECUTIONS TO SELL SHORT

| PREVIOUS ROUND-LOT TRANSACTION | TERMS | SUBSEQUENT ROUND-LOT TRANSACTIONS[a] | EXECUTION PRICE |
|---|---|---|---|
| 16¼ | Sell short at market | [16⅜,] 16¼, 16⅛ | 16¼ (16⅜ − ⅛) |
| 37⅝ | Sell short at market | 37½, 37⅜, [37½] | 37⅜ (37½ − ⅛) |
| 74 | Sell short at market | 73⅞, [74,] 74⅛ | 73⅞ (74 − ⅛) |
| 126¼ | Sell short at market | 126, 125½, [126½] | 126⅜ (126½ − ⅛) |

[a]Boxed price is the effective sale because exchange rules require execution of an odd-lot order based upon the first possible round-lot price.

**C5.**
**Odd-Lot Limit Orders**

In defining a limit order, the customer sets the maximum price to be paid as a buyer or the minimum price to be accepted as a seller.[14] A broker attempting to execute a limit order must do so within the framework of this restriction. Although the specialist certainly tries to "do better" (improve upon the limit price), no member of the NYSE can execute a limit order at a less favorable price than dictated in the instructions.

Therefore, in the case of an odd-lot limit order to

1. *buy*, the effective sale is the first round-lot transaction *below* the limit. When the differential is then added to that round-lot price, the execution terms do not exceed the customer's maximum designation.
2. *sell long*, the effective sale is the first round-lot transaction *above* the limit. When the differential is then subtracted from that round-lot price, the execution terms do not violate the customer's minimum designated price.

[14]Remember, for odd-lot limit orders, the stated prices must include the differential.

3. *sell short*, the effective sale is the first round-lot transaction that is *both*
   a. higher in value than the last different price; and
   b. above the limit.

Odd-lot limit orders have an advantage over round-lot limit orders in that they must all be executed on the first possible transaction. That is, because odd lots are never represented in the NYSE's auction market quotations, they do not have to wait their turn for execution and actively compete with each other as do round-lot orders. Their contra party is always the specialist who is obliged to satisfy all odd-lot orders at the first opportunity to do so. Table 5 lists some sample odd-lot limit order executions.

**TABLE 5**
SAMPLE ODD-LOT LIMIT ORDER EXECUTIONS

| PREVIOUS ROUND-LOT TRANSACTION | TERMS | SUBSEQUENT ROUND-LOT TRANSACTIONS [a] | EXECUTION PRICE |
|---|---|---|---|
| Not pertinent | Buy at 10½ | 10¾, 10⅝, 10½, [10⅜] | 10½ (10⅜ + ⅛) |
| " " | Buy at 21¾ | [21½,] 21⅝, 21¾, 21⅞ | 21⅝ (21½ + ⅛) |
| " " | Buy at 34⅜ | 34⅜, 34½, [34¼,] 34 | 34⅜ (34¼ + ⅛) |
| " " | Buy at 79 | 79, 80, 79, [78] | 78⅛ (78 + ⅛) |
| " " | Sell long at 86¼ | 86¼, [86½,] 86¾, 87 | 86⅜ (86½ − ⅛) |
| " " | Sell long at 5⅝ | 5½, [5¾,] 5⅝, 5⅞ | 5⅝ (5¾ − ⅛) |
| " " | Sell long at 38 | [38¼,] 38½, 38, 37¾ | 38⅛ (38¼ − ⅛) |
| " " | Sell long at 93⅞ | 93⅞, 93⅝, [94,] 94¼ | 93⅞ (94 − ⅛) |
| 138 | Sell short at 137½ | 137¾, [138,] 138¼, 137⅞ | 137⅞ (138 − ⅛) |
| 55 | Sell short at 55⅛ | 55⅛, 55, [55¼,] 55⅜ | 55⅛ (55¼ − ⅛) |
| 49⅞ | Sell short at 49¾ | [50,] 50⅛, 49⅞, 49¾ | 49⅞ (50 − ⅛) |
| 69 | Sell short at 69 | 68¾, 69, [69¼,] 69½ | 69⅛ (69¼ − ⅛) |

aThe effective sale (boxed in this table) is always the first possible round-lot transaction capable of satisfying the customer's instruction.

Bear in mind that because of the customer's restrictive price and the unknown variable of market fluctuation, it is possible that a customer's limit order will not be executed. If a round lot never trades low enough (for a buy order) or high enough (for a sell order) after entry, the odd-lot limit order cannot be executed. This is why many odd-lot orders are also entered with GTC time stipulations. Day or good-til-cancelled designations are acceptable adjuncts to odd-lot orders, just as they are for round-lot orders.

Open buy-limit and sell-stop orders are also reduced in value for forthcoming distributions, on the ex-dividend date, in a manner identical to that for round lots. However, there is no semiannual reconfirmation of orders between member organizations and specialists as is required with round-lot orders.

### *C6. Odd-Lot Stop Orders*

Remember that a stop order is not an immediate market order but rather a memorandum that becomes a market order when activated. If you keep this in mind, you will find it easy to handle odd-lot stop orders.

The price appearing on a stop order is *not* a restrictive instruction. It is only for information purposes and does not include the value of the odd-lot differential. It is simply a notice addressed to the specialist to buy (or sell) this odd lot at the market but *only* if and when a round-lot transaction occurs *at or through* the information price appearing on this notice. Thus, in the case of odd-lot stop orders, the round-lot transaction that activates a stop order, called the **electing sale**, is *not* the effective sale for this type of odd-lot transaction. The electing sale is a round-lot transaction that takes place at a price at or through the memorandum price. The effective sale is the *first* transaction following the electing sale. Sample odd-lot stop order executions are listed in Table 6.

**electing sale**

**TABLE 6**
SAMPLE ODD-LOT STOP ORDER EXECUTIONS

| ORDER | SUBSEQUENT ROUND-LOT TRANSACTIONS [a] | EXECUTION PRICE |
|---|---|---|
| Buy at 28⅞ stop | 28¾, **28⅞**, 29, 29⅛ | 29⅛ (29 + ⅛) |
| Buy at 45¼ stop | 45¼, **45½**, 45¾, 46 | 45⅝ (45½ + ⅛) |
| Buy at 80 stop | 79¾, **80¼**, 80¾, 81¼ | 80⅞ (80¾ + ⅛) |
| Sell long at 34½ stop | 34⅝, **34⅜**, 34⅛, 34 | 34 (34⅛ − ⅛) |
| Sell long at 13 stop | 13⅛, **13**, 13, 13⅛ | 12⅞ (13 − ⅛) |
| Sell long at 60¾ stop | 61, 60⅞, **60¾**, 60⅝ | 60½ (60⅝ − ⅛) |

[a] The electing sale is in boldface type and the effective sale is boxed.

### C7.
### *Odd-Lot Stop-Limit Orders*

Rather than be exposed to the "best available price" features of a market order once their stop order is elected, some customers prefer to enter stop-*limit* orders instead. Execution of such orders is almost the same as for ordinary stop orders. The difference is that once elected, the stop-limit order is treated as a normal limit instruction and is not necessarily executed based on the value of the following round-lot transaction. If a subsequent round-lot transaction is not at a price at least ⅛ point better than the customer's limit,[15] the odd-lot order cannot be executed. The risk, of course, is that the order may never be executed if the market continuously moves away from the customer's price. It could thereby defeat the intended purpose for use as a form of insurance. It is also permissible, however, to enter these orders with a limit pricing differing from the stop price and perhaps salvage an execution after all.

**example**

Buy 11 XYZ at 49 stop, limit 49½; or
sell long 31 TDQ at 75¼ stop, limit 75

Table 7 lists some sample odd-lot stop-limit orders to illustrate different orders, transactions, and execution prices.

[15] Lower for buy orders; higher for sell orders.

**TABLE 7**
SAMPLE ODD-LOT STOP-LIMIT ORDER EXECUTIONS

| ORDER | SUBSEQUENT ROUND-LOT TRANSACTIONS [a] | EXECUTION PRICE |
|---|---|---|
| Buy at 39 stop limit | 38½, **39,** 39½, 40 | Cannot be executed because the stock never traded below 39 *after* the stop order was elected. |
| Buy at 51½ stop limit | 51⅜, **51½**, 51½, 51⅜ | 51½ (51⅜ + ⅛) |
| Buy at 20¼ stop, limit 21 | **20¼**, 20⅜, 20½, 20⅝ | 20½ (20⅜ + ⅛) |
| Buy at 63⅞ stop, limit 64 | 63¾, **64,** 64, 63¾ | 63⅞ (63¾ + ⅛) |
| Sell long at 95¼ stop limit | 95½, **95,** 95½, 95 | 95⅜ (95½ − ⅛) |
| Sell long at 10⅝ stop limit | 10¾, **10⅝**, 10½, 10⅜ | Cannot be executed because the stock never traded above 10⅝ *after* the stop order was elected. |
| Sell long at 47⅛ stop, limit 47 | **47,** 46⅞, 47, 47⅛ | 47 (47⅛ − ⅛) |
| Sell long at 101 stop, limit 100 | 102, **101,** 100, 100½ | 100⅜ (100½ − ⅛) |

[a] The electing sale is in boldface type and the effective sale is boxed.

***C8. Short-Stop and Short-Stop-Limit Orders***

This next variety of stop or stop-limit orders is rarely encountered. Some registered representatives have never heard of short-stop and short-stop-limit orders even after many years of servicing customer accounts.

Nevertheless, there should be no confusion associated with short-stop or short-stop-limit orders if you remember the following facts and procedures.

1. The *stop* portion must be activated before there is an order to be executed. Therefore, the price represented applies *first* to the stop instruction. After this is eliminated, what remains is a simple short-sale order at the market or a short-sale limit order, as the case may be.
2. To determine the execution price once the stop has been activated, do the following:
   a. Seek the first transaction identified as a plus tick. This is the effective sale for the short-stop order.
   b. Compare that price with the limit set by the order. If that price is higher than the limit price specified in the order, it is also the effective sale for the short-stop-limit order. If it is not higher, continue searching for the first round-lot transaction that is both a plus tick *and* above the limit. This is the effective sale for the short-stop-limit order.

Let us illustrate how all this works. Assume that a customer entered an odd-lot order to sell short at 65¼ stop and that a round-lot sale eventually took place at 65¼ (or below). That trade would activate the stop portion of the order making it a market order to sell short. Now, we must look for the first round-lot sale higher than the electing sale. If the following sale occurred thereafter—65⅜, 65½, 65⅝—the effective sale would be 65⅜ because it is higher than the electing sale at 65¼. The stock would be sold short at 65¼ after the differential is subtracted.

*C9.*
***Summary of Odd-Lot Orders***

To illustrate the short-stop-limit order assume that the customer's odd-lot order had been to sell short at 65⅜ stop limit and had been elected when a round lot traded at 65¼. If the following sales occurred thereafter—65⅜, 65½, 65⅝—the first sale at 65⅜ is higher than the electing sale but *not* high enough to satisfy the limit instruction. Therefore, we must continue searching for the round-lot sale capable of satisfying that criterion, too (that is, a round lot at 65½ or above). The effective sale happens to be the following transaction. Therefore, the odd-lot order is sold short at 65⅜, the customer's limit, after the ⅛-point differential is subtracted from the effective sale at 65½. Table 8 summarizes some sample odd-lot short-stop and short-stop-limit order executions. Odd-lot orders in general are summarized in Table 9.

**TABLE 8**
SAMPLE ODD-LOT SHORT-STOP AND SHORT-STOP-LIMIT ORDER EXECUTIONS

| PREVIOUS ROUND-LOT TRANSACTION | TERMS | SUBSEQUENT ROUND-LOT TRANSACTIONS [a] | EXECUTION PRICE |
|---|---|---|---|
| 38⅝ | Sell short at 38⅝ stop | **38⅝**, 38½, 38⅜, 38¼ | Cannot be executed (no higher value sale than 38⅝): |
| 26¼ | Sell short at 26 stop | 26⅛, **26**, 25⅞, [26] | 25⅞ (26 − ⅛) The first plus tick after the electing sale is the second transaction thereafter, also at 26. That sale is the effective sale. The odd-lot short sale is completed at 25⅞. |
| 89⅜ | Sell short at 89¼ stop limit | 89⅜, **89⅛**, [89⅜,] 89⅝, | 89¼ (89⅜ − ⅛) |
| 57⅞ | Sell short at 57¾ stop limit | **57¾**, 57⅝, 57¾, [57⅞] | 57¾ (57⅞ − ⅛) After the stop order was elected at 57¾, the price declined to 57⅝, an ineligible short-sale price. Although the following sale at 57¾ solved that problem, it was not high enough in value to satisfy the limit requirement of 57¾. The first such sale to satisfy both requirements was the next transaction at 57⅞. Thus, the customer sells short at the limit of 57¾ after the differential is deducted from the effective sale. |
| 143 | Sell short at 142½ stop, limit 142 | 143, **142**, [142½,] 141½ | 142⅜ (142½ − ⅛) |
| 41⅞ | Sell short at 41¾ stop, limit 41½ | **41½**, 41⅜, [41⅝,] 41⅞ | 41½ (41⅝ − ⅛) |
| 18½ | Sell short at 18¼ stop, limit 18 | 18½, 18⅝, 18⅜, **18¼** | Cannot be executed from given information (no sales shown after electing sale at 18¼). |

[a] The electing sale is in boldface type and the effective sale is boxed.

*C10a.*

## *ON-THE-QUOTATION ODD-LOT ORDERS*

***C10.***
***Infrequent Odd-Lot Techniques***

It is not mandatory to base an odd-lot price upon an actual round-lot transaction, although that method overwhelmingly predominates. It is possible to use a *quotation rather than a transaction* as a basis for price determination. Odd-lot customers too impatient to wait for a round-lot transaction can enter their orders to buy or

**TABLE 9**
SUMMARY OF ODD-LOT ORDERS

| | MARKET ORDER | LIMIT ORDER | STOP ORDER | STOP-LIMIT ORDER |
|---|---|---|---|---|
| **BUY** | Customer pays the price of the first round-lot transaction plus the differential. | Customer pays the price of the first round-lot transaction that is *below* the limit, plus the differential. | *After the electing sale*, the customer pays the price of the first round-lot transaction, plus the differential. | *After the electing sale*, the customer pays the price of the first round-lot transaction *below* the limit, plus the differential. |
| **SELL LONG** | Customer receives the price of the first round-lot transaction minus the differential. | Customer receives the price of the first round-lot transaction that is *above* the limit, minus the differential. | *After the electing sale*, the customer receives the price of the first round-lot transaction, minus the differential. | *After the electing sale*, the customer receives the price of the first round-lot transaction *above* the limit, minus the differential. |
| **SELL SHORT** | Customer receives the price of the first round-lot transaction higher than the last different price, minus the differential. | Customer receives the price of the first transaction higher than the last different price that is *above* the limit, minus the differential. | *After the electing sale*, the customer receives the price of the first round-lot transaction higher than the last sale, minus the differential. | *After the electing sale*, the customer receives the price of the first round-lot transaction that is higher than the last sale and *above* the limit, minus the differential. |

sell immediately at a price related to the existing round-lot quotation on the floor of the exchange. The customer can buy at the prevailing offering price plus the differential, or sell long[16] at the prevailing bid price minus the differential.

This is no imposition upon the specialist because

1. the specialist alone acts as the accommodating principal on all odd-lot trades; and
2. the worst round-lot price that might occur is a transaction at the prevailing bid or offering, which would require the specialist to deal with the odd-lot customer at that time, anyway.

Besides, if that arrangement inconveniences the specialist's preference for a security position, there is nothing to prevent the specialist from buying a round lot from the offeror (or selling to the bidder) in that quotation to make adjustments thereto. In fact, quite often, in the act of adjusting inventory, the specialist creates the effective sale for a customer's order. In this way the specialist performs an important service for the customer. The SEC and the NYSE both recognize the value of this public service. To facilitate the specialist's flexibility of operation, they permit the specialist to sell short from inventory at a price *below* the last different price, if

1. the result of that sale does not create a short position of 100 shares or more; or
2. if forced into a short position by virtue of customer's orders.

In the latter event, there is no limitation on the number of shares sold short because the specialist does not act as the aggressor.

Let us illustrate this point. Assume that the specialist's position is even (that is, neither long or short). Then the specialist receives orders from four customers, each of whom wants to buy 50 shares of that issue at the market. But before the specialist can purchase two round lots for reallocation to those customers as odd

---

[16]Odd-lot customers are prohibited from selling short on a bid price. They require a bona fide round-lot sale above the last different price in order to qualify.

lots, two brokers trade a round lot of that issue on the exchange at a price below the previous sale. This transaction now

1. serves as the effective sale for each of those odd-lot orders;
2. requires the specialist to sell stock to those customers from an inventory that does not exist; and
3. leads to a short position in the specialist's account at a depressed value from the last transaction at a different price.

The specialist's transaction is permissible even though the specialist sells short and sells at a depressed value. This is so because the specialist acted because of the customers' orders.

### C10b.  AT-THE-CLOSE ODD-LOT ORDERS

Some customers prefer to buy or sell their stock as near as possible to the end of the trading day, probably on the supposition that they can achieve a more favorable execution price. The specialist is prepared to satisfy this eccentric belief without questioning the customer's motives, provided that this instruction is received before trading on the stock exchange ceases for the day. However, an at-the-close order to buy or sell is not executed on the last round-lot sale of the day. Rather, it is bought (or sold) on the final quotation of the day.[17]

When the closing bell (signaling the end of the trading that day) stops ringing, the prevailing highest bid and lowest offering prices become the closing quotation. This quotation is the determinant for executing at-the-close orders. Those customers will buy at the offering price plus the differential or sell long at the bid price minus the differential.

Some investors even attempt to hedge their instructions by entering limit orders with an ''or at-the-close'' stipulation. If their limit price cannot be satisfied during the normal trading session, they request an execution on the closing quotation, *at whatever price prevails*. This approach assures completion of their investment program that day.

### C10c.  BASIS PRICE ODD-LOT ORDERS

Executing an odd-lot order on a quotation may be inequitable for some investors who deal in relatively inactive stocks with a wide spread between their bid and offering prices. Upon request, the specialist will establish and permit execution of odd-lot orders at a **basis price**.

A basis price is an *artificial* round-lot transaction created at a price somewhere between the prevailing bid and offering if

1. that issue did not trade throughout the day; and
2. the spread between bid and offering prices equals at least 2 full points (for example, 141–143, 86½–89, 107–112, and so forth).

**basis price**

The price is set by the specialist at a level believed to be where that stock will eventually next trade. It is not necessarily

[17]Short sales at the close are prohibited.

directly in between the prevailing quotation. It could be on or close to the current bid or offering price. The specialist's judgment is influenced by such factors as the trend of prices in the rest of the market and knowledge of a large buy or sell interest overhanging this particular stock or industry. Each basis price, although established by the specialist, is subject to approval by a floor official to ensure fairness for the customer in view of market conditions.

Basis price executions are available only to customers who

1. deal in stock assigned 100-share trading units by the exchange;
2. enter their order at least 30 minutes before the market closes; and
3. instruct their orders be marked "on basis."

Table 10 lists some sample basic price odd-lot executions.

**TABLE 10**
SAMPLE BASIS PRICE ODD-LOT EXECUTIONS

|  | BASIS PRICE [a] | EXECUTION PRICE |
|---|---|---|
| Buy on basis | 147 | 147⅛ (147 + ⅛) |
| Sell long on basis | 87¾ | 87⅝ (87¾ − ⅛) |
| Buy at 111 or on basis [b] | 113½ | 113⅝ (113½ + ⅛) |
| Sell long at 130 or on basis [b] | 131 | 130⅞ (131 − ⅛) |
| Sell long at market or on basis [b] | 95⅝ | 95½ (95⅝ − ⅛) |

[a]Short sales are prohibited on a basis price.

[b]Because it is unknown at the time of entry whether the security will trade that day, most basis price orders include a provision for execution on an effective sale, too.

**BUNCHING ODD-LOT ORDERS**                                                C10d.

**bunching**
> Some customers and/or registered representatives can avoid paying the odd-lot differential by *combining two or more odd-lot orders* for entry and execution as a round lot. This practice, known as **bunching**, is acceptable provided each of the interested customers gives approval to this activity prior to the transaction. Obviously, it can be attempted only when the terms and conditions of the odd-lot orders are identical, and the total quantity amounts to a round lot.
>
> Bunched orders are executed on the floor of the exchange as a round lot, normally handled by a commission house broker, specialist, or two-dollar broker. However, once executed, the transaction must be split up into proper quantities and allocated among each of the participating customers. The odd-lot customer's saving is solely in avoiding payment of the odd-lot differential (⅛ point). Other expenses contingent to the transaction remain basically the same.

In an opposite vein, exchange regulations forbid customers from breaking up shares that make up round lots and entering them *simultaneously* as odd lots at identical prices. That practice is unfair to the specialist, who is obliged to execute all of them at the same time when a single effective sale occurs. Otherwise, the owner of several round lots of an issue subject to wide price fluctuation could be assured of a single favorable execution for the entire order

1. for the nominal fee of a ⅛-point differential; and
2. to the tactical detriment of the specialist's inventory cost position.

## C11.
### *Summary Guide to Odd-Lot Definitions*

*At-the-Close.* An odd-lot order to be executed on the final *quotation* of the day.

*Basis Price.* An artificial round-lot transaction created somewhere between the final bid and offer prices if a stock did not trade that day and had a spread in the closing quotation of at least 2 points.

*Bunching.* Combining two or more odd-lot orders for entry and execution as a round-lot transaction.

*Differential.* A fee charged by the specialist for execution of a customer's order.

1. The fee is added to the effective sale on purchase transactions.
2. The fee is subtracted from the effective sale on sale transactions.

On the New York Stock Exchange, if the effective sale is above 5/32, the odd-lot differential is ⅛ point.

*Effective Sale.* A round-lot transaction upon which a customer's odd-lot order is executed.

*Electing Sale.* A round-lot transaction that activates (triggers) a stop order.

*On-the-Quotation.* An odd-lot market order to be executed at the prevailing *offering or bid price* rather than at the price of a round-lot *transaction*.

## D.
## corporate bond transactions

### D1.
### *NYSE Bond Activity*

Most bond transactions take place over the counter; that is, away from the trading floor of the registered securities exchanges in the United States. This is only partly due to the fact that comparatively few debt issues are listed for trading there. The NYSE's lenient application of trading regulations has enabled most bond activity to take place over the counter. Nevertheless, those bonds that are listed represent a significant amount of dollar value and importance in the marketplace.

With some exceptions, NYSE member firms with orders for *listed stock* traditionally execute those orders on the floor of the Exchange. *Listed bond* orders have never been subject to that historical custom. This circumstance prevails because many bond traders and market-makers have always been nonmembers of the NYSE. Consequently, they have no ties to any Exchange rules or traditions. Moreover, the NYSE never really promoted itself as a bond marketplace for general public participants because, until recent years, the bond market was strictly for professionals whereas the stock market was principally for the less sophisticated smaller investor able to assume financial risk.

As might be expected in light of its position in the securities industry, the NYSE does have a rule designed to protect the interests of the small bond investor. It requires members to provide these investors with the advantages of the Exchange's centralized marketplace and prompt trade publicity.

D2.
*The Nine-Bond Rule*

Unless prior consent of the NYSE can be obtained, all orders handled by member firms for nine or fewer listed bonds must be sent to the floor of the exchange for a diligent attempt at execution.

Orders for ten or more bonds are not subject to these restrictive conditions. Nor are orders for less than 10 bonds that

1. mature within 12 months;
2. have been called prior to maturity and will be redeemed within 12 months;
3. are obligations of
   a. the United States, Puerto Rico, or the Philippine Islands, or
   b. any state, territory, or municipality therein;
4. will be executed as an *agency transaction* and the customer specifically directs the order to be executed elsewhere than on the exchange;[18]
5. is part of a primary distribution or part of a secondary distribution that was effected off the floor of the exchange;
6. are unrelated to the current market price if the intent of such order is to correct an error or make a gift;
7. are unregistered, as defined in the Securities Act of 1933;
8. are less than a normal unit of trading (that is, baby bonds, those bonds whose face value is less than $1,000).
9. are executed for persons situated outside the United States and before or after trading hours on the New York Stock Exchange.

Another permissible exception to the nine-bond rule allows execution of an order with a nonmember market-maker over the counter. The member organization is required to act only in an agency capacity in such transactions.

*D3.*
*The Bond Room Facilities*

Bond orders are sent to the floor of the NYSE under different conditions and procedures than those used to handle stock orders. The physical facilities are much smaller than any of the stock trading areas and lack the recognizable presence of a trading post. All trading activity must take place within the outline of an octagonal diagram imbedded into a rubberized flooring in the center of the room. It is generally referred to as a **trading ring**.

**trading ring**

Listed bonds are assigned trading privileges by either of two systems upon appropriate determination by the Floor Department of the NYSE.

### ACTIVE BONDS (THE "FREE" CROWD)

*D3a.*

Debt instruments expected to trade frequently on the trading floor are assigned privileges in this category. Included are most convertible bonds and substantial issues of well-known corporations. Brokers receiving orders to buy or sell such bonds step into the ring and make their bids or offerings *verbally*, provided they equal or improve upon the price terms of the prevailing quotation. Such information is furnished to them by a quotations clerk, a NYSE employee who maintains a record of best bids and offerings and posts them on a quotation board just outside the ring.

[18]Members may not solicit such instructions before attempting diligent execution on the floor.

> Orders to buy or sell 50 bonds or more may permissibly be entered as "all or none," thereby enabling a broker verbally to qualify this order in the trading crowd. This sharply contrasts with the manner in which all-or-none stock orders are handled, regardless of quantity involved in that order.

Acceptance of a bid or offering to consummate a transaction is accomplished within the confines of the ring by the statements, "Take it" or "Sold" in precisely the same fashion that stock orders are executed.

If no member accepts the verbal bid (or offering), that broker is free to use market judgment and withdraw from the trading ring. In other words, the broker can use personal discretion (but still be subject to the risk of missing the market). A broker is not bound to state or even restate the terms and conditions specified in an order if confident that the order can be executed at a better price. This is the origin and application of the expression "free crowd" for active bonds.

### D3b.  INACTIVE BONDS (THE "CABINET" OR "CAN" CROWD)

Inactive bonds are debt instruments traded infrequently because of such factors as

1. limited quantities outstanding;
2. concentrated long-term holdings by institutional investors; or
3. lack of investor popularity for that issuer's industry, causing the Floor Department to assign that bond to inactive status.

> Verbal bids or offerings would be futile in these instances, and so all bids and offerings are written on colored cards and filed in metal cabinets surrounding the trading ring. Hence, the significance of the expressions "cabinet" or "can" (a metal cabinet) crowd synonymous with inactive bonds.

Whereas only day or GTC orders may be entered on the floor in the stock trading room or active bond crowd, cabinet bond orders may also be entered as good-through-the-week or good-through-the-month as a convenience to investors that have an interest in dealing with them. Different colored cards indicate the effective lifetime of these orders.

### example

| | | |
|---|---|---|
| White | = | day orders |
| Blue | = | good-through-the-week |
| Salmon | = | good-through-the-month |
| Yellow | = | good-till-cancelled |

The absence of a specialist in the bond room precludes entry of stop orders in the active or inactive bond crowds. Normal market and limit orders, however, are acceptable and may be handled and executed in the fashion described.

Brokers with orders to buy or sell an issue assigned to the cabinets will first determine whether there is a contra order in the rack at an acceptable price. They inquire through a cabinet clerk (a NYSE employee responsible for maintaining the order cards in the proper cabinets). If no acceptable order is present, the brokers leave a card in the cabinet and go on about their business. If there is a satisfactory contra order card available, the card is removed from the rack and the original broker summoned. Both members step into the trading ring to consummate the transaction via verbal bid (offer) and acceptance.

Business is transacted in the cabinet crowd on a first-come, first-served basis. Priority belongs to each order in its entry time sequence. Although verbal bids or offers are permitted, any order in the cabinet at the same price has priority over a verbal competitor.

Members are held to terms and conditions specified on the order card and must consummate the transaction with the agreeable contra broker unless written cancellation is received by the cabinet clerk before preliminary acceptance by that broker.

In the final analysis, *all* NYSE bond transactions are completed within the trading ring. This is true for active and inactive bonds, even though the metal cabinets normally are used to facilitate entry and execution of inactive bond orders.

D4.
*Contract Settlement Terms*
D4a.

### REGULAR-WAY CONTRACTS

**regular way**

An overwhelming number of stock exchange bond contracts are executed **regular way**. But "regular way" has a different meaning for corporate or municipal bonds and U.S. government obligations.

Corporate and municipal transactions executed regular way require settlement between participating firms on the fifth business day after trade date.[19] Regular way for U.S. government bonds calls for settlement on the next business day after the trade date.

D4b.

### SELLER'S-OPTION CONTRACTS

If a selling broker is aware of the customer's inability to satisfy the delivery terms of a regular-way contract as prescribed, then the broker at the time of the offering must state the number of calendar days needed for completion of that contract. This is

**seller's option**

known as a **seller's option**. The buyer has a right to refuse acceptance of these unusual terms, but only at the time when the transaction is effected. Consequently, a selling broker under these circumstances generally must make a price concession of ¼ to ½ point to attract a buyer's willing participation.

## examples of sellers option offers

"10 XYZ 4¼s of 1991 at 82½, sellers 15"
"4 PDQ 7½s of 1998 at 94, sellers 28"
"8 CBA 8¼s of 2001 at 97⅝, sellers 39"

[19]Without benefit of an intervening holiday, this is the same as the seventh calendar date after the trade date; that is, Monday to Monday, Tuesday to Tuesday, Wednesday to Wednesday, and so forth. The presence of an exchange-recognized holiday extends settlement date by the holiday period itself.

Seller's-option contracts in corporate or municipal bonds are allowable under NYSE rules for any period of time running from 6 business to 60 calendar days; those for U.S. government issues, from 2 business to 60 calendar days. In other words, such contracts may be created for settlement beginning from the point at which a regular way ceases, but never for any longer than 60 calendar days after trade date.

> In the unlikely event that two or more seller's-option bond orders are entered at the same price, the offeror willing to settle soonest after trade date will assume priority for execution purposes.
>
> After execution, the seller has an option of delivering the bonds earlier than the specified settlement date. The purchasing firm must be prepared to pay for them. But the seller must give 24-hour written notice to the purchaser announcing the intention to deliver early. In no event may the seller give this written notice before the regular-way settlement of a contract effected on the day of the original transaction.
>
> In other words, the earliest possible *notification* date for a corporate or municipal bond seller's-option contract would be on the fifth business day after trade date; the earliest possible *physical delivery* of securities on the sixth business day. For U.S. government obligations, earliest notification can take place on the next business day after trade date and physical delivery can be arranged for the second business day.

### D4c.  CASH CONTRACTS

> A **cash contract**, stipulated in the bid or offer, calls for settlement on the same day as the trade itself. The terms are equally applicable to corporate, municipal, or U.S. government securities. In particular, trades effected before 2:00 P.M. (New York City time) must be settled by 2:30 P.M., whereas those executed after 2:00 P.M. must be settled within 30 minutes.

**cash contract**

### D4d.  WHEN-ISSUED/WHEN-DISTRIBUTED CONTRACTS

> A **when-issued (WI)/when-distributed (WD)** contract calls for settlement sometime in the future, on a date to be determined by the NYSE. These contracts relate only to securities that have not yet been distributed to stockholders by the issuing corporation.

**when-issued (WI)/ when-distributed (WD)**

The certificates can arise from bonds to be issued in payment for another company's securities in a merger proposition or from exchange offers of stock or convertible bonds for a new issue of a straight debt security.

Trading in these new securities often commences immediately upon agreement by management of the corporations but before final arrangements are made for physical delivery. Therefore, these transactions are effected literally on a when, as, and if issued basis for settlement. Should distribution arrangements be altered or terminated by the issuers, all pending trading contracts must be cancelled immediately, including contingent profits and losses. The credit department of a brokerage firm will, therefore, withhold any profits, losses, and contingent transaction fees from customers who trade in and out of when-issued/when-distributed contracts before the final terms are validated.

As an accommodation to investors, principally for tax reasons, the NYSE also permits next-day contracts in corporate and municipal securities traded on its premises toward the latter days of a calendar year. *Next-day contracts* call for settlement between purchasing and selling firm on the next business day after trade date. If the seller's settlement date falls within a calendar year, any *profit* on that transaction is taxed as a capital gain for that year.

This type of contract has little appeal for a seller establishing a capital loss, however. In calculating an annual *loss*, it is the *trade date* that counts. Therefore, losses can be taken through the last business day of the year under any contract settlement terms.

Contract settlement terms are summarized in Table 11.

**TABLE 11**
SUMMARY OF CONTRACT SETTLEMENT TERMS

| TYPE | SETTLEMENT DATE |
|---|---|
| REGULAR WAY (RW) | |
|   Corporate and municipal securities | = Fifth business day after trade date |
|   U.S. government obligations | = Next business day after trade date |
| SELLERS OPTION (S-?) | |
|   Corporate and municipal securities | = 6 business to 60 calendar days after trade date |
|   U.S. government obligations | = 2 business to 60 calendar days after trade date |
| CASH | = Same day as trade date |
| WHEN-ISSUED (WI)/WHEN-DISTRIBUTED (WD) | = On a date in the future to be determined |
| NEXT-DAY (ND) | = On the business day following trade date |

The final consideration in any bond contract concerns payment of interest. Interest is not included in the contract price. Unless specified to the contrary, all bonds trade in the marketplace "and interest." The amount of applicable accrued interest associated with a debt obligation constitutes an additional expense to the purchaser and additional proceeds for the seller of that security. The issuing corporation normally pays interest only twice each year. So, if the bond is traded in the interim period, the new owner must advance the interest accruable from the last payment and expect reimbursement with the usual semiannual distribution.

Those bonds that are in default of interest payments or that promise to pay interest only when and if earned (that is, income bonds), trade *flat* in the marketplace.[20] The contract price on these bonds is the only consideration exchanged between purchaser and seller. A purchaser has no future obligation to the former owner if the corporation eventually decides to make an interest distribution, either currently or cumulatively.

The four activities discussed in this chapter clearly show that the procedures for conducting business in the securities industry are

[20]On two days each year, even bonds that normally trade "and interest" will be traded flat (ex interest). This peculiarity occurs when the *settlement date* for a bond contract falls on the same day as the issuer's semiannual payment date for interest. The seller is then entitled to the interest accruable for the entire preceding period and will receive it from the corporation itself, instead of from the purchaser of that bond.

complex and detailed. We grant that some of your customers may not be interested in the intricate procedures for certificate borrowing, for managing of a specialist's book, for the timing of an odd-lot transaction, or for executing bond sales in the trading ring. Yet, these procedures have direct impact on the prices your customers obtain in investing in securities. For this reason, we have presented to *you*, your customer's contact with the securities industry, these inside procedures.

# processing securities transactions

**order room**

From previous discussions, you have learned that the people concerned with the actual execution of orders to buy and sell securities are members of the Order Department. If they are situated together in the same physical area, this section of the brokerage firm is likely to be called the **order room**[1] instead. However, that arrangement is not too practical for a large firm, and, in all likelihood, the Order Department may be located in different rooms, floors, or even buildings. The separation is determined on the basis of execution locale and/or security type. That is, handling of exchange transactions may take place in one area and over-the-counter transactions in another area. Or, corporate debt activities may be ministered to in one place, government and municipal securities in another, and equity issues in still another area.

Location is of relatively minor importance because of technological advances in modern data communication facilities. Many large brokerage firms use a technique known as *message switching*. It links sales, operations, and trading locales by computer, so that each order can be

1. routed from a sales office to a particular trader in the Order Department or directly to the trading floor of a designated stock exchange;
2. examined, following execution, as to trade details in order to ensure compliance with its terms and conditions; and
3. automatically relayed back to the appropriate sales office and to the firm's other operations departments for processing.

In a nonautomated firm, each buy or sell instruction is written on an order form, time-stamped per SEC rule, and telephoned or teletyped to the appropriate exchange for execution (or directed to the firm's traders in the over-the-counter market). After execution, the order form is time-stamped again to indicate the approximate minute of completion,[2] noting price, quantity, and perhaps information on the contra broker. Such information is then transmitted to the Purchase and Sales (P & S) Department for the start of operations departmental activity.

In summary, an Order Department

1. accepts customer instructions prepared by registered representatives; or
2. prepares its own order form for dealer-to-dealer trades initiated in behalf of the firm's account and risk (see Figure 1).

The Purchase and Sales Department, or the P & S Department, as it is better known, has two principal responsibilities:

1. To compare the terms and conditions of each transaction with the *contra brokerage firm*[3] or firms involved.

---

[1]Another name for this area is *wire room* because the room often serves as an electronic communications center between the firm's main office and its branch sales offices.

[2]SEC Rule 17a–3 necessitates both entry and execution times on order tickets so that, in the event of a dispute or inquiry, the problem can be pinpointed accurately in time. Computerized communication facilities are capable of making these time notations automatically.

[3]The contra broker is the firm that is on the opposite side of the transaction. If your firm buys, then the contra firm is the seller; if your firm sells, the contra firm is the buyer.

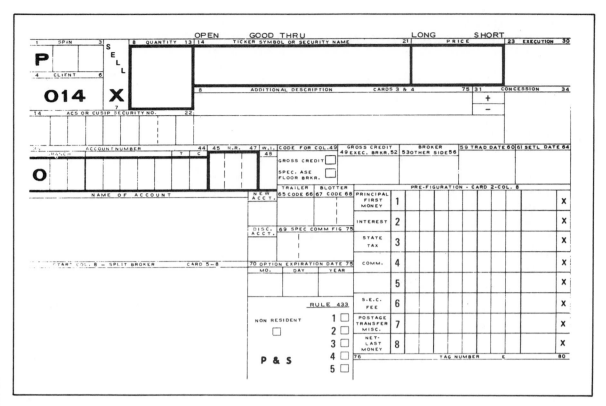

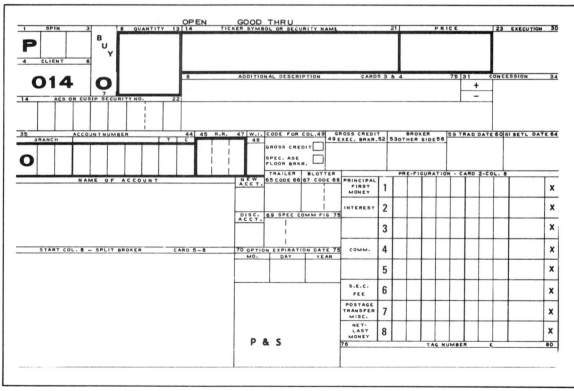

**FIGURE 1**
Sample Order Forms

2. To prepare a customer's confirmation notice. This is a bill for payment of a purchase or an advice for proceeds due the customer when selling.

*B1.*
*Comparison Procedures*

Comparison procedures between participating broker/dealers vary somewhat, by exchange locale and over-the-counter transactions. For New York Stock Exchange transactions, comparisons are arranged through Securities Industry Automation Corporation (SIAC), a computerized facility processing transactions in behalf of Stock Clearing Corporation (SCC), a wholly owned subsidiary of the NYSE. It also processes transactions on behalf of the American Stock Exchange Clearing Corporation (ASECC), a wholly owned subsidiary of the AMEX. Over-the-counter transactions are usually compared through the National Clearing Corporation (NCC), a subsidiary of the NASD. For exceptional reasons, with approval of both buying and selling firms, a trade may be processed "ex clearing house" (XCH),[4] but, by and large, round-lot activity is handled through the appropriate clearing facility.

On trade date plus one (that is, the next business day), each broker submits a list of its previous day's trades to SIAC. Such lists include:

1. buy or sell
2. quantity
3. description of issue
4. price
5. name of contra firm

**contract sheet**  SIAC then sorts the information and prepares a **contract sheet** that itemizes the information by issue on separate purchase and sales blotters (see Figure 2). By means of this computerized system, SIAC contract sheets are able instantly to identify, and advise each firm of, a "break" in information on the second business day after the trade. The system isolates differences in trade details submitted by participating firms, such as price or contra-party discrepancies. The computer even offers "good name" suggestions when a problem is caused by a mismatch in contra brokers. That is, when there is a mismatch, the computer will suggest the name of a firm that is possibly the correct one because that firm, too, is involved in a similar mismatch. Any disagreement must be resolved by the firms through direct communication or else promptly deleted from the contract sheets. This procedure allows sufficient time for adjustments and preparation of final notices to facilitate settlement on the fifth business day. New York Stock Exchange final notices are net balance summaries to receive from, or deliver to, the clearing corporation for deposit in that member organization's account, thus effecting a net settlement for each member. The National Clearing Corporation, employing a similar settlement procedure, advises each firm what its security balance or deposit requirement will be at the clearing house on settlement day. For ease in settling transactions, both SIAC and NCC interpose themselves into each intermember

[4]This phrase literally means "without clearing house participation." "Exceptional reasons" include in-house arranged "crosses," a need to obtain a new security certificate for tax-loss purposes, or a contract for other than regular-way settlement.

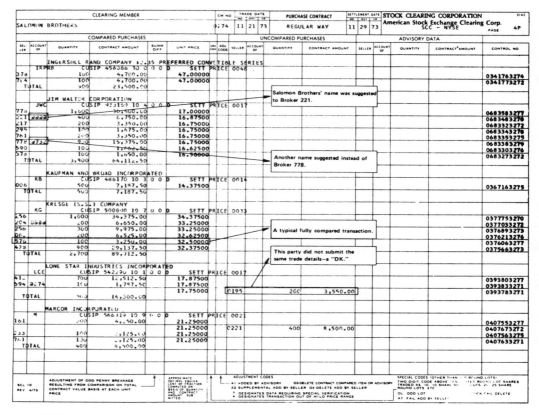

**FIGURE 2**
Purchase Contract Sheet

transaction, becoming the contra principal for receipt, delivery, and payment. The actual securities may then conveniently be maintained on account at Depository Trust Co. (DTC) for safe-keeping purposes.

Let us briefly examine three settlement procedures in terms of a single day's activities in one issue—American Motors Corporation—that is traded both on the NYSE and via NASDAQ in the over-the-counter market.

### B1a. SIAC's NET BALANCE SETTLEMENT

First, let us look at how SIAC prepares a net balance settlement. Suppose that on a single day, Broker A at different times:

| BOUGHT | SOLD |
|---|---|
| 100 shares @ 8 from Broker L | 200 shares @ 7⅞ to Broker R |
| 200 shares @ 8⅛ from Broker O | 300 shares @ 8 to Broker T |
| 300 | 500 |

Each member firm's activity per issue, including Broker A's trades in American Motors, is netted out by SIAC based upon fully compared information. That is, if there are no price or trade differences[5] between the participating firms, SIAC prepares a written notice to receive or deliver a net amount of shares.

[5]Each price or trade difference is commonly called a "DK," meaning, literally, "Don't know." If the disagreement cannot be resolved by the close of business on trade date plus two, the transaction must be deleted from the contract sheets and eventually satisfied ex clearing house.

For example, with Broker A's trade in American Motors, the 300 shares bought would be offset by the 500 shares sold, resulting in a net balance to deliver of only 200 shares. Instead of receiving 300 from Brokers L and O and delivering 500 to Brokers R and T, Broker A will

1.  pair off 300 shares of its own sales with 300 of its purchases during the day; and
2.  deliver the excess 200 shares of sales to its continuous settlement account at SIAC where it will be automatically transferred and credited to the appropriate purchasing member's account.

That firm may not even be Brokers R or T, the original trade participants. After all, due to the netting procedure, Brokers R and T may have completely paired off their purchases and sales internally. Nevertheless, because trading is conducted only with a small community of member firms, some broker(s) will need those shares and will be readily identified by the computerized facilities of SIAC. Money balances are determined, netted out, and settled via SIAC, too, from trade details submitted by each firm on the day after execution. A single check will be issued by SIAC if a member's credits exceed purchase costs, or by the firm to SIAC if the costs exceed sale proceeds (see Figure 3, SIAC's CNS Accounting Summary).

**FIGURE 3**
SIAC's CNS Accounting Summary

| CUSIP NUMBER | SECURITY DESCRIPTION | OPENING POSITION LONG/SHORT (−) | SETTLING TRADES BOUGHT/SOLD (−) | STOCK DIVIDEND AND MISC ACTIVITY REC/DEL (−) | RECEIPTS AND DELIVERIES REC/DEL (−) | CLOSING POSITION LONG/SHORT (−) | CURRENT MARKET PRICE | CURRENT MARKET VALUE LMV/SMV (−) |
|---|---|---|---|---|---|---|---|---|
| 963150107 000 | WHEELING PITTSBURGH STEEL CORP. | 175 | 1.000 | | 1.000 − | 175 | 14.000 | 2,450.00 |
| 964066104 000 | WHITE MOTOR CORPORATION | 565 − | 800 | 1.000 − | 200 | 565 − | 13.500 | 7,627.50 − |
| 966323107 001 | WHITING CORPORATION | 220 | 25 − | | | 195 | 15.750 | 3,071.25 |
| 980881106 000 | WOOLWORTH F W | 1,363 − | 200 − | | 1.000 | 563 − | 24.250 | 13,652.75 − |
| 984121103 000 | XEROX CORPORATION | 898 − | | | 500 | 398 − | 114.000 | 45,372.00 − |
| 989399100 000 | ZENITH RADIO OF DELAWARE | 373 | | | | 373 | 28.000 | 10,444.00 |

STOCK CLEARING CORPORATION
American Stock Exchange Clearing Corporation

CNS ACCOUNTING SUMMARY

MEMBER NUMBER 0002   MEMBER NAME ACME SECURITIES INC.

SETTLEMENT DATE 06-28-74   PAGE 001

| YESTERDAY'S EXCHANGE | 121,847.50 − | SETTLING TRADES | 21,537.50 | TODAY'S DIVIDEND | | TODAY'S MARKET | 15,965.25 | CNS SETTLEMENT | |
| YESTERDAY'S SETTLEMENT | 5,210.00 | DIVIDEND EXCHANGE | 100.00 | | | SHORT VALUE | 66,652.25 − | | 44,313.00 − |
| TODAY'S EXCHANGE | 116,637.50 − | MISC ACTIVITY | | TODAY'S EXCHANGE | 95,000.00 − | NET MARKET VALUE | 50,687.00 − | OWED BY MEMBER · DR DUE TO MEMBER · CR (−) | |

CNS

The second comparison procedure is NCC's net balance settlement. The comparison mechanics for the NCC are virtually identical to SIAC's procedures. Here, too, we find submission of trade details, contract sheets, DKs, and receipt/delivery advisories. No contra firm is cited in a balance notice because here, too, the NCC is always named as the contra party in the settlement process. Accordingly, each member firm's security account, by issue, is debited or credited with an appropriate number of shares from its net balance on settlement date. And, because this is accomplished on a cumulative basis

1. the number of fail-to-receive or fail-to-deliver contracts[6] for each member declines sharply; and
2. physical handling of securities certificates between firms is similarly curtailed.

The cumulative receipt and delivery of securities feature of NCC and SIAC is known as **continuous net settlement (CNS)**; it can be exemplified by using the American Motors situation cited above. After arriving at a net balance to deliver 200 shares to the NCC to satisfy its trade contracts for the day, Broker A may

**continuous net settlement (CNS)**

1. deliver 200 shares to the NCC on settlement day and thus complete its commitment;
2. reduce by 200 shares its long position unsegregated in the NCC certificate depository[7] (if it has such a position large enough to do so); or
3. be unable to deliver 200 shares on settlement date for various reasons and thus fail to meet its obligation as promised.

In the last situation, Broker A's account at NCC is set up as short 200 shares and marked to the market daily until the delinquency is eliminated. Furthermore, it becomes subject to the buy-in provisions of the NASD Uniform Practice Code if enough firms with long positions on NCC records want to withdraw their certificates physically from the depository. Each day of subsequent trading in American Motors by Broker A and its customers prompts an automatic adjustment in the firm's position record for that issue at NCC. Thus, on the following settlement date, if Broker A buys 600 shares and sells 300 shares of American Motors, its resulting 300-share net balance to receive will eliminate the 200-share short position and create a 100-share long position at NCC without ever making physical delivery to the clearing corporation.

*B1c.*   *OVER-THE-COUNTER PHYSICAL COMPARISON*

The third settlement procedure is the over-the-counter physical comparison. When one or both of the firms involved in a trade is

---

[6]A fail-to-receive or fail-to-deliver is a contract between two brokerage concerns that is not fulfilled by certificate delivery and payment on settlement date. Each day such contracts remain open interferes with that issue's market liquidity and, in prolonged instances, penalizes the responsible member firm's net capital position. The fail situation is often brought about by certificates registered in such a way, or in such denominations, that they do not qualify as a "good delivery."

[7]Officially called Free Account Net Settlement, the depository is more commonly referred to by its acronym, FANS.

not a member of the NCC, the participants cannot make use of the corporation's clearance facilities. They must prepare and exchange a written comparison no later than trade date plus one. This form, containing exact transaction details, may be mailed or hand delivered. It must be signed by the contra firm to evidence its acceptance and then returned to the sender prior to settlement date. Each transaction is a separate contract between the broker/dealers.

With this firm-by-firm procedure, a participating broker is unable to pair off its daily purchases and sales in the same issue so as to arrive at a net balance. This situation thus generates far more interfirm certificate shuffling on settlement date than results from a formal clearance system. (Clearance has been able to reduce the number of physical receipts and deliveries by as much as 75%.) Items to be handled with this procedure as well as noncleared items from a formal clearance system are settled in the office of the purchasing firm by means of delivery versus payment. The practice is known as a "**window settlement**" because the seller's messenger presents the security to a cashiering clerk through a barred teller's cage (similar to those found in a bank) and waits for payment.

**window settlement**

This laborious procedure can delay physical settlement of contracts past the fifth business day and may create serious fail problems for the brokerage firms involved. Steps are underway to compel all NASD members to clear through NCC in New York or via several of its satellite clearing facilities in major cities throughout the United States. When completed and coordinated with a national depository system, the program will allow for immediate nationwide electronic clearance and securities delivery.

As mentioned before, the P & S Department prepares customer confirmation notices from information furnished by the Order Department on an execution report. Most of the details are identical to those included in comparisons, and it is not surprising to see many brokers employing a confirmation model that is similar to, or even a duplicate of, their comparison forms. The information on a comparison form, along with each broker's transfer, reclamation, and delivery form, was standardized by BASIC[8] in 1972. It is to the firm's financial advantage to incorporate as many of these duplicated features as possible into the same illustrative scheme (see Figures 4 and 5).

*B2.*
*Confirmations*

Three items that *may* appear on a customer's confirmation but never on a broker/dealer comparison are

1. an SEC registration fee;
2. Florida transfer taxes; and
3. commission charges

They are inapplicable for a contra broker/dealer transaction because your firm does not act as its *agent*, and payment of appropriate transfer taxes and an SEC fee, if required, is fundamental with a brokerage firm's good delivery of securities, anyway. "May" is stressed for customer transactions because some or all

[8]BASIC is an acronym for Banking and Securities Industry Committee, a trade association of bankers and brokers dedicated to promoting economy in operating procedures by standardizing widely used industry forms.

## Confirmation 1

**AS PRINCIPAL**

**WE CONFIRM** the transaction described hereon, subject to the terms and conditions on the reverse side hereof.

**WE BOUGHT FROM YOU**

**Salomon Brothers**
Member of the New York Stock Exchange, Inc.
One New York Plaza, New York, N. Y. 10004
Telephone — (212) 747-7000

**CONTRACT ORIGINAL NO.** 654

| ORG # | TYPE | ACCOUNT NO. | MARKET | SALESMAN | INT. DAYS | TRANSACTION NO. | CODES TR | CAP | SETT | TRADE DATE | SETTLEMENT DATE |
|---|---|---|---|---|---|---|---|---|---|---|---|
| 274 | | 900433 | OTC | 818 | 047 | 1 WCTI | | | | 01/12/76 | 01/19/76 |

| IDENTIFICATION NO. | CONTRA PARTY | CH # | SPECIAL DELIVERY INSTRUCTIONS |
|---|---|---|---|
| | BUYEM & SELLEM, INC.<br>150 LINCOLN AVENUE<br>KINGSTON, N.Y. 12401 | | RVP<br>FIRST NATIONAL CITY BANK OF N.Y.<br>55 WALL STREET<br>NEW YORK, N.Y. 10005 |

| WE | QUANTITY | CUSIP NUMBER | SECURITY DESCRIPTION | NET AMOUNT |
|---|---|---|---|---|
| BOT | 50,000 | 909279AA9 | UNITED AIRLINES CVT  R* 5.000%<br>12/01/91      REGISTERED | 32,201.39 |

PRINCIPAL    31,875.00
INTEREST        326.39

**PRICE**

63 3/4

COMPARISON

On other than round lots (normally 100 shares) on all stock exchanges an amount may have been added to the price on purchases or deducted on sales. On the New York Stock Exchange that amount is 12½¢ per share. In all other cases an explanation will be provided upon request.

## Confirmation 2

**AS PRINCIPAL**

**WE CONFIRM** the transaction described hereon, subject to the terms and conditions on the reverse side hereof.

**WE BOUGHT FROM YOU**

**Salomon Brothers**
Member of the New York Stock Exchange, Inc.
One New York Plaza, New York, N. Y. 10004
Telephone — (212) 747-7000

**CONTRACT ORIGINAL NO.** 774

| ORG # | TYPE | ACCOUNT NO. | MARKET | SALESMAN | INT. DAYS | TRANSACTION NO. | CODES TR | CAP | SETT | TRADE DATE | SETTLEMENT DATE |
|---|---|---|---|---|---|---|---|---|---|---|---|
| 274 | | B00502 | OTC | 458 | | 1 WFY1 | | | | 02/05/76 | 02/13/76 |

| IDENTIFICATION NO. | CONTRA PARTY | CH # | SPECIAL DELIVERY INSTRUCTIONS |
|---|---|---|---|
| | STOCKUMBOND CORP.<br>200 WALL STREET<br>NEW YORK, N.Y. 10005 | 502 | |

| WE | QUANTITY | CUSIP NUMBER | SECURITY DESCRIPTION | NET AMOUNT |
|---|---|---|---|---|
| BOT | 127 | 170880108 | CHRISTIANA SECURITIES | 19,431.00 |

PRINCIPAL   19,431.00

**PRICE**

153

COMPARISON

On other than round lots (normally 100 shares) on all stock exchanges an amount may have been added to the price on purchases or deducted on sales. On the New York Stock Exchange that amount is 12½¢ per share. In all other cases an explanation will be provided upon request.

**FIGURE 4**
Sample Comparisons

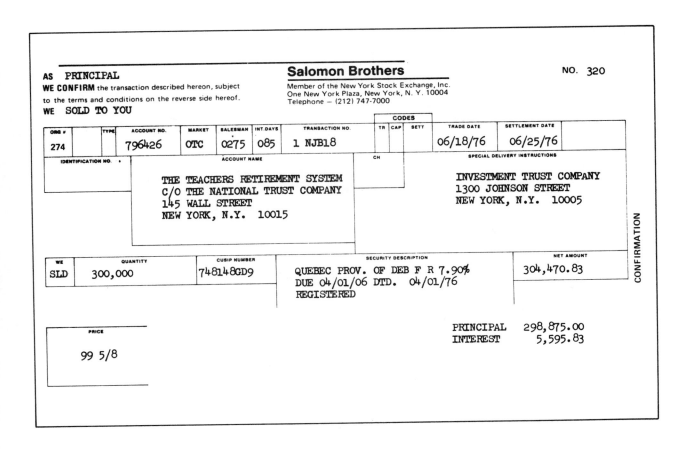

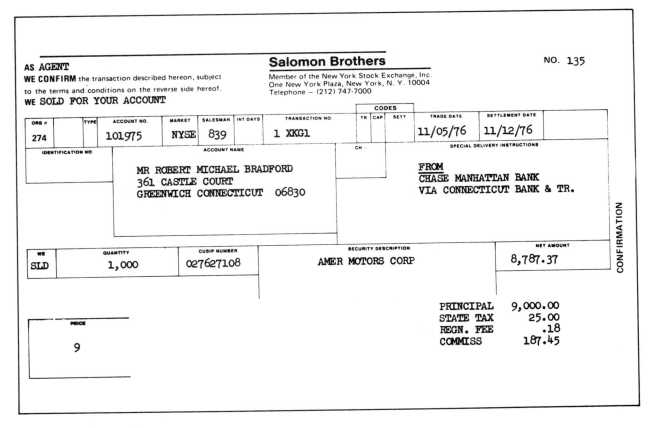

**FIGURE 5**
Sample Confirmations

of those charges do not even apply for customers under certain circumstances. For instance:

1. An SEC registration fee is paid normally by the seller of an equity security tradable on a national securities exchange whether the order is executed on the exchange or over the counter. However, the SEC has exempted the following sales transactions from imposition of that fee:

    a. sales of stock offered pursuant to an effective registration statement (spot secondaries and listed options sales remain liable for the SEC fee)
    b. private placements of stock by the issuing corporation
    c. the sale of securities pursuant to, and in consummation of, a tender or exchange offer
    d. The exercise of a warrant or subscription right or the conversion of a convertible security
    e. transactions executed outside the United States that are not reported, or required to be reported, to the Consolidated Tape Association.

    There is no fee charged to sellers of debt securities.

2. Florida tax is paid by *sellers of equity or debt securities*, but only when sale execution occurs within Florida's borders.

### B3a. ITEMIZING ACCRUED INTEREST

**B3.**
**Accrued Interest**

An important piece of information peculiar to transactions in most debt issues and essential for both comparisons and confirmations is the addition of accrued interest to the principal amount in the contract. Only contracts for income bonds, issues in a default status, or regular-way transactions in municipal or corporate bonds effected 5 business days prior to an interest payment date are exceptions. For purchasers, accrued interest represents another transaction expense, and for sellers, more proceeds. It must be shown as a separate item on the execution statement because of its taxable status as ordinary income for the recipient. It can never be entitled to favorable treatment for tax purposes in capital gains or loss transactions.

This out-of-pocket expense for the purchaser is only temporary. When the corporation next pays interest on its debt, the purchaser collects the entire amount, part of which is reimbursement for the earlier payment to the former bondholder and part is payment for the current holder's status as a creditor of that concern.

### B3b. CALCULATING ACCRUED INTEREST

Because most issuers of debt securities pay interest only semiannually, a precise method has been developed by the NASD and securities exchanges for determining amounts of accrued interest associated with transactions effected in the interim period.

Interest dollars accrue to the debt holder's benefit *from the date the issuer last paid interest* and continue up to, *but not including*, the settlement date of the regular-way or cash sale.[9] Thus, interest will *not* accrue for the seller through:

1. The fifth business day after trade date for corporate and municipal bonds executed regular way. Interest ceases to accrue after the day before the fifth business day. That is, if the trade day is May 9, the fifth business day falls on May 16 and interest ceases after May 15.

2. The next business day after trade date for U.S. government obligations executed regular way. Interest ceases to accrue after the day before the next business day. That is, if the trade date is May 13, the next business day falls on May 16 and interest ceases after May 15.

3. The day of the trade for a debt obligation executed as a cash contract. Interest ceases to accrue after the day before trade date. That is, if the trade date is May 16, interest ceases after May 15.

| | | | MAY | | | |
|---|---|---|---|---|---|---|
| S | M | T | W | T | F | S |
| 1 | 2 | 3 | 4 | 5 | 6 | 7 |
| 8 | 9 | 10 | 11 | 12 | 13 | 14 |
| 15 | 16 | 17 | 18 | 19 | 20 | 21 |
| 22 | 23 | 24 | 25 | 26 | 27 | 28 |
| 29 | 30 | 31 | | | | |

For calculation procedures:

1. in the case of corporate and municipal bonds, there are 30 days in each month and 360 days in the year;

2. in the case of U.S. government obligations, consideration is given to the actual number of days in each calendar month (365 days each year and 366 in leap years).

**examples**

Let us look at several examples with sample calendars provided to help you in your calculations based on the data provided.

(1) *Regular-Way Corporate Bond*
What are the interest dollars due the seller of a $10,000, 6.5% corporate bond traded regular way on Wednesday, October 13, with interest dates of January and July 1 (interest last paid on July 1)?

| | | OCTOBER | | | | |
|---|---|---|---|---|---|---|
| S | M | T | W | T | F | S |
| | | | | | 1 | 2 |
| 3 | 4 | 5 | 6 | 7 | 8 | 9 |
| 10 | 11 | 12 | [13] | 14 | 15 | 16 |
| 17 | 18 | 19 | 20 | 21 | 22 | 23 |
| 24 | 25 | 26 | 27 | 28 | 29 | 30 |
| 31 | | | | | | |

    30 days in July
    30 days in August
    30 days in September
    19 days in October (not including the fifth business day
               after October 13)
    109 *total days of interest*

The formula for calculating interest is:

principal × rate × time = interest $(P \times R \times T = I)$

Thus,

$$\frac{\$10,000}{1} \times \frac{6.5}{100} \times \frac{109}{360} = \frac{\$7,085,000}{36,000} = \$196.81 \text{ due the seller}$$

[9]In the case of seller's-option contracts, accrued interest is handled the same way it is with regular-way contracts, even though the purchaser may not anticipate receiving certificates until some future date.

| | | | JULY | | | |
|---|---|---|---|---|---|---|
| S | M | T | W | T | F | S |
| | | | | | | 1 |
| 2 | 3 | 4 | 5 | 6 | 7 | 8 |
| 9 | 10 | 11 | 12 | 13 | 14 | 15 |
| 16 | 17 | 18 | 19 | 20 | 21 | 22 |
| 23 | 24 | 25 | 26 | 27 | 28 | 29 |
| 30 | 31 | | | | | |

(2) *Regular-Way U.S. Government Bond*

What are the interest dollars due the seller of a $5,000, 3% U.S. Treasury bond traded regular way on Friday, July 14, with interest dates of February and August 15 (interest last paid on February 15)?

14 days in February (15 days in a leap year)
31 days in March
30 days in April
31 days in May
30 days in June
$\underline{\phantom{0}16}$ days in July
152 *total days of interest* (153 days in a leap year)

Before calculating the interest in this example, we must take into consideration two points about the $P \times R \times T = I$ formula. In calculating interest dollars for a U.S. government bond, a somewhat modified application of the usual formula is needed for greater accuracy. Although $P \times R \times T = I$ is still used

1. the *rate* is expressed as a percentage for that particular 6-month period alone, rather than as an annual percentage requirement; and

2. the *time* is expressed as the actual number of interest days related to the actual number of calendar days in that 6-month period under consideration.

In Example 2, therefore, interest dollars are calculated thus:

$$\begin{array}{ccccc} P & \times & R & \times & T & = & I \\ \dfrac{\$5,000}{1} & \times & \dfrac{1.5}{100} & \times & \dfrac{152a}{181b} & = & \dfrac{\$1,140,000}{18,100} & = & \$62.98 \text{ due the seller} \end{array}$$

[a]153 days in a leap year.
[b]182 days in a leap year and $63.05 total interest.

## examples

| | | | MARCH | | | |
|---|---|---|---|---|---|---|
| S | M | T | W | T | F | S |
| | | 1 | 2 | 3 | 4 | 5 |
| 6 | 7 | 8 | 9 | 10 | 11 | 12 |
| 13 | 14 | 15 | 16 | 17 | 18 | 19 |
| 20 | 21 | 22 | 23 | 24 | 25 | 26 |
| 27 | 28 | 29 | 39 | 31 | | |

(3) *Seller's-Option Corporate Bond*

What are the interest dollars due the seller of a $2,000, 5% corporate bond traded "sellers 21" on March 16, with interest dates of May and November 1 (interest last paid on November 1)?

30 days in November
30 days in December
30 days in January
30 days in February
22 days in March
142 *total days of interest*

Despite the fact certificate delivery may be expected on April 5 (21 calendar days after March 16), interest accrues up to, but not including the fifth business day after trade date. Interest calculation is:

$$\dfrac{\$2,000}{1} \times \dfrac{5}{100} \times \dfrac{142}{360} = \dfrac{\$1,420,000}{36,000} = \$39.44 \text{ due the seller}$$

**(4)** *Regular-Way Corporate Bond Traded Five Business Days before Interest Date*

What are the interest dollars due the seller of an $8,000, 4.25% corporate bond traded regular way on Thursday, September 24, with interest dates of April and October 1 (interest last paid on April 1)?

$$
\begin{array}{rl}
30 & \text{days in April} \\
30 & \text{days in May} \\
30 & \text{days in June} \\
30 & \text{days in July} \\
30 & \text{days in August} \\
30 & \text{days in September} \\
\hline
180 & \textit{total days of interest}
\end{array}
$$

Interest dollars are calculated thus:

$$\frac{\$8,000}{1} \times \frac{4.25}{100} \times \frac{180}{360} = \frac{\$6,120,000}{36,000} = \$170.00 \text{ due the seller}$$

Because the calculation procedure entitles the seller to the full 6 months of interest, the comparison/confirmation will appear "flat"; this means that when the seller delivers the certificates, they will be ex coupon.

| | | SEPTEMBER | | | | |
|---|---|---|---|---|---|---|
| S | M | T | W | T | F | S |
| | | 1 | 2 | 3 | 4 | 5 |
| 6 | 7 | 8 | 9 | 10 | 11 | 12 |
| 13 | 14 | 15 | 16 | 17 | 18 | 19 |
| 20 | 21 | 22 | 23 | [24] | 25 | 26 |
| 27 | 28 | 29 | 30 | | | |

**(5)** *Cash Transaction Municipal Bond.*

What are the interest dollars due the seller of a $5,000, 5.875 municipal bond traded for "cash" on Monday, January 19, with interest dates of March and September 1 (interest last paid on September 1)?

$$
\begin{array}{rl}
30 & \text{days in September} \\
30 & \text{days in October} \\
30 & \text{days in November} \\
30 & \text{days in December} \\
18 & \text{days in January (through the day before trade date)} \\
\hline
138 & \textit{total days of interest}
\end{array}
$$

The interest calculation is as follows:

$$\frac{\$5,000}{1} \times \frac{5.875}{100} \times \frac{138}{360} = \frac{\$4,053,750}{36,000} = \$112.60 \text{ due the seller}$$

| | | JANUARY | | | | |
|---|---|---|---|---|---|---|
| S | M | T | W | T | F | S |
| | | | | 1 | 2 | 3 |
| 4 | 5 | 6 | 7 | 8 | 9 | 10 |
| 11 | 12 | 13 | 14 | 15 | 16 | 17 |
| 18 | [19] | 20 | 21 | 22 | 23 | 24 |
| 25 | 26 | 27 | 28 | 29 | 30 | 31 |

**(6)** *Cash Transaction U.S. Government Bond*

What are the interest dollars due the seller of a $20,000, 7.70% U.S. government bond traded for "cash" on Tuesday, April 6, with interest dates of June and December 1 (interest last paid on December 1)?

$$
\begin{array}{rl}
31 & \text{days in December} \\
31 & \text{days in January} \\
28 & \text{days in February (29 days in leap year)} \\
31 & \text{days in March} \\
5 & \text{days in April} \\
\hline
126 & \textit{total days of interest (127 days in a leap year)}
\end{array}
$$

The interest calculation is:

$$\frac{\$20,000}{1} \times \frac{3.85a}{100} \times \frac{126b}{182c} = \frac{\$9,702,000}{18,200} = \$533.08 \text{ due the seller}$$

| | | APRIL | | | | |
|---|---|---|---|---|---|---|
| S | M | T | W | T | F | S |
| | | | | 1 | 2 | 3 |
| 4 | 5 | [6] | 7 | 8 | 9 | 10 |
| 11 | 12 | 13 | 14 | 15 | 16 | 17 |
| 18 | 19 | 20 | 21 | 22 | 23 | 24 |
| 25 | 26 | 27 | 28 | 29 | 30 | |

[a]See Example 2 above for modification of the $P \times R \times T = I$ formula.

[b]127 days in a leap year.

[c]183 days in a leap year and $534.37 total interest.

Multiple copies of each comparison/confirmation are prepared by the P & S Department. The actual number varies with the work flow peculiar to that brokerage concern and the preference of some customers to direct duplicates to an agent bank, accountant, or attorney.[10] In addition to a comparison for the contra dealer, and a confirmation for the customer and the registered representative, a detailed trade manifold is prepared for the Cashiering Department. This section of the firm is primarily responsible for movement and payment of securities to, or from, the opposite party in each transaction.

In some brokerage firms, a special credit unit serves in an advisory capacity as an agency of cashiering, and in others it is a separate entity known as the Margin Department.

This Margin Department (or credit unit) monitors all trade activities and ensures that payment and delivery are satisfied in accord with federal, exchange, and firm requirements. It advises cashiering *when* to complete its responsibilities—that is, after proper payment or acceptable delivery is accomplished.

The Margin Department's attention is focused principally upon customer activity because customers tend to be unfamiliar with, or rather casual about, regulations and customs of the securities industry. It is interesting and important to note that when the firm acts in an agency capacity, although customer payment for a purchase may be delayed, the Margin Department must still authorize its own firm's payment for the security as soon as it is received from the contra firm. The sacredness of a contract between members must be upheld despite the tardiness, or even the default, of a customer who precipitated the event.

In any event, the Margin Department maintains an account record for each customer and posts each activity on that card on a trade (activity) date basis. Informal entries are made in pencil and are sometimes posted on separate cards for each customer's specialized account, be it cash, margin, subscription, miscellaneous, and so on (see Figure 6).[11]

> In the case of a cash account, many customers want possession of their certificates instead of leaving them in care of the brokerage firm. After full payment is made for each purchase, the Margin Department gives the Cashiering Department instructions to *"transfer and ship."* This authorizes Cashiering to send that security to the issuer's transfer agent to have the customer's name inscribed on a new certificate and on that company's shareholder records.[12] When this is done, the brokerage firm delivers the certificate to the customer, completing this transaction.

Some knowledge of elementary bookkeeping is helpful for anyone employed in this area, because debits and credits are used to reflect securities positions and money balances. Thorough familiarity with Regulation T of the Federal Reserve Board is more than important; it is critical to compliance with securities laws and to the preservation of firm assets. Margin clerks must be

---

[10]Often, upwards of five copies are prepared, one each to the registered representative, Margin Department, Cashiering Department, Controller's Department, and to the firm's files.

[11]In highly automated firms, this record may be a computer printout or even tiny, computer-generated images on microfilm or microfiche.

[12]A transfer agent cancels old certificates and issues new ones reregistered in the new owner's name, a nominee name, or street name (in the name of a brokerage firm). A registrar maintains a record of all shareholder names and addresses and ensures that the transfer agent does not issue more shares than are cancelled.

| ACCOUNT: Harris Berg | | | | | 137846 Cash Account | | | |
|---|---|---|---|---|---|---|---|---|

| | | | | Account Executive | Max C. Mum | | #069 | |
|---|---|---|---|---|---|---|---|---|

| Date | Bought (Debit) | Sold (Credit) | Description | Date | Ledger Balance | | | |
|---|---|---|---|---|---|---|---|---|
| 8/12 | 3,685.09 | | 100 sh. U.S. Steel @ 36 1/4 | 8/19 | $3,685.09 Dr. | | | |
| 8/26 | | 3,625.00 | Check received | 8/26 | 60.09 Dr. | | | |
| 9/4 | | 6,828.83 | 200 sh. U.S. Steel @ 34 3/4 | 9/12 | 6,768.74 Cr. | | | |
| | | | | | | | | |
| | | | | | | | | |
| | | | | | | | | |
| | | | | | | | | |
| | | | | | | | | |
| | | | | | | | | |
| | | | | | | | | |

| Shares | Current | Long Positions | | PX | Value | Requirements |
|---|---|---|---|---|---|---|
| | | | | | | |
| | | | | | | |
| | | | | | | |
| | | | | | | |
| | | | | | | |
| | | | | | | |

| Shares | Current | Short Positions | | PX | Value | Requirements |
|---|---|---|---|---|---|---|
| 100 | U.S. Steel | | | 36 | 3600 — | |
| | | | | | | |
| | | | | | | |
| | | | | | | |
| | | Market value | | | | |
| | | Debit/Credit Balance | | | | |
| | | Equity | | | | |

CR-28

**FIGURE 6**
Account Record

able to analyze account postings and initiate corrective action if contra brokers or customers default in any aspect of their contracts.

For example, note in Figure 6 that Mr. Harris Berg bought 100 U.S. Steel Corporation at 36¼ on August 12, in a cash account for a total cost of $3,685.09. However, his check for payment did not arrive until August 26, thus necessitating an approved extension of time to defer mandatory liquidation proceedings. The Margin Department prepares these extension request forms after communicating with the registered representative to ascertain the customer's reason for failure to pay by the seventh business day after trade date. It must determine if approval was obtained for Harris Berg's extension. (If this were a margin account, the inquiry and request for extension would be submitted on the fifth business day following trade activity.) Furthermore, in margin accounts particularly, when sufficient collateral is not deposited on the trade date itself, the details of this deficiency must be posted in a separate firm ledger identified as *Federal Calls for Margin*. This record, available for New York Stock Exchange inspection for at least 1 year, indicates when and how customer margin calls are met.[13] No further action need be initiated in the customer's account until the fifth business day.

Note that Mr. Berg's check amounted to $3,625.00, $60 short of the total due; this $60 represents the commission fee. Because the account is delinquent by less than $100, no further federal action is necessary under Regulation T. However, the margin clerks should not issue instructions to register the certificate and send it to Mr. Berg until the additional money is deposited. Observe, too, that Harris Berg sold 200 U.S. Steel at 34¾ on September 4, 1976, for net proceeds of $6,828.83. One hundred shares are already in the account from the purchase in August. But where are the other 100 shares? If these are in Mr. Berg's possession, they must be deposited in this account by the fifth business day after trade date, and certainly not later than the seventh business day. If he procrastinates past the tenth business day *following settlement date*, Mr. Berg will run afoul of SEC Rule 15c3–3, which requires the brokerage concern to buy in that 100-share default. Competent and efficient margin clerks do not wait for this to occur. They communicate with the registered representative immediately after trade date to inquire about the 100-share deficiency, asking when they may expect to receive the certificate. Often enough, the clerks discover that the extra 100 shares was a mistake, or that this 100-share unit was a short sale and should be processed in the customer's margin account instead.

The point of the preceding discussion is merely to highlight the role of the Margin Department, underscoring its importance as

1. a liaison between registered representative sales efforts and cashiering responsibilities; and
2. the source of technical expertise in the subject of compliance with credit regulations governing securities transactions.

D.
**the cashiering department**

The Cashiering Department, which finalizes all transactions for the brokerage concern, is subdivided into three major sections:

[13]That is, by deposit of money or other securities, or by liquidation.

1. the Receive and Deliver Section, where money and securities come into or go out of the firm
2. the Box Section, where certificates are stored for a while
3. the Transfer Section, where arrangements are made to
   a. reregister certificates from one name to another, and/or
   b. provide desired certificate denominations

**the cage**

Collectively, these sections are commonly known as **the cage**, because they are physically situated in a locked-in area whose entrances and exits are continuously guarded. Strict security measures are necessary because of the presence and availability of money and of valuable stock and bond certificates.

*D1.*
*Receive and Deliver Section*

The Receive and Deliver Section (R & D) accepts certificates directly from customers, broker/dealers, and various securities depositories in the United States. It will make immediate payment for receipt of customer securities only if it is specifically instructed to do so by the Margin Department. This instruction is generally accomplished by means of a validated transaction manifold (comparison/confirmation) or via a specially prepared debit memorandum notice.

Receive and Deliver must first determine that securities are in transferable form[14] and, in the case of customers particularly, that they are accompanied by supporting documentation. This function is especially pertinent when certificates are registered in the name of a corporation, legal trust, estate of deceased person, incompetent, guardian, or person holding power of attorney over the owner of that issue. In the absence of a contingent comparison/confirmation of a trade, securities received *free* are usually given to the transfer section to reregister in the firm's own name. When they are returned from the transfer agent, the new certificates go to the Box Section for storage pursuant to regulatory requirements.

When the Receive and Deliver Section needs securities to deliver versus a sales transaction, it withdraws them from the Box (see Section D2) or from a securities depository, wherever they may be held. It dispatches them to the contra broker/dealer or bank against payment. The proceeds are then credited to the proper account or paid to the customer, as directed by the Margin Department. Securities to be delivered free, such as to a customer who paid for them and wants possession, normally go to the Transfer Section first. They should be reregistered into customer name before being sent out of the firm[15] Otherwise, there is a danger that the certificates may be lost or stolen and the broker may continue to receive interest or dividends without any evident justification for this money on the firm's records. The firm's bookkeeping, then, is likely to get bogged down with the need to maintain a **suspense account**.[16] The firm must then wait for

**suspense account**

---

[14]For brokers, dealers, and depositories, "transferable form" means that the certificates must meet the specifications for good delivery outlined in the New York Stock Exchange Constitution or in the NASD Uniform Practice Code, as the case may be.

[15]An important exception may be for delivery to a bank or to a sophisticated financial institution that can effect prompt registration out of street name.

[16]A special account created by a brokerage firm to reflect unreconciled money and securities differences on its books and records.

someone to claim those dollars or eventually surrender them to the state under prevailing escheat laws.[17]

**D2.**
*Box Section*

The term **Box**, which is used to identify the section of the cage where securities are temporarily stored, originated many years ago when certificates were actually kept in portable metal receptacles. Although boxes are not completely outmoded, many firms now use on-premises vaults, cabinets, and even desk drawers to serve the same purpose. More than ever before, brokerage firms are encouraged to store their securities in various industry-owned and industry-operated depositories. This lessens the risk of theft and, correspondingly, reduces the firm's fidelity insurance premiums. New York Stock Exchange member firms utilize the services of Depository Trust Company (DTC),[18] whereas NASD firms can turn to Free Account Net Settlement (FANS), a subsidiary of the over-the-counter National Clearing Corporation.

**Box**

---

Box clerks are responsible for the storage of securities in firm custody. They act upon orders issued by the Margin Department and the Receive and Deliver Section. Fully paid issues in cash accounts and excess collateral securing debit balances in margin accounts must be isolated from securities used by the firm in the conduct of its own business. This storage of securities held in cash accounts and registered in a customer's name is called **safekeeping**. The same situation for customer margin account securities registered in the broker's name is known as **segregation**. The two classifications demand almost identical physical treatment. The Box Section stores those protected securities in a bank vault,[19] identifying the true owners by means of

**safekeeping**

**segregation**

1. separate folders containing each customer's securities held in safekeeping; and
2. for issues held in segregation, a tag on each certificate with the underlying customer's name indicated (*individual identification*); or
3. a list serving as a cover for an envelope containing one or more certificates of the same issue for all customers in the same secure condition. Although each certificate is not individually earmarked, the outside list indicates the quantity set aside for each party with an interest in the securities inside the envelope (*bulk identification*).

---

Securities held by a brokerage firm that are eligible for use as collateral in financing arrangements are maintained collectively in a physical location known as the **open box** or **active box**. Such securities include the following:

**open box**
**active box**

---

[17]Laws that deal with a state's claim to abandoned property.

[18]Depository Trust Company is a member bank of the Federal Reserve System, founded specifically to safeguard securities and facilitate delivery between participating broker/dealers and banks. Although it is now wholly owned and organized by the New York Stock Exchange, it is expected that equity interest and control will eventually be divided as follows: 60% by the banking community members, 20% by the New York Stock Exchange, and 20% by the American Stock Exchange.

[19]Sometimes referred to as the "free box," indicating that the securities held within are owned by the underlying customers free and clear of encumbrances. Segregation responsibility may also be satisfied by specific instruction to Depository Trust Company or Free Account Net Settlement.

1. issues in proprietary accounts[20]
2. issues purchased in customer cash accounts not yet paid for and those past settlement date
3. issues in customer margin accounts whose value is necessary to finance debit balances in those accounts

Generally speaking, this means certificates with a market value equal to the debit balance are released from segregation if financing of a transaction is to be arranged via securities loans to brokers and dealers. When financing is arranged by means of a collateral loan at a bank, securities worth 140% of the customer's debit balance are rehypothecated. All other certificates in those accounts must be segregated.

This variation occurs simply because a bank demands a cushion of protective collateral value for its loan, whereas a broker loan is arranged on a dollar-for-dollar basis and is continuously marked to the market. Consequently, the firm that carries customer margin accounts has no ability to control those securities to its own advantage when conducting business in a dealer capacity. The Margin Department values each customer account in consideration of market price fluctuations and continuously advises the Box Section which securities to segregate and which to place in the active box. In some firms, daily pricing is required by management. In any event, no firm should undertake it *less* frequently than once a week or when activity occurs in that particular account, whichever happens first.

**D3.**
*Transfer Section*

> The Transfer Section of the cage is responsible for reregistering securities into a more desirable title of ownership and/or certificate denomination. This is accomplished by submitting the old certificate to the issuing corporation or to its authorized agent,[21] accompanied by written instructions as to the type of change required. Transfer is completed when the corporation or its agent cancels the old certificate, issues a new one, adjusts its ownership records accordingly, and returns the new document to the same brokerage firm. Due to the potential for error in this detailed process, many corporations preferably appoint two separate organizations to handle the necessary chores: one to facilitate reregistration and the other to adjust the company's record of ownership. The concern responsible for cancelling the old certificate and issuing a new one is called a **transfer agent**. The party responsible for adjusting the ownership record and ensuring that the transfer agent issues the same total quantity cancelled is called a **registrar**.

**transfer agent**

**registrar**

[20]Securities owned by the firm itself, and those in its principals' accounts if pledged as their capital contribution to the organization.

[21]Relatively few corporations reregister their own securities. Most use the specialized services of a commercial bank to act as transfer agent.

Normally the Transfer Section of the cage is given all registered securities received by its firm to reregister into either firm name, for segregation purposes, or into customer name, for safekeeping or delivery purposes, per instruction from the Margin Department or the Box Section.[22] Exceptions occur only in the case of securities sold soon after purchase or for delivery to a customer's agent bank or broker versus payment (COD transaction).

As a general rule, the Margin Department will not authorize registration of a security into customer name unless

1. it was a fully paid certificate in a cash account;
2. the customer did not owe the firm delivery of another security whose sale was pending; or,
3. the margin account (if the security was in a margin account) had no debit balance or a debit that was fully protected by other securities in the account.

If the third situation prevails, then, once reregistered into customer name, the security will be delivered to the customer or transferred from the margin account to a cash account and placed into safekeeping.

It is a bad business practice to segregate or hypothecate securities registered in the name of someone else, even though those certificates may be fully negotiable. Serious problems arise if the issuing corporation pays a dividend/interest or distributes an important communication to the holders whose names and addresses appear on its records. That distribution will obviously go to persons or brokers who legally disposed of their financial interest in the company some time ago. Any dividend or interest payment, in particular, must then be claimed by the rightful owner, entailing a lot of unnecessary paperwork, at best.

Sometimes, securities are in proper form for delivery but the available denominations are all wrong. In this case, the Transfer Section must request from the company's agent the right-sized pieces to make good delivery to the contra firm. It is to the firm's financial advantage to anticipate these problems in the original reregistration and request frequently needed denominations at that time. For example, if a brokerage firm receives a total of 1,000 shares registered in various names and wants to transfer them into its own name, it is probably wiser to do so by requesting several certificates in denominations such as the following:

$$
\begin{array}{rcr}
1 \times 500 = & 500 \\
3 \times 100 = & 300 \\
2 \times 50 = & 100 \\
2 \times 25 = & 50 \\
4 \times 10 = & 40 \\
2 \times 5 = & \underline{10} \\
& 1{,}000 \text{ shares}
\end{array}
$$

Otherwise, if the Transfer Section opts for an easy registration of 1,000 shares in a single piece, the firm will be hard pressed to

[22]Bearer certificates (that is, securities without an owner's name imprinted on the face of the documents or recorded on the issuer's books) are fungible instruments. They are, therefore, immediately placed into segregation or rehypothecation, as the case may be.

make prompt delivery unless it sells all 1,000 shares at the same time, and to the same contra party.

Denomination consideration is not a serious concern when deliveries between member firms are arranged via a national securities depository. The problem then belongs to the depository. However, when a firm deals directly with other firms or its own customers, its Transfer Section's good judgment is essential for efficient management of firm assets.

There are, depending on the particular firm, several other departments that offer ancillary, or auxiliary, services to your customers. These are the Dividend, Proxy, Reorganization, Stock Record, and Controller's Departments.

**E.
ancillary operations
procedures**

The title *Dividend Department*, something of a misnomer, refers to the area responsible for accepting, allocating, paying, and/or claiming dividends *and* interest distributions associated with securities in the firm's custody.

*E1.
The Dividend Department*

### SOURCES AND CORRECTIONS OF ERRORS

*E1a.*

The clerks in this department must be sure the firm receives all interest and dividends to which it is entitled. This involves reconciling a single check the firm receives from the corporation to the rate applicable for the number of shares or bonds registered in the firm's own name on the day the company closes its record book for payment purposes. Although this procedure sounds routine, it occasionally does not work out that way. Strange as it seems, the firm sometimes receives more than it should. This can be explained by

1. an error on the part of the company's disbursement agent; or, more likely,
2. a security, delivered to a contra firm or customer prior to the record date, which was not reregistered promptly by that party.

In the second case, the dividend clerk will hold the extra money or security in a suspense account waiting for the proper party to submit proof of claim for rightful payment. After an appropriate number of years have elapsed (the number varies from state to state), the broker must surrender unclaimed funds and securities to its own state of domicile.

Underpayments can be attributed to

1. an error on the part of the company's disbursement agent;
2. a mistake by the firm's own record-keeping department, an error which can now be corrected; or
3. failure by the firm's Transfer Section promptly to reregister certificates received by the firm before the record date.

In the third situation, the Dividend Department must claim the distribution from the delivering firm. The issuing corporation cannot be held at fault for sending a distribution to a party not technically entitled to it. After all, as far as the corporation is concerned, recognition was properly extended to the holder appearing on its ledger at the close of business on the official record date.

Occasionally, the selling firm is the cause of underpayment problems because it fails to deliver certificates promptly on settlement date. If this happens, the Dividend Department immediately notifies the Receive and Deliver Section of the cage to impose a condition of settlement to the contract in order to qualify as a good delivery. When the tardy shipment of securities finally arrives, it must be accompanied by a **due bill**. A due bill is an official authorization allowing the purchasing broker to make legal claim upon the selling broker for a future distribution to which it is entitled. Due bills for cash distributions are postdated checks (see Figure 7), while those for stock distributions entail use of a form similar to the one shown in Figure 8. The latter due bill is simply an I.O.U.-type contract that obligates the seller to present additional shares to the purchaser soon after the issuing corporation distributes them to holders of record. The appropriate exchange or NASD Uniform Practice Committee, as the case may be, establishes the date when a due bill becomes redeemable for the new shares.

Sometimes it *is* an action of the issuing corporation that gives rise to the use of a due bill in a typical transaction, particularly, in the case of a sizable stock dividend or any stock split. Extra time is needed for printing so many additional certificates and preparing for personalized registration and denomination requirements. In such a case, the corporation provides for a significant number of days between the time its entitled stockholders are identified and the time the distribution commences. But in the interim period, stock market trading continues in the old shares and at prices that include the value of the forthcoming distribution. Thus, to satisfy contracts made after the company has re-

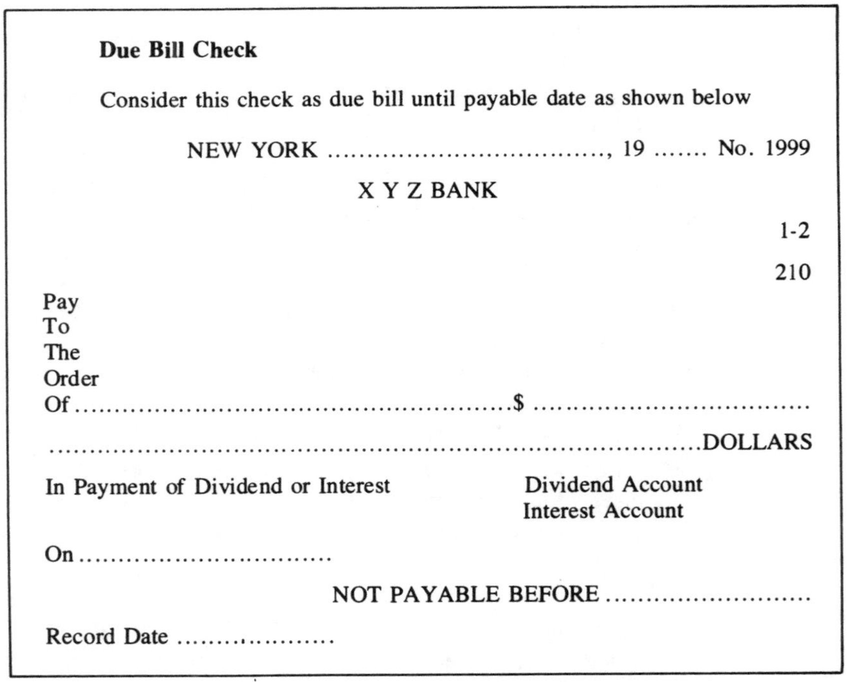

**due bill**

---

**Due Bill Check**

Consider this check as due bill until payable date as shown below

NEW YORK ................................., 19 ....... No. 1999

X Y Z BANK

1-2

210

Pay
To
The
Order
Of ...............................................$ ....................................

....................................................................DOLLARS

In Payment of Dividend or Interest      Dividend Account
Interest Account

On ...............................

NOT PAYABLE BEFORE ..........................

Record Date ...................

**FIGURE 7**
Due Bill Check

**Due Bill for Stock Dividend or Stock Distribution**

For value received, the undersigned hereby assigns, transfers and sets over to..............................................................the stock distribution of .......................................... (          ) shares of ......................... stock of ..............................................................to be issued on ...................to the registered holder of ........................................... (          ) shares of..................stock of ........................................... represented by certificate number ...................................., to which the undersigned is entitled as a stock dividend, and hereby irrevocably constitutes and appoints ..............................................................attorney to transfer the shares representing said stock dividend on the books of said corporation, with full power of substitution in the premises.

Dated............................

..........................................................

(Official Signature)

**FIGURE 8**
Due Bill for Stock Dividend or Stock Distribution

corded the names of holders to whom the new shares will be directed and before those new shares are actually distributed, the seller's broker must deliver the old certificates, accompanied by a due bill, to the purchasing firm.

If a customer is the underlying seller and delivers the old securities registered in his/her name, the Margin Department must withhold payment of sufficient proceeds[23] from the transaction until the new shares are distributed and sent to the broker to complete the obligation. Because they are unable to understand the record-keeping complexities involved in this corporate exercise, many customers erroneously believe that shares received from the company after the original sale automatically belong to them, not to the new purchaser. Withholding a portion of the sale proceeds guarantees the integrity of the transaction. Registered representatives should explain to these customers that the value of the shares was included in the original contract price.

### *FOUR ESSENTIAL CASH DISTRIBUTION DATES* *E1b.*

This whole situation points up the necessity for both investors and brokerage concerns to understand and act within the framework of four essential dates associated with corporate distributions. In chronological sequence, for cash dividends, these dates are:

1. *Date of declaration:* The day on which a corporation's board of directors convenes a meeting, decides upon a distribution, and makes public announcement of this fact.
2. *Ex-dividend (interest) date:* The day on which a security begins trading in the marketplace without the value of the dividend/interest distribution belonging to a purchaser of that issue. Because an overwhelming number of corporate

[23]For example, it might withhold 50% of the proceeds for a 2-for-1 split or 100% stock dividend, 33⅓% of the proceeds for a 3-for-2 split or 50% stock dividend, and so forth.

securities contracts are created regular way, the ex-dividend date consequently is normally the fourth business day prior to the record date.[24]

An exception to that rule of thumb involves certain foreign issues. This occurs when the transfer agent's principal office is located in the company's country of origin and there are definite communication difficulties. Interesting, too, is the fact that most mutual funds are also in the exceptional category. Because they don't really trade in the open market, their boards of directors set the ex-dividend date as well as all the other dates pertinent to a distribution.

3. *Record date:* The day on which a corporation closes its register of securities holders to determine the recipients of an announced distribution. This date is set by the directors of the issuing corporation. (See Section E1c.)

4. *Payment date:* The day on which a corporation or its disbursement agent makes payment of a distribution to its previously determined holders of record.[25]

### E1c.   *ILLUSTRATION OF EX-DIVIDEND AND RECORD DATE APPLICATION*

Assume a declaration of a distribution payable to holders of record on January 16 and realize that, technically speaking, a purchaser should become a holder of record on the settlement date of the contract.[26] The following conclusions may be drawn:

| JANUARY | | | | | | |
|---|---|---|---|---|---|---|
| S | M | T | W | T | F | S |
| | | 1 | 2 | 3 | 4 | 5 |
| 6 | 7 | 8 | 9 | 10 | 11 | 12 |
| 13 | 14 | 15 | 16 | 17 | 18 | 19 |
| 20 | 21 | 22 | 23 | 24 | 25 | 26 |
| 27 | 28 | 29 | 30 | 31 | | |

1. A regular-way contract made as late as January 9 settles on January 16, the record date, and entitles a purchaser of that security to the announced distribution.

2. Regular-way contracts made beginning on January 10 settle after January 16 and entitle sellers of that security to the announced distribution. Therefore, on January 10, the security begins trading ex dividend. A look at the calendar shows that January 10 is the fourth business day prior to the January 16 record date. (Note that for an atypical transaction—for example, a cash contract that settles on the same day as the trade itself—the ex-dividend date would be the day *after* the record date. Persons buying that stock in a cash contract on any day up to, and even including, the record date can have their names recorded on the company's books to get that dividend distribution.)

[24]If the company's sole transfer agent is a significant distance from the major marketplaces, or the corporation makes a late dividend announcement, the Uniform Practice Committee of the NASD may arbitrarily fix an ex date earlier than the fourth business day before record date. To do so gives entitled purchasers sufficient time to effect a reregistration and avoid the problem of subsequent dividend claims. The NYSE and AMEX require listed companies to maintain transfer agents, or their representatives, within the vicinity of the exchanges themselves; listed companies must be able to effect a reregistration within 24 hours, if necessary.

[25]A "holder of record" is a party whose name is inscribed in the corporation's register of stockholders, or creditors, as the case may be. These holders receive a distribution from the company if their names still appear on this list at the close of business on the record date.

[26]"Technically speaking," because, in reality, it may be physically impossible to accomplish this feat. The contract may settle in California and the company's transfer agent may have its office in New York.

To help you remember who gets the cash distribution, use the following rule of thumb: First, compare the settlement day of the contract to a company's record date. If the settlement day falls on any day up to and including the record date, the distribution belongs to the buyer. If the settlement day falls after the record date, it belongs to the seller.

### STOCK DISTRIBUTION DATES                                                  *E1d.*

As was mentioned earlier, stock dividends and stock splits may cause unique trading problems for the securities industry. The chronological sequence of dividend dates for cash distributions is inapplicable. The ex-dividend date, now called the "ex-distribution date," is positioned after the payment date instead of after the date of declaration. Thus, the chronological sequence for a stock distribution is as follows:

1. date of declaration
2. record date
3. payment date
4. ex-distribution date.

The rule of thumb is that the ex-distribution date will be the next business day following payment by the corporation.[27] Due bills are redeemable beginning on the fifth business day after the issuer's payment date.

For example, using the calendar in Section E1c, if the company declared a 5% stock dividend on January 2 for payment on January 24 to holders of record on January 10, the following analysis can be made:

1. All regular-way contracts in the marketplace will, therefore, trade with due bills attached from January 4 (settlement date is January 11) through January 24.
2. Commencing on January 25, that issue will trade "ex distribution" and all outstanding due bills may be redeemed for the additional stock on January 31.
3. Any delivery of stock to a purchasing firm after January 10 (through January 31) must be accompanied by a due bill for the stock dividend.

### ILLUSTRATIVE DIVIDEND SYNOPSIS                                            *E1e.*

Statistical information about dividends and dividend-payment policies of publicly held corporations can be found in the *Dividend Record*, a publication of Standard & Poors Corporation (S&P), New York City. Typical of the service provided by S&P is the following brief history of dividends paid by Georgia-Pacific Corporation, a large company listed principally on the New York Stock Exchange. That fact is noted by the identifying symbol (■) preceding its name.

[27]The procedural rules for handling subscription rights are identical to that for stock distributions and splits. It goes "ex" on the day after trading in them commences, which is also the day after payment.

| Divd $ | Declared | Ex-date | Stk Record | Payable |
|--------|----------|---------|------------|---------|
| ■**Georgia-Pacific—Com. p$0.80** | | | | |
| **Rate**— 0.20Q Pd'76 — new — 0.40: old — 0.50 | | | | |
| & stk '75 — old — 0.80 & stk. | | | | |
| 0.20 | Jan 26 | Jan 30 | Feb 5 | Mar 25 |
| 2% Stk | Jan 26 | Jan 30 | Feb 5 | Mar 25 |
| 0.30 | Apr 7 | May 17 | May 21 | Jun 21 |
| 3 for 2 Split | | Aug 13 | Jun 25 | Aug 12 |
| (After 3 for 2 Split) | | | | |
| 0.20 Init | Jul 26 | Aug 23 | Aug 27 | Sep 27 |
| 0.20 | Oct 25 | Nov 5 | Nov 12 | Dec 13 |

This detailed synopsis sets forth essential dates for cash and stock distributions made by the company in 1976, as well as its total payments in the preceding year. Next to the corporate title is a notice that the common stock of this issuer has an indicated dividend policy of $.80 per share annually (com. p$0.80). In the following two lines it presents the following information:

1.  The company's quarterly rate payment of $.20 per share (Rate—0.20Q).

2.  What it actually paid in 1976, both in terms of old shares and new shares owned by an investor (Pd '76—new—0.40: old—0.50 & stk). This dual presentation is necessary because Georgia-Pacific split its stock 3 for 2 during the year. This notice reveals that the corporation in 1976 paid $.40 per share on the "new" or split-up shares and $.50 per share plus a stock dividend on the "old" or pre-split shares of common stock.

3.  What it paid in 1975 by comparison to 1976 ('75—old—0.80 & stk.). It was $.80 per share on the pre-split shares plus a stock dividend.

If we read down column 1, titled "Divd $," we recognize that the corporation made six distributions in 1976; four cash payments, one stock dividend, and one stock split. Those distributions were declared by the board of directors on the dates shown in column 2. They were actually made on the dates shown in column 5 ("payable") to holders whose names were inscribed on the company's books on the record dates (column 4). Column 3 reflects the dates on which the stock began trading in the marketplace on a regular-way basis without the value of the distributions attached to the transaction price.

To apply this information to a practical example, assume you were a holder of 100 shares of Georgia-Pacific at the beginning of 1976. Now let's see what you received from the company for your investment:

1.  On March 25, you received $.20 per share, or $20 for your 100 shares.

2.  On the same date you received 2 additional shares of stock as a stock dividend.

3.  On June 21, you received $.30 per share and because you now owned 102 shares your check was for $30.60.

4.  On August 12, the company split its stock 3 for 2 (3 new shares for every 2 old shares already owned). This ratio is

also known as a 50% split because, when expressed on a per-share basis, it results in ½ of an additional share for each share currently held. Because you owned 102 shares before, you were entitled to 51 additional shares (102 × .50 = 51). Another way to formulate the result of this distribution is to multiply the shares already owned by the terms of the ratio. Thus, 102 × $^3/_2$ = 153 shares.

5. On September 27, Georgia-Pacific paid $.20 per share as an initial ("Init") dividend following the split. Because you now owned 153 shares your check amounted to $30.60;

6. The final distribution in 1976 was $.20 per share on December 13, and your payment was the same as the preceding one, $30.60.

As a result of the cash distributions during the year the company reported to the Internal Revenue Service payments to you of $111.80. The cash dividends are fully taxable to the shareholders, whereas the stock distributions serve merely to reduce the investor's per share acquisition cost.

### ALLOCATION OF MONEY AND SECURITIES

*E1f.*

**beneficial owners**

The Dividend Department must also allocate monies and/or securities received among the underlying owners entitled to them. Those customers whose securities are held by the brokerage firm but registered in the brokerage firm's name for reasons of convenience are called the **beneficial owners** of those shares. The issuing corporation does not know who they are, but the brokerage firm, acting as their agent, has a fiduciary responsibility to accord them full privileges of ownership. The distribution, allocated pro rata to the beneficial owners, must, of course, be equal to the amount received from the company. For example, if the Dividend Department receives a $1,500 check from an issuer for a payment rate of $.50 per share, and its position list shows the following beneficial owners and quantities on the record date, the pro rata allocation is:

|  | HOLDINGS | ALLOCATION |
| --- | --- | --- |
| Customer A | 250 shares | $ 125 |
| Customer B | 1,000 shares | 500 |
| Customer C | 1,300 shares | 650 |
| Customer D | 50 shares | 25 |
| Customer E | 400 shares | 200 |
|  | 3,000 shares | $1,500 |

Similar pro rata calculation and apportionment is needed when a corporate distribution is a stock dividend or a split-up. For example, using the record of customer holdings depicted above:

1. If the company pays a 2% stock dividend (two shares of new stock for each 100 shares owned), the brokerage firm receives one certificate of 60 shares (2% of 3,000) and must allocate it accordingly.

|            | STOCK DIVIDEND | NEW HOLDINGS   |
|------------|----------------|----------------|
| Customer A | 5 shares       | 255 shares     |
| Customer B | 20 shares      | 1,020 shares   |
| Customer C | 26 shares      | 1,326 shares   |
| Customer D | 1 share        | 51 shares      |
| Customer E | 8 shares       | 408 shares     |
|            | 60 shares      | 3,060 shares   |

2. If, *instead*, the company splits up its shares 4 for 3 (four new shares for every three old shares), the brokerage firm receives 1,000 additional shares. (The firm already has 3,000 shares, and $^4/_3 \times 3,000 = 4,000$.) The 1,000 additional shares are allocated accordingly.

|            | OLD HOLDINGS   | STOCK DIVIDEND | NEW HOLDINGS[28] |
|------------|----------------|----------------|------------------|
| Customer A | 250 shares     | 83⅓ shares     | 333⅓ shares      |
| Customer B | 1,000 shares   | 333⅓ shares    | 1,333⅓ shares    |
| Customer C | 1,300 shares   | 433⅓ shares    | 1,733⅓ shares    |
| Customer D | 50 shares      | 16⅔ shares     | 66⅔ shares       |
| Customer E | 400 shares     | 133⅓ shares    | 533⅓ shares      |
|            | 3,000 shares   | 1,000 shares   | 4,000 shares     |

In this illustration, because a brokerage firm often receives a full number of shares from the company, it credits its customer accounts with their full shares and acts as a dealer for the resolution of fractions per customer request.

3. If, *instead* of a stock split up, the company reorganizes by splitting down (a reverse split), and if it decides upon a ratio of 1 for 5 (one new share for every five shares), the brokerage firm must adjust its customer holding records for that issue accordingly.

|            | OLD HOLDINGS   | NEW HOLDINGS   |
|------------|----------------|----------------|
| Customer A | 250 shares     | 50 shares      |
| Customer B | 1,000 shares   | 200 shares     |
| Customer C | 1,300 shares   | 260 shares     |
| Customer D | 50 shares      | 10 shares      |
| Customer E | 400 shares     | 80 shares      |
|            | 3,000 shares   | 600 shares     |

**E2.**
**The Proxy Department**

Closely related to the work of the Dividend Department and frequently allied with that group in a typical brokerage concern is the Proxy Department. The Proxy Department distributes corporate publications, including financial reports, meeting notices, and voting information to the beneficial owners of shares. Because the corporation does not know the identity of these parties, the Proxy Department, acting under stock exchange and NASD regulations, obtains material sent directly to stockholders of record and mails it to customers for whom the firm holds securities in street name.

[28] If fractional shares result, the company, at its predetermined, stated option, may (1) pay cash in lieu of the fraction; (2) allow the holder to subscribe to the next highest full share; or (3) redeem the fraction at prevailing market values. Thus, if the fractional shares in the illustration were redeemed at a time when the stock was valued at 36, all but Customer D would be credited with $12 (⅓ of 36). Customer D would be paid $24 (⅔ of 36).

The most important of these distributions is an advisory and voting solicitation, generally sent at least once each year. It gives the stockholder a right to elect directors and decide upon other important matters brought before an annual or special meeting of the company. However, beneficial owners cannot cast their votes directly because the corporation recognizes only the brokerage firm as its stockholder from its street name registration of certificates. The Proxy Department sends a request form to each of the beneficial owners, soliciting instructions regarding casting of this ballot. The form is called a **proxy.** By definition, a proxy is simply an authorization or power to act for someone else. When the beneficial owners notify the Proxy Department about their preferences, the brokerage firm reflects their votes in the total cast in behalf of all of its customers at the company's meeting. It is as valid a participation in the company's affairs as if the customers had personally attended the meeting and cast their own votes. As a result of its customers' diverse opinions, brokerage firms usually submit split votes to reflect their instructions. Thus, if a broker was a stockholder of record of 7,180 shares, it might vote 4,130 shares for, and 3,050 shares against, a particular proposal (or some other such split vote). Sometimes, the beneficial owners do not bother to advise the Proxy Department about their preference, and, under certain conditions, that voting privilege may be wasted. In significant matters affecting the financial interest of stockholders in a public company, exchange regulations preclude members from voting unless specific instructions are received from the rightful owners of those shares. If routine matters are submitted to holders for a vote, *in the absence of customer instructions*, the brokerage firm is allowed to reflect its own judgment. It normally sides with management of the company, accepting its voting recommendations.

**proxy**

The Proxy Department also acts as agent for dissident shareholders or any other group anxious to communicate with, or solicit, the beneficial owners whose shares are in firm custody, if

1. that group has registered its proxy statement or solicitation with the SEC, per Section 14 of the Securities Exchange Act of 1934; and
2. the group agrees to reimburse the brokerage firm for postage and other out-of-pocket expenses.

A stockholder solicitation may be a simple plea for a vote to effect a reform or to overthrow the company's present management. Or, it may be a request for the beneficial owners to tender their shares in response to a purchase proposition. This often leads to another function of the Proxy Department, although in larger firms it is assigned to a separate unit known as a Reorganization Department.

*SIX FUNCTIONS*

The Reorganization Department is a service unit responsible for several functions:

1. *Obeying corporate calls for redemption of issues in custody of the brokerage firm*

*E3a.*

*E3.*
*The Reorganization*
*Department*

Most debt and preferred stock issues outstanding have call provisions written into their indentures or agreements, as the category may be. This means that the company may retire the issue at its option by repaying dollars to the owners of these securities. An absolute, or full, call of an issue requires all holders to submit their bonds or shares for redemption. A partial call necessitates only that the holders of specific certificate numbers do so. These certificate numbers are chosen at random by the company, often by electronic means. Frequently they include securities held by a brokerage firm in its own name, but on behalf of customers. If these securities are held in safekeeping or are segregated by owner through individual identification methods, the Reorganization Department simply submits the appropriate certificate to the company and credits that customer with the cash received. However, if the securities are segregated in bulk form, the firm must either

1.  maintain on its records the specific certificate numbers of each callable security set aside for each customer account; or

2.  adopt an impartial lottery system in which probability of selection is proportional to its holdings of all customers' certificates in that issue.

Partial calls at prices favorable to the holders when compared to current market value may not be allocated to accounts in which that brokerage firm's partners, officers, directors, approved persons, or employees have an interest until all bona fide customers have been satisfied.

Figure 9 is typical of a partial redemption of an outstanding bond pursuant to call. Holders of both bearer and registered bonds must compare the serial numbers on their certificates to the numbers cited in the Notice of Redemption. If their numbers match any of those in the advertisement, they must present those bonds to the Chase Manhattan Bank, N.A., in New York City or to two other banks situated outside the United States in order to claim the principal amount plus accrued interest to January 1, 1977. Interest will no longer accrue or be paid on the called certificates after January 1, 1977, and so if those bondholders delay redemption of their bonds, their investment funds will be idle after that date.

2.  *Converting appropriate securities into common stock upon request of their underlying owner*

The Reorganization Department processes conversion requests, too, exchanging convertible issues for the underlying common stock. Such appeals may sometimes result from a full or partial call in a convertible issue. The company literally forces the holders to exchange their securities for the common stock or else accept only the call price as their reward. Usually, at this time, the call price is significantly lower than the market value of the comparable shares.

Look at a typical redemption notice illustrated in Figure 10. Many technical facts are set forth in this advertisement, but the key points have been summarized in the six items positioned on the left side of the illustration. Note how often the bondholder is advised that unless some personal action is initiated before the close of business on December 23, 1976,

Notice of Redemption

# European Investment Bank

### 8¾% 15-Year Bonds of 1971 Due January 1, 1986

NOTICE IS HEREBY GIVEN that, pursuant to the provisions of the Paying Agency Agreement dated as of January 1, 1971 by and between the European Investment Bank and The Chase Manhattan Bank (National Association), as American Paying Agent, and Banca Commerciale Italiana S.p.A. and Banque Internationale à Luxembourg S.A., as European Paying Agents, $750,000 in principal amount of the above Bonds will be redeemed and prepaid on January 1, 1977 at the principal amount thereof together with accrued interest thereon to said redemption date.

The serial numbers of the coupon Bonds to be redeemed are as follows:

| | | | | | | | | | | | | | | |
|---|---|---|---|---|---|---|---|---|---|---|---|---|---|---|
| 75 | 2690 | 4669 | 6979 | 8518 | 10031 | 12269 | 14443 | 16915 | 19222 | 21564 | 23403 | 25126 | 27276 | 28698 |
| 102 | 2764 | 4671 | 7078 | 8534 | 10036 | 12295 | 14467 | 16931 | 19317 | 21638 | 23441 | 25148 | 27280 | 28735 |
| 131 | 2806 | 4681 | 7108 | 8637 | 10056 | 12365 | 14488 | 16952 | 19353 | 21656 | 23454 | 25280 | 27321 | 28739 |
| 160 | 2813 | 4723 | 7185 | 8638 | 10059 | 12434 | 14670 | 16954 | 19428 | 21661 | 23473 | 25303 | 27355 | 28753 |
| 161 | 2872 | 4724 | 7212 | 8652 | 10073 | 12517 | 14689 | 16958 | 19450 | 21664 | 23482 | 25353 | 27372 | 28865 |
| 224 | 2950 | 4738 | 7223 | 8716 | 10100 | 12528 | 14761 | 17012 | 19512 | 21732 | 23720 | 25429 | 27493 | 28894 |
| 301 | 3016 | 4753 | 7242 | 8730 | 10112 | 12565 | 14811 | 17023 | 19587 | 21797 | 23726 | 25461 | 27495 | 28925 |
| 390 | 3025 | 4773 | 7279 | 8741 | 10168 | 12601 | 14848 | 17027 | 19607 | 21806 | 23736 | 25480 | 27523 | 28934 |
| 444 | 3030 | 4800 | 7295 | 8825 | 10171 | 12609 | 14908 | 17062 | 19619 | 21812 | 23762 | 25514 | 27582 | 28965 |
| 494 | 3046 | 4856 | 7301 | 8888 | 10208 | 12684 | 14914 | 17078 | 19621 | 21844 | 23822 | 25516 | 27599 | 29077 |
| 602 | 3231 | 4870 | 7347 | 8931 | 10222 | 12712 | 15045 | 17096 | 19643 | 21850 | 23924 | 25610 | 27604 | 29083 |
| 648 | 3445 | 4886 | 7356 | 8942 | 10254 | 12814 | 15163 | 17111 | 19919 | 21919 | 23954 | 25656 | 27610 | 29093 |
| 680 | 3466 | 4899 | 7393 | 8956 | 10288 | 12822 | 15176 | 17146 | 19950 | 22011 | 23976 | 25680 | 27634 | 29145 |
| 758 | 3479 | 4917 | 7428 | 8977 | 10297 | 12873 | 15193 | 17149 | 19984 | 22038 | 23977 | 25702 | 27655 | 29205 |
| 763 | 3484 | 4955 | 7485 | 8987 | 10298 | 12905 | 15240 | 17164 | 20014 | 22046 | 24018 | 25758 | 27659 | 29247 |
| 880 | 3490 | 5007 | 7573 | 9045 | 10303 | 12993 | 15311 | 17208 | 20028 | 22051 | 24019 | 25781 | 27684 | 29359 |
| 900 | 3500 | 5077 | 7601 | 9100 | 10338 | 13033 | 15316 | 17247 | 20059 | 22193 | 24021 | 25788 | 27709 | 29369 |
| 937 | 3501 | 5093 | 7603 | 9130 | 10382 | 13078 | 15372 | 17314 | 20334 | 22271 | 24057 | 25845 | 27766 | 29378 |
| 1254 | 3518 | 5299 | 7606 | 9146 | 10384 | 13115 | 15392 | 17452 | 20344 | 22279 | 24147 | 25873 | 27797 | 29413 |
| 1268 | 3543 | 5303 | 7629 | 9153 | 10396 | 13181 | 15405 | 17463 | 20371 | 22338 | 24320 | 25982 | 27835 | 29481 |
| 1401 | 3594 | 5458 | 7645 | 9180 | 10455 | 13213 | 15457 | 17473 | 20378 | 22372 | 24322 | 25995 | 27842 | 29498 |
| 1418 | 3624 | 5468 | 7673 | 9241 | 10460 | 13222 | 15477 | 17528 | 20428 | 22389 | 24352 | 26008 | 27914 | 29502 |
| 1422 | 3644 | 5534 | 7793 | 9288 | 10465 | 13243 | 15484 | 17543 | 20441 | 22402 | 24388 | 26031 | 27967 | 29524 |
| 1489 | 3690 | 5571 | 7877 | 9299 | 10471 | 13269 | 15558 | 17570 | 20451 | 22404 | 24408 | 26104 | 27971 | 29561 |
| 1763 | 3717 | 5667 | 7880 | 9317 | 10568 | 13272 | 15623 | 17832 | 20474 | 22513 | 24417 | 26193 | 28032 | 29576 |
| 1770 | 3756 | 5726 | 7884 | 9332 | 10577 | 13298 | 15718 | 17861 | 20551 | 22591 | 24444 | 26201 | 28073 | 29585 |
| 1777 | 3758 | 5800 | 7963 | 9383 | 10586 | 13303 | 15757 | 17880 | 20564 | 22620 | 24452 | 26235 | 28074 | 29588 |
| 1779 | 3774 | 5837 | 7975 | 9425 | 10692 | 13386 | 15779 | 17893 | 20578 | 22637 | 24453 | 26374 | 28080 | 29600 |
| 1808 | 3776 | 5842 | 7976 | 9446 | 10819 | 13390 | 15819 | 18121 | 20652 | 22652 | 24467 | 26383 | 28100 | 29637 |
| 1835 | 3820 | 5881 | 8013 | 9491 | 10830 | 13454 | 15892 | 18125 | 20657 | 22709 | 24507 | 26454 | 28144 | 29740 |
| 1991 | 3888 | 5924 | 8020 | 9512 | 10901 | 13477 | 15893 | 18183 | 20686 | 22711 | 24518 | 26473 | 28169 | 29855 |
| 2081 | 3905 | 5952 | 8024 | 9570 | 10927 | 13495 | 16006 | 18186 | 20704 | 22723 | 24571 | 26493 | 28172 | 29888 |
| 2083 | 3985 | 5990 | 8028 | 9629 | 10932 | 13583 | 16008 | 18268 | 20727 | 22769 | 24662 | 26522 | 28179 | 29893 |
| 2161 | 4015 | 5991 | 8029 | 9636 | 10937 | 13799 | 16210 | 18386 | 20772 | 22826 | 24666 | 26619 | 28197 | 29932 |
| 2162 | 4056 | 6056 | 8086 | 9672 | 10950 | 13828 | 16253 | 18399 | 20861 | 22977 | 24717 | 26732 | 28288 | 29947 |
| 2187 | 4178 | 6183 | 8187 | 9727 | 11038 | 13850 | 16260 | 18412 | 20990 | 23001 | 24761 | 26875 | 28315 | |
| 2203 | 4190 | 6200 | 8189 | 9740 | 11359 | 13907 | 16262 | 18435 | 21044 | 23035 | 24764 | 26894 | 28329 | |
| 2231 | 4192 | 6304 | 8190 | 9783 | 11364 | 13928 | 16299 | 18446 | 21061 | 23042 | 24799 | 26928 | 28339 | |
| 2245 | 4257 | 6317 | 8224 | 9803 | 11389 | 13959 | 16303 | 18823 | 21114 | 23046 | 24815 | 26960 | 28354 | |
| 2253 | 4348 | 6434 | 8232 | 9806 | 11626 | 13999 | 16319 | 18870 | 21193 | 23055 | 24818 | 27006 | 28432 | |
| 2311 | 4356 | 6446 | 8236 | 9822 | 11637 | 14006 | 16336 | 18914 | 21217 | 23110 | 24886 | 27039 | 28458 | |
| 2424 | 4369 | 6616 | 8247 | 9832 | 11757 | 14019 | 16398 | 18919 | 21218 | 23193 | 24889 | 27045 | 28522 | |
| 2493 | 4393 | 6665 | 8262 | 9876 | 11841 | 14039 | 16441 | 18934 | 21224 | 23235 | 24900 | 27048 | 28534 | |
| 2502 | 4453 | 6776 | 8308 | 9931 | 12108 | 14098 | 16484 | 18947 | 21301 | 23235 | 24924 | 27067 | 28552 | |
| 2531 | 4519 | 6785 | 8311 | 9952 | 12146 | 14116 | 16493 | 19021 | 21355 | 23278 | 24947 | 27073 | 28573 | |
| 2535 | 4569 | 6830 | 8314 | 9995 | 12203 | 14181 | 16509 | 19049 | 21403 | 23288 | 25010 | 27133 | 28595 | |
| 2547 | 4585 | 6927 | 8327 | 10008 | 12220 | 14294 | 16527 | 19206 | 21430 | 23385 | 25010 | 27178 | 28596 | |
| 2665 | 4629 | 6967 | 8511 | 10010 | 12227 | 14322 | 16907 | 19220 | 21546 | 23392 | 25121 | 27221 | 28642 | |

The serial numbers of the registered Bonds to be redeemed in part and the principal amounts to be redeemed are as follows:

| Serial Number | Principal Amount to be Redeemed | Serial Number | Principal Amount to be Redeemed | Serial Number | Principal Amount to be Redeemed | Serial Number | Principal Amount to be Redeemed |
|---|---|---|---|---|---|---|---|
| R4 | $ 2,000 | R6 | $ 1,000 | R 9 | $13,000 | R12 | $ 3,000 |
| R5 | 13,000 | R7 | 2,000 | R11 | 9,000 | | |

In case of partial redemption of a fully registered Bond without coupons, the Authenticating Agent will authenticate and deliver Coupon Bonds or fully registered Bonds of authorized denominations in exchange for, and in aggregate principal amount equal to, the unredeemed portion of any fully registered Bond redeemed in part.

Interest on said Bonds shall cease to accrue on the redemption date and on said date the redemption price will become due and payable on each of said Bonds called for redemption.

Payment of Registered Bonds and Coupon Bonds to be redeemed will be made upon presentation and surrender thereof, together with all coupons, if any, appurtenant thereto maturing subsequent to the redemption date, at the principal office of The Chase Manhattan Bank (National Association) in the Borough of Manhattan, City and State of New York, or, at the option of the holder at the principal office of Banca Commerciale Italiana, S.p.A., Milan, Italy and, in the case of Coupon Bonds only, at the principal office of Banque Internationale à Luxembourg S.A., Luxembourg, Grand Duchy of Luxembourg. Such Bonds and coupons should be surrendered at The Chase Manhattan Bank, N.A. (Agency Division), 1 New York Plaza, New York, New York 10015 or, at the option of the holder, at Banca Commerciale Italiana, S.p.A., Sede di Milano, 6 Piazza della Scala, Milano, Italy or Banque Internationale à Luxembourg S.A., 2 Boulevard Royal, Luxembourg, Grand Duchy of Luxembourg.

Coupons which shall mature on, or shall have been matured prior to, said redemption date should be detached and surrendered for payment in the usual manner.

**EUROPEAN INVESTMENT BANK**

*By* The Chase Manhattan Bank (National Association),
*American Paying Agent*

in N. Y.
Dated: December 2, 1976.

**FIGURE 9**
Notice of Redemption Call

# GEORGIA-PACIFIC CORPORATION

## HAS CALLED FOR REDEMPTION ALL OF ITS
## 6¼% CONVERTIBLE SUBORDINATED DEBENTURES DUE 2000

**Conversion right terminates on December 23, 1976.**

1. Each Debenture is convertible into Common Stock of Georgia-Pacific Corporation until the conversion right expires at the close of business on December 23, 1976 at a conversion price of $29.80 per share, representing a conversion rate of 33.56 shares per $1,000 principal amount of Debentures.

From January 1, 1976 through November 22, 1976, the sale prices for Georgia-Pacific's Common Stock as reported on the New York Stock Exchange's consolidated transactions reporting system ranged from a high of $38.00 to a low of $27.45 per share. On November 22, 1976, the last reported price was $37.25 per share. As long as the price of the Common Stock is at least $32.625 per share, holders of Debentures will receive upon conversion Common Stock having a market value greater than the amount which would be received either upon redemption or purchase by certain Purchasers as described below.

2. The conversion right expires at the close of business on December 23, 1976. Failure to convert your Debentures by such date could result in a monetary loss to you by virtue of the above described facts.

3. Georgia-Pacific has entered into an agreement with Blyth Eastman Dillon & Co. Incorporated and certain other Purchasers, under which the Purchasers have agreed, on the terms and conditions set forth therein, to purchase Debentures submitted to them any time prior to the close of business on December 23, 1976 at $1,092.50 flat (without accrued interest) per $1,000 principal amount of Debentures. Please note that this price exceeds the price obtainable by surrendering Debentures for redemption by $3.24 for each $1,000 principal amount of Debentures.

4. Debentures not converted or submitted to the Purchasers by the close of business on December 23, 1976 will be redeemed for cash at the redemption price of $1,059.40 for each $1,000 principal amount of Debentures, plus $29.86 accrued interest to December 23, 1976.

---

## GEORGIA-PACIFIC CORPORATION
### 6¼% CONVERTIBLE SUBORDINATED DEBENTURES DUE MAY 15, 2000
### NOTICE OF REDEMPTION

November 23, 1976

Notice is hereby given, that Georgia-Pacific Corporation (G-P) has exercised its right, pursuant to Section 1101 of the Indenture, dated as of May 15, 1975, to redeem all of its 6¼% Convertible Subordinated Debentures due May 15, 2000 (the Debentures) on December 23, 1976, the date fixed for redemption.

**TERMS OF REDEMPTION.**

*Redemption Date.* December 23, 1976.

*Redemption Price.* The redemption price of the Debentures is 105.94% of the principal amount of the Debentures, plus interest accrued from July 1, 1976 to December 23, 1976 in the amount of $29.86 per $1,000 principal amount of Debentures, making a total of $1,089.26 payable on December 23, 1976 for each $1,000 principal amount of Debentures.

*Redemption Procedure.* Payment of the amount to be received on redemption will be made by G-P at Citibank, N.A., Agent, Receive and Deliver Department, 2nd Floor, 111 Wall Street, New York 10015, forthwith on presentation of the Debentures at any time on or after the Redemption Date.

*Cessation of Interest.* On and after December 23, 1976 interest on the Debentures will cease to accrue.

**CONVERSION RIGHTS.**

The principal amount of any Debenture may be converted at the option of the holder thereof, until the conversion right expires at the close of business on December 23, 1976, into shares of Common Stock of G-P at a conversion price of $29.80 per share, representing a conversion rate of 33.56 shares (rounded to the nearest 1/100th of a share) per $1,000 principal amount of Debentures.

*Price of Common Stock.* The last sale of G-P Common Stock as reported on the New York Stock Exchange's consolidated transactions reporting system on November 22, 1976 was at $37.25 per share. The market value of the shares of G-P Common Stock into which $1,000 principal amount of Debentures is convertible (and cash in lieu of fractional shares) was $1,250.11, based on such last sale price and a conversion rate of 33.56 shares per $1,000 principal amount, but such value is subject to change depending on changes in the market value of G-P's Common Stock. From January 1, 1976 through November 22, 1976, the sale prices for G-P's Common Stock have ranged from a high of $38.00 to a low of $27.45 per share (adjusted for all stock splits and dividends). As long as the price of G-P's Common Stock is at least $32.625 per share to the redemption date, the holders of Debentures will receive upon conversion Common Stock (and cash in lieu of fractional shares) having a market value greater than the amount which would be received either upon surrender of Debentures for redemption or purchase by the Purchasers as described below.

*Conversion Procedure.* Debentures may be surrendered for conversion during the usual business hours at Citibank, N.A., Agent, Receive and Deliver Department, 2nd Floor, 111 Wall Street, New York, New York 10015, together with a written notice of election to convert such Debentures in the form printed on the reverse side of the Debentures or in the form on the Letter of Transmittal enclosed herewith. Such notice shall state the name or names (with addresses) in which the certificate or certificates for Common Stock issuable on conversion shall be issued. If Common Stock is to be issued to other than the registered holder of a Debenture, such Debenture must be accompanied by proper instruments of transfer and by funds in the amount of any stock transfer tax which may be payable (see Instruction 3 under "Instructions if Debentures Are Surrendered for Conversion" in the Letter of Transmittal).

*Effective Date of Conversion.* Each conversion of Debentures will be deemed to have been made at the close of business on the date of receipt by such Bank of such Debentures accompanied by such written notice, and at such time the rights of the holders of such Debentures as such holders shall cease, and the person(s) entitled to receive the Common Stock issuable upon such conversion will be treated for all purposes as the record holder(s) of such Common Stock on that date.

*Adjustments, Fractional Shares, etc.* No adjustments in respect

---

**FIGURE 10**
Redemption Notice

5. You may obtain from Citibank, N.A., Agent, Receive and Deliver Department, 2nd Floor, 111 Wall Street, New York, N.Y. 10015 (tel. 212-558-5010), copies of a Letter of Transmittal which may be used to accompany Debentures surrendered for conversion into Common Stock or for purchase by the Purchasers.

6. You have, as a further alternative, the right to sell Debentures through brokerage facilities. You should consult your own broker as to this procedure.

*The conversion right terminates on December 23, 1976.*

Debentures remaining unconverted will be redeemed at the redemption price (including accrued interest) of $1,089.26 per $1,000 Debenture.

**BE SURE TO READ THE FORMAL NOTICE OF REDEMPTION**

*This advertisement is not and under no circumstances is to be construed as an offer to sell or as a solicitation of an offer to buy any of the securities of the Company.*

of interest or dividends will be made upon the conversion of any Debenture. No fractional shares or scrip representing fractional shares will be issued upon the conversion of any Debenture. If more than one Debenture is surrendered for conversion at any one time by the same holder, the number of full shares which will be issuable upon conversion thereof will be computed upon the basis of the aggregate principal amount of Debentures so surrendered. If the conversion of any Debenture results in a fractional share interest, G-P will pay a cash adjustment in respect of such fractional interest in an amount equal to the same fraction of the last sales price per share of Common Stock on the New York Stock Exchange on the business day which next precedes the day of conversion.

**SALE OF DEBENTURES TO PURCHASERS AT HIGHER THAN REDEMPTION PRICE.**

G-P has entered into an agreement with Blyth Eastman Dillon & Co. Incorporated and certain other purchasers (the Purchasers) under which the Purchasers have agreed to purchase all Debentures submitted to them at any time up to the close of business on December 23, 1976 at a price of $1,092.50 flat (without accrued interest) for each $1,000 principal amount thereof. This price is higher than the $1,089.26 for each $1,000 principal amount of Debentures payable upon redemption as described above.

The Purchasers have agreed to convert all Debentures so purchased into Common Stock, and G-P has agreed to pay the Purchasers a commission for their undertaking. G-P's agreement with the Purchasers also provides that if the Purchasers purchase Debentures on the open market, they will convert such Debentures into Common Stock.

G-P has been informed by the Purchasers that the Agreement Among Purchasers provides that, for the purpose of stabilizing the price of G-P's Common Stock or otherwise, the Purchasers may buy and convert Debentures, and may purchase and sell shares of Common Stock and other securities of G-P convertible into Common Stock, in the open market or otherwise, for either long or short account, at such times, in such amounts, on such terms and at such prices as Blyth Eastman Dillon & Co. Incorporated may determine, and may overallot in arranging sales. Any such transactions, if commenced, may be discontinued at any time.

Debentures may be surrendered for sale to Blyth Eastman Dillon & Co. Incorporated, as Representative of the several Purchasers, c/o Citibank, N.A., Agent for the Purchasers, Receive and Deliver Department, 2nd Floor, 111 Wall Street, New York, New York 10015, prior to the close of business on December 23, 1976, using the Letter of Transmittal enclosed herewith.

**FEDERAL INCOME TAXES.**

Counsel for G-P has advised that, under present law, for Federal income tax purposes:
(1) Conversion of the Debentures into Common Stock will not result in taxable gain or loss, and the tax basis of the Debentures will be allocated to the Common Stock.
(2) Taxable gain, loss or income will be recognized with respect to the receipt of cash for any fractional share interest.
(3) Taxable gain or loss will be recognized with respect to any Debentures sold to the Purchasers or surrendered to G-P for redemption.

G-P suggests that holders of the Debentures consult their own tax advisers regarding the Federal income tax treatment applicable to them resulting from the conversion of the Debentures into Common Stock and the receipt of cash in lieu of fractional shares.

**GEORGIA-PACIFIC CORPORATION**
By R. B. PAMPLIN
*Chairman*

The Representative of the Standby Purchasers is:

# BLYTH EASTMAN DILLON & CO.
### INCORPORATED

1. the conversion privilege will be revoked;
2. accrued interest on the bond will cease; and
3. the holder must accept the redemption price as an only choice between recovery of principal and idling of investment funds.

The corporation has allowed 1 month for the news to circulate and for the holders of these bonds to make a decision. In the interim, the Reorganization Department must communicate with the beneficial owners of the bonds held in this brokerage firm's custody and solicit instructions from them. During this period, too, Georgia-Pacific has contracted with Blyth Eastman Dillon to stabilize the price of the underlying common stock in the marketplace. This is done to ensure that the stock remains at a price that is continuously more advantageous for the holder to convert than to redeem each bond. Even so, for those holders who choose to sell the bond rather than convert, Blyth Eastman Dillon is prepared to pay $1,092.50 flat for each $1,000 par value debenture. In turn, it will convert each bond and probably sell the stock for its higher value in the marketplace. The intent of both actions taken by Blyth Eastman Dillon is to enable Georgia-Pacific to exchange its debt security for more outstanding equity with a minimal outlay of cash. The minimal cash requirement is necessary only to redeem any bonds of holders who neglect to act in time. They will be paid $1,059.40 plus $29.86 in accrued interest to December 23, 1976.

3. *Exchanging one class of security for another class of the same issuer, pursuant to a reorganization of the corporation*

Sometimes, with a corporation in dire financial straits, bondholders may be willing to accept an equity security in exchange for their debt instruments to avoid prolonged and expensive bankruptcy proceedings. Or, such an exchange may be directed as a result of judicial decision in a bankruptcy court. Either way, the Reorganization Department submits the old certificates on behalf of its owners and accepts the new security in satisfaction. A voluntary exchange request needs written instructions from the beneficial owner to accomplish this, whereas an involuntary exchange does not.

Figure 11 is an advertisement announcing a voluntary exchange of convertible debentures for convertible preferred stock in the same company. The Reorganization Department must therefore communicate with the beneficial owners of the 5¾% debentures held in custody by its firm to solicit instructions concerning the disposition of those securities. The offering circular and letters of transmittal must be sent promptly to those persons so that they can respond and appropriate action be taken before the offer's expiration date on January 14, 1977.

4. *Exchanging one company's securities for another company's securities or money, pursuant to a merger ratified by the shareholders of both companies*

In these circumstances, the Reorganization Department may submit shares held for its firm's customers for shares in the surviving company or in shares of a newly organized third company, according to terms of the merger agreement. Records of the holdings of the firm and its customers are adjusted subsdquent to completion of the exchange. If the merger is an outright acquisition for cash, the customer's account will be credited with the funds received after the Reorganization Department submits the old shares and obtains payment.

5. *Subscribing for new shares in a company, pursuant to a rights offering*

When a company gives its holders preemptive rights to subscribe to new stock, the Reorganization Department uses these rights,

# Notice of Exchange Offer to Holders of
## 5¾% Convertible Subordinated Debentures Due 1996
### of
# HALLCRAFT HOMES, INC.

Hallcraft Homes, Inc. ("Hallcraft") is offering to the holders of its 5¾% Convertible Subordinated Debentures due 1996 ("Debentures"), subject to the terms and conditions set forth in the Offering Circular dated December 10, 1976, to exchange for such Debentures, shares of newly authorized Series A Convertible Preferred Shares in the ratio of

**66⅔ Series A Convertible Preferred Shares for each
$1,000 principal amount of 5¾% Debentures
(without payment of accrued interest)**

---

**This Exchange Offer expires at 5:00 P.M., Phoenix Time,
on January 14, 1977, unless extended.**

---

Hallcraft is not obligated to accept any Debentures unless at least 90% of the $15,000,000 Principal Amount of the Debentures outstanding are validly tendered, and the other conditions of the Exchange Offer, as described in the Offering Circular, are met.

The Offering Circular (together with the Annual Report of Hallcraft) contains important information which should be read before any decision is made with respect to the Exchange Offer. Debentures may be tendered by delivering, before the Expiration Date, such Debentures and a properly executed Letter of Transmittal to the Exchange Agent: United States Trust Company of New York, Corporate Agency Department, 130 John Street, (20th Floor), New York, New York 10038.

---

Questions or requests for assistance or for additional copies of the Offering Circular (together with the Annual Report of Hallcraft) and the Letter of Transmittal may be directed to Hallcraft at (602-956-8440, collect) or the Information Agent:

## The Carter Organization, Inc.
55 Liberty Street, New York, New York 10005
(212) 962-6117 (collect)

---

December 13, 1976

**FIGURE 11**
Voluntary Exchange Announcement

along with supplementary funds from the customer's account, to acquire the new stock from the company. If additional rights are needed to satisfy the customer's written instructions, they, too, must be purchased, either from the company's agent or in the open market. Conversely, if certain customers decide not to subscribe or if they own rights in excess of the amount needed to subscribe for the number of shares they want to buy, the Reorganization Department disposes of the extra rights before they expire. It may either sell them to the company's agent bank or standby underwriter, or accept someone else's bid in the open market. Either way, the appropriate customer accounts are credited with the net proceeds of that sale.

Purchases via subscription warrants are handled in the same fashion as subscription rights. They, too, require written instructions from the beneficial owner before positive action may be taken by the Reorganization Department. They, too, require consideration of a ratio formula set by the company for purchase of the new shares. For example, the company may declare with issuance of its rights (or warrants) that four rights are needed for each new share at $45, or that each warrant entitles the holder to subscribe to two new shares at $24.50, and so forth.

6. *Transmitting securities to an intended purchaser under terms of a proxy statement and upon specific written instructions from its beneficial owner*

As an accommodation for customers, the Reorganization Department is also capable of submitting securities to financial institutions acting as agents for people who seek to acquire them pursuant to a proxy statement filed with the SEC. **Tender offers**, as such proxies are known, can be successful devices for acquiring large amounts of stock without upsetting the supply/demand equilibrium in the marketplace (see Figure 12). The tender offer is a method often used by corporations or large institutions to effect a merger with, or gain control of, a company at reasonable cost. If an insufficient number of shares are submitted, the offeror is denied its desired objective. The offeror usually reserves the right to refuse purchase of any shares tendered; this is a valuable privilege not available in open-market transactions. Similarly, if a tender offer brings forth an overabundance of shares for sale, the offeror can accept all the shares, any portion of them, or only that particular amount specified in the proxy statement. If either of the latter two courses are chosen, the statement must also describe the manner in which tendered shares will be accepted and paid for. For instance, it can be accomplished under either of two methods:

1. *First come, first served:* Preference is given to those holders who submitted their shares for sale earlier than did other tenderees.
2. *Pro rata allocation:* Tendered shares are accepted by means of a ratio formula developed by relating the total shares submitted to the total shares desired. For example, if a tender offer for exactly 500,000 shares resulted in stockholder submissions of 800,000 shares, the purchaser will accept ⅝, or 62½%, of each holder's offering.

The formula for calculating the pro rata acceptance is:

*This announcement is neither an offer to buy nor a solicitation of an offer to sell these securities. The offer is made solely by the Offer to Purchase which is being mailed to holders of Common Stock of General Development Corporation and is not being made to, and tenders will not be accepted from, holders of Common Stock in any State in which the making or acceptance thereof would not be in compliance with the securities laws of such State.*

## Notice of Offer
## by
# 1 General Development Corporation
## to Purchase
## up to 500,000 Shares of its Common Stock
## at $7.00 Per Share

GENERAL DEVELOPMENT CORPORATION (the "Company") is offering to purchase up to 500,000 shares of its Common Stock ("Common Stock") at a price of $7.00
per share, net to the seller in cash, without deduction of brokerage commissions, any
2 transfer taxes applicable to the transfer of shares directly to the Company or other
expenses. Such offer is subject to all of the terms and conditions set forth in the Offer to
Purchase ("Offer") and in the Letter of Transmittal. **All tenders of shares pursuant
to the Offer will be irrevocable, except that shares tendered prior to January 25,
4 1974 may be withdrawn until that time.**

5 **The Offer will terminate at 5:00 P. M., New York City Time, on February 6, 1974, unless extended.**

The Company will be obligated to purchase all shares validly tendered up to 500,000.
If more than 500,000 shares are tendered, the Company at its option may purchase all
6 or any of such additional shares, but in no event more than 1,000,000 shares. If the
Company purchases less than all of the shares tendered, purchases will be made on a
pro rata basis. The Offer may be extended by the Company from time to time. If the
Offer is extended, shares of Common Stock tendered prior to 5:00 P. M. New York City
Time on February 6, 1974 will be purchased in their entirety before additional shares
7 tendered during any extended period are purchased. If less than all shares tendered during any extended period are purchased, the shares will be purchased in the order tendered.
All shares tendered and not purchased will be returned as soon as practicable after
expiration of the Offer.

The Company will pay to any broker or dealer (including the Dealer Manager named
below) who is a member of the National Association of Securities Dealers, Inc.
("NASD") or any national securities exchange, to any foreign broker or dealer who
agrees to conform to the Rules of Fair Practice of the NASD or to any commercial bank
8 or trust company, whose name appears in the appropriate space in the Letter of Transmittal, a commission of $0.30 for each share of Common Stock tendered pursuant to
such Letter of Transmittal and purchased under the Offer, not to exceed $2,500 in
respect of all shares tendered by or on behalf of any single beneficial owner.

Copies of the Offer and the Letter of Transmittal may be obtained from the Depositary or the Dealer Manager. Facsimile copies of the Letter of Transmittal will be acceptable.

**The Offer contains important information which should be read before tenders are made.**

*Depositary:*

(By Hand)
CHEMICAL BANK
Corporate Tellers Window No. 32
9 2nd Floor, North Building
55 Water Street
New York, New York 10041

(By Mail)
CHEMICAL BANK
Corporate Agency Division
Cooper Station
P.O. Box 689
New York, New York 10003

*The Dealer Manager for the Offer is:*

## 10 Goldman, Sachs & Co.

3 January 17, 1974

FIGURE 12
Newspaper Announcement of a Tender Offer

$$\frac{\text{total shares to be purchased by the company}}{\text{total shares submitted to the company}} = \text{proportion of each tenderee's shares to be accepted}$$

Tender offers may also have a significant impact upon the conduct of activity in a customer's cash or margin account. From what we have already said, it should be obvious that mere submission of shares does not guarantee sale proceeds. So long as the purchaser has a right of full or partial refusal, no proceeds may be withdrawn or used for another investment. Only after official word is received about the purchaser's acceptance and payment procedures can the proceeds be applied against new commitments or used for substitution in the selling customer's account. This is the principal reason why there is still a significant amount of trading activity in the open market while the tender offer is pending. Stockholders, because they are unsure of how many shares will be accepted if tendered, often prefer to dispose of their shares at a slightly lower market price simply because an open-market contract is guaranteed to be binding for the full amount.

Tender offers also generate revenue for broker/dealers whose customers cooperate by offering their shares for sale. If the shares are accepted, the purchaser pays those firms significant fees for their help, separate and apart from proxy solicitation reimbursement expenses. This often amounts to more than a normal commission for far less work than that needed for stock exchange or usual over-the-counter transactions. There is no disadvantage to the customers. The firms deal with the purchaser on a net basis, meaning that all expenses are borne by the buyer.

### E3b. *DETAILED EXPLANATION OF TENDER OFFER ILLUSTRATION*

Although it is important for stockholders to read the entire solicitation statement carefully before deciding whether or not to tender their shares, much valuable information about the offer can be gleaned from the title page alone. This fact is obvious from the typical newspaper announcement appearing in Figure 12. Let's briefly analyze that advertisement. The following text explains the information to which the numbers in the figure refer.

1 General Development Corporation is making a tender offer for 500,000 shares of its own common stock at $7.00 per share. That stock will then be classified as *treasury stock* on the company's financial records, reducing the number of shares issued and outstanding.

2 The company will pay any brokerage expense or transfer tax normally borne by a seller of securities. This will result in net proceeds for the tenderee of exactly $7.00 per share for each share purchased by the company.

3, 4 The effective date of this offering (when solicitations may legally commence) is January 17, 1974. The offer enables tenderees between January 17 and January 24, 1974, the privilege of changing their minds and withdrawing their shares from consideration. But shares on deposit after January 24 cannot be withdrawn and will be returned to sellers only if the company chooses not to purchase them.

5 The tender offer will expire at 5:00 P.M. New York City time on February 6, 1974, unless the company, at its option,

chooses to extend it to some later date. Any shares not on deposit with the company's agent at that time may not be considered for purchase.

6 The company is required to accept 500,000 shares, if that many are tendered. If less than this amount are deposited, it must purchase them all. If more than this number are tendered it may, at its option, purchase as many as 1,000,000 shares at $7.00 per share. If the company chooses to purchase 500,000 or more shares, acceptance will be made on a pro rata basis. It is important to note that if these shares are tendered from a margin account in accord with that customer's request, the Margin Department must continue to price that security for collateral purposes at its current market value. Because there is no assurance how many shares will be accepted, the market price is usually somewhat lower than the tender price.

7 Should the company extend its offer past the original expiration date (February 6), all shares deposited by that time will be purchased. However, any additional shares tendered thereafter may be accepted, too, but only on a first-come, first-served basis.

8 General Development will pay any qualified broker/dealer, commercial bank or trust company a solicitation fee of $.30 per share for each share it purchases, if that institution was instrumental in arranging for the tender by the underlying owner. It has also imposed a limitation on the remuneration payable to such institution acting on behalf of a single beneficial shareowner. At the scheduled rate of $.30 per share, that ceiling of $2,500 will be reached when a single owner sells 8,333 shares to the company.

9 The company has set up two depositary addresses where shares may be presented for consideration. Both are in New York City and both are locations administered by Chemical Bank.

10 The company has retained the services of Goldman, Sachs & Co., a prominent broker/dealer and investment banker, to coordinate the efforts of securities firms and banks in contacting its stockholders and soliciting tender of their shares.

*E4.*
*The Stock Record Department*

The position lists used by the Dividend, Proxy, and Reorganization departments in performing their responsibilities are, in reality, documents prepared and maintained by the Stock Record Department. This unit serves as a control and easy reference department for monitoring securities under the brokerage firm's jurisdiction. Industry custom and tradition have bestowed upon this department the title *Stock Record*, although it does, in fact, keep records of all securities, stocks and bonds alike. Individual records are maintained for each issue in alphabetical order. For financial reasons, these records must be unquestionably current and accurate. The stock record ledger shows

1. the name of a security;
2. the owner of that security; and
3. the location of that certificate.

In terms of location, the stock record clerk should be able to identify whether that security is in

1. safekeeping;
2. segregation;

3. a loan arrangement at a bank (hypothecation);
4. a loan to another broker/dealer;
5. reregistration proceedings at the transfer agent;
6. transit to the customer's agent bank or broker versus payment; or
7. fail-to-receive status from a contra broker/dealer or customer.

In the course of business each day, entries are processed by different operations departments that bear upon the Stock Record Department's responsibilities. Changes in quantities and/or location are debited or credited to this group's records, and the daily totals must balance. A "break" in stock record balance figures indicates that a mistake was made in an entry somewhere along the way. Such a mistake must be corrected immediately before the problem compounds itself and defies resolution. An uncorrected break could ultimately lead to serious losses in firm capital and could jeopardize the assets of customers.

*E5.*
*The Controller's Department*

A surface examination of the controller's function in a brokerage firm doesn't generally reveal its involvement with customer trade processing. Most people think of this area in terms of accounts payable, employee payroll records, financial reporting to regulatory bodies, interest control, general accounting, and so forth. Although all this is obviously true, the Controller's Department is also involved in the very last step in customer operations activity—preparation of the statements of account. Under federal law, if there has been any transaction activity, security position, or money balance in a customer's account within the preceding calendar quarter, a statement of account must be prepared and presented to the customer. Many firms comply by sending their customers monthly statements instead of the mandatory quarterly report, particularly in the case of margin account customers. This affords the customers an opportunity to pay the monthly interest charge on their debit balance, and, as a result, they incur only the posted annual rate expense. Otherwise, because that annual rate is calculated daily and posted to the account each month, the interest dollars would compound themselves and cause the customer to pay interest upon interest. For example, the interest charge on a $10,000 debit balance for 30 days at an annual rate of 10% is $83.33.

$$\frac{\$10,000}{1} \times \frac{10}{100} \times \frac{30}{360} = \$83.33$$

Unless the customer pays the $83.33 when posted at the end of the month, that amount is added to the debit balance, increasing the new principal sum for the following month's calculations.

$$\frac{\$10,083.33}{1} \times \frac{10}{100} \times \frac{30}{360} = \$84.03$$

The monthly or quarterly statement is a summary of all that has occurred on the customer's behalf during the period of time under consideration. All purchase expenses are debited to the account, whereas sales proceeds are credited accordingly. However, each purchase and/or sales transaction is posted on contract *settlement date*, whereas all other activities are posted on the day those activities occur. For instance, a check received from a customer is credited to the account on the day it is received, and money delivered out of the account is debited on the actual day of disbursement. However, a regular-way sale of a corporate security on June 26 will not be posted until July 3, five business days later. This is often a point of confusion for many customers, especially toward the end of the month when they receive their statement of account for the month of June and fail to see that sale posted on it. The registered representative must be aware of this sequence of events in order to dispel customer allegations of impropriety in the handling of an account.

Despite the best efforts and intentions of the Controller's Department, occasional mistakes do occur. An issue may not be carried forward in the following month's position listing, or duplicate entries may be processed accidentally and both items posted in the account. Because there are so many opportunities for wrong entries, a typical customer statement often contains a protective hedge in the form of an abbreviated legend, "E & OE," which means, "errors and omissions excepted." This declaration is designed to allow the brokerage firm an opportunity subsequently to correct the mistake without legal liability. As a registered representative, you should, therefore, carefully review your copy of each of your customer's statements with a view toward prompt discovery and correction of errors before they become a problem that affects your business.

The statement of account may also carry a legend advising the customers of financial protection afforded them under SEC Rule 15c3–3. Free credit balances must be maintained in a "special reserve bank account for the exclusive benefit of customers," a rule that denies the brokerage firm the right to use those funds in speculative conduct of its own business. The Controller's Department, employing a formula approved by stock exchange or NASD authority, supervises firm compliance with this rule and ensures that customer money is used only for customer purposes.

**CONCLUDING COMMENTS**

The foregoing commentary briefly describes some activities behind the scenes at an average broker/dealer organization. Details and departmental structure may vary widely from firm to firm, depending on business/product mix and sophistication of its clientele. For example, it is unlikely that a "retail" firm's operations would be organized identically to those of a "wholesale" firm that does no business with public customers. A firm that clears its trade activities through another member's facilities would be structured still differently. But the basic operations concept and work flow is found throughout the industry. After execution of an order, certificate shuffling, payments, recordkeeping, and supervisory control procedures must prevail to some extent at all brokerage firms.

# principles of technical analysis: reading and understanding financial news

A. Averages and Indexes
- **A1.** Definition
- **A2.** The Dow Jones Averages
  - **A2a.** The Dow Jones Industrial Average
  - **A2b.** The Dow Jones Transportation Average
  - **A2c.** The Dow Jones Utility Average
  - **A2d.** The Dow Jones Composite Average
- **A3.** Standard & Poor's Index
- **A4.** The New York Stock Exchange Index
- **A5.** The NASDAQ-OTC Price Index
- **A6.** The American Stock Exchange Price Index

B. Market Theories
- **B1.** The Dow Theory
- **B2.** The Odd-Lot Theory
- **B3.** The Advance–Decline Theory
- **B4.** The Short Interest Theory (Cushion Theory)
- **B5.** The Confidence Theory
- **B6.** Formula Investing
  - **B6a.** Constant-Ratio Plan
  - **B6b.** Constant-Dollar Plan
- **B7.** Dollar Cost Averaging
- **B8.** Technical Analysis
  - **B8a.** What It Is
  - **B8b.** Point and Figure Charting
  - **B8c.** Vertical Line Charts
    - **B8c(1).** Head-and-Shoulders Pattern
    - **B8c(2).** Support and Resistance Levels
    - **B8c(3).** Double Tops and Bottoms
    - **B8c(4).** Climaxes

C. The Ticker Tape
- **C1.** Tape Language
  - **C1a.** Stock Symbols
  - **C1b.** Share Volume
  - **C1c.** Sequential Transactions
  - **C1d.** Delayed and Volatile Transaction Prints
  - **C1e.** Stopped Stock

An average and an index differ as to the number of components used. An average is based on a small number of securities, whereas an index uses a broader sampling. However, there isn't any clear line of demarcation between the two, and so, in some instances, one analyst's average may be another analyst's index.

An average adds the market value of selected stocks and divides either by the number of issues or by a divisor that allows for stock splits or other changes in capitalization. Criticism of averages is based on the small number of issues included in the sample and the resultant disproportionate effect that one company can have on the average. Also, the securities chosen are not always representative of the purpose of the average; for example, American Telephone & Telegraph, which is clearly a utility corporation, is a component of the Dow Jones *industrial* averages. Averages are, nonetheless, widely accepted and have provided a reliable market indicator for many years.

---

**THE DOW JONES INDUSTRIAL AVERAGE**

Three separate averages are prepared by Dow Jones. The *Industrial Average*, based on 30 stocks, is the most widely quoted market average or index. If one hears the phase, "The market was up 4 today," it means that this relatively small average has shown a rise of 4 points for the trading session in relation to the present overall total of about 1,200 points.

---

The Dow Jones Industrial Average (DJIA) is computed by totaling the market prices of all component issues and dividing the sum by a comparatively constant number to produce the arithmetic DJIA. The divisor is "comparatively constant" only in relation to the prices of the included securities. It, too, is adjusted (although only downward) from time to time to reflect stock splits and stock dividends that will affect the average by 5 or more points. That divisor is currently 1.132. If each security in the average moved 1 point in the same direction on a given day, the effect on the DJIA would be about 26½ points up or down, as the case may be. Note that the DJIA is not expressed in terms of dollars and cents. Rather, the DJIA is expressed only in points plotted against an overall numerical figure.

Despite competition from larger indexes, the popularity of the Dow remains undiminished. Its wide usage is due in part to the fact that its founder, Charles Dow, began his computations back in 1884, thus giving it the longest continuity in its field. The Dow Theory, which will be discussed later, is also based on this average. The 30 common stocks included in the *Dow Jones Industrial Average* are:

| | | | | |
|---|---|---|---|---|
| Allied Corporation | Chevron Corp. | Inco. Ltd. | Owens-Illinois Inc. | Westinghouse Electric Corp. |
| Aluminum Company of America | E.I. Du Pont de Nemours & Co. | International Business Machines Corp. | Procter & Gamble Co. | F.W. Woolworth Co. |
| American Brands, Inc. | Eastman Kodak Co. | International Harvester Co. | Sears Roebuck & Co. | |
| American Can Co. | Exxon Corp. | International Paper Co. | Texaco, Inc. | |
| American Express Co. | General Electric Co. | Merck & Co., Inc. | Union Carbide Corp. | |
| American Telephone & Telegraph Co. | General Foods Corp. | Minnesota Mining & Manufacturing Corp., Inc. | United States Steel Corp. | |
| Bethelehem Steel Corp. | General Motors Corp. | | United Technologies Corp. | |
| | Goodyear Tire & Rubber Co. | | | |

### A2b.   THE DOW JONES TRANSPORTATION AVERAGE

The *Dow Jones Transportation Average* contains 20 common stocks. Once known as the Rail Average, diminishing interest in, and declining growth of, railroads, together with a desire to reflect the importance of other forms of transportation, prompted the change. The list now includes six airlines and three trucking companies.

### A2c.   THE DOW JONES UTILITY AVERAGE

The *Dow Jones Utility Average* is made up of 15 major utility companies that service all parts of the United States.

### A2d.   THE DOW JONES COMPOSITE AVERAGE

The *Dow Jones Composite Average* consists of the 65 stocks included in the industrial, transportation, and utility indexes.

### A3. Standard & Poor's Index

The *Standard & Poor's 500* index has grown in stature and usage since its inception in 1957. This broad-based index is actually a composite of the four other indexes prepared by the service. 400 industrial, 20 transportation, 40 financial, and 40 public utility common stocks are computed separately and then combined to give the *500* stock figures. This index is a presentation in terms of movement in an overall total of about 103 points. It, like the DJIA, is not expressed as a dollars-and-cents fluctuation of market values.

The serious user of this tool considers it more representative of market activity and direction than the smaller-based averages. *Standard & Poor's* movements have not, however, shown a marked variation from its greatest competitor, the *Dow Jones Industrial Average*.

### A4. The New York Stock Exchange Index

The New York Stock Exchange publishes a composite index of *all its listed common stocks*. This index is further broken down into four groups—(1) industrial; (2) transportation; (3) utilities; (4) finance—and is printed on the tape every half-hour. This composite index is identified as the ''market.''

**example**

---

ON-THE-HOUR-TAPE

| FIVE. HOUR. APPROX. VOL | MARKET. UP CENTS..NYSE. INDEX | UP |
|---|---|---|
| 15,740,000 | 4 | 43.48    0.04 |

| ..INDU   UP | ..TRAN   UP | ..UTIL   DOWN | ..FINC   UP |
|---|---|---|---|
| 43.13   0.17 | 47.56    0.37 | 44.01 | 0.16   43.91    0.12 |

---

The five New York Stock Exchange indexes reflect the combined market-value changes in the component issues. Each index is weighted; this means that the price of each stock is multiplied by the number of listed shares in making the calculations. Wide price fluctuations in cyclical issues with a small number of shares will not distort the true value of the index, because both price and total value are used as determinants. Movements in the composite index (the "market") are shown in dollars and cents because most public investors find this form easier to understand. The group indexes are shown only in terms of point movements up or down from their previous values.

All five indexes were originally set at 50.00 as of the close of the market on December 31, 1965, because this was the approximate average price of listed shares at that time. If necessary, base market values are adjusted daily to allow for changes in capitalization, new listings, or delistings. If, for example, an issue is delisted, the base market value is decreased so that the level of the index will not be affected. The formula for computing the current index is:

$$\text{composite index} = \frac{\text{current market value}}{\text{base market value}} \times 50$$

If, for example, the base market value is \$800 billion and the current market value is \$700 billion, the current index will be 43.75.

$$\frac{700}{800} \times 50 = \frac{35,000}{800} = 43.75$$

A net money change in the average price of NYSE shares is derived from the net change in the NYSE Composite Index as follows:

$$\text{change in average price} = \frac{\text{average price of shares listed}}{\text{composite index value}a} \times \text{change in index}$$

**example**

Assume that the composite index value is 43.75, up .05 from 43.70 and that the average price of shares listed is 35.00. The ticker tape will show this as "Market up 4 cents."

$$\frac{35.00}{43.70a} \times .05 = .04, \text{ or 4 cents up}$$

aUse the *changed* composite index and reflect the change we use in the formula

### A5.
### The NASDAQ–OTC Price Index

In May 1971, a significant addition to stock market indexes was made with the announcement by the NASD of the NASDAQ–OTC Price Index (National Association of Securities Dealers Automated Quotations–Over The Counter Price Index). Made possible by developments that permit securities dealers to program over-the-counter stock prices into a central computer, this index gives a broad-based indication of activity in the unlisted securities market. It is updated every 5 minutes.

All domestic common stocks listed on NASDAQ have been divided into seven categories: (1) composite (all issues); (2) industrials; (3) banks; (4) insurance; (5) other finance; (6) transportation; (7) utilities. As new stocks are added to the system, they too are included. The system adjusts daily for capitalization changes, such as splits, rights to subscribe, new listings, and delistings, in order to prevent these changes from affecting the index value.

Each index was assigned a base value derived from the prevailing market prices on February 5, 1971. The total number of shares outstanding for each was multiplied by its median closing-bid price on that day. The total value for all stocks in each index was then arithmetically equated to a base of 100.

## A6.
### The American Stock Exchange Price Change Index

The American Stock Exchange computes an index that differs from the indexes prepared by the New York Stock Exchange. This index measures the average change in price for issues on the American Stock Exchange. All common stocks and warrants are included; no weighting is done, unlike the New York Stock Exchange measurements. Each issue is given equal consideration despite the number of shares outstanding. The total price change for all issues is simply divided by the number of issues to show the average change of price. If, on a given day, 1,000 different common stocks and warrants are traded and if each is up ½ point (50¢), the total price increase will be $500.00. By dividing this total by the 1,000 issues, or index will show + 0.50. This is a simple arithmetic computation that can be most useful in reading overall market direction.

A new issue admitted to dealings is included in the index after it trades for 1 hour. The number of issues used as a divisor is then increased by one for the next computation.

The index is first prepared at 10:30 A.M. (New York time) and then hourly from 11:00 A.M. to 3:00 P.M. It is shown again at the close. Changes are from the previous close, not from the previous hour.

## B.
### market theories

## B1.
### The Dow Theory

The Dow Theory is based on the writings of Charles Dow, an editor of the *Wall Street Journal* early in the twentieth century. His ideas on stock-price movements were later elaborated on by S. A. Nelson, who also wrote for the *Journal*. It was Nelson who named Dow's hypotheses the Dow Theory.

Using the Dow Jones averages as its base, the theory proposes that these market averages rise or fall in *advance* of similar changes in business activity. By properly reading the averages, you get a prediction of things to come and can accurately plan investments based on prior price movements. Although it was never considered a get-rich-quick scheme by its originators, the theory is claimed to be a reliable method of predicting future market direction.

There are three basic movements in the market listed here in order of importance:

1. The **primary movement** is long term and may last from 1 to 5 years. This is the overall trend of the market and is the most important reading. You must be able to differentiate between brief reversals of the major trend and reversals from a *bull* to a *bear* market and vice versa.     **primary movement**

2. **Secondary movements** reverse the primary movement and last for short periods, perhaps 1 to 3 months. As many as three to five of these shifts may occur during a bull or bear market before a trend reversal is indicated. The secondary     **secondary movements**

movements provide information for medium-term trading decisions. More important, they help you to anticipate the life expectancy of the primary movement. Experienced technicians measure the percentage of variance from the primary movement, correlate it with the time it takes to reach that level and, using historical precedent for that issue, project the duration potential of the primary movement.

Figure 1 shows a graph representing both primary and secondary movements. Note the primary movement illustrated between points A and B (upward), and then between B and F (downward). The temporary, short-lived reactions between A and B are secondary movements, as are the short rallies between B and F. The Dow theorists believe that an upward trend is not reversed until one of those secondary reactions penetrates the bottom of a previous reaction, such as that which occurred at point D in relation to C. Conversely, the downward trend is reversed when a secondary movement rally penetrates the top of a previous rally, such as what happened when point G rose above E. Analogies are often drawn between primary and secondary movements and the seas. Primary movements are comparable to the incoming and ebb tides, whereas secondary movements represent ocean waves influenced by those flows.

**FIGURE 1**
Dow Jones Primary and Secondary Movements

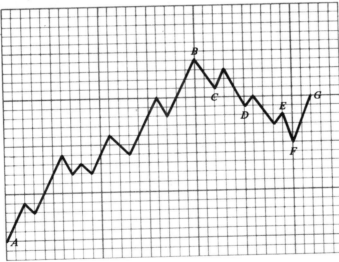

daily fluctuations

3. **Daily fluctuations** are of little consequence to longer-term market movements. They are not indicative of primary or secondary movements and are often emotional reactions. They are like ripples that appear on the waves of the sea, to use the analogy referred to earlier. Proponents of the Dow Theory hold that all factors concerning market conditions are built into the averages. It is unnecessary, therefore, to consider sales, earnings, dividends, production costs, or the hundreds of other factors included in fundamental analysis. These elements are implicit in the averages, and their effects can be clearly read.

The behavior of the small investor is a focal point of interest for

**B2.**
**The Odd-Lot Theory**

many market forecasters. Some go so far as to say, "The odd-lot customer is always wrong." This is an overstatement, but the investing patterns of the small investor have been refined into a number of interesting theories. The best-known of these was advanced by Garfield A. Drew, who noted that odd-lot customers frequently became heavy buyers as the market neared its top and reduced their buying in a down market prior to a rally. The changes in the odd-lot customer's buying can, therefore, be charted and used as an effective market signal.

Odd-lot purchases normally exceed sales. This results from the fact that clients often purchase an odd lot on a number of occasions until they accumulate a round lot. The subsequent sale will not, therefore, be reflected in the daily odd-lot figures but will become part of the normal round lot trading volume. Odd lots on the New York Stock Exchange are generally handled directly by the specialist. A customer wishing to purchase 50 shares of General Electric buys direct from the specialist, not from another client with a similar amount to sell. Total purchases and sales of odd lots, therefore, directly reflect the attitude of small investors and can easily be studied for changing trends. Working from the normal imbalance of purchases versus sales, we watch the behavior pattern of the odd-lot purchaser. When it indicates a significant change of direction, an adherent to this theory makes a commitment—in the opposite direction.

Figure 2 is an illustration of the way odd-lot statistics are released to the public, both on a daily and weekly basis. The daily figures are not as relevant for the followers of this theory. The daily release can be misleading because of a single unusual event that may have occurred on that day. In any event, it is incomplete. It does not include the odd-lot orders executed by Merrill Lynch, Pierce, Fenner & Smith, Inc., which undoubtedly constitute a considerable amount because of that firm's usually high volume of activity. Their figures, however, are included in the weekly statistics, which are also reported to the SEC. Based upon the weekly analysis depicted in Figure 2, twice as many odd-lot sellers than buyers indicate that the sophisticated round-lot investor should be buying stock.

## Weekly Odd-Lot Trading

New York Stock Exchange odd-lot trading statistics, as reported to the Securities and Exchange Commission for the week ended December 10, 1976 are:

|  | Shares | Values |
|---|---|---|
| Customers' Orders to Buy | 1,251,331 | $45,815,211 |
| Customers' Orders to Sell | 2,552,564 | $84,988,114 |

Week's short sales by customers totaled 8,301 shares.

## Odd-Lot Trading

NEW YORK—The New York Stock Exchange reported handling the following odd-lot transactions (in shares):

|  | Customer Purchases | Short Sales | Other Sales | Total Sales |
|---|---|---|---|---|
| December 21, 1976 | 149,693 | 1,764 | 409,497 | 411,261 |

FIGURE 2
Daily and Weekly Odd-Lot Trading

## B3.
### The Advance–Decline Theory

As indicated earlier, market averages and indexes include a limited number of components. Although averages are useful in many ways, some market analysts are more concerned with the *number* of stocks that advance in relation to the number that decline in order to gain a more detailed picture of market direction. It is not at all unusual for declines to exceed advances on a day on which other market indicators are pointing upward. This is a signal to the advance–decline theorist that the market will soon follow downward. Naturally, there is more to this theory than watching each day's picture. The follower of this theory keeps daily totals of advances and declines, subtracts the smaller from the larger figure to arrive at a net balance, and watches for pertinent changes.

The figures are often plotted on graph paper, as illustrated in Figure 3, and analyzed in conjunction with the number of issues actually traded that day. This is known as *the breadth of the market*. The breadth index is computed by taking the net of the advance–decline figure and dividing it by the total number of issues traded that day. If, on a given day, there are 1,350 different issues traded, and, of these, 712 advanced, 464 declined, and 174 remained unchanged:

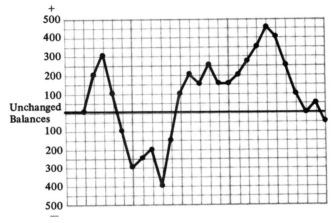

**FIGURE 3**
Advance and Declines

$$\frac{712 - 464}{1,350} = +18.4\%$$

If the day's results are:

374 issues up
598 issues down
426 issues unchanged
1,398 total issues traded.

Then $\dfrac{+374 - 598}{1,398} = -16.0\%$

The market as measured by other indicators may be approaching a low point. However, if the advance–decline net balance is cumulatively showing positive signs, the analyst concludes that the market will hold and reach for higher ground. A sell signal, on the other hand, occurs if, in a rising market, net declines continually surpass net advances.

Many sophisticated approaches have developed from the advance–decline theory. You should study them in detail if you wish to apply them in your own work. They have proved to be useful tools in judging market timing.

Figure 4, labeled "Market Diary," shows the number of issues advancing, declining, and remaining unchanged each day for the preceding six trading sessions. It includes the number of issues setting new highs and lows for the year during those sessions. This kind of overview should prove to be sufficient for followers of this theory to gauge market direction and spot changes in trends as soon as they occur.

**MARKET DIARY**

|  | Wed | Tues | Mon | Fri | Thur | Wed |
|---|---|---|---|---|---|---|
| Issues traded | 1,943 | 1,961 | 1,954 | 1,948 | 1,943 | 1,980 |
| Advances | 985 | 826 | 523 | 690 | 647 | 886 |
| Declines | 509 | 661 | 1,004 | 782 | 851 | 636 |
| Unchanged | 449 | 474 | 427 | 476 | 445 | 448 |
| New highs, 1976 | 120 | 92 | 77 | 110 | 106 | 156 |
| New lows, 1976 | 4 | 11 | 12 | 5 | 5 | 4 |

**FIGURE 4**
Market Diary

## B4.
### The Short Interest Theory (Cushion Theory)

A short sale is the sale of a security that one does not own or does not intend to deliver (short against the box). The seller arranges to borrow the security and delivers the borrowed stock to the purchaser. The usual reason for a short sale is an anticipated decline in the market value of the security shorted. The seller hopes to repurchase it at a lower price and realize a profit.

> A compilation of the short interest is made as of the fifteenth day of each month by the stock exchanges and reported to the media 4 business days later. At first glance, one would think that a sharp increase in short sales would presage a decline in the market. But the follower of this theory thinks otherwise. Short sellers at some future point become buyers of stock to cover their positions. This *cushion* of potential buyers will support a declining market and may even accelerate a rising one. Short sellers may repurchase when the market goes up to limit their losses and by doing so, give impetus to the advance.

The short interest theory can be applied to the overall market or to particular issues. The conclusions are based on the size of the short position as related to average daily volume. If the short interest exceeds 1 day's average volume, the picture begins to look bullish. Should short interest rise above 1½ times daily volume, this theory tells us that the cushion is now large enough to indicate a buy signal. If enough adherents begin to purchase, the stock will rise. The short seller may then be forced to cover, and a further rise will result.

Figure 5 shows a sampling of the monthly short-position statistics released by the New York Stock Exchange in December 1976. Observe that the information includes the current and previous month's figures as well as the average daily volume in each issue. This is designed to help cushion theorists make judgments about near-term price movements in these issues. Note, too, that some issues are marked to advise readers that these securities may be involved in an arbitrage transaction. That is, they have been sold short by traders who own another security and hope to close out that short position with the common stock receivable from the other security. It is a typical technique used in connection with mergers, acquisitions, and redemptions of convertible securities pursuant to call by the issuer. These short interest figures are thus temporarily inflated and are not indicative of potential buying interest by those sellers.

# New York Exchange Short Interest Registers Record

Short interest on the New York Stock Exchange in the month ended Dec. 15 rose to a record 27,510,879 shares from 24,777,197 shares a month earlier. The previous record was set last Jan. 15, when the short interest was 27,142,204 shares. The shares in the short interest are equal to one-tenth of 1 percent of the total shares listed on the Exchange.

On the American Stock Exchange the short interest increased 49,007 shares to 3,284,454 shares as of Dec. 15. A year ago the short interest was 3,155,234. Short position of 5,000 or more shares existed in 88 of the more than 120 stocks and warrants traded on the Exchange and some short position was shown in 496 issues.

The following figures show some of the important short positions and changes for companies on the New York Stock Exchange.

**SHORT INTEREST**

**NEW YORK STOCK EXCHANGE**

| | 12-15-76 | 11-15-76 | Avg. Daily Volume |
|---|---|---|---|
| Abbott Labs | 7,933 | 20,908 | 26,025 |
| ASA Ltd | 209,255 | 154,905 | 57,005 |
| Airco Inc | 30,844 | 17,644 | 8,055 |
| Aetna Life Casualty | 9,750 | 34,050 | 56,935 |
| Akzona Inc | 34,800 | 34,800 | 3,665 |
| Alcan Aluminium Ltd | 31,997 | 29,240 | 44,850 |
| tAmax Inc | 117,548 | 118,321 | 10,320 |
| Allied Stores | 4,685 | 19,502 | 9,910 |
| Aluminum Co America | 80,772 | 43,772 | 20,580 |
| tAmerada Hess Corp | 107,299 | 38,756 | 44,985 |
| American Credit Corp | 11,459 | 433 | 7,290 |
| Amer Broadcasting Cos | 38,891 | 58,562 | 59,270 |
| Amer Cyanamid Co | 63,800 | 61,706 | 22,185 |
| Amer Electric Power | 18,883 | 2,083 | 43,850 |
| Amer General Ins Co | 91,300 | 102,019 | 20,615 |
| Amer Home Products | 32,685 | 11,132 | 98,605 |
| Amer Hospital Supply | 63,369 | 118,272 | 21,670 |
| Amer Motors Corp | 71,567 | 71,267 | 32,945 |
| American Standard | 2,500 | 17,100 | 14,805 |
| tAmer Tel & Tel | 143,723 | 88,752 | 154,890 |
| AMP Inc | 247,484 | 258,174 | 29,415 |
| Anaconda Co | 39,417 | 32,218 | 26,365 |
| Apache Corp | 20,100 | 7,500 | 6,125 |
| Apco Oil Corp | 28,802 | 9,300 | 5,585 |
| Armstrong Cork Co | 43,420 | 14,820 | 31,770 |
| tAtlantic Richfield | 324,546 | 336,053 | 89,570 |
| Auto Data Processing | 50,093 | 24,752 | 13,150 |
| Avco Corp wts 78 | 63,900 | 67,200 | 3,410 |
| tAvery Intl Corp | 111,895 | 108,195 | 6,335 |
| Avco Corp | 24,155 | 15,905 | 23,765 |
| Avnet Inc | 8,440 | 21,365 | 35,770 |
| Avon Products Inc | 73,355 | 92,405 | 62,685 |
| Bandag Inc | 27,819 | 20,510 | 14,305 |
| Braun (C F) Co | 33,900 | 5,400 | 5,485 |
| Bates Mfg Co | 42,358 | 42,958 | 1,775 |
| Baker Intl Corp | 38,325 | 41,516 | 8,515 |
| Beatrice Foods | 47,751 | 32,262 | 43,035 |
| Beech Aircraft | 21,901 | 16,305 | 4,805 |
| Baxter Bravenol Lab | 27,700 | 46,191 | 27,560 |
| Beker Indus Inc | 85,999 | 67,809 | 8,895 |
| Bethlehem Steel | 16,744 | 44,998 | 35,005 |
| Black & Decker Mfg | 61,809 | 26,490 | 51,290 |
| Bally Mfg Corp | 52,796 | 46,200 | 25,510 |
| Best Products Co | 175,075 | 171,337 | 20,560 |
| H&R Block Inc | 23,388 | 18,140 | 37,180 |
| Blue Bell Inc | 30,150 | 29,500 | 28,715 |
| Boeing Co | 75,055 | 90,633 | 44,285 |
| Boise Cascade Corp | 46,816 | 41,922 | 45,200 |
| Braniff Intl Corp | 24,202 | 33,602 | 39,835 |
| British Pete Amer Sh | 207,814 | 98,950 | 51,725 |
| tContinental Group | 181,728 | 292,635 | 22,330 |
| tBrunswick Corp | 162,024 | 19,347 | 34,885 |
| CBS Inc | 23,866 | 24,384 | 23,510 |
| Budd Co | 97,232 | 73,585 | 8,495 |
| Emerson Elec Co | 30,327 | 33,161 | 25,295 |
| EMI Ltd Am Shs | 5,004 | 38,208 | 5,330 |
| Engelhard Min & Chem | 55,658 | 69,899 | 13,720 |
| Esquire Inc | 40,200 | 18,600 | 6,890 |
| Evans Products | 44,191 | 23,008 | 81,570 |
| Exxon Corp | 43,009 | 90,208 | 112,660 |
| Fairchild Cmra & Inst | 52,291 | 79,320 | 20,825 |
| Farah Mfg Co | 32,961 | 31,461 | 3,800 |
| Federal Nat Mtg | 29,101 | 92,970 | 61,930 |
| Federated Dept Stors | 97,092 | 121,833 | 37,580 |
| First Charter Fin Cp | 50,312 | 49,008 | 21,575 |
| Florida Power Corp | 900 | 16,000 | 9,090 |
| Ford Motor Co | 48,315 | 27,730 | 58,920 |
| tGulf & West Ind wts 78 | 972,688 | 831,491 | 35,010 |
| Golden West Fin Corp | 25,896 | 13,070 | 6,380 |
| Gardner & Denver | 25,020 | 16,020 | 26,590 |
| tGeneral Electric | 7,140,208 | | 63,470 |
| General Foods | 20,440 | 40,370 | 32,985 |
| Gneral Host Corp | 28,434 | 30,325 | 1,610 |
| General Mills | 62,200 | 61,661 | 17,385 |
| General Motors | 206,732 | 135,873 | 173,310 |
| Gen Tel & Electronics | 70,381 | 53,536 | 56,730 |
| tGenuine Parts Co | 145,470 | 119,970 | 9,265 |
| tGeorgia Pacific Corp | 324,413 | 130,986 | 64,125 |
| Getty Oil Co | 51,173 | 8,838 | 5,665 |
| Gibraltar Financial | 22,326 | 12,626 | 24,910 |
| xFrigitronics Inc | 70,200 | 73,900 | 6,565 |
| Global Marine Inc | 210,950 | 222,450 | 6,285 |
| Goodrich (B.F.) Co | 31,184 | 15,221 | 10,300 |
| Gould Inc | 53,353 | 59,521 | 18,945 |
| Grace (W.R.) & Co | 34,782 | 35,641 | 15,860 |
| tGreat Westrn Financl | 103,750 | 35,550 | 38,665 |
| Guardian Mtg Invest | 28,589 | 24,352 | 2,590 |
| Greyhound Corp wts 80 | 20,100 | 20,000 | 4,555 |
| Grumman Corp | 22,529 | 12,046 | 3,280 |
| Gulf Oil Corp | 68,738 | 19,908 | 99,355 |
| tGulf & Westrn Ind | 257,242 | 159,810 | 47,600 |
| Hall (Frank B.) & Co | 21,300 | 17,100 | 4,435 |
| Halliburton Co | 123,981 | 98,075 | 46,085 |
| Heinz (H.J.) Co | 32,545 | 21,695 | 16,060 |
| Hercules Inc. | 27,200 | 89,959 | 31,550 |
| Heublein Inc | 50,103 | 18,037 | 21,555 |
| Hewlett Packard Co | 95,385 | 173,022 | 22,750 |
| Holly Sugar | 75,828 | 43,979 | 5,000 |
| Homestake Mining | 69,878 | 69,794 | 27,370 |
| Honeywell Inc. | 50,345 | 27,063 | 41,930 |
| Horizon Corp | 10,400 | 400 | 3,890 |
| Houston Lighting & Pwr | 20,100 | 36,303 | 53,690 |
| Howard Johnson Co | 46,718 | 86,548 | 22,234 |
| House of Fabrics Inc | 30,710 | 20,300 | 6,205 |
| Hughes Tool Co | 46,225 | 15,100 | 33,555 |
| tIDS Realty Trust | 107,500 | 107,651 | 2,850 |
| Illinois Tool Works | None | 15,965 | 1,800 |
| Indianapolis Pwr & Lgt | 59,762 | 200 | 6,285 |
| Ingersoll Rand Co | 65,430 | 23,426 | 14,120 |
| Insilco Corp | 17,000 | 500 | 8,680 |
| Interco Inc | 21,593 | 16,270 | 6,250 |
| IC Industries Inc | 19,401 | 2,925 | 6,860 |
| Inter Business Mach | 39,034 | 36,737 | 71,675 |
| Int Flavors & Fragrnce | 83,623 | 87,451 | 28,450 |
| Inter Harvester | 44,400 | 20,250 | 19,060 |
| Inter Minerals & Chem | 25,181 | 49,370 | 18,075 |
| International Paper | 53,880 | 91,620 | 46,260 |
| Int Tel & Tel Pr Ser K | 38,503 | 21,511 | 6,610 |
| tInter Tel & Tel | 186,678 | 161,053 | 84,210 |
| tInt Tel & Tel Pr Ser N | 112,800 | 500 | 19,880 |
| IV Intl Corp | 50,332 | 27,152 | 21,775 |
| Itek Corp | 25,588 | 19,590 | 4,890 |
| Itel Corp | 64,005 | 28,050 | 9,110 |
| E. F. Johnson Co | 209,587 | 132,286 | 8,215 |
| Johns-Manville | 37,046 | 79,500 | 69,230 |
| Johnson & Johnson | 61,791 | 74,264 | 27,230 |
| Joy Mfg | 30,815 | 30,715 | 14,710 |
| tKaiser Alum & Chem | 251,003 | 249,727 | 7,100 |
| Kaiser Cement & Gypsum | 64,585 | 52,885 | 7,435 |
| Kaufman & Broad Inc | 45,900 | 44,700 | 56,190 |
| Kellogg Co | 36,832 | 54,917 | 22,745 |
| Kentucky Utilities | 22,020 | 17,200 | 7,325 |
| Kerr-McGee Corp | 20,390 | 54,410 | 18,765 |
| Kresge (S S) | 88,298 | 107,873 | 107,410 |
| Lear Siegler Inc | 29,227 | 26,159 | 13,785 |
| Levi Strauss & Co | 27,834 | 8,690 | 30,180 |
| LTV Corp | 39,204 | 41,533 | 18,865 |
| Litton Industries | 60,567 | 55,532 | 31,435 |
| Loews Corp | 36,836 | 15,643 | 15,920 |
| Louisiana L & Exp Co | 15,418 | 325 | 29,225 |
| Lubrizol Corp | 62,516 | 54,316 | 15,485 |
| Lucky Stores Inc | 31,766 | 40,182 | 20,710 |
| Melville Shoe Corp | 25,375 | 1,825 | 36,675 |
| Lykes Corp | 32,875 | 33,925 | 10,410 |
| Marriott Corp | 31,722 | 23,590 | 26,640 |
| Martin Marietta Corp | 36,317 | 15,434 | 13,555 |
| tRevlon Inc | r167,506 | s116,539 | 18,600 |
| tReynolds Metals | 101,065 | 94,790 | 16,815 |
| Reynolds Ind | 7,855 | 20,555 | 23,540 |
| Reynolds Ind $2.25 | 7,800 | 17,800 | 3,625 |
| Richardson-Merrell | 17,237 | 5,696 | 12,265 |
| Rite Aid Corp | 13,925 | 3,333 | 21,190 |
| Rohm & Haas Co | 28,425 | 36,260 | 6,145 |
| Royal Dutch Petr Co | 88,650 | 55,067 | 28,880 |
| Royal Industries | 22,027 | 420 | 38,885 |
| Ryder System Inc | 36,799 | 38,149 | 25,095 |
| St Joe Minerals Corp | 25,193 | 23,383 | 11,080 |
| Santa Fe Intrl | 31,335 | 25,135 | 24,060 |
| Schlitz (Jos) Brewing | 62,620 | 59,620 | 18,290 |
| Schlumberger N.V. | 88,132 | 113,252 | 43,875 |
| Savin Business Mach | 62,329 | 60,900 | 8,755 |
| Searle (G.D.) & Co | 41,500 | 25,700 | 53,030 |
| Sears Roebuck | 110,829 | 121,979 | 50,610 |
| xSambo's Restaurants | 34,704 | 25,699 | 25,575 |
| Seatrain Lines | 35,502 | 10,046 | 13,160 |
| Simplicity Pattern | 96,565 | 69,278 | 45,055 |
| Singer Co | 86,224 | 87,665 | 13,095 |
| Skyline Corp | 25,830 | 49,030 | 25,415 |
| SmithKline Corp | 35,361 | 31,339 | 14,950 |
| Southern Co | 103,625 | 38,400 | 92,305 |
| Southern Cal Edison | 395 | 57,095 | 29,640 |
| Southwestern Pub Ser | 14,120 | 1,200 | 14,805 |
| Sperry Rand Corp | 16,048 | 32,581 | 27,585 |
| Staley (A.B.) Mfg Co | 21,330 | 32,940 | 11,005 |
| Standard Oil Calif | 61,306 | 22,626 | 67,910 |
| Standard Oil (Indiana) | 65,570 | 12,184 | 51,975 |
| Stauffer Chem Co | 25,280 | 23,237 | 13,410 |
| Sterling Drug | 26,599 | 650 | 36,750 |
| Sun Co | 48,323 | 99,683 | 14,345 |
| Technicare Corp | 191,427 | 146,825 | 12,510 |
| Swank Inc | 15,900 | 5,300 | 6,280 |
| Sony Corp Am Sh | 111,666 | 54,015 | 68,920 |
| tTandy Corp | 222,244 | 88,064 | 63,155 |
| Tektronix Inc | 68,778 | 71,258 | 5,450 |
| Teledyne Inc | 64,904 | 58,784 | 28,525 |
| tTenneco Inc | 193,852 | 163,948 | 48,190 |
| Texaco Inc | 10,277 | 27,077 | 143,405 |
| Texas Intl Co | 38,900 | 28,700 | 42,440 |
| Texas Instruments | 125,132 | 134,059 | 37,280 |
| Texas Oil & Gas Corp | 23,930 | 22,830 | 28,115 |
| Tesoro Petroleum | 79,219 | 78,153 | 23,780 |
| Textron Inc | 2,908 | 61,896 | 9,800 |
| Thomas & Betts Corp | 19,900 | 9,050 | 2,320 |
| Tidewater Marine Ser | 22,309 | 21,621 | 7,515 |
| Timken Co | 40,798 | 15,290 | 5,055 |
| Transamerica Corp | 44,725 | 34,899 | 44,010 |
| Trans Union Corp | 90,000 | 90,000 | 5,340 |
| Trans World Airlines | 37,378 | 51,678 | 29,425 |
| TRW Corp | 64,958 | 7,445 | 27,480 |
| UAL Inc | 27,122 | 21,752 | 45,810 |
| Union Camp Corp | 14,803 | 112,306 | 20,230 |
| Union Corp | 37,800 | 37,800 | 6,690 |
| Union Pacific Corp | 42,129 | 23,399 | 19,550 |
| Untd Energy Res Inc | 75,370 | 58,300 | 13,640 |
| tUnited Tech Corp | 218,225 | 134,539 | 43,470 |
| United Tech Ser A pr | 10,225 | 162 | 3,190 |
| United Nuclear Corp | 31,202 | 27,947 | 21,915 |
| tUS Steel | 184,793 | 207,679 | 59,930 |
| United Telecomm Inc | 27,887 | 25,384 | 28,775 |
| Utah Intl Inc | 17,300 | 38,825 | 41,540 |
| Upjohn Co | 62,255 | 14,566 | 27,610 |
| xVard Inc | 15,877 | 27,235 | 18,100 |
| Valley Ind Inc | 66,600 | 67,200 | 6,445 |
| Vetco Inc | 161,140 | 134,440 | 25,730 |
| Wstn Co of N America | 117,969 | 147,859 | 4,715 |
| Wisconsin Pwr & Lt | None | 10,600 | 7,305 |
| Wal-Mart Stores Inc | 74,025 | 82,764 | 12,000 |
| Ward Foods Inc | None | 47,460 | 1,834 |
| Warner Communication | 46,602 | 9,078 | 83,485 |
| Webb (Del E) Corp | 28,871 | 4,200 | 20,115 |
| Western Air Lines | 27,854 | 31,704 | 11,180 |
| Western Union Corp | 9,490 | 33,590 | 13,725 |
| Westinghouse Elec | 32,749 | 47,478 | 64,385 |
| Weyerhaeuser Co | 87,994 | 106,174 | 41,040 |
| Whiting Corp | r21,356 | s10,175 | 1,710 |
| White Cons Ind | 61,935 | 21,431 | 30,990 |
| Whittaker Corp | 80,813 | 188,174 | 30,775 |
| Wisconsin El Power | 14,700 | 300 | 5,470 |
| Winnebago Ind Inc | 42,925 | 38,525 | 10,910 |
| Woolworth (F W) | 32,130 | 15,060 | 41,130 |
| tWyly Corp | 128,998 | 108,208 | 14,880 |
| Xerox Corp | 83,673 | 83,811 | 68,954 |
| Zapata Corp | 14,820 | 56,145 | 7,990 |
| Zenith Radio | 49,831 | 73,487 | 18,700 |

t-Possibly involved in arbitrage, depending on prices of the securities involved. r-New. s-Old. x-Issue dually traded on New York Stock Exchange and American exchange. Short interest is combined for both exchanges as reported by Big Board.

**FIGURE 5**
Short Interest Data

## B5.
*The Confidence Theory*

Two old and completely erroneous clichés are often used to explain sharp rises or falls in stock market prices: "more buyers than sellers" or "more sellers than buyers." Because every transaction requires both a buyer and a seller, one side can never outnumber the other. However, it would be correct to say that often one side becomes more anxious than the other. The double auction market employed by exchanges is built on the premise that competition among buyers and sellers will create the price. In the presence of competitors, potential buyers must raise their bids to fill their orders; hence, a market rise. If we measure this emotion, we have the basis of an interesting market technique.

The Confidence Theory proposes that price movements are based on an increase or decrease in the investor's confidence in the future trend of prices. Fundamentals are of little importance, because they do not reflect what the buyer is willing to pay. For example, in 1965, General Motors reported earnings of $5.25 per share, a 5-year high, yet the stock did not trade higher than 15 times those earnings during that year. Contrast this to 1961 when a 19 times multiple was reached and to 1970 when GM traded as high as 39 times earnings. If we follow the Confidence Theory, we hold that the investors' feeling for the future matters much more than their analysis of the present.

The difficulty with this theory is the method of measurement. How do we recognize the early signs of an increase or decrease in the emotions of the market movers? Can confidence be charted the way we chart earnings, volume, or prices? Some interesting answers to these questions have been advanced.

Barron's Confidence Index uses yields on bonds to measure the investor's willingness to take risks. This may seem a strange way to forecast stock prices, but bond yields have an excellent record for leading other indicators by many months. We hope to read the trend by comparing the yields on high-quality, lower-yield bonds with the yields of more speculative debt securities.[1] If the yield on lower-grade bonds declines, it shows that investors are leaving the safe harbor of high quality and speculating a bit more. An increase in yield on high-grade bonds tends to show that their attraction has diminished. This means that buyers have confidence; that is, they will take their chances with the higher yielding, less protected security. This confidence indicates a trend on which investors can base their decisions, hopefully months before those who read facts rather than emotions.

Many proponents of the Confidence Theory apply their study to public interest in speculative stocks. Low-priced issues, both listed and over the counter, as well as new securities offerings of untested companies, are the yardstick. When speculation in these securities reaches a fever pitch—beware! Confidence is reaching its peak and is probably spending its final energy seeking profit in the least likely areas. Because fundamentals have been put aside and emotions are ruling the marketplace, the bubble will burst, and new opportunities will soon be available—at much lower prices. Although not measured as formally as the Barron's Index, this method is followed by many professional traders and investors.

[1] Yields on all bonds move in the same *direction*. It is the comparative yield movements between high-quality and low-quality bonds upon which this theory is founded.

All market theories, in one way or another, are attempts to measure confidence. Although they take different paths, they seek an answer to one question: What will the investing public do next? Stock prices do not go up or down on their own; investor confidence reflects the eagerness to buy and sell, and prices move accordingly.

Although there are many approaches to formula investing, the basic tenets are the same: Devise a formula that reduces the guesswork of investing and stick with it. Many such plans are offered—a few will be discussed here. The advantage to all is that they relieve the investor from the continual decision making and interpretation required by other methods.

*B6.*
*Formula Investing*

**constant-ratio plan**

## CONSTANT-RATIO PLAN

*B6a.*

A **constant-ratio plan** simply requires you as an investor to maintain a percentage balance between stocks and bonds in your portfolio. The selection of the ratio would depend on the investment aim; the more conservative, the higher the percentage of bonds. Once established, the position is reviewed periodically and changes made as necessary to adjust the balance. To give an example: If you as an investor wish to maintain a constant ratio of 50% stocks and 50% bonds, an initial investment of $100,000 will be $50,000 in bonds and $50,000 in stocks. Assume that after a period of time your portfolio has increased in value by 10% but the entire increase has taken place in the stock portion. The value of your position now reads: stocks $60,000, bonds still $50,000. You now sell $5,000 of the stocks and purchase $5,000 of bonds. The result is a 50% constant ratio of $110,000, invested $55,000 each in stocks and bonds.

The concept of the constant ratio is at the heart of the *balanced mutual fund*. These investment companies state that they will maintain a ratio between their investments in common and preferred stocks and bonds. The ratio usually has a built-in option for variation, but the basic concept is the same.

## CONSTANT-DOLLAR PLAN

*B6b.*

Similar to the constant ratio plan is the *constant-dollar plan*. Here the measuring device is not a percentage but a dollar value. Perhaps you as an investor set a maximum of $75,000 in stocks. When the value of your holdings exceeds this figure, you sell the necessary amount and purchase more bonds. Should stock values decline, you put in additional funds to increase your holdings to the predetermined level. This method prevents staying too long with a rising market; of course, it may force you out long before a rally reaches its peak. It also requires you to purchase at low prices to keep your formula in operation. Many major institutions have developed their investment programs with variations of the constant-dollar plan. It can be adapted to meet individual needs, too, and it has many enthusiastic followers.

*B7.*
*Dollar Cost Averaging*

This program is followed by large and small investors alike. The client who purchases mutual funds on an accumulation or contractual basis or who uses a personal investment plan program is following this theory. Investment companies and other large institutions also apply it to their portfolios. It is based on investing fixed dollar amounts at periodic intervals, regardless of price. Over a period of time, the average *cost* per share will be less than the average of the purchase prices, providing an opportunity for profit over a long term. This program is not designed for short-term trading, and when opting for it, you as an investor choose an amount you can continue to invest for 5 years or more.

## example

This example of a dollar cost averaging program, of necessity, covers only a short period, but it demonstrates the inherent quality of dollar cost averaging—reducing average cost per share below the average of purchase prices.

| | AMOUNT INVESTED | MARKET PRICE PER SHARE | NUMBER OF SHARES PURCHASED |
|---|---|---|---|
| January 1977 | $100 | $ 50 | 2 |
| February 1977 | $100 | $ 40 | 2½ |
| March 1977 | $100 | $ 30 | 3⅓ |
| April 1977 | $100 | $ 40 | 2½ |
| May 1977 | $100 | $ 50 | 2 |
| | $500 Total investment | $210 Aggregate market prices | 12⅓ Shares owned |

$$\text{average price of investment} = \frac{\text{aggregate market prices of shares}}{\text{number of monthly investments}}$$

Therefore, $\frac{\$210}{5} = \$42.00$ average price of investment

$$\text{average cost per share} = \frac{\text{total money invested}}{\text{total shares and fractions owned}}$$

Therefore, $\frac{\$500}{12.33} = \$40.55$ Average cost per share

Our example also shows a nice profit for the client, as the most recent price is $50. This is not necessarily true in all cases. If we switch the order of prices and put $30.00 last, the average cost would still be $40.55. However, the investor will sustain a loss if the stock is sold at this time because the stock is now selling at $30 rather than at $50.

The average *cost* is lower than the average *price* because fewer shares are bought at the higher levels; many more shares are purchased when the price is low.

To get the true insight into dollar cost averaging, compare the periodic investment of equal-dollar amounts with the periodic purchases of equal-share amounts. You will quickly see that the investment of equal-dollar amounts gives a decided advantage over the investment of equal-share amounts. To do so, use the information from the example above, except that this investor will buy 2.467 shares of stock, regardless of price, instead of depositing $100 monthly. In the example, 2.467 shares is the average number of shares purchased each time. It is determined by dividing the total shares owned (12.33) by the total number of investments (5).

|  | NUMBER OF SHARES PURCHASED | MARKET PRICE PER SHARE | AMOUNT NEEDED FOR INVESTMENT |
|---|---|---|---|
| January 1977 | 2.467 | $50 | $123.35 |
| February 1977 | 2.467 | 40 | 98.68 |
| March 1977 | 2.467 | 30 | 74.01 |
| April 1977 | 2.467 | 40 | 98.68 |
| May 1977 | 2.467 | 50 | 123.35 |
|  | 12.33 Shares |  | $518.07 |

You quickly see that the investment of equal-dollar amounts gives a decided advantage over the investment of equal-share amounts. In the latter instance, the exercise resulted in the investment of more dollars and a higher average cost per share ($518.07 ÷ 12.33 = $42.02).

### WHAT IT IS

Technical analysis is the most popular method of forecasting price movements of securities. Most followers use charts that record price changes looked at in various ways over a period of time. Their methods differ, but they all subscribe to the theory that previous movements, properly interpreted, can indicate future patterns.

One point regarding technical analysis is important to all investors: if enough people *feel* that XYZ common stock is a good buy at $27 a share, it *will* become a good buy if that level is reached. The orders to purchase will cause a rise in the value of the stock independent of any basic changes in the fortunes of the company. The technical analyst is concerned with price, volume, timing, and trend. The analyst gives little consideration to those factors that are signposts to the fundamentalist. Earnings, dividends, and new product development can all be "read" in the price pattern. The technical analyst believes that all the necessary research can be gleaned from an interpretation of chart patterns. The basic belief is that what has happened in the past can forecast what will happen in the future. Compare the chartist to a doctor who specializes in cardiology: the doctor graphs the changing behavior of the heart and from it can tell what has happened. From the information in the graph, the doctor notes problems that have existed and concludes that they may well recur. The doctor can determine strength or weakness from past performance and then judge future prospects.

The chartist, too, believes in trends. Security prices tend to move in one direction for a long period of time. Interruptions will occur, but an interruption is not a reversal; it may provide an outstanding opportunity for profit. Charts are best used for discovering short-term potential. They are used to select levels that may indicate an upward or downward movement, as opposed to

*B8.*
*Technical Analysis*

*B8a.*

the Dow Theory, which concerns itself with long-term movements.

No complete study of technical analysis will be attempted here, but a brief look at some of the more indicative patterns will provide an introduction to this market-timing device.

*B8b.* **POINT AND FIGURE CHARTING**

> One method of technical analysis is called point and figure charting. It plots market direction through significant price changes, without regard to the timing of such movements. Through a

technique of posting *X*s on graph paper as prices rise and *O*s as they decline predetermined amounts, a skilled analyst can forecast anticipated price levels for an issue. A brief illustration of this technique appears in Figure 6.

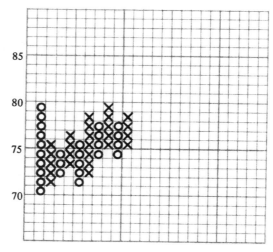

**FIGURE 6**
Point and Figure Chart

This chart plots 1-point price changes. Each square (not line) is a 1-point unit of change. In the first vertical column, the graph shows the price declining from 79 down to 70 before the movement reverses itself and begins to rise. The second column shows a move from 71 up to 75, the third column a decline from 74 to 72, and so forth. *When* those declines and rises occur is of no importance to point and figure chartists. These technical analysts are concerned only that changes did occur and that such movements were recorded when there were significant fluctuations in daily (or weekly) high and low prices. Closing prices are not posted on these charts unless they also happen to be the high or low levels required for transcription.

*B8c.* **VERTICAL LINE CHARTS**

Figures 7 through 13 are illustrative vertical line charts showing various patterns. This charting technique is simply a series of vertical lines plotted on graph paper, showing high and low prices reached during the day (or week). The horizontal line crossing the vertical line indicates the closing price. It is the simplest charting method used by technicians.

***Head-and-shoulders pattern***   This pattern can tell you when a trend reversal has occurred. As shown in Figure 7, a stock rises in price, then declines (left shoulder), and rises again far higher than before (head). Then the stock declines again to the neck. A third rise begins (right shoulder). The stock fails to reach the high achieved in forming the head, and it declines again. If the decline penetrates the neck line, it indicates an extended down trend in values. Although prices may return to the neck-line level before that happens, this reversal won't last long. A significant decline soon follows. | Head-and-shoulder *tops* are *bearish* indicators. |

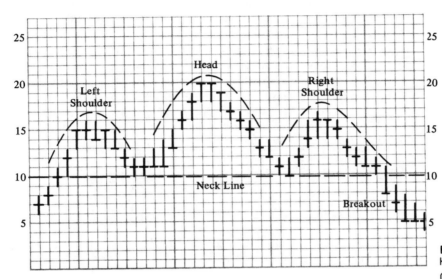

**FIGURE 7**
Head and Shoulders Top
(Downward Trend)

Upward trends can also be forecast from this pattern of head and shoulders. To read the upward trends you must recognize the pattern upside down, as shown in Figure 8. First comes the decline past the neck line and a rise back to the neck (left shoulder). This is followed by a decline to a much lower level (head) and a rally to the neck. Then comes another decline (right shoulder) but not as far. This upside-down head-and-shoulders pattern indicates an upward reversal. If the price manages to penetrate the neck-line level, an important trend reversal has occurred. Although a reaction sometimes drops prices back to the neck line, it is only

**FIGURE 8**
Head and Shoulders Bottom
(Upward Trend)

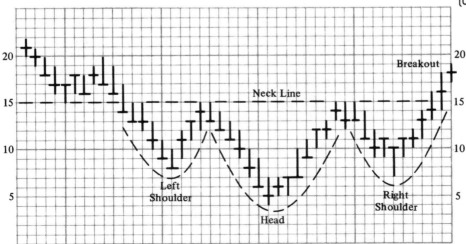

temporary. A major rally soon commences to move market values appreciably higher. Head-and-shoulder *bottoms* are *bullish* indicators.

**B8c(2).** *Support and resistance levels* Prices often move in a narrow range for a long period of time. Assume for XYZ stock that the stock moves between a low of 9 and a high of 14 for many months. This range is called the accumulation or distribution area. Levels of support and resistance are thus created. The low of 9 is considered a *support* level, whereas the high of 14 is considered a *resistance* level. The key for the technical analyst is a **breakout**, which is a decline through the support level or a rise through the resistance level. A decline to the support level of 9 will attract buyers eager to purchase at the appealing low price. If the stock rises to its recent high of 14, resistance to further price increases can be anticipated. Sellers skeptical of a breakout will show interest in disposing of the stock at this higher level. If XYZ stock penetrates the breakout barrier, the trend will continue (according to the technicians). Advantage can then be taken of this situation. See Figure 9 for a chart showing the support and resistance level pattern.

**breakout**

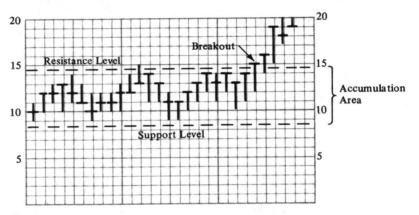

**FIGURE 9**
Support and Resistance Levels

**B8c(3).** *Double tops and bottoms* *Double tops* and *double bottoms* offer an excellent method of determining the levels of major supply and demand so as to avoid false signals. These two patterns are often referred to as *M* and *W* formations because they take the shape of those letters in a plotted chart (see Figures 10 and 11). In each case, a price has been reached twice but supply (tops) or demand (bottoms) caused a reversal. Chartists who see these patterns are alerted by them to determine if existing supply or demand has been satisfied. Does the price find support at the bottom? If so, a rise in price is indicated. Is resistance encountered at the top? If so, a decline will occur. Penetration of these levels leads to the conclusion that the price will continue in the upward or downward direction, and as a chartist you can make your investment decision.

Perfectly shaped *M*'s and *W*'s are rare. It is not uncommon to find triple or even quadruple tops or bottoms instead of doubles before the breakout takes place. A technician's consolation in these cases is that when the subsequent movement in that issue does occur, it is significant.

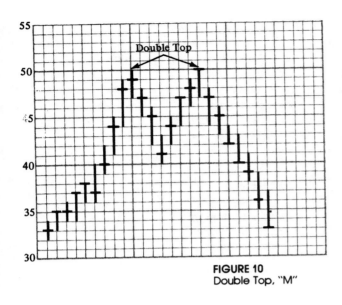

**FIGURE 10**
Double Top, "M"

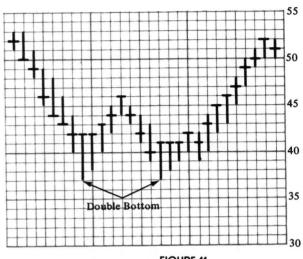

**FIGURE 11**
Double Bottom, "W"

Double tops and bottoms are based on support and resistance techniques and can be further analyzed to estimate the duration of a trend. Here, volume also becomes an important factor because it enables you to predict how much "steam" is left in the move. When volume contracts as prices rise, the forecast is for an imminent decline because the rally is apparently beginning to starve for want of anxious buyers. Conversely, if prices continue to fall as volume declines, be ready for a rally in the near future. This situation is indicative of a situation where those who wanted to sell have done so already and all who are left are holders with strong positive convictions about that stock's future. Consequently, the path of least resistance will soon point toward higher prices. On the other hand, rises or declines in prices of an issue, accompanied by high or increasing volume, signal a continuation of that upward or downward movement, as the case may be. The following grid summarizes forecasts based on price and volume:

|  |  | VOLUME | |
|---|---|---|---|
|  |  | Contracts | Increases |
| | Rises | Imminent decline | Continued rise |
| PRICE | | | |
| | Falls | Rally in near future | Continued fall |

*Climaxes* An expansion of the previous charting approach, | *B8c(4).*

which is also dependent upon a study of volume in conjunction with a continuing price trend, often results in what is known as a **climax**.[2] A climax usually arises when, after a slow but persistent trend in one direction, important news is announced affecting a company's fortunes. Maybe it is a large new business contract, or perhaps it is a dividend omission or a poor earnings statement. Sometimes there is no news at all. In any event, a high volume of trading suddenly develops to accelerate the decline (or rise) to such an extent that

**climax**

1. a price gap is created between the previous low (or high) sale and the next transaction; and/or

2. the vertical line chart illustrates an unusually large range between high and low prices for that period. See Figures 12 and 13 for illustrations of selling and buying climaxes.

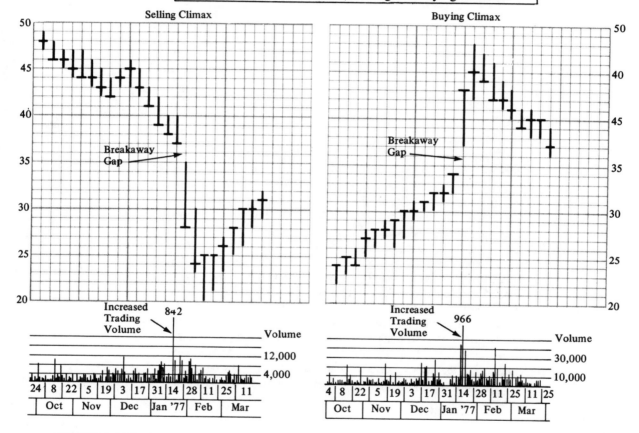

**FIGURES 12 AND 13**
Climaxes

When the increased selling (or buying) has been quickly completed, a reversal invariably and inevitably occurs. That is, prices rise (or decline) to the earlier level to close that gap.

Many highly regarded services follow the technical approach to market analysis. They differ sharply as to method but agree on the previously stated general premise. Instead of using charts, some services program their calculations into computers. The machine gives buy or sell signals based on the information it has been fed. The principle is the same; only the technique differs.

[2]Climaxes can happen on the buy side as well as the sell side. However, climaxes, or breakaway patterns, are more prevalent on the sell side of the market.

Technical analysis is an offshoot of statistics, and it has all the advantages and disadvantages of statistics. Its value is indicative only, not conclusive. On the other hand, it is the closest thing we have to the prediction of human behavior in the marketplace on a short-term basis.

C.
the ticker tape

Important to a technical analyst's interpretation of market trends is an understanding of transaction reports appearing on the stock exchange ticker tape. The tape is a report of activity in each exchange-traded issue moments after execution has been completed. Experienced technicians are able to recognize changing trends by developing a feel for the market from ticker-tape readings.

Actually, the term *ticker tape* is something of a misnomer that stems from the original mechanical device invented and implemented in 1867 by the New York Stock Exchange to publicize transactions. Despite many technological improvements in the paper-tape system, relatively few professional broker/dealers now use it. Most member firm subscribers use an electronic display device connected to the exchange's ticker mechanism. A paper tape is used primarily by nonmember brokers and dealers as well as by wealthy individuals. Regardless of which device is used to display trades, the reporting system is called a ticker tape.

The ticker mechanism is capable of printing up to 900 characters per minute, which is about as much as the eye can recognize and the human brain can translate into understandable information. This high-speed system, introduced in 1964, resulted from an effort to display current activity in a growing marketplace dominated by high volume and rapidly changing prices. Because time and space are limited, a tape language was developed and is utilized to provide maximum transaction details.

C1.
*Tape Language*

C1a.

### STOCK SYMBOLS

Each issue traded on an exchange is assigned a unique letter symbol to identify that security's transactions on the ticker tape. Care is taken to ensure that this symbol has not been assigned to another issue on another exchange or has not been used for some company recently deprived of exchange trading privileges through merger, liquidation, delisting, or similar actions. To better understand how this space-conserving system operates, examine the symbols assigned to the first ten corporations that comprise the Dow Jones Industrial Average, listed earlier in this chapter.

| CORPORATE TITLE | TICKER SYMBOL |
| --- | --- |
| Allied Corporation | ALD |
| Aluminum Company of America | AA |
| American Brands, Inc. | AB |
| American Can Company | AC |
| American Express Company | AXP |
| American Telephone & Telegraph Company | T |
| Bethlehem Steel Corp. | BS |
| E.I. duPont de Nemours & Company | DD |
| Eastman Kodak Company | EK |
| Exxon Corp. | XON |

Most New York or American Stock Exchange issues have one, two, or three letters assigned to them as a symbol. A few have as many as four letters, although four-letter symbols are generally used only to distinguish a preferred stock from the common stock of the same issuer or to differentiate between a voting and nonvoting class of common stock. For example, the symbol for Monongahela Power Company is MPN, whereas its 4.40% preferred stock is MPNA. Or, Harvey Hubbell Company's Class A's symbol is HUBA, whereas its voting Class B stock has been assigned the letters HUBB. This method compares with NASDAQ's use of four-letter symbols for over-the-counter issues registered in the system and five letters (ending with a ''Y'') for ADRs.

When a listed company petitions the federal court system for protection from its creditors under the bankruptcy laws of the United States, this fact is disclosed on the ticker tape by the letter ''Q'' preceding that company's usual ticker symbol. Consequently, no securities traded on stock exchanges are assigned symbols beginning with ''Q''. Thus, there is no confusion about this symbol's meaning when it appears on the tape.

*C1b.* ## SHARE VOLUME

Each depicted trade on the ticker tape is comprised of two lines of information.[3] The top line is the stock symbol; below that and to the right is the share volume and execution price. Because the typical trading unit for NYSE stocks is 100 shares, no special identification is needed to indicate a 100-share transaction. The absence of quantity means that the tape report is for a single, round-lot execution. The prints in the following example reflect 100-share trades.

**example**

| T | AC |
|---|---|
| 50 1/2 | 27 7/8 |

Multiple trading-unit executions show the actual quantity separated from the price by the letter ''S'' but ignore the zeroes in the number of units. The prints in the following example are for a 200-share trade, an 800-share trade, and a trade involving 4,200 shares:

**example**

| DD | BS | XON |
|---|---|---|
| 2s160 1/4 | 8s32 | 42s36¼ |

[3]Some electronic display machines illustrate the entire transaction on a single line of print.

Ten-share trading-unit stocks are recognizable on the ticker tape by means of a double "s" in vertical order between quantity and execution price. The following example illustrates reports of transactions involving stocks that trade in 10-share units.

example

PE pr
$1\S47\ 1/2$

AB pr
$6\S55$

The volume totals are actually 10 shares in the first illustration and 60 shares in the second. Most 10-share-unit stocks are preferred stock issues; this is shown by the letters "pr" after the company's usual ticker symbol.

## SEQUENTIAL TRANSACTIONS

*C1c.*

When a series of trades occurs in the same issue at the same time at the same or varying prices, the whole number of the price is dropped from the ticker prints after the initial transaction in that series; only the fractional digit and corresponding quantities appear, in order of execution.[4] Once again the letter "S" is used to separate data.

example

AA
40s 43 3/4. 3/4. 2s 3/4. 7/8. 5s 7/8. 10s 44
  (1)    (2)  (3)  (4)  (5)    (6)

The sequence in this example is translated as follows:

1. 4,000 shares of Aluminum Co. of America traded at 43¾; followed by
2. 100 shares at 43¾; followed by
3. 200 shares at 43¾; followed by
4. 100 shares at 43⅞; followed by
5. 500 shares at 43⅞; followed by
6. 1,000 shares at 44.

[4]Unless, of course, executions occurred at a whole number price. In that case, the full price and quantities are printed.

After completing a transaction on the trading floor of the stock exchange, it is the selling broker's responsibility to advise an exchange employee (a reporter) at that post about the terms of the execution. That clerk records the transaction data on a card and inserts the card into a scanning device that transmits impulses of what it "reads" to a ticker-tape information-collection and coordination room above the trading floor. Within a few moments, the transaction terms are published for subscribers to view throughout the United States and in several foreign countries, too.

Sometimes, either the selling broker or the reporter doesn't act promptly enough. As a result, subsequent transactions in that issue are printed before the oversight is realized. Or, perhaps the delay causes a transaction's appearance on the ticker tape to be significantly separated from the prints of other issues executed at approximately the same time. Should either of these events occur, the errant transaction is published nevertheless, but with the letters "SLD" following the ticker symbol and before the quantity and execution price. This designation is officially called a *sold sale*, and it simply means this transaction notice was delayed and is appearing out of its proper place.

**example**

CRO. SLD
3s 12 1/2

Closely akin to a sold sale in external semblance, but with an entirely different meaning, is a *sold last sale*. In order to avoid any misunderstanding, "SLD LAST SALE" is printed on the bottom line of trade information after the execution price. This expression identifies a transaction that has fluctuated volatilely, either up or down, from the last sale in that issue. Specifically, this announcement is made when a stock previously selling at 19⅞ or below trades one or more points from the last sale. If the stock previously traded at 20 or above, the "SLD LAST SALE" designation is made when the price fluctuates two or more points away from the last sale.

**example**

MAR
913s 19 1/2 SLD LAST SALE

IBM
40s 248 SLD LAST SALE

The high degree of marketability experienced by exchange-listed issues makes prints of this kind an infrequent occurrence. But if a temporary inequity between supply and demand does develop, it generally occurs prior to the daily opening of that issue on the exchange. It may stem from an overnight build-up of orders relating to an important international or business announcement. When an opening price of stock falls within the categories mentioned above, the initial transaction for that day is identified by the letters "OPD" following the ticker symbol, in lieu of "SLD LAST SALE."[5]

example

CB. OPD
815s 10⅛

## STOPPED STOCK

*Cle.*

After a broker has been "stopped"[6] by a specialist, the broker has an opportunity to try for a better price. The broker does not incur personal liability if unsuccessful in this effort and another person usurps the original prevailing price. If there is no improvement over the guaranteed price available, the broker is stopped out and required to accept an execution at the figure. This transaction is characterized by the letter "S" set above the letter "T" on the second line of print following the execution price.

example

GM
50¼ $\frac{S}{T}$

This type of transaction is printed in its proper place on the ticker tape *unless* to do so might embarrass another broker who is attempting to execute an order for another customer at the same time. How can a ticker tape report embarrass another broker? Suppose, for instance, that Broker A was stopped at 27 and Broker B bought 200 shares at the market, 100 at 27 and 100 at 27⅛. Broker B's customer might claim foul play if the tape were to report these transactions as shown in our next example.

example

XYZ
27.27$\frac{S}{T}$.27⅛

[5]"OPD" is also used to announce an opening trade in an issue whose ticker print does not get published for some time after execution. Clerical delays are not always indicative of transaction volatility.

[6]Guaranteed an execution price while attempting to improve upon it.

Broker B's customer might insist that his market order should have purchased 200 shares at 27. It is difficult for a lay person to understand how someone can come in between the execution of a market order for multiple round lots. Because the ticker tape should, nevertheless, be an accurate indicator of volume and activity in each listed issue, stopped stock in these instances is printed after trading ceases for the day; akin to a sold sale but identified with the stopped stock symbol.

### C1f.  BIDS AND OFFERS

In a difficult market situation, such as

1.  a sudden imbalance of orders,
2.  a delay in the opening of a particular issue, or
3.  a resumption of trading after a suspension,

it is often tactically advantageous to advise viewers of prevailing conditions in order to solicit their orders. This is accomplished by printing bid and offering prices prevailing for the affected issue. In extreme circumstances, only an "indicated" quotation is disclosed. Both situations are recognizable as quotations by the letter "B" on the lower line of information. The first price given in the print is the bid; the bid is separated from the offering price by a dot.

**example**

| XRX | PRD.INDICATION |
|---|---|
| B115.118 | B75.85 |

### C1g.  WHEN-ISSUED OR WHEN-DISTRIBUTED STOCK

Soon after a listed corporation announces a forthcoming distribution of stock and before the security is actually allocated, the appropriate stock exchanges commence trading in that issue. These contracts carry no specific settlement terms until a distribution date can be ascertained; hence the name "when-issued" or "when-distributed." To distinguish these transactions from the activity in the old shares, the letters "WI" or "WD" appear in vertical order after the execution price.

**example**

| LPX | SQB |
|---|---|
| 2s 19¼ $_W^I$ | 41 $_W^D$ |

*EX DIVIDEND, EX RIGHTS, EX WARRANTS, OR EX DISTRIBU-*
*TION*

C1h.

On the first day a listed security begins trading without the value of the forthcoming cash or security distribution in its market price, the ticker tape makes that fact known by means of an identifying code after the issue's symbol. The code is:

XD    for ex dividend
XRT   for ex rights
XW    for ex warrants
XDIS  for ex distribution

The announcement appears only for the first three or four transactions in that issue. After that, it is assumed that the viewer has been adequately informed and can make intelligent interpretations of price fluctuations.

**example**

| SCE.XRT | GE.XD |
|---------|-------|
| 19⅝ | 3s57¾ |

*CONDITIONS*

C2.
*The Late Tape*

C2a.

There are occasions when the pace of activity on the trading floor exceeds the capacity of the ticker tape's ability to provide current information. They may occur at the opening of the exchange in the morning, or late in the afternoon at the close as traders adjust their portfolio positions, or, for that matter, at any time during the day, especially after important news is made public. New reporting procedures are then implemented into the ticker system to signify that the tape is falling behind actual trading activity, every effort is made to maintain continuous and relevant information.

*DIGITS & VOLUME DELETED (DELETE MODE 1)*

C2b.

In the initial stage of increasing activity, when it appears that trade information is falling behind the trading floor and is likely to slip further, the announcement "DIGITS & VOLUME DELETED" is made on the ticker tape. It means only the last digit and fraction, if any, of an execution price is printed, and quantity figures for trades of less than 5,000 shares are eliminated; thus conserving space on the tape and speeding up reports. It is necessary for the tape watcher to be familiar with the issue to realize what the first digit(s) should be.

**example**

| TX | S | DD |
|----|---|-----|
| 7⅞. | 8¼. | 3½. |

As these items appear, it is essential for the viewer's understanding to realize that "TX" is Texaco Inc. and its price is 27⅞; "S" is Sears Roebuck at 88¼; and "DD" is E.I. duPont de Nemours at 163½. There are two important exceptions to this procedure, however. Both require complete price prints, although digits are otherwise deleted.

1. An opening transaction is always announced with its full terms.
2. An execution price ending in a zero is always printed in its entirety (for example, 20½ is not depicted as 0½).

When conditions permit, normal reporting procedures are employed following the announcement, "DIGITS & VOLUME RESUMED."

### C2c. *REPEAT PRICES OMITTED*

If the ticker tape should fall *further* behind trading activity, the words "REPEAT PRICES OMITTED" are published. From that point on until the tape is clear again, sequential repeat transactions at the same price are dropped from the tape. This practice conserves valuable space and time and avoids printing a string of transactions all at the same time and price, a condition typical of active issues and active markets. Here, too, accurate daily volume figures are properly recorded and maintained by the exchange.

As a prelude to the much discussed and highly automated central market system (CMS) of the future, a computerized system was implemented in 1974 to promptly report securities transactions effected in various marketplaces on a single ticker tape. The participants include all regional stock exchanges, Instinet, "third market" NASD member dealers as well as the New York and American Stock exchanges, both of whose ticker-tape facilities are utilized for this arrangement.

Under the Consolidated Tape System, all transactions in NYSE-listed securities are reported on the NYSE ticker tape as they occur (Network A), whereas those issues listed on the AMEX, or traded exclusively on the regional exchanges, are published on the AMEX ticker tape (Network B).

---

[7]The issues representative of current market conditions are frequently components of the Dow Jones Industrial Average.

Most investors are unable to scan the ticker tape to keep informed about market activity and price trends in their favorite issues. In many instances, it is physically impossible to do so simply because some kinds of securities transactions are not publicized on a ticker tape system. Such transactions include over-the-counter executions,[8] especially transactions in U.S. government, federal agency, municipal, and numerous corporate issues not traded on a securities exchange. Investors interested in these as well as exchange-traded securities rely primarily upon the daily newspapers for relatively current market information about their favorite stocks and bonds. The newspapers provide a synopsis of the previous day's financial industry activity; information obtained from the various stock exchanges, the NASD, OTC market-makers, and government securities dealers. Due to space limitations, some newspapers provide less detailed and less comprehensive coverage of financial information than others. On a national level, *The Wall Street Journal,* a daily publication of Dow Jones & Company, Inc., is well known and respected for the depth and accuracy of its coverage; its presentation is, therefore, utilized in this section. However, at least one newspaper in each major city in the United States devotes some space to quality financial reporting, too. The prime difference among them is the extent of coverage devoted to local issues of interest to each paper's readers.

*D1.*
*The Listed Stock Tables*

The style and statistical information tables used for stocks listed on the New York and American Stock exchanges are provided by the Associated Press, a major news wire service. The format is, therefore, uniform throughout the country. Issues that have traded each day are recorded in alphabetical order and appear as shown in Figure 14.

From this segment of the page you can determine—

1. the stock exchange whose activity is highlighted;
2. the date of such activity;
3. top volume in equity issues broken down by share and warrant quantities and by marketplace;
4. cumulative and historical comparison of trading volume;
5. the ten most active stocks that day, showing each one's trading and volume statistics;

From this portion of the tables, let us isolate the facts for Cabot Corporation (abbreviated Cabot C) to explain their meaning (highlighted in Figure 14):

[8] Except for Instinet and "third market" transactions.

FIGURE 14
Newspaper List of Stock Transactions on the NYSE

# NYSE-Composite Transactions

*Wednesday, February 13, 1980*

Quotations include trades on the American, Midwest, Pacific, Philadelphia, Boston and Cincinnati stock exchanges and reported by the National Association of Securities Dealers and Instinet

| 52 Weeks High | Low | Stock | Div. | Yld % | P-E Ratio | Sales 100s | High | low | Close | Net Chg. |
|---|---|---|---|---|---|---|---|---|---|---|
| 45½ | 36 | Benef | pf4.30 | 12. | .. | 3 | 35½ | d35¼ | 35¼ | – ¾ |
| 26½ | 20 | Benef | pf2.50 | 13. | .. | z70 | 20 | 20 | 20 | ..... |
| 19⅝ | 2⅞ | BengtB | | .. | 36 | 1231 | 12⅛ | 11½ | 11½ | – ⅝ |
| 7¼ | 3 | BerkeyP | | .. | 14 | 134 | 5⅛ | 4⅞ | 5 | ..... |
| 29⅛ | 18¾ | BestPd | .24 | 1.3 | 6 | 500 | 19½ | d18½ | 19 | – ⅞ |
| 25⅞ | 19½ | BethStl | 1.60 | 6.3 | 4 | 1471 | 25¾ | 24½ | 25⅜ | + ⅞ |
| 47¾ | 32⅝ | BigThr | .88 | 1.8 | 15 | 160 | 47¾ | 47 | 47¾ | +1 |
| 33⅝ | 14⅝ | Binney | .92 | 4.2 | 10 | 56 | 22⅞ | 22⅛ | 22⅛ | – ⅜ |
| 29¼ | 16⅞ | BisFSL | s.80 | 3.9 | 6 | 43 | 20¾ | 20¼ | 20⅝ | – ⅞ |
| 25¼ | 18½ | BlackDr | .76 | 3.4 | 9 | 578 | 22¼ | 21⅝ | 22¼ | + ¼ |
| 24½ | 18½ | BlairJn | s 1 | 5.3 | 6 | 64 | 19¼ | 18¾ | 18¾ | – ⅜ |
| 25½ | 15⅝ | BlissL | 1.10 | 5.5 | 6 | 45 | 20 | 19¾ | 20 | + ⅛ |
| 27¼ | 21¼ | BlckHR | 1.60 | 6.2 | 10 | 245 | 26⅜ | 25½ | 26 | + ⅜ |
| 37⅝ | 22⅝ | BlueB | 1.80 | 4.8 | 7 | 243 | 37⅜ | 36⅜ | 37⅛ | + ⅞ |
| 5¾ | 3⅝ | BobbieBr | | .. | 5 | 137 | 4 | 3¾ | 3⅞ | + ⅛ |
| 68⅞ | 37¼ | Boeing | s1.80 | 2.8 | 8 | 4346 | 64⅜ | 62¾ | 63¼ | –1 |
| 42½ | 29¾ | BoiseC | 1.50 | 3.7 | 6 | 675 | 41⅞ | 40¾ | 40⅞ | – ⅞ |
| 27⅞ | 23 | Borden | 1.82 | 7.9 | 5 | 322 | 23¾ | 23 | 23 | – ⅝ |
| 40⅞ | 27⅛ | BorgW | 2.30 | 5.4 | 6 | 1095 | u42⅞ | 40⅞ | 42⅝ | +2 |
| 8⅜ | 4⅛ | Bormns | .20e | 4.4 | 8 | 23 | 4⅝ | 4½ | 4½ | ..... |
| 24¼ | 19⅞ | BosEd | 2.72 | 13. | 6 | 46 | 21¼ | 21 | 21 | + ⅛ |
| 84¾ | 69 | BosE | pf8.88 | 13. | .. | z460 | 70 | 69 | 70 | ..... |
| 11⅛ | 9 | BosE | pr1.17 | 13. | .. | 11 | 9⅛ | 9⅛ | 9⅛ | – ⅛ |
| 14 | 11 | BosE | pr1.46 | 13. | .. | 22 | 11⅛ | 11 | 11⅛ | + ⅛ |
| 13¾ | 6¾ | Braniff | .20 | 2.2 | .. | 447 | 9⅜ | 9⅛ | 9¼ | ..... |
| 29⅞ | 23⅜ | BrigSt | 1.20a | 5.0 | 7 | 68 | 24⅛ | 23¾ | 24 | ..... |
| 39¼ | 31 | BristM | 1.44 | 4.2 | 10 | 1673 | 35⅜ | 34¼ | 34½ | – ⅝ |
| 44¼ | 35½ | BristM | pf 2 | 5.1 | .. | 4 | 39½ | 39 | 39½ | +1⅛ |
| 37⅞ | 19 | BritPet | 1.02e | 2.7 | 8 | 987 | u38½ | 37⅝ | 38¼ | +1⅛ |
| 19½ | 12½ | BrkwGl | 1.08 | 7.3 | 7 | 263 | 15⅛ | 14⅝ | 14⅞ | – ¼ |
| 25 | 18¾ | BkyUG | 2.22 | 11. | 6 | 41 | 20⅜ | 20 | 20 | – ¼ |
| 30⅛ | 16¾ | BwnSh | 1 | 3.5 | 6 | 94 | 28⅞ | 28⅜ | 28⅞ | + ¼ |
| 30 | 9⅝ | Brown | .30 | 1.1 | 8 | 133 | 28¼ | 28 | 28¼ | + ¼ |
| 28¾ | 22½ | BwnGp | 2 | 7.8 | 4 | 20 | 26 | 25⅝ | 25⅝ | – ⅛ |
| 17⅞ | 11⅝ | BwnFer | .70 | 4.1 | 10 | 355 | 17⅝ | 17 | 17 | ..... |
| 15⅜ | 10⅞ | Brnswk | .90 | 6.2 | 6 | 428 | 15 | 14½ | 14⅝ | – ⅜ |
| 30 | 24⅝ | Brnsk | pf2.40 | 8.1 | .. | 55 | 30 | 29½ | 29½ | – ⅜ |
| 33½ | 17½ | BrushW | s 1 | 3.2 | 10 | 148 | 31½ | 30⅞ | 31 | + ⅝ |
| 25 | 16½ | BucyEr | .88 | 4.2 | 8 | 1000 | 21½ | 20½ | 21 | + ¾ |
| 19½ | 15⅞ | BufFor | s 1 | 6.3 | 8 | 26 | 16⅝ | 16 | 16 | –1 |
| 16⅜ | 9¼ | Bundy | 1 | 9.2 | 7 | 23 | 10⅞ | 10⅝ | 10⅞ | + ¼ |
| 19½ | 15⅛ | BunkrH | 1.96 | 13. | .. | 21 | 15⅝ | 15⅛ | 15¼ | + ⅛ |
| 32⅜ | 19 | BunkR | 1.20 | 4.0 | 8 | 161 | 30⅜ | 29⅜ | 29¾ | ..... |
| 32 | 22⅞ | BnkR | pf1.50 | 5.1 | .. | 13 | 30 | 29⅝ | 29⅝ | – ⅜ |
| 20 | 15 | BurlInd | 1.40 | 7.8 | 7 | 784 | 18⅛ | 17⅞ | 17⅞ | – ⅛ |
| 80¾ | 38 | BurlNo | 2.10 | 2.8 | 6 | 1182 | 76⅞ | 73⅛ | 74⅛ | –1⅜ |
| 7½ | 5⅝ | BrlNo | pf .55 | 11. | .. | 7 | 5⅞ | d 5 | 5 | – ⅞ |
| 71½ | 37½ | BrlNo | pf2.85 | 4.3 | .. | 103 | 67½ | 65¾ | 65¾ | –1¼ |
| 35½ | 21¼ | Burndy | 1 | 2.8 | 10 | 37 | 35⅜ | 35⅛ | 35⅜ | + ⅛ |
| 8⅞ | 3 | BrnsRL | | .. | 23 | 1022 | 8½ | 7⅞ | 8⅛ | – ¼ |
| 87½ | 64⅜ | Burrgh | 2.60 | 3.3 | 10 | 851 | 79⅞ | 76¾ | 77¾ | –1 |
| 30¼ | 14 | Butlrln | s.80 | 2.9 | 7 | 34 | 28⅜ | 27¾ | 28 | ..... |
| 18 | 8⅜ | Buttes | | .. | 97 | 462 | u18¼ | 17⅜ | 17⅜ | + ⅛ |
| | | – C–C–C – | | | | | | | | |
| 43⅞ | 27 | CBI Ind | s1a | 2.4 | 15 | x109 | 42¼ | 41⅝ | 42 | + ¾ |
| 56¾ | 44⅛ | CBS | 2.80 | 5.3 | 8 | 666 | 53¼ | 52⅝ | 52⅝ | + ½ |
| 37½ | 30½ | CBS pf | 1 | 2.8 | .. | 2 | 35⅞ | 35⅞ | 35⅞ | + ⅞ |
| 11¼ | 6 | CCI | | .. | 6 | 303 | 10⅝ | 9¾ | 10 | ..... |
| 12⅞ | 6⅞ | CLC | | .. | 37 | 82 | 10¾ | 10 | 10⅜ | – ¼ |
| 18¾ | 10⅛ | CNA Fn | | .. | 4 | 775 | 17¾ | 17⅜ | 17¾ | + ⅝ |
| 22¾ | 15¼ | CNA pf | 1.10 | 5.1 | .. | 14 | 21½ | 21½ | 21½ | + ½ |
| 11⅞ | 9⅛ | CNAI | 1.14a | 12. | .. | 34 | 9¾ | 9⅝ | 9⅝ | – ⅛ |
| 71 | 48⅛ | CPC | 3 | 4.5 | 9 | 666 | 68¼ | 67 | 67¼ | – ½ |
| 16¾ | 14⅛ | CP Nat | 1.88 | 12. | 9 | 14 | 15⅛ | 14¾ | 15⅛ | + ¼ |
| 28½ | 16¼ | CTS | .80 | 3.8 | 9 | 157 | 21⅜ | 20¼ | 20⅞ | – ⅛ |
| 64¾ | 34 | CabotC | 2 | 3.1 | 8 | x190 | u65½ | 62¾ | 65¼ | +2¾ |
| 21⅝ | 9⅝ | Cadence | | .. | 6 | 22 | 16¾ | 16⅜ | 16⅜ | – ⅛ |
| 36⅛ | 13¼ | Caesars s | | .. | 24 | 1198 | 16⅞ | 16¼ | 16¼ | – ⅝ |

| 52 Weeks High | Low | Stock | Div. | Yld % | P-E Ratio | Sales 100s | High | low | Close | Net Chg. |
|---|---|---|---|---|---|---|---|---|---|---|
| 20 | 13⅝ | DanRiv | 1.12 | 6.0 | 5 | 121 | 18⅞ | 18⅝ | 18⅝ | ..... |
| 30¼ | 22⅞ | DanaCp | 1.56 | 5.9 | 5 | 139 | 26⅝ | 26¼ | 26½ | ..... |
| 28⅞ | 16⅜ | Daniel | .30 | 1.1 | 13 | 58 | 28⅜ | 27⅞ | 27⅞ | – ⅜ |
| 49⅝ | 37¼ | DartInd | 2 | 4.7 | 6 | 262 | 43¼ | 42¾ | 42⅞ | ..... |
| 49¼ | 37 | Dart pf | 2 | 4.8 | .. | 5 | 42½ | 42 | 42 | – ¼ |
| 74½ | 46 | DataGen | | .. | 14 | 704 | 66¼ | 65⅛ | 65⅝ | +1⅝ |
| 48⅛ | 27⅝ | DataTer | .30 | 1.0 | 9 | 275 | 30⅛ | 28½ | 28⅝ | –1⅛ |
| 119 | 67¾ | Datapnt | | .. | 19 | 65 | u120 | 118 | 118⅛ | – ⅞ |
| 18½ | 13½ | Dayco | .56b | 4.1 | 3 | 30 | 13¾ | 13½ | 13¾ | + ⅛ |
| 49¼ | 36½ | DaytHd | 1.80 | 3.8 | 7 | x495 | 48⅝ | 47⅞ | 47⅞ | – ⅜ |
| 17¼ | 13¾ | DaytPL | 1.74 | 13. | 7 | 141 | 13⅞ | d13⅝ | 13¾ | ..... |
| 76 | 57⅜ | DPL pf | 7.37 | 12. | .. | z100 | 60 | 60 | 60 | –1 |
| 41½ | 33¼ | Deere | 1.80 | 5.4 | 7 | 1358 | 36⅛ | 35⅜ | 35¾ | + ¼ |
| 14 | 11½ | DelmP | 1.48 | 13. | 6 | 97 | 11¾ | 11½ | 11¾ | ..... |
| 47⅜ | 36 | DeltaA | 1.20 | 3.3 | 7 | 827 | 36½ | 36⅛ | 36¼ | – ¼ |
| 8¾ | 5⅜ | Deltec | 2.50c | .. | .. | 21 | 8 | 8 | 8 | + ¼ |
| 17 | 8⅝ | Deltona | | .. | 5 | 329 | 16¼ | 15½ | 15¾ | + ¼ |
| 21¾ | 16⅛ | DenMf | s1.16 | 5.8 | 7 | 78 | 20½ | 20 | 20 | ..... |
| 23⅜ | 13⅜ | Dennys | .88 | 6.0 | 6 | 197 | 14⅞ | 14½ | 14¾ | – ⅛ |
| 20 | 14⅝ | Dentsply | .88 | 5.0 | 10 | 124 | 17½ | 17 | 17½ | + ½ |
| 14 | 10 | DeSoto | 1 | 6.9 | 8 | 95 | u14⅝ | 14 | 14½ | + ½ |
| 15⅞ | 12¼ | DetEd | 1.60 | 13. | 7 | 941 | 12⅝ | 12¼ | 12⅝ | + ⅛ |
| 68½ | 56¼ | DetE | pf5.50 | 9.6 | .. | 1 | 57¼ | 57¼ | 57¼ | + ¼ |
| 76¾ | 58¼ | DetE | pf7.68 | 13. | .. | z100 | 59½ | 59½ | 59½ | –1½ |
| 25¾ | 21 | DE | pfF 2.75 | 13. | .. | 5 | 21⅜ | 21⅜ | 21⅜ | – ⅛ |
| 25⅞ | 20⅞ | DE | pfB 2.75 | 13. | .. | 4 | 21¼ | 21⅛ | 21⅛ | + ¼ |
| 21¾ | 16½ | DetE | pr2.28 | 14. | .. | 5 | 16¾ | 16½ | 16⅝ | ..... |
| 25⅝ | 19¾ | Dexter | 1 | 4.2 | 9 | 12 | 23¾ | 23¾ | 23¾ | + ¼ |
| 15⅛ | 8⅛ | DiGior | .56 | 4.7 | 7 | 141 | 12⅜ | 11¾ | 12 | – ¼ |
| 25 | 14 | DiGior | pf.88 | 4.6 | .. | z30 | 19¼ | 19¼ | 19¼ | –1¾ |
| 27 | 20⅝ | DiGior | pf2.25 | 9.2 | .. | 18 | 24⅝ | 24¼ | 24⅜ | + ⅛ |
| 26½ | 16⅝ | DialCp | 1.20 | 6.6 | 5 | 30 | 18⅜ | 17⅝ | 18⅛ | + ¼ |
| 47½ | 32½ | DiaInt | 2.20b | 5.0 | 10 | 85 | 44¼ | 42¾ | 44¼ | +1¼ |
| 21¼ | 16⅛ | DiaInt | pf1.20 | 6.0 | .. | 8 | 20 | 20 | 20 | ..... |
| 36¾ | 19⅛ | DiamS | 1.60 | 4.6 | 10 | x916 | 35¾ | 34¾ | 35 | – ¾ |
| 38⅝ | 18¾ | Diebold | .70 | 1.9 | 12 | 97 | 37¾ | 36¾ | 37¼ | + ½ |
| 77⅞ | 48⅝ | DigitalEq | | .. | 17 | 1392 | u79⅝ | 77⅞ | 78⅝ | + ¾ |
| 15⅜ | 8½ | Dillingm | .60 | 4.3 | 7 | 268 | 14⅜ | 13¾ | 14 | – ¼ |
| 27¾ | 22 | Dillingm | pf2 | 7.5 | .. | 1 | 26½ | 26½ | 26½ | ..... |
| 23¼ | 15½ | Dillon | s 1.08 | 6.5 | 9 | 51 | 16½ | 16¼ | 16½ | – ⅜ |
| 48⅛ | 33 | Disney | .72 | 1.5 | 12 | 854 | 47⅛ | 46⅜ | 46½ | +1½ |
| 8¾ | 2⅝ | Divrsfdln | | .. | 11 | 185 | 7⅝ | 7⅜ | 7⅜ | ..... |
| 6⅞ | 3⅜ | DivrsMtg | | .. | .. | 137 | 4⅝ | 4⅜ | 4⅝ | + ⅛ |
| 19¼ | 10 | DrPeppr | .68 | 4.6 | 13 | 555 | 15 | 14⅝ | 14⅞ | + ⅛ |
| 27 | 12⅝ | Documat | | .. | 17 | 45 | 13⅝ | 13⅜ | 13½ | + ¼ |
| 73¾ | 34⅜ | Dome g | s.50 | .7 | .. | 109 | 72⅞ | 71¾ | 71¾ | – ¼ |
| 24 | 18¾ | Donald | n.60 | 2.8 | 8 | 6 | 21¼ | 21 | 21⅛ | + ⅛ |
| 6½ | 3¼ | DonLJ | .14 | 2.2 | 15 | 625 | 6⅜ | 6⅛ | 6¼ | – ⅛ |
| 31 | 25½ | Donnly | 1.14 | 3.7 | 9 | 87 | 30¾ | 30⅜ | 30½ | – ¼ |
| 20 | 12⅛ | Dorsey | .75 | 5.2 | 5 | 67 | 14½ | 14⅜ | 14½ | ..... |
| 40⅝ | 27¾ | Dover s | .86 | 2.2 | 12 | 24 | 39⅛ | 38¼ | 38¼ | – ¾ |
| 39 | 24⅜ | DowCh | 1.60 | 4.2 | 9 | 6415 | u39¼ | 38 | 38 | – ½ |
| 49½ | 32½ | DowJn | 1.60 | 3.7 | 13 | 29 | 43¾ | 43⅛ | 43½ | ..... |
| 38⅜ | 23⅞ | Dravo | 1.36 | 3.6 | 11 | 213 | u38¾ | 38 | 38⅛ | + ⅜ |
| 62¾ | 36¼ | Dressr | 1.10 | 1.7 | 11 | 1220 | u63½ | 61½ | 63 | +2¼ |
| 17¼ | 14¼ | DrexB | 1.72 | 12. | .. | 11 | 14⅝ | 14⅝ | 14⅝ | ..... |

| 52 Weeks High | Low | Stock | Div. | Yld % | P-E Ratio | Sales 100s | High | low | Close | Net Chg. |
|---|---|---|---|---|---|---|---|---|---|---|
| 5¾ | 3⅜ | Genesco | | .. | 100 | 100 | 4⅛ | 4 | 4 | – ⅛ |
| 28⅝ | 17¼ | Genst | g s1.60 | .. | .. | 168 | 28¼ | 27½ | 27⅝ | – ¼ |
| 26⅞ | 21 | GenuPt | s.88 | 3.8 | 10 | 165 | 23¾ | 23¼ | 23¼ | – ¼ |
| 33⅞ | 23½ | GaPac | 1.20 | 3.6 | 11 | 2851 | u34⅞ | 33 | 33½ | – ⅜ |
| 36 | 30 | GaPac | pf2.24 | 6.2 | .. | 60 | u36⅜ | 35¾ | 36 | + ¾ |
| 34¾ | 30 | GaPac | pfB | 6.2 | .. | 37 | u36 | 34⅞ | 36 | +1¼ |
| 24⅝ | 19⅝ | GaPw | pf2.56 | 13. | .. | 21 | 19¾ | d19½ | 19½ | – ⅜ |
| 25 | 18⅝ | GaPw | pf2.52 | 13. | .. | 7 | 19⅝ | 19½ | 19½ | ..... |
| 27¼ | 22 | GaPw | pf2.75 | 12. | .. | 4 | 23⅛ | 23 | 23 | – ⅜ |
| 77¼ | 58 | GaPw | pf7.72 | 13. | .. | z20 | 58¼ | 58¼ | 58¼ | – ¾ |
| 66½ | 27¾ | Geosrc | .80 | 1.2 | 16 | 104 | 65¼ | 64¼ | 64¼ | – ¾ |
| 30⅞ | 23 | GerbPd | 1.62 | 6.8 | 7 | 93 | 24¼ | 23⅝ | 24 | + ⅜ |
| 97¾ | 36 | Getty | 1.50e | 1.6 | 13 | 705 | 94⅜ | 92½ | 92½ | –1 |
| 18¼ | 14¾ | Getty | pf1.20 | 7.9 | .. | 1 | 15¼ | 15¼ | 15¼ | ..... |
| 11⅞ | 6¼ | GiantPC | | .. | 14 | 66 | 6¾ | 6½ | 6¾ | + ¼ |
| 16⅝ | 10 | GlbrFn | .60 | 5.9 | 5 | 213 | 10⅛ | d 9¾ | 10⅛ | + ⅛ |
| 37 | 14 | GidLew | 1 | 3.1 | 6 | 343 | 33⅜ | 31¾ | 32¾ | – ¼ |
| 19½ | 12 | GiffHill | .92 | 5.1 | 5 | 226 | 18⅛ | 18 | 18⅛ | – ⅛ |
| 28 | 23⅜ | Gillette | 1.72 | 7.2 | 6 | 2153 | 24⅜ | 23½ | 23¾ | – ¾ |
| 13¼ | 6⅞ | GinosInc | .40 | 3.2 | .. | 87 | 12⅝ | 12¼ | 12½ | + ⅛ |
| 25¾ | 16 | GleasW | .80 | 3.1 | 7 | 32 | 25¾ | 25½ | 25½ | – ¼ |
| 53⅞ | 14⅞ | GlobMar | .20 | .4 | 13 | 187 | u55⅜ | 54¼ | 54¾ | +1⅛ |
| 17 | 10⅝ | GldWFn | .54 | 4.1 | 5 | 396 | 13⅛ | 13 | 13⅛ | + ⅛ |
| 24 | 17½ | Gdrich | 1.44 | 7.2 | 4 | 75 | 20¼ | 19⅞ | 19⅞ | – ⅛ |
| 92⅜ | 79⅛ | Gdrich | pf7.85 | 9.9 | .. | z50 | 79⅛ | 79⅛ | 79⅛ | ..... |
| 18⅛ | 11⅞ | Goodyr | 1.30 | 10. | 6 | 1588 | 13 | 12¾ | 13 | + ⅛ |
| 29 | 16⅞ | GordJw | .72 | 2.6 | 5 | 37 | 27½ | 27¼ | 27¼ | + ¼ |
| 29¼ | 22 | Gould | 1.72 | 7.1 | 6 | 263 | 24¼ | 23¾ | 24⅛ | – ¼ |

## Wednesday's Volume
## 72,185,250 Shares; 372,300 Warrants

## TRADING BY MARKETS

| | Shares | Warrants |
|---|---|---|
| New York Exchange | 65,230,000 | 372,200 |
| American Exchange | .... | .... |
| Midwest Exchange | 2,904,200 | .... |
| Pacific Exchange | 1,702,100 | .... |
| Nat'l Assoc. of Securities Dealers | 901,450 | 100 |
| Philadelphia Exchange | 964,900 | .... |
| Boston Exchange | 237,700 | .... |
| Cincinnati Exchange | 227,300 | .... |
| Instinet System | 17,600 | .... |

**NYSE – Composite**

| Volume since Jan. 1: | 1980 | 1979 | 1978 |
|---|---|---|---|
| Total shares | 1,837,261,110 | 957,966,682 | 704,758,240 |
| Total warrants | 10,475,200 | 4,093,049 | 3,288,000 |

**New York Stock Exchange**

| Volume since Jan. 1: | 1980 | 1979 | 1978 |
|---|---|---|---|
| Total shares | 1,629,566,840 | 844,175,032 | 615,205,130 |
| Total warrants | 10,474,900 | 3,963,900 | 3,287,900 |

## MOST ACTIVE STOCKS

| | Open | High | Low | Close | Chg. | Volume |
|---|---|---|---|---|---|---|
| Colg Palm | 13½ | 13¾ | 12⅞ | 13¼ | – ⅛ | 1,356,400 |
| Capit Hold | 20 | 20⅛ | 19 | 19¼ | – ¾ | 1,036,700 |
| IBM s | 70 | 70½ | 69¼ | 69⅜ | + ½ | 807,000 |
| GulfWstn | 22 | 22⅛ | 21⅛ | 21⅜ | – ⅛ | 667,100 |
| DowChem | 39⅛ | 39¼ | 38 | 38 | – ½ | 641,500 |
| Texaco Inc | 39½ | 39⅝ | 37¾ | 38 | –1¼ | 640,600 |
| Baxt Travnl | 43⅛ | 43¼ | 40¼ | 40⅝ | –2½ | 504,700 |
| Tesoro Pet | 27¾ | 27⅞ | 26⅝ | 26¾ | – ⅜ | 502,600 |
| Gulf Oil | 47½ | 47⅞ | 46⅜ | 46½ | – ½ | 480,100 |
| Int T&T | 28⅜ | 29¼ | 28⅜ | 29¼ | +1⅛ | 478,600 |
| ValeroEnr n | 23 | 23⅛ | 21⅛ | 21¼ | –1 | 473,200 |
| SearsRoeb | 17⅝ | 17⅝ | 17¼ | 17⅜ | ..... | 449,500 |
| Boeing s | 64⅜ | 64⅜ | 62¾ | 63¼ | –1 | 434,600 |
| Exxon | 67⅜ | 67½ | 64⅛ | 66⅞ | + ⅜ | 403,500 |
| ScovillInc | 18⅛ | 18⅛ | 17¼ | 17½ | – ⅜ | 401,300 |

### EXPLANATORY NOTES

(For New York and American Exchange listed issues)

Sales figures are unofficial.

The 52-Week High and Low columns show the highest and the lowest price of the stock in consolidated trading during the preceding 52 weeks plus the current week, but not the current trading day.

u–Indicates a new 52-week high. d–Indicates a new 52-week low.

s–Split or stock dividend of 25 per cent or more in the past 52 weeks. The high-low range and dividend begin with the date of split or stock dividend, and do not cover the entire 52-week period.

n–New issue in the past 52 weeks. The high-low range begins with the start of trading in the new issue and does not cover the entire 52-week period.

g–Dividend or earnings in Canadian money. Stock trades in U.S. dollars. No yield or PE shown unless stated in U.S. money.

Unless otherwise noted, rates of dividends in the foregoing table are annual disbursements based on the last quarterly or semi-annual declaration. Special or extra dividends or payments not designated as regular are identified in the following footnotes.

a–Also extra or extras. b–Annual rate plus stock dividend. c–Liquidating dividend. e–Declared or paid in preceding 12 months. i–Declared or paid after stock dividend or split up. j-Paid this year, dividend omitted, deferred or no action taken at last dividend meeting. k–Declared or paid this year, an accumulative issue with dividends in arrears. r–Declared or paid in preceding 12 months plus stock dividend. t–Paid in stock in preceding 12 months, estimated cash value on ex-dividend or ex-distribution date.

x–Ex-dividend or ex-rights. y–Ex-dividend and sales in full. z–Sales in full.

wd–When distributed. wi–When issued. ww–With warrants. xw–Without warrants.

vj–In bankruptcy or receivership or being reorganized under the Bankruptcy Act, or securities assumed by such companies.

From this portion of the tables, let us isolate the facts for Cabot Corporation (abbreviated Cabot C) to explain their meaning (highlighted in Figure 14):

| 1 | | 2 | 3 | 4 | 5 | 6 | 7 | 8 | 9 | 10 |
|---|---|---|---|---|---|---|---|---|---|---|
| 52 Weeks | | | | | P.E. | Sales | | | | Net |
| High | Low | Stocks | Div. | Yld | Ratio | 100s | High | Low | Close | Chg. |
| 64¾ | 34 | Cabot Corp. | 2 | 3.1 | 8 | x190 | u65½ | 62¾ | 65¼ | +2¾ |

1 The first columns indicate both the highest and lowest prices at which this issue traded in the past year. Past year encompasses a span of 52 weeks preceding the current week. This practice avoids hundreds of meaningless daily announcements of "new" highs and lows at the beginning of each year until a reasonable amount of price fluctuation has established itself.

2 This column briefly identifies the issue, citing its full name or abbreviated title. If it is one of several preferred stocks issued by that company, some means of distinguishing this item from the others also appears. It may be a designation of "a," "b," or "c" preferred or, if the issues carry different dividend rates, that associated rate may be used instead.

3 If the company habitually makes a dividend distribution to its stockholders, or has made an unexpected one thus far this year, that information appears next to the corporation title or abbreviation. Thus, Cabot Corp. has established a policy of paying a $2. per share dividend annually. Because of the unique character of some distributions, they appear with a footnote designation. The meaning of the footnote is recorded at the end of the stock tables in a box labeled "Explanatory Notes." For example, if the dividend amount is followed by the letter "e," a glance at those notes reveals that this sum was paid in the preceding 12 months but is not indicative of a fixed or habitual rate. Although it was not the case with Cabot Corporation, stock splits or stock dividends of 25% or more paid in the past 52 weeks are also identified in these stock tables. Between the name and the cash dividend amount per share would be a small "s." That identifier is shown for Dover Corporation which is listed in the column next to Cabot Corporation.

4 Yield is the percentage rate of return for someone purchasing this stock at the current price. It is calculated by dividing the annual cash dividend per share by the last sale price ($2 dividend by 65¼).

5 The P.E. ratio, meaning price-earnings ratio, is an equation used by some investors to gauge the relative value of a particular security. It compares the current market price of an issue to the latest 12-month earnings announcement on a per share basis. Thus, because the number 8 appears in this column and the stock is selling at about $64, simple arithmetic advises that 12-month earnings are approximately $8. per share (64 ÷ 8). No figure appears in this column if the issue is preferred stock or if the company has no earnings or deficit income to report. Negative P.E. ratios are meaningless.

6 Daily quantity figures are recorded only in terms of the number of round lots traded. Because the typical trading unit is 100 shares, the actual share volume is derived by adding two zeroes to the number of round lots shown. Thus, a figure of 190

actually means 19,000 shares changed hands today. One important exception to this statement concerns 10-share trading unit stocks. The quantity figure for these issues is always stated in full and is recognizable by the letter ''z'' preceding the volume. Sales indicated as ''z100'' mean, in fact, that a total of 100 shares traded today. The ''x'' preceding the volume figure signifies that this issue began trading ex-dividend today.

**7** *High* refers to the highest priced transaction for that issue this day.

**8** *Low* refers to the lowest priced transaction for that issue this day. Both these columns are included for the benefit of readers interested in determining the extent of the security's daily fluctuation. Note: the letter ''u'' next to 65½ signifies that this price is a new high for the year. If the stock had traded at a yearly low price the letter ''d'' would appear next to that price in the column labeled low.

**9** *Close* is the final sale price of that security on the exchange today. In the interest of conserving newsprint, some papers omit the high and low prices, but all of them publish the closing price because of its importance. It is the basis upon which collateral value is determined for loans arranged under Federal Reserve Board Regulations T, U. G, and other financing procedures. It is the item most investors refer to when discussing a security's current price.

---

**10** Net change *(Net Chg.)* is the difference between yesterday's closing price and today's closing price. It is an indicator of daily price trend, and it enables you to determine a monetary result of activity upon an issue you particularly favor. Sometimes, the numerical difference between the two closing prices appears illogical. Some investors may wonder why a stock closing at 28 yesterday and 26¾ today shows a net change of only ''—¾'' instead of an apparently obvious ''—1¼.'' The answer lies in the fact that this issue is trading ex dividend one-half point today. A price reduction resulting from a corporate distribution is not calculated in the net change column. Net change is designed to consider *trading* factors only, not to reflect internal corporate affairs.

---

Over-the-counter stock information is furnished to the major newspapers by United Press International (UPI). It is limited to NASDAQ issues and is further categorized into the most active and less active lists. The most active list is identified as *Over-the-Counter Markets* (see Figure 15). It is composed of about 1,400 issues that have the highest dollar value of average weekly volume.

*D2.*
*The Over-the-Counter Stock Tables*

Let us examine the statistical detail published for Alaska International Corp., a NASDAQ issue framed in the stock table for purposes of easy identification.

| Stock & Div. | 1 | 2 Sales 100s | Bid | 3 | Asked | 4 Net Chg. |
|---|---|---|---|---|---|---|
| Alaska Intl. | .24 | 92 | 6 | | 7 | + ¼ |

**1** This is the name of the issuer and the annual dividend rate per share established by the board of directors of the company. The dividend is ordinarily paid in quarterly installments (that is 6¢ per share every 3 months). If the company has no fixed

**FIGURE 15**
Newspaper List of OTC Stock Transactions

# Over-the-Counter Markets

**4:00 p.m. Eastern Time Prices, Thursday, December 30, 1976**

*All over the counter prices printed on this page are representative quotations supplied by the National Association of Securities Dealers through NASDAQ, its automated system for reporting quotes. Prices don't include retail markup, markdown or commission. Volume represents shares that changed ownership during the day. Figures include only those transactions effected by NASDAQ market makers but may include some duplication where NASDAQ market makers traded with each other.*

**Volume, All Issues, 9,729,900**

**SINCE JANUARY 1**

| | 1976 | 1975 | 1974 |
|---|---|---|---|
| Total sales ...... | 1,675,010,581 | 1,390,411,700 | 1,179,708,948 |

**MARKET DIARY**

| | Thur | Wed | Tues | Mon | Thur |
|---|---|---|---|---|---|
| Issues traded ....... | 2,557 | 2,556 | 2,557 | 2,556 | 2,555 |
| Advances .......... | 682 | 487 | 607 | 617 | 496 |
| Declines ........... | 226 | 339 | 303 | 273 | 302 |
| Unchanged ........ | 1,649 | 1,730 | 1,647 | 1,666 | 1,757 |
| xNew highs ......... | 104 | 93 | 121 | 96 | 83 |
| xNew lows .......... | 7 | 5 | 7 | 8 | 10 |

x-Based on 4 p.m. Eastern time bid quote.

**ACTIVE STOCKS**

| | Volume | 4:00 Bid | Chg. |
|---|---|---|---|
| Amer Express Co .............. | 231,300 | 40¼ | + ¾ |
| Anheuser Busch Inc ........... | 153,900 | 22⅜ | + ¾ |
| Tosco Corp .................... | 153,000 | 4½ | + ¼ |
| De Beers Consol ADR ......... | 128,000 | 2⅜ | +3-16 |
| Govt Employee Ins ............ | 127,300 | 7⅛ | + ⅛ |
| Penn Offshore Gas B .......... | 122,600 | 14⅜ | + ¼ |
| Rank Organisation ADR ....... | 121,600 | 2⅛ | + ⅛ |
| Energy Reserves Grp .......... | 91,900 | 1⅞ | +1-16 |
| Amer Pacific Intl ............. | 89,100 | 5¼ | + ⅛ |
| St Paul Companies ............ | 87,600 | 35¾ | + ¼ |

| Stock & Div. | Sales 100s | Bid | Asked | Net Chg. |
|---|---|---|---|---|
| --A A-- | | | | |
| AaronBro .10d | 2 | 7¼ | 8 | ... |
| AccelratnC .80 | 32 | 14¼ | 15 | ... |
| Accelrators In | 42 | 2¼ | 2⅝ | + ⅛ |
| AcetoChm 5.5i | 8 | 15½ | 16¼ | + ¼ |
| ACMAT Corp | 3 | 1⅛ | 1⅝ | ... |
| AcmeElc .40g | 4 | 12⅝ | 13⅛ | + ⅜ |
| AddWesley .40 | 17 | 6¾ | 7¼ | + ⅛ |
| Advance Ross | 52 | 3¾ | 4⅛ | + ⅛ |
| Advan MicroD | 137 | 25¼ | 26 | + ⅜ |
| AeroSystem 5i | 65 | 1 | 1⅜ | ... |
| Aerosonc .06d | 6 | 2⅛ | 2½ | ... |
| Aerotron Incp | 14 | 2½ | 2⅞ | ... |
| Advent Corp | 40 | 10⅛ | 10⅝ | + ¼ |
| Affil Bnksh .84 | 13 | 16½ | 17½ | ... |
| AgMet Incorp | 93 | 10⅛ | 10⅝ | + ⅛ |
| Agnico Eagle | 91 | 3¾ | 4 | + ⅛ |
| AlaBncp 1.32g | 38 | 25¾ | 26¾ | ... |
| Alanthus C .25 | 2 | 3½ | 4 | ... |
| Alaska Gold | 9 | 3¼ | 4 | + ⅛ |
| Alaska Intl .24 | 92 | 6 | 7 | + ¼ |
| Alberts Inc .20 | 8 | 7½ | 8¼ | ... |
| AlexandA 1.06 | 42 | 38⅛ | 38⅝ | – ⅛ |
| Alex Bald 1.20 | 51 | 14½ | 15 | + ⅛ |
| AlicoIncp .17d | 163 | 9¾ | 10¼ | ... |
| Allegheny Bv | 35 | 3¾ | 4⅛ | ... |
| Allergn Ph .10 | 10 | 24 | 24¾ | ... |
| AlliedBncs .84 | 69 | 29⅜ | 29⅞ | – ¼ |
| Allied Leisure | 19 | 3½ | 4¼ | ... |
| Allied Tele .56 | 50 | 13 | 13½ | + ⅛ |
| AlliedVnLin B | 1 | 3¾ | 4½ | ... |

| Stock & Div. | Sales 100s | Bid | Asked | Net Chg. |
|---|---|---|---|---|
| Charles Rv .20 | x1 | 16½ | 17½ | + ⅛ |
| CharmSh .10d | 2 | 12¾ | 13¾ | ... |
| Chart Hous .72 | 60 | 26⅞ | 27⅜ | + ⅜ |
| ChathamM .80 | 33 | 11⅜ | 11⅞ | – ⅛ |
| Chef Pierre In | 9 | 16¼ | 17 | ... |
| ChmLeaTk .80 | 10 | 10¾ | 11¾ | ... |
| ChemedCorp 1 | 36 | 24½ | 25½ | + 1 |
| Chemineer .20 | 11 | 11¾ | 12¼ | ... |
| ChiBridge 1.40 | 86 | 54½ | 56½ | – ½ |
| Ch NW Trans | 12 | 4½ | 4¾ | ... |
| Chilton Cp .20 | 18 | 6¼ | 6¾ | – ⅛ |
| ChrisSec 5.58 | 2 | 123 | 127 | ... |
| Christensn .40 | 33 | 18½ | 19 | + ⅛ |
| ChubbCrp 1.48 | 116 | 39⅝ | 40⅛ | + ⅜ |
| Cinevideo Intl | 10 | 3 | 3¾ | ... |
| Cinn FclC .64g | 2 | 19¾ | 20¼ | ... |
| Circl Seal .40d | 1 | 16⅞ | 17⅝ | ... |
| Circle In 1.24d | 12 | 15⅝ | 16⅛ | ... |
| CitzSthnCp .96 | 16 | 17¼ | 18¼ | ... |
| CitSoNBGa .52 | 369 | 7⅞ | 8¼ | – ⅛ |
| CitizenFid 1.44 | 5 | 32 | 33 | ... |
| CitznUtils B 2 | 13 | 31⅜ | 31⅞ | ... |
| CitzUtil A 3.5i | 8 | 33⅜ | 33⅞ | ... |
| City Natl Cp 1 | 5 | 17½ | 19 | ... |
| Clabir Cp .06d | 22 | 1⅞ | 2¼ | ... |
| ClarkJL Mf 1a | 54 | 31¾ | 32¾ | + 1 |
| ClevTrust Rlt | 22 | 2⅜ | 2⅞ | ... |
| Clevetrust 2.60 | 18 | 51¼ | 52¼ | ... |
| Clow Corp .40 | 2 | 6½ | 7 | ... |
| CoastlStCp .28 | 27 | 4⅝ | 5 | – ¼ |
| Cobe Labrator | 7 | 22¼ | 23 | + ½ |

| Stock & Div. | Sales 100s | Bid | Asked | Net Chg. |
|---|---|---|---|---|
| Fidelity Co Va | 98 | 2¾ | 3 | ... |
| FidelityUnLf 1 | 41 | 24⅜ | 24⅞ | + ⅛ |
| 5th 3rd Bc 1.80 | z50 | 30 | 30¾ | ... |
| Fingerhut Cp | 266 | 6½ | 6⅞ | + ¼ |
| Finnigan Corp | 29 | 10½ | 11¼ | ... |
| 1stAla Bcsh 1g | 27 | 20¾ | 21¾ | ... |
| FirstAmFn .32 | 20 | 13¼ | 14¼ | ... |
| 1st Amtenn .40 | 35 | 9 | 9½ | ... |
| 1stBcgAla .65d | z95 | 13¼ | 14 | ... |
| 1stBGOh 1.20g | 12 | 25¾ | 26¾ | – ¼ |
| 1st Bncshr Fla | 35 | 5¾ | 6¼ | ... |
| 1stBks SC 1.10 | 15 | 22½ | 23½ | ... |
| 1stBnkSys 1.52 | 81 | 44¼ | 45 | – ¼ |
| 1st Boston 2 | 20 | 23½ | 24¼ | ... |
| 1st Colony .48 | 15 | 12⅜ | 12⅞ | + ⅛ |
| 1stComRI .47b | 12 | 4¼ | 5¼ | – ¼ |
| 1stCmlBkInc 1 | 17 | 13¼ | 13¾ | – ⅛ |
| FstCnnBc 1.80 | 5 | 22½ | 24 | ... |
| 1stCtlRIE .70d | 21 | 8 | 8½ | |

| Stock & Div. | Sales 100s | Bid | Asked | Net Chg. |
|---|---|---|---|---|
| K C LfIns 1.40 | 5 | 35¾ | 36¾ | – ¼ |
| Kar Prodct .24 | 17 | 17 | 17¾ | – ¼ |
| Kayot Incorp | 14 | 4¼ | 5 | – ¼ |
| K D I Corptn | 190 | ¾ | 15-16 | ... |
| KearnyNat .48 | 12 | 6 | 6½ | ... |
| KearneyTr .40 | 96 | 9¼ | 9⅝ | ... |
| KeithClark .50 | 1 | 9 | 10 | ... |
| Kelly Serv .80 | 5 | 24 | 24¾ | ... |
| Kemper C 1.20 | 89 | 31½ | 32¼ | ... |
| Kenai Drilling | 174 | 3⅜ | 3¾ | + ¼ |
| Kenington Ltd | 21 | 5 | 5¾ | + ¼ |
| Ky CenLife .20 | 21 | 7⅝ | 8 | ... |
| Keuffl & E .80 | 6 | 13 | 14 | + ¼ |
| Key Pharmcal | 29 | 4¾ | 5¼ | + ⅛ |
| Keyes Fibr .72 | 25 | 16⅜ | 16¾ | ... |
| KeystCus FdA | 21 | 7¼ | 7¾ | ... |
| Keystn Foods | 48 | 7¾ | 8¼ | + ⅛ |
| Keyst Intl .50a | 30 | 19 | 19¾ | + ¼ |
| Keystone OTC | 27 | 6⅝ | 7⅛ | ... |
| Keystn PCmt | 2 | 10½ | 11¼ | ... |
| Kimball Intl B | 24 | 10 | 10½ | ... |
| KnapeVogt .90 | 9 | 17¾ | 18¾ | ... |
| KnudsenC .60g | 3 | 10⅞ | 11⅜ | – ⅛ |
| KogerPrp .10d | 56 | 10 | 10¾ | – ¼ |
| KossCorp .20a | 23 | 4⅝ | 5⅛ | + ¼ |
| KRM Petrolm | 206 | 4⅛ | 4½ | + ⅛ |
| Krueger W .60 | 27 | 13 | 14 | ... |
| Kuhlman .50a | 39 | 10⅞ | 11¼ | ... |
| --L L-- | | | | |
| LacledeSteel 1 | 6 | 15¼ | 16 | ... |
| LakeSDisPw 1 | 10 | 11¼ | 11¾ | ... |
| LncstrCol .56a | 49 | 16⅝ | 17⅛ | ... |
| Lance Inc .88a | 8 | 22¼ | 23 | ... |
| Lanchart Ind | 8 | 3⅝ | 3⅞ | ... |
| LandmBFI .36 | 82 | 5¼ | 5¾ | + ⅛ |
| LaneComp .60 | 7 | 19¾ | 20¾ | + ¼ |
| Lawrys Fd .24 | 201 | 24 | 25 | ... |
| Lawson Pr .24 | 3 | 13 | 14½ | ... |
| La ZBoyCh .56 | 25 | 20¼ | 21 | ... |
| LearPetrol 10i | 22 | 9⅜ | 9⅞ | + ⅛ |
| Leggett Plt .40 | 42 | 12⅜ | 12¾ | ... |
| LeonarSil .10d | 10 | 9⅝ | 10⅛ | + ⅜ |
| Lexitron Corp | 69 | 4⅛ | 4⅝ | + ⅛ |
| LewisPalm .12 | 3 | 8¾ | 9¼ | ... |
| Liberty Home | 32 | 2¾ | 3⅛ | ... |
| LibNatLife .80 | 119 | 25¼ | 25¾ | + ¼ |
| Life InvInc .10 | 112 | 6⅝ | 7⅛ | + ⅜ |
| Lil ChFd .20e | 8 | 5⅜ | 5⅞ | ... |
| Ltd Stores .08 | 62 | 23¼ | 24 | + ¼ |
| Lin Broadcast | 38 | 17⅜ | 17¾ | ... |
| Lin 1st Bk 1.88 | 23 | 23¾ | 24½ | + ½ |
| LinFstBpf 1.05 | 9 | 12¼ | 13 | ... |
| LincTel&Tel 2 | 4 | 28¼ | 29¼ | ... |
| Lindberg .80a | 6 | 12¾ | 13¼ | + ⅜ |
| Lion Cntry Saf | 107 | ⅝ | 1 | + ⅛ |
| LiqAirNA 1.40 | 9 | 32¾ | 33½ | + ½ |

**EXPLANATORY NOTES**

z-Sales in full.

a-Annual rate plus cash extra or extras. b-Paid last year. c-Declared or paid since stock dividend or split, no regular rate. d-Paid this year, no regular rate. e-Declared or paid in 1975 plus stock. f-Declared or paid in 1976 plus stock. g-Annual rate plus stock dividend. h-Paid this year, latest dividend omitted. i-Paid in stock in 1976. k-Percent paid in stock in 1975. r-Ex-rights. x-Ex-dividend. y-Ex-distribution. (z)-No representative quote.

yearly rate, this amount is followed by a letter code whose meaning can be found in the "Explanatory Notes" at the bottom of the tables.

2 This figure is yesterday's sales volume for the issue in terms of the number of 100-share units traded by registered NASDAQ market-makers. Thus, the figure 92 equals 9,200 shares of stock. Trades between customers and NASD members who are not NASDAQ market-makers in this issue are reported weekly to the NASD in Washington, D.C. Those figures do not appear in the newspapers.

3 Due to the nature of OTC activity and the lack of a central marketplace, specific high, low, and last-sale trade information is superseded in the list by a closing quotation. These prices are representative of bids and offers submitted by registered NASDAQ market-makers in this issue.

4 In this table, net change is related to the closing bid prices on a day-to-day basis because the bid is the most meaningful indicator of value in a quotation. Thus, a change of + ¼ next to the quotation of 6–7 indicates that yesterday's closing bid was 5¾.

An additional OTC–NASDAQ securities list composed of

approximately 950 less active issues is published daily, too (see Figure 16). These tables are in abbreviated form, however; they lack dividend information, trading volume, and net-change disclosures. Quotations are represented as of 2:00 P.M. (New York time), as opposed to the active list, whose prices are shown as of 4:00 P.M. (New York time), the usual market closing time.

# Additional OTC Quotes

Thursday, December 30, 1976

Representative bid-asked ranges for less actively traded issues as of 2 p.m. Eastern time.

| | Bid | Asked |
|---|---|---|
| --A A-- | | |
| Aaronson Br Str | 1 | 1⅜ |
| A B A Indust | 5¾ | 6½ |
| Abkco Industrie | 2¾ | 3½ |
| Acady Ins Grup | 1¼ | 1½ |
| Acme Gen Corp | 8 | 8¾ |
| AcmeUntd Corp | 5¾ | 6¼ |
| A D A Resourcs | 2¼ | 2⅝ |
| Addmaster Crp | 1¼ | 1¾ |
| Adobe Bldg Cnt | 1⅜ | 1¾ |
| Advanced Comp | 1¾ | 2¼ |
| Advanced Chem | ⅞ | 1⅜ |
| Advertisg Unltd | 1¼ | 2 |
| AEL Industr A | 2⅝ | 3 |
| Aid Auto Stores | 1⅝ | 2⅛ |
| AID Inc Cla A | 7 | 7½ |
| Air Calfornia | 11½ | 12½ |
| Air Florida Syst | 2 | 2½ |
| A E S Technolg | ⅞ | 1⅛ |
| AFA Protective | 5¾ | 6½ |
| Alabama Oxygn | 2 | 2½ |
| Aldon Industr | 1⅜ | 1⅞ |
| Algorex Corptr | 1¼ | 1¾ |
| Allegheny Bv pf | 4½ | 5 |
| Allen Organ B | 9 | 9½ |
| Allied Capitl Cp | 8¼ | 9 |
| Allied Farm Ec | 3⅜ | 3⅞ |
| Allied Food Inc | 1 | 1½ |
| Cutler Federal | 1¾ | 2¼ |
| Cybermatics | ½ | ⅞ |
| --D D-- | | |
| D A B Indust | 11¼ | 12¼ |
| DairyQueen Str | 3¼ | 3¾ |
| DallasBus Captl | 7½ | 8 |
| Danker& Wohlk | 1⅞ | 2⅜ |
| Danly Machine | 8½ | 9½ |
| Danners Incorp | 6 | 6½ |
| Data Dimensn | 4½ | 4⅞ |
| Dataram Corp | 1¾ | 2½ |
| Data Technolgy | 3¼ | 3¾ |
| Datatab Incorp | 1⅜ | 1⅞ |
| Dauphn Deposit | 31½ | 33½ |
| DavisWater Wst | 3⅝ | 4⅛ |
| Del Electronics | 3½ | 4½ |
| Delw ValRlty ut | 11½ | 13 |
| Delta California | 4¼ | 4¾ |
| Dellwood Furn | 6⅛ | 6⅝ |
| Dentalloy Ijcrp | 3 | 4 |
| Detection Syst | 1⅞ | 2⅝ |
| Det Can Tunnel | 12¼ | 13¼ |
| DetroitInt Bridg | 31½ | 33½ |
| Devcon Intl Crp | ½ | 1¼ |
| Dewey Electrn | 1⅛ | 1⅝ |
| Dickey WS Clay | 17⅝ | 18⅜ |
| DigiLog Systms | 1⅜ | 1⅞ |
| --K K-- | | |
| Kahler Corprtn | 14 | 16 |
| Kaibab Industrs | 1¾ | 2⅛ |
| Kane Furniture | 3½ | 4 |
| Kan St Network | 4¾ | 5⅛ |
| Kaysam Cp Am | 3 | 3½ |
| Kenai Drill wts | ⅝ | 1 |
| Kentucky Invst | 5¼ | 5⅝ |
| Kewaunee SciE | 8 | 9½ |
| Keydata Corp | 1⅝ | 2⅛ |
| Kiddie Products | 3¾ | 4½ |
| KindCare Learn | 7⅞ | 8⅜ |
| King Intl Corp | 1½ | 1⅞ |
| KingKullen Grc | 8¾ | 9¾ |
| K M C Mtg Inv | ⅞ | 1¼ |
| Knogo Corportn | 2⅝ | 3⅛ |
| Kobacker Store | 19½ | 20½ |
| Kodicor Incorp | 3 | 3½ |
| Koger Prp 79wt | 1¾ | 2¼ |
| KogerPropt wts | 8¼ | 9¼ |
| Kroy Industries | 6¼ | 6¾ |
| Kustom Electns | 2⅛ | 2⅝ |
| Kulicke Soffa In | 3 | 3½ |
| KV Pharmaceut | 4¼ | 4¾ |
| --L L-- | | |
| Lafayette Unitd | 1¼ | 1⅝ |
| Lamar Life Cp | 14¼ | 15¼ |
| LamstonMH Inc | 11½ | 13½ |
| Land Resources | 1⅜ | 1¾ |
| Lane Wood Incp | 1⅛ | 1⅜ |
| Larsen Compny | 23½ | 24½ |
| Latham Proces | 1¾ | 2¼ |
| Lazare Kaplan | 5¼ | 5¾ |
| LaserLink Corp | 1½ | 2 |
| Laufr Company | 5 | 5¾ |
| Leisure Dynmic | 2½ | 2⅞ |
| Leisure Group | 3-16 | ⅜ |
| LiberianIron Or | 14¾ | 15¾ |
| LibertyNtBk Tr | 33½ | 35½ |
| Life Sciences | ½ | 1 |
| Lifesurance Cp | 3⅛ | 3⅝ |
| Lincoln Inc Life | 9½ | 10¼ |
| RamapoFncl Cp | 3½ | 4 |
| RandCapital Cp | 1⅜ | 1⅞ |
| Raven Industris | 4⅛ | 4⅝ |
| Ratner Corp | 3¾ | 4¾ |
| Rayne Industris | ⅜ | ¾ |
| Real Estat Data | 2⅞ | 3¼ |
| Realist Incorpr | 2¾ | 3½ |
| Realty Indust | 2 | 2½ |
| RealtyRefnd wt | 1¼ | 1½ |
| Recoton Corpn | 3⅝ | 4⅛ |
| Refac Tech Dev | 3⅜ | 3⅞ |
| ReidProvdt Lab | 3½ | 4 |
| Reinell Indust | 3¼ | 3¾ |
| Reliable Lfelns | 12 | 12¾ |
| Rem Metals Cp | ⅝ | ⅞ |
| Rentex Services | 2¼ | 2⅝ |
| RepublVan Line | 1½ | 2¼ |
| Research Fuels | ⅞ | 1¼ |
| Research Incp | 9 | 9¾ |
| Resers FineFds | 1⅜ | 1¾ |
| Respirtory Care | 4¼ | 5 |
| Retail Merchnt | ¾ | 1½ |
| Reuter Incorp | 1⅜ | 1⅞ |
| Revell Incorptd | 6¼ | 7 |
| Ridgeway Incp | 7¼ | 8¼ |
| Ripley Compny | 3¾ | 4¾ |
| R L I Corprtion | 8¼ | 9 |
| R M I C Corp | 13¼ | 14 |
| Roanna Togs In | 1¾ | 2¾ |
| Roberts Porter | x7 | 7¾ |
| RobinexIntl Ltd | 1 | 1¾ |
| Rochester Instr | 7¼ | 8 |
| RockyMtNat Gs | 2¾ | 3¼ |
| RockyMt Nat pf | 9¾ | 10¼ |
| Rodale Electron | 3¾ | 4½ |
| Roffler Ind Inc | 1⅝ | 2⅛ |
| RooseveltNatl A | 2¼ | 3 |
| Roper Industrs | 8¾ | 9¾ |
| Roselon Industr | 3½ | 4¼ |
| Rowe Furniture | 5¼ | 5¾ |
| RoyalCastle Sys | 1 | 1½ |
| RoyalDutch Pet | 85¾ | 86¾ |

**FIGURE 16**
Newspaper List of Additional OTC Stock Transactions

About every 6 months, the National NASDAQ Committee of the NASD meets to determine what revisions are necessary in each of these listings. Some stocks are downgraded due to lack of trading volume, whereas others are promoted to the higher-prestige category. Any issue deleted from the NASDAQ system at any time is immediately dropped from its appropriate listing.

***D3. The Listed Bond Tables***

### *CORPORATE BONDS*

*D3a.*

The format for the tables of bonds listed on the New York and American stock exchanges differs from the listed stock tables in that

1. instead of dividend information, the corporate description reveals interest rate and maturation year.
2. instead of price-earnings information, there is a column to represent the issue's current yield;[9]
3. instead of volume represented in terms of the number of 100-share round lots, it is shown in terms of $1,000 par value bonds traded that day; and
4. bond prices are shown as a percentage figure of $1,000, par

[9] With the exception of convertible bonds, for which this detail is of little significance to an investor.

value, whereas stock prices are listed in actual dollars and fractions thereof. For example, a bond price shown as 106 means 106% of $1,000, or $1,060 per bond. A stock listed at 106 means $106 per share

To practice reading these tables, let us turn our attention to a Mobil Corporation debenture listed on the New York Stock Exchange. It is framed in the segment of the bond tables pictured as Figure 17.

# New York Exchange Bonds
## Thursday, December 30, 1976

**Total Volume, $30,640,000**

**SALES SINCE JANUARY 1**

| 1976 | 1975 | 1974 |
|---|---|---|
| $5,239,215,900 | $5,178,337,500 | $4,052,123,400 |

|  | Domestic | | All Issues | |
|---|---|---|---|---|
|  | Thurs | Wed | Thurs | Wed |
| Issues traded | 847 | 841 | 866 | 855 |
| Advances | 437 | 391 | 451 | 398 |
| Declines | 196 | 217 | 196 | 223 |
| Unchanged | 214 | 233 | 219 | 234 |
| New highs, 1976 | 190 | 162 | 198 | 166 |
| New lows, 1976 | 0 | 0 | 0 | 1 |

## Dow Jones Bond Averages

|  | —1974— | | —1975— | | —1976— | | ---THURSDAY--- | | |
|---|---|---|---|---|---|---|---|---|---|
|  | High | Low | High | Low | High | Low |  | —1976— | —1975— |
| 20 Bonds | 91.70 | 78.52 | 88.05 | 81.03 | 93.07 | 85.68 | 93.07 + .48 | | |
| 10 Utilities | 80.82 | 70.81 | 79.05 | 74.51 | 98.58 | 87.46 | 98.58 + .70 | close 81.03 + .23 |
| 10 Industrial | | | | | 87.57 | 78.58 | 87.57 + .26 | close 74.68 + .05 |

**FIGURE 17**
Newspaper Lists of NYSE and AMEX Bond Transactions

| | 1 | 2 Cur Yld | 3 Vol | 4 High | 5 Low | 6 Close | 7 Net Chg. |
|---|---|---|---|---|---|---|---|
| Bonds | | | | | | | |
| Mobil 8½ 01 | | 8.0 | 166 | 106¼ | 106 | 106⅛ | + ¼ |

1 The bond description sets forth the abbreviated name of the issuer, the interest rate, and the year of maturity. In this illustration the issuer of the bond is the Mobil Corporation, the interest rate is 8½% of the bond's $1,000 face value, and the bond must be redeemed in the year 2001. The specific month and day of maturation cannot be determined from these tables. Interested investors must refer to the bond's indenture or to a research service that provides such information.

2 The current yield is a function of the investor's annual interest dollars and the latest value of the bond. The analytical formula is the annual interest divided by the current market value shown in column 6. Therefore, the current yield for this debenture is:

$$\frac{\$85 \quad (8½\% \text{ of } \$1,000)}{\$1,061.25 \ (106⅛\% \text{ of } \$1,000)} = .08, \text{ or } 8\%$$

The current yield of a convertible bond is not calculated in this bond table. It is identified by the letters "cv" appearing in this column. Investors do not normally buy convertible bonds for their yield. They look for a movement in the underlying stock to provide them with capital gains. Interest income is of secondary importance.

3 Volume figures are expressed in the number of $1,000 face value bonds traded today. Simply add three zeros to the number in this column to find that $166,000 worth of face value Mobil bonds changed hands on the NYSE.

4 *High* indicates the highest value at which these bonds traded today (106¼% of $1,000 = $1,062.50). You cannot determine from this information how many bonds traded at that price. It could have been a single bond, 100 bonds, or maybe even more.

5 *Low* is the minimum value at which the Mobil bonds traded today on the NYSE. It is not apparent here, either, how many of these debentures changed hands at this price.

6 The *Close* is the last price at which a transaction took place today in the Mobil 8½% bonds on the NYSE. One or more bonds may have been involved in that transaction, which took place sometime between 10:00 P.M. and 4:00 P.M. Eastern time on this date. Just because a sale is the last transaction of the day does not mean it must occur at or close to the end of the trading day on the exchange.

7 *Net Chg.*, representing net change in value between day-to-day closing prices, is expressed as a percentage of a bond's $1,000 typical face value. Thus, a change of + ¼ means an increase in value of ¼% of $1,000 ($2.50 per bond) over the previous closing price of that issue. The Mobil debentures due 2001 obviously closed yesterday at 105⅞ (106⅛ − ¼).

A portion of the business section in the daily newspaper is often used to present price information for most U.S. government, government agency, and quasi-government debt securities (see Figure 18). Some local papers may publish such information weekly only, although the major ones print daily quotations solicited from market-makers in those issues. The listings are categorized by issuer. In the case of U.S. government securities, they are categorized by type (such as bills, notes, bonds) and arranged in order of maturity. The earliest maturation dates are first, without regard to interest rate or yield. As with securities traded over the counter, only bid and asked prices are shown, defined in increments as small as $1/32\%$ of the issue's par value.[10] The figure in the column labeled *Yield* is a yield to maturity, not a current yield. Yield to maturity gives a more relevant number for institutional investors for whom the securities have greatest appeal.

In analyzing Figure 18, let us focus upon the 4½s of May 1975–85 outlined in the section headed "Treasury Bonds and Notes."

| 1 | 2 | 3 | 4 | 5 | 6 |
|---|---|---|---|---|---|
|  |  |  |  | Bid. |  |
| Rate | Mat. Date | Bid | Asked | Chg. | yld. |
| 4¼s | 1975–85 May | 86.4 | 87.4 | + .12 | 6.25 |

**1** These bonds pay 4¼% interest. The small letter "s" following the interest rate is the traditional way these securities are identified; that is, in the plural form. It means that there is more than one debt instrument outstanding in this series to represent the obligation characterized by this issue. The absence of an "n" after the maturation month informs us that this is a bond and not a government note. That is, its maturation date was set for more than 10 years after the date of issuance.

**2** What appears to be a double maturation date (1975–85) is, in reality, how the reader is advised that this issue is a term bond. The earlier year signifies that anytime after May 1975 until the time the bond must be redeemed in May 1985, the government can retire it at par by exercising its option to call this issue pursuant to such privilege stated in the indenture. In 1977, it seems unlikely to do so because it cannot borrow medium-term funds at better than the 4¼% it is paying on this bond now. This is also why the Treasury Department did not call the bond in 1975 or 1976 either.

**3** A holder anxious to sell this bond must accept the bid price of 86.4 which is 86 4/32% of $1,000, or $861.25 per bond.

**4** An investor interested in buying the bond must pay the offering price of 87.4 which is 87 4/32% of $1,000, or $871.25 per bond.

**5** This issue was up .12 or 12/32% of $1,000 ($3.75) from yesterday's bid. Net changes are always measured from day to

[10] Treasury bills, of course, are traditionally presented in terms of an annualized percentage discount from par value; hence the peculiarity of their numerically higher bid than asking price.

# *Government, Agency and Miscellaneous Securities*

Thursday, December 30, 1976

Over-the-Counter Quotations: Source on request.
Decimals in bid-and-asked and bid changes represent 32nds; 101.1 means 101 1-32. a-Plus 1-64. b-Yield to call date. d-Minus 1-64.

## Treasury Bonds and Notes

| Rate | Mat. Date | | Bid | Asked | Bid Chg. | Yld. |
|---|---|---|---|---|---|---|
| 3s, | 1977 | Feb n | 100.12 | 100.14 | .... | 4.11 |
| 6s, | 1977 | Feb n | 100.5 | 100.9 | .... | 4.08 |
| 6½s, | 1977 | Mar n | 100.14 | 100.18 | + .1 | 4.06 |
| 7⅜s, | 1977 | Apr n | 100.26 | 100.30 | − .2 | 4.37 |
| 6⅞s, | 1977 | May n | 100.25 | 100.29 | .... | 4.31 |
| 9s, | 1977 | May n | 101.14 | 101.18 | − .2 | 4.58 |
| 6¾s, | 1977 | May n | 100.28 | 101 | + .2 | 4.23 |
| 6½s, | 1977 | Jun n | 100.27 | 100.31 | .... | 4.48 |
| 7½s, | 1977 | Jul n | 101.18 | 101.22 | .... | 4.50 |
| 7¾s, | 1977 | Aug n | 101.27 | 101.31 | .... | 4.48 |
| 8¼s, | 1977 | Aug n | 102.7 | 102.11 | .... | 4.58 |
| 8⅜s, | 1977 | Sep n | 102.17 | 102.21 | .... | 4.69 |
| 7½s, | 1977 | Oct n | 102.3 | 102.7 | .... | 4.72 |
| 7¾s, | 1977 | Nov n | 102.12 | 102.16 | .... | 4.77 |
| 6⅝s, | 1977 | Nov n | 101.16 | 101.20 | .... | 4.77 |
| 7¼s, | 1977 | Dec n | 102.8 | 102.12 | + .2 | 4.77 |
| 6⅜s, | 1978 | Jan n | 101.13 | 101.17 | + .1 | 4.90 |
| 6¼s, | 1978 | Feb n | 101.9 | 101.13 | + .1 | 4.95 |
| 8s, | 1978 | Feb n | 103.8 | 103.12 | .... | 4.98 |
| 6¾s, | 1978 | Mar n | 101.29 | 102.1 | + .1 | 5.09 |
| 6½s, | 1978 | Apr n | 101.22 | 101.26 | − 1 | 5.07 |
| 7⅛s, | 1978 | May n | 102.17 | 102.21 | + .1 | 5.09 |
| 7⅛s, | 1978 | May n | 102.18 | 102.22 | + .1 | 5.12 |
| 7⅞s, | 1978 | May n | 103.17 | 103.21 | + .1 | 5.07 |
| 6⅞s, | 1978 | Jun n | 102.11 | 102.15 | + .1 | 5.14 |
| 6⅞s, | 1978 | Jul n | 102.12 | 102.16 | + .1 | 5.20 |
| 6⅝s, | 1978 | Aug n | 102.1 | 102.5 | + .1 | 5.25 |
| 7⅝s, | 1978 | Aug n | 103.16 | 103.20 | + .1 | 5.28 |
| 8¾s, | 1978 | Aug n | 105.7 | 105.11 | + .1 | 5.26 |
| 6¼s, | 1978 | Sep n | 101.16 | 101.20 | + .3 | 5.26 |
| 5⅞s, | 1978 | Oct n | 100.29 | 101.1 | + .2 | 5.27 |
| 5¾s, | 1978 | Nov n | 100.23 | 100.25 | + .2 | 5.31 |
| 6s, | 1978 | Nov n | 101.4 | 101.8 | + .2 | 5.29 |
| 8⅛s, | 1978 | Dec n | 105.1 | 105.5 | .... | 5.36 |
| 5¼s, | 1978 | Dec n | 99.26 | 99.28 | + .2 | 5.32 |
| 7s, | 1979 | Feb n | 103.1 | 103.9 | + .1 | 5.34 |
| 7⅞s, | 1979 | May n | 105.1 | 105.9 | + .2 | 5.47 |
| 7¾s, | 1979 | Jun n | 104.30 | 105.6 | + .1 | 5.49 |
| 6¼s, | 1979 | Aug n | 101.11 | 101.19 | + .4 | 5.59 |
| 6⅞s, | 1979 | Aug n | 102.27 | 103.3 | .... | 5.59 |
| 8½s, | 1979 | Sep n | 107 | 107.8 | + .2 | 5.61 |
| 6¼s, | 1979 | Nov n | 101.20 | 101.24 | + .3 | 5.58 |
| 6⅝s, | 1979 | Nov n | 102.16 | 102.24 | + .3 | 5.58 |
| 7s, | 1979 | Nov n | 103.12 | 103.20 | + .1 | 5.61 |
| 7½s, | 1979 | Dec n | 104.23 | 104.31 | + .1 | 5.67 |
| 4s, | 1980 | Feb | 95 | 95.16 | + .4 | 5.59 |
| 7½s, | 1980 | Mar n | 104.26 | 105.2 | + .4 | 5.77 |
| 6⅞s, | 1980 | May n | 103.1 | 103.9 | + .1 | 5.79 |
| 7⅝s, | 1980 | Jun n | 105.11 | 105.19 | + .3 | 5.83 |
| 9s, | 1980 | Aug n | 109.17 | 109.25 | + .3 | 5.95 |
| 6⅞s, | 1980 | Sep n | 103.6 | 103.14 | + .5 | 5.84 |
| 3½s, | 1980 | Nov | 100.3 | 100.7 | +8.3 | 5.81 |
| 5⅞s, | 1980 | Dec n | 99.30 | 100.2 | .... | 5.86 |
| 7s, | 1981 | Feb n | 103.16 | 103.24 | + .4 | 5.96 |
| 7⅜s, | 1981 | Feb n | 104.25 | 105.1 | + .5 | 5.97 |
| 7⅜s, | 1981 | May n | 104.24 | 105 | + .5 | 6.06 |
| 7⅝s, | 1981 | Aug n | 105.25 | 106.1 | + .6 | 6.11 |
| 7s, | 1981 | Aug | 104.2 | 105.2 | + .4 | 5.74 |
| 7s, | 1981 | Nov n | 103.22 | 103.30 | + .6 | 6.05 |
| 7¾s, | 1981 | Nov n | 106.14 | 106.22 | + .6 | 6.14 |
| 6⅜s, | 1982 | Feb | 100.30 | 101.14 | +1.7 | 6.04 |
| 8s, | 1982 | May n | 107.18 | 107.26 | + .8 | 6.26 |
| 8⅛s, | 1982 | Aug n | 108.4 | 108.12 | + .6 | 6.33 |
| 7⅞s, | 1982 | Nov n | 107.4 | 107.12 | + .6 | 6.35 |
| 8s, | 1983 | Feb n | 107.30 | 108.6 | + .8 | 6.36 |
| 3¼s, | 1978-83 | Jun | 85.2 | 86.2 | + .8 | 5.88 |
| 7s, | 1983 | Nov n | 103.13 | 103.17 | + .3 | 6.36 |
| 6⅜s, | 1984 | Aug | 99.26 | 100.26 | + .6 | 6.24 |
| 3¼s, | 1985 | May | 83.20 | 84.20 | + .4 | 5.57 |
| 4¼s, | 1975-85 | May | 86.4 | 87.4 | + .12 | 6.25 |
| 7⅞s, | 1986 | May n | 107.20 | 107.23 | + .11 | 6.72 |
| 8s, | 1986 | Aug n | 108.20 | 108.24 | + .10 | 6.75 |
| 6⅛s, | 1986 | Nov | 98.8 | 99.8 | + .16 | 6.23 |
| 3½s, | 1990 | Feb | 83.22 | 84.22 | + .14 | 5.11 |
| 8¼s, | 1990 | May | 111.4 | 111.20 | + .26 | 6.93 |
| 4¼s, | 1987-92 | Aug | 84.26 | 85.26 | + .8 | 5.63 |
| 4s, | 1988-93 | Feb | 84.24 | 85.24 | + .2 | 5.33 |
| 6¾s, | 1993 | Feb | 98.20 | 99.20 | + .18 | 6.79 |
| 7½s, | 1988-93 | Aug | 104.4 | 105.4 | + .26 | 6.86 |
| 4⅛s, | 1989-94 | May | 84.10 | 85.10 | + .12 | 5.45 |
| 3s, | 1995 | Feb | 83.18 | 84.18 | + .8 | 4.23 |
| 7s, | 1993-98 | May | 99.10 | 100.10 | + .18 | 6.97 |
| 3½s, | 1998 | Nov | 83.20 | 84.20 | + .12 | 4.63 |
| 8½s, | 1994-99 | May | 112.8 | 112.24 | + .24 | 7.20 |
| 7⅞s, | 1995-00 | Feb | 107 | 107.8 | + .26 | 7.16 |
| 8⅜s, | 1995-00 | Aug | 111.14 | 111.30 | + .28 | 7.19 |
| 8s, | 1996-01 | Aug | 108.10 | 108.18 | + .26 | 7.17 |
| 8¼s, | 2000-05 | May | 110.24 | 111.8 | + .26 | 7.24 |

n— Treasury notes.

**U.S. Treas. Bills**

| Mat | Bid Discount | Ask Discount | Mat | Bid Discount | Ask Discount |
|---|---|---|---|---|---|
| 12-30 | 4.31 | 4.13 | 4-21 | 4.45 | 4.39 |
| 1- 6 | 4.32 | 4.10 | 4-28 | 4.47 | 4.39 |
| 1-11 | 4.30 | 4.10 | 5- 3 | 4.50 | 4.42 |
| 1-13 | 4.28 | 4.10 | 5- 5 | 4.50 | 4.42 |
| 1-20 | 4.25 | 4.09 | 5-12- | 4.50 | 4.42 |
| 1-27 | 4.25 | 4.11 | 5-19- | 4.50 | 4.44 |
| 2- 3 | 4.27 | 4.17 | 5-26 | 4.51 | 4.43 |
| 2- 8 | 4.28 | 4.18 | 5-31 | 4.51 | 4.43 |
| 2-10 | 4.32 | 4.22 | 6- 2 | 4.52 | 4.44 |
| 2-17 | 4.33 | 4.23 | 6- 9 | 4.52 | 4.44 |
| 2-24 | 4.33 | 4.23 | 6-16 | 4.52 | 4.44 |
| 3- 3 | 4.33 | 4.25 | 6-23 | 4.52 | 4.46 |
| 3- 8 | 4.35 | 4.25 | 6-28 | 4.50 | 4.42 |
| 3-10 | 4.35 | 4.27 | 6-30 | 4.50 | 4.46 |
| 3-17 | 4.35 | 4.27 | 7-26 | 4.58 | 4.48 |
| 3-24 | 4.36 | 4.30 | 8-23 | 4.60 | 4.52 |
| 3-31 | 4.34 | 4.30 | 9-20 | 4.63 | 4.55 |
| 4- 5 | 4.40 | 4.32 | 10-18 | 4.64 | 4.56 |
| 4- 7 | 4.40 | 4.32 | 11-15 | 4.64 | 4.56 |
| 4-14 | 4.43 | 4.35 | 12-13 | 4.60 | 4.56 |

**Fed. Home Loan Bank**

| Rate | Mat | Bid | Asked | Yld |
|---|---|---|---|---|
| 7.20 | 2-77 | 100.10 | 100.14 | 4.05 |
| 8.05 | 2-77 | 100.14 | 100.18 | 4.02 |
| 6.95 | 5-77 | 100.22 | 100.80 | 4.50 |
| 8.70 | 5-77 | 101.12 | 101.20 | 4.47 |
| 7.15 | 8-77 | 101.10 | 101.18 | 4.65 |
| 8.80 | 8-77 | 102.10 | 102.18 | 4.70 |
| 6.75 | 11-77 | 101.8 | 101.24 | 4.72 |
| 7.45 | 11-77 | 101.28 | 102.12 | 4.70 |
| 9.15 | 11-77 | 103.12 | 103.28 | 4.67 |
| 7.25 | 2-78 | 102 | 102.16 | 4.98 |
| 9.38 | 2-78 | 104.12 | 104.28 | 4.95 |
| 7.60 | 5-78 | 102.24 | 103.8 | 5.15 |
| 9.10 | 11-78 | 106.8 | 106.24 | 5.31 |
| 8.65 | 2-79 | 105.20 | 106.4 | 5.58 |
| 9.45 | 2-79 | 107.8 | 107.24 | 5.58 |
| 8.65 | 5-79 | 106.4 | 106.20 | 5.65 |
| 8.75 | 5-79 | 106.8 | 106.24 | 5.69 |
| 9.50 | 8-79 | 108.20 | 109.4 | 5.75 |
| 7.50 | 11-79 | 104 | 104.16 | 5.79 |
| 8.15 | 11-79 | 105.24 | 106.8 | 5.77 |
| 7.05 | 2-80 | 102.20 | 103.4 | 5.94 |
| 7.75 | 2-80 | 104.16 | 105.16 | 5.81 |
| 7.30 | 8-80 | 103.16 | 104 | 6.06 |
| 7.80 | 10-80 | 104.24 | 105.24 | 6.07 |
| 6.70 | 11-80 | 102.2 | 102.10 | 6.02 |
| 7.75 | 11-80 | 105.4 | 105.20 | 6.10 |
| 7.60 | 2-81 | 104.16 | 105 | 6.21 |
| 8.65 | 11-81 | 109.8 | 109.24 | 6.30 |
| 6.60 | 11-81 | 101 | 102 | 6.12 |
| 3.63 | 2-82 | 108.16 | 109.16 | 6.42 |
| 7.30 | 5-83 | 103.4 | 104.4 | 6.50 |
| 7.38 | 11-83 | 103.24 | 104.8 | 6.60 |
| 9.75 | 5-84 | 110.12 | 111.12 | 6.77 |
| 7.75 | 5-84 | 104.28 | 105.12 | 6.81 |
| 7.85 | 8-84 | 105.20 | 106.4 | 6.81 |
| 7.38 | 11-84 | 103.4 | 103.12 | 6.81 |
| 8.10 | 11-85 | 106.28 | 107.12 | 6.97 |
| 7.38 | 11-93 | 99.20 | 100.20 | 7.28 |

**World Bank Bonds**

| Rate | Mat | Bid | Asked | Yld |
|---|---|---|---|---|
| 6.38 | 1-77 | 100 | 100.4 | 2.22 |
| 6.40 | 3-77 | 100.4 | 100.16 | 3.77 |
| 8.40 | 9-77 | 102 | 102.16 | 4.70 |
| 7.00 | 3-78 | 101.4 | 101.20 | 5.57 |
| 4.25 | 5-78 | 97.28 | 98.12 | 5.53 |
| 6.88 | 9-78 | 101.12 | 101.28 | 5.69 |
| 4.25 | 1-79 | 96.24 | 97.8 | 5.70 |
| 8.00 | 1-80 | 104.8 | 104.24 | 6.24 |
| 8.30 | 7-80 | 105.8 | 105.24 | 6.45 |
| 4.75 | 11-80 | 94.28 | 95.12 | 6.12 |
| 8.35 | 12-80 | 105.24 | 106.8 | 6.53 |
| 8.00 | 7-81 | 104.12 | 104.28 | 6.72 |
| 3.25 | 10-81 | 95.24 | 96.24 | 4.01 |
| 4.50 | 2-82 | 90.4 | 90.20 | 6.71 |
| 8.15 | 1-85 | 104 | 104.16 | 7.39 |
| 5.00 | 2-85 | 86.28 | 87.12 | 7.07 |
| 8.60 | 7-85 | 106.4 | 106.20 | 7.53 |
| 8.85 | 12-85 | 107.24 | 108.8 | 7.56 |
| 8.38 | 7-86 | 105.16 | 106 | 7.48 |
| 7.80 | 12-86 | 102.4 | 102.16 | 7.44 |
| 4.50 | 2-90 | 75.16 | 76 | 7.39 |
| 5.38 | 7-91 | 80.12 | 80.28 | 7.57 |
| 5.38 | 4-92 | 79.16 | 80 | 7.61 |
| 5.88 | 9-93 | 83 | 83.24 | 7.61 |
| 6.50 | 3-94 | 87.20 | 88.4 | 7.76 |
| 6.38 | 10-94 | 86.16 | 87 | 7.73 |
| 8.63 | 8-95 | 104 | 104.16 | 8.15 |
| 8.13 | 8-96 | 100.16 | 101 | 8.02 |
| 9.35 | 12-00 | 108.24 | 109.16 | 8.42 |
| 8.85 | 7-01 | 105.24 | 106.8 | 8.25 |
| 8.38 | 12-01 | 102.24 | 103.8 | 8.07 |

**Bank for Co-ops**

| Rate | Mat | Bid | Asked | Yld |
|---|---|---|---|---|
| 6.15 | 1-77 | 100 | 100.1 | 2.33 |
| 5.80 | 2-77 | 100 | 100.4 | 4.09 |
| 5.65 | 3-77 | 100.3 | 100.7 | 4.20 |
| 7.70 | 4-77 | 100.22 | 100.30 | 3.88 |
| 5.60 | 4-77 | 100.6 | 100.10 | 4.29 |
| 5.25 | 5-77 | 100.4 | 100.8 | 4.48 |
| 5.20 | 6-77 | 100.5 | 100.9 | 4.48 |
| 4.75 | 7-77 | 99.31 | 100.1 | 4.69 |
| 8.55 | 10-78 | 105 | 105.16 | 5.21 |
| 8.00 | 10-79 | 105.4 | 105.20 | 5.75 |
| 7.75 | 1-86 | 105 | 105.16 | 6.92 |

**Inter-Amer. Devel. Bk.**

| Rate | Mat | Bid | Asked | Yld |
|---|---|---|---|---|
| 4.25 | 12-82 | 88.16 | 89.16 | 6.40 |
| 4.50 | 4-84 | 87 | 88 | 6.61 |
| 4.50 | 11-84 | 86.8 | 87.8 | 6.61 |
| 8.25 | 1-85 | 104.24 | 105.8 | 7.37 |
| 8.00 | 3-85 | 103.12 | 103.28 | 7.36 |
| 8.38 | 2-86 | 105.16 | 106 | 7.45 |
| 5.20 | 1-92 | 79 | 80 | 7.43 |
| 6.50 | 11-92 | 89 | 90 | 7.59 |

**FNMA Issues**

| Rate | Mat | Bid | Asked | Yld |
|---|---|---|---|---|
| 4.50 | 2-77 | 99.24 | 100.4 | 3.22 |
| 6.30 | 3-77 | 100.4 | 100.12 | 4.19 |
| 7.05 | 3-77 | 100.8 | 100.16 | 4.25 |
| 8.30 | 3-77 | 100.16 | 100.24 | 4.13 |
| 6.38 | 6-77 | 100.16 | 100.24 | 4.60 |
| 6.50 | 6-77 | 100.18 | 100.26 | 4.58 |
| 7.20 | 6-77 | 100.28 | 101.4 | 4.55 |
| 6.88 | 9-77 | 101.4 | 101.16 | 4.63 |
| 7.38 | 9-77 | 101.16 | 101.28 | 4.57 |
| 7.85 | 9-77 | 101.24 | 102.4 | 4.68 |
| 7.25 | 12-77 | 101.24 | 102.8 | 4.77 |
| 7.55 | 12-77 | 102 | 102.16 | 4.89 |
| 8.45 | 3-78 | 103.12 | 103.28 | 5.03 |
| 6.70 | 3-78 | 101.12 | 101.28 | 5.04 |
| 7.15 | 6-78 | 102.4 | 102.20 | 5.23 |
| 7.45 | 6-78 | 102.20 | 103.4 | 5.17 |
| 7.15 | 9-78 | 102.16 | 103 | 5.26 |
| 7.45 | 9-78 | 103 | 103.16 | 5.25 |
| 6.75 | 12-78 | 102.12 | 102.28 | 5.17 |
| 8.95 | 12-78 | 106.4 | 106.20 | 5.31 |
| 7.25 | 3-79 | 103 | 103.16 | 5.53 |
| 7.85 | 6-79 | 104.16 | 105 | 5.63 |
| 9.80 | 6-79 | 108.16 | 109.16 | 5.58 |
| 6.40 | 9-79 | 101.12 | 101.28 | 5.63 |
| 7.80 | 9-79 | 104.16 | 105 | 5.78 |
| 8.50 | 10-79 | 106.12 | 106.28 | 5.77 |
| 6.55 | 12-79 | 101.24 | 102.8 | 5.70 |
| 7.75 | 12-79 | 104.24 | 105.8 | 5.78 |
| 6.88 | 3-80 | 101.24 | 102.24 | 5.91 |
| 7.25 | 3-80 | 103.4 | 103.20 | 5.98 |
| 7.38 | 4-80 | 103.16 | 104 | 6.00 |
| 8.50 | 6-80 | 107.4 | 107.20 | 6.01 |
| 7.50 | 9-80 | 103.16 | 104.16 | 6.11 |
| 8.75 | 9-80 | 108.4 | 108.20 | 6.10 |
| 6.60 | 12-80 | 101 | 102 | 6.02 |
| 8.00 | 12-80 | 105.28 | 106.12 | 6.15 |
| 7.05 | 3-81 | 102.8 | 103.8 | 6.15 |
| 7.35 | 3-81 | 103.20 | 104.4 | 6.21 |
| 7.25 | 6-81 | 103.4 | 104.4 | 6.17 |
| 7.95 | 6-81 | 106 | 106.16 | 6.25 |
| 7.25 | 9-81 | 103.8 | 104.8 | 6.19 |
| 9,70 | 9-81 | 112.20 | 113.20 | 6.29 |
| 6.45 | 12-81 | 100.24 | 101 | 6.21 |
| 7.30 | 12-81 | 103.12 | 104.12 | 6.25 |
| 8.88 | 3-82 | 109.28 | 110.28 | 6.38 |
| 6.65 | 6-82 | 100.12 | 101.12 | 6.35 |
| 6.80 | 9-82 | 100.28 | 101.28 | 6.40 |
| 8.60 | 10-82 | 109.4 | 109.20 | 6.57 |
| 7.35 | 12-82 | 103 | 104 | 6.52 |
| 7.75 | 3-83 | 105.4 | 105.20 | 6.62 |
| 6.75 | 6-83 | 100.12 | 101.12 | 6.48 |
| 7.30 | 6-83 | 102.24 | 103.24 | 6.57 |
| 8.10 | 6-83 | 106.24 | 107.8 | 6.69 |
| 6.75 | 9-83 | 100.12 | 101.12 | 6.49 |
| 8.00 | 12-83 | 106.20 | 107.20 | 6.61 |
| 8.40 | 12-83 | 108.8 | 109.8 | 6.71 |
| 6.25 | 6-84 | 97.12 | 98.12 | 6.53 |
| 8.20 | 7-84 | 106.2 | 107.20 | 6.88 |
| 7.95 | 9-84 | 105.20 | 106.20 | 6.82 |
| 6.90 | 12-84 | 100 | 101 | 6.73 |
| 7.65 | 3-85 | 103.8 | 104.8 | 6.86 |
| 7.90 | 10-85 | 105.12 | 105.28 | 6.99 |
| 7.95 | 7-86 | 105.12 | 105.28 | 7.08 |
| 7.90 | 9-86 | 105.4 | 105.20 | 7.08 |
| 7.30 | 12-86 | 101.30 | 102.6 | 6.99 |
| 7.80 | 10-91 | 103.24 | 104.8 | 7.32 |
| 7.00 | 3-92 | 97.8 | 98.8 | 7.19 |
| 7.05 | 6-92 | 97.24 | 98.24 | 7.18 |
| 7.10 | 12-97 | 96.16 | 97.16 | 7.33 |

**Federal Land Bank**

| Rate | Mat | Bid | Asked | Yld |
|---|---|---|---|---|
| 7.45 | 1-77 | 100 | 100.4 | 4.64 |
| 8.25 | 4-77 | 100.28 | 101.4 | 4.34 |
| 6.25 | 7-77 | 100.20 | 100.28 | 4.61 |
| 7.50 | 7-77 | 101.10 | 101.18 | 4.57 |
| 6.35 | 10-77 | 100.28 | 101.12 | 4.56 |
| 6.60 | 10-77 | 101.8 | 101.16 | 4.65 |
| 6.70 | 10-77 | 101.10 | 101.18 | 4.67 |
| 6.10 | 1-78 | 101.2 | 101.10 | 4.81 |
| 8.70 | 1-78 | 103.16 | 104 | 4.76 |
| 4.13 | 2-78-73 | 98.8 | 99.8 | 4.81 |
| 5.13 | 4-78 | 99.8 | 100.8 | 4.92 |
| 7.60 | 4-78 | 102.16 | 103 | 5.17 |
| 6.40 | 7-78 | 100.28 | 101.28 | 5.12 |
| 9.15 | 7-78 | 105.8 | 105.24 | 5.23 |
| 7.35 | 10-78 | 102.24 | 103.8 | 5.42 |
| 5.00 | 1-79 | 98.28 | 99.12 | 5.32 |
| 7.10 | 1-79 | 102.20 | 103.4 | 5.47 |
| 6.85 | 4-79 | 101.28 | 102.28 | 5.50 |
| 8.55 | 4-79 | 105.28 | 106.12 | 5.56 |
| 7.15 | 7-79 | 103.4 | 103.20 | 5.61 |
| 6.80 | 10-79 | 102 | 103 | 5.63 |
| 6.70 | 1-80 | 101.20 | 102.20 | 5.75 |
| 7.35 | 4-80 | 103.20 | 104.4 | 5.95 |
| 7.50 | 7-80 | 103.28 | 104.28 | 5.95 |
| 8.70 | 10-80 | 107.28 | 108.12 | 6.19 |
| 7.10 | 1-81 | 103.4 | 103.12 | 6.14 |
| 6.70 | 4-81 | 101.20 | 102.20 | 5.99 |
| 9.10 | 7-81 | 110.16 | 111.16 | 6.16 |
| 7.45 | 10-81 | 104.15 | 105 | 5.22 |
| 7.80 | 1-82 | 105.28 | 106.12 | 5.30 |
| 6.90 | 4-82 | 101.20 | 102.20 | 6.31 |
| 8.15 | 4-82 | 106.24 | 107.8 | 6.51 |
| 7.30 | 10-82 | 103.12 | 104.12 | 6.38 |
| 8.20 | 1-83 | 107.12 | 107.28 | 6.60 |
| 7.30 | 10-83 | 103 | 104 | 6.56 |
| 8.10 | 7-85 | 106.24 | 107.8 | 6.96 |
| 7.95 | 10-85 | 105.28 | 106.12 | 6.94 |
| 8.80 | 10-85 | 110.16 | 111 | 7.09 |
| 7.85 | 1-88 | 105 | 105.16 | 7.11 |
| 7.95 | 4-91 | 105.24 | 106.8 | 7.24 |
| 7.95 | 10-96 | 104.4 | 104.20 | 7.50 |

| | | | | |
|---|---|---|---|---|
| 6.63 | 11-93 | 88.24 | 89.24 | 7.72 |
| 8.63 | 10-95 | 104 | 104.16 | 8.15 |
| 9.00 | 2-01 | 106.8 | 107 | 8.32 |
| 8.75 | 7-01 | 105 | 105.16 | 8.22 |

**FIGURE 18**
Newspaper List of Government, Agency, and Miscellaneous Debt Securities Transactions

day based upon the bid price. Therefore, yesterday's bid was 85.24 (86 4/32 − 12/32), equal to $857.50 per bond.

6 The $871.25 offering price per bond is equivalent to a yield to maturity of 6.25% when one takes into account the guaranteed appreciation if held until 1985, plus the interest coupon of $42.50 ($1,000 × 4¼%) per year.

With the exception of the U.S. Treasury bills, identical analysis can be accorded to all of the other debt instruments listed in this table. Treasury bills, which range in duration up to 1 year from date of issuance, are listed in order of maturity month and day. There is no column for yield because bill prices are already discounted and expressed in terms of that security's yield-to-maturity. Hence, the bid price is always numerically higher than its offering price. The higher percentage discount from par value always means a lower dollar price.

For example, look at the January 20 bill noted in the tables. Its remaining lifetime is just 21 days from December 30, 1976. This bill is offered at a dollar value, discounted from its face amount. If purchased on December 30, 1976 the average rate of return for that investor, on an annualized basis, would be 4.09%. Because it is purchased for less than face amount and redeemed at maturity for its face amount, the difference in dollars, based upon the money actually invested, equals 4.09%.

## D4.
### Tables for Investment Companies (Mutual Funds)

The *Wall Street Journal*'s financial stock and bond tables additionally include market statistics for the most popular investment companies. Information about the larger mutual funds is published daily, whereas figures for the smaller funds, closed-end companies, specialty funds, and dual-purpose funds appear weekly in the Monday edition of the newspaper (See Figure 19). From the segment of the daily table in this figure, we can see that the funds are arranged in alphabetical order and by management group,[11] also in alphabetical order.

The bid price in the quotation of a mutual fund is identified as its net asset value (NAV). As is the case with any OTC security, the holder of these shares can, in most instances, dispose of them at the bid price, albeit via redemption rather than to another investor or to a market-maker. The offering price is a fixed price dependent upon the bid. It is inclusive of the *maximum* sales charge employed to sell those shares to the investing public.[12] Observe the many offering prices without a number, just the letters "N. L." "N. L." means "no load" and indicates that

1. there is no sales charge for this fund; and
2. the offering price is the same as the bid price.

Let us briefly analyze the quotation for the Audax Fund (highlighted in Figure 19.). It is shown as $7.93 bid and offered at $8.67, up $.04 from yesterday's closing bid price. Change in NAV is figured on the basis of closing-to-closing prices. The difference between current bid and offer prices is a sales charge of

[11]The entity that controls several funds, each fund with different investment objectives. Because of these centralized control relationships, they are referred to in the industry as "families of funds."

[12]This price is subject to sales-charge discounts made available to quantity purchasers (breakpoint transactions).

$.74 ($8.67 − $7.93). If that charge is then divided by the offering price itself, the result is the percentage of sales load levied. This percentage equals 8½%, the maximum amount permitted under current NASD rules.

$$\frac{\$\ .74}{\$8.67} = .085, \text{ or } 8\frac{1}{2}\%$$

> The funds represented in the top two weekly listings in Figure 19 are closed-end investment companies. Those listed in the bottom table are open-end funds. The most unique feature about the closed-end funds is that their market prices are not tied directly to their net asset values. This point is brought forth dramatically in these tables when both the NAV and open-market price of each fund's stock are presented side by side. The right-hand column shows the percentage premium (+) or discount (−) at which the stock sells in comparison to that fund's net asset value. In all but one instance, the closed-end companies are selling at discounts from net asset values. Some funds are selling by as much as 35–37% below what each share would be worth if the company liquidated itself. Historically, that situation is typical for most closed-end investment company shares.

D5.
*Stock Option Tables*

No discussion of newspaper financial tables would be complete without reviewing the transaction reporting techniques of the listed options marketplace. (Early in 1977 only call options were traded on exchanges and consequently references to items shown in Figure 20 refer to calls exclusively.) The few put option classes that will trade during its pilot program are identifiable in the tables by the letter "p" between the option name and exercise price. For example IBM p 70. These tables list separately the options transactions on each exchange, including those that are traded on more than one exchange (dually listed). The presentation is organized first horizontally, categorizing listed options by expiration month, and then vertically, for alphabetic listings of underlying stocks and exercise prices available for those issues.

To explain how to read these tables, let us analyze the activity that took place in $30 call options of Houston Oil and Minerals Corp. (as highlighted in two places in Figure 20). Houston Oil and Minerals options are dually listed and are traded on the Chicago Board Options Exchange (CBOE) and the Pacific Stock Exchange (PSE).

| 1 | 3 | | CBOE | | | | 2 |
|---|---|---|---|---|---|---|---|
| Option & | JAN | | APR | | JUL | | N.Y. |
| Price | Vol. | Last | Vol. | Last | Vol. | Last | Close |
| Hou OM 30 | 147 | 16¾ | 3 | 17¾ | 2 | 17¼ | 46½ |
| | 4 | 5 | | | | | |

| | 3 | | PSE | | | | 2 |
|---|---|---|---|---|---|---|---|
| Option & | JAN | | APR | | JUL | | N.Y. |
| Price | Vol. | Last | Vol. | Last | Vol. | Last | Close |
| Hou OM 30 | 30 | 16⅜ | 2 | 17⅛ | a | a | 46½ |
| | 4 | 5 | | | | 6 | |

# Mutual Funds

Thursday, December 30, 1976

Price ranges for investment companies, as quoted by the National Association of Securities Dealers. NAV stands for net asset value per share; the offering includes net asset value plus maximum sales charge, if any.

| | Offer NAV | | | | Offer NAV | |
|---|---|---|---|---|---|---|
| | NAV | Price Chg. | | | NAV | Price Chg. |
| Acorn Fnd | 13.94 | N.L.+ .11 | | Growth | 8.66 | 9.46+ .05 |
| Adv Invest | 11.18 | N.L.+ .06 | | Income | 10.73 | 11.73+ .02 |
| Aetna Fnd | 7.95 | 8.69+ .01 | | Resrch | 16.06 | 17.55+ .03 |
| Aetna InSh | 13.26 | 14.49+ .05 | | LifeIns Inv | 7.40 | 8.09— .25 |
| Afuture Fd | 9.62 | N.L.+ .07 | | **Lincoln National Funds:** | | |
| AGE Fund | 5.40 | 5.51+ .11 | | Selct Am | 7.34 | N.L.+ .03 |
| Allstate | 9.55 | 10.27+ .04 | | Selct Spl | 13.69 | N.L.+ .06 |
| Alpha Fnd | 11.43 | (z) + .04 | | **Loomis Sayles Funds:** | | |
| Am Birthrt | 9.75 | 10.66+ .05 | | Cap Dev | 10.94 | N.L.+ .07 |
| Am Equity | 5.36 | 5.87+ .03 | | Mutual | 13.89 | N.L.+ .08 |
| **American Funds Group:** | | | | **Lord Abbett:** | | |
| Am Bal | 8.32 | 9.09+ .03 | | Affilatd | 8.44 | 9.10+ .05 |
| Amcap F | 5.67 | 6.20+ .05 | | Bond Deb | 11.48 | 12.55+ .03 |
| Am Mutl | 10.11 | 11.05+ .05 | | Income | 3.55 | 3.83+ .02 |
| Bnd FdA | 15.21 | 16.62 | | **Lutheran Brotherhd Fds:** | | |
| Cap FdA | 6.70 | 7.32+ .04 | | Broth Fd | 10.92 | 11.93+ .02 |
| Gth FdA | 4.66 | 5.09+ .04 | | Broh Inc | 9.45 | 10.33— .07 |
| IncF Am | 16.85 | 18.42+ .06 | | Bro MBd | 10.08 | 11.02+ .01 |
| I C A | 14.60 | 15.96+ .08 | | Broth US | 10.07 | 11.01 ... |
| Nw Prsp | 16.49 | 18.02+ .09 | | **Mass. Company:** | | |
| Wash Mt | 7.21 | 7.88+ .03 | | Freedm | 8.25 | 9.02+ .03 |
| **American General Group:** | | | | Indep Fd | 7.60 | 8.31+ .03 |
| A GenBd | 8.99 | 9.83+ .01 | | Mass Fd | 10.97 | 11.99+ .05 |
| A GC Gr | 4.35 | 4.75+ .01 | | **Mass Financial Svcs:** | | |
| A Gn Inc | 6.73 | 7.36+ .01 | | MIT | 11.41 | 12.30+ .07 |
| A GnVen | 11.20 | 12.24+ .13 | | MIG | 9.21 | 9.93+ .03 |
| Eqty Gth | 7.01 | 7.66+ .04 | | MID | 15.07 | 16.25+ .07 |
| Fd Amer | 6.89 | 7.53+ .03 | | MFD | 12.40 | 13.37+ .04 |
| Prov Inc | 3.93 | 4.24+ .01 | | MCD | 13.22 | 14.25+ .06 |
| Am Grwth | 5.39 | 5.81+ .04 | | MFB | 16.08 | 17.34+ .04 |
| Am Ins Ind | 4.98 | 5.44+ .03 | | Mather Fd | 13.24 | N.L.+ .08 |
| Am Invest | 5.44 | N.L.+ .07 | | ML CapFd | 14.07 | 15.05+ .04 |
| AmNat Gw | 2.79 | 3.05+ .01 | | ML RdyAs | 1.00 | N.L. ... |
| **Anchor Group:** | | | | Mid Amer | 5.32 | 5.81+ .04 |
| Daily Inc | 1.00 | N.L. ... | | Money Mkt | 1.00 | N.L. ... |
| Growth | 7.29 | 7.86+ .03 | | MONY Fd | 9.91 | 10.83+ .06 |
| Income | 7.71 | 8.31+ .03 | | MSB Fund | 15.24 | N.L.+ .03 |
| Reserv | 10.22 | N.L.+ .01 | | Mutl BnFd | 9.64 | 10.54+ .04 |
| Spectm | 5.01 | 5.40+ .02 | | M I F Fd | 9.02 | 9.75+ .04 |
| Fund Inv | 7.38 | 7.96+ .03 | | M I F Gro | 4.02 | 4.35+ .01 |
| Wa Natl | 10.68 | 11.51+ .06 | | **Mutual of Omaha Funds:** | | |
| Audax Fnd | 7.93 | 8.67+ .04 | | Amer | 11.96 | 12.14+ .02 |
| **Axe-Houghton:** | | | | Growth | 4.41 | 4.79+ .02 |
| Fund B | 8.06 | 8.76+ .04 | | Income | 9.65 | 10.49+ .04 |
| Income | 5.02 | 5.46+ .01 | | Mutl Shars | 29.34 | N.L.+ .23 |
| Stock Fd | 6.38 | 6.97+ .01 | | Natl Indust | 11.29 | N.L.+ .01 |
| BLC Gwth | 10.87 | 11.88+ .01 | | **National Securities Funds:** | | |
| Babsn Inc | 1.82 | N.L. ... | | Balanc | 9.89 | 10.66+ .03 |
| Babsn Inv | 9.99 | N.L.+ .05 | | Bond | 4.67 | 5.04+ .01 |
| Beacon Hll | 8.75 | N.L.+ .03 | | Dividnd | 4.17 | 4.50+ .02 |
| Beacon Inv | 9.77 | N.L.+ .05 | | Preferd | 7.54 | 8.13+ .02 |
| **Berger Group Funds:** | | | | Income | 5.53 | 5.96+ .03 |
| 100 Fund | 7.45 | N.L.+ .06 | | Stock | 8.48 | 9.14+ .04 |
| 101 Fund | 9.31 | N.L.+ .03 | | Grwth | 5.94 | 6.40+ .01 |
| Brksh Cap | 8.43 | 9.21+ .07 | | **New Eng Life Fds:** | | |
| Bondsk Cp | 5.03 | 5.50+ .03 | | Equity | 17.85 | 19.40+ .11 |
| Bos Found | 9.67 | 10.57+ .02 | | Grwth | 9.14 | 9.93+ .05 |
| Brown Fnd | 3.57 | 3.85+ .03 | | Income | 14.36 | 15.61+ .04 |
| **Calvin Bullock Funds:** | | | | Side | 14.35 | 15.60+ .07 |
| Bullock | 13.45 | 14.70+ .07 | | | | |
| Canadn | 7.85 | 8.58+ .03 | | | | |
| Div Shrs | 3.26 | 3.57+ .02 | | z-Quote not available. NL- | | |
| Income | 15.04 | 16.44+ .04 | | No load. x-Ex-dividend. r- | | |
| Ntwide | 10.34 | 11.30+ .05 | | Ex-rights. d Ex-distribution | | |
| NY Vent | 11.52 | 12.59+ .05 | | a-funds redemption price. | | |
| C G Fund | 10.48 | 11.33+ .04 | | | | |
| CG Inc Fd | 8.73 | 9.44+ .03 | | | | |
| Cap Presv | 1.00 | N.L. ... | | | | |
| Century Sh | 11.98 | 12.92+ .10 | | | | |
| Chalng Inv | 10.41 | 11.38+ .03 | | | | |
| Charter Fd | 13.92 | 15.21+ .09 | | | | |

# Closed-End Funds

Thursday, December 23, 1976

Following is a weekly listing of unaudited net asset values of closed-end investment fund shares, reported by the companies as of Friday's close. Also shown is the closing listed market price or a dealer-to-dealer asked price of each fund's shares, with the percentage of difference.

| | N.A. Value | Stk Price | % Diff |  | N.A. Value | Stk Price | % Diff |
|---|---|---|---|---|---|---|---|
| **Diversified Funds** | | | | ChaseCvB | z | z | z |
| AdmExp | 15.68 | 12¾ | —18.7 | CLIC | (—7.92) | ... | ... |
| BakerFen | 56.21 | 35 | —37.7 | Diebold | 9.07 | 6⅛ | —32.5 |
| Carriers | 17.87 | 14⅜ | —19.6 | Japan | 12.48 | 9 | —27.9 |
| CentSec | 8.69 | 5⅞ | —32.3 | KeysnOTC | 10.03 | 7⅛ | —29.0 |
| GenAInv | 13.85 | 11¾ | —15.2 | NatlAvia | 23.49 | 15⅝ | —33.5 |
| Lehman | 14.72 | 12¼ | —16.8 | NewAmFd | 16.80 | 12 | —28.6 |
| Madison | 16.93 | 12⅝ | —25.4 | PetroCp | 26.76 | 27½ | + 2.8 |
| NiagaraSh | 13.88 | 12⅜ | —10.8 | RETIncC | z | z | z |
| OseasSec | 4.57 | 3⅞ | —15.2 | S-GSecInc | 1.59 | 1¼ | —21.4 |
| Tri-Contl | 27.00 | 21⅝ | —19.9 | Source | 16.99 | 13¼ | —22.0 |
| United | 11.57 | 10⅜ | —10.3 | StdSh | 38.59 | 24¾ | —35.9 |
| US&For | z | z | z | ValueLn | z | z | z |
| **Specialized Equity and Convertible Funds** | | | | a-Ex-Dividend. z-Not Available. b-as of Thursdays close. | | | |
| AmUtllS | 14.90 | 11½ | —22.8 | | | | |
| bASA | z | z | z | | | | |
| BancrftCv | 22.38 | 17 | —24.0 | | | | |
| Castle | 23.29 | 17¾ | —23.8 | | | | |

# Dual-Purpose Funds

Thursday, December 23, 1976

Following is a weekly listing of the unaudited net asset values of dual-purpose, closed-end investment funds' capital shares as reported by the companies as of Friday's close. Also shown is the closing listed market price or the dealer-to-dealer asked price of each fund's capital shares, with the percentage of difference.

| | Cap. Shs. Price | N.A. Val. Cap. Shs. | % Diff. |
|---|---|---|---|
| Am DualVest | 7¾ | 9.44 | —17.9 |
| Gemini | 18¼ | 24.63 | —25.9 |
| Hemisphere | | 1.66 | — 2.1 |
| Income and Cap | 7⅛ | 10.59 | —32.7 |
| Leverage | 12⅛ | 17.00 | —28.7 |
| Pegasus Inco&Cap | 8¾ | 9.56 | — 8.5 |
| Putnam Duo Fund | 7⅜ | 10.27 | — 8.2 |
| Scudder Duo-Vest | 7⅝ | 10.44 | —26.9 |
| Scudder D-V Exch | 20 | 31.16 | —35.8 |
| Lipper Analytical Distributors. | | | |

# Weekly Mutual Funds

| | | | | | | |
|---|---|---|---|---|---|---|
| AmFd Govt Sec | 25.53 | 25.98 | | Lincoln Nat Inc | (z) | (z) |
| Am Gen Growth | (z) | (z) | | LordAbt Dev Gr | 10.55 | 11.53 |
| BLC Income Fd | 11.87 | 12.97 | | | | |
| Capital ExchFd | 30.60 | (z) | | MassFund Incm | 15.67 | 17.13 |
| Congress Str Fd | 31.80 | (z) | | MoneyMkt Oplv | 17.36 | 18.42 |
| Constitution Fd | x46.55 | N.L. | | Nassau Fund | 12.63 | N.L |
| Daily IncomeFd | (z) | (z) | | Ocean TechnFd | (z) | (z) |
| Deposit FndBos | 22.78 | (z) | | | | |
| Devnshire St Fd | 11.83 | N.L. | | Safeco IncomeF | (z) | (z) |
| Divesifcatn Fd | 36.22 | (z) | | Scudder Dev Fd | 47.62 | 48.59 |
| Exchang FdBos | 42.38 | (z) | | 2nd Fiduciary | 30.59 | (z) |
| Exeter Fund | 41.67 | (z) | | SecurtyBond Fd | 10.10 | 10.39 |
| Federal StFund | (z) | (z) | | Sentinel Trustes | 10.70 | 11.63 |
| Fiduciary ExFd | 24.32 | (z) | | S & P Liq Asset | (z) | (z) |
| Josten GrwthFd | (z) | (z) | | Sun Growth Fd | 9.40 | 10.05 |
| | | | | Vance Sandr Fd | 52.13 | (z) |

**FIGURE 19**
Mutual Funds Tables

1 Houston Oil and Minerals Corporation is abbreviated in the table as "Hou OM." Each option gives you as holder a right to buy 100 shares of the underlying stock at $30 per share anytime up to 5 P.M. (Eastern time) on the expiration date.

2 The closing price of the underlying stock on the New York Stock Exchange is given in the last column to allow you to compare prices of the option and the stock. On this day Houston Oil and Minerals closed at 46½ on the NYSE. The call privilege therefore has a conversion value of $16.50. (The conversion value is the difference between 46½ for the underlying stock and 30, the exercise price of the option.) The actual value of this call option is determined by the forces of supply and demand as reflected in the

# Chicago Board

| Option & price | | Jan Vol. | Jan Last | Apr Vol. | Apr Last | Jul Vol. | Jul Last | N.Y. Close |
|---|---|---|---|---|---|---|---|---|
| Alcoa | 45 | 8 | 12⅞ | b | b | b | b | 57⅛ |
| Alcoa | 50 | 21 | 7 | a | a | a | a | 57⅛ |
| Alcoa | 55 | 32 | 2¾ | b | b | b | b | 57⅛ |
| Alcoa | 60 | 67 | ⅜ | 8 | 1⅝ | 7 | 2⅝ | 57⅛ |
| Am Tel | 55 | 30 | 9 | 9 | 9¼ | a | a | 63⅞ |
| Am Tel | 60 | 275 | 4 | 72 | 4⅝ | 25 | 5 | 63⅞ |
| Am Tel | 65 | b | b | 187 | 1⅜ | 208 | 1 15-16 | 63⅞ |
| Atl R | 40 | 6 | 18½ | b | b | b | b | 58⅜ |
| Atl R | 45 | 14 | 12⅜ | a | a | b | b | 58⅜ |
| Atl R | 50 | 79 | 8⅜ | 33 | 9¼ | a | a | 58⅜ |
| Atl R | 60 | 290 | 1 | 239 | 3 | 51 | 4⅛ | 58⅜ |
| Avon | 40 | 164 | 9 | 113 | 9⅞ | 6 | 10⅜ | 49 |
| Avon | 45 | 933 | 4¼ | 311 | 5¾ | 35 | 6¾ | 49 |
| Avon | 50 | 958 | 15-16 | 621 | 2 11-16 | 105 | 3⅝ | 49 |
| BankAm | 25 | 34 | 4⅞ | 111 | 5 | 46 | 5⅜ | 29⅞ |
| BankAm | 30 | 139 | ⅝ | 122 | 1⅝ | 57 | 2⅛ | 29⅞ |
| Beth S | 35 | 12 | 5¾ | 7 | 6⅜ | 5 | 6⅝ | 40⅝ |
| Beth S | 40 | 148 | 1⅛ | 156 | 2 5-16 | 22 | 3 | 40⅝ |
| Beth S | 45 | 7 | 1-16 | 52 | 11-16 | b | b | 40⅝ |
| Bruns | 10 | 11 | 6 | b | b | b | b | 16 |
| Bruns | 15 | 174 | 1⅜ | 75 | 2⅛ | 142 | 2 9-16 | 16 |
| Bruns | 20 | 15 | 1-16 | 127 | 7-16 | 60 | ¾ | 16 |
| Burl N | 40 | 59 | 5½ | 16 | 7¼ | 4 | 7½ | 44¾ |
| Burl N | 45 | 116 | 1⅛ | 49 | 3⅛ | 42 | 4 | 44¾ |
| Burl N | 50 | 102 | 1-16 | 36 | 1 | b | b | 44¾ |
| Citicp | 25 | 34 | 7⅜ | 2 | 7⅞ | 35 | 8 | 32½ |
| Citicp | 30 | 102 | 2 7-16 | 101 | 3½ | 77 | 4¼ | 32½ |
| Citicp | 35 | 174 | 1-16 | 128 | ⅞ | 48 | 1½ | 32½ |
| Citicp | 40 | 2 | 1-16 | 40 | ⅛ | b | b | 32½ |
| Delta | 35 | 49 | 3⅞ | 18 | 4⅞ | 26 | 6 | 38¼ |
| Delta | 40 | 92 | ⅝ | 139 | 2 | 106 | 3 | 38¼ |
| Delta | 45 | 3 | 1-16 | 109 | ½ | b | b | 38¼ |
| Dow Ch | 40 | 692 | 3½ | 305 | 4⅞ | 64 | 6¼ | 43½ |
| Dow Ch | 45 | 733 | ½ | 592 | 2¼ | 105 | 3⅛ | 43½ |
| Dow Ch | 50 | 74 | 1-16 | 294 | ¾ | b | b | 43½ |
| Eas Kd | 80 | 867 | 7½ | 257 | 10⅜ | 145 | 12⅜ | 86⅜ |
| Eas Kd | 90 | 1405 | ⅞ | 887 | 4½ | 190 | 6½ | 86⅜ |
| Eas Kd | 100 | 301 | 1-16 | 812 | 1⅜ | b | b | 86⅜ |
| Eas Kd | 110 | 18 | 1-16 | 27 | 5-16 | b | b | 86⅜ |
| Exxon | 45 | 88 | 8¼ | 14 | 8½ | 2 | 9 | 53½ |
| Exxon | 50 | 311 | 3½ | 173 | 4½ | 25 | 5⅛ | 53½ |
| Exxon | 55 | 216 | ½ | 295 | 1½ | b | b | 53½ |
| Exxon | 60 | 20 | 1-16 | 2 | 7-16 | 36 | 13-16 | 53½ |
| F N M | 15 | 1089 | 2 1-16 | 425 | 2⅜ | 349 | 2 9-16 | 17⅛ |
| F N M | 20 | 103 | 1-16 | 471 | 5-16 | 742 | ½ | 17⅛ |
| Fluor | 30 | 6 | 8⅜ | a | a | a | a | 38⅜ |
| Fluor | 35 | 43 | 3⅞ | 58 | 5⅛ | 2 | 6 | 38⅜ |
| Fluor | 40 | 59 | 9-16 | 112 | 2¼ | 40 | 3⅛ | 38⅜ |
| Fluor | 45 | 2 | 1-16 | 27 | 1 | b | b | 38⅜ |
| Ford | 50 | 139 | 11⅝ | 38 | 12⅛ | 96 | 12¾ | 61½ |
| Ford | 60 | 698 | 2 5-16 | 580 | 4 | 209 | 5¼ | 61½ |
| Gen El | 50 | 1120 | 4⅞ | 174 | 6⅛ | 53 | 6⅞ | 54⅞ |
| Gen El | 55 | 717 | 1 1-16 | 571 | 2 13-16 | 78 | 3⅞ | 54⅞ |
| Gen El | 60 | 76 | 1-16 | 243 | 15-16 | b | b | 54⅞ |
| G M | 60 | 319 | 18½ | 65 | 18⅝ | b | b | 78¼ |
| G M | 70 | 743 | 8½ | 209 | 9 | 97 | 9⅞ | 78¼ |
| G M | 80 | 1489 | 1⅛ | 613 | 2 15-16 | 213 | 4 | 78¼ |
| Gt Wst | 15 | 8 | 8¼ | 2 | 8⅞ | 1 | 8⅝ | 23⅜ |
| Gt Wst | 20 | 69 | 3⅝ | 77 | 4¼ | 2 | 4½ | 23⅜ |
| Gt Wst | 25 | 22 | ¼ | 108 | 1 5-16 | 51 | 2 | 23⅜ |
| Glf Wn | 15 | 88 | 3¼ | 92 | 3⅞ | 199 | 4¼ | 18¼ |
| Glf Wn | 20 | 425 | ⅛ | 549 | ⅞ | 299 | 1⅜ | 18¼ |
| GfWn O | 16 | 102 | 2⅜ | b | b | b | b | b |
| GfWn O | 20 | 30 | 3-16 | b | b | b | b | b |
| Halbtn | 60 | 49 | 6 | 46 | 7⅞ | a | a | 65⅞ |
| Halbtn | 70 | 122 | ⅜ | 101 | 2¼ | 9 | 3¼ | 65⅞ |
| Homstk | 25 | 15 | 11⅞ | 5 | 11½ | b | b | 36¾ |
| Homstk | 30 | 53 | 6⅞ | 43 | 7½ | 2 | 7½ | 36¾ |
| Homstk | 35 | 242 | 2 7-16 | 213 | 3⅞ | 25 | 4⅞ | 36¾ |
| Homstk | 40 | 193 | 5-16 | 97 | 1⅝ | 31 | 2½ | 36¾ |
| Hou OM | 30 | 147 | 16¾ | 3 | 17¾ | 2 | 17¼ | 46½ |
| Hou OM | 35 | 221 | 11¾ | 158 | 13 | 150 | 13⅞ | 46½ |
| Hou OM | 40 | 733 | 6⅝ | 338 | 8⅝ | 119 | 9⅞ | 46½ |
| Hou OM | 45 | b | b | 1051 | 5 | 240 | 6⅝ | 46½ |
| I N A | 35 | 22 | 12¼ | a | a | b | b | 47⅛ |
| I N A | 40 | 64 | 7¼ | 10 | 7⅜ | a | a | 47⅛ |
| I N A | 45 | 92 | 2¼ | 60 | 3½ | 29 | 4 | 47⅛ |
| I B M | 240 | 875 | 40¼ | b | b | b | b | 278½ |
| I B M | 260 | 4832 | 20⅝ | 1269 | 27½ | 661 | 33½ | 278½ |
| I B M | 280 | 6221 | 4½ | 2087 | 12⅝ | 596 | 18¾ | 278½ |
| In Har | 25 | 55 | 7⅝ | 16 | 7¾ | 26 | 7⅞ | 32¾ |
| In Har | 30 | 454 | 2 11-16 | 213 | 3⅜ | 78 | 3⅞ | 32¾ |
| In Min | 35 | 20 | 5⅛ | 8 | 5¾ | 2 | 6⅜ | 39¾ |
| In Min | 40 | 146 | 13-16 | 175 | 2 1-16 | 39 | 2¾ | 39¾ |
| In Pap | 60 | 38 | 9⅛ | 6 | 9½ | a | a | 68¾ |
| In Pap | 70 | 145 | 1⅛ | 68 | 3⅜ | 9 | 4⅜ | 68¾ |
| I T T | 25 | 21 | 9 | 7 | 9⅜ | b | b | 34 |
| I T T | 30 | 642 | 4 | 163 | 4½ | 77 | 5 | 34 |
| I T T | 35 | 480 | 7-16 | 420 | 1 5-16 | 130 | 1⅞ | 34 |
| John J | 70 | b | b | 38 | 9⅝ | 11 | 10¾ | 76⅛ |
| John J | 80 | 270 | 9-16 | 245 | 3⅛ | 71 | 4½ | 76⅛ |
| John J | 90 | a | a | 73 | ½ | 35 | 1 7-16 | 76⅛ |
| Kenn C | 25 | 38 | 2¾ | 121 | 4 | 32 | 4⅝ | 27 |

# Listed Options Quotations

Tuesday, December 28, 1976

Closing prices of all options. Sales unit usually is 100 shares. Security description includes exercise price. Stock close is New York Stock Exchange final price.

# American Exchange

| Option & price | | Jan Vol. | Jan Last | Apr Vol. | Apr Last | Jul Vol. | Jul Last | N.Y. Close |
|---|---|---|---|---|---|---|---|---|
| Aetna | 25 | 43 | 11 | 33 | 11⅛ | b | b | 35⅞ |
| Aetna | 30 | 402 | 5⅞ | 48 | 6⅝ | 51 | 7⅜ | 35⅞ |
| Aetna | 35 | 300 | 1⅜ | 212 | 2 11-16 | 69 | 3½ | 35⅞ |
| Am Cya | 25 | 90 | 2⅝ | 46 | 3 | 20 | 3¼ | 27¾ |
| Am Cya | 30 | 27 | ⅛ | 88 | ½ | 30 | ¾ | 27¾ |
| Am Hom | 30 | 243 | 2 3-16 | 102 | 2 13-16 | 84 | 3½ | 32 |
| Am Hom | 35 | 38 | ⅛ | 69 | ¾ | 108 | 1⅛ | 32 |
| Am Hom | 40 | 6 | 1-16 | a | a | b | b | 32 |
| Asarco | 15 | 44 | 1 1-16 | 4 | 1⅞ | 41 | 2⅛ | 15⅞ |
| Asarco | 20 | 4 | 1-16 | 30 | ⅜ | 44 | 11-16 | 15⅞ |
| Beat F | 25 | 181 | 3¼ | 24 | 3½ | 20 | 4 | 28⅛ |
| Beat F | 30 | 112 | ⅛ | 110 | ½ | 8 | 15-16 | 28⅛ |
| Burrgh | 80 | 76 | 10¾ | 50 | 13¼ | 57 | 15¼ | 90½ |
| Burrgh | 90 | 313 | 2⅝ | 180 | 6¾ | 168 | 9½ | 90½ |
| Burrgh | 100 | 36 | ⅛ | 78 | 2¼ | b | b | 90½ |
| Burrgh | 110 | a | a | 56 | ⅝ | b | b | 90½ |
| Chase | 25 | 21 | 4¾ | 6 | 5⅛ | 14 | 5⅜ | 29⅝ |
| Chase | 30 | 337 | 7-16 | 229 | 1 3-16 | 245 | 1⅝ | 29⅝ |
| C Tel | 15 | 41 | 2 3-16 | 64 | 2¼ | 11 | 2½ | 17¼ |
| C Tel | 20 | b | b | 9 | 3-16 | 40 | ⅜ | 17¼ |
| Deere | 30 | 46 | 1⅝ | 31 | 2⅝ | 18 | 3⅜ | 31 |
| Deere | 35 | 60 | 1-16 | 37 | 11-16 | 14 | 1¼ | 31 |
| Dig Eq | 45 | 178 | 9¼ | 99 | 11 | 103 | 11¾ | 54 |
| Dig Eq | 46⅝ | 79 | 8 | 58 | 10 | 8 | 10¾ | 54 |
| Dig Eq | 50 | 511 | 5 | 127 | 7⅝ | 72 | 9¼ | 54 |
| Dig Eq | 53⅜ | 451 | 2 7-16 | 118 | 5⅜ | 78 | 7 | 54 |
| Dig Eq | 56⅝ | 592 | 15-16 | 145 | 3½ | b | b | 54 |
| Dig Eq | 60 | 194 | ¼ | 947 | 2⅛ | 474 | 3½ | 54 |
| Disney | 38⅞ | 55 | 10 | 3 | 11 | 4 | 12 | 48⅞ |
| Disney | 43¾ | 386 | 5⅛ | 313 | 6⅞ | 23 | 8¼ | 48⅞ |
| Disney | 45 | b | b | 131 | 6 | 105 | 7¼ | 48⅞ |
| Disney | 48½ | 771 | 1⅝ | 267 | 3⅝ | 129 | 5 | 48⅞ |
| Disney | 50 | b | b | 397 | 2 13-16 | 136 | 4 | 48⅞ |
| Disney | 58¼ | 8 | 1-16 | 308 | 11-16 | b | b | 48⅞ |
| du Pnt | 120 | 111 | 15⅛ | 34 | 17¾ | 116 | 20½ | 135 |
| du Pnt | 130 | 341 | 6 | 115 | 9⅜ | 74 | 12 | 135 |
| du Pnt | 140 | 377 | 1⅛ | 215 | 4⅝ | 30 | 6¾ | 135 |
| du Pnt | 160 | 8 | 1-16 | b | b | b | b | 135 |
| Fst Ch | 9½ | 200 | 7⅜ | b | b | b | b | 16½ |
| Fst Ch | 14¼ | 38 | 2 13-16 | 105 | 3⅛ | b | b | 16½ |
| Fst Ch | 15 | 105 | 1 13-16 | 56 | 2¾ | b | b | 16½ |
| Fst Ch | 19 | 1 | ⅛ | b | b | b | b | 16½ |
| Fst Ch | 15 | b | b | b | b | 261 | 3¼ | 16½ |
| Fst Ch | 19 | b | b | 113 | 15-16 | b | b | 16½ |
| Fst Ch | 20 | 47 | 1-16 | 116 | ¾ | 189 | 1¼ | 16½ |
| G Tel | 25 | 206 | 6¾ | 3 | 6¾ | a | a | 31⅝ |
| G Tel | 30 | 566 | 1 11-16 | 162 | 1 15-16 | 169 | 2¼ | 31⅝ |
| Gillet | 25 | 123 | 2⅛ | 198 | 2 15-16 | 45 | 3½ | 27¼ |
| Gillet | 30 | 529 | 1-16 | 125 | 13-16 | 59 | 1 3-16 | 27¼ |

# Philadelphia Exchange

| | | — Feb — | | — May — | | — Aug — | | |
|---|---|---|---|---|---|---|---|---|
| Abbt L | 45 | 5 | 6 | 5 | 7¼ | a | a | 50¼ |
| Abbt L | 50 | 48 | 2⅜ | a | a | a | a | 50¼ |
| Abbt L | 60 | 8 | ¼ | a | a | b | b | 50¼ |
| A Hess | 19½ | 2 | 10 | b | b | b | b | 29½ |
| A Hess | 20 | 12 | 9¾ | 84 | 9⅝ | 2 | 9⅞ | 29½ |
| A Hess | 24⅜ | 5 | 5⅜ | b | b | b | b | 29½ |
| A Hess | 25 | 180 | 4¾ | 30 | 5¼ | 22 | 6¼ | 29½ |
| A Hess | 30 | 174 | 1½ | 116 | 2½ | 58 | 3¼ | 29½ |
| Bois C | 25 | 25 | 8½ | a | a | a | a | 33½ |
| Bois C | 30 | 15 | 3¾ | a | a | a | a | 33½ |
| Bois C | 35 | a | a | 25 | 1 9-16 | 10 | 2 5-16 | 33½ |
| Firstn | 20 | 3 | 3½ | a | a | a | a | 23¾ |
| Firstn | 25 | 14 | ¼ | 7 | 11-16 | 20 | 1⅛ | 23¾ |
| Joy | 40 | 1 | 6¼ | a | a | a | a | 46⅛ |
| Joy | 45 | 13 | 2⅞ | 6 | 4⅛ | 1 | 4⅜ | 46⅛ |
| Joy | 50 | 6 | ⅝ | 3 | 2 | b | b | 46⅛ |
| La Lnd | 25 | 17 | 3⅞ | 13 | 4½ | 2 | 4¾ | 28⅜ |
| La Lnd | 30 | 79 | 11-16 | 42 | 1⅜ | 16 | 2 | 28⅜ |
| Mariot | 15 | 28 | ⅝ | 50 | 1¼ | 3 | 1⅝ | 14 |
| Mc Der | 45 | 7 | 4¼ | 6 | 5¼ | 3 | 7 | 46½ |
| Mc Der | 50 | 42 | 1 5-16 | 37 | 2⅞ | a | a | 46½ |
| P P G | 55 | 15 | 2¾ | a | a | a | a | 56 |
| Pttstn | 35 | 39 | 3⅜ | 1 | 4½ | a | a | 38 |
| Pttstn | 40 | 103 | 15-16 | 86 | 2⅛ | 9 | 3 | 38 |
| Sun Co | 35 | a | a | 4 | 12¼ | a | a | 46¾ |
| Sun Co | 40 | 6 | 7¼ | 4 | 8¼ | a | a | 46¾ |
| Sun Co | 45 | 17 | 2¾ | 9 | 4 | 5 | 5⅛ | 46¾ |
| Trnsam | 10 | 19 | 4⅜ | 59 | 4½ | a | a | 14⅛ |
| Trnsam | 15 | 120 | 7-16 | 78 | 13-16 | 95 | 1⅛ | 14⅛ |
| Wlwrth | 20 | 16 | 5⅛ | 7 | 5¼ | 3 | 5½ | 24⅞ |
| Wlwrth | 25 | 129 | 1 | 50 | 1⅝ | 42 | 2 3-16 | 24⅞ |
| Total volume | | 6,903 | | Open interest | | | | 220,237 |

# Pacific Exchange

| Option & price | | Jan Vol. | Jan Last | Apr Vol. | Apr Last | Jul Vol. | Jul Last | N.Y. Close |
|---|---|---|---|---|---|---|---|---|
| BankAm | 25 | a | a | 14 | 5 | 9 | 5⅜ | 29⅞ |
| BankAm | 30 | 4 | ⅝ | 26 | 1 9-16 | 10 | 2 | 29⅞ |
| Clorox | 15 | a | a | 10 | ⅜ | a | a | 12⅛ |
| Cr Zel | 40 | 4 | 4¼ | a | a | a | a | 44⅞ |
| Cr Zel | 45 | a | a | 1 | 1⅝ | a | a | 44⅞ |
| D Sham | 30 | 85 | 5⅛ | a | a | b | b | 34⅞ |
| D Sham | 35 | 71 | 1 | 42 | 2 | 13 | 3¼ | 34⅞ |
| D Sham | 40 | 6 | 1-16 | 26 | 1 | b | b | 34⅞ |
| Disney | 43¾ | 18 | 5⅛ | a | a | 11 | 8¼ | 48⅞ |
| Disney | 48½ | 26 | 1 11-16 | a | a | 22 | 5 | 48⅞ |
| Disney | 50 | b | b | 16 | 2 13-16 | a | a | 48⅞ |
| Disney | 58¼ | 4 | 1-16 | a | a | b | b | 48⅞ |
| Hou OM | 30 | 30 | 16⅜ | 2 | 17⅛ | a | a | 46½ |
| Hou OM | 35 | 67 | 12 | 28 | 13 | a | a | 46½ |
| Hou OM | 40 | 210 | 6¾ | 205 | 8⅞ | 17 | 10 | 46½ |
| Hou OM | 45 | b | b | 389 | 5 | 125 | 6⅝ | 46½ |
| Levi | 20 | 18 | 7⅜ | 5 | 7¾ | a | a | 26¾ |
| Levi | 22½ | 114 | 4½ | 15 | 5⅛ | b | b | 26¾ |
| Levi | 25 | 67 | 2 5-16 | 80 | 3⅛ | 9 | 4¼ | 26¾ |
| Levi | 30 | b | b | 29 | 1 1-16 | 7 | 1 15-16 | 26¾ |
| Merril | 20 | 3 | 5½ | a | a | 1 | 6¾ | 25⅛ |
| Merril | 25 | 23 | 1¼ | 32 | 2¾ | a | a | 25⅛ |
| Merril | 30 | a | a | 10 | 1 | b | b | 25⅛ |
| J Morg | 50 | a | a | 10 | 7 | 13 | 7⅝ | 56¼ |
| J Morg | 60 | a | a | 2 | 1½ | a | a | 56¼ |
| N C R | 35 | 4 | 1¾ | 2 | 3½ | a | a | 36½ |
| Polar | 30 | 14 | 8⅞ | b | b | b | b | 38⅝ |
| Polar | 35 | 6 | 4⅛ | 10 | 5⅞ | 3 | 7 | 38⅝ |
| Polar | 40 | 61 | 1 1-16 | 4 | 2 15-16 | a | a | 38⅝ |
| Polar | 45 | a | a | 3 | 1 7-16 | b | b | 38⅝ |
| R C A | 20 | 20 | 7 | a | a | a | a | 26⅞ |
| R C A | 30 | 19 | ⅛ | a | a | b | b | 26⅞ |
| Sambos | 10 | 52 | 7½ | 2 | 7⅞ | a | a | 17½ |
| Sambos | 15 | 295 | 2⅝ | 141 | 3⅛ | 10 | 3⅞ | 17½ |
| Sambos | 20 | 115 | ⅛ | 249 | ¾ | 93 | 1 5-16 | 17½ |
| San Fe | 30 | 40 | 14½ | 6 | 13⅝ | b | b | 44⅜ |
| San Fe | 35 | 317 | 9½ | 55 | 9⅞ | 51 | 11 | 44⅜ |
| San Fe | 40 | 700 | 4½ | 327 | 6¼ | 103 | 7⅛ | 44⅜ |
| San Fe | 45 | b | b | 598 | 3 | 115 | 4¼ | 44⅜ |
| Teldyn | 60 | 58 | 10⅜ | 4 | 13 | 7 | 15⅜ | 69¾ |
| Teldyn | 70 | 117 | 2 9-16 | 56 | 6⅜ | 47 | 8½ | 69¾ |
| Teldyn | 80 | 30 | ⅜ | 60 | 2 11-16 | b | b | 69¾ |
| Un Oil | 50 | 100 | 8¼ | 4 | 8¾ | a | a | 58⅛ |
| Un Oil | 55 | 7 | 3¾ | 2 | 4½ | 7 | 5⅝ | 58⅛ |
| Un Oil | 60 | 44 | 9-16 | 27 | 1¾ | 7 | 2⅝ | 58⅛ |
| U S St | 50 | a | a | a | a | 1 | 3⅞ | 49½ |
| U S St | 55 | a | a | 3 | 1⅛ | a | a | 49½ |
| Xerox | 50 | 4 | 9⅛ | 71 | 10⅝ | a | a | 58⅝ |
| Xerox | 60 | 43 | 1 3-16 | 7 | 3¾ | 140 | 5⅜ | 58⅝ |
| Xerox | 70 | a | a | 10 | 1 | b | b | 58⅝ |
| | | — Feb — | | — May — | | — Aug — | | |
| A B C | 30 | 4 | 9½ | b | b | b | b | 39⅝ |
| A B C | 35 | 44 | 5½ | 8 | 6⅛ | 3 | 6⅝ | 39⅝ |
| A B C | 40 | 152 | 1⅝ | 64 | 2⅞ | 13 | 3⅝ | 39⅝ |
| F Stor | 45 | 20 | 4⅜ | a | a | a | a | 49 |
| F Stor | 50 | 43 | 1½ | a | a | a | a | 49 |
| Heubln | 40 | 8 | 4⅝ | 4 | 4¾ | 13 | 7 | 42 |
| Heubln | 45 | 8 | 1¼ | 31 | 3 | a | a | 42 |
| Heubln | 50 | 2 | ⅛ | 4 | ⅞ | b | b | 42 |
| Hilton | 20 | 6 | 3½ | a | a | a | a | 23 |
| Hilton | 25 | 6 | 9-16 | a | a | a | a | 23 |
| Mc D D | 25 | 3 | ¾ | 21 | 1 11-16 | 16 | 2⅛ | 23⅝ |
| RynMtl | 35 | 2 | 4⅜ | 1 | 5¼ | a | a | 39½ |
| RynMtl | 40 | 1 | 1⅛ | 1 | 2⅛ | 2 | 3⅛ | 39½ |
| Scher | 40 | 14 | 6 | 31 | 7¼ | a | a | 44¾ |
| Scher | 45 | 140 | 2⅜ | 69 | 3⅞ | 1 | 4½ | 44¾ |
| Scher | 50 | 4 | ½ | 73 | 1½ | b | b | 44¾ |
| Scher | 60 | 10 | 1-16 | 10 | ¼ | b | b | 44¾ |
| Travel | 30 | 18 | 6¾ | b | b | b | b | 36⅜ |
| Travel | 35 | 15 | 2½ | 11 | 4 | 8 | 4⅛ | 36⅜ |
| Travel | 40 | 5 | ½ | 5 | 1¼ | 2 | 1¾ | 36⅜ |
| Total volume | | 7,096 | | Open interest | | | | 396,051 |

# Midwest Exchange

Tuesday, Dec. 28

| Option & price | | Mar Vol. | Mar Last | Jun Vol. | Jun Last | Sep Vol. | Sep Last | N.Y. Close |
|---|---|---|---|---|---|---|---|---|
| BrisMy | 60 | 11 | 9⅛ | 28 | 2⅜ | a | a | 68½ |
| BrisMy | 70 | 38 | 2⅜ | a | a | 4 | 4⅛ | 68½ |
| Crrier | 20 | 102 | 1 1-16 | 55 | 1⅜ | 47 | 2¼ | 19½ |
| Chamln | 25 | 1 | 3 | a | a | a | a | 27¼ |
| Chamln | 30 | 66 | 9-16 | 25 | 15-16 | 4 | 1¼ | 27¼ |
| CornGl | 70 | 48 | 5 | 5 | 6½ | a | a | 72⅝ |
| CornGl | 80 | 4 | 1 | 8 | 2⅜ | a | a | 72⅝ |
| Frpt M | 25 | 5 | 5 | a | a | a | a | 29½ |
| Frpt M | 30 | 38 | 1⅛ | 28 | 1 9-16 | 13 | 2¼ | 29½ |
| Litton | 10 | a | a | a | a | 1 | 5½ | 14⅞ |
| Litton | 15 | 147 | 1⅛ | 35 | 1 11-16 | 16 | 2⅛ | 14⅞ |
| Nw Ind | 45 | 62 | 1¾ | a | a | a | a | 44¼ |
| Nw Ind | 50 | 2 | ½ | 22 | 1⅛ | b | b | 44¼ |
| Ow Ill | 50 | 31 | 6¼ | 1 | 7½ | a | a | 55¾ |
| Ow Ill | 55 | 32 | 2⅞ | 7 | 4⅞ | a | a | 55¾ |
| Ow Ill | 60 | 1 | 1 | a | a | a | a | 55¾ |
| Revlon | 40 | 70 | 5¼ | 8 | 6¼ | 1 | 6½ | 44½ |
| Revlon | 45 | 230 | 2⅛ | 84 | 3¼ | 1 | 4⅛ | 44 |
| Rockwl | 25 | 1 | 6¼ | a | a | b | b | 30¾ |
| Rockwl | 30 | 8 | 2¼ | 7 | 2¾ | 8 | 3⅛ | 30¾ |
| Rockwl | 35 | 36 | ½ | 28 | ¾ | 7 | 1⅛ | 30¾ |
| Safewy | 40 | 1 | 10¼ | a | a | a | a | 49¼ |
| Safewy | 50 | 7 | 1⅞ | 1 | 2 | 5 | 3½ | 49¼ |
| Total volume | | 1,390 | | Open interest | | | | 5,344 |

a-Not traded. b-No option offered.

**FIGURE 20**
Stock Options Tables

prices listed at the left for the call options. If you exercise a January 30 call option for Houston Oil and Minerals you do not automatically make a profit of $16.50 per share, your profit, if any, is the amount you paid for the option privilege plus the aggregate exercise price ($30 × 100 shares = $3,000) subtracted from the net proceeds from the sale of the stock itself. Another way to profit from this option transaction is to sell the option privilege for more money than your original cost to acquire it.

3  The expiration month appears at the top of every two columns of trading information for an option series. Although listed options have fixed *quarterly* expiration dates, only the next nearest three dates are made available for trading at one time. Therefore, on December 28, 1976, only options set to expire in January, April, and July 1977 are available; or February, May, and August 1977 (see Philadelphia Exchange table); or March, June, and September 1977 (see Midwest Exchange table). When the January options expire, the exchanges will list the October series; after February expires, the November series; and after March expires, the December series.

4  The volume figure indicates the total number of contracts traded today in that particular series. On the CBOE, 147 contracts for the January 30 call options were traded, while on the PSE 30 contracts were traded. Because each contract usually commands at least 100 shares of underlying stock, 147 options on the CBOE equals 14,700 shares of stock: and 30 options on the PSE, 3,000 shares.

5  The column labeled *Last* is the final transaction price for option premiums on this day. Due to space limitations, the tables do not show opening-, high-, or low-priced transactions for premiums paid. Note the interesting oddity between the CBOE and PSE January 30s. The CBOE closed at 16¾, a premium over its conversion value of 16½, while the PSE series closed at 16⅜, a discount. Why? The aggressiveness of supply versus demand can sometimes cause price aberrations. In this case, too, remember the PSE is open for trading later than is the CBOE (5:30 P.M. Eastern time versus 4 P.M. Eastern time) and one late but anxious seller might have created that disparity.

6  The footnote at the bottom of the Listed Options Quotation tables reveals that while the July 30s were available for trading on the PSE, no buyers and sellers agreed upon a transaction price this day. Two contracts in that series did trade on the CBOE and closed at 17¼

Two final points to highlight in these tables are items that appear at the very bottom of each exchange's daily transaction record. They are *Total Volume* and *Open Interest*. (The CBOE and American Exchange's information does not appear because their trade statistics were clipped to conserve space in this figure.

*Total volume* is the aggregate number of option contracts traded on the exchange that day. It encompasses all classes of options as well as all series with activity that day. The total volume of 7,096 contracts on the PSE is comparable to 709,600 shares of stock traded on the NYSE. *Open interest* is the aggregate number of exercisable contracts existing on the records of the Options Clearing Corporation from cumulative activities. Any opening writing transaction in a PSE option would increase the figure of 396,051 options, whereas a closing writing transaction would reduce it.

In addition to daily quotations and transaction prices, the *Wall Street Journal* also publishes financial news that influences values of these securities. Such information includes earnings reports released by corporations publicly owned and registered with the SEC. Admittedly, these reports are just thumbnail sketches of the actual financial statements. Nevertheless, they do serve an important function for stockholders and potential investors. The announcements are simple to read and understand. Without comment or excuse, they are published quickly and gain wide circulation. Moreover, they are isolated in the *Wall Street Journal* each day in a section called "Digest of Earnings Reports" (see Figure 21) and therefore can't easily be overlooked. When used in conjunction with dividend and transaction news, which is also in this newspaper, these reports can be employed as a basis for making certain fundamental analyses about a company's stock.

The typical earnings report compares the previous year's and the current year's net sales (revenues), net income (or loss), per share earnings (primary and fully diluted), and extraordinary items taken into consideration during these fiscal periods.

*D6.*
*Digest of Earnings Reports*

### INFORMATION LISTED

*D6a.*

Let us now concentrate upon Figure 21 and see how much pertinent information can be recognized or gleaned from a typical Digest of Earnings Report. Next to the corporate title is a letter designation advising you about the principal marketplace where this issue is traded. In referring to the legend at the base of the figure, we realize that Altamil Corp. is traded primarily on the American Stock Exchange (A), Argus Corp. is on the Toronto Stock Exchange (T), Bassett Furniture Industries is over-the-counter (O), and so forth.

You should realize that the earnings reports are for varying fiscal periods, and so care should be taken before impetuous conclusions are drawn. Some reports are annual, but many are often just semiannual, or for the preceding quarter, or even for the last 9 months or 30 weeks. Note, too, that comparisons between 1975 and 1976 are facilitated because the figures for both fiscal periods are positioned side by side. Footnotes are kept to a minimum but play an important role. They help you in making a worthwhile analysis should the company's report contain extraordinary and nonrecurring income or write-offs. Commonwealth Holiday Inns of Canada, Forum Restaurants, and Prochemco Inc., among others, made such announcements in their reports.

You should also recognize when a company reports its earnings both on a primary and on a fully diluted basis. This double reporting means that the company has convertible securities outstanding and may also have securities classified as common stock equivalents. Under present accounting regulations, corporations with convertible securities outstanding are required to state their earnings both before and after consideration for conversion of those issues into common stock. Altamil Corp., Cooper Labs, Inc., and Shoney's Inc., fall into this category.

### DETERMINATIONS TO BE MADE

*D6b.*

Now let us see what else you can often determine from these earnings reports.

# Digest of Earnings Reports

**ALTAMIL CORP. (A)**

| Quar Nov 30: | 1976 | 1975 |
|---|---|---|
| Sales | $12,995,751 | $10,155,316 |
| Net income | 546,418 | 391,292 |
| Avg shares | 1,535,000 | 1,670,000 |
| Shr earns (primary): | | |
| Net income | .34 | .22 |
| Shr earns (fully diluted): | | |
| Net income | .30 | .20 |

**ARGUS CORP. (T)**

| Year Nov 30: | 1976 | 1975 |
|---|---|---|
| Net income | $11,380,000 | $12,138,000 |
| aShr earns: | | |
| Net income | 1.16 | 1.25 |

a-Based on common and Class C shares.

**BASSETT FURNITURE INDS (O)**

| Year Nov 30: | 1976 | 1975 |
|---|---|---|
| Sales | $226,447,812 | $160,882,934 |
| Net income | 17,259,619 | 9,891,935 |
| Shr earns: | | |
| Net income | 2.26 | 1.30 |

**BOC INT'L LTD. (F)**

| Year Sept 30: | 1976 | 1975 |
|---|---|---|
| Sales | $1,024,100,000 | $817,600,000 |
| Income | 45,500,000 | 30,200,000 |
| Ext cr | 500,000 | 500,000 |
| Net inco | 46,000,000 | 30,700,000 |

The above results have been computed at the pound's current rate.

**BOMBARDIER-MLW LTD. (Mo)**

| 9 mo Oct 31: | 1976 | a1975 |
|---|---|---|
| Sales | $180,010,000 | $172,386,000 |
| Income | 53,000 | 1,216,000 |
| Extrd cred | 113,000 | 446,000 |
| Net income | 116,000 | 1,662,000 |
| Shr earns: | | |
| Income | .01 | .31 |
| Net income | .04 | .43 |

a-Restated to reflect the acquisition of MLW-Worthington.

**BRODY (B.) SEATING CO. (A)**

| Quar Nov 30: | 1976 | 1975 |
|---|---|---|
| Sales | $4,754,200 | $4,325,000 |
| Net income | 45,700 | 31,000 |
| Shr earns: | | |
| Net income | .06 | .04 |

**BROOKS FASHION STORES (O)**

| Quar Nov 27: | 1976 | 1975 |
|---|---|---|
| Sales | $15,694,115 | $13,434,755 |
| Net income | 1,312,790 | 1,086,948 |
| Shr earns: | | |
| Net income | .35 | a.29 |
| 9 months: | | |
| Sales | 44,973,063 | 35,773,447 |
| Net income | 3,273,251 | 2,926,327 |
| Shr earns: | | |
| Net income | .87 | a.78 |

a-Adjusted for a 50% stock dividend in April 1976.

**COMMONWLTH HOL INNS-CAN (T)**

| Year Oct 31: | 1976 | 1975 |
|---|---|---|
| Revenues | $156,374,200 | $120,694,700 |
| Income | 425,100 | 412,900 |
| Extrd chg | a3,500,000 | |
| Net loss | 3,074,900 | b412,900 |
| Shr earns: | | |
| Income | c | c |
| Net loss | c | c |

a-Write-down of investment in Caribbean. b-Income. c-No earnings for common shares after deduction of preferred dividend requirements.

---

**COOPER LABS INC. (N)**

| Year Oct 31: | 1976 | 1975 |
|---|---|---|
| Sales | $95,170,000 | $88,256,000 |
| Income | 4,631,000 | 2,025,000 |
| Extr credit | a4,771,000 | |
| Net income | 9,402,000 | 2,025,000 |
| Shr earns (primary): | | |
| Income | .70 | .31 |
| Net income | 1.43 | .31 |
| Shr earns (fully diluted): | | |
| Income | .70 | .... |
| Net income | 1.35 | .... |
| Quarter: | | |
| Sales | 26,092,000 | 24,134,000 |
| Income | 1,812,000 | 800,000 |
| Extrd credit | a4,265,000 | |
| Net income | 6,077,000 | 800,000 |
| Shr earns (primary): | | |
| Income | .28 | .12 |
| Net income | .93 | .12 |
| Shr earns (fully diluted): | | |
| Income | .28 | .... |
| Net income | .85 | .... |

a-Consists of a gain from a debenture exchange and tax-loss carry-forwards.

**FORUM RESTAURANTS (O)**

| Year Aug 29: | 1976 | a1975 |
|---|---|---|
| Sales | $22,878,000 | .... |
| Loss cnt op | 201,000 | .... |
| Loss dis op | b388,000 | .... |
| Net loss | 589,000 | .... |

a-Comparable figures unavailable; company changed its fiscal year ending from May 31 to the last Sunday in August. b-Includes loss of $409,000 on disposal of discontinued operations.

**GILBERT-ROBINSON INC (O)**

| Quar Nov 27: | 1976 | 1975 |
|---|---|---|
| Sales | $7,164,322 | $5,472,943 |
| Net income | 334,165 | 261,459 |
| Avg shares | 1,548,878 | a1,376,000 |
| Shr earns: | | |
| Net income | .22 | a.19 |
| 6 months: | | |
| Sales | 14,684,456 | 10,966,684 |
| Net income | 799,029 | 487,769 |
| Avg shares | 1,491,209 | a1,394,000 |
| Shr earns: | | |
| Net income | .54 | a.35 |

a-Adjusted for a 20% stock dividend in April 1976.

**HY-GAIN ELECTRONICS (O)**

| Quar Nov 27: | 1976 | 1975 |
|---|---|---|
| Sales | $12,311,655 | $18,617,986 |
| Net loss | 2,034,598 | a4,409,409 |
| Shr earns: | | |
| Net loss | .... | a1.41 |

a-Income.

---

---

**IMPERIAL INDUSTRIES (A)**

| Quar Sept 30: | 1976 | a1975 |
|---|---|---|
| Sales | $8,488,000 | $6,551,000 |
| Loss cnt op | 141,000 | 257,000 |
| Loss dis op | .... | 147,000 |
| Net loss | 141,000 | 404,000 |
| 9 months: | | |
| Sales | 22,721,000 | 19,868,000 |
| Loss cnt op | 458,000 | 603,000 |
| Loss dis op | .... | 489,000 |
| Net loss | 458,000 | 1,092,000 |

a-Restated to reflect discontinued operations.

**PACESETTER BUILDING SYS (O)**

| Year Oct 31: | 1976 | 1975 |
|---|---|---|
| Sales | $18,342,833 | $14,522,432 |
| Net income | 1,338,010 | 988,377 |
| Shr earns: | | |
| Net income | 1.40 | 1.01 |
| Quarter: | | |
| Sales | 5,434,453 | 4,355,662 |
| Net income | 402,224 | 362,125 |
| Shr earns: | | |
| Net income | .42 | .37 |

**PAY'N PAK STORES INC. (O)**

| Quar Nov 30: | 1976 | 1975 |
|---|---|---|
| Revenues | $22,577,874 | $20,183,015 |
| Net income | 894,525 | 746,979 |
| Shr earns: | | |
| Net income | .55 | a.45 |
| 9 months: | | |
| Revenues | 62,414,299 | 57,792,126 |
| Net income | 2,357,565 | 2,082,372 |
| Shr earns: | | |
| Net income | 1.46 | a1.25 |

a-Adjusted to reflect 10% stock dividend in May, 1976.

**PROCHEMCO INC. (O)**

| Year Oct 31: | a1976 | 1975 |
|---|---|---|
| Revenues | $42,375,000 | $40,306,000 |
| Net income | b780,000 | d150,000 |
| Shr earns: | | |
| Net income | .54 | .... |

a-Includes a new cotton machinery division, acquired July 1, 1976. b-Includes a nonrecurring gain of $225,000 on the sale of ranch property in Mississippi. d-Loss.

**REAL EST INV TRUST (A)**

| Year Nov 30: | 1976 | 1975 |
|---|---|---|
| Income | $1,861,072 | $2,201,770 |
| Cap gain | 21,702 | 130,988 |
| Net income | 1,882,774 | 2,332,758 |
| Shr earns: | | |
| Income | 1.14 | 1.35 |
| Net income | 1.15 | 1.43 |
| Quarter: | | |
| Income | 413,562 | 515,220 |
| Cap loss | .... | 2,136 |
| Net income | 413,562 | 513,084 |
| Shr earns: | | |
| Income | .25 | .32 |
| Net income | .25 | .32 |

**SHONEY'S INC. (O)**

| Year Oct 31: | 1976 | 1975 |
|---|---|---|
| Revenues | $95,290,593 | $70,018,911 |
| Net income | 5,446,786 | 3,906,696 |
| Shr earns (com & com equiv): | | |
| Net income | 1.40 | 1.03 |

**SILVER KING MINES (O)**

| Quar Oct 31: | 1976 | 1975 |
|---|---|---|
| Net loss | $211,205 | $517,182 |
| 6 months: | | |
| Net loss | 480,009 | 666,992 |

**SOUTHWEST FACTORIES (O)**

| Year Sept 30: | 1976 | 1975 |
|---|---|---|
| Revenues | $21,300,000 | $22,600,000 |
| Net income | 263,423 | 536,037 |
| Shr earns: | | |
| Net income | .04 | .11 |

**FIGURE 21**
Digest of Earnings Reports

---

**D6b(1).** *Net profit margin (after-tax)* To calculate the percentage of net income available for stockholders from net sales, simply divide net income by net sales. In the case of Pacesetter Building Systems, the after-tax profit margin for fiscal 1976 was about 7.3% ($1,338,010 ÷ $18,342,833). If a company reports a loss, there is, understandably, no profit margin.

**D6b(2).** *Approximate number of common shares outstanding* To determine the common shares outstanding, divide net income by the per share earnings figure presented. As long as the share earnings are not fully diluted or adjusted for common stock equivalents, the result will be a good approximation of common stock outstanding. In the case of Prochemco, Inc. you divide $780,000 by .54 to find that there are about 1,444,444 shares outstanding.

*Percentage increase in per share earnings*  To calculate the percentage increase in per share earnings subtract last year's per share earnings from this year's figure. Then divide the difference by last year's earnings per share. For Bassett Furniture Industries, the percentage increase is almost 74%.

*D6b(3).*

$$\frac{(\$2.26 - \$1.30)}{1.30} = \frac{\$ .96}{\$1.30} = .738, \text{ rounded to } .74, \text{ or } 74\%$$

If the company projects the same percentage increase over each of the next 3 years, the same arithmetic formula can determine those earnings for those years. For example:

| YEAR 1 | YEAR 2 | YEAR 3 |
|---|---|---|
| $\dfrac{(x - \$2.26)}{\$2.26} = \dfrac{.74}{1}$ | $\dfrac{(y - \$3.93)}{\$3.93} = \dfrac{.74}{1}$ | $\dfrac{(z - \$6.84)}{\$6.84} = \dfrac{.74}{1}$ |
| $x - \$2.26 = .74(2.26)$ | $y - \$3.93 = .74(3.93)$ | $z - \$6.84 = .74(6.84)$ |
| $x - \$2.26 = 1.6724$ | $y - \$3.93 = 2.9082$ | $z - \$6.84 = 5.0616$ |
| $x = 1.6724 + \$2.26$ | $y = 2.9082 + \$3.93$ | $z = 5.0616 + \$6.84$ |
| $x = \$3.93$ | $y = \$6.84$ | $z = \$11.90$ |

At that percentage rate of increase, earnings will have moved spectacularly in a short period of time.

*Sales growth*  To calculate sales growth, subtract last year's sales from this year's sales. Then divide the difference by last year's sales. For Imperial Industries the percentage increase is almost 30%.

*D6b(4).*

$$\frac{\$8,488,000 - \$6,551,000}{\$6,551,000} = \frac{\$1,937,000}{\$6,551,000} = .295, \text{ rounded to } .30, \text{ or } 30\%$$

The increase is notable despite the fact the company reported a net loss of capital from unprofitable operations. This type of analysis is really more relevant over a longer period of time, say 5 to 10 years, than it is over a 2-year period. The longer period is better because on a short-term basis management is capable of temporarily inflating sales revenues or deferring them to a succeeding fiscal period. A brief comparison is meaningful only when it signals a departure from a well-established pattern of growth (or lack of it). It thus alerts the prospective investor to look deeper into the situation for valid reasons.

*Price-earnings ratio*  The calculation of a price-earnings ratio from an earnings report can be done only in conjunction with the price of the issue appearing in the stock transaction tables. Just divide the price per share by the earnings per share. The result is a ratio often used by investors as an indicator of value. For example, for Cooper Labs, Inc., use the fully diluted annual net income per share of $1.35 and its current price of 11. The price-earnings

*D6b(5).*

EXCHANGE STOCK TRANSACTIONS

| | | | | | | | | | |
|---|---|---|---|---|---|---|---|---|---|
| 92 | 75½ | ConPow | pf 6 | .. | 2 | 92½ | 92½ | 92½ | + ½ |
| 9¾ | 5¼ | ContAir | Lin | 14 | 160 | 7⅜ | 7⅛ | 7⅛ | – ⅛ |
| 8⅛ | 4⅞ | ContCop | .50 | .. | 31 | 5⅞ | 5⅝ | 5⅞ | + ¼ |
| 13¼ | 11¼ | CtCop | pf1.25 | .. | z100 | 13⅛ | 13⅛ | 13⅛ | + ⅛ |
| 57½ | 41⅝ | ContlCp | 2.80 | 19 | 548 | 54⅜ | 53¼ | 53¼ | – 1¼ |
| 62¾ | 45¼ | CtlC | pfA2.50 | .. | 3 | 59 | 59 | 59 | – ½ |
| 34⅜ | 26¾ | CntlGrp | 2 | 9 | 98 | 33⅞ | 33½ | 33⅞ | ...... |
| 58⅛ | 35⅝ | ConllCp | 2.40 | 8 | 110 | 57¾ | 57⅛ | 57½ | – ⅛ |
| 17¼ | 9⅞ | ContllP | 1.28 | 8 | 16 | 16⅞ | 16¾ | 16⅞ | ...... |
| 3 | 1¼ | Contll | Rlty | .. | 13 | 2¼ | 2⅛ | 2¼ | ...... |
| 40⅞ | 33 | Cont Oil | 1.20 | 9 | 876 | 38 | 36⅞ | 37 | – ⅝ |
| 17⅝ | 12¼ | ContTel | 1.08 | 12 | 629 | 17⅝ | 17⅜ | 17⅝ | + ⅛ |
| 27⅛ | 17⅝ | Control | Dat | 10 | 403 | 26⅜ | 25¼ | 25¼ | – ⅞ |
| 48 | 40¾ | CnDt | pf 4.50 | .. | z1000 | 47¼ | 46½ | 46½ | – ¾ |
| 35⅝ | 26¾ | Conwd | 2.20 | -8 | 31 | 36 | 35¾ | 35¾ | + ⅛ |
| 6 | 2½ | CookUn | .30t | 6 | 30 | 4⅝ | 4½ | 4½ | – ⅛ |
| 42¾ | 29 | CooperIn | .84 | 11 | 121 | 40½ | 40 | 40⅛ | – ⅜ |
| 11½ | 4⅞ | Cooper | Lab.20 | | 151 | 11⅛ | 10¾ | 10⅞ | – ¼ |
| 16¾ | 9⅛ | CoopTR | .70 | 3 | 48 | 16¼ | 15⅞ | 16¼ | + ½ |
| 17¼ | 12 | CopT | pf 1.25 | .. | 2 | 16⅞ | 16⅞ | 16⅞ | + ⅛ |
| 20⅛ | 10¾ | Copelnd | .68 | 10 | 29 | 19¾ | 19⅜ | 19¾ | + ⅜ |
| 25¾ | 17½ | CoppRg | | .. | 124 | 20⅛ | 19¾ | 19¾ | – ⅛ |
| 3¾ | 1½ | Cordura | Cp.10e | .. | 391 | 3¼ | 3⅛ | 3¼ | ...... |
| 80 | 43⅝ | CornG | 1.52a | 16 | 123 | 71 | 70⅝ | 70⅝ | – ⅜ |
| 4 | 1¼ | Cousins | Mtg | .. | 68 | 2 | 1⅞ | 1⅞ | ...... |
| 12¾ | 6⅛ | Cowles | .56 | 15 | 1 | 12½ | 12½ | 12½ | ...... |
| 37⅞ | 27½ | CoxBdct | .55 | 11 | 14 | 33½ | 33¼ | 33¼ | – ⅛ |
| 16⅜ | 8¼ | Craig | .30 | 4 | 110 | 15⅜ | 14⅞ | 15 | ...... |
| 39¾ | 23¼ | Crane | 1.20 | 5 | 90 | 29½ | 29¼ | 29⅜ | + ¼ |
| 6¼ | 3¼ | CreditF | .24 | 11 | 63 | 6¼ | 5⅞ | 5⅞ | – ⅜ |
| 28¾ | 21⅝ | CrockN | 1.66 | 8 | 45 | 27⅞ | 27½ | 27½ | – ½ |
| 46½ | 35½ | CrockN | pf 3 | .. | 18 | 46 | 45¾ | 45¾ | – ¼ |
| 15¾ | 10½ | CrompK | .80 | 8 | 24 | 14 | 13⅝ | 13⅝ | – ⅜ |
| 33⅛ | 18⅞ | CrouHi | 1 | 12 | x16 | 30⅝ | 30½ | 30½ | ...... |
| 88 | 51¾ | CroHi | pf 3.35 | .. | x1 | 81 | 81 | 81 | + ¼ |
| 22⅛ | 16⅞ | Crown | Cork | | 86 | 21¾ | 21 | 21 | – ⅝ |
| 49 | 35⅝ | CrwZel | 1.80 | 11 | 66 | 45 | 44½ | 44⅞ | – ⅛ |
| 21½ | 13⅝ | Culbro | 1.32 | 7 | 60 | 22⅜ | 21⅝ | 22¼ | + ⅞ |
| 11 | 7⅝ | Culligan | .44 | 10 | 21 | 10¾ | 10½ | 10½ | – ¼ |
| 48¾ | 19⅝ | CummEng | 1.20 | 11 | 178 | 48⅜ | 47½ | 47½ | – ¾ |
| 131½ | 79 | Cum | pf 7.50 | .. | z2080 | 131½ | 130 | 130 | – 1 |
| 9⅝ | 6½ | CunnDrg | .25 | 8 | 17 | 8⅛ | 8 | 8⅛ | ...... |
| 12⅝ | 11 | Currlnc | 1.08 | .. | 20 | 12⅝ | 12½ | 12⅝ | + ⅛ |
| 17⅝ | 10 | CurtisWr | .60 | 10 | 138 | 17⅜ | 17¼ | 17¼ | ...... |
| 40¾ | 26⅝ | CutlerH | 1.80 | 8 | 120 | 38¾ | 37⅞ | 38 | – ½ |
| 25⅜ | 15⅝ | Cyclops | 1.20a | 5 | 66 | 24 | 23⅜ | 23½ | – ⅜ |
| 31⅞ | 21½ | Cyprus | 1.40 | 25 | 51 | 25⅝ | 25⅜ | 25½ | + ¼ |

***D6b(6).***

OVER-THE-COUNTER MARKETS

| | | | | | |
|---|---|---|---|---|---|
| | --B B-- | | | | |
| BairdAtomc | 2i | 20 | 4¾ | 5¼ | ... |
| BairdWr | 1.08d | 1 | 6¾ | 7¼ | ... |
| Baker | Brothrs | 11 | 3½ | 3⅞ | ... |
| BakerFentr | 1a | 5 | 35½ | 36½ | – ¼ |
| Baldw Ly | .30d | 41 | 14 | 14½ | + ⅛ |
| Baltek | Corp | 2 | 5¼ | 6 | ... |
| BancoCred | .80 | 9 | 5¾ | 6½ | ... |
| BancoPop | 1.20 | 8 | 16¼ | 17¼ | ... |
| Bncohio | 1.20a | 24 | 19 | 20 | – ¼ |
| BancOklahm | 1 | 1 | 16¾ | 17¾ | ... |
| BncshrNJ | 2.20 | 32 | 23½ | 25½ | ... |
| BangorHy | 1.40 | 2 | 14½ | 15 | ... |
| BnkamRl | .25d | 99 | 10⅛ | 10⅝ | + ⅛ |
| Bank Build | .83 | 10 | 11⅜ | 11⅞ | + ⅛ |
| Bnk of | Comwl | 10 | ⅜ | ⅞ | ... |
| BankDela | 2.20 | 3 | 25½ | 27½ | + ½ |
| BnkrSec Lf | .35 | 58 | 8¼ | 8¾ | + ⅝ |
| BnkrTrSC | 1.20 | 1 | 15¼ | 16¼ | ... |
| Bnks ofla | 1.04 | 1 | 22 | 23½ | ... |
| BantaGeor | .48 | 9 | 8¼ | 8¾ | ... |
| BarbGreen | .80 | 44 | 21¾ | 22¼ | – ⅝ |
| Barden Cp | .50 | 82 | 12¾ | 13¼ | – ⅛ |
| BarnettFla | .72 | 83 | 15¼ | 15¾ | – ¼ |
| Basco | Incorp | 35 | 5¾ | 6¾ | – ¼ |
| BasicEarth | Sc | 14 | 1⅝ | 2⅛ | ... |
| Basic | Resourc | 5 | 9 | 9½ | ... |
| Baset Furn | .80 | 284 | 18 | 18¾ | + ¼ |
| BayBanks | 2.10 | 12 | 30 | 30¾ | ... |
| BaylessMk | .60 | 3 | 8⅛ | 8⅝ | – ⅛ |
| Beard | Oil Co | 20 | 6⅝ | 7⅛ | ... |
| BBDOIntl | 1.80 | 35 | 22½ | 23¼ | ... |
| Beck Arnly | Cp | 1 | 3⅝ | 4⅜ | ... |
| Beehive | Intl | 38 | 10¾ | 11¼ | – ⅛ |
| BeelineFsh | .50 | 35 | 6⅞ | 7⅜ | + ⅛ |
| Bekins Co | .50 | 70 | 8 | 8½ | ... |

ratio (P/E) is about 8.1 ($11 ÷ $1.35). However, a few months ago the stock was trading at 5. Its P/E at that time (predicated upon current earnings) was therefore only 3.7 ($5 ÷ $1.35). An analyst who realized that this was an inordinately low ratio could have bought the stock and profited handsomely today as a result.

Knowledge of this formula and a little arithmetic can also enable you to solve for any one of the components, given two of the three basic ingredients: ratio, price, and earnings per share. For example, given a P/E ratio of 15 for Argus Corp., its price must be about 17¼. The formula and procedure is as follows:

$$\frac{x \text{ (price)}}{\$1.16 \text{ (earnings)}} = \frac{15 \text{ (ratio)}}{1}$$

$$x = 15\ (\$1.16)$$

$$x = \$17.40$$

Or, given a P/E ratio of 7.97 for Bassett Furniture Industries and a bid price $18, its annual earnings must be $2.26 per share.

$$\frac{\$18.00 \text{ (price)}}{x \text{ (earnings)}} = \frac{7.97 \text{ (ratio)}}{1}$$

$$7.97\,x = \$18.00$$

$$x = \frac{\$18.00}{7.97}$$

$$x = \$2.26 \text{ (rounded)}$$

***Dividend payout ratio*** To determine the dividend payout ratio you must also refer to another information source in conjunction with the Digest of Earnings Reports. That source can be the stock transactions tables in the newspaper, if the issue is on an exchange. It can be the Over-the-Counter Markets tables, if the stock is registered in NASDAQ. If the stock is traded elsewhere, the source of supplementary information used can be the Dividend Record, published by Standard & Poor's Corporation. The additional information needed is the indicated annual dividend payment. If the stock is listed in the newspapers, the figure appears next to the name of the issue in the stock tables.

The dividend payout ratio is calculated by dividing the annual dividend distribution per share by the net income per share. Thus, for Bassett Furniture Industries, with an 80¢ indicated annual dividend, the payout ratio is 35%.

$$\frac{\$\ .80}{\$2.26} = .35, \text{ or } 35\%$$

In other words, this company paid out 35% of what it had available from current earnings in dividends to its common stockholders. The remainder of its earnings was reinvested in the business. Industrial corporations in a growing stage of development generally have low percentage dividend payout ratios, if any at all. Their profits are primarily plowed back into the company. Mature corporations, such as well-established electric and gas utilities concerns, have high percentage dividend payouts. Some are even in the neighborhood of 80–90% of their net earnings each year.

The *Wall Street Journal* does not have a monopoly on published financial news. Other fine newspapers, such as the *New York Times*, also offer a variety of statistical market information to interested readers. Typical of this is its "Market Indicators" table shown in Figure 22. It is a synopsis of technical information about the preceding day's activities on the New York Stock Exchange and in other key marketplaces. In one centralized section of the financial news, the average investor or a sophisticated technical analyst can do the following:

*D7.*
***The New York Times Market Indicators***

1. Examine chart plottings of the New York Stock Exchange's (NYSE) Market Index, Market Volume of the past 3 months, and even the NYSE 12-Month Trend of prices over the past year (see Figure 23). The Market Index is a vertical line chart showing daily highs, lows, and closings in terms of the NYSE's index of all common stocks on the exchange. Market Volume is a vertical bar chart designed to measure the level of investor interest in NYSE stocks. When used in conjunction with advance-decline analysis, Market Volume becomes a valuable tool for forecasting the duration of a trend once established. The 12-Month Trend is a line-analysis chart connecting postings of just the weekly closing value of the NYSE Market Index over 1 year. The portion of the chart below the connecting lines is shaded for effect and to emphasize even minor changes in trend over this extended period.

2. Compare the previous day's statistics for the Dow Jones Stock Averages, Standard & Poor's (S&P) Index, the New York and the American Stock Exchange indexes, and NASDAQ's Index, too (see Figure 24). It is important to note that while all these indexes and averages are good tools for recognizing long-term changes in stock values, they do differ somewhat on a short-term basis. For example, the Dow Jones Industrials, the NYSE Industrials, and the Standard & Poor's Industrials are computed from separately selected NYSE listed stocks. On the one day illustrated in Figure 24, all industrial indicators showed advances. The Dow Jones Industrial Average was up .19%, the NYSE Index was up .28%, and S&P Index was up .20%.[13] It is amazing that they were even that close when you realize how different the number of samplings are in each institution's computations. The Dow uses only 30 stocks, the NYSE uses over 1,400, and S.&.P. uses 400. On a longer-term basis, these indicators have shown even closer results, performing in an almost identical fashion.

3. Gather information for charting an advance-decline line (A/D) for the NYSE, AMEX, and NASDAQ marketplaces and calculating a Breadth Index (see Figure 25).

4. Determine the most active stocks on the New York and the American Stock Exchanges and in NASDAQ, too. Heavy activity often heralds penetration of a support or resistance level and precedes significant movement in the price of that particular stock. In the case of the NYSE, the tables also list

[13]These percentages are calculated by dividing the net changes by the previous day's closing figures.

# New York Stock Exchange Issues

CONSOLIDATED TRADING

**MARKET INDICATORS**

MONDAY, JANUARY 3, 1977

## N.Y.S.E. Index

| | High | Low | Last | Chg |
|---|---|---|---|---|
| Index | 57.92 | 57.63 | 57.69 | −0.19 |
| Industrial | 63.27 | 63.06 | 63.09 | −0.27 |
| Transportation | 42.94 | 42.53 | 42.94 | +0.37 |
| Utility | 41.28 | 41.20 | 41.28 | +0.01 |
| Finance | 59.02 | 58.88 | 58.99 | −0.24 |

## Up-Down Volume

| | Advanced | Declined |
|---|---|---|
| NYSE | 9,286,670shares | 8,521,570shares |
| AMEX | 1,755,780shares | 656,825shares |

## Odd-Lot Trading

purchases of 131,426 shares; sales of 316,937 shares including 564 shares sold short.

## S.&P. Index

| | High | Low | Close | Chg. |
|---|---|---|---|---|
| 400 Indust | 120.02 | 118.31 | 118.92 | -.54 |
| 20 Transport | 15.45 | 15.20 | 15.36 | +.02 |
| 40 Utilities | 54.56 | 53.86 | 54.29 | +.05 |
| 40 Financial | 12.81 | 12.61 | 12.67 | -.12 |

## Amex Index

| High | Low | Close | Chg. |
|---|---|---|---|
| 110.61 | 109.84 | 110.60 | +0.76 |

## NASDAQ Index

| Index | Close | Chg. | Week Ago. | Month Ago. |
|---|---|---|---|---|
| Composite | 97.69 | − 0.19 | 95.68 | 92.31 |
| Industrial | 100.02 | − 0.10 | 97.24 | 94.22 |
| Financial | 101.29 | − 0.28 | 100.13 | 94.97 |
| Insurance | 104.65 | + 0.56 | 103.15 | 101.57 |
| Utilities | 87.04 | + 0.13 | 85.15 | 81.57 |
| Banks | 92.82 | + 0.10 | 91.42 | 88.04 |
| Transport | 101.75 | − 0.53 | 97.32 | 94.29 |

## Dow Jones Stock Averages

| | Open | High | Low | Close | Chg |
|---|---|---|---|---|---|
| 30 Industrials | 1005.40 | 1007.81 | 994.18 | 999.75 | − 4.90 |
| 20 Transport | 236.80 | 238.91 | 234.78 | 237.52 | + 0.49 |
| 15 Utilities | 108.64 | 109.22 | 107.91 | 108.64 | + 0.26 |
| 65 Stocks | 325.68 | 327.15 | 322.49 | 324.86 | − 0.63 |

## Consolidated Trading for N.Y.S.E. Issues

### Changes – Up

| | Name | Last | Chg | | Pct. |
|---|---|---|---|---|---|
| 1 | LionelCorp | 2⅞ | + ⅜ | Up | 15.0 |
| 2 | ElectAssoc | 3 | + ⅜ | Up | 14.3 |
| 3 | SCASvc | 3 | + ⅜ | Up | 14.3 |
| 4 | CollinsFd | 8¾ | + 1 | Up | 12.9 |
| 5 | HarmanIntl | 25½ | + 2⅞ | Up | 12.7 |
| 6 | HemispCap | 2¼ | + ¼ | Up | 12.5 |
| 7 | ToddShipyd | 9¼ | + 1 | Up | 12.1 |
| 8 | ChockFON | 3⅝ | + ⅜ | Up | 11.5 |
| 9 | RaA2.25pf | 21¾ | + 2¼ | Up | 11.5 |
| 10 | ACentMtg | 2½ | + ¼ | Up | 11.1 |
| 11 | GlfMtgRlty | 2½ | + ¼ | Up | 11.1 |
| 12 | ElixirInd | 8⅞ | + ⅞ | Up | 10.9 |
| 13 | JusticeMtg | 2⅝ | + ¼ | Up | 10.5 |
| 14 | EastnAirL | 9¼ | + ⅞ | Up | 10.4 |
| 15 | AticoMtg | 2¾ | + ¼ | Up | 10.0 |

### Changes – Down

| | Name | Last | Chg | | Pct. |
|---|---|---|---|---|---|
| 1 | MtgeTrAm | 4⅛ | − ½ | Off | 10.8 |
| 2 | UVInl.26pf | 38 | − 3½ | Off | 8.4 |
| 3 | UnBrndpfA | 13¼ | − 1⅛ | Off | 7.8 |
| 4 | CorduraCp | 3¼ | − ¼ | Off | 7.1 |
| 5 | UnitBrands | 9¾ | − ¾ | Off | 7.1 |
| 6 | BenfStdMtg | 2 | − ⅛ | Off | 5.9 |
| 7 | Fairmontpf | 14¼ | − ¾ | Off | 5.0 |
| 8 | NthgateEx | 4¾ | − ¼ | Off | 5.0 |
| 9 | JapanFnd | 9¾ | − ½ | Off | 4.9 |
| 10 | BaldwinDH | 13 | − ⅝ | Off | 4.6 |
| 11 | FstPaMtg | 2⅝ | − ⅛ | Off | 4.5 |
| 12 | FtBcpTex | 35½ | − 1⅝ | Off | 4.4 |
| 13 | Emp4.75pf | 5½ | − ¼ | Off | 4.3 |
| 14 | InexcoOil | 12⅛ | − ½ | Off | 4.0 |
| 15 | BekerInd | 9¼ | − ⅜ | Off | 3.9 |

### N.Y.S.E. Issues—Volume by Exchanges

| Markets | Shares |
|---|---|
| NYSE | 21,280,000 |
| Pacific | 693,400 |
| Midwest | 993,500 |
| NASD | 739,140 |
| Boston | 94,500 |
| Cinci | 157,700 |
| Amex | 4,100 |
| Phila | 253,100 |
| Other | 13,900 |
| Total | 24,229,340 |

### Most Active

| Name | Vol | Last | Net Chg |
|---|---|---|---|
| Texac Inc | 367,800 | 27½ | − ¼ |
| PhilipMorr | 323,600 | 59⅞ | − 1⅞ |
| RamadaIn | 214,000 | 4¼ | − ⅛ |
| Chrysler | 200,700 | 21⅛ | + ¾ |
| OccidenPet | 184,200 | 24¼ | + ¼ |
| GenMotors | 157,100 | 78 | − ½ |
| AmTel&Tel | 154,700 | 63⅜ | − ⅛ |
| HughesTool | 152,300 | 39½ | + ¼ |
| NCRCorp | 151,900 | 38⅛ | + ⅝ |
| SouthernCo | 147,500 | 16⅝ | + ¼ |
| KresgeSS | 144,800 | 40 | − ¾ |
| Weyerhsr | 141,300 | 45⅞ | − ⅝ |
| DowCh | 139,800 | 42¾ | − ⅝ |
| AmT&Tpf-b | 136,000 | 51 | + ¼ |
| Exxon | 135,500 | 53⅝ | ..... |

### Market Diary

| | Today | Prev. day |
|---|---|---|
| Advances | 861 | 1125 |
| Declines | 645 | 394 |
| Unchanged | 438 | 393 |
| TotalIssues | 1944 | 1912 |
| New1976-77highs | 205 | 190 |
| New1976-77lows | ..... | ..... |

### Dollar Leaders

| Name | Tot ($1000) | Sales (hds) | Last |
|---|---|---|---|
| PhilMorr | $19,537 | 3236 | 59⅞ |
| IBM | $19,467 | 699 | 276½ |
| GnMot | $12,273 | 1571 | 78 |
| Texaco | $10,160 | 3678 | 27½ |
| AmT&T | $9,804 | 1547 | 63⅜ |
| EasKd | $8,347 | 972 | 85⅜ |
| Exxon | $7,283 | 1355 | 53⅝ |
| ATTpfB | $6,885 | 1360 | 51 |
| Weyerhr | $6,517 | 1413 | 45⅞ |
| AtlRich | $6,410 | 1110 | 58 |
| HughsTl | $6,053 | 1523 | 39½ |
| DowCh | $6,011 | 1398 | 42¾ |
| KresgeS | $5,846 | 1448 | 40 |
| ATTpfA | $5,815 | 1166 | 49⅞ |
| NCRCp | $5,734 | 1519 | 38⅛ |

### N.Y.S.E. Volume Comparisons

| | |
|---|---|
| Day's Sales | 21,280,000 |
| Friday's Sales | 19,170,000 |
| Year Ago | 21,960,000 |
| 1977 to Date | 21,280,000 |
| 1976 to Date | 10,300,820 |

## Consolidated Trading for Amex Issues Most Active

| Name | Vol | Last | Net Chg |
|---|---|---|---|
| ChampHo | 145,500 | 3⅞ | ..... |
| SyntexCorp | 115,600 | 24⅛ | +1 |
| HouOilM | 90,400 | 48⅞ | +1¼ |
| KewaneeIn | 62,200 | 34¾ | + ⅝ |
| SundanceO | 42,500 | 16¾ | +1⅛ |
| FlyDiaOil | 41,400 | 21⅞ | +1¼ |
| MitchIED | 41,100 | 42¼ | +2⅝ |
| InstrumSys | 40,200 | 1¼ | + ¼ |
| IntlBnknot | 36,200 | 2¾ | ..... |
| PGE7.84pf | 36,100 | 23½ | − ⅛ |

## Amex Market Diary

| | Today | Prev. day |
|---|---|---|
| Advances | 488 | 566 |
| Declines | 227 | 213 |
| Unchanged | 257 | 307 |
| TotalIssues | 972 | 1086 |
| New1976-77highs | 66 | 56 |
| New1976-77lows | ..... | ..... |

## O.T.C. Most Active

| Name | Vol | Bid | Asked | Chg. |
|---|---|---|---|---|
| Daylin | 179,800 | 1 9-16 | 1 11-16 | +1-16 |
| RankOrg | 163,400 | 2¼ | 2⅜ | + ⅛ |
| AnheusB | 125,200 | 23⅛ | 23⅜ | + ¼ |
| USBncrp | 86,600 | 29½ | 30 | ..... |
| PabstBr | 70,900 | 23¾ | 24¼ | + ¼ |
| GovEmp | 69,800 | 6⅞ | 7¼ | − ¼ |
| DeBeer | 69,100 | 2 7-16 | 2 9-16 | +1-16 |
| AmExp | 66,200 | 40⅛ | 40⅝ | − ½ |
| CoorsB | 52,800 | 21⅛ | 21⅝ | + ⅞ |
| PnzlOG | 52,800 | 14¼ | 14½ | − ⅛ |

## O.T.C. Market Diary

| | |
|---|---|
| Advanced | 516 |
| Declined | 408 |
| Unchanged | 1,633 |
| TotalIssues | 2,557 |
| Newhighs | 124 |
| Newlows | 3 |
| Totalsales | 7,249,700 |

**MARKET INDEX**

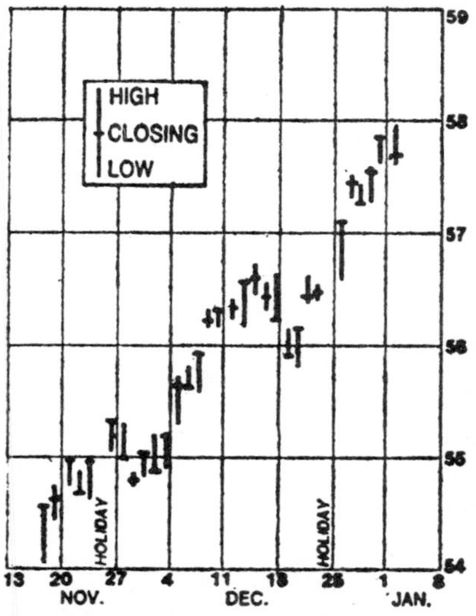

HIGH
CLOSING
LOW
59
58
57
56
55
54
HOLIDAY
HOLIDAY
13
20
27
4
11
18
25
1
8
NOV.
DEC.
JAN.


**MARKET VOLUME**

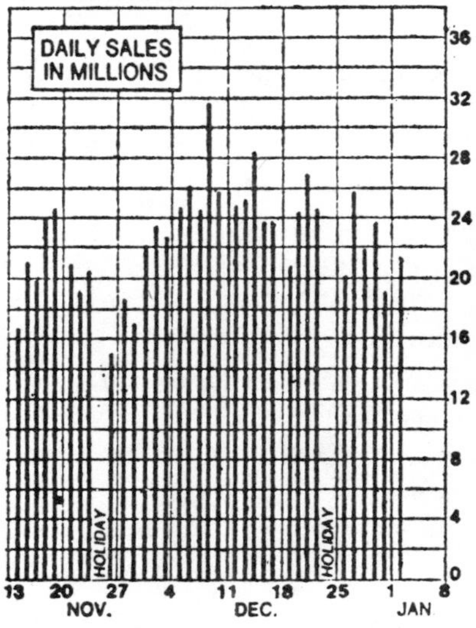

DAILY SALES
IN MILLIONS
36
32
28
24
20
16
12
8
4
0
HOLIDAY
HOLIDAY
13
20
27
4
11
18
25
1
8
NOV.
DEC.
JAN


**12-MONTH TREND**

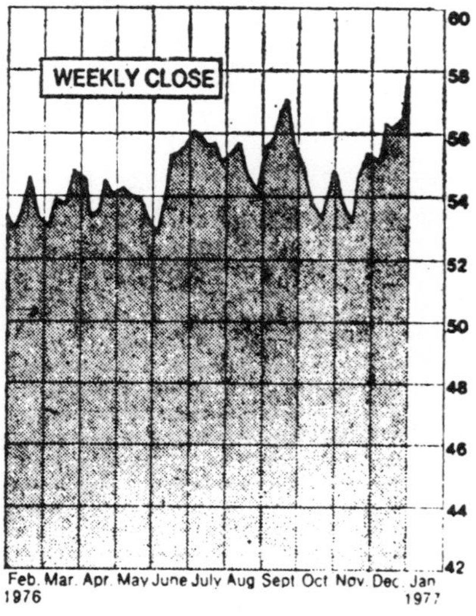

WEEKLY CLOSE
60
58
56
54
52
50
48
46
44
42
Feb. Mar. Apr. May June July Aug Sept Oct Nov. Dec. Jan
1976
1977


FIGURE 22
The New York Times Market Indicators

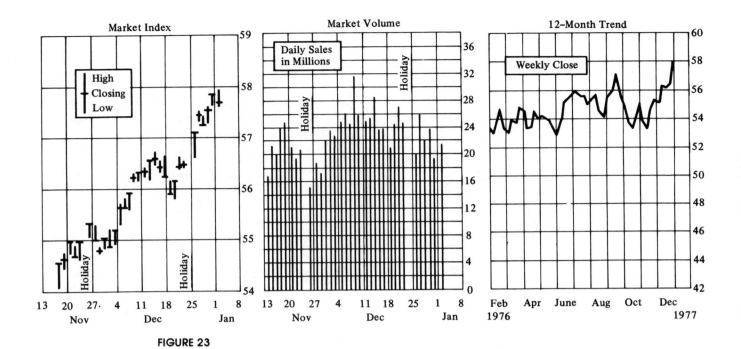

Market Index

| | High |
| | Closing |
| | Low |

Holiday

Holiday

13 20 27· 4 11 18 25 1 8
Nov        Dec        Jan

**FIGURE 23**

Market Volume

Daily Sales
in Millions

Holiday

Holiday

13 20 27 4 11 18 25 1 8
Nov        Dec        Jan

12-Month Trend

Weekly Close

Feb   Apr   June   Aug   Oct   Dec
1976                              1977

## Dow Jones Stock Averages

| | Open | High | Low | Close | Chg |
|---|---|---|---|---|---|
| 30 Industrials | 980.14 | 989.03 | 974.07 | 979.89 | + 1.83 |
| 20 Transport | 233.17 | 235.95 | 232.18 | 234.61 | + 1.40 |
| 15 Utilities | 107.65 | 108.35 | 107.07 | 107.75 | + 0.16 |
| 65 Stocks | 319.16 | 322.15 | 317.38 | 319.66 | + 0.91 |

### N.Y.S.E. Index

| | High | Low | Last | Chg. |
|---|---|---|---|---|
| Index | 56.93 | 56.74 | 56.75 | +0.16 |
| Industrial | 62.11 | 61.88 | 61.88 | +0.16 |
| Transport | 42.39 | 42.24 | 42.36 | +0.17 |
| Utility | 41.10 | 41.04 | 41.07 | +0.10 |
| Finance | 58.50 | 58.27 | 58.39 | +0.29 |

**FIGURE 24**

### S. & P. Index

| | High | Low | Close | Chg. |
|---|---|---|---|---|
| 400 Indust | 117.56 | 115.93 | 116.59 | +0.23 |
| 20 Transport | 15.18 | 14.98 | 15.11 | +0.05 |
| 40 Utilities | 54.13 | 53.52 | 53.84 | +0.06 |
| 40 Financial | 12.59 | 12.39 | 12.49 | +0.06 |
| 500 Stocks | 105.86. | 104.40 | 105.02 | +0.26 |

### Amex Index

| High | Low | Close | Chg. |
|---|---|---|---|
| 110.42 | 109.61 | 110.34 | +0.68 |

### NASDAQ Index

| Index | Close | Chg. | Week Ago | Month Ago |
|---|---|---|---|---|
| Composite | 97.29 | +0.40 | 97.05 | 92.63 |
| Industrial | 99.55 | +0.58 | 99.02 | 94.43 |
| Financial | 100.85 | +0.21 | 100.81 | 95.60 |
| Insurance | 103.65 | +0.19 | 104.79 | 101.68 |
| Utilities | 87.91 | +0.73 | 86.36 | 81.88 |
| Banks | 92.97 | +0.31 | 92.15 | 88.43 |
| Transport | 101.14 | +0.23 | 100.44 | 94.28 |

## N.Y.S.E. Issues Market Diary

| | Today | Prev. day |
|---|---|---|
| Advances | 949 | 491 |
| Declines | 548 | 1047 |
| Unchanged | 461 | 397 |
| Totalissues | 1958 | 1935 |
| New 1976-77 highs | 129 | 113 |
| New 1976-77 lows | ............ | |

## Amex Market Diary

| | Today | Prev. day |
|---|---|---|
| Advances | 420 | 291 |
| Declines | 246 | 342 |
| Unchanged | 273 | 329 |
| Totalissues | 939 | 962 |
| New 1976-77 highs | 47 | 36 |
| New 1976-77 lows | .......... | 1 |

## O.T.C. Market Diary

| | |
|---|---|
| Advanced | 576 |
| Declined | 269 |
| Unchanged | 1,711 |
| Totalissues | 2,556 |
| Newhighs | 109 |
| Newlows | 1 |
| Totalsales | 8,617,500 |

**FIGURE 25**

yesterday's 15 stocks that rose and 15 that declined by the largest percentage amount as well as those that traded in the greatest dollar values, either up or down (see Figure 26).

FIGURE 26

**N.Y.S.E. Issues Most Active**

| Name | Vol | Last | Net Chg |
|---|---|---|---|
| OccidenPet | 444,200 | 23⅝ | + ¾ |
| VaElPow | 377,800 | 15½ | + ¼ |
| CapitHold | 327,800 | 18⅞ | − ⅞ |
| GenMotors | 317,200 | 76½ | +1⅜ |
| AmTel&Tel | 311,300 | 63⅜ | + ⅜ |
| TexacoInc | 263,700 | 27 | − ¼ |
| GenElec | 258,700 | 52⅝ | − ¼ |
| KresgeSS | 242,900 | 40 | + ⅜ |
| PhilaElec | 239,100 | 17⅛ | ..... |
| AmHome | 217,300 | 29⅛ | + ¼ |
| SonyCorp | 207,100 | 9½ | + ¼ |
| Exxon | 178,800 | 51⅞ | + ¼ |
| DeereCo | 164,000 | 31 | ..... |
| NorStaPw | 163,000 | 29⅞ | + ⅛ |
| NatSemicn | 159.300 | 26 | +1⅛ |

**Consolidated Trading for Amex Issues Most Active**

| Name | Vol | Last | Net Chg |
|---|---|---|---|
| HeitmMtgI | 118,000 | 1½ | ..... |
| DixilynCp | 95,200 | 11¼ | +1⅞ |
| SyntexCorp | 81,100 | 21 | + ⅛ |
| HouOilM | 70,600 | 43½ | +2⅛ |
| GtBasPet | 67,000 | 5⅜ | + ¼ |
| KaiserInd | 61,500 | 14 | + ⅛ |
| BrownForB | 51,100 | 13⅜ | − ⅜ |
| IntSysCont | 46,700 | 17¼ | −1¼ |
| SCE7.58pf | 40,000 | 94 | +1½ |
| PrentHall | 35,600 | 23¾ | + ⅛ |

**O.T.C. Most Active**

| Name | Vol | Bid | Asked | Chg. |
|---|---|---|---|---|
| GovEmp | 233,000 | 5⅝ | 6 | + ⅛ |
| AmExp | 116,300 | 39¼ | 39¾ | + ¾ |
| HondaM | 103,600 | 24¾ | 25¼ | + ¾ |
| AnheusB | 90,300 | 22¾ | 23¼ | − ¼ |
| GovEmppf. | 89,000 | 12⅞ | 13¼ | + ½ |
| RankOrg | 87,000 | 1 15-16 | 2 1-16 | .... |
| AdvMicr | 64,000 | 22 | 22½ | +1½ |
| BetzLab | 59,000 | 27¼ | 28 | −2½ |
| OrionCap | 56,000 | 5½ | 5⅞ | ..... |
| Microfo | 53,200 | 2¾ | 3⅛ | + ⅛ |

**Changes – Up**

| | Name | Last | Chg | Pct. | |
|---|---|---|---|---|---|
| 1 | ChockFON | 3½ | + ⅜ | Up | 12.0 |
| 2 | AppldMag | 3⅝ | + ⅜ | Up | 11.5 |
| 3 | MonroeEq | 11¾ | + 1⅛ | Up | 10.6 |
| 4 | NoNG6.40pf | 85 | + 8⅛ | Up | 10.6 |
| 5 | ConAgra | 13⅛ | + 1⅛ | Up | 9.4 |
| 6 | ReliancpfB | 59 | + 4¾ | Up | 8.8 |
| 7 | ElMemMg | 3½ | + ¼ | Up | 7.7 |
| 8 | CadenceInd | 4 | + ¼ | Up | 6.7 |
| 9 | QuestrpfA | 23¾ | + 1½ | Up | 6.7 |
| 10 | CollinsAik | 12⅞ | + ¾ | Up | 6.2 |
| 11 | OneidaLtd | 17⅝ | + 1 | Up | 6.1 |
| 12 | AmInvest | 5 | + ¼ | Up | 5.3 |
| 13 | SCASvc | 2½ | + ⅛ | Up | 5.3 |
| 14 | PlesseyLtd | 10⅛ | + ½ | Up | 5.2 |
| 15 | PSEG7.70pf | 90¾ | + 4⅜ | Up | 5.1 |

**Changes – Down**

| | Name | Last | Chg | Pct. | |
|---|---|---|---|---|---|
| 1 | GlfWindwt | 3⅜ | − ⅜ | Off | 10.0 |
| 2 | Filtrol | 9⅛ | − ⅞ | Off | 8.8 |
| 3 | ChaseMTr | 2⅞ | − ¼ | Odf | 8.0 |
| 4 | AlliedSuper | 3 | − ¼ | Off | 7.7 |
| 5 | PSInd4.32pf | 13 | − 1 | Off | 7.1 |
| 6 | SavAStop | 3¼ | − ¼ | Off | 7.1 |
| 7 | JusticeMtg | 2 | − ⅛ | Off | 5.9 |
| 8 | RexnrdpfA | 56 | − 3½ | Off | 5.9 |
| 9 | Munfordpf | 6⅛ | − ⅜ | Off | 5.8 |
| 10 | AticoMtg | 2⅛ | − ⅛ | Off | 5.6 |
| 11 | WolverWW | 4¼ | − ¼ | Off | 5.6 |
| 12 | DeltonaCp | 4½ | − ¼ | Off | 5.3 |
| 13 | Warnaco | 6¾ | − ⅜ | Off | 5.3 |
| 14 | InexcoOil | 11⅜ | − ⅝ | Off | 5.2 |
| 15 | LTVCorp | 11⅜ | − ⅝ | Off | 5.2 |

**Dollar Leaders**

| Name | Tot ($1000) | Sales (hds) | Last |
|---|---|---|---|
| IBM | $13,779 | 519 | 265¾ |
| UtahInt | $13,305 | 1946 | 68⅝ |
| GenEl | $12,182 | 2315 | 52⅞ |
| GnMot | $12,142 | 1619 | 75⅛ |
| AmT&T | $11,789 | 1864 | 63 |
| Exxon | $11,289 | 2171 | 51⅝ |
| TandyCorp | $7,877 | 2073 | 38¾ |
| CocaCol | $7,697 | 1035 | 73½ |
| DowCh | $7,571 | 1819 | 41¾ |
| TexInst | $7,478 | 777 | 96⅛ |
| DigitalEq | $7,165 | 1433 | 50¼ |
| Hallibrtn | $7,145 | 1132 | 63 |
| EasKd | $7,143 | 862 | 81¾ |
| KresgeS | $6,581 | 1661 | 39⅝ |
| Texaco | $6,223 | 2284 | 27¼ |

5. Collect odd-lot trading figures each day on the NYSE and pertinent round-lot volume comparisons, too (see Figure 27). Followers of the Cushion Theory are most interested in these statistics to help them foretell major movements in the market (a movement down to enable them to sell short and a movement up to cover those short positions).

**N.Y.S.E. Issues—Volume by Exchanges**

| Markets | Shares |
|---|---|
| NYSE | 24,390,000 |
| Pacific | 1,026,600 |
| Midwest | 1,374,100 |
| NASD | 1,642,280 |
| Boston | 247,000 |
| Cinci | 294,900 |
| Amex | 2,900 |
| Phila | 402,000 |
| Other | 2,300 |
| Total | 29,382.080 |

**N.Y.S.E. Volume Comparisons**

| | |
|---|---|
| Day's Sales | 24,390,000 |
| Monday's Sales | 20,690,000 |
| Year Ago | 17,750,000 |
| 1976 to Date | 5,197,885,438 |
| 1975 to Date | 4,589,096,268 |

**Odd-Lot Trading**

purchases of 162,504 shares; sales of 385,633 shares including 1,194 shares sold short.

FIGURE 27

## E. standard and poor's stock reports

Another source of market information is published by Standard and Poor's Corporation (S&P). It is subscribed for and referred to extensively by broker/dealers and their registered representatives. In fact, it often serves as a miniature and inexpensive research department for brokers and their customers. The publication is known as *Standard Stock Reports*. Subscription is offered for NYSE, AMEX, and many OTC stocks popular with investors.

The NYSE stock reports are printed on yellow paper, the AMEX's on blue paper, and OTC on green paper. Thus, at a glance, you can tell where the principal marketplace is for that issue. The reports are updated frequently, often every 3 months.

Figure 28 illustrates the usual stock report presentation and format. It is printed front and back on a 6¼″ × 9¼″ loose-leaf page and is frequently referred to by brokers as a "tear sheet."

The following discussion confines itself to a specific Standard NYSE Stock Report dealing with General Mills, as shown in Figure 28. It is designed to enable you to recognize and analyze the wealth of information contained in a typical report. Let us analyze this stock report section by section according to the numbering inserted for ease in describing the content as we go along.

**1** This is the NYSE ticker symbol for this issue. The footnote also cites the other exchanges where the issue is also traded.

**2** The number 976 is the page number in the book where this particular report is filed. The NYSE Stock Report service is composed of four volumes with report pages numbered consecutively from Volume 1.

**3** This section provides thumbnail statistics for this stock using earnings reported in the last 12 months and the company's indicated dividend rate.

**4** The "Summary" paragraph contains S&P's general comments about the company and its recommendations for investors.

**5** This vertical line chart plots the monthly highs, lows, and closing prices over the last 4 years. It also shows the annual highs and lows for the 5 years prior to this time. Technical chart patterns are sometimes easier to recognize over a 10-year period than when the period covered is 5 years or less. Many investors like to see an issue's market performance over a long period to determine how the stock reacts under different economic conditions and under different managements. Superimposed over the General Mills chart and drawn to the same proportionate scale is the course of S&P's Composite Index for those same years. Investors can compare and determine now whether the stock equaled, underperformed, or outperformed the general market during this time. Some technicians believe this comparison is a reflection of management's ability to cope with the changing times.

**6** Monthly trading volume is presented for the last 5 years to enable technicians to relate changes in volume to subsequent market-price movements. It is a way of recognizing advantageous buying and selling opportunities before they become apparent to everybody.

**7** Net sales statistics are broken down on a quarterly basis for each fiscal year ending in May. They are then presented in a format designed to facilitate comparison between the same reporting periods for each of the preceding 3 years.

**8** Earnings per common share (E.P.S.) are recorded in the same fashion as net sales, that is, quarterly for comparison purposes. From these last two tables and with the number of outstanding shares (49,459,808) taken from the back side of this report in section **16**, we can examine management's efficiency by computing an after-tax profit margin. First, multiply the shares outstanding by the $.65 E.P.S. to arrive at net income ($32,148,875). Then, divide net income by net sales ($32,148,875 ÷ $720,000,000) to arrive at an after-tax profit margin of 4.5%.

# General Mills

| Stock— | Price Oct. 29'76 | *P-E Ratio | Dividend | Yield |
|---|---|---|---|---|
| COMMON .......................... | 30¾ | 14 | [2]$0.76 | [2]2.5% |

**SUMMARY:** This leading factor in the packaged food industry has, through acquisition, diversified into a number of unrelated areas, including apparel, crafts, games and toys, furniture, specialty chemicals, and restaurants. Strong established lines, new products, and planned expansion should maintain earnings in an upward course in the years ahead.

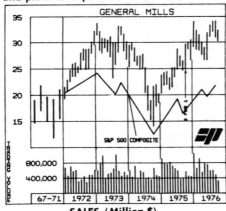

### SALES (Million $)

| Quarter: | 1976-7 | 1975-6 | 1974-5 | 1973-4 |
|---|---|---|---|---|
| Aug. ........ | 720 | 625 | 544 | 464 |
| Nov. ........ | | 763 | 678 | 556 |
| Feb. ........ | | 606 | 522 | 498 |
| May ........ | | 651 | 564 | 483 |

Aided by good growth in volume, sales for the fiscal year ended May 30, 1976 (53 weeks) rose 14.6%, year to year. Despite a $7.0 million plant conversion charge and a $4.0 million loss on the sale of a facility, margins widened. The improvement was attributed to the higher volume and lower raw material costs. Operating income increased 28.7%. Non-operating charges were up less than proportionately, and pretax income rose 37.5%. After taxes at 49.9%, against 48.5%, and adjustments for partially owned companies, net income advanced 31.9%.

Further gains in volume contributed to a 15.2% year-to-year increase in sales for the first quarter of 1976-7. Margins widened in response to cost controls, lower agricultural prices, and the prior elimination of unprofitable and marginal operations. Net income increased 30.9%.

### PROSPECTS

**Near Term**—Sales for the fiscal year ending May 29, 1977, should post a moderate increase from the $2.64 billion of the prior year, with progress expected at both food and non-food operations. Major emphasis on new food products, along with volume gains from established lines and further expansion of the Red Lobster Inns restaurant chain should contribute importantly. In non-food activities, craft, game and toy operations should have another strong year. Fashion and specialty retailing should also do better.

Margins in 1976-7 should be at least maintained on the expected growth in volume, and the absence of plant conversion costs and losses on the sale of a facility. Non-recurring charges during the first quarter and charges to be taken during the second quarter to reflect the devaluation of the Mexican peso will be limiting, but share profits for all of 1976-7 should progress well from the $2.04 of the prior year. Dividends should continue at $0.19 quarterly.

**Long Term**— Increasing reliance on newer, innovative products offering wider margins, and continued diversification through acquisitions augur well for the future.

### RECENT DEVELOPMENTS

Although detailed terms and conditions had yet to be finalized, GIS announced in October 1976 an agreement in principle to acquire York Steak House Systems, an operator of 45 family steak restaurants.

In September, the company reported that it was withdrawing from two ventures involving the production of xanthum gum, and that it had closed the Brown-Saltman furniture production facilities. A $2.1 million net charge was taken in the 1976-7 first quarter to reflect these actions.

### DIVIDEND DATA

A dividend reinvestment plan is available. Payments in the past 12 months were:

| Amt. of Divd. $ | Date Decl. | Ex-divd. Date | Stock of Record | Payment Date |
|---|---|---|---|---|
| 0.17... | Dec. 15 | Jan. 5 | Jan. 9 | Feb. 2'76 |
| 0.17... | Mar. 22 | Apr. 5 | Apr. 9 | May 1'76 |
| 0.19... | Jun. 28 | Jul. 2 | Jul. 9 | Aug. 2'76 |
| 0.19... | Sep. 27 | Oct. 4 | Oct. 8 | Nov. 1'76 |

### [3]COMMON SHARE EARNINGS ($)

| Quarter: | 1976-7 | 1975-6 | 1974-5 | 1973-4 |
|---|---|---|---|---|
| Aug. ........ | 0.65 | 0.50 | 0.41 | 0.40 |
| Nov. ........ | | 0.70 | 0.55 | 0.53 |
| Feb. ........ | | 0.43 | 0.31 | 0.32 |
| May ........ | | 0.41 | 0.32 | 0.34 |

[1]Listed N.Y.S.E.; also listed Midwest S. E. & traded Boston, Pacific & Philadelphia S.Es.   [2]Indicated rate.   [3]Based on com. shs. & com. sh. equivalents (stk. options & contingent shs. were applicable); reflects partial adoption of LIFO acctg. aft. 1973–4; adj. for 2-for-1 split in Nov. 1975.   *Based on latest 12 mos. earns.

Vol. 43, No. 214          Friday, November 5, 1976

**FIGURE 28**
Standard Stock Report (Front)

# GENERAL MILLS, INCORPORATED

## [1]INCOME STATISTICS (Million $) AND PER SHARE ($) DATA

| [2]Year Ended May 31 | [4]Net Sales | [7]% Oper Inc. of Sales | [7]Oper Inc. | [8]Depr. & Amort. | Net bef. Taxes | [4]Net Inc. | [6]Common Share ($) Data: [4]Earns. | *Funds Generated | Divs. Paid | [3]Price Range | Price Earns. Ratios HI LO |
|---|---|---|---|---|---|---|---|---|---|---|---|
| 1976-- | ----- | -- | ---- | ---- | ----- | ----- | --- | --- | 0.38 | 34¼-26⅝ | ----- |
| 1975-- | 2,645.0 | 10.0 | 264.5 | 46.71 | 200.26 | 100.54 | 2.04 | 3.11 | 0.66 | 30½-20⅜ | 15-10 |
| 1974-- | 2,308.9 | 8.9 | 205.5 | 41.79 | 145.63 | 76.21 | 1.59 | 2.60 | 0.58½ | 30 -14⅛ | 19- 9 |
| 1973-- | 2,000.1 | 9.9 | 198.6 | 36.35 | 150.16 | 75.14 | 1.59 | 2.46 | 0.53 | 33⅞-23¼ | 21-15 |
| 1972-- | 1,662.0 | 10.8 | 180.2 | 34.76 | 135.19 | 66.14 | 1.41 | 2.39 | 0.50 | 32¼-19⅜ | 23-14 |
| 1971-- | 1,343.2 | 11.3 | 151.3 | 32.11 | 108.93 | 54.67 | 1.19 | 2.01 | 0.48 | 21 -15½ | 18-13 |
| 1970-- | 1,120.1 | 11.0 | 123.5 | 27.46 | 88.67 | 43.86 | 0.99 | 1.72 | 0.45 | 19¼-11⅞ | 19-12 |
| 1969-- | 1,033.6 | 11.1 | 114.3 | 25.89 | 86.97 | 41.62 | 0.94 | 1.61 | 0.44 | 19⅝-15 | 21-16 |
| 1968-- | 922.4 | 11.3 | 104.3 | 22.78 | 79.94 | 38.13 | 0.89 | 1.47 | 0.40 | 21⅞-17 | 25-19 |
| 1967-- | 748.9 | 11.5 | 86.3 | 17.98 | 66.73 | 32.54 | 0.84 | 1.36 | 0.39½ | 19 -14⅝ | 23-18 |
| 1966-- | 628.4 | 11.7 | 73.5 | 12.59 | 59.32 | 30.06 | 0.86 | 1.39 | 0.37½ | 16⅝-13 | 19-15 |

## [1]PERTINENT BALANCE SHEET STATISTICS (Million $)

| [2]May 31 | Gross Prop. | [5]Capital Expend. | Cash Items | Inven-tories | Receiv-ables | Current Assets | Current Liabs. | Net Workg. Cap. | Cur. Ratio | Long Term DEbt | Share-hldrs. Equity | [6]($) Book Val. Com. Sh. |
|---|---|---|---|---|---|---|---|---|---|---|---|---|
| 1975-- | 739.26 | 94.44 | 81.8 | 353.7 | 216.0 | 672.8 | 377.7 | 295.1 | 1.8-1 | 281.76 | 640.25 | 9.88 |
| 1974-- | 685.24 | 99.83 | 10.0 | 345.9 | 213.6 | 590.4 | 313.5 | 276.8 | 1.9-1 | 304.91 | 560.49 | 8.43 |
| 1973-- | 593.98 | 92.24 | 19.9 | 353.3 | 186.5 | 580.5 | 312.4 | 268.1 | 1.9-1 | 298.18 | 483.44 | 7.41 |
| 1972-- | 529.57 | 57.49 | 17.4 | 242.9 | 154.9 | 428.0 | 248.0 | 180.0 | 1.7-1 | 213.52 | 426.88 | 5.48 |
| 1971-- | 502.22 | 51.28 | 34.8 | 179.8 | 128.3 | 354.4 | 204.7 | 149.7 | 1.7-1 | 227.89 | 377.87 | 4.31 |
| 1970-- | 470.19 | 60.40 | 11.2 | 153.7 | 113.4 | 291.4 | 150.8 | 140.5 | 1.9-1 | 252.43 | 332.68 | 3.32 |
| 1969-- | 419.65 | 60.39 | 14.1 | 129.6 | 99.6 | 254.6 | 119.6 | 135.1 | 2.1-1 | 237.32 | 307.67 | 2.81 |
| 1968-- | 378.98 | 31.01 | 24.8 | 112.4 | 90.8 | 236.5 | 112.7 | 123.7 | 2.1-1 | 214.68 | 294.55 | 2.10 |
| 1967-- | 349.19 | 23.05 | 29.6 | 88.3 | 70.4 | 195.9 | 97.9 | 98.0 | 2.0-1 | 190.52 | 227.18 | 1.53 |
| 1966-- | 278.88 | 26.70 | 64.9 | 58.5 | 42.0 | 171.5 | 75.5 | 96.0 | 2.3-1 | 92.25 | 119.42 | 3.02 |

[1]Data for 1973 & thereafter as originally reported; data for each yr. prior to 1973 as taken from subsequent yr.'s Annual Report; reflects partial adoption of LIFO acctg. aft. 1973. [2]Of the foll. cal. yr. [3]Cal. yrs. [4]Aft. $0.16 a sh. reduction from partial adoption of LIFO acctg. in 1974; bef. spec. cr. of $0.03 a sh. in 1968 & spec. chgs. of $0.15 in 1971 & $0.32 in 1969; sh. earns. based on com. shs. & equivalents (stk. options & contingent shs. where applicable & prior to 1973 conv. pref. stk.). [5]Net expend. prior to 1969. [6]Adj. for 2-for-1 splits in Nov. 1975 & Aug. 1967. [7]Aft. deducting interest expense on grain opers. [8]Depr. only in 1966.

*As computed by Standard & Poor's.

### Fundamental Position

In fiscal 1975-6, breakfast and snack items accounted for 26.3% of sales and 38.3% of pretax income (before unallocated expenses); mixes, family flour, seafoods, etc. 25.2% and 18.4%; commercial foods and ingredients 10.3% and 3.1%; restaurants 6.8% and 9.3%; crafts, games and toys 13.1% and 16.3%; fashions, furniture and specialty retailing 14.4% and 11.7%; and specialty chemicals 3.9% and 2.9%. International operations accounted for 16.4% of sales and 14.9% of net income.

The following comprise the company's food operations: Big G ready-to-eat breakfast cerals, headed by Cheerios, Wheaties and Total; Tom's snack items; GoodMark sausage products and beef jerky; Donruss bubblegum; and Mrs. Bumby's potato chips. Others include Betty Crocker prepared cake mixes; Bisquick baking mix; Betty Crocker instant potato products and packaged casseroles; Hamburger Helper and Tuna Helper; Gold Medal flour; Gorton's seafoods; GoodMark breakfast sausages, frankfurters and luncheon meats; imitation bacon chips; frozen pizza; cake decorations; and birthday and party favors. General Mills also operates 185 Red Lobster Inns seafood restaurants, six Betty Crocker Pie Shops, and six Hannahan's restaurants.

The Craft, Games and Toys group consists of the Parker Brothers division, the Kenner Products division, and the Fundimensions division. Fashion operations include David Crystal, Alligator Co., Kimberly Knitwear, Lord Jeff Knitting, Foot-Joy, and Monet Jewelers.

General Interiors produces furniture under the names Pennsylvania House, Shaw, Cushman, Kittinger, Biggs and Dunbar. Specialty retailing is carried out by LeeWards Creative Crafts, Eddie Bauer, David S. Reid, The Talbots, and Olson-Travelworld. The company also makes a variety of specialty chemicals.

Dividends, paid each year since 1898, averaged 34% of earnings in the five years through May 30, 1976.

Employees: 51,778. Shareholders: 29,200.

### Finances

In April, 1976, GIS announced a major expansion program for its packaged foods operations. This would include capital spending of about $125 million in 1976-7.

On April 26, 1972 the Federal Trade Commission issued a complaint alleging that GIS and three others shared an illegal monopoly in the dry cereal market. These charges have been formally denied by all of the companies involved, and a period of lengthy litigation, which began April 28, 1976, is expected.

### CAPITALIZATION

LONG TERM DEBT: $280,344,000.
MINORITY INTEREST: $5,217,000.
COMMON STOCK: 49,459,808 shs. ($0.75 par).

**Incorporated** in Del. in 1928. **Office**—9200 Wayzata Blvd., Minneapolis, Minn. 55440. **Tel**—(612) 540-2311. **Pres**—E. R. Kinney. **Secy**—J. M. Neville. **VP-Fin. & Treas**—H. H. Porter, Jr. **Dirs**—J. P. McFarland (Chrmn), H. B. Atwater, Jr., C. H. Bell, T. M. Crosby, K. N. Dayton, J. W. Feighner, P. B. Harris, S. F. Keating, E. R. Kinney, L. W. Menk, J. W. Morrison, G. A. Newkirk, M. Perlmutter, C. F. Phillips, E. S. Reid, W. G. Smith, J. A. Summer, D. F. Swanson, R. L. Terrell. **Transfer Agents**—Company's Office, Minneapolis; Citibank, NYC. **Registrars**—Northwestern National Bank, Minneapolis; Citibank, NYC.



FIGURE 28
Standard Stock Report (Back)

**9** This is the date on which this report has been prepared. Updated, future information will be published in the next report, probably 3 months hence.

**10** This is S&P's analysis of the company's business plans. Information is derived from General Mills' news releases and from interviews the S&P analysts have had with the company.

**11** Important business and financial news announced by the company since publication of the last Stock Report appears under "Recent Developments."

**12** General Mills' dividend information for the preceding 12 months is listed in this table and will also appear in Standard & Poor's Dividend Record book for 1976. Note that this company is one of a growing number of companies that offers stockholders a convenient plan for automatically reinvesting their dividends in additional shares of stock. These additional shares do not come from unissued stock purchased directly from the company. Rather, it is outstanding stock purchased in the open market and allocated to the plan subscribers according to their cash dividend contributions.

**13** Relevant details have been culled from the company's balance sheets and income statements over the past 10 years and are presented in tabular form to facilitate comparisons. Technical market information such as trading ranges and P/E ratios have been included by S&P for analytical reasons. This information helps investors make value judgments based on the financial statement statistics.

---

**14** "Fundamental Position" is an analysis of the corporation's operating divisions and their percentage contribution to the consolidated sales and pretax income of General Mills. It also identifies these subsidiaries and affiliated companies by name. This section also sets forth, without further comment, the average dividend payout ratio for the last 5 years and the number of current employees and stockholders.

**15** Any news with potential for having a material effect upon the company's capital, current or long term, appears here. This includes such items as business expansion programs, anticipated new financings, debt retirements, and pending litigation or regulatory agency penalties.

**16** Capitalization consists of the total par values of outstanding bonds plus the interest of the common shareholder, as shown on the current balance sheet. Note the item labeled "Minority Interest." Like most large concerns, General Mills has significant ownership interests in one or more other corporations, organizations that may provide General Mills with services, raw materials, or finished merchandise, for resale. Although General Mills enjoys management control over these companies by virtue of its majority equity holdings, it does not own all the stock outstanding in these corporations. Nevertheless, General Mills has chosen to consolidate their balance sheet items and operating results into its own financial statements. Consequently, it "owes" the minority stockholders in those concerns a proportionate share of benefits although, in fact, it is a liability that will never be paid. Therefore, minority interest is included, like long-term debt, as part of General Mills' total capitalization.

**17** This small but important section is often of great interest to analysts and stockholders. It provides

---

1. the address and phone number of the company's main office;
2. the names of the company's senior officers;
3. the names of the directors serving on its board; and
4. the names and locations of the company's transfer agent(s) and registrar(s).

Such information enables you to direct inquiries and correspondence, including complaints, to the appropriate parties. For instance, to correct the spelling of a name on your stock certificate you can submit it to either the company itself in Minneapolis, Minnesota, or to Citibank (its transfer agent) in New York City. Or, to change your address for dividend and company report purposes, write a letter to either of the registrars, Northwestern National Bank in Minneapolis, Minnesota, or Citibank in New York City.

## CONCLUDING COMMENTS

Whether you accept one of the market theories described in this chapter or any other market theory, including your own personal mixture of theories, it is necessary to stay abreast of stock market developments constantly. The primary means of doing so is the regular reading of financial news as it appears in your local newspaper or the national financial daily, *The Wall Street Journal*. Obviously you must be able to read and refer to the many graphs and tables that provide a wealth of financial information despite their compact form. Similarly, the ticker tape flashes on-the-spot developments when trading is in progress.

Reading and interpreting financial news is critical to your function as an effective member of the securities industry. Your ability to read and understand the news will improve when you read financial news regularly and discuss what you read with colleagues and customers. The more informed you are, the more efficiently you can function.